W0008494

caravan
AND camping
BRITAIN & IRELAND

 Lifestyle Guides

Produced by AA Publishing

This edition published 2001

© The Automobile Association Developments Limited 2001

The Automobile Association retains the copyright in the current edition and in all subsequent editions, reprints and amendments to editions

The directory is generated from the AA's establishment database, Information Research and Control, AA Hotel and Touring Services

Maps prepared by the AA Cartographic Department
© The Automobile Association Developments Limited 2001

The contents of this publication are believed correct at the time of printing. Nevertheless, the publishers cannot be held responsible for any errors or omissions or for changes in the details given in this guide or for the consequences of any reliance on the information provided by the same. Assessments of the campsites are based on the experience of the AA Caravan & Camping Inspectors on the occasion of their visit(s) and therefore descriptions given in this guide necessarily contain an element of subjective opinion which may not reflect or dictate a reader's own opinion on another occasion. We have tried to ensure accuracy in this guide but things do change and we would be grateful if readers would advise us of any inaccuracies they may encounter.

Advertisements
This guide contains display advertisements in addition to the editorial features and line entries. For further information contact:
Advertisement Production: Karen Weeks, telephone 01256 491545

Typeset and colour origination by Avonset, 11 Kelso Place, Bath
Printed in Italy by Rotilito Lombarda SpA

Editor: Denise Laing

Cover Photograph World Pictures Ltd.

The Automobile Association wishes to thank the following photographers for their assistance in the preparation of this book.

All photographs listed below are held in the Association's own photo library (AA PHOTO LIBRARY) and were taken by the following:

3, H. Williams; 5, E Bownes; 11, C. Lees; 12, W. Voysey; 13, R. Weir; 16, T. Souter; 17a, R. Moss; 17b, P. Trenchard; 18, M. Short; 19, K. Paterson; 28a, J. Carnie; 28b, S. Day; 29a, S. Day; 29b, V. Bates; 34, R.Elliot.

A CIP catalogue record for this book is available from the British Library
ISBN 0 7 4952 5983

Published by AA Publishing, a trading name of Automobile Association Developments Limited, whose registered office is Norfolk House, Priestley Road, Basingstoke, Hampshire RG24 9NY.
Registered number 1878835

CONTENTS

36 great ways to enjoy your FREE time.

GRANNIE'S HEILAN' HAME
NAIRN LOCHLOY
TUMMEL VALLEY

FREE pools, sports and leisure facilities.

SUNDRUM CASTLE
CRAIG TARA   RIVERSIDE

WHITBY
BLUE DOLPHIN
PRIMROSE VALLEY
REIGHTON SANDS
BARMSTON BEACH

BEACON FELL VIEW

PRESTHAVEN SANDS
TY MAWR

GOLDEN SANDS
HEACHAM BEACH

CHERRY TREE
WILD DUCK
KESSINGLAND BEACH

BRYNOWEN

SUFFOLK SANDS

STEEPLE BAY
SHEERNESS

FREE family entertainment.

DONIFORD BAY
ST MINVER   DEVON CLIFFS   WEST BAY
PERRAN SANDS
SEAVIEW
LITTLESEA
TRELAWNE MANOR   CHESIL BEACH
WEYMOUTH BAY

THORNESS BAY
NODES POINT
LOWER HYDE

FREE children's clubs.

With 36 Touring Parks across Britain, you're closer to Haven than you think. Whether it's an all-action holiday you want, or something a little more leisurely and relaxing, Haven has the touring holiday that's exactly right for you. All our Parks offer superb facilities — many of them **FREE** — and provide a perfect base for your touring break. For your **FREE** 2001 Haven Touring Brochure, call now on

0870 242 4444

quoting TMA01. Or see your Travel Agent. www.havenholidays.com

Haven
Touring

HOW TO USE
THIS GUIDE

Whether you are a new-comer to camping and caravanning or an old hand, it is probable that what attracted you in the first place was the 'go-as-you-please' freedom of being able to set off on the merest whim. However, in practice, especially during holiday periods, parks in popular parts of the country get dreadfully crowded, and if you choose somewhere off the beaten track, you may go for miles without finding a suitable park.

When you do find somewhere, how do you know that it will have the facilities you need? How do you know whether they will be maintained to an acceptable standard? This is where you will find the AA guide invaluable in helping you to choose the right park. Please also read the section on the Pennant Classification Scheme so that you know what the classification symbols used in this guide mean.

The directory of parks is organised in county order with locations listed in alphabetical order. The Scottish Islands have their own section and are not listed in county order. The Channel Islands and Isle of Man appear between England and Scotland. Parks are listed in descending order of pennant classification.

DIRECTORY ENTRIES

If the name of a park is printed in italics this indicates that we have not been able to get details or prices confirmed by the owners. An asterisk (*) in front of the prices means that we only have information about the previous year's prices.

LOCATIONS · 1

Each location in the directory has a map reference, starting with the map page number and followed by a number based on the National Grid and can be used in conjunction with the 16-page atlas at the back of the guide, or with any AA Atlas of Britain. To find a location, read the first figure horizontally and the second figure vertically within a lettered square. In order to find the precise location of a site, each entry in the directory has a 6-figure map reference also based on the National Grid.

PENNANT RATING · 2

Sites are rated from 1-pennant parks offering a fairly simple standard of facilities to 5-pennant Premier Parks that are of an award-winning standard. For a fuller explanation of the AA Scheme see page 11

DIRECTIONS · 3

We also give route directions as supplied by the site, but as space in the directory is limited we cannot go into great detail.

CHARGES · 4

Charges given immediately after the appropriate symbol (caravan, tent, motorvan) are the overnight cost for one tent or caravan, one car and two adults, or one motor caravan and two adults. The price may vary according to the number of people in your party, but some parks have a fixed fee per pitch regardless of the number of people.

Please note that some parks may charge separately for some of the park's facilities, including the showers.

Please also note that prices have been supplied to us in good faith by the park operators and are as accurate as possible. They are, however, only a guide and are subject to change at any time during the currency of this book.

When parks have been unable to forecast their 2001 prices, those for 2000 may be quoted, prefixed by an asterisk. See also 'Directory Entries' above.

BOOKING · 5

It is advisable to book in advance during peak holiday seasons and in school or public holidays. Where an individual park requires advance booking, 'advance bookings accepted' or 'booking advisable' (followed by dates) appears in the entry. It is also wise to check whether a reservation entitles you to a particular pitch. It does not necessarily follow that an early booking will get you the best pitch; you may just have the choice of what is available at the time you check in.

The words 'Advance bookings not accepted' indicate that a park does not accept reservations. Some parks may require a deposit on booking which may well be non-returnable if you have to cancel your holiday. If you have to cancel, notify the proprietor at once because you may be held legally responsible for partial or full payment unless the pitch can be re-let. Do consider taking out insurance such as AA Travel Insurance to cover lost deposit or compensation. Some parks will not accept overnight bookings unless payment for a full minimum period (e.g. two or three days) is made. If you are not sure whether your camping or caravanning equipment can be used at a park, check beforehand.

Please note: The AA does not undertake to find accommodation or to make reservations.
Last Arrival – Unless otherwise stated, parks will usually accept arrivals at any time of the day or night but some have a special 'late arrivals' enclosure where you have to make temporary camp so as not to disturb other people on park. Please note that on some parks access to the toilet block is by key or pass card only, so if you know you will be late, do check what arrangements can be made.
Last Departure – As with hotel rooms and self-catering accommodation, most parks will specify their overnight period – e.g. noon to noon. If you overstay the departure time you can be charged for an extra day. Do make sure you know what the regulations are.

TOURING PITCHES & STATIC VAN PITCHES · 6

The brief description of the site includes the number of touring pitches. We give the number of static van pitches available in the entries in our guide in order to give a picture of the nature and size of the park. The AA pennant classification is based on an inspection of the touring pitches and facilities only. AA inspectors do not visit or report on fixed types of accommodation. The AA takes no responsibility for the condition of rented caravans or chalets and can take no action whatsoever about complaints relating to them.

ADDITIONAL INFORMATION · 7

We include in the entry any further or more specific information about facilities, supplied by the campsite, that is not represented by a symbol.

SYMBOLS & ABBREVIATIONS · 8

See page 10 and each page in the directory for explanation of symbols and abbreviations used in entries. Please note that any symbol appearing after the arrow symbol → represents facilities found within 3 miles of the site.

CREDIT/CHARGE CARDS · 9

Most of the larger parks now accept payment by credit or charge card. We use the following symbols at the end of the entry to show which cards are accepted

▬	Access/Mastercard
▭	Barclaycard/Visa
▣	Switch

▬	Connect
▼	Delta

IMPORTANT NOTE ON RESTRICTIONS

Many parks in our guide are selective about the categories of people they will accept on their parks. In the caravan and camping world there are many restrictions and some categories of visitor are banned altogether.

On many parks in this guide, unaccompanied young people, single-sex groups, single adults, and motorcycle groups will not be accepted. The AA takes no stance in this matter, basing its pennant classification on facilities, quality and maintenance.

On the other hand, some parks cater well for teenagers with magnificent sporting and leisure facilities as well as discos; others have only very simple amenities.

Most parks accept dogs, but some have no suitable areas for exercise, and some will refuse to accept certain large breeds, so you should always check with the park before you set out.

Always telephone the park before you travel.

Explanation of a Directory Entry
(see also The AA Pennant Classification Scheme)

(1) ANY TOWN — Map 1 3XS
(2) ►► **Name Caravan Park** SW8627281
PL28 8PN ☎ 01841 520230
(3) *Dir:* Off B3Z76 Padstow-Newquay road 2m SW of village.
(4) 🚐 £5-£8 🚐 £5-£8 ▲ £5-£8
(5) Open Apr-Oct 1st Apr-Whit & mid Sep-Oct shop closed Booking advisable Jul-Aug. Last departure 14.00hrs. Last arrival 21.00hrs Last departure noon
(6) *A working farm site with better than average facilities. The very well converted farm buildings look purpose built. A 3-acre site with 40 touring pitches.*
(7) Sports field & pitch n putt
(8) Leisure: ⚃ ♦ /Ⅲ⌂ Facilites: ➡🐾 📞🌠🏛🏕🐎
Services: 🅱️♀️🔆🚐🚽 →∪ ✚🎵
(9) ▬ 🅳 🅲 ▬

CHILD-FREE PARKS

A small number of parks in our guide have decided to concentrate on the adults-only market, aiming to attract holiday makers who are in search of total peace and quiet. They advertise themselves as child-free parks, and those in our guide who have informed us about their policy are:

Cornwall: Resparva House Camping & Caravanning, Summercourt Chacewater Park, Truro
Cumbria: Larches Caravan Park, Mealsgate
Derbyshire: Longnor Wood C. P, Longnor
Dorset: Bingham Farm Touring C P, Bridport
Greater Manchester: Gelder Wood Country Park, Rochdale
Norfolk: Little Haven Camping & Caravanning Park, Erpingham
Norfolk: Two Mills Touring Park, North Walsham
Shropshire: Beaconsfield Farm Caravan Park, Shrewsbury (July-Aug)
Somerset: Chew Valley . P, Bishop Sutton
Suffolk: Lonely Farm, Saxmundham
North Yorkshire: Hollybrook Caravan Park, Easingwold
West Yorkshire: Moor Lodge Park, Bardsey
Powys: Daisy Bank C P, Church Stoke Riverside Caravan & Camping Park, Crickhowell

CHEMICAL CLOSET DISPOSAL POINT (CDP)

You will usually find one on every park, except those catering only for tents. It must be a specially constructed unit, or a WC permanently set aside for the purpose with adjacent rinsing and soak-away facilities. However, some local authorities are concerned about the effect of chemicals on bacteria in cesspools etc, and may prohibit or restrict provision of CDPS in their areas.

COLD STORAGE

A fridge and/or freezer or icepacks for the use of holidaymakers.

COMPLAINTS

Speak to the park proprietor or supervisor immediately if you have any complaints, so that the matter can be sorted out on the spot. If this personal approach fails, you may decide, if the matter is serious, to approach the local authority or tourist board. AA members may write to:

The Editor,
The AA Caravan & Camping Guide,
AA Lifestyle Guides,
Fanum House, Basing View
Basingstoke, Hants RG21 4EA

The AA will look into any reasonable complaints from its members but will not in any circumstances act as negotiator or undertake to obtain compensation or enter into further correspondence. The AA will not guarantee to take any specific action.

ELECTRIC HOOK-UP

This is becoming more generally available at parks with three or more pennants, but if it is important to you, you must check before booking. The voltage is generally 240v AC, 50 cycles, although variations between 200v and 250v may still be found. All parks in the AA scheme which provide electrical hook-ups do so in accordance with International Electrotechnical Commission regulations. Outlets are coloured blue and take the form of a lidded plug with recessed contacts, making it impossible to touch a live point by accident. They are also waterproof. A similar plug, but with protruding contacts which hook into the recessed plug, is on the end of the cable which connects the caravan to the source of supply, and is dead.

These cables can usually be hired on site, or a plug supplied to fit your own cable. You should ask for the male plug; the female plug is the one already fixed to the power supply. This supply is rated for either 5, 10 or 16 amps and this is usually displayed on a triangular yellow plate attached to source of supply. If it is not, be sure to ask at Reception. This is important because if you overload the circuit, the trip switch will operate to cut off the power supply. The trip switch can only be reset by a park official, who will first have to go round all the hook-ups on park to find the cause of the trip. This can take a long time and will make the culprit distinctly unpopular with all the other caravanners deprived of power, to say nothing of the park official.

It is a relatively simple matter to calculate whether your appliances will overload the circuit. The amperage used by an appliance depends on its wattage and the total amperage used is the total of all the appliances in use at any one time. See the table below.

Portable black & white TV	
50 watts approx.	0.2 amp
Small colour TV	
90 watts approx.	0.4 amp
Small fan heater	
1000 (kW) approx.	4.2 amp
One-bar electric fire	
NB each extra bar rates	1000 watts
60 watt table lamp	
approx.	0.25 amp
100 watt light bulb	
approx.	0.4 amp
Battery charger	
100 watts approx.	0.4 amp
Small refrigerator	
125 watts approx.	0.4 amp
Domestic microwave	
600 watts approx.	2.5 amp

MOTOR CARAVANS

At some parks motor caravans are only accepted if they remain static throughout the stay. Also check that there are suitable level pitches at the parks where you plan to stay.

PARKING

Some park operators insist that cars be put in a parking area separate from the pitches; others will not allow more than one car for each caravan or tent.

PARK RULES

Most parks display a set of rules which you should read on your arrival. Dogs may or may not be accepted on parks, and this is entirely at the owners' or wardens' discretion. Even when parks say they accept dogs, it is still discretionary and we most strongly advise that you check when you book. Dogs should always be kept on a lead and under control. Dogs sleeping in cars is not encouraged by most proprietors.

Most parks will not accept the following categories of people: single-sex groups, unsupervised youngsters and motorcyclists whether singly or in groups, even adults travelling on their own are sometimes barred. A handful will not accept children. See Child-Free Parks on page 7. If you are not a family group or a conventional couple, you would be well advised to make sure what rules apply before you try to book.

PITCHES

Campsites are legally entitled to use an overflow field which is not a normal part of their camping area for up to 28 days in any one year as an emergency method of coping with additional numbers at busy periods. When this 28 day rule is being invoked site owners should increase the numbers of sanitary facilities accordingly when the permanent facilities become insufficient to cope with extra numbers. In these circumstances the extra facilities are sometimes no more than temporary portacabins.

SHOPS

The range of food and equipment in shops is usually in proportion to the size of the park. As far as our pennant requirements are concerned, a mobile shop calling several times a week, or a general store within easy walking distance of the park entrance is acceptable.

TELEPHONE NUMBERS

The telephone authorities are liable to change some telephone numbers during the currency of this guide. If you have any difficulty please check with Directory Enquiries.

IMPORTING ANIMALS

The importation of animals into the UK is subject to strict controls. Penalties for trying to avoid these controls are severe. However, the introduction of the Pet Travel Scheme (PETS) on 28 February 2000 allows cats and dogs coming from the EU (and certain other countries and rabies-free islands) to enter the UK without quarantine provided certain conditions are met. These conditions include having the animal microchipped and vaccinated and obtaining appropriate documentation; a process which takes a minimum of six months.

Pets resident in the Channel Islands, Isle of Man or the Republic of Ireland are only subject to quarantine or the PETS rules when entering the UK from outside the British Isles.

Visitors intending to bring a cat or dog into the UK from an EU country should consult a vet in their country of residence. Details of other qualifying countries and further information is available on the Ministry of Agriculture, Fisheries and Food (MAFF) website:
www.maff.gov.uk/animalh/quarantine

USEFUL ADDRESSES

Camping and Caravanning Club
Greenfields House
Coventry
CV4 8JH
Tel: 02476 694995

Caravan Club
East Grinstead House
East Grinstead
West Sussex
RH19 1UA
Tel: 01342 326944

British Holiday &
Homes Parks Association Ltd
6 Pullman Court
Great Western Road
Gloucester
GL1 3ND
Tel: 01452 526911

National Caravan Council Ltd
Catherine House
Victoria Road
Aldershot
Hampshire
GU11 1SS
Tel: 01252 318251

Symbols & Abbreviations

LEISURE

- Boats for hire
- Fishing
- 9/18-hole golf course
- Mini-golf
- Stables
- Swimming Pool, Indoor
- Swimming Pool, Outdoor
- Tennis Court
- Watersports
- Children's Playground
- Cinema
- Games Room
- Separate TV room

FACILITIES

- Bath(s)
- Shower(s)
- Electric Shaver points
- Hairdryer
- Ice Pack Facility

- Public Telephone
- Shop on Site or within 200yds
- Mobile Shop (calls at least 5 days a week)
- BBQ Area
- Picnic Area
- Dog Exercise Area
- Disabled facilities

SERVICES

- Electric Hook Up
- Calor Gaz
- Camping Gaz
- Battery Charging
- Toilet Fluid
- Launderette
- Licensed Bar
- Cafe/Restaurant
- Fast Food/Takeaway
- Baby Care

- AA Pennant Classification
- Touring Caravans
- Motor Caravans
- Tents
- Facilities within 3 miles
- No dogs
- 2000 prices

Credit/Charge cards

Etr	Easter
Whit	Whitsun
dep	Depature
fr	From
hrs	Hours
m	Mile
mdnt	midnight
rdbt	roundabout
rs	restricted service
wk	week
wknd	weekend

THE AA PENNANT

CLASSIFICATION
SCHEME

AA parks are classified on a 5-point scale according to their style and the range of facilities they offer. As the pennant rating increases, so the quality and variety of facilities and amenities must be greater. All AA parks must meet a minimum standard: they should be clean, well-maintained and welcoming.

In addition they should have a local authority site licence (unless specially exempted), and satisfy local authority fire regulations.

► One Pennant Parks

These parks will offer a fairly simple standard of facilities, including:

- No more than 30 pitches per acre
- At least 6 pitches or 10% of total (if more than 60 pitches) allocated to tourers
- An adequate drinking water supply and reasonable drainage
- Washroom with flush toilets and toilet paper provided, unless no sanitary facilities in which case this should be clearly stated
- Chemical disposal arrangements, ideally with running water
- Adequate refuse disposal arrangements, clearly signed
- Well-drained ground, and some level pitches
- Entrance and access roads of adequate width and surface
- Whereabouts of emergency telephone displayed

►► Two Pennant Parks

Parks in this category will meet all of the above basic requirements, but offer a good level of facilities, services, customer care, security and ground maintenance. They should include the following:

- Separate washrooms, including 2 WCs and 2 washbasins per sex per 30 pitches
- Hot and cold water direct to each basin
- Urgent telephone numbers signed
- Externally-lit toilet blocks
- Warden available during day, times to be indicated
- Whereabouts of chemist/shop clearly signed
- Dish-washing facilities, covered and lit

►►► Three Pennant Parks

Most parks come within this rating, and the range is therefore quite wide. However, all three-pennant parks will be of a very good standard, and will offer most of the following in addition to the above:

- Facilities, services and park grounds very clean and well maintained, buildings in good repair, and attention paid to customer care and security
- Evenly-surfaced roads and paths

- Decent, modern or modernised toilet blocks, all-night lit, to contain:
    mirrors, shelves and hooks
    shaver/hairdryer points
    lidded waste bins in ladies toilets
    uncracked toilet seats
    soap and hand dryer/towels
- A reasonable number of modern shower cubicles with hot water
- Electric hook-ups
- Some hardstandings/wheel runs/firm, level ground
- Laundry with drying facilities, separate from toilets
- Children's playground with some equipment
- Public telephone on site, available 24 hours
- Warden's hours and 24-hour contact number clearly signed

►►►► Four Pennant Parks

These parks have achieved an extremely high standard in all areas, including landscaping of grounds, natural screening and attractive park buildings,

► ► ► ► ► **Five Pennant Premier Parks**

Premier Parks are of an award-winning standard, and are set in attractive surroundings with superb landscaping. Facilities, security and customer care are of an exceptional quality. As well as the above, they will offer:

- first-class cubicled washing and toilet facilities, at least 1 per sex per 20 pitches
- some fully-serviced pitches
- electric hook-ups to most pitches

Many Premier parks will also provide:

- Heated swimming pool
- Well-equipped shop
- Café or restaurant as well as bar
- Serious catering indoors and outdoors for young people
- A designated walking area for dogs (if accepted)

but also customer care and security. Toilets are smartly modern and immaculately maintained, and offer the following:

- Spacious vanitory-style washbasins, at least 2 per 25 pitches per sex
- Fully-tiled shower cubicles with dry areas, shelves and hooks, at least one per 30 pitches per sex
- Some fully-serviced toilet cubicles

Other requirements are:

- Shop on site, or within a reasonable distance
- Warden available 24 hours
- Reception area open during the day, with tourist information available
- Internal roads, paths and toilet blocks lit at night
- 25 pitches per campable acre (maximum)
- Toilet blocks heated October to Easter
- 50% electric hook-ups
- 10% hardstandings where necessary a late arrivals enclosure

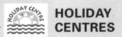 **HOLIDAY CENTRES**

In this category we distinguish parks which cater for all holiday needs. Anyone staying on one of these parks will have no need to go elsewhere for meals or entertainment. They provide:

- A wide range of on-site sports, leisure and recreational facilities.
- Supervision and security of a very high level
- A choice of eating outlets
- Touring facilities of equal importance to statics
- A maximum density of 25 pitches per acre.
- Clubhouse with entertainment provided
- Automatic laundry

THE TOP PARKS IN ENGLAND, SCOTLAND AND WALES

Listed below, in county order, are those parks that have achieved a five-pennant rating - the AA's highest category. To qualify for this top rating parks should not only have facilities of the highest quality, they must also maintain them to an extremely high standard, and landscape their grounds attractively to provide screening and privacy. Two of the parks that have been selected as Best Campsites of the Year for 2001 are Premier Parks, and their listing is preceded by an asterisk.

ENGLAND

CORNWALL

Sea View International Caravan & Camping Park, Boswinger
Wooda Farm Park, Bude
Sun Valley Holiday Park, Pentewan
Polmanter Holiday Park, St Ives

CUMBRIA

Wild Rose Park, Appleby-in-Westmorland
Fallbarrow Park, Windermere
Limefitt Park, Windermere

DERBYSHIRE

Darwin Forest Country Park, Matlock

DEVON

Stowford Farm Meadows, Combe Martin
Ross Park, Newton Abbot
Hidden Valley Coast & Country Park, West Down

DORSET

Highlands End Farm Holiday Park, Bridport
Hoburne Park, Christchurch
Merley Court Touring Park, Wimborne Minster
Wilksworth Farm Caravan Park, Wimborne Minster

HAMPSHIRE

Bashley Park, New Milton

ISLE OF WIGHT

Orchards Holiday Caravan Park, Newbridge
Southland Camping Park, Newchurch
Adgestone Camping Park, Sandown

LANCASHIRE

Holgate's Caravan Park, Silverdale

NORTHUMBERLAND

Ord House Country Park, Berwick-upon-Tweed

OXFORDSHIRE

Lincoln Farm Park, Standlake

SHROPSHIRE

Beaconsfield Farm Caravan Park, Shrewsbury

SOMERSET

Broadway House Holiday Caravan & Camping Park, Cheddar
The Old Oaks Touring Park, Glastonbury

SUFFOLK

Grange Country Park, East Bergholt
Moon and Sixpence, Woodbridge

YORKSHIRE, EAST

Low Skirlington Leisure Park, Skipsea

YORKSHIRE, NORTH

Ripley Caravan Park, Harrogate
*Rudding Holiday Park, Harrogate

SCOTLAND

DUMFRIES & GALLOWAY

Brighouse Bay Holiday Park, Brighouse Bay
Castle Cary Holiday Park, Creetown
Hoddom Castle Caravan Park, Ecclefechan

EAST LOTHIAN

Thurston Manor Holiday Home Park, Dunbar

FIFE

Craigtoun Meadows Holiday Park, St Andrews

HIGHLAND

Linnhe Lochside Holidays, Corpach
Glen Nevis Caravan & Camping Park, Fort William
Grantown on Spey Caravan Park, Grantown-on-Spey
Torvean Caravan Park, Inverness

PERTH & KINROSS

Blair Castle Caravan Park, Blair Atholl
River Tilt Caravan Park, Blair Atholl

STIRLING

*Trossachs Holiday Park, Aberfoyle
Glendochart Caravan Park, Luib

WALES

CARMARTHENSHIRE

Cenarth Falls Holiday Park, Newcastle Emlyn

A COMPLETE HOLIDAY EXPERIENCE

Listed below are the parks that are classified by the AA as Pennanted Holiday Centres, a designation outside the range of the ordinary pennant awards. These parks have an outstanding range of leisure and sports facilities and enable people to enjoy a self-contained holiday on the park, with everything a family needs for its recreation

ENGLAND

CORNWALL

Bude
Sandymouth Bay Holiday Park
Hayle
St Ives Bay Holiday Park
Holywell Bay
Trevornick Holiday Park
Looe
Tencreek Caravan & Camping Park
Mullion
Mullion Holiday Park
Newquay
Hendra Holiday Park
Newquay
Newquay Holiday Park
Pentewan
Pentwan Sands Holiday Park
Polperro
Killigarth Manor Holiday Estate
St Minver
St Minver Holiday Park

Torpoint
Whitsand Bay Holiday Park
Whitecross
White Acres Holiday Park
Widemouth
Bay Widemouth Bay Caravan Parc

CUMBRIA

Flookburgh
Lakeland Leisure Park
Silloth
Stanwix Park Holiday Centre

DEVON

Chudleigh
Finlake Holiday Park
Dawlish
Golden Sands Holiday Park
Dawlish
Lady's Mile Touring & Caravan Park
Paignton
Beverley Parks Caravan & Camping Park
Paignton
Grange Court Holiday Centre

ESSEX

Mersea Island
Waldegraves Holiday Park

GLOUCESTERSHIRE

South Cerney
Cotswold Hoburne

HAMPSHIRE

Fordingbridge
Sandy Balls Holiday Centre

LANCASHIRE

Blackpool
Marton Mere Holiday Village
Cockerham
Cockerham Sands Country Park
Heysham
Ocean Edge Caravan Park
Morecambe
Regent Caravan Park

LINCOLNSHIRE

Cleethorpes
Thorpe Park Holiday Centre
Mablethorpe
Golden Sands Holiday Park
Woodhall Spa
Bainland Country Park

NORFOLK

Great Yarmouth
Vauxhall Holiday Park
Hunstanton
Searles of Hunstanton

NORTHUMBERLAND

Berwick-upon-Tweed
Haggerston Castle

SUSSEX, WEST

Selsey
Warner Farm Touring Park

WIGHT, ISLE OF

Whitecliff Bay
Whitecliff Bay Holiday Park

YORKSHIRE, EAST RIDING

Skipsea
Far Grange Park

YORKSHIRE, NORTH

Filey
Flower of May Holiday Park

SCOTLAND

DUMFRIES & GALLOWAY

Gatehouse-of-fleet
Auchenlarie Holiday Park
Southerness
Southerness Holiday Village

EAST LOTHIAN

Longniddry
Seton Sands Holiday Village

HIGHLAND

Dornoch
Grannie's Heilan Hame Holiday Park
Nairn
Nairn Lochloy Holiday Park

PERTH & KINROSS

Tummel Bridge
Tummel Bridge Holiday Park

WALES

PEMBROKESHIRE

Tenby
Kiln Park Holiday Centre

REPUBLIC OF IRELAND

KERRY

Killarney
Fossa Caravan Park

AWARD WINNERS
CAMPSITE OF THE YEAR AWARD 2001

We are often asked what special qualities we look for in our Campsites of the Year, and the answer is usually another question along the lines of 'How long is a piece of string?' Obviously the selection process cannot be entirely objective, although many criteria have to be met before a park can be considered

for an award. When inspectors nominate their candidates, they choose parks which demonstrate a consistently high standard in all of the key areas: care and courtesy, sanitary facilities, environment and setting, general maintenance of buildings and grounds etc etc. Usually there is something extra special, in addition to a rigorous achievement of high standards, that sets a park apart from its fellows. We always look for the personal touch, which even very large parks with many staff members can offer, and which demonstrates that every visitor is important. This willingness on behalf of park management to go the extra mile in their bid to provide the best for their customers really counts. And it shows, as we discover each year when we finally come up with our winners.

OVERALL WINNER OF BEST CAMPSITE OF THE YEAR 2001

RUDDING HOLIDAY PARK
HARROGATE, NORTH YORKSHIRE

A peaceful parkland setting with an imaginatively spacious layout and beautiful views is the superb setting for our overall national winner. The private country estate of Rudding Park offers much more than a centre for touring caravans and tents, however. Within the 50-acres of woodland, open parkland and attractive, colourful gardens there is also a hotel, a golf driving range and, a recent addition, an 18-hole golf course. Viewers of the television 'soap' will recognise the static caravans and holiday chalets where many of the series' episodes are located. Other facilities include a supervised heated open-air swimming pool, and the comfortable Deer House bar and restaurant. Visitors to the campsite can choose between standard pitches-all generously-sized and equipped with electricity - or, in a separate area, super pitches with hardstanding, picnic table, mains water and drainage, and satellite TV channels, all surrounded by laurel hedging. Pitches are located in open parkland, or on wide terraces amongst mature trees; others are enclosed within a walled garden, and

most have a very pleasant outlook. When it comes to its toilet facilities, Rudding Park is totally deserving of its AA Premier status. The centrally-heated sanitary blocks are immaculate, with their fully-tiled walls, cubicled washbasins, showers and even baths and special baby facilities. This splendid holiday park is close to the spa town of Harrogate, and not far from historic York. We unconditionally recommend it to our readers as a park of exceptional quality, with innovative facilities and enthusiastic, courteous staff.

TROSSACHS HOLIDAY PARK,

ABERFOYLE, PERTH & KINROSS

With its glorious situation beside the Queen Elizabeth Country Park, and its Gold David Bellamy award for outstanding conservation, it is easy to see why Trossachs Holiday Park is a natural winner with lovers of the countryside. It is possible to lose yourself

park with touring pitches cleverly sited on terraces which offer superb panoramic views of the countryside, and the hills beyond. All pitches face south, and receive the maximum amount of sun. Behind them is a natural oak and bluebell wood which is a haven for wildlife, and there is open parkland to be enjoyed, and nature trails. The touring pitches are fully serviced, with TV and mains electricity, fresh and waste water points, and hardstandings. The toilet block fully deserves its five pennant premier rating, with its glossy, sparkling appearance and thoughtful

completely in this area of southern Scotland-nicknamed 'the Highlands in miniature', and walk or cycle for hours without meeting anything other than deer or buzzards. Joe and Hazel Norman always knew how they wanted to develop their park, and it was not with swimming pools, leisure centres, or noisy bars and restaurants. Instead they capitalised on the peace, quiet and beauty of their location, and concentrated on getting the most out of their surroundings. The result is a 40-acre

facilities which include cubicled washing as well as showering units. The park is also a mountain biker's paradise, with its rental, sales and repair shop catering for the newcomer to the sport as well as the seasoned cyclist. And there are miles and miles of unspoilt tracks and paths to explore on foot or on two wheels, taking in the nearby hills and lochs of the eye-opening Trossachs scenery. This is truly a magnificent park, and one we are proud to recommend as one of our top pennant-rated parks.

HENDRE MYNACH TOURING CARAVAN AND CAMPING PARK,

BARMOUTH, GWYNEDD

Even in a country as renowned as Wales is for its beautiful and dramatic scenery, the setting of Hendre Mynach is blessed indeed. Nestling between the mountains and the sea, it offers the best of both world: the fun and excitement of the beach just a stone's throw away and extending northwards for seven miles, and the peace and silence of the hills. The resort town of Barmouth is just a 20 minute walk away along the promenade, and the area offers many opportunities for sports and leisure activities, including sea, river, lake and beach fishing, hill walking, and bird watching in the nearby Mawddach estuary. Cycling and mountain bikes are also popular activities in this hilly countryside. Alun and Lesley Williams have carried on the camping and caravanning tradition begun by his father over 30 years ago, and the park has steadily developed under their watchful eyes. It now offers all-weather pitches so that the intrepid caravanner can take a break right up to the first week in January without fear of being swamped in sodden grass. The heated toilet block also makes winter holidays more pleasant, and throughout most of the season there is a well-equipped shop and off-licence, and a takeaway. Other amenities include a children's play area, a laundrette, and a designated dog walk. The friendliness and consideration of the Williams help to make this an outstanding park, and their many return visitors are happy to agree.

WINNER OF BEST CAMPSITE OF THE YEAR FOR THE CHANNEL ISLANDS

FAUXQUETS VALLEY FARM,

CASTEL, GUERNSEY

Hidden away in a world of its own, and surrounded by lush countryside, Fauxquets Valley Park is the perfect holiday base for the true camper. Owners Carol and Roland Guille often spend their own holidays under canvas, and are therefore very sensitive to the needs of their visitors. Their ongoing programme of upgrading the park, renewing existing facilities and providing new ones, has resulted in an excellent camping centre for the whole family. The pièce de résistance at Fauxquets, and source of much pride, is the superb swimming pool which is surrounded by sun-bathing area, lawns and flowering shrubs. Naturally this is the focus of much enjoyment, but other parts of the park have not been neglected in its favour. Another popular feature here is the nature trail which meanders along the river valley. This area was once filled with flowers grown for commercial use, as Fauxquets Valley Park used to be part of Guernsey's floral export business. Nowadays wild flowers and animals have reclaimed the land, and there is much of the natural world to see in this peaceful valley. On higher ground, the several camping areas rise out of the sloping

land on one side of the valley, and terracing has provided them with level surfaces. Landscaping has further given each pitch individual screening, and there are tall hedges around each camping field to give an added impression of seclusion and privacy. The thoughtfulness of the Guille Family extends to other areas of the park as well. One of the two toilet blocks is brand new, and boasts the sort of high class finishing touches often found on much larger parks. There is also a small laundry, an ironing-cum-hair drying room, and telephones. Some of the old farm buildings have been delightfully converted into a shop, a smart reception, and the Haybarn restaurant and licensed bar where meals and drinks can be enjoyed alfresco on one of the two terraces, or in the beamed barn itself. A small playground with purpose-built equipment provides enjoyment for young children, and for adults and older youngsters there is a huge field with nets for football and volleyball, and bicycles for hire. All of this is situated within a mile and a half of coast.

Looking for the best sites?

Troutbeck Head Club Site near Ullswater

HOBURNE
Holiday Parks of Distinction

Hoburne is the most successful family owned holiday park group in the country.

Our five superb touring parks can be found in some of the most scenic locations in the South and South West. They have all been graded 'Excellent' ☆☆☆☆ and ☆☆☆☆☆ by the English Tourist Board. Whether you require an action-packed peak season holiday with nightly entertainment, or a peaceful retreat where you can relax and unwind, there is sure to be a Hoburne Park to meet your needs. Facilities include indoor leisure pools, outdoor pools, licensed club houses* with seasonal entertainment, tennis courts, adventure playgrounds, restaurants and Bashley Park even has its own golf course!

And remember our tariffs are for up to 6 people and inclusive of electricity, toilet blocks with hot showers, awning space where available, and where applicable membership of the Park club.

*There is no clubhouse at Blue Anchor Park

Major investment programme for 2001 - see brochure for full details

For more information or a brochure please visit our website or call the park of your choice:

www.hoburne.co.uk

Bashley Park
New Milton, Hampshire
Tel: 01425 612340

Hoburne Park
Christchurch, Dorset
Tel: 01425 273379

Cotswold Hoburne
Cirencester, Gloucestershire
Tel: 01285 860216

Grange Court
Goodrington,
Paigton, Devon
Tel: 01803 558010

Blue Anchor Park
Blue Anchor Bay,
Nr Minehead, Somerset
Tel: 01643 821360

THE DAVID BELLAMY
CONSERVATION
AWARDS

Concern for the environment and an awareness of how to help protect it for future generations is clearly on the increase. The good news is that caravan and camping parks are at the forefront of the effort to protect our natural surroundings. This is reflected in the huge growth in the number of parks receiving a David Bellamy Conservation Award - more than double those which were recognised in 1998. These innovative awards are jointly organised by Dr Bellamy and the British Holiday & Home Parks Association. We are very proud to report that AA-Pennant Parks accounted for more than half of all awards made in 1999. Any small or large project which encourages wildlife to flourish makes parks eligible for an award, and we thought our readers would like to know which AA-recognised parks have been praised for their outstanding contribution to the environment. We list the prize-winners here, alphabetically by location within county.

For details of companies which won awards in 2000, please contact the BH & HP Association direct on tel: 01452 526911

Berkshire

Hurley Farm Caravan & Camping Park, Hurley

Cornwall

Sea View International, Boswinger
Trevella Tourist Park, Crantock
Maen Valley Holiday Park, Falmouth
Silverbow Park, Goonhavern
Holywell Bay Holiday Park, Holywell Bay
Silver Sands Holiday Park, Kennack Sands
Calloose Caravan & Camping Park, Leedstown

Croft Farm, Luxulyan
Penhaven Touring Park, Mevagissey
Mullion Holiday Park, Mullion
Newquay Holiday Park, Newquay
Penhaven Touring Park, Pentewan
Sun Valley Holiday Park, Pentewan
Polruan Holiday Centre, Polruan
Ayr Holiday Park, St Ives
Polmanter Tourist Park, St Ives
Carnon Downs Caravan & Camping Park, Truro

Ringwell Valley Holiday Park, Truro

Cumbria

Skelwith Fold Caravan Park, Ambleside
Lakeland Leisure Park, Flookburgh
Castlerigg Hall Caravan & Camping Park, Keswick
Wild Rose Park, Appleby-in-Westmorland
Fallbarrow Park, Windermere

Derbyshire

Rivendale Touring Caravan & Leisure Park, Ashbourne
Darwin Forest Country Park, Matlock

Sycamore Caravan &
  Camping Park, Matlock

Devon

Parkers Farm Holidays,
  Ashburton
Clifford Bridge Park, Clifford
  Bridge
Peppermint Park, Dawlish
Forest Glade Holiday Park,
  Kentisbeare
Channel View Caravan &
  Camping Park, Lynton
Moor View Touring Park,
  Modbury
Warcombe Farm Camping
  Park, Mortehoe
Dornafield, Newton Abbot
Ross Park, Newton Abbot
Beverley Park, Paignton
Widend Touring Park,
  Paignton
Oakdown Touring & Holiday
  Home Park, Sidmouth
Ramslade Touring Park,
  Stoke Gabriel
Harford Bridge Holiday Park,
  Tavistock
Higher Longford Farm
  Caravan Site, Tavistock

Dorset

Rowlands Wait Touring Park,
  Bere Regis
Freshwater Beach Holiday
  Park, Bridport
Highlands End Holiday Park,
  Bridport
Newlands Holiday Park,
  Charmouth
Golden Cap Holiday Park,
  Chideock
Sandford Holiday Park,
  Holton Heath

Beacon Hill Touring Park,
  Poole
Rockley Park, Poole
Ulwell Cottage Caravan Park,
  Swanage
Warmwell Country Touring
  Park, Warmwell
Merley Court Touring Park,
  Wimborne Minster
Wilksworth Farm Caravan
  Park, Wimborne Minster

Essex

Waldegraves Holiday Park,
  Mersea Island

Gloucestershire

Tudor Caravan & Camping,
  Slimbridge

Greater Manchester

Gelder Wood Country Park,
  Rochdale

Hampshire

Sandy Balls Holiday Centre,
  Fordingbridge

Kent

Sandwich Leisure Park,
  Sandwich

Lancashire

Marton Mere Holiday Village,
  Blackpool
Mosswood Caravan Park,
  Cockerham

Claylands Caravan Park,
  Garstang
Holgate's Caravan Park,
  Silverdale
Knepps Farm Holiday Park,
  Thornton Cleveleys

Lincolnshire

Thorpe Park Holiday Centre,
  Cleethorpes
Heron's Mead Fishing Lake &
  Touring Park, Orby
Foremans Bridge Caravan
  Park, Sutton St James

Norfolk

The Old Brick Kilns, Barney
Clippesby Holidays,
  Clippesby
Forest Park Caravan Site,
  Cromer
Searles of Hunstanton
Two Mills Touring Park,
  North Walsham

Northumberland

Waren Caravan Park,
  Bamburgh
Haggerston Castle, Berwick-
  upon-Tweed
Ord House Caravan Park,
  Berwick-upon-Tweed

Shropshire

Mill Farm Holiday Park,
  Hughley
Fernwood Caravan Park,
  Lyneal
Oxon Touring Park,
  Shrewsbury

Somerset

Broadway House Holiday
  Caravan & Camping Park,
  Cheddar
Westermill Farm, Exford
The Old Oaks Touring Park,
  Glastonbury
Halse Farm Caravan &
  Camping Park, Winsford

Suffolk

Cliff House, Dunwich
Heathland Beach Caravan
  Park, Kessingland

Sussex, East

Bayview Caravan & Camping Park, Pevensey Bay

Warwickshire

Island Meadow Caravan Park, Aston Cantlow

Wight, Isle of

Heathfield Farm Camping, Freshwater
The Orchards Holiday Caravan & Camping Park, Newbridge
Whitecliff Bay Holiday Park, Whitecliff Bay

Worcestershire

Ranch Caravan Park, Honeybourne

Yorkshire, East Riding

Thorpe Hall Caravan & Camping Site, Rudston
Far Grange Park, Skipsea
Weir Caravan Park, Stamford Bridge

Yorkshire, North

Vale of Pickering Caravan Park, Allerston
Allerton Park Caravan Site, Allerton Park
Ripley Caravan Park, Harrogate
Rudding Holiday Park, Harrogate

Riverside Caravan Park, High Bentham
Upper Carr Touring Park, Pickering
Jasmine Caravan Park, Snainton
Knight Stainforth Hall Caravan & Campsite, Stainforth
Woodnook Caravan Park, Threshfield
Ladycross Plantation Caravan Park, Whitby
Northcliffe Holiday Park, Whitby

Central Scotland

Trossachs Caravan Park, Aberfoyle
Blair Castle Caravan Park, Blair Atholl
Twenty Shilling Wood Caravan Park, Comrie
Argyll Caravan Park, Inveraray
Seton Sands Holiday Village, Longniddry
Craigtoun Meadows Holiday Park, St Andrews

Southern Lowlands & Borders

Brighouse Bay Holiday Park, Brighouse Bay
Park of Brandedleys, Crocketford
Sandgreen Caravan Park, Gatehouse of Fleet
Auchenlarie Holiday Park, Gatehouse of Fleet

Springwood Caravan Park, Kelso
Kippford Caravan Park, Kippford
Loch Ken Holiday Park, Parton
Galloway Point Holiday Park, Portpatrick
Sands of Luce Caravan Park, Sandhead

Highlands

Rothiemurchus Camping & Caravan Park, Aviemore
Linnhe Lochside Holidays, Corpach
Glen Nevis Caravan & Camping Park, Fort William
Silver Sands Leisure Park, Lossiemouth

Mid Wales

Fforest Fields Caravan & Camping Park, Builth Wells
Disserth Caravan & Camping Park, Llandrindod Wells

North Wales

Ty Hen, Rhosneigr

South Wales

Acorn Camping & Caravan Site, Llantwit Major

For further information on these awards, please contact the British Holiday & Home Parks Association Ltd, Chichester House, 6 Pullman Court, Great Western Road, Gloucester GL1 3ND. Tel: (01452) 526911.

Hints for a Hassle-free Caravanning Holiday

By Derek Emmott, Alec Grundy and Roger Almond

Undoubtedly, one of the major attractions of the camping and caravanning holiday is the sense of adventure it inspires. There is something about piling belongings into the van, or loading the tent and all of its accoutrements into a trailer or car, and heading off into the blue yonder that brings out the old pioneer spirit in everyone. After all, sleeping under canvas or in a caravan is not so very different from roughing it in one of the old covered wagons of the Wild West, give or take the odd luxury like polar sleeping bags, and satellite television. Even if getting away from it all means parking the family in a neat line next to other families, with little separating you apart from a flapping awning, every caravan park still represents the 'great outdoors', and is increasingly sought after.

Given the escapist nature of this kind of holiday, the temptation to leave the plans on the drawing board and just go off with little preparation might be hard to resist. Even those who plan ahead and try to anticipate every conceivable eventuality might miss the obvious in their forecast. Our campsite inspectors spend many months of every year out in the field, travelling around the countryside on our behalf. When they are not working for the AA they are often touring on their own account, both at home and abroad, and between them they have amassed years of experience. We asked some of them to offer their favourite tips to stress-free holidaying, and how to get the best out of this guidebook and the parks it recommends.

Roger and Marion Almond have camped, caravanned, and worked as wardens at one of the best parks in the country, and for the past 13 years Roger has inspected sites for the AA. They are the first to acknowledge how fast this industry has changed, and how advances in technology have turned tents, caravans and motorhomes into mini but very upmarket versions of home. Nevertheless, they say, try taking one of these little palaces to a remote part of the British Isles only to discover that you are missing just one essential item, and see how quickly the dream turns to disappointment. With plenty of forethought, and a glimpse of the shared experiences of the experts, many commonly-occurring problems can be averted.

Roger and Marion advise contacting several parks in the region you want to visit before making any bookings. While the AA guide book does its best to describe each park objectively according to how the inspectors see them, and to list all of the amenities offered on-site and nearby, this information might not tell you everything you want to know. The AA categorises parks by a pennant rating according to the quality of their facilities and amenities, and based on an increasing list of requirements. It also details the number of static and touring pitches and the acreage of each park, so if for example small is good for you, and individually-screened pitches plus a dog-walking area are what you seek, the guide will help to narrow down your search. Inevitably, though, not all similar-sounding parks will appeal to all people. Once you have compiled a shortlist, ring, e-mail, fax or use the AA web site where applicable to find out everything you want to know about each park, and choose the right one for you. Order a copy of their brochure, and scrutinise it to see what it offers, and whether or not it will suit your needs. Check your timing as the deserted beach you pitch your tent on one day, may be packed with bank holiday party-goers the next.

Once you have made your choice and embarked on your holiday, don't be afraid to ask for assistance to make sure you get the most out of your stay. And if something goes wrong, or you are not happy with some aspect of the park or the running of it, discuss it there and then with the owners, managers or wardens. In Roger's experience, most difficulties can be sorted out face to face, and stressful situations can be defused by discussion.

Alec Grundy and his partner Judith leave nothing to chance when they set off on a trip in their motorvan, and experience has shown them how to minimise the things that can go wrong. Cooking their evening meal on one trip to Ireland, they were astonished when the gas ran out. They had not checked their spare bottle before leaving home, and too late they remembered loaning it to a friend. In England they could have easily located a replacement, but gas bottles in Ireland are not compatible with their UK counterparts, and they ended up being grateful

for the camper's kitchen on site where they were able to finish off their dinner.

At one holiday park, Alec and Judith were amused to see a smart couple with a very expensive motor home trying to fill their fresh water tank with a jug. Apparently the van did not have a hose, and the taps on site didn't have one either. It is a good idea to always carry a hose, and also a funnel attached to a small length of hose, as well as at least one bottle of water. Alec and Judith always keep a thermos of hot water, as well as a carton of long life milk, a loaf of long life bread, and two tins of baked beans. This small supply has provided a hot meal on more than one occasion when the pair have been stranded in the back of beyond.

Waterproof duck tape has saved their van from flooding when one of the roof covers was lost in the middle of a deluge in Scotland. A tool kit consisting of the usual implements is a good idea, but other suggestions include a roll of insulating tape, a tube of impact adhesive, and an ordinary stapler, all of which can help with instant repairs. A short length of cable to convert your hook-up to a standard 13 amp plug is also very handy, and this can be attached to the mains supply in, for example, the warden's garage, if all hook-ups have been taken by the time you arrive at a site. Alec's last piece of advice is simple but vital: don't leave your electric hook-up cable in the garage at home when you depart, which is easy to do if you've been charging up the fridge prior to filling it with food.

Derek Emmott is notorious for losing keys, and had it not been for the sensible presence of his wife Pat who carries a spare set on most of his caravanning expeditions, he would have often found himself in serious trouble. His primary tip, and one he tries to remember himself, is to keep a spare set somewhere accessible, and not locked inside a car or caravan which you cannot get inside. Apart from ways to avoid the embarrassing glitches brought on by temporary forgetfulness, Derek strongly recommends taking out membership of a good roadside assistance and rescue scheme (like the AA). He points out that small problems can be put right or even avoided by a little preparation and planning, but for peace of mind in the event of serious problems, it is always a good idea to let the experts take over.

With full insurance cover, major headaches can be quickly smoothed away with just a little inconvenience. Disaster caused by the failure of a small but vital parts of a vehicle or caravan can also be avoided. Derek always carries a spare wheel for caravan as well as car, as well as spare road light bulbs, fuses, and batteries for portable equipment not powered from elsewhere. Packing a spare pressure switch and a water pump for the caravan water system can get you out of a tight spot, as it did Derek on one occasion when the alternative was to make a 140-mile round trip through the mountains of North Wales.

Our inspectors always recommend compiling a useful checklist to work from some weeks before setting off, and another one to keep tabs on things right up to the moment of departing, as this practice can eliminate many errors. The lists vary for tents, caravans and motor vans, and we show the key points:

Tents

✓ Check the tent a few weeks before your holiday by erecting it. Any missing poles, pegs, guy ropes etc will be discovered before it is too late

✓ Ensure the car will take the extra weight, and that any roof rack is securely fitted

✓ Before leaving, make sure the park's confirmation and the AA Caravan & Camping Guide are on the dashboard

✓ Gas bottles should be charged and secure

✓ Store some drinking water in container

Caravans

✓ Everything inside the caravan should be secured

✓ The hook-up to the car must be correct, and the safety chain fitted

✓ All lights must be working

✓ Close windows and roof lights

✓ Unhook electric hook-ups

✓ Remove wheel chocks

✓ Wind up corner steadies

✓ Empty and stow fresh/waste water containers

✓ Empty chemical toilet

✓ Lock caravan door

✓ Wind jockey wheel up to car height

✓ Fix caravan to car and attach safety chain

✓ Connect and check electrics and signals

✓ Move forwards 10 yards and then stop and check that nothing has been left

Motor caravans

✓ Have some fresh water in tank

✓ Ensure that the gas tank bottle is charged and turned off

✓ Check engine oil, water, battery are OK

✓ Ensure all bedding, towels, dish cloths and food supplies are on board

✓ Disconnect electric hook-ups

✓ Secure doors

✓ Close roof vents

✓ Set fridge on battery operation.

✓ Pack some sort of marker to leave on your pitch while you are off-site

Planning and preparation are half the battle, as you can see, when taking to the road with your temporary home. Even the experts pack plenty of spares as a precaution, so be prepared, and have a great holiday!

ISLAND CAMPING

SCOTLAND

The Shetland Islands

These are the farthest-flung outpost of the British Isles, taking 14 hours to reach by boat from Aberdeen. The archipelago of Shetland consists of over 100 islands and skerries (reefs of rock), though only 15 are permanently inhabited. At no point on the mainland are you more than three miles from the sea, and the impressively rugged coastline is stunning.

Campers and caravanners are welcome, the only restrictions being on Noss and Fair Isle, and the Tresta Links in Fetlar, where camping is not allowed at all. Elsewhere there are four official campsites, but visitors can stray into the wilds, provided that they seek permission to stay from the owner of the land. Caravans and motor caravans must stick to the public roads. Drivers are strongly advised to check maps and routes carefully so that they don't find themselves in a difficult or dangerous situation.

Camping 'Böds' are a good way of seeing Shetland on a budget as long as you don't mind a unisex dormitory as sleeping accommodation. The böd was traditionally a building for fishermen and their gear during the fishing season, and the idea has been adopted to provide low-cost, basic accommodation, with the emphasis on 'basic'. Some have no electricity, and none has hot water. You need your own sleeping bag and bed roll, camping stove and cooking utensils. What you get is a toilet, table and benches, and a roof over your head.

The Orkney Isles

Closer to the mainland of Scotland, the Orkneys are far less rugged and wild than the Shetlands. There are no restrictions on access for camping and caravanning, and plenty of beautiful spots to pitch camp. Here it is an easy matter to avoid the crowds, although the Orkneys' incredible bird population is never very far away. Only on the tiny island of Fair Isle between Shetland and Orkney is camping not allowed, and there is no car ferry.

The Western Isles (Outer Hebrides)

These are a group of over 200 islands – only 13 of them inhabited - linked by a network of ferries and causeways. Most of the population live on Lewis, with Harris, home of the famous tweed, being another major centre. That leaves miles and miles of spectacular mountains, golden beaches and rolling hills to explore. There are official campsites, but 'wild' camping is allowed within reason, and with the landowner's prior permission.

The Inner Hebrides and other Scottish Islands

Tucked in against the mainland behind North and South Uist is that most nostalgic of islands, Skye. With its sister isles of Rhum and Eigg. These days there is the road bridge from Kyle of Lochalsh, and still a car ferry from Mallaig in the summer. No such ferry goes to Rhum and Eigg, so the only camping possible on these islands is for the backpacker.

The Isle of Bute is tucked into the west coast of Scotland only 30 miles

from Glasgow. Official camping is permitted at Rothesay, and wild camping is discouraged.

The islands of Mull, Islay, Coll and Arran have official campsites, and caravan and motor caravans are welcome as are tenters. Offsite camping is also allowed, provided the usual permission is sought. Iona is car-free, and a backpackers' paradise, while Tiree does not accept either caravans or motor caravans, and has no official sites.

Colonsay and Cumbrae allow no camping or caravanning, though organised groups such as the Scouts and Guides may stay with official permission; Jura and Gigha allow no camping or caravanning; Lismore bans caravans but permits camping, although there are no official sites and few suitable places anyway.

THE CHANNEL ISLANDS

The tightest controls are on the Channel Islands, because of the narrowness of the mainly rural roads. On all the Channel Islands you can hire tents on recognised campsites.

Jersey

On this, the largest of the islands, only islanders may own and use towed caravans; visitors are not allowed to bring either caravans or motor caravans, but tents and trailer tents are allowed, as long as you stay on a recognised campsite, and booking is strongly advised during July and August. The AA-approved sites which appear in this guide are attractively located and maintained to a very high standard

Guernsey

The same rules apply as on Jersey, except that motor caravans are allowed under certain strict conditions.

1. You must apply for and receive a permit in advance.
2. You may not use your motor caravan for sleeping but merely as a means of transport.
3. When not being used for transport, the motor caravan must be left under cover on a camping park with prior permission from the owner.

Herm and Sark

These two small islands are traffic-free. Sark is not part of the UK but the smallest independent and feudal state in the commonwealth. Both islands are surrounded by breathtaking stretches of golden sand. Herm is privately owned, with one hotel, a few shops and pubs, a handful of self-catering cottages and a small campsite. You can either hire a tent or pitch your own on a terrace overlooking the sea.

Sark has three campsites and offers a more dramatic landscape. New arrivals are met off the boat by a tractor to carry both themselves and their luggage up the steep hill from the harbour. After that all travel is by foot, on bicycle, or by horse and cart. The island is a natural fortress, being surrounded by cliffs and set high above sea level. There are some excellent beaches, but many of them are a long way down, and a long climb back up again.

Alderney

The third largest Channel Island is the closest to France and small enough to get around on foot for those who relish a slow pace of life. The island is a haven for flora and fauna. The clear seas are ideal for snorkelling, and sailboarding and surfing are popular in the sandy bays. As on Jersey, neither caravans nor motor caravans are allowed and campers must have a confirmed booking on the one official camp site before they arrive.

ISLE OF MAN

Trailer caravans are only allowed on the Isle of Man if they are to be used in connection with trade shows and exhibitions, or for demonstration purposes. They must not be used for living accommodation. Written application for permission should be made to the Secretary, Planning Committee, Isle of Man Local Government Board, The Government Offices, Murray House, Mount Havelock. The shipping line cannot accept a caravan without this written permission. Motor caravans may enter without prior permission.

ISLES OF SCILLY

Caravans and motor caravans are not allowed, and campers must stay at officially licensed sites. Booking is advisable on all sites, especially during school holidays.

For details about licensed sites on St Mary's write to: Mr and Mrs Ted Moulson, Garrison Farm, St Mary's.
For Bryher write to: Mrs J Stedeford, Jenford Bryer.
For St Agnes write to: Mrs S J Hicks, Troy Town, St Agnes.
For St Martin's write to: Mr C A Savill, Middletown, St Martin's.

Please note that strict control is kept on the landing of animals on these islands.

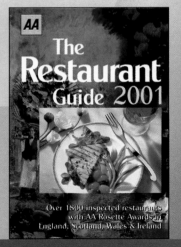

England

England

ENGLAND

FORESTRY COMMISSION CARAVAN AND CAMPSITES Forestry Commission sites which come within the scope of the Automobile Association's Caravan and Campsite classification scheme are listed in this guide. For a Forestry Commission brochure telephone 0131 334 0066. In addition there are entries for minimum-facility sites suitable for the camper or caravanner who prefers to be self-sufficient and carries his own chemical toilet.

ISLE OF Places incorporating the words 'Isle of' or 'Isle' will be found under the actual name, eg Isle of Wight is listed under Wight, Isle of. Channel Islands and Isle of Man, however, are between England and Scotland and there is a section containing Scottish Islands at the end of the Scotland gazetteer.

BERKSHIRE

FINCHAMPSTEAD   Map 04 SU76

▶ ▶ ▶ *California Chalet & Touring Park (SU788651)*
Nine Mile Ride RG40 4HU ☎ 0118 973 3928
Dir: From A321 S of Wokingham, turn right onto B3016 to Finchampstead, and follow Country Park signs along Nine Mile Ride to site
🚐 🚙 Å
Open Mar-Oct Booking advisable Last arrival 20.00hrs Last departure noon
Peaceful woodland site, with secluded pitches among the trees, adjacent to country park. A 5.5-acre site with 30 touring pitches.
Facilities: 🏕 ⊙ ᖇ ᛒ 🐕 **Services:** 🔌 Ⓣ
→ ∪ ▶ ⊚ ♪

HURLEY   Map 04 SU88

▶ ▶ ▶ *Hurley Farm Caravan & Camping Park (SU826839)*
Estate Office, Hurley Farm SL6 5NE
☎ 01628 823501 & 824493
Dir: Signed off A4130 Henley to Maidenhead road, just W of Hurley village
🚐 🚙 Å

Open all year Booking advisable bank hols, school hols & Henley Regatta
Large Thames-side site with good touring area close to river. Level grassy pitches in small, sectioned areas, and a generally peaceful setting. A 15-acre site with 200 touring pitches and 450 statics.
Facilities: 🏕 ⊙ ᖇ ✳ ᛒ ᖇ 🐕 **Services:** 🔌 ◻ 🛢 ⊘ 🏧 Ⓣ
→ ∪ ▶ ⊚ ♨ ♪ 🚌 ▱ ▨ 🗓

NEWBURY   Map 04 SU46

▶ ▶ ▶ *Oakley Farm Caravan & Camping Park (SU458628)*
Andover Rd, Washwater RG20 0LP ☎ 01635 36581
Dir: From rdbt S of Newbury on A34, take A343. Site 300yds past Hants/Berks boundary bridge. Left at car sales garage into Penwood Rd. Site on left
★ 🚙 £6.50 🚗 £6.50 Å £6.50
Open Mar-Oct Booking advisable bank hols
An open farmland site, well maintained and clean. A 3-acre site with 30 touring pitches.
Leisure: ⚲ ◣ ⚲ ▱ **Facilities:** 🏕 ⊙ ✳ ᖇ
Services: 🔌 ◻ 🛢 ⊘
→ 🚌 ▨

RISELEY   Map 04 SU76

▶ ▶ ▶ *Wellington Country Park (SU728628)*
RG7 1SP ☎ 0118 9326445
Dir: Signed off A33 between Reading and Basingstoke, 4m S of M4 junct 11

🚐 🚙 🛆
Open Mar-8 Nov Booking advisable peak periods
Last departure 14.00hrs
A peaceful woodland site set within extensive country park, which comes complete with lakes, nature trails, deer farm and boating. Ideal for M4 travellers. A 350-acre site with 70 touring pitches. Boating & fishing.
Leisure: 🅰 Facilities: 🕅 ⊙ ⚲ 🌡 Services: 🔌 🖥
→ ◎ 🛆 ⅍ 🗲 🍴 ▬ ▩ 🔌

BUCKINGHAMSHIRE

CHALFONT ST GILES   Map 04 SU99

▶ ▶ ▶ **Highclere Farm Country Touring Park** (SU977927)
Highclere Farm, Newbarn Ln, Seer Green HP9 2QZ
☎ 01494 874505 & 875665
Dir: 2m E of Beaconsfield between Chalfont St Giles and Seer Green
★ 🚐 £10-£12 🚙 £10-£12 🛆 £8-£14

Open Mar-Jan Booking advisable Last departure noon
A small farm park surrounded by pasture, and sheltered on one side by trees. A 2.5-acre site with 60 touring pitches.
Leisure: 🅰 Facilities: 🕅 ⊙ ⚲ ✻ ⅚ ⚲ 🌡 🎋 🐾
Services: 🔌 🖥 ℹ ⌀ 🔋 🔲 ⊤
→ ∪ ▶ 🞧 🍴 ▬ ■ ▩ 🔌

CAMBRIDGESHIRE

BURWELL   Map 05 TL56

▶ ▶ ▶ *Stanford Park (TL578675)*
Weirs Drove CB5 0BP
☎ 01638 741547 & 0802 439997
Dir: Signed from B1102
🚐 🚙 🛆
Open all year Booking advisable bank hols Last arrival 20.30hrs Last departure noon
A secluded site on outskirts of Burwell with modern amenities including purpose-built disabled facilities. A 20-acre site with 100 touring pitches and 3 statics.
Leisure: 🅰 Facilities: 🕅 ⊙ ⚲ ✻ ⅚ ⚲ 🌡
Services: 🔌 ℹ ⌀ 🔋 ⊤
→ ∪ ▶ ⅍ 🗲 🖥

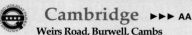

CAMBRIDGE   See **Burwell & Comberton**

COMBERTON   Map 05 TL35

▶ ▶ ▶ ▶ **Highfield Farm Touring Park (TL389572)**
Long Rd CB3 7DG ☎ 01223 262308
Dir: From M11 junct 12, take A603 (Sandy) for 0.5m, then right onto B1046 to Comberton
🚐 £7.50-£9 🚙 £7.50-£8.75 🛆 £7.50-£8.75
Open Apr-Oct Booking advisable bank hols wknds
Last arrival 22.00hrs Last departure 14.00hrs
Run by a very efficient and friendly family, the park is on a hilltop but well sheltered, with spacious pitches including a cosy backpacker's/cyclists area, and separate sections for couples and families. The layout is interesting, and there is a 1.5m marked walk around the family farm, with stunning views. An 8-acre site with 120 touring pitches.
Postbox.
Leisure: 🅰 Facilities: 🕅 ⊙ ⚲ ✻ ⚲ 🌡 🔲 🎋
Services: 🔌 🖥 ℹ ⌀ 🔋 ⊤
→ ∪ ▶ 🗲

See advert on page 40

GRAFHAM   Map 04 TL16

▶ ▶ ▶ ▶ **Old Manor Caravan Park (TL160269)**
Church Rd PE28 0BB ☎ 01480 810264
Dir: Signposted off A1 S of Huntingdon at Buckden and from A14 W of Huntingdon.
★ 🚐 £10-£12 🚙 £10-£12 🛆 £10-£12

contd.

England

Highfield Farm Touring Park

Comberton, Cambridge CB3 7DG
Tel/Fax: 01223 262308

A popular award-winning park with excellent facilities. Close to the historic university city of Cambridge, the Imperial War Museum, Duxford and ideally situated for touring East Anglia

Please write or phone for colour brochure

Open all year (rs Nov-Feb Shower block closed) Booking advisable weekends & peak times Last arrival 21.30hrs Last departure 18.00hrs
A secluded, well screened park in attractive gardens surrounding a 17th-century cottage. Pitches have lovely views of the countryside and Grafham Water is only a mile away. A 5-acre site with 84 touring pitches and 8 statics.
Leisure: ↘ /A **Facilities:** ♠ ⊙ ☜ ☀ ⓗ ⛄ ☍ ≧ ♠ **Services:** ♥ ⓘ ∅ ⊞ ⛽ ⇄
→ ∪ ⚠ ☇ ↙ ⛟ ⊞ ⇆ ☑

▶ ▶ ▶ **Camping & Caravanning Club Site (TL455539)**
19 Cabbage Moor CB2 5NB
☎ 01223 841185
Dir: From junct 11 of M11 onto B1309 signposted Cambridge. At 1st set of lights turn right. After 0.5m site sign on left pointing down lane
★ ☗ £11.80-£14.90 ☗ £11.80-£14.90 ▲ £11.80-£14.90
Open 10 Mar-01 Nov Booking advisable bank hols & Jul-Aug Last arrival 21.00hrs Last departure noon
An attractive site with good landscaping and excellent toilet blocks. Please see the advertisement on page 14 for details of Club Members' benefits. An 11-acre site with 120 touring pitches.
Leisure: /A **Facilities:** ♠ ⊙ ☜ ☀ ⓗ ⛄ ☍
Services: ♥ ⓘ ⓐ ∅ ⊞
→ ∪ ▶ ☇ ☄ ↙ ⛟ ⛽ ⇄

▶ ▶ **Quiet Waters Caravan Park (TL283712)**
PE28 9AJ ☎ 01480 463405
Dir: Situated on A14, 4m from Huntingdon, 13m from Cambridge
★ ☗ £8.50-£10 ☗ £8.50-£10 ▲ £8.50-£10

Open Apr-Oct Booking advisable high season Last arrival 20.00hrs Last departure noon
This attractive little riverside site is found in a charming village just 1m from the A14 making an ideal centre to tour the Cambridgeshire area. A 1-acre site with 20 touring pitches and 40 statics. Fishing & boating.
Facilities: ♠ ⊙ ☜ ☀ ☍ **Services:** ♥ ⓘ ⓐ ∅
→ ∪ ▶ ☄ ☸ ↙ ⛟ ⛽ ⇆ ☒ ☑

▶ ▶ ▶ *Huntingdon Boathaven & Caravan Park (TL249706)*
The Avenue, Godmanchester PE29 8AF
☎ 01480 411977
Dir: S of town off B1043
☗
Open Mar-Oct
Small, well laid out site overlooking a boat marina and the River Ouse, set close to the A14 and within walking distance of Huntingdon town centre. Clean, well kept toilets. A 2-acre site with 23 touring pitches.

▶ ▶ ▶ *The Willows Caravan Park (TL224708)*
Bromholme Ln, Brampton PE18 8NE
☎ 01480 437566 & 454961
Dir: Leave A14/A1 signed Brampton, follow signs for Huntingdon. Site on right close to Old Mill pub
☗ ☗ ▲
Open Mar-Oct Booking advisable bank hols, weekends & school hols Last arrival 23.00hrs Last departure 19.00hrs
A small, friendly site with a pleasant situation beside the River Ouse, on the Ouse Valley Walk. A 4-acre site with 50 touring pitches.
Facilities: ♠ ⊙ ☀ ⛄ ☍ **Services:** ♥ ⊞
→ ▶ ☄ ☸ ↙ ⛟

ST NEOTS   Map 04 TL16

▶ ▶ ▶ **Camping & Caravanning Club Site**
(TL182598)
Rush Meadow PE19 2PR ☎ 01480 474404
Dir: From A1 take A428 to Cambridge-2nd rdbt left to
Tesco's-past Sports Centre. International Camping signs
to site
★ ⊞ £11.80-£14.90 ⊞ £11.80-£14.90 ▲ £11.80-£14.90
Open 20 Mar-1 Nov Booking advisable bank hols &
peak periods Last arrival 21.00hrs Last departure
noon
A level meadowland site adjacent to the River Ouse
on the outskirts of St Neots, with well maintained
and modern facilities, and helpful, attentive staff.
Please see the advertisement on page 14 for details
of Club Members' benefits. A 10-acre site with 180
touring pitches.
Coarse fishing.
Facilities: ⋒⊙☜✳⛐℄⅊✝ **Services:** ⚡⬚🛢∅⊞⊤
→➤▲↘↙ ⬤ ▭▭

WILLINGHAM   Map 05 TL47

▶ ▶ ▶ *Roseberry Tourist Park (TL408728)*
Earith Rd CB4 5LT ☎ 01954 260346
Dir: Signposted between Earith and Willingham on
B1050
⊞ ⊞ ▲
Open Mar-Oct Booking advisable bank hols Last
arrival 22.00hrs Last departure 13.00hrs
A pleasant site in an old pear orchard, surrounded
by peace and seclusion, but next to the B1050
which can be noisy. The park has well-maintained
pitches, and clean though dated toilets. A 9.5-acre
site with 80 touring pitches and 10 statics.
Leisure: ⚠ **Facilities:** ⋒⊙☜✳℄⅊✝
Services: ⚡🛢∅⊞⊤
→∪➤◎◬↙↘

CHESHIRE

CHESTER   Map 07 SJ46

▶ ▶ *Chester Southerly Caravan Park (SJ385624)*
Balderton Ln, Marlston-Cum-Lache CH4 9LB
☎ 0976 743888
Dir: Just off A55/A483 rdbt
⊞ ⊞ ▲
Open Mar-Nov (rs Dec-Feb open for caravan rallies
only) Booking advisable for periods of 1 wk or more
& bank hols Last arrival 23.00hrs Last departure
noon
A well-tended site in rural area, on S side of city
close to the bypass. An 8-acre site with 90 touring
pitches.
Duck pond & breeding cage.
Leisure: ⚠ **Facilities:** ⋒⊙☜✳℄⅊⅊⊞⌂⊓
Services: ⚡🛢∅⊤
→∪➤◬↙⊞↘

KNUTSFORD   Map 07 SJ77

▶ ▶ ▶ *Woodlands Park (SJ743710)*
Wash Ln, Allostock WA16 9LG
☎ 01565 723429 & 0976 702490
Dir: From Holmes Chapel take A50 N for 3m, turn into
Wash Lane by Boundary Water Park. Site 0,25m on left
⊞ ⊞ ▲
Open Mar-6 Jan Booking advisable Bank Holidays
Last arrival 21.00hrs Last departure 11.00hrs
A very attractive park in the heart of rural Cheshire,
and set in 16 acres of mature woodland. 3m from
Joddrell Bank. A 16-acre site with 50 touring pitches
and 100 statics.
Facilities: ⊙⅊℄ **Services:** ⚡⬚🛢
→➤↘⅊

MACCLESFIELD   Map 07 SJ97

▶ ▶ **Capesthorne Hall (SJ840727)**
Siddington SK11 9JY ☎ 01625 861779 & 861221
Dir: Situated on A34, 3m S of Alderley Edge
⊞ £11.50-£13.50 ⊞ £11.50-£13.50
Open Mar-Oct Booking advisable public hols Last
arrival dusk Last departure noon
Set in grounds and gardens of Capesthorne Hall in
the heart of the Cheshire countryside. The pitches
are on level ground close to the Hall. Immaculate
toilets in old stable block. A 5.5-acre site with 30
touring pitches.
Capesthorne Hall, gardens, fishing, laundry room.
Facilities: ⋒⊙℄✝ **Services:** ⚡
→↙⅊

RIXTON   Map 07 SJ69

▶ ▶ ▶ **Holly Bank Caravan Park (SJ693904)**
Warburton Bridge Rd WA3 6HU ☎ 0161 775 2842
Dir: From junct 21 of M6, turn E on A57 to Irlam. After
2m turn right at lights. Site immediately on left
★ ⊞ £11-£13 ⊞ £11-£13 ▲ £10-£11
Open all year Booking advisable bank hols & wknds
Apr-Oct Last arrival 21.00hrs Last departure noon
Attractive site with spotlessly clean facilities. A 9-
acre site with 75 touring pitches.
Lending library.
Leisure: ♣ ⚠ **Facilities:** ⋒⊙✳℄⅊✝
Services: ⚡⬚🛢∅⊞⊤
→∪➤◬⚏↙

CORNWALL &
ISLES OF SCILLY

ASHTON   Map 02 SW62

▶ ▶ ▶ **Boscrege Caravan Park (SW595305)**
TR13 9TG ☎ 01736 762231
Dir: Take A394 Helson-Penzance Rd. Turn at Ashton
Post Office. 1m to site
★ ⊞ £6-£12.50 ⊞ £6-£12.50 ▲ £6-£12.50
Open Apr-Oct Booking advisable Jul-Aug Last
arrival 22.00hrs Last departure 11.00hrs

contd.

A quiet and bright little touring park divided into small paddocks with hedges, and offering plenty of open spaces for children to play in. The family-owned park offers clean, well-painted toilets facilities and neatly trimmed grass. In an Area of Outstanding Natural Beauty at the foot of Tregonning Hill. A 4-acre site with 50 touring pitches and 26 statics.
Recreation field. Microwave facility.
Leisure: ◖ ⋀ ⊡ Facilities: ♠ ☉ ⚒ ✳ ℄ ⊡ ⊞ 🛪
Services: ♨ ◙ ⓘ ⊘ ⊞ ⊡ ➘
→ ∪ ⏵ ☺ ⤬ ⤻ ⤻ ℥ ⬤ ☰ ⬛ ▣

BLACKWATER   Map 02 SW74

► ► ► **Chiverton Caravan & Touring Park**
(SW743468)
East Hill TR4 8HS ☎ 01872 560667
Dir: Leave A30 at Three Burrows/Chiverton rdbt onto unclass rd signed Blackwater (3rd exit). Take 1st right and 300yds to site
★ ♨ £5-£7 ♨ £5-£8 ⅄ £5-£7
Open Good Fri/Apr-Oct (rs Apr-May & mid Sep-Oct limited stock kept in shop) Booking advisable mid Jul-Aug Last arrival 22.00hrs Last departure noon
A small, well maintained, level, grassy site midway between Truro and St Agnes. Some mature hedges divide pitches, and the toilet block is nicely painted and clean. This neat site makes an ideal touring centre, being midway between St Agnes and Truro. A 4-acre site with 30 touring pitches and 38 statics.
Covered sink area, drying lines.
Leisure: ◖ ⋀ Facilities: ♠ ☉ ⚒ ✳ ℄ ℥ ⊞
Services: ♨ ◙ ⊘ ⊞
→ ∪ ⏵ ⤻ ⚇ ⤻

► ► ► **Trevarth Holiday Park** *(SW744468)*
TR4 8HR ☎ 01872 560266
Dir: Leave A30 at Chiverton rdbt onto unclass rd signed Blackwater. Site on right in 200mtrs
♨ ♨ ⅄

Open Etr or Apr-Oct Booking advisable Jul-Aug Last arrival 22.00hrs Last departure noon
A compact, well screened site on high ground adjacent to A30/A39 junction. A 2-acre site with 30 touring pitches and 21 statics.
Leisure: ◖ ⋀ Facilities: ♠ ☉ ⚒ ✳ ℄
Services: ♨ ◙ ⓘ ⊘ ⊞
→ ∪ ⤻ ℥ ⬤ ☰ ▣

BODINNICK   Map 02 SX15

► ► ► **Yeate Farm Camp & Caravan Site**
(SX134526)
PL23 1LZ ☎ 01726 870256
Dir: From A390 at East Taphouse take B3359 signed Looe and Lanreath. Follow signs for Bodinnick on unclass rd
♨ ♨ ⅄
Open Apr-Oct Booking advisable mid Jul-mid Aug Last arrival 21.30hrs Last departure 11.00hrs
A small, level grass site adjacent to a working farm overlooking the River Fowey. The park has its own deep water moorings and slipway, and facilities are well kept. A 1-acre site with 33 touring pitches and 2 statics.
Private slipway/quay, storage of small boats.
Facilities: ♠ ☉ ⚒ ✳ 🛪 Services: ♨ ◙ ⓘ ⊘ ⊞
→ ∪ ⌂ ⤬ ⤻ ℥

BODMIN   Map 02 SX06

► ► ► **Camping & Caravanning Club Site**
(SX081676)
Old Callywith Rd PL31 2DZ ☎ 01208 73834
Dir: A30 from N, at sign for Bodmin turn right crossing dual carriageway in front of industrial estate, turn left at international sign, site left
★ ♨ £9.80-£12.40 ♨ £9.80-£12.40 ⅄ £9.80-£12.40
Open all year Booking advisable bank hols & Jul-Aug Last arrival 21.00hrs Last departure noon
Undulating grassy site with trees and bushes set in meadowland close to the town of Bodmin with all its attractions. The site is close to A30 and makes a very good touring base. Please see the advertisement on page 14 for details of Club Members' benefits. An 11-acre site with 175 touring pitches.
Leisure: ⋀ Facilities: ♠ ☉ ⚒ ✳ ℄ 🛪
Services: ♨ ◙ ⓘ ⊘ ⊞
→ ∪ ⏵ ⤻ ℥ ⬤ ☰

BOLVENTOR   Map 02 SX17

► ► ► ► **Colliford Tavern Campsite** *(SX171740)*
Colliford Lake, St Neot PL14 6PZ ☎ 01208 821335
Dir: Leave A30 1.25m W of Bolventor onto unclass rd signed Colliford Lake. Site 0.25m on left
♨ ♨ ⅄
Open Etr-Sep Booking advisable bank hols & Jul-Aug Last arrival 22.30hrs Last departure 11.00hrs
An oasis on Bodmin Moor, a small site with spacious grassy pitches and very good quality facilities. A 3.5-acre site with 40 touring pitches.
Facilities: ♠ ☉ ⚒ ✳ ℄ ⓺ ℄ ⊡ 🛪 Services: ♨ ⅄ ⓘ ⊘ ✗ ➘
→ ⤻ ⬤ ⬛ ☰ ▦ ▣ ▣

England

BOSWINGER   Map 02 SW94

PREMIER PARK

► ► ► ► ► **Sea View International Caravan & Camping Park (SW990412)**
PL26 6LL ☎ 01726 843425
Dir: From St Austell take B3273 signed Mevagissey. Turn right before entering village and follow brown tourist signs to site
★ 🏕 £5-£17.50 🚐 £5-£17.50 ⚠ £5-£17.50
Open Mon before Good Fri-Sep No Shop until May Booking advisable Aug Last arrival 22.00hrs Last departure 11.00hrs
This level, grassy site has been colourfully landscaped with flowers and shrubs and overlooks Veryan Bay. Many times a winner of AA awards in previous years for its beautiful environment and its dedication to high standards of maintenance. 0.5m from beach and sea. A 28-acre site with 165 touring pitches and 38 statics.
Crazy golf, volleyball, badminton courts, putting.
See advertisement under MEVAGISSEY
Leisure: 🏊 🎾 🎣 ⛰ **Facilities:** 🚽 🏪 ⊙ 🍴 ✳ ♿ 📞
🎰 🏛 🎪 🐕 **Services:** 🔌 🗑 🅿 🛢 🍴 🚿 📮
→ ◎ 🛒 ↯ 🍴 💷 💺 ▓ 🔋 🔵

BUDE   Map 02 SS20

Sandymouth Bay Holiday Park (SS214104)
Sandymouth Bay EX23 9HW
☎ 01288 352563 & 0831 213932
Dir: Signed off A39 approx 0.5m S of Kilkhampton, 4m N of Bude
🏕 🚐 ⚠
Open Apr-Oct Booking advisable Jul & Aug Last arrival 22.00hrs Last departure 10.00hrs
A friendly holiday park with glorious and extensive sea views. Many on-site facilities, and an on-site entertainment programme for all ages. A 4-acre site with 100 touring pitches and 125 statics.
Sauna & solarium.
Leisure: 🏊 🎣 ⛰ 🎱 **Facilities:** 🚽 ⊙ 🍴 ✳ ♿ 📞 🎰 🏛
Services: 🔌 🗑 🅿 🛢 🛒 🚰 🔋 🍴 🚿
→ ∪ ▶ 🛒 ↯ ↯ ↯ 🍴 💷 💺 ▓ 🔋 🔵

PREMIER PARK

► ► ► ► ► **Wooda Farm Park (SS229080)**
Poughill EX23 9HJ ☎ 01288 352069
Dir: 2m E. From A39 at edge of Stratton follow unclass Coombe Valley road
★ 🏕 £7.50-£11 🚐 £7.50-£11 ⚠ £7.50-£11
Open Apr-Oct (rs Apr-end May & mid Sep-end Oct shop hrs, laundrette/restaurant limited) Booking advisable Jul-Aug Last arrival 20.00hrs Last departure noon

contd.

Services: 🚰 Toilet Fluid   ✗ Café/ Restaurant   🍴 Fast Food/Takeaway   📮 Baby Care   🔌 Electric Hook Up   🗑 Launderette   💺 Licensed Bar   🛢 Calor Gaz   ⊘ Camping Gaz   🔋 Battery Charging

Attractive park set on raised ground overlooking Bude Bay, with lovely sea views. The park is divided into paddocks by hedges and mature trees, and offers high quality facilities and a variety of activities. The sandy surfing beaches are a short drive away. A 12-acre site with 160 touring pitches and 55 statics.
Coarse fishing, clay pigeon shoots, pets corner.

Leisure: ♦ ⋒ ▭ **Facilities:** ➡ ⋔ ☉ ♋ ⋇ ᕦ ℄
ᕳ ⋔ ↟ **Services:** ♨ ⊟ ♈ ⋒ ⊟ ⊡ ✕ ♨ ➡
→ ∪ ┠ ◎ ⟁ ⋋ ⅗ ⅃   ▱ ▱ ▱ ▱ ▱

▶ ▶ ▶ ▶ **Budemeadows Touring Holiday Park**
(SS215012)
EX23 0NA ☎ 01288 361646
Dir: 3m S of Bude on A39
★ ⌗ £8.90-£11.98 ⌗ £8.90-£11.98 ▲ £8.90-£11.98

Open all year (rs Oct-Spring bank hol shop & pool closed) Booking advisable Jul-Aug Last arrival 21.00hrs Last departure noon
A very well kept site of distinction, with good quality facilities. Budemeadows is set on a gentle sheltered slope in nine acres of naturally landscaped parkland, surrounded by mature hedges. Just one mile from the surf and sand of Widemouth Bay, and three miles from the unspoilt resort town of Bude. A 9-acre site with 146 touring pitches.
Outdoor table tennis & giant chess. Baby changing.

Leisure: ⋌ ♦ ⋒ ▭ **Facilities:** ➡ ⋔ ☉ ♋ ⋇ ᕦ ℄
ᕳ ⋒ ↟ ↟ **Services:** ♨ ⊟ ♈ ⊟ ♨
→ ∪ ┠ ◎ ⟁ ⋋ ⅗ ⅃   ▱ ▱ ▱ ▱ ▱

Facilities: ➡ Bath ⋔ Shower ☉ Electric Shaver ♋ Hairdryer ⋇ Ice Pack Facility ᕦ Disabled Facilities ℄ Public Telephone ᕳ Shop on Site or within 200yds ⊟ Mobile Shop (calls at least 5 days a week) ⋒ BBQ Area ↟ Picnic Area ↟ Dog Exercise Area

England

▶ ▶ ▶ *Willow Valley Holiday Park (SS236078)*
Bush EX23 9LB ☎ 01288 353104
Dir: On A39, 0.5m N of junct with A3072 at Stratton
🚐 🚙 ⚠

Open Mar-Dec Booking advisable Jul & Aug Last
arrival 21.00hrs Last departure noon
*Small sheltered park in Strat Valley with stream
running through. Level grassy pitches and direct
access off A39. A 3-acre site with 41 touring pitches
and 4 statics.*
Leisure: ⚙ Facilities: ℝ ⊙ ♥ ✳ ⭑ 🎣 🏧 🐾
Services: 🔌 🖲 🔋 ⊘ 🗲 Ⓣ
→ ∪ ℙ ☺ ⚠ ☇ ⏷ ⚃ 🍴 ➖ 🔀 🔳 🔳

CAMELFORD   Map 02 SX18

▶ ▶ ▶ *Lakefield Caravan Park (SX095853)*
Lower Pendavey Farm PL32 9TX ☎ 01840 213279
*Dir: From A39 in Camelford turn right onto B3266, then
right at T-junct and site 1.5m on left*
★ 🚐 £6-£11 🚙 £6-£11 ⚠ £6-£11
Open Etr or Apr-Oct Booking advisable Jul-Aug Last
arrival 22.00hrs Last departure noon
*Set in a rural location, this friendly park is part of a
specialist equestrian centre, and offers good quality
services. Riding lessons and hacks always available,
with BHS qualified instructor. A 5-acre site with 40
touring pitches.*
Own lake & full Equestrian Centre.
Leisure: ⚙ Facilities: ℝ ⊙ ♥ ✳ ⭑ ⭑ 🐾
Services: 🔌 🔋 ⊘ Ⓣ ✕
→ ℙ ☇ ⚃
See advertisement on page 65

CARBIS BAY   Map 02 SW53

▶ ▶ ▶ *Little Trevarrack Tourist Park (SW525379)*
Laity Ln TR26 3HW ☎ 10736 797580
*Dir: From A30 take A3074 signed 'Carbis Bay & St Ives',
and turn left onto unclass rd at Carbis Bay village*
🚐
Open May-Oct
*A pleasant grassy park set in countryside but close
to local amenities, and lovely nearby beaches.
A 20-acre site with 254 touring pitches.*

CARLEEN   Map 02 SW63

▶ ▶ ▶ *Lower Polladras Touring Park (SW617308)*
TR13 9NX ☎ 01736 762220
*Dir: From A394 turn onto B3302 Hayle road at Hilltop
Garage, then take 2nd turning on left to Carleen for site
2m on right*
🚐 🚙 ⚠

Open Apr-Oct Booking advisable Jul-Aug Last
arrival 22.00hrs Last departure noon
*A rural park with extensive views of the
surrounding fields, appealing to families who enjoy
the quiet countryside. The keen owners keep their
park immaculately clean and trimmed, and the
grassy pitches are spacious. A 4-acre site with 60
touring pitches.*
Leisure: ⚙ Facilities: ℝ ⊙ ♥ ✳ ⭑
Services: 🔌 🖲 🔋 ⊘ ⊞ Ⓣ
→ ∪ ℙ ⭑ ⚃

▶ ▶ ▶ *Poldown Caravan Park (SW629298)*
Poldown TR13 9NN ☎ 01326 574560
*Dir: From Helston follow Penzance signs for 1m then
right onto B3302 to Hayle, 2nd left to Carleen, continue
0.5m to site.*
🚐 £6.50-£9.50 🚙 £6.50-£9.50 ⚠ £6.50-£9.50
Open Apr-Oct (rs Apr & Oct Statics only) Booking
advisable Jul-Aug Last arrival 22.00hrs Last
departure noon
*A small, quiet site set in attractive countryside with
bright, newly painted toilet facilities. All of the level
grass pitches have electricity, and the sunny park is
sheltered by mature trees and shrubs. A 2-acre site
with 13 touring pitches and 7 statics.*
Leisure: ⚙ Facilities: ℝ ⊙ ♥ ✳ ⭑ 🐾
Services: 🔌 🖲 🔋 ⊘ ⊞
→ ∪ ℙ ☺ ⭑ ⚃

CARLYON BAY   Map 02 SX05

▶ ▶ ▶ ▶ *Carlyon Bay Caravan & Camping Park
(SX052526)*
Bethesda, Cypress Av PL25 3RE
☎ 01726 812735
*Dir: Off A390 W of St Blazey, turn left on A3092 for Par,
and right again in 0.5m. On private road to Carlyon
Bay*
🚐 🚙 ⚠
Open Etr-3 Oct (rs Etr-mid May & mid Sep-3 Oct
swimming pool/take-away/shop closed) Booking
advisable mid Jul-mid Aug Last arrival anytime Last
departure 11.00hrs
*An attractive, secluded site set amongst a belt of
trees with background woodland. The spacious
grassy park offers plenty of on-site attractions, with
occasional family entertainment, and is less than
0.5m from sandy beach. A 35-acre site with 180
touring pitches.*
Crazy golf, childrens entertainment in Jul & Aug.
Leisure: ⌇ ☘ ⚲ ⚙ 🎱 Facilities: ℝ ⊙ ♥ ✳ ⭑ 🎣 🏧 🐾
Services: 🔌 🖲 🔋 ⊘ ⊞ Ⓣ 🍴 ➡
→ ∪ ℙ ☺ ⚠ ⭑ ⚳ ⚃ 🍴 ➖ 🔀 🔳 🔳

▶ ▶ ▶ *East Crinnis Camping & Caravan Park
(SX062528)*
Lantyan, East Crinnis PL24 2SR
☎ 01726 813023
*Dir: From A390 Lostwithiel-St Austell road take A3082
signed Fowey, site on left*
🚐 ⚠
Open Etr-Oct Booking advisable Jul & Aug Last
arrival 23.00hrs Last departure noon
contd.

England

EAST CRINNIS CAMPING & CARAVAN PARK

East Crinnis is a spacious and landscaped park, set in secluded rural countryside on the beautiful south coast of Cornwall, ideal for a quiet relaxing holiday.

Lantyan, East Crinnis, Par, Cornwall PL24 2SQ
Tel: 01726 813023

Small rural park with spacious pitches set in individual bays about 1m from beaches and sea at Carlyon Bay. A 2-acre site with 25 touring pitches.

Leisure: ⚠ **Facilities:** ⚑☉✳ 🐕 **Services:** 🖸
→ ∪ ▶ ♨ ❊ 🕿 🎵 🖸 ♨

COVERACK   Map 02 SW71

► ► ► *Little Trevothan (SW772179)*
Trevothen TR12 6SD ☎ 01326 280260
Dir: *From A3083 turn left onto B3293 signed Coverack, approx 2m after Goonhilly ESS right at Zoar Garage on unclass rd. Take 3rd on left, site 0.5m on left*
🏕 🚐 🅰

Open Apr-Oct (rs Mar tents & tourers only) Booking advisable Aug Last arrival 21.00hrs Last departure noon
A level grassy park with mature hedging for shelter, in a peaceful rural location, close to unspoilt fishing village of Coverack. A 10.5-acre site with 65 touring pitches and 25 statics.
Leisure: ♦ ⚠ ☐ **Facilities:** ⚑☉🔍✳🕻💺⊞🖸 🐕
Services: 🖸 🏧 ⊞🖸
→ ♨ 🎵 🖸

CRANTOCK (Near Newquay) Map 02 SW76

► ► ► ► *Trevella Tourist Park (SW801599)*
TR8 5EW ☎ 01637 830308
Dir: *Between Crantock and A3075*
★ 🚐 £6.60-£11.80 🚐 £6-£11 🅰 £6.60-£11.80
Open Etr-Oct Booking advisable bank hols & Jul-Aug
A well established and very well run family site, with outstanding floral displays in rural area close to Newquay. This attractive park boasts three teeming fishing lakes for the experienced and novice angler, and a superb outdoor swimming pool and paddling area. All areas are neat and clean, and the facilities are spacious and comfortable. A 15-acre site with 295 touring pitches and 50 statics.
Crazy golf, fishing & badminton.
See advertisement under NEWQUAY
Leisure: ➘ ♦ ⚠ ☐ **Facilities:** ⚑☉🔍✳🕻💺⊞ 🐕
Services: 🖸 🖥🏧🖸⊞🖸✕ 🔌
→ ∪ ▶ ☺ ♨ ❊ 🕿 🎵 ● ■ 🔲 🔲 🔲 🖸

► ► ► *Crantock Plains Touring Park (SW805589)*
TR8 5PH ☎ 01637 830955 & 831273
Dir: *From A3075 take 3rd turning right signed Crantock. Site on left along a narrow lane*
★ 🚐 £4.50-£9 🚐 £4.50-£9 🅰 £4.50-£9
Open Etr/Apr-Sep Booking advisable Jul-Aug Last arrival 22.00hrs Last departure noon
A small farm site with level grassy touring pitches on two sides of a narrow lane, and surrounded by mature trees for shelter. The family-run park offers clean but fairly basic facitilies. A 6-acre site with 60 touring pitches.
Leisure: ♦ ⚠ **Facilities:** ⚑☉🔍✳🕻💺⊞ 🐕
Services: 🖸🖥🏧🖸
→ ∪ ▶ ♨ ❊ 🎵

► ► ► *Treago Farm Caravan Site (SW782601)*
TR8 5QS ☎ 01637 830277 & 830522
Dir: *From A3075 W of Newquay turn right for Crantock. Site signed beyond village*
🚐 🚐 🅰
Open mid May-mid Sep (rs Apr-mid May & Oct no shop or bar) Booking advisable Jun-Aug Last arrival 22.00hrs Last departure 18.00hrs
Grass site in open farmland in a south-facing sheltered valley. This friendly family park has direct access to Crantock and Polly Joke beaches, National Trust Land and many natural beauty spots. A 4-acre site with 92 touring pitches and 7 statics.
Leisure: ♦ ☐ **Facilities:** ⚑☉🔍✳🕻💺⊞🖸 🐕
Services: 🖸🖥🏧🖸⊞🖸
→ ∪ ▶ ☺ ♨ ❊ 🎵

CUBERT   Map 02 SW75

► ► ► *Cottage Farm (SW786589)*
Treworgans TR8 5HH ☎ 01637 831083
Dir: *From A392 towards Newquay, left onto A3075 towards Redruth. In 2m turn right signed for Cubert, right again in 1.5m signed Crantock and left in 0.5m*
🚐 🚐 🅰
Open Apr-Sep Booking advisable Last arrival 22.30hrs Last departure noon ❀
A small grassy touring park nestling in the tiny hamlet of Treworgans, in sheltered open countryside close to a lovely beach at Holywell Bay. This quiet family-run park boasts very good quality facilities. A 2-acre site with 45 touring pitches and 1 static.
Facilities: ⚑☉🔍✳🕻💺 **Services:** 🖸🖥🏧🖸⊞🔌
→ ∪ ▶ ☺ ♨ ❊ 🎵

Facilities: ➾ Bath ⚑ Shower ☉ Electric Shaver 🔍 Hairdryer ✳ Ice Pack Facility 🕻 Disabled Facilities 🕻 Public Telephone
💺 Shop on Site or within 200yds ⊞ Mobile Shop (calls at least 5 days a week) 🍴 BBQ Area 🔲 Picnic Area 🐕 Dog Exercise Area

DAVIDSTOW — Map 02 SX18

► ► ► *Inny Vale Holiday Village (SX170870)*
PL32 9XN ☎ 01840 261248 & 261740
Dir: Signed off A395 on single track road to Tremail, approx 1m from junct with A39
♨ ♨ 🅰
Open Etr-Oct Booking advisable

A level sheltered park with stream running through, adjacent to and enjoying benefit from small holiday bungalow village. A 2-acre site with 27 touring pitches.
shop
Leisure: ৎ ९ ⚠ Facilities: ⎚ ৭ ✳ ᵹ ৻ ⴾ ⊞ ⊓
Services: ⊕ ⎚ ⚲ 🛈 ⌀ ⊞ ⊤ ✕ 🖤
→ ► ᴊ

EDGCUMBE — Map 02 SW73

► ► ► Retanna Holiday Park (SW711327)
TR13 OEJ ☎ 01326 340643
Dir: 100mtrs off A394, signposted
♨ £5-£7.50 ♨ £5-£7.50 🅰 £5-£7.50
Open Apr-Oct Booking advisable Jul & Aug Last arrival 22.00hrs Last departure 11.00hrs
A small family-owned and run park in a rural location midway between Falmouth and Helston. Its well-sheltered grassy pitches make this an ideal location for visiting the lovely beaches and towns nearby. An 8-acre site with 24 touring pitches and 35 statics.
Leisure: ৻ ⚠ ⊓ Facilities: ⎚ ⊙ ৭ ✳ ৻ ⴾ ⊓ ⵟ
Services: ⊕ ⎚ 🛈 ⌀ ⊞ ⊤ 🖤
→ ∪ ► ⊚ ⚠ ᴊ ⚫ ⊟ ⵟ 🔲

FALMOUTH — Map 02 SW83

See also **Perranarworthal**
► ► ► ► Maen Valley Holiday Park (SW789311)
Roscarrick Rd TR11 5BJ ☎ 01326 312190
Dir: Leave A39 at Hillhead rdbt on Penryn bypass and follow signs to Maenporth and industrial estate. Site in 1.5m
★ ♨ £8-£12 ♨ £8-£12
Open Etr-Oct Booking advisable Jul & Aug Last arrival 22.00hrs
Set in a picturesque valley with a stream, this site offers rural tranquillity and well-kept facilities. The small touring area is at the top of the mainly holiday and residential park which is within walking distance of Swanpool Beach. A 16-acre site with 20 touring pitches and 94 statics.
Crazy golf.

Leisure: ৎ ৻ ⚠ Facilities: ⎚ ⊙ ✳ ৻ ⴾ ⊓ ⵟ
Services: ⊕ ⎚ ⚲ 🛈 ⌀ ⊞ ⊤ ✕ 🖤
→ ∪ ► ⊚ ⚠ ᴊ ✳ ⵟ ᴊ ⚫ ⊟ ⵟ 🔲

► ► ► Pennance Mill Farm Touring Park (SW792307)
Maenporth TR11 5HJ ☎ 01326 317431 & 312616
Dir: From A39 Truro-Falmouth follow brown 'Camping' signs towards Maenporth Beach
★ ♨ £2.50-£3 ♨ £2.50-£3 🅰 £2.50-£3
Open Etr-Xmas (rs Jan-Etr) Booking advisable Jan-Etr Last arrival 22.00hrs Last departure 10.00hrs
Set approximately half a mile from the safe, sandy Bay of Maenporth this is a mainly level, grassy, family-run farm park. A rural location sheltered by mature trees and shrubs and divided into three meadows. The farm has a large dairy herd and there is a milking parlour with viewing gallery. A 6-acre site with 75 touring pitches and 4 statics.
Leisure: ৎ ৻ ⚠ Facilities: ⎚ ⊙ ৭ ✳ ৻ ⴾ ⵟ
Services: ⊕ ⎚ 🛈 ⌀ ⊞ 🖤
→ ∪ ► ⊚ ⚠ ✳ ⵟ ᴊ

► ► ► *Tremorvah Tent Park (SW798313)*
Swanpool TR11 5BA
☎ 01326 318311 & 07977056432
Dir: In Falmouth follow signs to 'Beaches' and on to Swanpool. Site signed on right
♨ 🅰
Open mid May-Oct Booking advisable Jul-Aug Last arrival 22.00hrs Last departure 10.00hrs
A secluded tent park in a meadowland setting overlooking Swanpool Beach. No towed caravans. A 3-acre site with 72 touring pitches.
Dishwashing sinks & electric cooking hob.
Leisure: ৻ Facilities: ⎚ ⊙ ৭ ✳ ৻ ⴾ ⵟ
Services: ⎚ 🛈 ⌀ ⊞
→ ∪ ► ⊚ ⚠ ᴊ

FOWEY — Map 02 SX15

► ► ► *Penhale Caravan & Camping Park (SX104526)*
PL23 1JU ☎ 01726 833425
Dir: Off A A3082, 0.5m before junct with B3269
♨ ♨ 🅰
Open Etr/Apr-Oct Booking advisable for electric hook-ups

contd.

Services: ⊤ Toilet Fluid ✕ Café/ Restaurant 🖤 Fast Food/Takeaway ⵟ Baby Care ⊕ Electric Hook Up
⎚ Launderette ⚲ Licensed Bar 🛈 Calor Gaz ⌀ Camping Gaz ⊞ Battery Charging

England

Set on a working farm 1.5 m from sandy beach and town of Fowey, this grassy park has stunning coastal and country views. A 4.5-acre site with 56 touring pitches and 14 statics.
Leisure: ♦ Facilities: 🖳⊙🖳✳ Services: 🖵🖩🛢⌀
→ ∪ ▶ ♨ ↯ ♨ 🛒

GOONHAVERN   Map 02 SW75

► ► ► ► *Silverbow Park (SW782531)*
Perranwell TR4 9NX ☎ 01872 572347
Dir: Adjacent to A3075, 0.5m S of village
🚐 🚐 Å
Open mid May-mid Sep (rs mid Sep-Oct & Etr-mid May swimming pool & shop closed) Booking advisable Jul-Aug Last arrival 22.00hrs Last departure noon
This park has a quiet garden atmosphere, and appeals to families with young children. The landscaped grounds and good quality toilet facilities are maintained to a very high standard with attention paid to detail. No unaccompanied teenagers. A 14-acre site with 100 touring pitches and 15 statics.
Badminton courts, short mat bowls rink.
Leisure: ⚲ ♦ ♦ 🅰 Facilities: 🛠🖳⊙🖳✳🖖🛒🖵🖻🛒
Services: 🖵🖩🛢⌀🔲🔲
→ ∪ ▶ ↯

See advert on page 65

► ► ► *Perran Springs Touring Park (SW796535)*
TR4 9QG ☎ 01872 540568
Dir: Leave A30 right onto B3285 to Perranporth. Follow tourist signs marked Perran Springs for 1.5m, entrance clearly marked
★ 🚐 £7-£11 🚐 £7-£11 Å £7-£11
Open Apr-Oct Booking advisable Jul-Aug Last arrival anytime Last departure 10.00hrs
A grassy open park in a quiet position offering comfortable, modern facilities. The park has its own fishing lake which is open to all visitors for coarse fishing, and the family owners are constantly improving the amenities. A 21-acre site with 120 touring pitches and 1 static.
Coarse fishing lake
Leisure: 🅰 Facilities: 🖳⊙🖳✳🖖🛒🛒
Services: 🖵🖩🛢⌀🔲🔲✕🖖
→ ∪ ▶ ♨ ↯

► ► ► *Roseville Holiday Park (SW787540)*
TR4 9LA ☎ 01872 572448
Dir: From mini rdbt in Goonhavern follow B3285 towards Perranporth, site 0.5m on right
🚐 🚐 Å
Open Whit-Oct (rs Etr-Whit shop) Booking advisable Jul-Aug Last arrival 21.30hrs Last departure 11.00hrs
Recently upgraded to a very high standard, this family park is set in a rural location, with sheltered, mostly level pitches. An attractive swimming pool complex has been added, plus a new shop, and the friendly owners keep everything spotlessly clean and tidy. A 7-acre site with 95 touring pitches.
Off-licence in shop.

See advert on page 65

Leisure: ⚲ ♦ 🅰 🖵 Facilities: 🖳⊙🖳✳🖳🖖🛒🛒
Services: 🖵🖩🛢⌀🔲🔲🖖🛒
→ ∪ ▶ ⊙ ↯

GORRAN   Map 02 SW94

► ► ► *Tregarton Park (SW984437)*
PL26 6NF ☎ 01726 843666
Dir: From St Austell travel south on B3273, at top of Pentewan Hill turn right towards Gorran and follow tourist signs
★ 🚐 £6-£13 🚐 £6-£13 Å £6-£13

Open Etr-Oct Booking advisable Jun-Sep Last arrival 22.00hrs Last departure 11.00hrs
A sheltered park set in lovely countryside lying two miles from the sea and off a minor road to Gorran Haven. Many of the facilities have been upgraded and improved, and this friendly park attracts couples and families who want a quiet holiday. A 12-acre site with 125 touring pitches.
Camping equipment for sale, Off Licence.
Leisure: ⚲ 🅰 Facilities: 🖳⊙🖳✳🖖🛒🖻🛒
Services: 🖵🖩🛢⌀🔲🔲🖖🛒
→ ∪ ▶ ♨ ↯ 🔲🔲🔲🔲🔲🔲

► ► ► *Treveor Farm Caravan & Camping Site (SW988418)*
PL26 6LW ☎ 01726 842387
Dir: St Austell bypass left onto B3273 for Mevagissey. On hilltop before descent to village turn right on unclass for Gorran. Right in 3.5m, site on right
🚐 £7-£13 🚐 £7-£13 Å £7-£13
Open Apr-Oct Booking advisable ASAP Last arrival 20.00hrs Last departure 11.00hrs
A small family run camping park with good facilities, situated on a working farm. There is a large coarse fishing pond, and this quiet park is close to the beaches. A 4-acre site with 50 touring pitches.
Coarse fishing.
Leisure: 🅰 Facilities: 🖳⊙🖳✳ Services: 🖵🖩🔲
→ ∪ ↯ ↯ 🛒

GORRAN HAVEN   Map 02 SX04

► ► *Trelispen Caravan & Camping Park (SX008421)*
PL26 6HT ☎ 01726 843501
Dir: From St Austell bypass take B3273 for Mevagissey. At X-rds signed 'No caravans beyond this point', right on unclass rd through Gorran to site on left
🚐 £8-£12 🚐 £8-£10 Å £8-£10

Facilities: 🛠 Bath 🖳 Shower ⊙ Electric Shaver 🖳 Hairdryer ✳ Ice Pack Facility 🖖 Disabled Facilities 🛒 Public Telephone
🛒 Shop on Site or within 200yds 🔲 Mobile Shop (calls at least 5 days a week) 🖻 BBQ Area 🖵 Picnic Area 🛒 Dog Exercise Area

Open Etr & Apr-Oct Booking advisable Last arrival 22.00hrs Last departure noon
A very basic site in a beautiful, quiet location within easy reach of beaches. A 2-acre site with 40 touring pitches.
A 30 acre nature reserve may be visited.
Leisure: /⚲\ Facilities: ⌐⊙✳☪ Services: ⊞⊡⋮∅
→⚱✦♪

HAYLE   Map 02 SW53

St Ives Bay Holiday Park (SW577398)
73 Loggans Rd, Upton Towans
TR27 5BH ☎ 01736 752274
Dir: Exit A30 at Hayle. Immediate right at mini-rdbts. Park entrance 0.5m on right
★ ⊞ £6-£17 ⊞ £6-£17 ▲ £6-£17
Open 3 May-27 Sep (rs Etr-3 May & 27 Sep-25 Oct no entertainment, food & bar service)
Booking advisable Jan-Mar Last arrival 23.00hrs
Last departure 09.00hrs
An excellently maintained holiday park with a relaxed atmosphere, built on sand dunes adjacent to a three-mile long beach. The touring section forms a number of separate locations in amongst the statics. A 90-acre site with 240 touring pitches and 250 statics.
Crazy golf, video room.
Leisure: ₹ ⚲ /⚲\ ▭ Facilities: ⌐⊙⚑✳⌂♨☪↟
Services: ⊞⊡⊻⋮∅⊞⊤✖⛟
→∪▶♪ ☎▦▦▦ ▧⑤

▶ ▶ ▶ *Higher Trevaskis Caravan Park (SW611381)*
Gwinear Rd, Conner Downs TR27 5JQ
☎ 01209 831736
Dir: At Hayle rdbt on A30 take 1st exit signed Connor Downs, in 1m turn right signed Carnhell Green. Site 0.75m just past level crossing
⊞ ⊞ ▲
Open mid Apr-mid Oct Booking advisable May-Sep
Last arrival 20.00hrs Last departure 11.00hrs
Rural grassy park divided into sheltered paddocks, and with views towards St Ives. Fluent German spoken. A 6.5-acre site with 82 touring pitches.
Leisure: /⚲\ Facilities: ⌐⊙⚑✳⌂☪↟
Services: ⊞⊡⋮∅⊞⊤
→▶⊚⚱✦♪

▶ ▶ ▶ *Parbola Holiday Park (SW612366)*
Wall, Gwinear TR27 5LE ☎ 01209 831503
Dir: At Hayle rdbt on A30 take Connor Downs exit. In 1m turn right signed Carnhell Green. In village right to Wall and site in village on left
★ ⊞ £7.50-£13 ⊞ £7.50-£13 ▲ £7.50-£13
Open Etr-Sep (rs Etr-spring bank hol & Sep shop & takeaway closed) Booking advisable Jul-Aug Last arrival 22.00hrs Last departure noon ⌦
A level grassy site in Cornish downland, with pitches in both woodland and open grassy areas. A 17.5-acre site with 110 touring pitches and 28 statics.
Crazy golf, bike hire & table tennis

contd.

Services: ⊤ Toilet Fluid ✖ Café/ Restaurant ⛟ Fast Food/Takeaway � Baby Care ⊞ Electric Hook Up
⊡ Launderette ⊻ Licensed Bar ⋮ Calor Gaz ∅ Camping Gaz ⊞ Battery Charging

Leisure: ⚡ ◣ ⚠ ▢ Facilities: ☺ ⊙ ® ☀ ♿ ☎ ⚑ ♨
Services: 🔌 🗑 🛈 🚿 ⊞ ⊤ ⚓
→ ∪ ► ⊙ ♪ ● ▬ ▨ ▨

HELSTON   Map 02 SW62

► ► ► **Trelowarren Caravan & Camping Park**
(SW721238)
Mawgan TR12 6AF ☎ 01326 221637
*Dir: From Helston on A3083 turn left past Culdrose
Naval Air Station on to B3293. Site signed on left in
1.5m*
★ 🚐 £6.50-£8 🚐 £6.50-£8 ⛺ £6.50-£8
Open Apr-Sep Booking advisable bank hols & Jul-
Aug Last departure noon
*A very attractive setting in the extensive park of
Trelowarren House. A 20-acre site with 225 touring
pitches.*
Leisure: ◣ ⚠ ▢ Facilities: ➼ ® ⊙ ® ☀ ♿ ☎ ⚑ ♨ �🎋 🐕
Services: 🔌 🗑 🍴 🛈 ⌀ ⊞ ⊤ ✕ ⚓ ➼
→ ∪

HOLYWELL BAY   Map 02 SW75

Trevornick Holiday Park (SW776586)
TR8 5PW ☎ 01637 830531
*Dir: 3m from Newquay off A3075
Newquay to Redruth road. Follow signs to Cubert
and Holywell bay*
★ 🚐 £6.80-£12.30 🚐 £6.80-£12.30 ⛺ £6.80-£12.30
Open Etr & mid May-mid Sep Booking advisable
Jul-Aug Last arrival 21.00hrs Last departure
10.00hrs
*A large seaside holiday complex with excellent
facilities and amenities. There is plenty of
entertainment including a children's club and an
evening cabaret, on a park which offes a full
family holiday experience. A sandy beach is a
15-minute footpath walk away. A 20-acre site
with 450 touring pitches and 60 statics.*
Fishing, golf course, entertainment.

See advertisement under NEWQUAY

Leisure: ⚡ ◣ ⚠ Facilities: ➼ ® ⊙ ® ☀ ♿ ☎
⚑ 🎋 🐕 Services: 🔌 🗑 🍴 🛈 ⌀ ⊞ ⊤ ✕ ⚓
→ ∪ ► ⊙ ♨ ↘ ♪ ● ▬ ▨ ▨

► ► ► ► **Holywell Bay Holiday Park (SW773582)**
TR8 5PR ☎ 01637 871111
*Dir: Leave A30 onto A392, take A3075 signed Redruth,
then left in 2m signed Holywell/Cubert. Follow road
through Cubert past Trevornick to park on left*
★ 🚐 £6.80-£12.80 🚐 £6.80-£12.80 ⛺ £6.80-£12.80
Open mid May-mid Sep Booking advisable Jun-Aug
Last arrival 21.00hrs Last departure 10.00hrs ⌘
*Close to lovely local beaches in a rural location, this
level grassy park borders on National Trust land,
and is only a short distance from the Cornish
Coastal Path. The park provides a family
entertainment programme for young and old. Some
pitches are rather small and cramped. A 2.5-acre
site with 75 touring pitches and 149 statics.*
Leisure: ⚡ ⚠ Facilities: ® ⊙ ☎ 🎋 ♨ ⚑
Services: 🔌 🗑 🍴 🛈 ⌀ ⊞ ⊤ ⚓
→ ∪ ► ⊙ ♨ ♪ ● ▬ ▨

Enjoy the real warmth of Cornwall

VOTED ONE OF THE TOP 100 Touring Parks

among our sheltered orchards and walled
gardens, on a 1000 acre Cornish manor close to
Frenchman's Creek on the Helford river.

Electric hook-ups, Hard standings (electric), Rallies welcome,
Gas, Take-away & Pub, Heated toilets & showers

SOME SEASONAL PITCHES AVAILABLE

TRELOWARREN
Touring Caravan & Camping Park

Trelowarren, Mawgan, Helston, Cornwall TR12 6AF.
Telephone: 01326 221637

INDIAN QUEENS   Map 02 SW95

► **Gnome World Touring Park (SW890599)**
Moorland Rd TR9 6HN ☎ 01726 860812
*Dir: Signed from slip road at A30 and A39 rdbt at village
of Indian Queens - park is on old A30, now unclass*
🚐 🚐 ⛺
Open Etr-Oct (rs Nov-Mar) Booking advisable Jul-
Aug Last arrival 22.00hrs Last departure noon
*A level grassy park set in extensive farmland.
A 4.5-acre site with 50 touring pitches.
Nature trail.*
Leisure: ⚠ Facilities: ® ⊙ ® ☀ ♿ ☎ 🎋 🐕
Services: 🔌 ⌀ ⊞
→ ∪ ♪ 🗑

JACOBSTOW   Map 02 SX19

► ► ► **Edmore Tourist Park (SX187955)**
Edgarrd, Wainhouse Corner EX23 0BJ
☎ 01840 230467
★ 🚐 £6-£7 🚐 £6-£7 ⛺ £6-£7
Open Etr-Oct Booking advisable peak periods Last
departure noon
*Small, family run, rural campsite in good location,
just off main A39 at Wainhouse Corner, and signed.
A 3-acre site with 28 touring pitches and 2 statics.*
Leisure: ⚠ ▢ Facilities: ® ⊙ ® ☀ ☎
Services: 🔌 🗑 🛈 ⌀ ⊞
→ 🏕 🎋

KENNACK SANDS — Map 02 SW71

▶ ▶ ▶ *Chy-Carne Holiday Park (SW725164)*
Kuggar, Ruan Minor TR12 7LX ☎ 01326 290200
Dir: From A3083 turn left on B3293 after Culdrose Naval Air Station. At Goonhilly ESS right into unclass road signed Kennack Sands. Left in 3m at junct
🚐 Å
Open Etr-Oct Booking advisable Aug
Small but spacious park in quiet, sheltered spot, with extensive sea and coastal views from the grassy touring area. A 6-acre site with 14 touring pitches and 18 statics.
Leisure: ♣ Facilities: ⋒⊙🖤✳&⋐🐾⊱
Services: 🔌🗑🛢🖋⊞

▶ ▶ ▶ *Gwendreath Farm Caravan Park (SW738168)*
TR12 7LZ ☎ 01326 290666
Dir: From A3083 turn left past Culdrose Naval Air Station onto B3293. Right past Goonhilly ESS signed Kennack Sands and left in 1m
🚐🚐Å

Open Etr-Oct Booking advisable all times Last departure 10.00hrs
A grassy park in elevated position with extensive sea and coastal views. A short walk through woods to the beach. A 5-acre site with 10 touring pitches and 30 statics.
Leisure: ⚠ Facilities: ⋒⊙✳⋐🐾🔥⊱
Services: 🔌🗑🛢🖋⊞T➡
→ ⋃ ⊢ ⊙ ♠ ✦

▶ ▶ ▶ *Silver Sands Holiday Park (SW727166)*
Gwendreath TR12 7LZ ☎ 01326 290631
Dir: From Helston take A3083, then B3293, after 4m right at X-roads signed Kennack Sands, continue 1.5m, left at sign for Gwendreath, park 0.5m down lane
★ 🚐 £6-£7.50 🚐 £6-£7.50 Å £6-£7.50
Open May-Sep Booking advisable Jul-Aug Last arrival 22.00hrs Last departure 11.00hrs
A small park in a remote location with individually screened pitches providing sheltered sun-traps. This family-owned park has access to the shop, bar/restaurant and takeaway at an adjacent park. A 9-acre site with 34 touring pitches and 16 statics.
Leisure: ⚠ Facilities: ⋒⊙🖤✳⋐🐾🔥⊱
Services: 🔌🗑🛢🖋⊞
→ ⋃♠✦ ✦

KILKHAMPTON — Map 02 SS21

▶ ▶ ▶ ▶ *Penstowe Caravan & Camping Park (SS230100)*
Penstowe Manor EX23 9QY
☎ 01288 321601 & 321354
Dir: 5m N of Bude, 200yds off A39
★ 🚐 £6.50-£12.50
Open Mar-mid Nov Booking advisable August Last arrival 23.00hrs Last departure noon
Newly opened in 2000, this all touring park has high quality facilities. Located approximately two miles from Sandymouth Bay with its sandy beaches and surf, this park has all level hardstanding and grassy pitches. It has the advantage of the adjoining Penstone Leisure Club which is just 0.25 mile away, on a private road through the estate. Some of the amenities require a small membership charge. A 6-acre site with 65 touring pitches.
Leisure: ⚡ ⚡♣⚠🏊 Facilities: ⊙🖤✳&⋐🐾🔥⊱
Services: 🔌🗑🍸🛢🖋✕🔌
→ ⋃⊢✦ 🍴 🚂 📠 🗄

LANDRAKE — Map 02 SX36

▶ ▶ ▶ *Dolbeare Caravan & Camping Park (SX363616)*
St Ive Rd PL12 5AF ☎ 01752 851332
Dir: A38 to Landrake, 4m W of Saltash. At footbridge over A38 turn N following signs to the site, located 0.75m from A38
🚐 £7.50-£8.50 🚐 £7.50-£8.50 Å £2.50-£8.50
Open all year Booking advisable peak periods only Last arrival 23.00hrs
A mainly level grass site with trees and bushes set in meadowland. A 4-acre site with 60 touring pitches.
Volley ball pitch, Boules pitch, Info Centre.
Leisure: ⚠ Facilities: ⋒⊙🖤✳⋐🐾🔥🔥⊱
Services: 🔌🗑🛢🖋⊞T
→⊢✦♨✦

LAND'S END — Map 02 SW32

▶ ▶ ▶ *Sea View Holiday Park (SW356253)*
TR19 7AD ☎ 01736 871266
Dir: 0.5m from Land's End, with direct access from A30
🚐
Open all year (rs Nov-Feb not all shower blocks open) Booking advisable bank holidays & Aug
Grassy park with sea views from all areas. This rather basic park is being upgraded gradually by friendly family owners, who have just added a heated outdoor swimming pool. A 6-acre site with 100 touring pitches and 75 statics.
Leisure: ⚠ Facilities: ⋒🖤✳⋐🐾🔥🔥
Services: 🔌🗑🛢🖋⊞T✕🔌
→ ⋃♠✦ 🍴 🚂 🗄

LAUNCELLS — Map 02 SS20

▶ ▶ ▶ *Red Post Holiday Park (SS264052)*
EX23 9NW ☎ 01288 381305
Dir: At junct of A3072/B3254, 4m from Bude
🚐 £6.50-£8.50 🚐 £6.50-£8.50 Å £4-£8.50 *contd.*

Open 31 Mar-Oct Booking advisable Jul & Aug Last arrival 23.00hrs Last departure 11.00hrs
A basic site at rear of a country inn. A 4-acre site with 50 touring pitches.
Leisure: ⚙ **Facilities:** ⓝ☉✳✆⚑⎈⊓
Services: ⊕◉⓪⊡⊺✕♨
→ ∪ ⍑ ☺ ♨ ♪

LEEDSTOWN (NEAR HAYLE) Map 02 SW63

► ► ► ► *Calloose Caravan & Camping Park (SW597352)*
TR27 5ET ☎ 01736 850431
Dir: *Follow B3302 from Duke of Leeds pub in village centre for 0.5m*
⌂⌂🅰
Open Apr-Oct (rs Apr-mid May & late Sep swimming pool) Booking advisable Etr, May bank hols & Jun-Aug Last arrival 22.00hrs Last departure 11.00hrs
A comprehensively equipped leisure park in a remote rural setting in a small river valley. A 12.5-acre site with 120 touring pitches and 17 statics. Crazy golf, skittle alley & fishing

See advertisement under HAYLE

Leisure: ⌇✎♠⚙⌷ **Facilities:** ⓝ☉⍨✳✆⚑⎈⊞⌸
Services: ⊕◉⓪⚿⊡⊺✕♨
→ ♪ ⬤ 💱 📧 🏧 🈂

LISKEARD   Map 02 SX26

► ► ► **Pine Green Caravan & Camping Site (SX195646)**
Doublebois PL14 6LE ☎ 01579 320183
Dir: *From M5 join A38 to Plymouth, head for Dobwalls through 2 sets of lights and take B3360 Lostwithiel to St Austell road. Site 200yds on right*
★ ⌂ £6-£10 ⌂ £6-£10 🅰 £5-£8
Open all year Booking advisable high season Last arrival 22.00hrs Last departure noon
A well-kept terraced site in a good touring location with scenic views over surrounding countryside and Fowey River Valley. A 3-acre site with 50 touring pitches and 1 static.
Facilities: ⓝ☉⍨✳✆⊓⚓ **Services:** ⊕◉⚿⊘
→ ⍑♨⚞♪⚓

LOOE   Map 02 SX25

Tencreek Holiday Park (SX233525)
PL13 2JR ☎ 01503 262447 & 01831 411843
Dir: *Take A387 1.25m from Looe. Site on left*
★ ⌂ £7.50-£13.50 ⌂ £7.50-£13.50 🅰 £7.50-£13.50
Open all year Booking advisable Jul & Aug Last arrival 23.00hrs Last departure 10.00hrs
Occupying a lovely position with extensive countryside and sea views, this holiday centre is in a rural spot but close to Looe and Polperro. There is a full family entertainment programme, with indoor and outdoor swimming pools and

Facilities: ⇥ Bath ⓝ Shower ☉ Electric Shaver ⍨ Hairdryer ✳ Ice Pack Facility ✆ Disabled Facilities ⎈ Public Telephone ⚑ Shop on Site or within 200yds ⊡ Mobile Shop (calls at least 5 days a week) ⊞ BBQ Area ⊓ Picnic Area ⚓ Dog Exercise Area

an adventure playground. Families and couples only accepted. A 14-acre site with 254 touring pitches and 85 statics.
Nightly entertainment & solarium. 45m Flume in Pool
Leisure: ⤳ ⤳ ⚑ ⚜ **Facilities:** ⌂⊙🌂☀⚒🛒⚞🛒🐾
Services: 🔌🗑🍷🔒⌀⊞🚽✗♨
→ ∪ 🍴⚐⚒ 🐾 🍽 🚮 ⟷ ▦ ▦ 🎮

▶ ▶ ▶ *Camping Caradon (SX218539)*
Trelawne PL13 2NA ☎ 01503 272388
Dir: Signed off B3359 near junc with A387, between Looe and Polperro
🔌 🚐 ⚑
Open Etr-Oct Booking advisable Jul-Aug Last arrival 20.00hrs Last departure 11.00hrs
A quiet touring park in a grassy, rural setting, midway betweeen Looe and Polperro. The park is kept clean and tidy, and there is a licensed bar and clubhouse. A 4-acre site with 85 touring pitches and 1 static.
Leisure: ⚜ ⛱ **Facilities:** ⌂⊙🌂☀⚒🛒
Services: 🔌🗑🍷🔒⌀⊞🚽✗♨
→ ∪⊙⚐⚒ 🐾 🍽

▶ ▶ ▶ *Polborder House Caravan & Camping Park (SX283557)*
Bucklawren Rd, St Martins PL13 1QR
☎ 01503 240265
Dir: On approaching Looe from E on A387, follow B3253 for 1m, then bear left at signpost to Polborder & Monkey Sanctuary. Site 0.5m on right
★ 🚐 £6-£9.50 🚐 £6-£9.50 ⚑ £6-£9.50
Open Etr or Apr-Oct Booking advisable Jul-Aug Last arrival 22.00hrs Last departure noon
A very neat and well-kept small grassy site on high ground above Looe in a peaceful rural setting. Friendly and enthusiastic owners. A 3-acre site with 36 touring pitches and 5 statics.
Washing/food prep sinks, Off-licence, Info Centre
Leisure: ⚜ **Facilities:** ⌂⊙🌂☀⚒🛒🛒
Services: 🔌🗑🔒⌀⊞🚽↩
→ ∪🍴⊙⚐⚒ 🍽 ▦

▶ ▶ ▶ *Talland Barton Caravan Park (SX220510)*
Talland Bay PL13 2JA ☎ 01503 272715
Dir: 1m from A387 on unclass road to Talland Bay
★ 🚐 £7-£14 🚐 £7-£11
Open Apr-Oct Booking advisable School hols

Overlooking the sea just 300 yards from Talland Bay's two beaches, this quiet park has an elevated grassy touring area with sea views. Surrounded by unspoilt countryside and with direct access to the coastal footpath it is approximately halfway between Looe anmd Polperro. A 4-acre site with 80 touring pitches and 46 statics.
Leisure: ⚜ **Facilities:** ⊙☀⚒🛒🛒🎗🗂🐾
Services: 🔌🗑🍷🔒⌀⊞🚽✗♨
→🍴⚐⚒⚒ 🐾 🍽 ⟷ 🚮 🎮

▶ ▶ ▶ *Tregoad Farm Touring Caravan & Camping Park (SX272560)*
St Martin's PL13 1PB ☎ 01503 262718
Dir: Signed with direct access from B3253, or from E on A387 follow B3253 for 1.75m towards Looe and site on left
🔌 🚐 ⚑
Open Apr-Oct Booking advisable Jul & Aug Last arrival 21.00hrs
A terraced grassy site with fine sea and rural views, approx 1.5m from Looe. This quiet family-run park has a relaxed, friendly atmosphere. A 10-acre site with 150 touring pitches and 4 statics.
Fishing lake.
Leisure: ⚑ ⚜ **Facilities:** ⌂⊙🌂☀⚒🛒🗂🗂🐾
Services: 🔌🗑🍷🔒⌀⊞🚽✗♨
→ ∪ 🍴⊙⚐⚒⚒ 🐾 🍽 ⟷ ◯ 🚮 🎮

▶ ▶ ▶ *Trelay Farmpark (SX219545)*
PL13 2JX ☎ 01503 220900
Dir: On B3359 towards Pelynt, 1m on right
★ 🚐 £7-£8.50 🚐 £6-£8.50 ⚑ £6-£8.50
Open Apr-Oct Booking advisable Jul & Aug Last arrival 21.00hrs
A slightly sloping, grass site in a rural area with extensive views. 3m from Looe and Polperro. A 3-acre site with 55 touring pitches and 20 statics.
Facilities: ⌂⊙🌂☀⚒🛒🗂🗂 **Services:** 🔌🗑🔒⌀⊞↩
→ ∪⚐⚒ 🐾 🍽 🛒

LOSTWITHIEL   Map 02 SX15
▶ ▶ ▶ *Powderham Castle Tourist Park (SX083593)*
PL30 5BU ☎ 01208 872277
Dir: 1.5m SW of Lostwithiel on A390 turn right at brown/white signpost in 400mtrs
★ 🚐 £6.90-£9.80 🚐 £6.90-£9.80 ⚑ £6.90-£9.80
Open Apr-Oct Booking advisable peak periods Last arrival 22.00hrs Last departure 11.30hrs   *contd.*

Services: 🅣 Toilet Fluid ✗ Café/ Restaurant ♨ Fast Food/Takeaway ↩ Baby Care 🔌 Electric Hook Up
🗑 Launderette 🍷 Licensed Bar 🔒 Calor Gaz ⌀ Camping Gaz ⊞ Battery Charging

A very quiet and well-run site in a good touring location, set in mature parkland and well screened. A 12-acre site with 70 touring pitches and 38 statics. Badminton, soft tennis, children's paddling pool.

Leisure: ⚓ ⚁ ⌷ **Facilities:** ⌐ ☉ ⚑ ✳ ⚲ ⊞ ⋔ **Services:** ☎ 🅑 🅰 ⌀ ⊞
→ ∪ ⌐ ♣ ↙ ✦ ⚲

LUXULYAN · Map 02 SX05

▶ ▶ ▶ Croft Farm Holiday Park (SX044568)
PL30 5EQ ☎ 01726 850228
Dir: From A30 left off Bodmin bypass onto A391, left at lights at Bugle onto B3374, turn left at Penwithick signed Trethurgy/Luxulyan. In 1.75m turn left at T-junct and site on left in 0.5m. Do not take any other routes signed Luxulyan or Luxulyan Valley.
🚐 🚐 ▲
Open Apr-Oct Booking advisable Jul & Aug Last departure noon
A peaceful, picturesque setting at the edge of a wooded valley, and only 1m from 'The Eden Project', Cornwall's new biodomes. A 5-acre site with 45 touring pitches and 8 statics.
Mother & baby room.
Leisure: ⚓ ⚁ **Facilities:** ⌐ ☉ ⚑ ✳ ⚲ ⚞ ⤳ ⋔
Services: ☎ 🅑 🅰 ⌀ ⊞ ⊤
→ ✦ ⊞ ⌦ ⊟ 🔲

MARAZION · See St Hilary

MAWGAN · See Helston

MAWGAN PORTH · Map 02 SW86

▶ ▶ ▶ ▶ Sun Haven Valley Holiday Park (SW861669)
TR8 4BQ ☎ 01637 860373
Dir: From B3276 at Mawgan Porth take unclass road along Vale of Lanherne for 1m. Site on left
★ 🚐 £8.50-£12.50 🚐 £8.50-£12.50 ▲ £8.50-£12.50
Open all year (rs Oct-Mar Chalets only) Booking advisable Jul-Aug Last arrival 22.00hrs Last departure 11.00hrs

An attractive site set on the side of a river valley with a camping area alongside the stream with level pitches. The very high quality facilities include a TV lounge and games room in a Swedish-style chalet, a well-kept adventure playground and a good shop.

Trees and hedges fringe the park, and the grounds are well-drained and level. Not far from the golden beach and other amenities of Mawgan Porth. A 5-acre site with 118 touring pitches and 36 statics.
See advertisement under NEWQUAY

Leisure: ⚓ ⚁ ⌷ **Facilities:** ➡ ⌐ ☉ ⚑ ✳ ⚲ ⚲ ⚞ ⊞ ⋔
Services: ☎ 🅑 🅰 ⌀ ⊤
→ ∪ ⌐ ☉ ✦ 🔘 ⌦ ⊠ 🔲

▶ ▶ ▶ Trevarrian Holiday Park (SW853661)
TR8 4AQ ☎ 01637 860381 & 01637 860495
Dir: From A39 at St Columb rdbt turn right onto A3059 towards Newquay. Fork right in approx 2m for St Mawgan onto B3276. Turn right and site on left
🚐 🚐 ▲
Open Etr-Sep Booking advisable Jun-Aug Last arrival 22.00hrs Last departure 11.00hrs
A well-established and well-run holiday park overlooking Mawgan Porth beach. This park has a wide range of attractions including a free entertainment programme in peak season. A 7-acre site with 185 touring pitches.
Sports field & pitch n putt.
See advertisement under NEWQUAY

Leisure: ⚐ ⚐ ⚓ ⚁ ⌷ **Facilities:** ➡ ⌐ ☉ ⚑ ✳ ⚲ ⚞
Services: ☎ 🅑 🅨 🅰 ⌀ ⊞ ⊤ ✕
→ ∪ ⌐ ☉ ✤ ☸ ✦ ⌦ ⊠

MEVAGISSEY

See Gorran, Boswinger & Pentewan

MULLION · Map 02 SW61

Mullion Holiday Park (SW699182)
Lizard Peninsula, A3083 TR12 7LJ
☎ 01326 240000 & 240428
Dir: Adjacent to A3083 Helston road
🚐 🚐 ▲
Open Etr & May-mid Sep Booking advisable Jul-Aug Last arrival 21.00hrs Last departure 10.00hrs
A comprehensively equipped leisure park geared mainly for self-catering holidays, set in rugged moorland on the Lizard peninsula. A 10-acre site with 150 touring pitches and 347 statics.
Adventure playgrounds, sandpit, amusement arcade.
Leisure: ⚐ ⚐ ⚓ ⚁ ⌷ **Facilities:** ⌐ ☉ ✳ ⚲ ⚞
⚞ ⤳ ⤳ ⋔ **Services:** ☎ 🅑 🅨 🅰 ⌀ ⊞ ✕ 🚿 ✦
→ ∪ ⌐ ✦ ⊞ ⌦ 🔘 ⊠ 🔲
See advert on page 56

▶ ▶ ▶ 'Franchis' Holiday Park (SW698203)
Cury Cross Lanes TR12 7AZ ☎ 01326 240301
Dir: Off A3088 on left 0.5m past Cury, between Helston & The Lizard
★ 🚐 £8-£9 🚐 £8-£9 ▲ £8-£9
Open Wed before Etr-Sep (rs low season shop open on request) Booking advisable end Jul-Aug Last arrival 22.00hrs Last departure noon

---

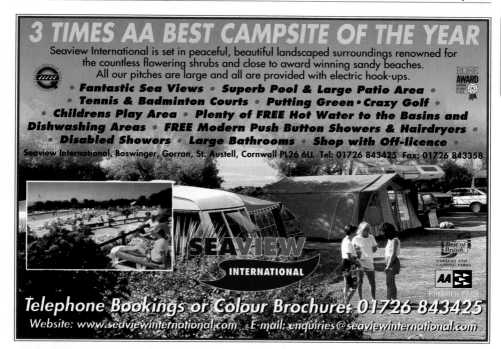

A level grassy site surrounded by hedges and coppices, and divided into two paddocks for tourers, in an ideal position for exploring the Lizard peninsula. A 4-acre site with 70 touring pitches and 12 statics.
Licensed shop
Facilities: ℞ ⊙ ⌁ ※ ⌂ ⛷ ➟ **Services:** ♨ 🛢 ∅ 🔋 🅃
➝ ∪ ▶ 🔺 🍴 ♨ 🛢 💳 ☎ 🛒 🔋

▶ ▶ Criggan Mill (SW670179)
Mullion Cove TR12 7EU ☎ 01326 240496
Dir: From A3083 Helston road take B3296 to Mullion Cove. Follow signs to "The Cove"
★ ♨ £7-£11 🚐 £7-£11 ▲ £7-£11
Open Apr-Oct Booking advisable Jul-Aug Last arrival 22.00hrs Last departure 10.00hrs ⊗
A secluded site with level pitches in a combe near to Mullion Cove. A 1-acre site with 5 touring pitches.

Facilities: ℞ ⊙ ※ ⌂ ⛷ 🛢 🔋 **Services:** ♨ 🛢 ✕
➝ ∪ ▶ 🍴 💳 🛒 🔋 🔋

NANCEGOLLAN   **Map 02 SW63**

▶ ▶ Pengoon Farm Touring Caravan Park (SW632309)
TR13 0BH ☎ 01326 561219
Dir: Direct access off B3302, 3m from Helston and 6m from Hayle. Do not take any signs for Nancegollan village
A grass park divided into two paddocks on a small working farm. In a very rural location, with friendly owners. A 3-acre site with 25 touring pitches.

Services: 🅃 Toilet Fluid ✕ Café/ Restaurant 🍴 Fast Food/Takeaway ➡ Baby Care ♨ Electric Hook Up
🅁 Launderette ⚲ Licensed Bar 🛢 Calor Gaz ∅ Camping Gaz 🔋 Battery Charging

England

England

Fantastic Family Fun

Newquay

Excellent Camping and Touring Facilities Luxury Static Caravans

Cabaret Entertainment • Licensed Bars Restaurants • Takeaway • Supermarket Amusements • Games Fields • Children's Hippo Club • Toddlers Pirate Den • Train Rides Pitch n Putt • Adventure Playgrounds

Open February onwards

Hendra
HOLIDAY PARK

Oasis Hendra's New Water Fun Park

where wetter is better whatever the weather!

Fabulous outdoor pool complex • Superb indoor fun pool • 3 fantastic water flumes • River rapid ride
Water cannon • Geyser • Fountain • Waterfall • Toddlers area

Freephone Brochure Hotline 0500 242523

Hendra Holiday Park, Newquay, Cornwall TR8 4NY Tel: 01637 875778 e.mail: hendra.uk@dial.pipex.com www.hendra-holidays.com

England

England

England

NEWQUAY — Map 02 SW86

Hendra Holiday Park (SW833601)
TR8 4NY ☎ 01637 875778
Dir: *Leave A30 onto A392 signed Newquay. At Quintrell Downs over rdbt, signed Lane, and park 0.5m on right.*
Open Feb-Oct (rs Apr-Spring bank hol) Booking advisable Jul-Aug Last arrival dusk Last departure noon
A large, long-established complex with mature trees and bushes set in downland, with superb leisure facilities and a newly opened indoor fun pool complex. These amanities are open to the general public. A 46-acre site with 600 touring pitches and 188 statics.
Solarium, fish bar, sauna, kids club, train rides.
Leisure: **Facilities:** **Services:**
See advert on page 57

Newquay Holiday Park (SW853626)
TR8 4HS ☎ 01637 871111
Dir: *A30 from Exeter, through Victoria village. Continue & turn right after RAF St Mawgan sign. Carry on 3m. At rdbt take A3059 to Newquay. Signed after 4m*
★ £6.80-£12.60 £6.80-£12.60 £6.80-£12.60
Open 13 May-15 Sep Booking advisable Jun-Aug Last arrival 21.00hrs Last departure 10.00hrs
A well-managed and maintained site with a wide range of indoor and outdoor activities. A 14-acre site with 259 touring pitches and 137 statics.
Snooker/Pool tables, 9hole pitch & putt, crazy golf.
Leisure: **Facilities:**
Services:
See advert on page 58

►►►► **Trencreek Holiday Park (SW828609)**
Hillcrest, Higher Trencreek TR8 4NS ☎ 01637 874210
Dir: *A392 to Quintrell Downs, turn right in direction of Newquay, turn left at 2 mini rdbts into Trevenson Road to Trencreek*
★ £7.30-£11.50 £7.30-£11.50 £7.30-£11.50
Open Whit-mid Sep (rs Etr, Apr-May & late Sep swimming pool, cafe & bar closed) Booking advisable Jul-Aug Last arrival 22.00hrs Last departure noon
Slightly sloping grassy site with excellent facilities, set in meadowland in the village of Trencreek. The on-site evening entertainment at the licensed clubhouse is a popular amenity. A 10-acre site with 194 touring pitches and 6 statics.
Coarse fishing on site.
Leisure: **Facilities:**
Services:
See advert on page 61

Sun Haven Valley
HOLIDAY PARK
Mawgan Porth, Newquay, Cornwall TR8 4BQ.
Tel: St Mawgan (01637) 860 373

• FREE hot showers • Children's adventure playground
• Games room • Free hot washing-up facilities
• TV Lounge • Electric showers
Extremely high standards. Sheltered level pitches. Tents and tourers. Well-behaved pets allowed strictly on leash. Golden beach within walking distance. Personally supervised by resident proprietors. Families and couples only.

►►► ***Porth Beach Tourist Park (SW834629)***
Porth TR7 3NH ☎ 01637 876531
Dir: *1m NE off B3276 towards Padstow*
Open Mar-Oct Booking advisable Jul-Aug Last arrival 21.00hrs Last departure 10.00hrs
This attractive, popular park offers level, grassy pitches in neat and tidy surroundings, and has the benefit of a new toilet block. A well-run site set in meadowland and adjacent to sea and a fine sandy beach. A 6-acre site with 201 touring pitches and 12 statics.
Leisure: **Facilities:**
Services:

►►► **Riverside Holiday Park (SW829592)**
Ln TR8 4PE ☎ 01637 873617
Dir: *From A30 take A392 signed Newquay, at Quintrell Downs cross rdbt signed Lane. 2nd left in 0.5m onto unclass rd signed Gwills. Park in 400yds.*

Facilities: Bath · Shower · Electric Shaver · Hairdryer · Ice Pack Facility · Disabled Facilities · Public Telephone · Shop on Site or within 200yds · Mobile Shop (calls at least 5 days a week) · BBQ Area · Picnic Area · Dog Exercise Area

★ ⊞ £10-£12.50 ⊞ £10-£12.50 ▲ fr £10
Open Mar-Dec Booking advisable Jul-Aug Last departure 10.00hrs
A lightly wooded park set alongside a river, with level grass pitches. This family park has a new toilet block, and offers a good range of amenities. An 11-acre site with 140 touring pitches and 20 statics. Fishing.
Leisure: ⌇ ◣ ⅏ ⎚ **Facilities:** ⋔⊙⛌✳⛐⚓⚑↟
Services: ◪⊟⊠⚡▤⌀⊞Ⓣ⚱
→∪⚑◉⚠⚒⚙ ▦▥▨▩▧⚑

▶ ▶ ▶ *Trebellan Park (SW790571)*
Cubert TR8 5PY ☎ 01637 830522
Dir: 4m S of Newquay, turn W off A3075 at Cubert signpost and turn left in 0.75m onto unclass road
⊞ ⊞ ▲
Open Etr-Oct

A terraced grassy rural park within a picturesque valley with views of Cubert Common, and adjacent to the Smuggler's Den, a 16th-century thatched inn. This park welcomes families and couples only, and has some excellent coarse fishing on site. An 8-acre site with 150 touring pitches.
Three well stocked coarse fishing lakes.
Leisure: ⌇◣⅏⎚ **Facilities:** ⋔⊙⛌✳⛐⚓
Services: ◪⊡

▶ ▶ ▶ Treloy Tourist Park (SW858625)
TR8 4JN ☎ 01637 872063 & 876279
Dir: From A30 turn right onto A3059 signed St Columb, & after 3m at rdbt follow A3059 sign to Newquay. Site signed in 4m
★ ⊞ £6-£10.40 ⊞ £6-£10.40 ▲ £6-£10.40
Open Apr-Oct (rs Apr & Sept swimming pool & bar closed) Booking advisable Jul-Aug Last arrival mdnt Last departure 11.00hrs   *contd.*

Services: Ⓣ Toilet Fluid ✗ Café/ Restaurant ⚱ Fast Food/Takeaway ⚓ Baby Care ◪ Electric Hook Up
⊡ Launderette ⚲ Licensed Bar ⚐ Calor Gaz ⌀ Camping Gaz ⊞ Battery Charging

Attractive site with fine countryside views, within easy reach of resorts and beaches. The park caters for couples and for families. A 12-acre site with 119 touring pitches.
Golf, entertainment, children's club.
Leisure: ⬧ ✦ ⚙ ▢ **Facilities:** ⬧⊙⬧✳ ✆ ⬧ ➤
Services: ⬧⬧⬧ ⬧ ⬧ ▢ ✖ ⬧
→ ∪ ➤ ⬧ ⬧ ✦ ⬧ ⬤ ⬧ ⬧ ⬧

► ► ► **Trenance Caravan & Chalet Park (SW818612)**
Edgcumbe Av TR7 2JY ☎ 01637 873447
Dir: Off A3075 near viaduct. Entrance by boating lake rdbt
★ ⬧ £7.50-£13.50 ⬧ £7.50-£13.50 ▲ £7.50-£13.50
Open 26 May-Oct (rs Apr-25 May no showers or take-away restaurant) Booking advisable Jul-Aug Last arrival 22.00hrs Last departure 10.00hrs ✧
Principally a static park with a small area for tourers and tents, set on high ground in an urban area of Newquay. This park is for families and couples only. A 12-acre site with 50 touring pitches and 190 statics.
Dishwashing facilities.
Leisure: ✦ **Facilities:** ⬧⊙⬧✳ ✆ ⬧ **Services:** ⬧⬧⬧
⬧▢✖⬧
→ ∪ ➤ ⊙ ⬧ ✦ ⬧ ⬤ ⬤ ⬧ ⬧ ⬧ ⬧

► ► ► **Trethiggey Touring Park (SW846596)**
Quintrell Downs TR8 4LG ☎ 01637 877672
Dir: 2m SE A392
⬧ £7-£12 ⬧ £6-£11 ▲ £6-£9.80

Facilities: ⬧ Bath ⬧ Shower ⊙ Electric Shaver ⬧ Hairdryer ✳ Ice Pack Facility ⬧ Disabled Facilities ✆ Public Telephone
⬧ Shop on Site or within 200yds ⬧ Mobile Shop (calls at least 5 days a week) ⬧ BBQ Area ⬧ Picnic Area ➤ Dog Exercise Area

Open Mar-Dec Booking advisable Jul-Aug
This family-owned park is in a rural setting, and
ideal for touring this part of Cornwall. It is a
pleasant, improving site divided into paddocks with
maturing trees and shrubs. A 15-acre site with 145
touring pitches and 12 statics.
Off licence, recreation field, fishing
Leisure: ◣ ⋀ ☐ Facilities: ⋒ ☉ ☜ ✳ ⅃ ⚲ 🛒 ⊞ ㄫ ♜
Services: ☎ 🖥 🛢 ⌀ ⊞ Ⅱ ⚒
→ ∪ ▶ ◎ ◬ ⤳ ⅃ 🅟 🈂 🔳 🔟

NOTTER BRIDGE   Map 02 SX36

▶ ▶ ▶ **Notter Bridge Caravan & Camping Park**
(SX384608)
PL12 4RW ☎ 01752 842318
Dir: On A38, 3.5m W of Tamar Bridge
🚐 £5-£7 🚐 £5-£7 ⅄ £5-£7
Open Etr-Sep Booking advisable peak periods Last
arrival 22.00hrs Last departure 11.00hrs

Small, level grassy riverside site in wooded Lynner
Valley. Fishing licences available. A 6.25-acre site
with 33 touring pitches and 23 statics.
Salmon & trout fishing, Country Pub/Food opposite
Leisure: ⋀ Facilities: ⋒ ☉ ✳ ☜ 🛒 ♜ Services: ☎ 🖥
→ ▶ ◬ ⤳ ⅃ 🈂

OTTERHAM   Map 02 SX19

▶ ▶ ▶ **St Tinney Farm Holidays (SX169906)**
PL32 9TA ☎ 01840 261274
Dir: Signposted 1m off A39 via unclass road signed
Otterham
🚐 🚐 ⅄
Open Etr-Oct Booking advisable Spring bank hol &
Jul-Aug Last arrival 21.00hrs Last departure
11.00hrs
A family-run farm site in a rural area, with nature
trails, lakes, valleys and complete seclusion. Visitors
are free to walk around the 34-acre farmland lakes.
A 5-acre site with 20 touring pitches and 9 statics.
Coarse fishing, horse & donkey rides, farm animals
Leisure: ◣ ⋀ Facilities: ⋒ ☉ ✳ ☜ 🛒 ㄫ ♜
Services: ☎ 🖥 ⅄ 🛢 ⌀ ⊞ ✕ ⚒
→ ∪ 🈂 ⅃ 🅟 🔳 🔟

PADSTOW   Map 02 SW97

▶ ▶ ▶ **Dennis Cove Camping (SW920744)**
Dennis Farm, Dennis Cove PL28 8DR
☎ 01841 532349
Dir: Approach Padstow on A389 and turn right into
Sarah's Lane *contd.*

Services: ⊞ Toilet Fluid ✕ Café/ Restaurant 🍴 Fast Food/Takeaway 🍼 Baby Care ☎ Electric Hook Up
🖥 Launderette ⅄ Licensed Bar 🛢 Calor Gaz ⌀ Camping Gaz ⊞ Battery Charging

★ ⚏ £8.85-£12.35 ⚏ £8.85-£12.35 ▲ £8.85-£12.35
Open Whit-Sep (rs Apr & Sep onwards swimming
pool & club closed) Booking advisable before Etr
Last arrival 23.00hrs Last departure noon
*Level and slightly sloping site with mature trees set
in meadowland, overlooking Padstow Bay with
access to River Camel estuary and Padstow Bay
beach. A 4.5-acre site with 63 touring pitches.*
Leisure: ⚒ **Facilities:** ⚒⊙✳⚒⊞ **Services:** ⚒⚒⚒⚒⊞
→ ∪ ⚒ ⊙ ⚒ ⚒ ⚒ ⚒ ⚒ ⚒

▶ ▶ ▶ **Trerethern Touring Park (SW913738)**
PL28 8LE ☎ 01841 532061
*Dir: Situated 2m S of Padstow on the eastern side of
A389 Padstow to Wadebridge road*
★ ⚏ £7-£10 ⚏ £7-£10 ▲ £7-£10
Open Apr-mid Oct Booking advisable Jul-Aug Last
arrival 19.00hrs Last departure 16.00hrs
*Set in open countryside above the quaint fishing
town of Padstow which can be approached by
footpath directly from the park. This level grassy
site is divided into paddocks by maturing bushes
and hedges. A 13.5-acre site with 100 touring
pitches.*
Leisure: ⚒ **Facilities:** ⚒⊙⚒✳⚒⚒⚒⚒
Services: ⚒⚒⚒⚒⊞⚒
→ ∪ ⚒ ⚒ ⚒ ⚒ ⚒

PENTEWAN   Map 02 SX04

**Pentewan Sands Holiday Park
(SX018468)**
PL26 6BT ☎ 01726 843485
Dir: On B3273 4m S of St Austell
★ ⚏ £6.25-£15.95 ⚏ £6.25-£15.95 ▲ £6.25-£15.95
Open May-Oct (rs Apr-14 May & 15 Sep-Oct
shop, snacks, pool, clubhouse ltd or closed)
Booking advisable Jul-Aug Last arrival 22.00hrs
Last departure 10.30hrs ⚒
*A large camping site with a wide range of
amenities, set on the dunes adjacent to a private
beach, well equipped for aquatic activities. A
short stroll on a private footpath leads to the
pretty village of Pentewan, and other attractions
are a short drive away. A 32-acre site with 480
touring pitches and 120 statics.*
Mini golf, cycle hire, boat launching, water
sports.
Leisure: ⚒⚒⚒⚒ **Facilities:** ⚒⚒⊙⚒✳⚒⚒⚒
Services: ⚒⚒⚒⚒⚒⊞⚒✕⚒
→ ∪ ⚒ ⊙ ⚒ ⚒ ⚒ ⚒ ⚒ ⚒ ⚒ ⚒

PREMIER PARK

▶ ▶ ▶ ▶ ▶ **Sun Valley Holiday Park
(SX005486)**
Pentewan Rd PL26 6DJ
☎ 01726 843266 & 844393
*Dir: From St Austell take B3273 towards
Mevagissey. Park is 2m on right*
⚏ £8-£22 ⚏ £8-£22 ▲ £8-£22
Open Apr (or Etr if earlier)-Oct Booking
advisable May-Sep Last arrival 22.00hrs Last

departure noon
*In a picturesque valley and set amongst
woodland, this neat park is presented to an
exceptionally high standard throughout. The
owners are constantly upgrading and improving
the park, and the extensive amenities include
tennis courts, indoor swimming pool, licensed
clubhouse and restaurant. The sea is 1m away,
and can be accessed via a footpath and cycle
path along the river bank. A 4-acre site with 22
touring pitches and 75 statics.*
Leisure: ⚒⚒⚒⚒ **Facilities:** ⚒⊙⚒✳⚒
⚒⚒⚒⚒ **Services:** ⚒⚒⚒⚒⚒⊞✕⚒
→ ∪ ⚒ ⚒ ⚒ ⚒ ⚒ ⚒ ⚒ ⚒ ⚒

▶ ▶ ▶ *Pengrugla Caravan Park (SW998470)*
PL26 6BT ☎ 01726 842714
*Dir: From A390 take B3273 for Mevagissey at X-roads
signed 'No caravans beyond this point'. Right onto
unclass road towards Gorran, site 0.75m on left*
⚏
Open Apr-1 Nov
*A pleasant peaceful park adjacent to Lost Gardens
of Heligan with views over St Austell Bay, and well-
maintained facilities. Guests at Pengrugla can also
use the extensive amenities at the sister park,
Pentewan Sands. A 12-acre site with 30 statics.*

▶ ▶ ▶ **Penhaven Touring Park (SX008481)**
PL26 6DL ☎ 01726 843687
*Dir: S from St Austell on B3273 towards Mevagissey.
Site on left 1m after village of London Apprentice*
★ ⚏ £8.80-£18 ⚏ £8.80-£18 ▲ £8.80-£13.90
Open Apr-Oct Booking advisable public hols & end
Jul-Aug Last arrival 22.00hrs Last departure 10.00hrs
*Level, landscaped site in wooded valley, with river
running by and 1m from sandy beach at Pentewan.
A 13-acre site with 105 touring pitches.*
Off-licence.
Leisure: ⚒⚒ **Facilities:** ⚒⊙⚒✳⚒⚒⚒⚒
Services: ⚒⚒⚒⚒⊞⚒⚒
→ ∪ ⚒ ⚒ ⚒ ⚒ ⚒ ⚒ ⚒ ⚒ ⚒ ⚒

PENZANCE   Map 02 SW43

▶ ▶ ▶ **Bone Valley Caravan & Camping Park
(SW472316)**
Heamoor TR20 8UJ ☎ 01736 360313
*Dir: A30 to Penzance then towards Lands End, at 2nd
rdbt right into Heamoor, 300yds right into Josephs
Lane, 1st left Bone Valley and site is 50yds on left*
★ ⚏ £8.50-£10.50 ⚏ £8.50-£9.50 ▲ £8.50-£10
Open Mar-7 Jan Booking advisable Jul-Aug Last
arrival 22.00hrs Last departure 11.00hrs ⚒
*A compact grassy park on the outskirts of Penzance,
with well maintained facilities. It is divided into
paddocks by mature hedges, and a small stream
runs alongside. A 1-acre site with 17 touring pitches
and 1 static.*
Leisure: ⚒ **Facilities:** ⚒⊙⚒✳⚒⚒
Services: ⚒⚒⚒⚒⊞
→ ∪ ⊙ ⚒ ⚒ ⚒ ⚒

Facilities: ⚒ Bath ⚒ Shower ⊙ Electric Shaver ⚒ Hairdryer ✳ Ice Pack Facility ⚒ Disabled Facilities ⚒ Public Telephone
⚒ Shop on Site or within 200yds ⊞ Mobile Shop (calls at least 5 days a week) ⚒ BBQ Area ⚒ Picnic Area ⚒ Dog Exercise Area

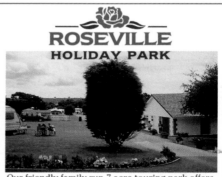
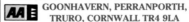
Services: T Toilet Fluid ✗ Café/ Restaurant 🍔 Fast Food/Takeaway 🍼 Baby Care 🔌 Electric Hook Up
🧺 Launderette ⚲ Licensed Bar 🛢 Calor Gaz ⊘ Camping Gaz ⊞ Battery Charging

PERRANARWORTHAL   Map 02 SW73

▶ ▶ ▶ **Cosawes Caravan Park** (SW768376)
TR3 7QS ☎ 01872 863724 & & 863717
Dir: Leave A38 at Trerulefoot rdbt onto A387, through Looe, over Looe Bridge signed Polperro. Left past bus shelter/phone box. Park 400yds on left
★ 🚐 £8-£10 🚐 £7-£9 ▲ £6.50-£7
Open all year Booking advisable mid Jul-mid Aug
A small touring park in a peaceful wooded valley, midway between Truro and Falmouth. Its stunning location is ideal for visiting the many nearby hamlets and villages on the Carrick Roads, a stretch of tidal water which is a centre for sailing and other boats. A 2-acre site with 40 touring pitches and 100 statics. Squash court.
Facilities: 🍴 ⊙ ※ 🐕 🖃 🌀 🎋 🎠 **Services:** 🕯 🖾 🛢 ⌀ 🖽 🆃
→ ∪ 🅿 ◎ ♨ ↘ ♪ 🐾

PERRANPORTH   Map 02 SW75

▶ ▶ ▶ *Perranporth Camping & Touring Site (SW768542)*
Budnick Rd TR6 0DB ☎ 01872 572174
Dir: 0.5m E off B3285
🚐 🚐 ▲
Open Whit-Sep (rs Etr-Whit & mid Sep-end Sep shop & club facilities closed) Booking advisable Jul-Aug Last arrival 23.00hrs Last departure noon
A mainly tenting site with few level pitches but adjacent to a fine sandy beach. A 6-acre site with 180 touring pitches and 9 statics.
Leisure: ↘ ⚲ 🎡 ⬜ **Facilities:** 🍴 🍴 ⊙ ☜ ※ ⚓ 🐾 🎋 🐕
Services: 🕯 🖾 🍽 🛢 ⌀ 🖽 🆃 ⚓
→ ∪ 🅿 ◎ ♨ ↘ ♪ 🍺 💳 ⊠ 🔄 🐾

See advert on page 65

POLPERRO   Map 02 SX25

Killigarth Manor Holiday Estate (SX214519)
PL13 2JQ ☎ 01503 272216 & 272409
🚐 🚐 ▲
Open Etr-Oct Booking advisable 3rd wk Jul-Aug Last arrival 20.00hrs Last departure noon ✂
A well-ordered site on high ground on the approach to a historic fishing village on the A387. A large touring and holiday complex with many amenities and facilities. A 7-acre site with 202 touring pitches and 147 statics. Amusement arcade, pool table & table tennis.
Leisure: ↘ ⚲ ⚓ 🎡 ⬜ **Facilities:** 🍴 ⊙ ☜ ※ ⚓ 📞
🐾 🎋 🎠 **Services:** 🕯 🖾 🍽 🛢 ⌀ 🖽 🆃 ✕ ⚓
→ ∪ 🅿 ↘ 🍽 ♪ 💳 ⊠ ▦ 🔄 🐾

POLRUAN   Map 02 SX15

▶ ▶ ▶ **Polruan Holidays-Camping & Caravaning** (SX133509)
Polruan-by-Fowey PL23 1QH ☎ 01726 870263
Dir: A38 to Dobwalls, left onto A390 to East Taphouse then left onto B3359. After 4.5m turn right signposted Polruan
🚐 £6.75-£10.75 🚐 £6.75-£10.75 ▲ £4.25-£10.75
Open Etr-Oct Booking advisable Jul, Aug & bank hols Last arrival 21.00hrs Last departure noon

A very rural and quiet site in a lovely elevated position above the village, with good views. River Fowey passenger ferry close by. A 3-acre site with 32 touring pitches and 11 statics. Tourist information.
Leisure: 🎡 **Facilities:** 🍴 ⊙ ☜ ※ 🐕 🎋 🎠 🐾
Services: 🕯 🛢 ⌀ 🖽 🆃 → ∪ ♨ ↘ ♪

POLZEATH   Map 02 SW97

▶ ▶ ▶ *South Winds Caravan & Camping Park (SW948790)*
Polzeath Rd PL27 6QU ☎ 01208 863267 & 862646
Dir: Leave B3314 on unclass road signed Polzeath, park on right just past turn to New Polzeath
🚐 🚐 ▲

Open Mar-Oct Booking advisable Jul & Aug Last arrival 23.00hrs Last departure 11.00hrs
A peaceful site with beautiful sea and panoramic rural views, within walking distance of new golf

complex, and 0.75m from beach and village.
A 6-acre site with 50 touring pitches.
Facilities: ⌇⊙⚲⚹✻🖪🖭🛒🅃 ♉
Services: ⚡🖳📱⌀🔲🅃
→∪▸◉♨✚☎🚽🌙🍴 ⬤🚊

► ► ► *Tristram Caravan & Camping Park (SW936790)*
PL27 6UG ☎ 01208 862215 & 863267
Dir: From B3314 take unclass road signed Polzeath. Through village and up hill, site 2nd turn on right
🚐🚙 Å

Open Mar-Oct Booking advisable Jul, Aug & All School Hols Last arrival 23.00hrs Last departure 10.00hrs
An ideal family site, positioned on a gently-sloping cliff with grassy pitches and glorious sea views. Direct gated access to the beach, where surfing is very popular. A 10-acre site with 100 touring pitches.
Private footpath onto beach
Facilities: ⌇⊙⚲⚹✻⚓🛒🖭🖃🛒🅃 ♉
Services: ⚡🖳❄📱⌀🔲🅃✕🖌
→∪▸◉♨✚☎🚽🌙 ⬤■🔲⊙🈺🎮🕹

PORTHTOWAN   Map 02 SW64

► ► ► ► *Rose Hill Touring Park (SW693466)*
Rose Hill TR4 8AR ☎ 01209 890802
Dir: From A30 follow B3277 signposted St Agnes. After 1m turn left signed Porthtowan. Site 100yds past beach road
🚐 £8-£12.50 🚙 £8-£12.50 Å £8-£12.50
Open end Mar-end Oct Booking advisable Jun-Aug Last arrival 21.30hrs Last departure 11.00hrs
A small, well-kept park in an attractive position, set into the hillside and terraced. The park is quiet and sheltered, hidden away in a wooded valley, with some hardstandings among many level pitches. New toilet facilities are of a high standard. The park offers 'bake-off' oven for fresh bread in its well-stocked shop. Only a short way away is a popular sandy beach and surf centre, plus village pubs and restaurants. A 2.5-acre site with 50 touring pitches.
Tourist information, Site Shop
Facilities: ⌇⊙⚲⚹✻⚓🛒🖭🖃
Services: ⚡🖳📱⌀🔲✕🖌🥤
→∪▸♨✚☎🚽🌙 ⬤■🔲⊙🈺🎮🕹

► ► ► *Porthtowan Tourist Park (SW693473)*
Mile Hill TR4 8TY ☎ 01209 890256
Dir: Leave A30 at rd signed Redruth/Portreath onto B3047 signed Camborne. Approx 0.75m at rdbt turn right signed Porthreath. 3m turn right onto unclass rd.
🚐 £5-£9 🚙 £5-£9 Å £5-£9
Open Etr-Oct Booking advisable Jul-Aug Last departure noon
A neat, level grassy site on high ground above Porthtowan, with plenty of shelter from mature trees and shrubs. This rural park in a peaceful location offers good facilities, and is almost midway between the small seaside resorts of Porthreath and Porthtowan, with their beaches and surfing. A 5.5-acre site with 50 touring pitches.
Leisure: ⚓ ⚲ **Facilities:** ⌇⊙⚲⚹✻⚓🛒🖭🖃🛒
Services: ⚡🖳📱⌀🔲🅃
→∪▸◉♨✚☎🚽🌙⌀

PORTSCATHO   Map 02 SW83

► ► *Treloan Farm Holidays (SW876348)*
Treloan Ln TR2 5EF ☎ 01872 580989
Dir: Take unclass road to Gerrans off A3078 Tregony-St Mawes. Immediately after Gerrans church road divides - take section beside Royal Standard pub
🚐🚙 Å
Open all year (rs Nov-Feb Touring) Booking advisable High Season Last departure 11.00hrs
A quiet and well-screened coastal site with mature trees and bushes, and three secluded nearby beaches. A 5-acre site with 49 touring pitches and 8 statics.
Coastal Foot Path on site
See advertisement under TRURO
Leisure: ⚓ ⚲🖵 **Facilities:** ⌇⊙⚲⚹✻⚓🛒🖭🖃🛒 ♉
Services: ⚡🔲🅃
→∪♨✚🌙⌀

REDRUTH   Map 02 SW64

► ► ► *Cambrose Touring Park (SW684453)*
Portreath Rd TR16 4HT ☎ 01209 890747
Dir: Leave A30 onto B3047 towards Camborne. Approx 0.75m at 1st rdbt R onto B3300. Take unclas rd on R signed Porthtowan. Site 200yds on L
🚐🚙 Å
Open Apr-Oct Booking advisable Jul-Aug Last arrival 22.00hrs Last departure 11.30hrs

Situated in a rural setting surrounded by trees and shrubs, this park is divided into grassy paddocks. About two miles from the harbour village of Portreath. A 6-acre site with 60 touring pitches. contd.

Leisure: ⬚ ⬚ ⬚ Facilities: ⬚⊙⬚✳⬚⬚⬚⬚
Services: ⬚⬚⬚⬚⬚⬚⬚⬚⬚
→⬚⬚⬚⬚⬚⬚

▶ ▶ ▶ *Lanyon Park (SW684387)*
Loscombe Ln, Four Lanes TR16 6LP ☎ 01209 313474
*Dir: Signed 0.5m off B2397 on Helston side of Four
Lanes village*
⬚ ⬚ A
Open Mar-Oct & mid Jan-mid Feb Booking
advisable Jul & Aug Last departure noon
*Small, friendly rural park in elevated position with
fine views to distant St Ives Bay. This family owned
and run park is being upgraded in all areas, and is
close to a new cycling trail. Stithian's Reservoir for
fishing, sailing and windsurfing is two miles away.
A 10-acre site with 25 touring pitches and 49 statics.*
Leisure: ⬚ Facilities: ⬚⬚⬚✳⬚⬚⬚
Services: ⬚⬚⬚✕⬚
→⬚

▶ ▶ ▶ **Tehidy Holiday Park (SW682432)**
Harris Mill, Illogan TR16 4JQ
☎ 01209 216489 & 314558
*Dir: Leave A30 at Redruth/Portreath exit, continue on
A3047 to 1st rdbt. Right onto B3300, approx 1m left
onto unclass rd. Site 1m on left and signed*
★ ⬚ £6.50-£8 ⬚ £6.50-£8 A £6.50-£8
Open Apr-Oct Booking advisable Jul-Aug Last
arrival 20.00hrs Last departure 10.00hrs

*An attractive wooded location in a quiet rural area
only 2.5m from popular beaches. Mostly level
pitches on tiered ground. A 1-acre site with 18
touring pitches and 32 statics.*
Badminton, off-licence.
Leisure: ⬚⬚⬚ Facilities: ⬚⊙⬚✳⬚⬚⬚
Services: ⬚⬚⬚⬚⬚⬚
→⬚⬚⬚⬚⬚⬚⬚⬚⬚⬚

REJERRAH   Map 02 SW75

▶ ▶ ▶ ▶ **Newperran Tourist Park (SW801555)**
TR8 5QJ ☎ 01872 572407 in season & 01637 830308
Dir: 4m SE of Newquay & 1m S of Rejerrah on A3075
★ ⬚ £6.60-£11.80 ⬚ £6-£11 A £6.60-£11.80
Open mid May-mid Sep Booking advisable Jul-Aug
*A very good family site in a lovely rural position,
central for several beaches and bays. It occupies an
airy position in the centre of unspoilt countryside,
and there is some screening around the pitches.
This park offers plenty to occupy all members of the*

*family, and work carried out to upgrade the facilities
has left it looking very bright and well-maintained.
Newperran is equidistant from Newquay and
Perrenporth. A 25-acre site with 270 touring pitches.
Crazy golf, adventure playground, pool &
badminton.*
Leisure: ⬚⬚⬚⬚ Facilities: ⬚⬚⊙⬚✳⬚⬚⬚⬚
Services: ⬚⬚⬚⬚⬚⬚⬚✕⬚
→⬚⬚⬚⬚⬚⬚⬚ ⬚ ⬚ ⬚ ⬚ ⬚

▶ ▶ ▶ **Monkey Tree Touring Park (SW803545)**
Scotland Rd TR8 5QR ☎ 01872 572032
Dir: Access from Rejerrah-Zelah road off A3075
★ ⬚ £3.50-£12 ⬚ £3.50-£12 A £3.50-£12
Open Mar-Oct Booking advisable Jul & Aug Last
arrival 22.00hrs Last departure from 10.00hrs
*A quiet, open moorland setting, well-screened by
mature hedges on high ground near the north
Cornwall coast. An 18-acre site with 295 touring
pitches and 22 statics.*
Sauna, solarium, mountain bike hire & football
pitch
Leisure: ⬚⬚⬚⬚ Facilities: ⬚⊙✳⬚⬚⬚⬚⬚
Services: ⬚⬚⬚⬚⬚⬚⬚✕⬚
→⬚⬚⬚⬚⬚ ⬚ ⬚ ⬚ ⬚ ⬚

▶ ▶ ▶ *Perran-Quay Tourist Park (SW800554)*
Hendra Croft TR8 5QP ☎ 01872 572561
⬚ ⬚ A
Dir: W of Rejerrah village off unclass road.
Open Apr-Oct Booking advisable Jul-Aug Last
arrival anytime Last departure 10.00hrs
*Level grassy site with young trees and bushes, set
in meadowland, with access to the sea, Holywell
beach and A3075 Newquay road. The park is
divided into paddocks by mature trees and shrubs,
which also act as a shelter. It has its own pub on
site serving food and drink. A 5.5-acre site with 135
touring pitches.*
Leisure: ⬚⬚⬚⬚ Facilities: ⬚⊙⬚✳⬚⬚⬚
Services: ⬚⬚⬚⬚⬚⬚⬚✕⬚
→⬚⬚⬚⬚⬚⬚⬚

RELUBBUS   Map 02 SW53

▶ ▶ ▶ ▶ **River Valley Country Park (SW565326)**
TR20 9ER ☎ 01736 763398
*Dir: From A30 take signpost for Helston A394. At next
rbdt 1st left signposted Relubbus*
★ ⬚ £6-£11 ⬚ £6-£11 A £6-£11
Open Mar-Dec (rs Nov-4 Jan hardstanding only)
Booking advisable Jul-Aug Last arrival 20.00hrs Last
departure 11.00hrs
*A quiet, attractive site of quality in a picturesque
river valley with direct access to shallow trout
stream. This level park has a good mix of grass and
hard pitches, and is partly wooded with pleasant
walks. It is surrounded by farmland, and just a few
miles from the sandy beaches of both the north and
south coasts, as well as St Michael's Mount at
Marazion. An 18-acre site with 150 touring pitches
and 48 statics.*

Facilities: ⬚ Bath ⬚ Shower ⊙ Electric Shaver ⬚ Hairdryer ✳ Ice Pack Facility ⬚ Disabled Facilities ⬚ Public Telephone
⬚ Shop on Site or within 200yds ⬚ Mobile Shop (calls at least 5 days a week) ⬚ BBQ Area ⬚ Picnic Area ⬚ Dog Exercise Area

THE PERFECT PEACEFUL COUNTRY LOCATION FOR A RELAXING HOLIDAY

18 acres of beautifully landscaped partly wooded park set in one of the most picturesque valleys in Cornwall - for those looking for peace and tranquillity in the countryside yet close to many of Cornwall's glorious beaches and sheltered coves.

- **SPACIOUS PITCHES FOR TENTS, TOURERS AND MOTORHOMES**
- **SHOP & LAUNDERETTE**
- **SPOTLESSLY CLEAN HEATED TOILET/ SHOWER BLOCKS WITH FREE HOT WATER**
- **LUXURY HOLIDAY HOMES & LODGE AVAILABLE**

RIVER VALLEY COUNTRY PARK

Relubbus, Penzance, Cornwall. TR20 9ER
Tel:(01736) 763398
www.rivervalley.co.uk

Fishing.
Facilities: ⁿ⊙◖☀︎ℂ☎︎⌕ **Services:** 🔌🖥🛢⌀⊞⊤
→ ∪ ▸ ◎ ♪ 🍴 🎮

ROSUDGEON   Map 02 SW52

► ► ► **Kenneggy Cove Holiday Park (SW562287)**
Higher Kenneggy TR20 9AU ☎ 01736 763453
Dir: On A394 between Penzance & Helston, turn S down signed lane to site & Higher Kenneggy
★ 🚐 £5-£8.50 🚐 £5-£8.50 ▲ £5-£8.50

Open Apr-Nov Booking advisable Jul-Aug Last arrival 21.00hrs Last departure 11.00hrs
An attractive and neatly-kept site within a short walk of a sheltered, sandy beach and with lovely sea views. A converted milking parlour houses the well equipped games room, and there is a good shop and takeaway. A 4-acre site with 60 touring pitches and 9 statics.

Leisure: ◆ ⚠ **Facilities:** ⁿ⊙◖☀︎ℂ☎︎⌕🐾
Services: 🔌🖥🛢⌀⊞⊤⌕
→ ∪ ▸ △ ┿ ♪

RUTHERNBRIDGE   Map 02 SX06

► ► ► **Ruthern Valley Holidays (SX014665)**
PL30 5LU ☎ 01208 831395
Dir: From A30 just past W end of Bodmin bypass. Site signed on right on unclassified road to Ruthernbridge
★ 🚐 £7.75-£11.25 🚐 £7.75-£11.25 ▲ £7.75-£11.25
Open Apr-Oct Booking advisable high season Last arrival 21.00hrs Last departure noon
An attractive woodland site in a remote, small river valley south of Bodmin Moor. This away-from-it-all park is ideal for those wanting a quiet holiday, and the young owners work hard to keep their facilities in order. A 2-acre site with 29 touring pitches and 6 statics.
Off-licence.
Leisure: ⚠ **Facilities:** ⁿ⊙☀︎ℂ☎︎⌕
Services: 🔌🖥🛢⌀⊞
→ ∪ ▸ ♪

ST AGNES   Map 02 SW75

► ► ► **Beacon Cottage Farm Touring Park (SW705502)**
Beacon Dr TR5 0NU ☎ 01872 552347 & 553381
Dir: From A30 at Threeburrows rdbt, take B3277 to St Agnes, then left into Beacon Road
★ 🚐 £5-£14 🚐 £5-£14 ▲ £5-£14
Open end May-Oct (rs Etr-Whitsun shop closed) Booking advisable Jul-Aug Last arrival 20.00hrs Last departure noon
A neat and compact site utilizing a cottage and outhouses, an old orchard and adjoining walled paddock. Unique location on a headland looking NE along the coast. A 4-acre site with 50 touring pitches and 1 static.
Leisure: ⚠ **Facilities:** ⁿ⊙◖☀︎ℂ☎︎⌕
Services: 🔌🖥🛢⌀⊞↩
→ ∪ ▸ ◎ △ ┿ ♪

► ► ► *Presingoll Farm Caravan & Camping Park (SW721494)*
TR5 0PB ☎ 01872 552333
Dir: From A30 Chiverton rdbt (Little Chef) take B3277 towards St Agnes. Park 3m on right
🚐 🚐 ▲
Open Etr/Apr-Oct Booking advisable Jul & Aug Last departure 10.00hrs
An attractive rural park adjoining farmland, with extensive views of the coast beyond. Family owned and run, with level grass pitches, and modernised toilet block in smart converted farm buildings. A 3-acre site with 90 touring pitches.
Leisure: ⚠ **Facilities:** ⁿ⊙◖☀︎� ℂ☎︎⌕🖥☐⌕🐾
Services: 🔌🖥⊞
→ ∪ ♪

Services: ⊤ Toilet Fluid ✕ Café/ Restaurant 🍴 Fast Food/Takeaway ↩ Baby Care 🔌 Electric Hook Up
🖥 Launderette 🍺 Licensed Bar 🛢 Calor Gaz ⌀ Camping Gaz ⊞ Battery Charging

England

ST AUSTELL   Map 02 SX05

▶ ▶ ▶ *River Valley Holiday Park (SX010503)*
London Apprentice PL26 7AP ☎ 01726 73533
Dir: Direct access to park signed on B3273 from St Austell at London Apprentice
⊞ ⊞ ⋏
Open end Mar-Sep Booking advisable Jul-Aug Last arrival 22.00hrs Last departure 11.00hrs
A neat, well-maintained family-run park set in a pleasant river valley with cycle trail to Pentewan Beach alongside. A 2-acre site with 45 touring pitches and 40 statics.
Cycle trail.
Leisure: ⚡ ◀ ⚠ Facilities: ⋔ ☉ ♦ ✳ ╰ ⚏ ⋔
Services: ⊠ ⓑ ◀
➔ ▶ ♨ ⚘ ⚑ ⚙ 🍴 ⊞ ⊞ ⑤

▶ ▶ ▶ *Trencreek Farm Holiday Park (SW966485)*
Hewas Water PL26 7JG ☎ 01726 882540
Dir: Off B3287, 1m from junct with A390
★ ⊞ £6-£12 ⊞ £6-£12 ⋏ £6-£12
Open Spring bank hol-13 Sep (rs Etr-Spring bank hol & 14 Sep-Oct restricted shop hours & pool closed) Booking advisable Jul-Aug Last arrival 21.00hrs Last departure noon
A working farm site with mature trees and bushes, close to river and lake. Animals roam around this friendly family park, and there are organised activities for children indoors and out. An 8-acre site with 184 touring pitches and 37 statics.
Fishing, fitness & agility course & mini golf.

Holiday bungalows, caravans and a fully serviced touring park. All with country views and within easy reach of the sea. No bar or gaming machines, but a heated swimming pool, tennis court and fishing lake etc. We provide a supervised Kids Club in the main season and the park is safely situated a quarter of a mile off the main road, down our own private lane. **Special Offers:** Easter to mid July. Self catering: second week half price. Touring: £42.00 per pitch, per week, including electric.

**Trencreek Farm Holiday Park,
Hewaswater, St Austell,
Cornwall PL26 7JG
Telephone: 01726 882540
www.trencreek.co.uk**

Leisure: ⚡ ◀ ◀ ⚠ ⌨ Facilities: ➡ ⋔ ☉ ♦ ✳ ╰ ⚏ ⋔
Services: ⊠ ⓑ ▮ ⌗ ⊞ ⓣ ⛀
➔ ⊙ ▶ ♨ ⚘ ⚑ ⚙ ⊞ ⊞ ⑤

▶ ▶ ▶ *Trewhiddle Holiday Estate (SX010508)*
Trewhiddle, Pentewan Rd PL26 7AD ☎ 01726 67011
Dir: Take B3273 from St Austell towards Mevagissey. Trewhiddle is 0.75m from the rdbt
★ ⊞ £6-£12 ⊞ £6-£12 ⋏ £6-£12
Open all year Booking advisable July & August
Secluded wooded site with well-kept gardens, lawns and flower beds, set in the grounds of a mature estate, and with country club facilities. A 16.5-acre site with 105 touring pitches and 74 statics.
Leisure: ⚡ ◀ ⚠ Facilities: ⋔ ✳ ╰ ⚏ ⌗
Services: ⊠ ⚐ ▮ ⌗ ⊞ ⌗ ✕ ⛀
➔ ⊙ ▶ ♨ ⚘ ⚑ ⚙ ⊞ ⊞ Ⓓ ⊞ ⊠ ⑤

ST BURYAN   Map 02 SW42

▶ ▶ ▶ *Camping & Caravanning Club Site (SW378276)*
Higher Tregiffian Farm TR19 6JB ☎ 01736 871588
Dir: Follow A30 towards Lands End. Turn right onto A3306 St Just/Pendeen Rd. Site 50yds on left
★ ⊞ £10.60-£13.90 ⊞ £10.60-£13.90 ⋏ £10.60-£13.90
Open 07 Apr-25 Sep Booking advisable bank hols & Jul-Aug Last arrival 21.00hrs Last departure noon
A level grassy park in a rural area with distant views of Carn Brae and the coast, situated just 2m from Land's End. Please see the advertisement on page 14 for details of Club Members' benefits. A 4-acre site with 75 touring pitches.
Leisure: ⚠ Facilities: ⋔ ☉ ♦ ✳ ╰ ⚏ ⋔
Services: ⊠ ⓑ ▮
➔ ⊙ ▶ ⊙ ♨ ⚙ ⊞ ⊞

▶ ▶ ▶ *Cardinney Caravan & Camping Park (SW401278)*
Crows an Wra, Main A30 TR19 6HX ☎ 01736 810880
Dir: Site has direct access from A30, 4m from Penzance
⊞ ⊞ ⋏
Open Feb-Nov Booking advisable Jul & Aug Last arrival 23.30hrs Last departure noon
A pleasant grassy park set in farmland with an open aspect, midway between Penzance and Land's End. A 4.5-acre site with 105 touring pitches.
Leisure: ◀ ⌨ Facilities: ⋔ ☉ ♦ ✳ ╰ ⚏
Services: ⊠ ⓑ ⚐ ▮ ⌗ ⊞ ⌗ ✕ ⛀
➔ ⊙ ♨ ⚘ ⚑ ⚙ ⊞ ⊞ ⊞ ⊠ ⑤

▶ ▶ ▶ *Lower Treave Caravan & Camping Park (SW388272)*
Crows-an-Wra TR19 6HZ ☎ 01736 810559
Dir: Direct access off A30 approx 0.25m before Crows-an-Wra & just after unclass rd to St Buryan
★ ⊞ £6.50-£8.50 ⊞ £6.50-£8.50 ⋏ £6.50-£8.50
Open Apr-Oct Booking advisable Jul-Aug Last arrival 22.30hrs Last departure 11.00hrs
A terrced grass site sheltered by mature trees and bushes but with extensive meadowland views. A 5-acre site with 80 touring pitches and 5 statics.
Facilities: ⋔ ☉ ♦ ✳ ╰ ⚏ Services: ⊠ ⓑ ▮ ⌗ ⊞ ⓣ
➔ ⊙ ▶ ⚙ ⊞ ⊞ ⊞ ⊠ ⑤

Facilities: ➡ Bath   ⋔ Shower   ☉ Electric Shaver   ♦ Hairdryer   ✳ Ice Pack Facility   ╰ Disabled Facilities   ╰ Public Telephone
⚏ Shop on Site or within 200yds   ⊞ Mobile Shop (calls at least 5 days a week)   ⌗ BBQ Area   ⋔ Picnic Area   ⋔ Dog Exercise Area

► ► ► **Tower Park Caravans & Camping** (SW406263)
TR19 6BZ ☎ 01736 810286
Dir: 4m from Sennen Cove & Porthcurno. Situated off A30 & B3283
★ ♥ £6-£8.50 ♥ £6-£8.50 ▲ £6-£8.50
Open 8 Mar-Oct (rs Mar-Whit shop & cafe closed)
Booking advisable Jul-Aug Last arrival 22.00hrs Last departure noon
A rural site sheltered by mature trees, and close to village amenities. A 6-acre site with 102 touring pitches and 5 statics.
Leisure: ♠ ⚑ ▢ **Facilities:** ♠ ⊙ ♈ ※ ♿ ℃ ♨ ♠ ♒ ♅
Services: ♨ ⚘ ⓘ ∅ ⊞ ⊤ ✕ ⚲
→ ∪ ♪

► ► ► **Treverven Touring Caravan & Camping Site** (SW410237)
Treverven Farm TR19 6DL
☎ 01736 810200 & 871221
Dir: Leave A30 onto B3283 1.5m after St Buryan, left onto B3315. Site on right in 1m
♥ ♥ ▲

Open Etr-Oct Booking advisable Jul-Aug Last departure noon
An isolated tidy farm with panoramic views including the ocean. A quiet family-owned park off a traffic-free lane which leads directly to a coastal path. A 6-acre site with 115 touring pitches.
Facilities: ♠ ⊙ ♈ ※ ℃ ♨ ♅ **Services:** ♨ ⚘ ⓘ ∅
→ ♪ ⚈ ▦ ▨

ST COLUMB MAJOR   Map 02 SW96

► ► ► *Southleigh Manor Tourist Park* (SW918623)
TR9 6HY ☎ 01637 880938
Dir: Leave A30 at sign to RAF St Mawgan and St Columb onto A3059. Park 3m on left
♥ ♥ ▲
Open mid Apr-mid Sep Booking advisable Jul & Aug Last arrival 20.00hrs Last departure noon
A very well maintained naturist park in the heart of the Cornish countryside, catering for families and couples only. Seclusion and security are very well planned, and the lovely gardens provide a calm setting. A 2.5-acre site with 50 touring pitches. Sauna, Spa bath & croquet lawn.
Leisure: ⚐ ⚑ **Facilities:** ♠ ⊙ ♈ ※ ℃ ♨ ♒
Services: ♨ ⚘ ⓘ ∅ ⊞ ⊤
→ ∪ ♪

ST DAY   Map 02 SW74

► ► ► **Tresaddern Holiday Park** (SW733422)
TR16 5JR ☎ 01209 820459
Dir: From A30 at Scorrier onto B3298 towards Falmouth. St Day 2m, site signed, access on right
★ ♥ £6-£7 ♥ £6-£7 ▲ £6-£7
Open Etr & Apr-Oct Booking advisable Jul-Aug
A tidy grass park, with friendly owners who keep it well maintained. Situated in a quiet spot in a rural area between Falmouth & Newquay, and within close walking distance of the attractive village of St Day. A 2-acre site with 15 touring pitches and 17 statics.
Facilities: ♠ ⊙ ※ ℃ ♨ ♅ **Services:** ♨ ⚘ ⓘ ∅ ⊞
→ ∪ ▶ ⚊ ♪

ST GENNYS   Map 02 SX19

► ► ► **Camping & Caravanning Club Site** (SX176943)
Gillards Moor EX23 0BG ☎ 01840 230650
Dir: From S on A39 site on right in lay-by, 9m from Bude. From N on A39 site on left in lay-by 9m from Camelford. Approx 3m from B3262 junct
★ ♥ £11.80-£14.90 ♥ £11.80-£14.90 ▲ £11.80-£14.90
Open 20 Mar-27 Sep Booking advisable bank hols & Jul-Aug Last arrival 21.00hrs Last departure noon
A well-kept, level grass site with good quality facilities. Located midway between Bude and Camelford in an area full of sandy coves and beaches with good surfing.Please see the advertisement on page 14 for details of Club Members' benefits. A 6-acre site with 106 touring pitches.
Recreation Hall
Leisure: ⚑ ▢ **Facilities:** ♠ ⊙ ♈ ※ ℃ ♨ ♒ ♅
Services: ♨ ⚘ ⓘ ♈ ∅ ⊞ ⇥
→ ∪ ▶ ⚼ ♪ ⚈ ▦

ST HILARY   Map 02 SW53

► ► ► **Trevair Camping & Caravan Park** (SW548326)
South Treveneague TR20 9BY ☎ 01736 740647
Dir: 2m NE of Marazion off B3280
★ ♥ £6-£8
Open Etr-Oct
Set in a rural location adjacent to woodland, this secluded, level, grassy touring park is approximately three miles from the famous St Michael's Mount at Marazion. The friendly owners live in the farmhouse on the park. A 3-acre site with 40 touring pitches and 2 statics.
※ **Services:** ⊞
→ ▶ ♪ ♒

► ► ► **Wayfarers Caravan & Camping Park** (SW558314)
Relebbus Ln TR20 9EF ☎ 01736 763326
Dir: Turn left off A30 onto A394 towards Helston. Turn left at rdbt onto B3280 after 2m. Site is 1.5m on the left
♥ £6-£9 ♥ £6-£9 ▲ £6-£9
Open 5 Mar-5 Jan Booking advisable Jul & Aug Last arrival 23.00hrs Last departure 11.00hrs   *contd.*

England

A quiet sheltered park in a peaceful rural setting within 2.5m of St Michael's Mount. It offers spacious, well-drained pitches and very well cared for facilities. A 4.75-acre site with 54 touring pitches and 6 statics.
Tourist Info Room, Family Room
Leisure: ⚙ **Facilities:** ⬤☉❄✳✢❤⬛⊟▥ ㅠ
Services: ▦⊟ℹ∅⊞▦▦➡
→ ∪ ► ☉ ⬥ ⁘ ♨ ♪

ST ISSEY   Map 02 SW97

▶ ▶ ▶ ▶ ▶ *Trewince Farm Holiday Park*
(SW937715)
PL27 7RL ☎ 01208 812830
Dir: From Wadebridge on A39 towards St Columb take A389 signed Padstow. Site 2m on left
⊞ ⊞ Å
Open Etr-Oct Booking advisable anytime Last departure 11.00hrs
A family-owned park run to high standards amongst rolling farmland close to the coast. Although part of a working farm, Trewince has been beautifully landscaped with many trees, shrubs and colourful plants, and offers all the facilities of a holiday park. This comfortable and friendly park has a relaxed feel, and is only three miles from Padstow. A 6-acre site with 120 touring pitches and 35 statics.
Crazy golf, farm rides in summer, near Camel trail
See advertisement under PADSTOW
Leisure: ⸜ ♠ ⚙ **Facilities:** ➡⬤☉❄✳⬤❤⬛⊟▥ ㅠ
Services: ▦⊟ℹ∅
→ ∪ ► ☉ ⬥ ⁘ ♨ ♪ ⬛ 💳 🗺 📰 🖼

ST IVES   Map 02 SW54

PREMIER PARK

▶ ▶ ▶ ▶ ▶ *Polmanter Tourist Park*
(SW510388)
Halsetown TR26 3LX ☎ 01736 795640
Dir: Signed off B3311 at Halestown
★ ⊞ £9-£14 ⊞ £9-£14 Å £9-£14
Open Whit-10 Sep (rs Mar-Whit & 12 Sep-Dec shop, pool, bar & takeaway food closed)
Booking advisable Jul-Aug Last arrival 21.00hrs
Last departure 10.00hrs
A well-developed touring park on high ground, with distant views of the sea in St Ives Bay. Polmanter offers high quality in all areas, from the immaculate modern toilet blocks to the outdoor swimming pool and hard tennis courts. Pitches are individually marked and sited in meadows, and the park has been tastefully landscaped. The fishing port and beaches of St Ives are just 1.5m away, and there is a bus service in high season. A 20-acre site with 240 touring pitches.
Putting, sports field, two family shower rooms.
Leisure: ⸜ ♧ ♠ ⚙ **Facilities:** ⬤☉❄✳⬤❤⬛ ㅠ
Services: ▦⊟▦ℹ∅⊞▦✕▦➡
→ ∪ ► ☉ ⬥ ⁘ ♨ ♪ ⬛ 💳 🗺 📰 🖼

▶ ▶ ▶ *Ayr Holiday Park (SW509408)*
TR26 1EJ ☎ 01736 795855
Dir: From A30 follow St Ives 'Large Vehicles' route via B3311 through Halestown on to B3306. Park signed towards St Ives town centre
⊞ ⊞ Å
Open Apr-Oct (rs Apr-mid May & Oct shop closed)
Booking advisable Jun-Aug Last arrival 22.00hrs
Last departure 10.00hrs
A well-established park on a cliffside overlooking St Ives Bay. A 4-acre site with 40 touring pitches and 43 statics.
Leisure: ♠ ⚙ **Facilities:** ⬤☉❄✳⬤❤
Services: ▦⊟ℹ∅⊞▦
→ ∪ ► ⬥ ⁘ ♨ ♪ ⬤ 💳 🗺 📰 🖼

▶ ▶ ▶ *Trevalgan Holiday Farm Park (SW490402)*
Trevalgan TR26 3BJ ☎ 01736 796433
Dir: From A30 follow St Ives 'large vehicles' route via B3311 through Halestown. Turn left at junct with B3306 and site 0.5m on the right
★ ⊞ £7.50-£11.50 ⊞ £7.50-£11.50 Å £7.50-£11.50
Open May-Sep Booking advisable mid Jul-mid Aug
Last arrival 23.30hrs Last departure noon
An open, level grass site on a working farm with very good facilities. A 4.75-acre site with 120 touring pitches.
Farm trail, pets corner, mini golf
Leisure: ♠ ⚙ ▭ **Facilities:** ⬤☉❄✳⬤❤⬛ ㅠ ㅠ
Services: ▦⊟ℹ∅⊞▦✕▦
→ ∪ ► ⁘ ♪ ⬛ 💳 🗺 📰 🖼

ST JUST (Near Land's End)   Map 02 SW33

► ► ► **Kelynack Caravan & Camping Park (SW374301)**
Kelynack TR19 7RE ☎ 01736 787633
Dir: 1m S of St Just 5m N of Land's End on B3306
★ ⊞ £6 ⊞ £6 ▲ £6
Open Apr-Oct Booking advisable Jul-Aug Last arrival 22.00hrs Last departure noon
A small, secluded site in an old walled garden, surrounded by open countryside. This well-appointed park offers neat a laundry and a small but well-stocked shop. A 2-acre site with 20 touring pitches and 13 statics.
Leisure: ♣ ⚠ **Facilities:** ℝ⊙ ⊛ ☀ ⚲ ℄ ⚍ ⚘ ⋒ ≒
Services: ⊕ ▮ ⊘ ⊞ Ⓣ
→ ► ⤳ ▣

► ► ► **Roselands Caravan Park (SW387305)**
Dowran TR19 7RS ☎ 01736 788571
Dir: 1.25m E on unclass rd, off A3071
⊞ £6.50-£9.50 ⊞ £6.50-£9.50 ▲ £5-£8
Open Jan-Oct Booking advisable Jun-Sep Last arrival 23.00hrs Last departure 11.00hrs

A small recently upgraded park in a sheltered rural setting, with an indoor games room, and an attractive little bar. An ideal location for a quiet family holiday. A 3-acre site with 12 touring pitches and 15 statics.
Leisure: ♣ ⚠ **Facilities:** ℝ⊙ ⊛ ☀ ℄ ⚍ ⚘ ⋒ ≒
Services: ⊕ ▣ ⚤ ▮ ⊘ ✕ ⚒
→ ∪ ► ⤳

► ► *Bosavern Secret Garden Park (SW370305)*
TR19 7RD ☎ 01736 788301
Dir: Turn off A3071 near St Just onto B3306 Land's End road. Park 0.5m on left
⊞ ⊞ ▲
Open Mar-Oct Booking advisable Jul-Aug Last arrival 22.00hrs Last departure 14.00hrs
A small, neat site in a walled garden behind a guest house. The fairly sheltered location has all grassy pitches. A 2-acre site with 12 touring pitches.
Leisure: ⚍ **Facilities:** ℝ⊙ ⊛ ☀ ℄ ⚘
Services: ⊕ ⚤ ⊞ ⚒
→ ∪ ► ⚙ ⤳ ⚒ ⚍ ⚌ ⚏ ⚏ ⚍ Ⓖ

ST JUST-IN-ROSELAND   Map 02 SW83

► ► ► **Trethem Mill Touring Park (SW860365)**
TR2 5JF ☎ 01872 580504
Dir: From Tregony follow A3078 to St Mawes. 2m after passing through Trewithian look out for signs to park
⊞ £7-£11 ⊞ £7-£11 ▲ £7-£11
Open Apr-Oct Booking advisable Jul-Aug Last arrival 21.00hrs Last departure 11.00hrs

A carefully tended and sheltered park in a rural setting. This quiet park is personally run by a very keen family. An 11-acre site with 80 touring pitches. Info centre, Wet suit hire.
Leisure: ♣ ⚠ ⚍ **Facilities:** ℝ⊙ ⊛ ☀ ℄ ⚘ ≒
Services: ⊕ ▣ ▮ ⊘ ⊞ Ⓣ ⤳
→ ∪ ◭ ⤳ ⤳ ⚌ ⚏ ⚍ Ⓖ

ST KEW HIGHWAY   Map 02 SX07

► ► **Lanarth (SX033751)**
PL30 3EE ☎ 01208 841215
Dir: 3m NE of Wadebridge off A39, just before entering the village
★ ⊞ £6-£10
Open Etr/Apr-Oct Booking advisable Last departure noon
New owners are in the process of upgrading this park, a sheltered site with level grassy pitches in the grounds of a country hotel. The hotel amenities are available to those staying on the site. Situated three miles from Wadebridge and in the centre of a famous cycle trail. A 9-acre site with 86 touring pitches.
Facilities: ℝ ⊛ ☀ ℄ ⚘ ≒ **Services:** ⊕ ⚤ ▮ ⊞ ✕
→ ∪ ► ⚤ ⤳ ▣

ST MABYN   Map 02 SX07

► ► ► *Glenmorris Park (SX055733)*
Glenmorris PL30 3BY ☎ 01208 841677
Dir: Signed on unclass road off B3266 towards St Mabyn, at Longstone village
⊞ ⊞ ▲
Open Etr-Oct Booking advisable bank hols & Jul-Aug Last arrival 22.00hrs Last departure 10.30hrs
A very good, mainly level park in a peaceful rural location offering clean and well-maintained facilities - a small games room, heated outdoor swimming pool and sunbathing area, and shop. An ideal location for visiting this unspoilt area. A 10-acre site with 80 touring pitches and 6 statics.
Off licence
Leisure: ↖ ♣ ⚠ **Facilities:** ℝ⊙ ⊛ ☀ ℄ ⚍ ⚘ ⋒ ≒
Services: ⊕ ▣ ▮ ⊘ ⊞ Ⓣ
→ ∪ ► ◭ ⤳ ⚌ ⚏ ⚍

ST MERRYN (Near Padstow) Map 02 SW87

► ► ► **Carnevas Farm Holiday Park (SW862728)**
Carnevas Farm PL28 8PN ☎ 01841 520230 & 521209
Dir: *Take B3276 towards Porthcothan Bay, 2m SW of village*
★ ⚘ £6-£10 ⚘ £6-£10 ▲ £6-£10

Open Apr-Oct (rs Apr-Whit & mid Sep-Oct shop, bar, restaurant closed) Booking advisable Jul-Aug
This slightly sloping site is divided into four areas with central toilet facilities, and offers good shopping and a well-equipped laundry. An 8-acre site with 195 touring pitches and 14 statics.
Leisure: ◆ ⚏ **Facilities:** ↟⊙ᕦ✳᛬↖⛾ᑫ
Services: ⛽⛳♀ᵢ⌀⊞⊤✕
➔∪▶♨⚓⚒♪

► ► **Tregavone Touring Park (SW898732)**
Tregavone Farm PL28 8JZ ☎ 01841 520148
Dir: *1m off A389 on unclass road to church*
⚘⚘▲
Open Mar-Oct Booking advisable end Jul-beg Aug
This rather open grassy park on a working farm has good facilities in well-converted farm buildings. Run by friendly owners, and handy for the beaches and surfing areas on the north Cornish coast. A 3-acre site with 40 touring pitches.
Facilities: ↟⊙✳↖ **Services:** ⛽⛳⊞
➔∪▶◉♨⚓⚒♪ᕇ

► ► **Trevean Caravan & Camping Park (SW875724)**
Trevean Ln PL28 8PR ☎ 01841 520772
Dir: *From St Merryn village take B3276 to Newquay for 1m. Turn left for Rumford. Site 0.25m on the right*
★ ⚘ £6-£8 ⚘ £6-£8 ▲ £6-£8

Open Apr-Oct Booking advisable mid Jul-Aug Last arrival 22.30hrs Last departure noon

A small working farm site with level grassy pitches in rather open countryside. A 1.5-acre site with 36 touring pitches and 3 statics.
Leisure: ⚏ **Facilities:** ↟⊙ᕦ✳᛬↖⛾ᑫ↖
Services: ⛽⛳ᵢ⌀⊞
➔∪▶♨⚒♪

ST MINVER   Map 02 SW97

     St Minver Holiday Park (SW965772)
PL27 6RR ☎ 01208 862305
Dir: *From A39 N of Wadebridge take the B3314 Port Isaac road. Site signed on left in 3m*
★ ⚘ £4.25-£17.50 ⚘ £4.25-£17.50 ▲ £4.25-£17.50
Open Etr-5 Oct Booking advisable Jul-Sep Last arrival mdnt Last departure 10.00hrs
A large holiday park set around St Minver House in sylvan surroundings. The park offers a wide range of holiday activites, including crazy golf, table tennis and large indoor fun pool and waterslide. A programme of family entertainemnt is offered during evenings in the high season, and there is an adult-only bar. A 5-acre site with 120 touring pitches and 300 statics.
Crazy golf, free evening entertainment, amusements.
Leisure: ⚲ ◆ ⚏ **Facilities:** ↟⊙ᕦ✳↖⛾↖
Services: ⛽⛳♀ᵢ⌀⊞⊤✕♨
➔▶♨⚒ ⬤ ▦▦ ⛽

► ► ► *Gunvenna Touring Caravan & Camping Park (SW969782)*
PL27 6QN ☎ 01208 862405
Dir: *From A39 N of Wadebridge take Port Isaac road B3314, park 4m on right*
⚘⚘▲
Open Etr-Oct Booking advisable Jul-Aug Last arrival mdnt Last departure 11.00hrs

Attractive park with extensive rural views in a quiet country location, yet within three miles of Polzeath. This popular park is family owned and run, and provides good facilities in an ideal position for touring north Cornwall. A 10-acre site with 75 touring pitches and 20 statics.
Leisure: ⚲ ⚲◆⚏ **Facilities:** ↦↟⊙ᕦ✳↖⛾⌂↖↖
Services: ⛽⛳♀ᵢ⌀✕↦
➔∪▶♨⚓⚒♪

SCILLY, ISLES No sites on the island hold AA classification. See Island Camping on page 34

SCORRIER   Map 02 SW74

▶ ▶ ▶ *Wheal Rose Caravan & Camping Park* *(SW717449)*
Wheal Rose TR16 5DD ☎ 01209 891496
Dir: Leave A30 at Scorrier sign and follow signs on unclass road to Wheal Rose. Park 0.5m on left
⚑ ⚐ Å
Open Mar-Dec Booking advisable Aug Last arrival 23.00hrs Last departure 11.00hrs

A quiet, peaceful park in secluded valley setting, central for beaches and countryside. The friendly owners work hard to keep this park immacualte, with bright toilet block and well-trimmed pitches. A 6-acre site with 50 touring pitches and 1 static.
Leisure: ◆ ⚑ Facilities: ⬤⊙❄✲↖▥⊞☴
Services: ⬤⊟▤⊘⊞⊺◆
→ ∪ ▶ ⊙ ⚌ ⚇ ⊿

SUMMERCOURT   Map 02 SW85

▶ ▶ ▶ *Resparva House Camping & Caravanning* *(SW881557)*
Chapel Town TR8 5AH ☎ 01872 510332
Dir: Signed off A30 to Chapel Town and Summerscourt, 1.5m past McDonald's and just beyond Kessels Volvo. Do not take 1st sign for Summerscourt
⚑ ⚐ Å
Open May-Sep Booking advisable Jul/Aug Last arrival 20.00hrs Last departure noon
A small, grassy park with good facilities, almost in the centre of Cornwall. This adults-only site is edged by hedgebanks, and is almost entirely surrounded by farmland. A 2-acre site with 15 touring pitches.
Facilities: ⬤⊙❄✲▥⊞ Services: ⬤▤⊘⊞
→ ∪ ▶ ⊿ ↖

TINTAGEL

See **Camelford**

TORPOINT   Map 02 SX45

Whitsand Bay Holiday Park *(SX410515)*
Millbrook PL10 1JZ ☎ 01752 822597
Dir: Leave Torpoint on A374 and turn left at Anthony onto B3247 for 1.25m to T-junct. Turn left for 0.25m then right on to Cliff Road. Site 2m on left
⚑ ⚐ Å

Whitsand Bay Holiday Park

In Cornwall and only six miles from the historic city of Plymouth, and twelve miles from Looe. South East Cornwall's award winning holiday centre. Set in grounds of an historic hilltop ancient fortification with spectacular views over the Tamar estuary and Dartmoor. Minutes walk to unspoilt sandy beaches. Luxury self-catering chalets and caravans. Touring pitches for caravans and tents. Extensive range of facilities including heated pool; licensed family club with entertainment; cafe-bar; shop; playback; park; sauna; arcade; crazy golf and much more!!!!
indoor heated swimming pool and sun terrace
For free colour brochure/bookings
Tel: 01752 822597 Fax: 01752 823444
www.whitsandbayholidays.co.uk
E-mail: enquiries@whitsandbayholidays

Open all year (rs Oct-Feb some facilities closed)
Booking advisable Last arrival 24.00hrs Last departure 10.00hrs
A very well-equipped site with panoramic views from its tiered pitches, and plenty of on-site entertainment. A 27-acre site with 100 touring pitches and 40 statics.
Sauna, sunbed, entertainment, putting.
Leisure: ⚡ ◆ ⚑ ▱ Facilities: ⬤⊙❄✲⬤◆⬤
↖▥⊞✦ Services: ⬤⊟▤⊘⊞✕▤
→ ∪ ▶ ⊙ ⚌ ⚇ ⊿ ⬛ ▦

TREGURRIAN   Map 02 SW86

▶ ▶ ▶ *Camping & Caravanning Club Site* *(SW853654)*
TR8 4AE ☎ 01637 860448
Dir: From A3059 to Newquay. 1.5m on, after service station, right to Newquay Airport. Continue to junct then left to Tregurrian. Follow Watergate Bay signs
★ ⚑ £11.80-£14.90 ⚐ £11.80-£14.90 Å £11.80-£14.90
Open 7 Apr-25 Sep Booking advisable bank hols & Jul-Aug Last arrival 21.00hrs Last departure noon
A level grassy site close to the famous beaches of Watergate Bay, with a modern amenity block. This upgraded club site is an excellent touring centre for the Padstow-Newquay coast. Please see the advertisement on page 14 for details of Club Members' benefit. A 4.25-acre site with 90 touring pitches.
Parent & child room, Motor caravan service area.
Facilities: ⬤⊙❄✲⬤◆ Services: ⬤⊟▤⊘⊞⊺
→ ∪ ▶ ⊙ ⚌ ⊿ ↖ ⬛ ▦

Services: ⊺ Toilet Fluid ✕ Café/ Restaurant ⬛ Fast Food/Takeaway ➴ Baby Care ⬤ Electric Hook Up
▤ Launderette ♀ Licensed Bar ⬤ Calor Gaz ⊘ Camping Gaz ⊞ Battery Charging

England

TRURO   Map 02 SW84

► ► ► ► Leverton Place (SW774453)
Greenbottom, Chacewater TR4 8QW
☎ 01872 560462
Dir: 3.5m W of city centre. Off A390 at Threemilestone rdbt
★ ⚲ £7.50-£16 ⚲ £7.50-£16 ▲ £7.50-£16
Open all year (rs Oct-May not all facilities open all year round) Booking advisable Spring bank hol & Jun-early Sep Last arrival 22.00hrs Last departure noon
An attractive park divided into paddocks with mature hedging, in a pleasant location on the rural fringes of Truro. There are 15 en-suite unisex facilities in addition to the normal segregated ones, and all pitches are of a generous size. In high season there is a small lounge bar, a bistro and a takeaway. A 9.75-acre site with 107 touring pitches and 13 statics.
Hairdrying room, children's heated pool.
Leisure: ⌇ ◖ ⚲ ◻ Facilities: ⬥◉❄⬥⬥◖ ⬥ ⬥
Services: ⬥⬥⬥⬥⬥⬥⬥◻✕⬥
→ ∪ ▶ ⬥ ⬥ ⬥ | ⬥ ⬥ ⬥ ⬥ ⬥

► ► ► ► Ringwell Valley Holiday Park (SW805408)
Bissoe Rd, Carnon Downs TR3 6LQ
☎ 01872 862194 & 865409
Dir: 3m SW off A39
⚲ £8-£14 ⚲ £8-£14 ▲ £8-£14
Open Etr-Sep Booking advisable Jul & Aug Last arrival 21.30hrs Last departure noon
A well-run park nestling in a tranquil valley with open countryside views. Four separate touring areas are allocated for caravans, tents and motor vans, with the freedom to pitch on a favoured spot. The park is set in 12 acres of lush parkland, and at the bottom of the valley in a sheltered sun-trap is the swimming pool, next to the pub. A 12-acre site with 34 touring pitches and 44 statics.
Leisure: ⌇ ◖ ⚲ Facilities: ⬥◖◉❄⬥◖⬥⬥⬥
Services: ⬥⬥⬥⬥⬥⬥◻✕⬥
→ ∪ ▶ ⬥ ⬥ ⬥ ⬥ | ⬥ ⬥ ⬥ ⬥ ⬥

► ► ► Camping & Caravanning Club Site (SW934414)
Tretheake Manor, Veryan TR2 5PP ☎ 01872 501658
Dir: Left off A3078 at filling station signed Veryan/Portloe on unclass road. Site signed on left
★ ⚲ £11.80-£14.90 ⚲ £11.80-£14.90 ▲ £11.80-£14.90
Open 20 Mar-1 Nov Booking advisable Jul-Aug Last arrival 21.00hrs Last departure noon
A quiet park situated on slightly undulating land with pleasant views of the surrounding countryside. Please see the advertisement on page 14 for details of Club Members' benefits. A 9-acre site with 150 touring pitches.
Leisure: ◖ ⚲ Facilities: ◖◉❄⬥⬥⬥⬥
Services: ⬥⬥
→ ∪ ⬥ ⬥ | ⬥ ⬥

► ► ► Carnon Downs Caravan & Camping Park (SW805406)
Carnon Downs TR3 6JJ ☎ 01872 862283
Dir: Take A39 from Truro towards Falmouth. Located just off the main Carnon Downs rdbt, on the left
★ ⚲ £7.25-£12.75 ⚲ £7.25-£12.75 ▲ £6.25-£12.75
Open Etr or Apr-Oct Booking advisable Jul-Aug Last arrival 23.00hrs Last departure 11.00hrs
A mature park with a high standard of landscaping set in meadowland and woodland just outside the urban area. An 11-acre site with 150 touring pitches. Baby & child bathroom. Three family bathrooms.
Leisure: ⚲ ◻ Facilities: ⬥◖◉❄⬥⬥◖⬥⬥
Services: ⬥⬥⬥⬥◻◻
→ ∪ ▶ ⬥ ⬥ ⬥ ⬥ | ⬥ ⬥ ⬥ ⬥ ⬥

► ► ► Chacewater Park (SW740438)
Coxhill, Chacewater TR4 8LY ☎ 01209 820762
Dir: From A30 take A3047 to Scorrier, after 400yds left at Crossroads Motel. Join B3298 for 1.25m. At X-roads left to Chacewater & continue 0.75m
★ ⚲ £9 ⚲ £9 ▲ £9
Open May-Sep Booking advisable May-Sep Last arrival 21.00hrs Last departure 11.00hrs
A level grassy site with young trees set in meadowland. Ideal for couples over 30 seeking a relaxing rural holiday, with well-maintained facilities and open space. A 6-acre site with 94 touring pitches and 6 statics.
Facilities: ◖◉❄⬥⬥◖⬥ Services: ⬥⬥⬥⬥◻◻
→ ∪ ▶ | ⬥ ⬥ ⬥ ⬥ ⬥

► ► ► Liskey Touring Park (SW772452)
Greenbottom TR4 8QN ☎ 01872 560274
Dir: Off A390 at Threemilestone rdbt onto unclass road towards Chacewater. Signed on the right in 0.5m
★ ⚲ £6.50-£10.50 ⚲ £6.50-£10.50 ▲ £6.50-£10.50
Open Apr-Oct Booking advisable Jul-Aug Last arrival 20.00hrs Last departure noon
A small, south facing park of exceptional attractiveness, on the edge of an urban area. The cleanliness of the facilities cannot be faulted, and the pitches are always well manicured. The keen and friendly owners have created a warm and relaxed atmosphere. A 4.5-acre site with 60 touring pitches.
Serviced pitches, undercover playbarn.
Leisure: ⚲ ◻ Facilities: ⬥◖◉❄⬥◖⬥
Services: ⬥⬥⬥⬥◻◻
→ ∪ ▶ ⬥ ⬥ ⬥ ⬥ | ⬥ ⬥ ⬥ ⬥ ⬥

► ► ► Summer Valley (SW800479)
Shortlanesend TR4 9DW ☎ 01872 277878
Dir: 3m NW off B3284
★ ⚲ £6.50-£9.50 ⚲ £6.50-£9.50 ▲ £6.50-£9.50
Open Apr-Oct Booking advisable Jul-Aug Last arrival 22.00hrs Last departure noon

---

Facilities: ⬥ Bath ◖ Shower ◉ Electric Shaver ❄ Hairdryer ❄ Ice Pack Facility ⬥ Disabled Facilities ◖ Public Telephone
⬥ Shop on Site or within 200yds ◻ Mobile Shop (calls at least 5 days a week) ⬥ BBQ Area ⬥ Picnic Area ⬥ Dog Exercise Area

A very attractive and secluded site in a rural setting, and very well-maintained. A 3-acre site with 60 touring pitches.
Campers lounge.
Leisure: ⚠ **Facilities:** ➡ ⊙ ⚹ ✳ ⚿ ⚑ ⊪
Services: ⚑ ⬛ ⓘ ⬧ ⊞ ⓣ
→ ∪ ▶ ⚎ ⬥ ⬤ ⬛ 🔲

Crazy golf, water shute/splash pool & pets corner.
Leisure: ⚘ ⚘ ⚠ **Facilities:** ➡ ⚑ ⊙ ⚹ ✳ ⬧ ⚿ ⚑ ⊪
Services: ⚑ ⬛ ⚑ ⓘ ⬧ ⊞ ⓣ ✗ ⬤
→ ∪ ▶ ⬤ ⬧ ⚎ ⬥ ⬤ 🔲 🔲 🔲

WADEBRIDGE   Map 02 SW97

▶ ▶ ▶ **The Laurels (SW957715)**
Whitecross PL27 7JQ
☎ 01208 813341 & 07799 777715
Dir: Off A389 Padstow road nr junct with A39
⚑ £9-£14 ⚑ £9-£14 ⚠ £9-£11
Open Apr/Etr-Oct Booking advisable Jul-Sep Last arrival 20.00hrs Last departure noon
A small family owned and run park that is centrally located for the Camel Trail cycle way (2.75m), the famous town of Padstow and all the sandy, surfing beaches. A 2.25-acre site with 30 touring pitches.
Leisure: ⚠ **Facilities:** ⚑ ⊙ ⚹ ⚿ ⬛ ⊓ **Services:** ⚑ ⬛ ⊞
→ ∪ ▶ ⬥ ⚎ ⚎ ⬥ ⚑ ⬤ 🔲

▶ ▶ ▶ *Little Bodieve Holiday Park (SW995734)*
Bodieve Rd PL27 6EG ☎ 01208 812323
Dir: From A39 rdbt on Wadebridge by-pass take B3314 signed Rock/Port Isaac, site 0.25m on right
⚑ ⚑ ⚠
Open Apr-Oct (rs early & late season pool & shop closed) Booking advisable Jul-Aug Last arrival 20.00hrs Last departure 11.00hrs
An established and well-organised gently-sloping park in a rural area with good touring facilities. There is a sun terrace around the swimming pool with direct access from the bar and entertainment lounge. A 20-acre site with 195 touring pitches and 75 statics.

WATERGATE BAY   Map 02 SW86

▶ ▶ ▶ **Watergate Bay Tourist Park (SW850653)**
Watergate Bay TR8 4AD ☎ 01637 860387
Dir: 4m N of Newquay on B3276 coast road at Watergate Bay
★ ⚑ £7-£12.50 ⚑ £7-£12.50 ⚠ £7-£12.50
Open 22 May-12 Sep (rs Mar-21 May & 13 Sep-Nov restricted bar, cafe, shop & swimming pool)
Booking advisable Jul-Aug Last arrival 22.00hrs Last departure noon

A well-established park on high ground above Watergate Bay with its acres of golden sands, and lots of rock pools. This park has a regular entertainment programme in the clubhouse. A 32-acre site with 171 touring pitches.
Entertainment, free minibus to beach.
Leisure: ⚘ ⚘ ⚠ ⬜ **Facilities:** ➡ ⚑ ⊙ ⚹ ✳ ⬧ ⚿ ⚑ ⬛ ⊪
Services: ⚑ ⬛ ⚑ ⓘ ⬧ ⊞ ⓣ ✗ ⬤
→ ▶ ⊙ ⬤ ⚎ ⬤ 🔲 🔲 🔲 🔲

Services: ⊤ Toilet Fluid ✗ Café/ Restaurant ⬛ Fast Food/Takeaway ⚎ Baby Care ⚑ Electric Hook Up
⬛ Launderette ⚑ Licensed Bar ⬛ Calor Gaz ⬧ Camping Gaz ⊞ Battery Charging

WHITECROSS   Map 02 SW85

White Acres Holiday Park (SW890599)
TR8 4LW
☎ 01726 860220 & 0800 389 3845
Dir: From A30 at Indian Queens take A392 signed Newquay. Site 2m on the right
★ 🏕 £8-£23 🚐 £8-£23 ▲ £8-£23
Open end Mar-end Oct Booking advisable Jul-Aug Last arrival midnight Last departure 10.00hrs
A large holiday complex, partially terraced, in a rural setting, with one of the best coarse fishing centres in the South West on site.The centre covers 100 acres of woodland, water and grass, and there is a wide range of leisure activities. 115-acre site with 140 touring pitches and 210 statics.
Entertainment, sauna, solarium, fishing lakes, gym, spa
Leisure: ≷ ◆ ⚠ Facilities: ♠⊙ℚ✳�&ℂ▨▦🎋
Services: ⊟🗑♨🖍☎⊞⊤✕🪣
→∪⊙♪ ●🚊🏧📶🔤📳

▶ ▶ ▶ **Summer Lodge Holiday Park (SW890597)**
TR8 4LW ☎ 01726 860415
Dir: From Indian Queens on A30 take A392 to Newquay. Site on left at Whitecross in 2.5m
★ 🏕 £6-£10 🚐 £6-£10 ▲ £6-£10
Open Whit-Oct (rs Etr-Whit & Sep-Oct shop cafe closed) Booking advisable Jul-Aug Last arrival 20.00hrs Last departure noon ⚥
Small holiday complex offering use of good facilities. This park has a nightly cabaret in the licensed pub, plus other on-site entertainment. A 26-acre site with 75 touring pitches and 114 statics.
Leisure: ≷ ◆ ⚠ Facilities: ♠⊙ℚ✳�&ℂ▨▦🎋
Services: ⊟🗑♨🖍☎⊞⊤✕🪣
→∪♪ ●🚊🏧📶🔤📳

WIDEMOUTH BAY   Map 02 SS20

Widemouth Bay Caravan Parc (SS199008)
EX23 0DF
☎ 01288 361208 & 01271 866766
Dir: take Widemouth Bay coastal road off A39, turn left. Park on left
🚐🏕▲
Open Mar-Oct Booking advisable Last arrival 23.00hrs Last departure 10.00hrs
A partly sloping rural site set in countryside overlooking the sea and one of Cornwall's finest beaches. Nightly entertainment in high season with emphasis on children's and family club programmes. This park is located less than half a mile from the sandy beaches of Widemouth Bay. A 10-acre site with 100 touring pitches and 150 statics.
See advertisement under BUDE
Leisure: ≷ ◆ ⚠ Facilities: ♠⊙ℚ✳ℂ▨▦🎋🐕
Services: ⊟🗑♨🖍⚚✕🪣
→∪⊙◭☘☂🐾♪ ●🚊🏧📶🔤📳

▶ ▶ ▶ *Penhalt Farm Holiday Park (SS194003)*
EX23 0DG ☎ 01288 361210
Dir: From Bude take Widemouth Bay road off A39, left at end of road signed Millook onto Cornish coastal footpath. Site 0.75m on left
🚐🚐▲
Open Etr-Oct Booking advisable Jul & Aug
Splendid views of the sea and coast can be enjoyed from all pitches on this sloping but partly level site, set in a rural area on a working farm. An 8-acre site with 100 touring pitches and 2 statics.
Pool table.
See advertisement under BUDE
Leisure: ◆ ⚠ Facilities: ♠⊙ℚ✳�&ℂ▨🎋
Services: ⊟🗑♨⊞🖍
→∪⊙◭☘☂🐾♪

CUMBRIA

AMBLESIDE   Map 07 NY30

▶ ▶ ▶ ▶ *Skelwith Fold Caravan Park (NY355029)*
LA22 0HX ☎ 015394 32277
Dir: Leave Ambleside on A593 towards Coniston, turn left at Clappersgate on 1m onto B5286 Hawkshead road. Park 1m on right
🚐🚐
Open Mar-15 Nov Booking advisable public hols & Jul-Aug Last departure noon
In the grounds of a former mansion, this park is in a beautiful setting close to Lake Windermere. Approached up a grand private driveway, the park is set in 130 magnificent acres. Touring areas are dotted in paddocks around the extensively wooded grounds, and the all-weather pitches are set close to the many facility buildings. The park is enhanced by many azaleas, rhododendrons and both evergreen and broad-leaf trees, and there is a 5-acre family recreation area which has spectacular views of Loughrigg Fell. A 10-acre site with 150 touring pitches and 300 statics.
Family recreation area.
Leisure: ⚠ Facilities: ♠⊙ℚ✳�&ℂ▨▦🎋🐕
Services: ⊟🗑♨🖍⊞⊤
→∪⊙◭☘☂🐾♪

▶ ▶ ▶ *Low Wray National Trust Campsite (NY372013)*
Low Wray LA22 0JA ☎ 015394 32810
Dir: 3m SW via A583 to Clappersgate, then B5286 and unclass road
▲
Open wk before Etr-Oct Booking advisable Last arrival 23.00hrs no cars by caravans no cars by tents
A site for tenters on the banks of Lake Windermere, divided naturally into areas for families and for young people. A 10-acre site with 200 touring pitches.
Launching for sailing.
Leisure: ⚠ Facilities: ♠⊙&ℂ▨ Services:
→◭☘☂♪🗑 ●🚊🏧📶🔤📳

APPLEBY-IN-WESTMORLAND   Map 12 NY62

PREMIER PARK

▶ ▶ ▶ ▶ ▶ **Wild Rose Park (NY698165)**
Ormside CA16 6EJ ☎ 017683 51077
Dir: Signposted on unclass road to Great Ormside off B6260
🚐 £7.80-£13.20 🚐 £7.80-£13.20 ▲ £7.80-£13.20
Open all year (rs Nov-Mar shop, swimming pool & restaurant closed) Booking advisable bank & school hols Last arrival 22.00hrs Last departure noon
Situated in the Eden Valley, this large family-run park has been carefully landscaped and offers superb facilities maintained to an extremely high standard. There are several individual pitches, and extensive views from most areas of the park. Traditional stone walls and the planting of lots of indigenous trees help it to blend into the environment, and wildlife is actively encouraged. A 40-acre site with 240 touring pitches and 240 statics.
Tourist Information, bike hire & pitch and putt.
Leisure: ⚛ ⚓ ⚖ ⬜ Facilities: ⬤⊙⬤✳⬤⬤⬤⬤
Services: ⬤⬤⬤⬤⬤⬤⬤✕⬤
→ ▶ ✔ ⬤ ⬤ ⬤ ⬤ ⬤

▶ ▶ ▶ *Low Moor Caravan Site (NY624259)*
CA10 1XQ ☎ 017683 61231
Dir: On A66, 7m SE of Penrith, close to Kirby Thore
🚐 🚐 ▲

Open Apr-Oct Booking advisable high season Last arrival 23.00hrs
A small farm site with well cared for grounds and clean sanitary facilities. There are extensive views over the surrounding countryside. A 2-acre site with 12 touring pitches and 25 statics.
Leisure: ⚛ Facilities: ⬤⊙⬤✳⬤⬤⬤⬤⬤ Services: ⬤⬤⬤⬤

▶ **Hawkrigg Farm (NY659203)**
Colby CA16 6BB ☎ 017683 51046
Dir: In Colby turn left signed Kings Meadburn and Newby. Site 800yds on right
🚐 £4 🚐 £4 ▲ £2-£4
Open all year Booking advisable Jul-Aug Last arrival 23.30hrs
Attractive level farm site in a pleasant and quiet location on the edge of the small village of Colby. A 1-acre site with 15 touring pitches and 4 statics.
Facilities: ⬤⊙✳⬤ Services: ⬤
→ ▶ ✔ ⬤ ⬤

AYSIDE   Map 07 SD38

▶ ▶ ▶ **Oak Head Caravan Park (SD389839)**
LA11 6JA ☎ 015395 31475
Dir: From M6 junct 36, follow A590 towards Newby Bridge, 14m. Park sign on L, 1.25m past High Newton
★ 🚐 £10 🚐 £8-£10 ▲ £8-£10
Open Mar-Oct Booking advisable bank hols Last arrival anytime Last departure noon

contd.

Services: Ⓣ Toilet Fluid ✕ Café/ Restaurant 🍟 Fast Food/Takeaway 🍼 Baby Care ⬤ Electric Hook Up
🔲 Launderette ♀ Licensed Bar 🛢 Calor Gaz ⊘ Camping Gaz ⬤ Battery Charging

England

A tiered grassy site with some hardstandings set in hilly country with woodland. A 3-acre site with 60 touring pitches and 71 statics.
Facilities: ℟ ⊙ ⚲ ⚹ ᗜ ᘳ 𝑇 **Services:** ᕸ ᐃ ᒷ ⊘ ⊞
➔ ∪ ᐃ ⚵ ⤷ ᔱ

BARROW-IN-FURNESS   Map 07 SD26

► ► ► **South End Caravan Park (SD208628)**
Walney Island LA14 3YQ ☎ 01229 472823 & 471556
Dir: In Barrow follow signs for Walney Island. Turn left after crossing bridge. 4m S
★ ᕸ £8-£12 ᕸ £8-£12 ▲ £8-£12

Open Mar-Oct Booking advisable Jul-Aug Last arrival 22.00hrs Last departure noon
Mainly level grass site adjacent to sea, and close to a nature reserve, on southern end of Walney Island. This friendly family-owned and run park offers an extensive range of good quality amenities and high standards of cleanliness and maintenance. A 7-acre site with 60 touring pitches and 100 statics. Bowling green.
Leisure: ⚲ ⚮ ⚲ ⊡ **Facilities:** ℟ ⊙ ⚹ ᗜ ᘳ 𝒟 𝑇
Services: ᕸ ᐃ ᒷ ⚲ ᒷ ⊘ ⊞ ⚱
➔ ∪ ⌖ ⊚ ᕧ ᕷ ᕹ ᕙ ᘆ ᕨ

BASSENTHWAITE LAKE   Map 06 NY23

See map for locations of sites in the vicinity

BOTHEL   Map 11 NY13

► ► ► **Skiddaw View Holiday Park (NY180366)**
CA5 2JG ☎ 016973 20919
Dir: Signed on unclass road off A591 towards Sunderland, 12m from Keswick
ᕸ ᕹ ▲
Open Etr-Oct Booking advisable bank holidays Last arrival 20.00hrs Last departure noon
A picturesque park with elevated touring pitches and extensive views towards Bassenthwaite Lake and Skiddaw. Sauna available for guests. A 10-acre site with 20 touring pitches and 76 statics.
Sauna
Leisure: ⚮ **Facilities:** ℟ ⊙ ⚲ ⚹ ᘳ 𝑇
Services: ᕸ ᐃ ᒷ ⊞
➔ ∪ ⌖ ᕷ ᔱ ᕹ ᕙ ᘆ ᕵ ᕨ

BOUTH   Map 07 SD38

► ► ► **Black Beck Caravan Park (SD335855)**
LA12 8JN ☎ 01229 861274
Dir: Take A590 at Newby Bridge, turn right at Bouth sign onto unclass road. Left at T-junct to park signed on right. Road is 1st right after railway museum
ᕸ ᕹ ▲

Open Mar-Nov Booking advisable bank hols Last arrival 20.00hrs Last departure 13.00hrs
A quiet site surrounded by attractive woodlands and fields close to southern Cumbria and the Lake District. The 38 acres of private grounds has a beck running through, and Windermere is only two miles away. A 2-acre site with 75 touring pitches and 235 statics.
Leisure: ⚮ **Facilities:** ℟ ⊙ ⚲ ⚹ ᗜ ᘳ ᔱ
Services: ᕸ ᐃ ᒷ ⊘ ⊞
➔ ∪ ᕷ

BOWNESS-ON-WINDERMERE

Sites are listed under **Windermere**

BRAITHWAITE   Map 11 NY22

► ► ► **Scotgate Holiday Park (NY235235)**
CA12 5TF ☎ 017687 78343
Dir: At junct of A66 and B5292, 2m from Keswick
ᕸ ᕹ ▲
Open Mar-Oct Last arrival 22.00hrs Last departure 11.00hrs

A pleasant rural site with dramatic views towards Skiddaw and the northern Fells. Close to the starting point for lots of popular fell-walking routes, and popular with tenters, with its level grass pitches. An 8-acre site with 165 touring pitches and 35 statics.
Leisure: ⚲ ⚮ **Facilities:** ℟ ⊙ ⚲ ⚹ ᔱ ᔱ
Services: ᕸ ᐃ ᒷ ⊘ ⊡ ✕
➔ ∪ ⊙ ⚵ ᕱ ᕷ

Facilities: ⇥ Bath ℟ Shower ⊙ Electric Shaver ⚲ Hairdryer ⚹ Ice Pack Facility ᗜ Disabled Facilities ᘳ Public Telephone
ᔱ Shop on Site or within 200yds ⊞ Mobile Shop (calls at least 5 days a week) ᕱ BBQ Area ⊼ Picnic Area 𝑇 Dog Exercise Area

BRAMPTON   Map 12 NY56

▶ ▶ ▶ **Irthing Vale Holiday Park (NY522613)**
Old Church Ln CA8 2AA ☎ 016977 3600
Dir: Approaching on A69, take A6071 to site 0.5m outside the town
★ ⊞ fr £8 ⊞ fr £8 ▲ fr £8

Open Mar-Oct Booking advisable public hols & Jul-Aug Last arrival 23.30hrs Last departure noon
A grassy site on the outskirts of the market town on the A6071. A 4.5-acre site with 30 touring pitches and 26 statics.
Leisure: ⚓ Facilities: ♠⊙☀✆☎ Services: ☎🔋🅰⊞
→ ∪ ▶ ⌴ ⤴

CARLISLE   Map 11 NY35

▶ ▶ ▶ **Dandy Dinmont Caravan & Camping Park (NY399620)**
Blackford CA6 4EA ☎ 01228 674611
Dir: Leave M6 at junct 44 and continue N on A7. Site 1.5m on right, signposted after Blackford sign
⊞ £7.75-£8 ⊞ £7.75-£8 ▲ £6.50-£6.75
Open Etr-Oct (rs Mar showers not available) Booking advisable Last arrival anytime Last departure 15.00hrs
A level, sheltered site, screened on two sides by hedgerows. A 4-acre site with 47 touring pitches and 15 statics.
Dog area off site - Country Lanes
Facilities: ♠⊙☀✆⌇☎ Services: ☎🅰🔋🅰
→ ∪ ▶ ◎ ☎

▶ ▶ ▶ *Green Acres Caravan Park (NY416614)*
High Knells, Houghton CA6 4JW
☎ 01228 577403 & 675418
Dir: Leave M6/A74(M) at junct 44, take A689 towards Brampton for 1m. Left at Scaleby sign and site 1m on left
⊞ ⊞ ▲

Open Etr-Oct Booking advisable Bank Holidays Last arrival 21.00hrs Last departure 14.00hrs
A small family touring park in rural surroundings with distant views of the fells. This pretty park is run by keen, friendly owners who maintain high standards throughout. A 1.5-acre site with 30 touring pitches.
Leisure: ⚓ Facilities: ♠⊙☎ Services: ☎
→ ▶ ☎

▶ ▶ ▶ **Orton Grange Caravan & Camping Park (NY355519)**
Orton Grange, Wigton Rd CA5 6LA ☎ 01228 710252
Dir: 4m W of Carlisle
★ ⊞ £7.40-£8.80 ⊞ £7.40-£8.80 ▲ £7.40-£8.80
Open all year Booking advisable bank hols & Jul-Aug Last arrival 22.00hrs Last departure noon
Mainly grassy site in rural surroundings close to A595, with hardstanding pitches for motorhomes, and an extensive camping shop. A 6-acre site with 50 touring pitches and 22 statics.
Cafe & Fast food facilities in Apr-Sep only.
Leisure: ⚓ ♠ ⚓ ▢ Facilities: ♠⊙🔋☀⌇✆☎🅰🔊
Services: ☎🅰🅰🔋⊞🕀✕⚓
→ ∪ ▶ ☎ ⤴ ⊞ ⊞ ⊞ ⊞ ⊞ ⊞ ⊞

CARTMEL   Map 07 SD37

▶ ▶ ▶ *Greave Farm Caravan Park (SD391823)*
Prospect House, Barber Green LA11 6HU
☎ 015395 36329 & 36587
Dir: M6 junct 36 onto A590 signed Barrow. Approx 1m before Newby Bridge, turn left at X-roads signed Cartmel/Staveley. Site 1m on left just before church
⊞ ⊞ ▲
Open Mar-Oct Booking advisable Last arrival 21.00hrs Last departure noon
A small family-owned park close to working farm in peaceful rural area. The well-tended grass and flower gardens distinguish this carefully nurtured park, and there is always a sparkle to the toilet facilities. A 3-acre site with 3 touring pitches and 20 statics.
Facilities: ♠🔋☀✆⊞ Services: ☎🅰
→ ∪ ▶ ⚓ ⌴ ⤴ ☎

COCKERMOUTH   Map 11 NY13

▶ ▶ ▶ *Violet Bank Holiday Home Park (NY126295)*
Simonscales Ln, Lorton Rd CA13 9TG
☎ 01900 822169
Dir: Approach on B5292 Lorton Road via town centre
contd.

Services: ⊞ Toilet Fluid ✕ Café/ Restaurant ⊞ Fast Food/Takeaway ⤴ Baby Care ☎ Electric Hook Up
⊞ Launderette ⚓ Licensed Bar 🅰 Calor Gaz ⊘ Camping Gaz ⊞ Battery Charging

England

🚐 🚐 👤
Open Mar-15 Nov Booking advisable Spring bank hol & Jul-Aug Last arrival mdnt Last departure noon
Well-maintained site, with a slightly sloping touring area, in a pleasant rural setting affording excellent views of Buttermere Hills. 1m from the town centre. An 8.5-acre site with 30 touring pitches and 86 statics.
Leisure: 🅰 Facilities: ⋔ ☉ ✳ ⋏ 🐾 ℡
Services: 🔌 🗊 🛢 🔋 🎛
→ ∪ ▶ ⤴

CROOKLANDS   Map 07 SD58

► ► ► *Waters Edge Caravan Park (SD533838)*
LA7 7NN ☎ 015395 67708 & 67414
Dir: From M6 Follow signs for Kirkby Lonsdale A65, at 2nd rdbt follow signs for Crooklands/Endmoor. Site 1m on right
🚐 🚐 👤
Open Mar-14 Nov Booking advisable bank hols Last arrival 22.00hrs Last departure noon
A small rural site, close to junction 36 of M6 yet in a very peaceful setting. The facilities are housed in smart buildings, and the park is bordered on two sides by clear running water. A 3-acre site with 30 touring pitches and 9 statics.
Leisure: 🎣 🎠 Facilities: ⋔ ☉ ♋ ✳ ♿ ⋏ 🐾 🍖 ⊓
Services: 🔌 ♀ 🛢 ⤴ 🎛
→ ∪ ⤴ 🍴 💳

CROSTHWAITE   Map 07 SD49

► ► ► *Lambhowe Caravan Park (SD422914)*
LA8 8JE ☎ 015395 68483
Dir: On A5074 between Lancaster and Windermere, opposite Damson Dene Hotel.
🚐 £10-£12 🚐 £10-£12
Open Mar-mid Nov Booking advisable Etr, Spring bank hol & Jul-Aug Last arrival 21.00hrs Last departure noon
A secluded, wooded site in a peaceful location at the hub of Windermere, where the excellent touring pitches are not overwhelmed by the statics. The friendly warden keeps the place attractively maintained. Ideal for touring the Lake District National Park. No tents. A 1-acre site with 14 touring pitches and 112 statics.
Facilities: ⋔ ☉ ⋏ Services: 🔌 🗊 ♀ 🛢
→ ▶ 🛒

CUMWHITTON   Map 12 NY55

► ► ► *Cairndale Caravan Park (NY518523)*
CA4 9BZ ☎ 01768 896280
Dir: Off A69 at Warwick Bridge on unclass rd through Great Corby to Cumwhitton, turn left at village sign, site 1m
🚐 £5-£5.50 🚐 £5-£5.50
Open Mar-Oct Booking advisable school & public hols Last arrival 22.00hrs

Lovely grass site set in tranquil Eden Valley with good views to distant hills. The all-weather touring pitches have electricity, and are located close to the immaculate toilet facilities. A 2-acre site with 5 touring pitches and 15 statics.
Facilities: ⋔ ☉ ✳ Services: 🔌 🛢 🎛
→ ▶ 🛶 ⤴ ⤴ 🛒

DALSTON   Map 11 NY35

► ► ► **Dalston Hall Caravan Park** (NY378519)
Dalston Hall Estate CA5 7JX
☎ 01228 710165
Dir: On B5299
★ 🚐 £7-£7.50 🚐 £7-£7.50 👤 £6-£6.50
Open Mar-Oct Booking advisable Jul-Aug Last arrival 21.00hrs Last departure 13.00hrs
A neat, well-maintained site, situated in the grounds of an estate located between Carlisle and Dalston. Ideal position for touring northern Lake District, Carlisle and surrounding country. A 3-acre site with 60 touring pitches and 17 statics.
9 hole golf course & fly fishing.
Leisure: 🅰 Facilities: ⋔ ☉ ♋ ✳ ⋏ 🐾 🍖 ⊓ ℡
Services: 🔌 🗊 ♀ 🛢 ⤴ 🎛 ⊓ ✗ ♨
→ ▶ 🍴 ⤴

ESKDALE   Map 07 SD19

► ► ► **Fisherground Farm Campsite** (NY152002)
Fisherground CA19 1TF ☎ 019467 23319
Dir: Leave A595 at Gosforth or Holmrook, follow signs on unclass road to Eskdale Green, on towards Boot. Site signed on left
🚐 £8-£9 👤 £8-£9
Open 8 Mar-14 Nov

A mainly level grassy site on farmland amidst beautiful scenery, in Eskdale Valley below Hardknott Pass, between Eskdale and Boot. Own railway halt on the Eskdale-Ravenglass railway, 'The Ratty'. A 3-acre site with 30 touring pitches and 5 statics.
Adventure playground and miniature railway.
Leisure: 🅰 Facilities: ⋔ ☉ ♋ ✳ ⋏ 🍖 ⋏
Services: 🔌 🗊 🎛
→ ⤴ 🛒

Facilities: 🛁 Bath   ⋔ Shower   ☉ Electric Shaver   ♋ Hairdryer   ✳ Ice Pack Facility   ♿ Disabled Facilities   ℡ Public Telephone
🛒 Shop on Site or within 200yds   🚐 Mobile Shop (calls at least 5 days a week)   🍖 BBQ Area   🍽 Picnic Area   🐾 Dog Exercise Area

FLOOKBURGH   Map 07 SD37

Lakeland Leisure Park (SD372743)
Moor Ln LA11 7LT ☎ 015395 58556
Dir: Approach on B5277 through Grange-over-Sands to Flookburgh, turn left at village square and park 1m

Open late Mar-early Nov Booking advisable May-Oct Last arrival 21.00hrs Last departure 11.00hrs
A complete leisure park with full range of activities and entertainments, making this flat, grassy site ideal for families. The touring area is quietly situated away from the main amenities, but the swimming pools, all-weather bowling green and evening entertainment are just a short stroll away. A 105-acre site with 125 touring pitches and 740 statics.
Horse riding.

Leisure: Facilities: Services:

GRANGE-OVER-SANDS

See **Cartmel & Holker**

GREYSTOKE   Map 12 NY43

► ► ► **Hopkinsons Whitbarrow Hall Caravan Park (NY405289)**
Berrier CA11 OXB ☎ 01768 483456
Dir: M6 junction 40 take A66 to Keswick, after 8m turn right and follow tourist signs to 'Hopkinsons'
£8.50 £8.50 £8.50
Open Mar-Oct Booking advisable bank hols & for electric hook up Last arrival 22.00hrs Last departure 23.00hrs
A rural park in a peaceful location surrounded by mature trees and shrubs. This family owned and run park on the fringe of the Lake District National Park offers plenty of grassy pitches and a good number of hardstandings. An 8-acre site with 81 touring pitches and 167 statics.
Table tennis, pool table & video games.

Leisure: Facilities: Services:

HAVERTHWAITE   Map 07 SD38

► ► ► **Bigland Hall Caravan Park (SD344833)**
LA12 8PJ ☎ 01539 531702 & 723339
Dir: From A592 in Haverthwaite turn left opposite steam railway, left at T-junct signed B5278, park on left after 1.5m
£10-£12 £10-£12
Open Mar-Oct Booking advisable public hols Last arrival 22.30hrs Last departure 13.00hrs
A wooded site in lovely countryside 3m from the southern end of Lake Windermere and near the Haverthwaite Steam Railway. The various touring areas are dotted around this large park, and the three toilet blocks are strategically placed. A 30-acre site with 86 touring pitches and 29 statics.
Off-licence on site.

Facilities: Services:

HAWKSHEAD   Map 07 SD39

► ► **Camping & Caravanning Club Site (SD337943)**
Grizedale Hall LA22 0GL ☎ 01229 860257
Dir: Take A590. Right A5092 to Greenodd 0.5m to Penny Bridge. Take minor road and follow signs for Grizedale Visitors' Centre through Satterthwaite
★ £9.80-£12.40 £9.80-£12.40 £9.80-£12.40
Open 20 Mar-26 Sep Booking advisable Spring bank hol & Jul-Aug Last arrival 21.00hrs Last departure noon
A peaceful, sloping site with level pitches set in Grizedale Forest, with lots of marked walks. Close to the visitors' centre with its shop and gallery. Please see the advertisement on page 14 for details of Club Members' benefits. A 5-acre site with 60 touring pitches.

Leisure: Facilities: Services:

HOLKER   Map 07 SD37

► ► ► *Old Park Wood Caravan Park (SD335784)*
LA11 7PP ☎ 015395 58266
Dir: 2m W of Cark in Cartmel, off B5278; follow signs for Holker Hall
Open Mar-Oct Booking advisable bank hols Last departure 17.30hrs
contd.

Services: Ⓣ Toilet Fluid ✗ Café/ Restaurant Fast Food/Takeaway Baby Care Electric Hook Up Launderette Licensed Bar Calor Gaz Camping Gaz Battery Charging

England

Terraced park gently sloping towards the River Leven estuary, surrounded on three sides by woodland; very well maintained and with good facilities. The park is adjacent to Holker Hall house and gardens which are open to the public. A 4-acre site with 50 touring pitches and 325 statics.

See advertisement under GRANGE-OVER-SANDS

Leisure: ？ ⚠   **Facilities:** ⋒ ⊙ ⚲ ℓ ⚏

Services: ⊟ ⚉ ⓘ ⊘ ⊞ ✕

→ ∪ ⏵

KENDAL   Map 07 SD59

► ► ► ► **Ashes Lane Caravan & Camping Park (SD478962)**

Ashes Ln LA8 9JS ☎ 01539 821119

Dir: *Signed off A591, 0.75m from rdbt with B5284 towards Windermere*

⚏ ⚏ Å

Open mid Mar-mid Jan (rs 14 Nov-14 Jan Reduced space) Booking advisable bank hols Last arrival 22.00hrs Last departure noon

A family-run park set in 22 acres of open and undulating countryside with lovely views, in a naturally secluded Lake District area. There are level hardstandings with grassed awning areas for caravans, and well-drained grassy pitches for tents. Most of the facilities have been recently upgraded, including the family room with TV and pool table, the lounge bar, and the attractive children's play area. A 22-acre site with 160 touring pitches and 68 statics.

Leisure: ◆ ⚠ ▢   **Facilities:** ⋒ ⊙ ⚲ ✳ ⚲ ℓ ⚏ ⚏ ₸ ⚲

Services: ⊟ ⚉ ⚏ ⓘ ⊘ ✕ ⛟

→ ∪ ⏵ ⚏ ⚏ ⌡ ⚏ ▦ ⚏ ⚏

► ► ► **Camping & Caravanning Club Site (SD526948)**

Millcrest, Shap Rd LA9 6NY ☎ 01539 741363

Dir: *On A6 1.5m N of Kendal. Site entrance is 100yds N of nameplate 'Skelsmergh'*

★ ⚏ £11.80-£14.90 ⚏ £11.80-£14.90 Å £11.80-£14.90 Open 20 Mar-1 Nov Booking advisable bank hols & high season Last arrival 21.00hrs Last departure noon

Sloping grass site, set in hilly wood and meadowland, with some level all-weather pitches. Please see advertisement on page 14 for details of Club Members' benefits. A 3-acre site with 53 touring pitches.

Leisure: ⚠   **Facilities:** ⋒ ⊙ ⚲ ✳ ℓ ⚏ ₸

Services: ⊟ ⚉ ⓘ ⊘ ⊞

→ ∪ ⏵ ⚏ ⌡ ⚏ ⚏

KESWICK   Map 11 NY22

► ► ► **Camping & Caravanning Club Site (NY258234)**

Derwentwater CA12 5EP ☎ 01768 772392

Dir: *Take A5271 into Keswick town centre, turn R at mini-rdbt, right past bus stn, right past rugby club into narrow road to site*

★ ⚏ £13.90-£14.90 ⚏ £13.90-£14.90 Å £13.90-£14.90 Open Feb-29 Nov Booking advisable all season Last arrival 21.00hrs Last departure noon

---

A well-situated lakeside site within walking distance of the town centre. Boat launching is available from the site onto Derwentwater, and this level grassy park also offers a number of all-weather pitches. Please see advertisement on page 14 for details of Club Members' benefits. A 14-acre site with 250 touring pitches.

Leisure: ⚠   **Facilities:** ⋒ ⊙ ⚲ ✳ ⚲ ℓ ⚏ ₸

Services: ⊟ ⚉ ⓘ ⊘ ⊞

→ ∪ ⏵ ⚏ ⚏ ⌡ ⚏ ⚏

► ► ► *Castlerigg Hall Caravan & Camping Park (NY282227)*

Castlerigg Hall CA12 4TE ☎ 017687 72437

Dir: *300yds along unclass road off A591, approx 1.5m SE of Keswick towards Ambleside, signed in direction of Heights Hotel*

⚏ ⚏ Å

Open Etr-mid Nov Last arrival 21.00hrs Last departure 11.30hrs

A family-run site with tiered pitches and spectacular views over Derwent Water to the mountains beyond. All caravan and motorhome hardstanding pitches have electrics, and the grassy camping field is well sheltered by mature trees and shrubs. An 8-acre site with 173 touring pitches and 30 statics.

Facilities: ⋒ ⊙ ⚲ ✳ ℓ ⚏   **Services:** ⊟ ⓘ ⊘ ⊞ ⊤

→ ⏵ ⚏ ⚏ ⌡ ⊟ ⚏ ⚏ ⚏

► ► ► **Derwentwater Caravan Park (NY257234)**

Crowe Park Rd CA12 5EN ☎ 017687 72579

Dir: *Signposted off B5289 in town centre*

★ ⚏ £9.40-£10.20 ⚏ £9.40-£10.20

Open Mar-14 Nov Booking advisable at all times Last arrival 21.00hrs Last departure noon

A peaceful location close to Derwentwater for this well-managed park which is divided into two areas for tourers. A 4-acre site with 50 touring pitches and 160 statics.

Leisure: ⚠   **Facilities:** ⋒ ⊙ ⚲ ℓ ⚏ ₸

Services: ⊟ ⚉ ⓘ ⊘

→ ∪ ⏵ ⊙ ⚏ ⚏ ⌡ ⚏ ⚏ ⚏ ⚏ ⊙ ⚏ ⚏

► ► ► *Gill Head Farm Caravan & Camping Park (NY380269)*

Troutbeck CA11 0ST ☎ 017687 79652

Dir: *From junct 40 on M6 avoiding Kirkstone Pass. Site 200yds from A66/A5091*

⚏ ⚏ Å

Open Apr-Oct Booking advisable bank hols Last arrival 22.30 hrs Last departure noon

---

Facilities: ➡ Bath ⋒ Shower ⊙ Electric Shaver ⚲ Hairdryer ✳ Ice Pack Facility ⚲ Disabled Facilities ℓ Public Telephone ⚏ Shop on Site or within 200yds ⊞ Mobile Shop (calls at least 5 days a week) ⊞ BBQ Area ₸ Picnic Area ⚲ Dog Exercise Area

England

This level family-run park is part of a hill farming business. An attractive and well-maintained site, with spacious and comfortable facilities, set against a backdrop of Blencathra and the northern fells. A 5.5-acre site with 42 touring pitches and 17 statics.
Facilities: ⚑☉☜☼☾🛒📶☂🐕 Services: 🔌📺🗑🍴
→ ∪ ▶ 🔺 ✈ 🍴

KIRKBY LONSDALE   Map 07 SD67

▶ ▶ ▶ ▶ **Woodclose Caravan Park** (SD618786)
Casterton LA6 2SE ☎ 01524 271597
Dir: On an A65, 0.25m beyond Kirkby Lonsdale, heading to Skipton
★ ⚑ fr £10 ⚑ fr £10 Å fr £4
Open Mar-Oct Booking advisable bank hols, Jul-Aug & Sep Last arrival 21.00hrs Last departure 13.00hrs
A pleasant park site in a rural area with a mix of grass and hardstanding pitches. Although the ground is undulating, all the pitches are level. Two well-placed toilet blocks serve the tourers. The traditional market town of Kirkby Lonsdale is less than 0.5m walk over the famous Devil's Bridge. A 9-acre site with 50 touring pitches and 50 statics. Dog area off site
Leisure: ⚘ Facilities: ⚑☉☜☼☾🛒🐕
Services: 🔌📺🗑🍴
→ ▶ 🍴

▶ ▶ ▶ *New House Caravan Park* (SD628774)
LA6 2HR ☎ 015242 71590
Dir: 1m SE of Kirkby Lonsdale on A65
⚑ ⚑ Å
Open Mar-Oct Booking advisable
A recently developed park around a former farm, set on part grass and part hardstanding in a rural area. A 3-acre site with 50 touring pitches.
Facilities: ⚑☉☜☼☾🐕 Services: 🔌📺🗑🍴⚗🔋
→ ∪ ▶ 🍴🛒

LAMPLUGH   Map 11 NY02

▶ ▶ ▶ **Inglenook Caravan Park** (NY084206)
Fitzbridge CA14 4SH ☎ 01946 861240
Dir: On the left of A5086 in the direction of Egremont
★ ⚑ £8-£9 ⚑ £8-£9 Å £4.50-£9
Open all year Booking advisable bank hols Last arrival 20.00hrs Last departure noon

An ideal touring site, well-maintained and situated in beautiful surroundings. The picturesque village of Lamplugh is close to the western lakes of Ennerdale, Buttermere and Loweswater, and a short drive from sandy beaches. A 3.5-acre site with 30 touring pitches and 29 statics.
Leisure: ⚘ Facilities: ⚑☉☜☼☾🛒
Services: 🔌🗑⚗🔋
→ 🍴

LEVENS   Map 07 SD48

▶ ▶ ▶ *Sampool Caravan Park* (SD479844)
LA8 8EQ ☎ 015395 52265
Dir: Turn off A6 at Levens Bridge onto A590, then left on unclass lane to park in 1m
⚑ ⚑
Open 15 Mar-Oct Booking advisable bank hols & Jul-Aug

A pleasantly landscaped park adjacent to the River Kent. The small touring area is conveniently close to the toilet facilities, and the part hardstanding and part grassy pitches are neatly kept. A 1.5-acre site with 20 touring pitches and 200 statics.
Leisure: ⚘ Facilities: ⚑☉☼☾🛒🐕
Services: 🔌📺🗑
→ 🍴

LONGTOWN   Map 11 NY36

▶ ▶ ▶ **Camelot Caravan Park** (NY391666)
CA6 5SZ ☎ 01228 791248
Dir: Leave M6 junct 44. Site 5m N on A7, 1m S of Longtown
★ ⚑ fr £7 ⚑ fr £7 Å £3-£7
Open Mar-Oct Booking advisable Jul-Aug Last arrival 22.00hrs Last departure noon   *contd.*

England

Very pleasant level grassy site in a wooded setting near junction 44 of the M6, with direct access from the A7. This park is an ideal stopover site. A 1.5-acre site with 20 touring pitches and 1 static.

Facilities: **Services:**

► ► ► *High Gaitle Caravan & Camping Park (NT360684)*
High Gaitle Bridge CA6 5LU ☎ 01228 791819
Dir: *0.5m W of Longtown on A6071. Can also be approached from S at junct 44 of M6 and A7 through Longtown*

Booking advisable all times Last arrival 23.00hrs Last departure 13.00hrs
A level grassy park with modern, spacious sanitary facilities. A 6-acre site with 30 touring pitches.

Facilities: **Services:**

► ► *Oakbank Lakes Country Park (NY369700)*
CA6 5NA ☎ 01228 791108
Dir: *Leave Longtown on A7 towards Langholm/Galashiels. Turn left after 1m signed Corries Mill Chapelknowe and site in 200yds*

Booking advisable Last arrival 20.00hrs Last departure 14.00hrs
Set alongside three fishing lakes, and adjacent to the River Esk, this park has many established and newly planted trees, and a bird sanctuary. A 60-acre site with 22 touring pitches and 4 statics.
Fishing (course, salmon & trout).

Leisure: **Facilities:**
Services:

MEALSGATE — Map 11 NY24

► ► ► ► Larches Caravan Park (NY205415)
CA7 1LQ ☎ 016973 71379 & 71803
Dir: *Situated on A595 Carlisle to Cockermouth road*

Open Mar-Oct (rs early & late season) Booking advisable Etr Spring bank hol & Jul-Aug Last arrival 21.30hrs Last departure noon

This adult-only park (over 18) is set in wooded rural surroundings on the fringe of the Lake District National Park. Touring units are spread out over two sections with well-maintained en-suite facilities. The friendly family-run parks offers well cared for facilities, and a delightful small indoor swimming pool which is ideal for a quiet swim. A 5-acre site with 73 touring pitches and 100 statics.
En suites with toilets, shower, washbasin, shaverpoint

Leisure: **Facilities:**
Services:

MILNTHORPE — Map 07 SD48

► ► ► ► Fell End Caravan Park (SD505780)
Slackhead Rd, Hale LA7 7BS
☎ 015395 62122 & 01524 781918
Dir: *Exit M6 at junct 35. Follow A6 N signposted Kendal Milnthorpe. Left at Esso garage/Wildlife oasis. Follow signs to park*
★ £12.50-£14.50 £12.50-£14.50 £7.50-£14.50
Open all year Booking advisable school & bank hols Last arrival 21.00hrs Last departure 17.00hrs
A well-kept park pleasantly sited in a very picturesque natural position, surrounded by woodland. High standards are constantly reached at this park, and there is a continual improvement programme. The nearby Forestry Commission land can be easily and directly accessed from the touring area, and there are plenty of walks to be enjoyed. All pitches have hardstandings, and they are also linked to satellite TV hook-up points. An 8-acre site with 68 touring pitches and 215 statics.
Off-licence, TV aerial hook ups, kitchen facility.

Leisure: **Facilities:**
Services:

► ► ► Hall More Caravan Park (SD502771)
Hale LA7 7BP ☎ 015395 63383
Dir: *Leave M6 at junct 35 onto A6 towards Milnthorpe for 3.5m. Take 1st left after crossing Cumbrian border & site is signed after 0.75m*
★ £9.50-£12.50 £9.50-£12.50 £6.50-£11.50
Open Mar-Oct Booking advisable bank hols & wknds Last arrival 22.00hrs
A mainly level grassy site in meadowland, adjacent to main road, with all hardstanding pitches and unsophisticated facilities. Close to farm and stables offering pony trekking, and there is trout fishing nearby. A 6-acre site with 50 touring pitches and 65 statics.

Leisure: **Facilities:**
Services:

PATTERDALE — Map 11 NY31

► ► ► *Sykeside Camping Park (NY403119)*
Brotherswater CA11 0NZ
☎ 017684 82239
Dir: *Off A592 Windermere to Ullswater road; not suitable for caravans*

Open all year Booking advisable bank hols & Jul-Aug Last arrival 22.30hrs Last departure 14.00hrs

Facilities: Bath Shower Electric Shaver Hairdryer Ice Pack Facility Disabled Facilities Public Telephone Shop on Site or within 200yds Mobile Shop (calls at least 5 days a week) BBQ Area Picnic Area Dog Exercise Area

Sykeside
CAMPING PARK

**Brotherswater,
Patterdale, Penrith,
Cumbria CA11 0NZ**
Tel: 017684 82239
Fax: 017684 82558
Web: www.sykeside.co.uk

A stunning backdrop for camping, with Dove Crag, Hart Crag and Fairfield to watch over you and tranquil Brotherswater adjacent, there can be few more inspiring locations in which to pitch than Sykeside Camping Park.

All the facilities you need

On site you will find a large toilet block with wash basins, showers, shaving sockets, hand dryers and a 24-hour supply of hot water. Our well-stocked shop offers all the provisions you will need to make your stay even more comfortable. Relax in our Barn End Bar at the end of the day where we have tasty home cooked food and a well stocked bar – including over 150 whiskies!

*A camper's delight, this family-run park is situated halfway up Kirkstone Pass, under the 2000ft Hartsop Dodd in a spectacular area with breathtaking views. The park has mainly level grassy pitches with a few hardstandings, and for those campers without a tent there is bunkhouse accommodation.
A 5-acre site with 86 touring pitches.*

Facilities: ⌂⊙☂✳⌧⌸♨️⛺
Services: ⌀⛽☿ℹ️⌀⊞Ⓣ✕
→◬⊁♪ ⊙▬▦▩▦▨

PENRITH   Map 12 NY53

See also **Greystoke**
► ► ► ► *Lowther Caravan Park (NY527265)*
Eamont Bridge CA10 2JB
☎ 01768 863631
Dir: 3m S of Penrith on A6
⌂⛺△
Open mid Mar-mid Nov Booking advisable bank hols Last arrival 21.00hrs
A secluded natural woodland site with lovely on-site riverside walks and glorious surrounding countryside. The park is home to a rare colony of red squirrels, and trout fishing is available on the 2-mile stretch of the River Lowther which runs through it. A 10-acre site with 150 touring pitches and 407 statics.

Leisure: ⚠ **Facilities:** ⌂⊙☂✳⌸♨️⛺
Services: ⌀⛽☿ℹ️⌀⊞Ⓣ✕⛟
→∪▸⊙☺♪ ⊙▬▦▩▦▨

Services: Ⓣ Toilet Fluid ✕ Café/ Restaurant ⛟ Fast Food/Takeaway ⛟ Baby Care ⌀ Electric Hook Up ⌀ Launderette ☿ Licensed Bar ⌀ Calor Gaz ⌀ Camping Gaz ⊞ Battery Charging

► ► ► **Thacka Lea Caravan Site (NY509310)**
Thacka Ln CA11 9HX ☎ 01768 863319
Dir: 1.5m from juncts 40/41 of M6, at N end of Penrith, and just off A6 at petrol station and Grey Bull Hotel into Robinson St, and signed
★ 📷 fr £6.50 📷 fr £6.50
Open Mar-Oct Booking advisable public hols
A sheltered, tiered park, family owned and run, and maintained to a very good standard. The level grass and hardstanding pitches are mainly equipped with electricity, and the park is on the edge of this attractive market town. An ideal base from which to tour the Lake District. A 2-acre site with 25 touring pitches.
Facilities: ⋒ ⊙ ❋ **Services:** 🛢 🛆 ⌀ ⊞
→ ∪ ▶ 🕱 🎵 🖳

PENRUDDOCK   Map 12 NY42

► ► ► **Beckses Caravan Park (NY419278)**
CA11 0RX ☎ 01768 483224
Dir: Leave M6 junct 40 onto A66 towards Keswick. Approx 6m at caravan park sign turn right onto B5288, site on right in 0.25m
★ 📷 fr £7 📷 fr £7 🛆 fr £5
Open Etr-Oct Booking advisable public hols Last arrival 20.00hrs Last departure 11.00hrs
A small, pleasant site on sloping ground with level pitches and views of distant fells, on the edge of the National Park. This sheltered park is in a good location for touring the North Lakes. A 4-acre site with 23 touring pitches and 18 statics.
Leisure: ⚠ **Facilities:** ⋒ ⊙ 🏳 ❋ ᰣ ⚲
Services: 🛢 🛆 ⌀ ⊞ ⊤
→ ∪ 🎵 🖳

POOLEY BRIDGE   Map 12 NY42

► ► ► ► **Park Foot Caravan & Camping Park (NY469235)**
Howtown Rd CA10 2NA
☎ 017684 86309
Dir: M6 junct 40 onto A66 towards Keswick, then A592 to Ullswater. Turn left for Pooley Bridge, right at church, right at X-roads signed Howtown
📷 📷 🛆
Open Mar-Oct Booking advisable bank hols Last arrival 22.00hrs Last departure noon
A mainly tenting park on gently sloping ground, with access to Lake Ullswater and lovely views. This well-maintained park caters for campers of all ages, and has a separate field for group camping. A

footpath from the park leads to the village of Pooley Bridge, and there is also direct access to the fells. Another feature is the park's own boat-launching facility. An 18-acre site with 323 touring pitches and 131 statics.

Lake access with boat launch, pony treking.
Leisure: ⚲ ⚓ ⚠ 🏳 **Facilities:** ⋒ ⊙ 🏳 ❋ ᰣ ⚲ 🖳 ⚘ ᰣ
Services: 🛢 ⊞ 🛢 🛆 ⌀ ⊞ ⊤ ✕ ⚕
→ ∪ ▶ 🛆 ᰣ 🎵

► ► ► **Hillcroft Caravan & Camping Site (NY478241)**
Roe Head Ln CA10 2LT ☎ 017684 86363
Dir: From A592 fork left just before Pooley Bridge and site is signed on the left
📷 £12 📷 £12 🛆 £9
Open 7 Mar-14 Nov Booking advisable bank hols
A pleasant rural site close to the village and Ullswater with good fell views and spacious grassy pitches. Also six hardstandings for caravans. An ideal touring base. A 10-acre site with 125 touring pitches and 200 statics.
Leisure: ⚠ **Facilities:** ⋒ ⊙ 🏳 ❋ ᰣ ⚲ 🖳 ᰣ
Services: 🛢 ⊞ 🛆 ⌀ ⊞ ⊤
→ ∪ 🛆 ᰣ 🎵

RAVENGLASS   Map 06 SD09

► ► ► **Walls Caravan & Camping Park (SD087964)**
CA18 1SR ☎ 01229 717250
Dir: On the coast, midway between Millom and Whitehaven. Leave A595 to village of Ravenglass. Left at 30mph sign. Site located on the left
📷 £9-£9 📷 £8.50-£8.50 🛆 £3.50-£9
Open Mar-Oct Booking advisable bank hols & summer Last arrival 22.00hrs Last departure noon
A well-maintained site in a woodland park with all hardstandings for vans, and grassy area for tents.

BECKSES CARAVAN PARK
Penruddock, Penrith, Cumbria CA11 0RX
Telephone: Greystoke (017684) 83224
CARAVANS TO LET
A small pleasant site on the fringe of the Lake District National Park, within easy reach of the M6 Motorway (6 miles) Ullswater (4 miles), Keswick (12 miles). Modern facilities for those wishing to pitch their own caravan or tent, or hire a luxury fully equipped static caravan. Telephone enquiries before 6.30p.m. please.

Facilities: ⬛ Bath ⋒ Shower ⊙ Electric Shaver 🏳 Hairdryer ❋ Ice Pack Facility ᰣ Disabled Facilities ⚲ Public Telephone 🖳 Shop on Site or within 200yds ⊞ Mobile Shop (calls at least 5 days a week) ⊞ BBQ Area ᰣ Picnic Area ᰣ Dog Exercise Area

Close to Ravenglass-Eskdale narrow gauge railway service. A 5-acre site with 50 touring pitches. Washing up sinks with free hot water.
Facilities: 🐾⊙🏧☀🔌⚓🚿 Services: 🔌🔲🍴🔋➕
→�🎣

SEDBERGH   Map 07 SD69

► ► ► **Pinfold Caravan Park (SD665921)**
Garsdale Rd LA10 5JL
☎ 01539 620576 01524 781918
Dir: Follow A684 through Sedbergh, turn right after Police/Fire station over Dales bridge. Site on left
★ 🚐 £10-£12 🚲 £10-£12 ⚑ £10-£12
Open Mar-Oct Booking advisable bank hols & Jul-Aug Last arrival 21.30hrs Last departure 13.30hrs
A mature site amongst beautiful scenery on a river bank. A 4-acre site with 28 touring pitches and 56 statics.
Barbeques are allowed
Facilities: 🐾⊙🏧🔌⚓ Services: 🔌🔲🍴🔋➕
→🔤🎣 🍴🍔🔲

SILECROFT   Map 06 SD18

► ► ► **Silecroft Caravan Site (SD124811)**
LA18 4NX ☎ 01229 772659
Dir: Turn off A595 at Silecroft onto A5039 towards Millom, right onto unclass road, park after level crossing. 7m W of Broughton-in-Furness
🚐 £8.50-£9.50 🚲 £8-£9 ⚑ £8-£9
Open Mar-15 Nov Booking advisable

Quietly situated close to the shore 4m N of Millom, in a beautiful, little-known area of the Lake District with lovely beach nearby. A 5-acre site with 60 touring pitches and 124 statics.
Sauna, gym & Jacuzzi.
Leisure: 🏊 ♦ ⚙ Facilities: 🐾🔌☀🔌⚓
Services: 🔌🔲🔋
→🔤🔤🔔ᴧ🎣

SILLOTH   Map 11 NY15

Stanwix Park Holiday Centre (NY108527)
Green Row CA7 4HH ☎ 016973 32666
Dir: 1m SW on B5300
★ 🚐 £13.60-£16.70 🚲 £13.60-£16.70
⚑ £13.60-£16.70
Open all year (rs Nov-Feb no mid week entertainment) Booking advisable Etr, Spring bank hol & Jul-Aug Last arrival 21.00hrs Last departure 11.00hrs
A large well-run family park within easy reach of the Lake District. Attractively laid-out, with lots of amenities to ensure a lively holiday, including a 4-lane automatic ten-pin bowling alley. A 4-acre site with 121 touring pitches and 212 statics.
Pony trekking, Ten-pin Bowling, Bars
Leisure: 🏊 🎯🔤♦⚙🖥 Facilities: ➡🐾⊙🏧
☀♿🔌⚓ Services: 🔌🔲🔲🍴🔋🔌🔲✖👜
→🔤🔔⊙🎣 🍴🍔🔲 🔲🔲🔲

Services: 🔲 Toilet Fluid ✖ Café/ Restaurant 🍔 Fast Food/Takeaway 🔌 Baby Care 🔌 Electric Hook Up
🔲 Launderette 🍴 Licensed Bar 🔌 Calor Gaz 🔌 Camping Gaz 🔋 Battery Charging

► ► ► *Tanglewood Caravan Park (NY131534)*
Causewayhead CA5 4PE ☎ 016973 31253
Dir: Adjacent to B5302 Wigton-Silloth
🚐 🚐 Å
Open Mar-Oct Booking advisable Etr, Whit & Jul-
Aug Last arrival 23.00hrs Last departure 10.00hrs
Mainly level grass site sheltered by a variety of
trees and bushes, and set in meadowland. A 7-acre
site with 31 touring pitches and 58 statics.

Leisure: ◄ ⚠ ▢ Facilities: ⋒ ⊙ ⊠ ☀ ⚲ ⛏
Services: 🖳 🗄 ♀ 🛢 🎁
→ ∪ ⏵ ◎ ✇ 🔧

TEBAY   Map 07 NY60

► ► ► **Tebay Caravan Site (NY609060)**
Orton CA10 3SB ☎ 015396 24511
Dir: Leave M6 1m N of junc 38, accessed through Tebay
service area both N & S/bound. Follow Caravan park
signs
★ 🚐 £8.50-£9.50 🚐 £8.50-£9.50

Open 14 Mar-Oct Booking advisable Jul-Aug Last
departure noon no cars by tents
An ideal stopover site adjacent to the Tebay service
station on the M6, and handy for touring the Lake
District. The park is screened by high grass banks,
bushes and trees, and is within walking distance of
a shop and restaurant. A 4-acre site with 77 touring
pitches and 8 statics.
Facilities: ⋒ ⊙ ⊠ ☀ ⚲ ⚲ 🖳 🎁 📷 ⛏
Services: 🖳 🗄 ♀ 🛢 ⊘ ✕ ⚱
→ ∪ ✇

ULVERSTON   Map 07 SD27

► ► ► *Bardsea Leisure Park (SD292765)*
Priory Rd LA12 9QE ☎ 01229 584712
Dir: Off A5087
🚐 🚐 Å
Open all year Booking advisable bank hols & Jul-
Aug Last arrival 21.00hrs Last departure 18.00hrs
Attractively landscaped former quarry making a
quiet and very sheltered site, with generously-sized
pitches, many of which offer all-weather full
facilities. On southern edge of town, convenient for
both the coast and the Lake District. A 5-acre site
with 83 touring pitches and 73 statics.
Leisure: ⚠ Facilities: ⋒ ⊙ ⊠ ☀ ⚲ 🖳 📷 ⛏
Services: 🖳 🗄 🛢 ⊘ 🎁 ⊤
→ ∪ ⏵ 🎿 ✇

WATERMILLOCK   Map 12 NY42

► ► ► *Cove Caravan & Camping Park (NY431236)*
Ullswater CA11 0LS ☎ 017684 86549
Dir: From M6 junct 40 follow signs for Ullswater (A592).
Turn right at lake junct, then right at Brackenrigg Hotel.
Site 1.5m on right
🚐 🚐 Å
Open Etr-Oct Booking advisable bank & school hols
Last arrival 21.00hrs Last departure noon
A peaceful family site in an attractive and elevated
position with extensive fell views and glimpses of
Ullswater Lake. This grassy park with some sloping
areas is popular with tenters. A 3-acre site with 50
touring pitches and 38 statics.
Drinks machine.
Leisure: ⚠ Facilities: ⋒ ⊙ ⊠ ☀ ⚲ 🖳 🎡 📷 ⛏
Services: 🖳 🗄 🛢 ⊘ 🎁 ⊤
→ ∪ 🎿 ✇

► ► ► **The Quiet Site (NY431236)**
Ullswater CA11 0LS ☎ 01768 486337
Dir: Leave M6 at junct 40 following signs to
Ullswater (A592). Turn right at lake junct, then right at
Brackenrigg Hotel. Site is 1.5m on right
★ 🚐 £9-£11 🚐 £8-£10 Å £8-£10
Open Mar-Oct Booking advisable bank hols & Jul-
Aug Last arrival 22.00hrs Last departure noon
A well-maintained site in a lovely, peaceful location,
with very good facilities, including a charming olde-
worlde bar. A 6-acre site with 60 touring pitches and
23 statics.
Pets corner. Pool & darts (adults only).
Leisure: ◄ ⚠ ▢ Facilities: ⋒ ⊙ ⊠ ☀ ⚲ 🖳
Services: 🖳 🗄 ♀ 🛢 ⊘ 🎁 ⊤ ↩
→ ∪ 🎿 ✇

► ► ► **Ullswater Caravan Camping Site & Marine
Park (NY438232)**
High Longthwaite CA11 0LR ☎ 017684 86666
Dir: M6 junct 40, turn W for Ullswater (A592) for 5m.
Right alongside Ullswater for 2m, then right at
telephone box. Site 0.5m on right
★ 🚐 £10 🚐 £9 Å £9

Open Mar-Nov Booking advisable public hols Last
arrival 21.00hrs Last departure noon
A pleasant rural site with own nearby boat
launching and marine storage facility making it
ideal for sailors. The family-owned and run park
enjoys fell and lake views, and there is a bar and
café on site. A 9-acre site with 155 touring pitches
and 55 statics.   *contd.*

Facilities: ⊷ Bath ⋒ Shower ⊙ Electric Shaver ⊠ Hairdryer ☀ Ice Pack Facility ⚲ Disabled Facilities ⚲ Public Telephone
🖳 Shop on Site or within 200yds ⊡ Mobile Shop (calls at least 5 days a week) 🎡 BBQ Area 📷 Picnic Area ⛏ Dog Exercise Area

'BEST IN BRITAIN' 1996/97

★★★★★ *AA 'Premier Park'*

'Award winning caravan & self-catering holiday

fallbarrow park
...on the shore of Lake Windermere

'We would love to welcome you to our family owned park and do our very best to ensure that you have a really enjoyable and relaxing holiday'. Paul Whiteley

● Luxury *Rose Award* holiday 'caravans' that will probably amaze you!

● 'State-of-the-art' touring pitches with individual connections for water, waste, TV and electric.

● Friendly reception and tourist information centre. Welcoming 'Boathouse' pub with bar meals and delightful beer garden.

● Lake-side lawns Picnic areas Boat launching - and much more.

● Whilst a five minute stroll brings you to the Lakeland village of Bowness with its shops, local inns and lake cruises.

DAVID BELLAMY CONSERVATION AWARD
GOLD

..on the shore of the Lake
www.fallbarrow.co.uk

Fallbarrow Windermere LA23 3DL Tel: 015394 44422   (ref T41)

Boat launching & moorings.
Leisure: ♦ ⚠ ☐ Facilities: ↿⊙🔍※⚓⛎⛏️
Services: ⊞⛽⛴⚑⊘⊟⊡✕
➜ ∪△↘⌥ ⊿ 🔲⬛📷 📼 🔳

WESTWARD　　　　　　Map 11 NY24

▶ ▶ ▶ *Clea Hall Holiday Park (NY279425)*
CA7 8NQ ☎ 016973 42880
Dir: From M6 (S), junct 41, take B5305 signed Wigton, turn left at X-roads onto B5299 towards Keswick and Caldbeck. Right at 2nd X-roads. Park 2m on right
🔲 🔲 ▲
Open Mar-Nov Booking advisable bank hols & Jul-Aug Last departure noon
A slightly sloping grassy site surrounded by woods, moorland and hills. Clea Hall is set on the edge of the Lake District National Park, in quiet rural surroundings within easy reach of Carlisle and Keswick. A 10-acre site with 16 touring pitches and 90 statics.
Leisure: ⟋ ♦ ⚠ ☐ Facilities: ↿⊙🔍※⚓⛎⛏️
Services: ⊞⛽⛴

WINDERMERE　　　　　Map 07 SD49

PREMIER PARK

▶ ▶ ▶ ▶ *Fallbarrow Park (SD401973)*
Rayrigg Rd LA23 3DL ☎ 015394 44422
Dir: 0.5m N of Windermere on A591. At mini rdbt take road to Bowness Bay & The Lake. Fallbarrow 1.3m on the right
🔲 £14.50-£20.50 🔲 £14.50-£20.50
Open mid Mar-Oct Booking advisable bank hols & Jul-Aug Last arrival 23.00hrs Last departure 13.00hrs
A very high quality park with excellent facilities, a few minutes' walk from Bowness on shore of Lake Windermere. Many of the individual pitches enjoy good views of the lake, and there is direct access to Windermere through the wooded park. A restaurant with a specialist chef is a popular innovation, and there is a pets' corner to delight children and adults alike. A 32-acre site with 38 touring pitches and 258 statics. Boat launching, lakeside picnic area, pet corner
Leisure: ♦ ⚠ ☐ Facilities: ↿⊙🔍※⚓⛎⛏️
Services: ⊞⛽⛴⚑⊘⊡✕⛽🛒
➜ ∪▶⊙△↘⌥ ⊿ 🔲⬛ ▥🔳 🔳

See advert on page 91

PREMIER PARK

▶ ▶ ▶ ▶ ▶ Limefitt Park (NY416032)
LA23 1PA ☎ 015394 32300
Dir: From Windermere take A592 to Ullswater. Limefitt is 2.5m on right
🔲 £9.50-£13 🔲 £9.50-£13 ▲ £9.50-£13
Open Apr-Oct Booking advisable bank hols & Jul-Aug Last arrival 22.00hrs Last departure noon ⊘
A lovely family site with superb facilities in a beautiful location in the Lake District National Park. Buildings are tastefully integrated into the landscape, and the River Troutbeck runs through

the parkland. From the spectacular valley setting there are stunning views of the surrounding hills, with direct access to the fells and plenty of walks. This park is a family park, and does not accept single sex pairs or groups. A 12-acre site with 165 touring pitches and 45 statics. Riverpool for paddling & swimming (with beach)
Leisure: ♦ ⚠ ☐ Facilities: ↿⊙🔍※⚓⛎▥
Services: ⊞⛽⛴⚑⊘⊡✕⛽🛒
➜ ∪▶△↘⛟ ⊿ 🔲⬛ ▥🔳 🔳

▶ ▶ ▶ ▶ Park Cliffe Camping & Caravan Estate (SD391912)
Birks Rd, Tower Wood LA23 3PG ☎ 01539 531344
Dir: Leave M6 at junct 36 onto A590. Turn right at Newby Bridge onto A592. After 4m turn right into site. This is only advised route for caravans/trailers
★ 🔲 £13-£19 🔲 £13-£19 ▲ £10-£12.80
Open Mar-15 Nov Booking advisable bank hols & Aug Last arrival 22.00hrs Last departure noon
A lovely hillside park set in 25 secluded acres of fell land which blend in with the surrounding countryside. The camping areas are well drained, and sheltered by a mixture of trees, shrubs and dry stone walls, and some pitches have spectacular views of Lake Windermere and the Langdales. There is easy access up a well-surfaced lane, and despite its proximity to the main road there is plenty of wildlife to be seen. The park is very well equipped for families, and there is no loud entertainment to spoil the peace and tranquillity. A 25-acre site with 250 touring pitches and 50 statics.

Off-licence.
Leisure: ♠ /Λ **Facilities:** ➡ ⋒ ⊙ �ⓠ ✳ ⅍ ₡ ⅀ ⟊ ★
Services: 🗷 🗟 ♀ 🅐 ⌀ ⊞ ⓣ ✕ ⚖
→ ∪ ⌐ ◎ ▲ ♣ ☷ ✦ ⬤ ▥ ▦ ▧ 🔊

DERBYSHIRE

ASHBOURNE   Map 07 SK14

▶ ▶ ▶ **Rivendale Touring Caravan & Leisure Park**
(SK162566)
Buxton Rd, Alsop en le Dale DE6 1QU
☎ 01335 310311 01332 843000
*Dir: Off A515 (Ashbourne-Buxton) opposite turn for
Biggin*
★ 🚐 £6.20-£8.20 🚐 £6.20-£8.20 ▲ £4.80-£8.20
Open Mar-Jan Booking advisable
*A sheltered site built in a long-closed quarry with all
hardstandings. A 37-acre site with 105 touring
pitches and 20 statics.*
Leisure: ♠ /Λ ☐ **Facilities:** ⋒ ⊙ ✳ ⅍ ₡ ⅀ ⚏ ⟊ ★
Services: 🗷 🗟 ♀ 🅐 ⌀ ⓣ ✕
→ ∪ ⬤ ▥ ▧ 🔊

▶ ▶ **Sandybrook Country Park (SK179481)**
Buxton Rd DE6 2AQ
☎ 01335 300000 & 01629 732428
*Dir: Take A515 out of Ashbourne towards Buxton.
Sandybrook 1.5m on right*
🚐 fr £7 🚐 fr £7 ▲ fr £7
Open Apr-Oct Booking advisable public hols,
weekends & Jul-Aug Last arrival 22.00hrs Last
departure 10.00hrs
*A family-run touring site on mostly sloping grass.
An 8-acre site with 50 touring pitches and 6 statics.*
Facilities: ⋒ ⊙ ⓠ ₡ ★ **Services:** 🗷 🅐 ⌀
→ ∪ ⌐ ▲ ⌀ ⅀ ⬤ ▥ ▧ 🔊

BAKEWELL   Map 08 SK26

See also Youlgreave
▶ ▶ ▶ **Greenhills Caravan Park (SK202693)**
Crow Hill Ln DE45 1PX ☎ 01629 813052
*Dir: 1m NW of Bakewell on A6. Signed before Ashford
in the Water, 50yds along unclass rd on right*
★ 🚐 £9-£10.50 🚐 £8-£9.50 ▲ £7.50-£10.50
Open May-Sep (rs Oct, Mar & Apr bar & shop
closed) Booking advisable Etr-Sep Last arrival
21.00hrs Last departure noon
*A well-established family-run park with a separate
tenting field, and easy access to all facilities. The*

*tenting field is well cut with path of shorter grass to
the toilet block. An 8-acre site with 60 touring
pitches and 60 statics.*
Leisure: /Λ **Facilities:** ⋒ ⊙ ⓠ ✳ ⅍ ₡ ⅀ ⚏ ★
Services: 🗷 🗟 ♀ 🅐 ⌀ ⊞ ⓣ ➡
→ ∪ ⌐ ♪ ⬤ ▥ ▧ 🔊

BUXTON   Map 07 SK07

See also Longnor (Staffordshire)
▶ ▶ ▶ ▶ **Lime Tree Park (SK070725)**
Dukes Dr SK17 9RP ☎ 01298 22988
Dir: 1m S, between A515 & A6
★ 🚐 £8-£10 🚐 £8-£10 ▲ £8-£10
Open Mar-Oct Booking advisable bank hols & Jul-
Aug Last arrival 21.00hrs Last departure noon
*A most attractive and well-designed site, set on the
side of a narrow valley in an elevated situation of
gently sloping land with views. A 10.5-acre site with
99 touring pitches and 43 statics.*
Leisure: ♠ /Λ ☐ **Facilities:** ⋒ ⊙ ⓠ ✳ ⅍ ₡ ⅀ ★
Services: 🗷 🗟 🅐 ⌀ ⊞ ⓣ
→ ∪ ⌐ ◎ ▲ ♣ ⬤ ▥ ▧ 🔊

▶ ▶ ▶ *Cottage Farm Caravan Park (SK122720)*
Blackwell in the Peak SK17 9TQ ☎ 01298 85330
*Dir: 6m E of Buxton off A6 and B6049, signed Blackwell
in the Peak*
🚐 🚐 ▲
Open mid Mar-Oct (rs Nov-Mar hook up and water
tap only) Booking advisable Last arrival 21.30hrs
*A small terraced site overlooking farm buildings
with good views. Ideal for touring/walking in the
Peak Park. Vans are parked on hardstandings, and
there is a separate field for tents. 30 touring pitches.*
Facilities: ⋒ ⊙ ✳ ₡ ⅀ **Services:** 🗷 🅐 ⌀ ⓣ

▶ ▶ **Thornheyes Farm Campsite (SK084761)**
Thornheyes Farm, Longridge Ln, Peak Dale
SK17 8AD ☎ 01298 26421
*Dir: 1.5m from Buxton on A6 turn E for Peak Dale. After
0.5m S at X-rds to site on right*
★ 🚐 £5.50 🚐 £5.50 ▲ £5.50
Open Etr-Oct Booking advisable bank hols & high
season Last arrival 21.30hrs Last departure
evenings
*A pleasant farm site run by a friendly family team,
in the central Peak District. A 2-acre site with 10
touring pitches.*
Facilities: ⋒ ✳ **Services:** 🗷 🅐 ⊞
→ ∪ ⌐ 🗟 ⅀

Greenhills Caravan Park is on the A6 1 miles NW of Bakewell. A well established touring site in the heart of the Peak District National Park. Bakewell is an historic and lively country market town, interesting all year round. Greenhills affords an ideal base for exploring this lovely area, four miles from Chatsworth House and Haddon Hall, within minutes of the Monsal Trail, eight miles of former Midland Railway line now a spectacular level walk or cycle ride. Bikes for hire nearby. The site overlooks the beautiful Wye Valley with the village of Ashford in the Water a short walk away. We have full facilities, shop and bar (both seasonal), children's playground and ample walking for dogs. Open 1st March-31st October..
**GREENHILLS CARAVAN & CAMPING PARK
CROWHILL LANE, BAKEWELL, DERBYSHIRE
Telephone: 01629 813052 Fax: 01629 815131**

Services: ⓣ Toilet Fluid ✕ Café/ Restaurant ⚏ Fast Food/Takeaway ➡ Baby Care 🗷 Electric Hook Up
🗟 Launderette ♀ Licensed Bar 🅐 Calor Gaz ⌀ Camping Gaz ⊞ Battery Charging

England

CROWDEN — Map 07 SK09

► ► **Camping & Caravanning Club Site (SK072992)**
SK14 1HZ ☎ 01457 866057
Dir: A628 Manchester to Barnsley Rd. At Crowden follow sign for car park Youth Hostel and Camp site. Site approx 300yds from main road
★ **Å** £9.80-£12.40
Open 7 Apr-25 Sep Booking advisable bank hols & Jun-Aug Last arrival 21.00hrs Last departure noon
A beautifully located moorland site, overlooking the reservoirs and surrounded by hills. Tents only, with backpackers' drying room. Please see advertisement on page 14 for details of Club Members' benefits. A 2.5-acre site with 45 touring pitches.
Facilities: ⋔ ⊙ ⍾ ✳ **Services:** ❷ ∅
→ ✕ ♪ ≗ ⬛ 💳

EDALE — Map 07 SK18

► ► *Coopers Caravan Site (SK121859)*
Newfold Farm, Edale Village S30 2ZD
☎ 01433 670372
Dir: From A625 at Hope take minor road for 4m to Edale. Site 800yds on right
⬛ ⬛ Å
Open all year Booking advisable bank hols Last arrival 23.30hrs Last departure 15.00hrs

Rising grassland behind a working farm, divided by a wall into two fields, culminating in the 2062ft Edale Moor. Facilities converted from original farm buildings, and include a new cafe for backpackers with all-day meals. A 6-acre site with 135 touring pitches and 11 statics.
Facilities: ⋔ ⊙ ⍾ ✳ ℂ ≗ **Services:** ❷ ❶ ∅ ⊞ ✕
→ ∪

FENNY BENTLEY — Map 07 SK14

► ► ► **Bank Top Farm (SK181498)**
DE6 1LF ☎ 01335 350250
Dir: 1m N of Ashbourne turn off A515 onto B5056, at Bentley Brook pub, immediately right into farm drive.
★ ⬛ £5.90-£6.90 ⬛ £5.90-£6.90 Å £5.90-£6.90
Open Mar/Etr-Sep Booking advisable peak periods Last arrival 22.00hrs Last departure 14.00hrs
A dairy farm with good new toilet facilities including a laundry. The gently sloping grass site has some level pitches. A 2-acre site with 36 touring pitches and 15 statics.

Working dairy farm with viewing gallery.
Facilities: ⋔ ⊙ ⍾ ✳ ≗ **Services:** ❷
→ ▶ ♪

HAYFIELD — Map 07 SK08

► ► **Camping & Caravanning Club Site (SK048868)**
Kinder Rd SK22 2LE ☎ 01663 745394
Dir: Off A624, Glossop to Chapel-en-le-Frith (Hayfield by-pass). Well signed into the village, follow wooden carved signs to site
★ ⬛ £10.60-£13.90 Å £10.60-£13.90
Open 20 Mar-1 Nov Booking advisable bank hols & peak periods Last arrival 21.00hrs Last departure noon
Pleasant site bordered by trees near the River Sett. No caravans. Please see advertisement on page 14 for details of Club Members' benefits. A 7-acre site with 90 touring pitches.
Facilities: ⋔ ⊙ ⍾ ✳ ℂ **Services:** ❶ ∅
→ ∪ ▶ ≗ ⬛ 💳

HOPE — Map 07 SK18

► ► *Pindale Farm Outdoor Centre (SK163825)*
Pindale Rd S33 6RN ☎ 01433 620111
Dir: From A625 in Hope turn into Pindale Lane between church and Woodroffe Arms. Pass cement works over bridge, and site in 400yds and well signed
Open all year Booking advisable

An ideal base for walking, climbing and various outdoor pursuits, offering good facilities for campers and with a self-contained bunkhouse for up to 60 people.
Facilities: ⋔ ⛯ **Services:** ❷ ▣
→ ∪ ▶ ♪ ≗

MATLOCK — Map 08 SK35

PREMIER PARK

► ► ► ► ► **Darwin Forest Country Park (SK302649)**
Darley Moor, Two Dales DE4 5LN
☎ 01629 732428
Dir: A632 to Matlock. Turn onto B5057 to Darley Dale. Park is on the right. Caravans must approach from A632 to avoid difficult bends on a very steep hill
★ ⬛ £10-£12 ⬛ £10-£12
Open Mar-Oct Booking advisable bank hols & Jul-Aug Last arrival 20.00hrs Last departure 10.00hrs

Facilities: ➤ Bath ⋔ Shower ⊙ Electric Shaver ⍾ Hairdryer ✳ Ice Pack Facility ♿ Disabled Facilities ℂ Public Telephone
≗ Shop on Site or within 200yds ⊞ Mobile Shop (calls at least 5 days a week) ⛯ BBQ Area 🎋 Picnic Area 🐕 Dog Exercise Area

A mostly level woodland site set amongst tall pines in the heart of the Derbyshire Dales. The park has an excellent indoor swimming pool complex, and good facilities for children both indoors and out. There is also a licensed bar and restaurant, and the area is ideal for touring and walking. A 9-acre site with 50 touring pitches and 90 statics.

Leisure: ⚓ ⚘ ◆ /𝔸 Facilities: 𝄢 ⊙ ☜ ◔ ℄
🐾 ⊞ ♒ 🛒 Services: 🔌 🗓 ♈ 🚪 ⌀ ✕ 🧺
→ ∪ ⌕ ⊙ ⤙ ♨ 🥄 💳 ▦ 🔋 💧

▶ ▶ ▶ *Sycamore Caravan & Camping Park (SK329615)*
Lant Ln, Tansley DE4 5LF ☎ 01629 55760
Dir: 2.5m NE of Matlock off A632
🚐 🚙 🛖
Open 15 Mar-Oct Booking advisable bank hols & summer hols Last arrival 21.00hrs Last departure noon
An open grassland site with mainly level touring pitches in two fields. A 6.5-acre site with 55 touring pitches and 52 statics.
Leisure: /𝔸 Facilities: 𝄢 ⊙ ☜ ❄ ℄ Services: 🔌 🗓 ⌀ 🔋
→ ∪ ⌕ ⚙ ⤙ ♈ 🥄 🚪 🛒 💳 ▦ 🎪 🧺

▶ ▶ ▶ *Wayside Farm Caravan Park (SK361620)*
Chesterfield Rd, Matlock Moor DE4 5LF
☎ 01629 582967
Dir: From Matlock on Chesterfield road, site on right in 2m opposite golf course
🚐 🚙 🛖
Open all year (rs Nov-Feb showers turned off) Booking advisable all year Last arrival 22.00hrs Last departure flexible
A small hilltop farm overlooking Matlock with two camping fields and good facilities. A 1.5-acre site with 30 touring pitches.
Leisure: /𝔸 Facilities: 𝄢 ⊙ ☜ ❄ ◔ ℄ 🐾 ⊞ ♒
Services: 🔌 🛖 ⌀ 🔋 🗓 ✕
→ ∪ ⌕ ⊙ ⚙ ⤙ 🚪 🗓

▶ ▶ *Packhorse Farm (SK323617)*
Tansley DE4 5LF ☎ 01629 582781
Dir: 2m NE of Matlock off A632 at the Tansley signpost
🚐 🚙 🛖
Open all year Booking advisable bank hols Last arrival 22.30hrs Last departure noon

A pleasant, well-run farm site in a quiet situation with good views of Riber Castle and Matlock. A 2-acre site with 39 touring pitches.
Facilities: 𝄢 ⊙ ❄ ♒ Services: 🔌 🔋
→ ∪ ⌕ 🚪 ♈ 🥄 🗓 🧺

▶ ▶ *Pinegroves Caravan Park (SK345585)*
High Ln, Tansley DE4 5BG ☎ 01629 534815
Dir: From Matlock take A615 for 3m, then 2nd right at X-roads. Site is 400yds on the left
★ 🚐 fr £7 🚙 fr £7 🛖 fr £7
Open Apr or Etr-Oct Booking advisable bank hols & Jul-Aug Last arrival 21.00hrs Last departure 16.00hrs
A beautiful hilltop location overlooking Matlock and Riber Castle. Very secluded site in a former plant nursery. A 23-acre site with 60 touring pitches and 14 statics.
Area of woodland for walks.
Facilities: 𝄢 ⊙ ❄ ◔ ℄ ⊞ ♒ Services: 🔌 🗓 ⌀ 🔋
→ ∪ ⌕ ⤙ 🚪 🥄

NEWHAVEN Map 07 SK16

▶ ▶ ▶ *Newhaven Holiday Camping & Caravan Park (SK167602)*
SK17 0DT ☎ 01298 84300
Dir: Halfway between Ashbourne and Buxton at junct with A5012
🚐 £7.25-£8.50 🚙 £7.25-£8.50 🛖 £7.25-£8.50
Open Mar-Oct Booking advisable public hols Last arrival 23.00hrs Last departure anytime

Pleasantly situated within the Peak District National Park. Well-maintained and immaculate site. A 30-acre site with 125 touring pitches and 73 statics.
Leisure: ◆ /𝔸 Facilities: 𝄢 ⊙ ☜ ❄ ◔ ℄ 🐾 ⊞ ♒ ♒
Services: 🔌 🗓 🛖 ⌀ 🔋 ⊞
→ ∪ ⤙ ⤙ 🥄

ROWSLEY Map 08 SK26

▶ ▶ ▶ *Grouse & Claret (SK258660)*
Station Rd DE4 2EL ☎ 01629 733233
★ 🚐 fr £8.50 🚙 fr £8.50
Open all year Booking advisable wknds, bank hols & peak periods Last arrival 20.00hrs Last departure noon
A well-designed, purpose-built park at the rear of an eating house on A6 between Bakewell and Chatsworth, and adjacent to the New Peak Shopping Village. The park comprises a level grassy area running down to the river, and all pitches have

contd.

Services: ⊞ Toilet Fluid ✕ Café/ Restaurant 🍟 Fast Food/Takeaway 🍼 Baby Care 🔌 Electric Hook Up
🧺 Launderette ♈ Licensed Bar 🛖 Calor Gaz ⌀ Camping Gaz 🔋 Battery Charging

hardstandings and electric hook-ups. A 2.5-acre site with 29 touring pitches.

Leisure: ♦ ⚙ **Facilities:** ⬚⊙✳✎⬚⊓

Services: ⊟♀✕♨

→ ∪ ▶ ♫ ⚑ ⬚ ⬚ ⬚ ⬚ ⬚

SHARDLOW   Map 08 SK43

▶ ▶ ▶ **Shardlow Marina Caravan Park (SK444303)**
London Rd DE72 2GL ☎ 01332 792832
*Dir: M1 junct 24, take A6/A50 Derby southern bypass,
take exit for Shardlow. Site 0.5m on right*
★ ⊞ £7-£10.75 ⊞ £7-£10.75 ▲ £7-£8.75
Open Mar-Oct Booking advisable bank hols Last
arrival 20.00hrs Last departure 14.00hrs
*A large marina site with good toilet and restaurant
facilities. Situated on the Trent/Mersey Canal. A 25-
acre site with 70 touring pitches.*

Leisure: ⚙ **Facilities:** ⬚⊙✳⬚

Services: ⊟♀⬚⬚⬚⊓✕

→ ▶ ⬚ ♫ ⬚

YOULGREAVE   Map 07 SK26

▶ **Camping & Caravanning Club Site (SK206632)**
c/o Hopping Farm DE45 1NA ☎ 01629 636555
*Dir: A6/B5056, after 0.5m turn right to Youlgreave. Turn
sharp left after church down Bradford Lane, opposite
George Hotel. 0.5m to sign turn right*
★ ⊞ £8.60-£9.60 ⊞ £8.60-£9.60 ▲ £8.60-£9.60
Open 20 Mar-27 Sep Booking advisable bank hols &
peak periods Last arrival 21.00hrs Last departure
noon
*Ideal for touring and walking in the Peak District
National Park, this gently sloping grass site is
accessed through narrow streets and along
unadopted hardcore. Own sanitary facilities
essential. Please see the advertisement on page 14
for details of Club Members' benefits. A 14-acre site
with 100 touring pitches.*

Leisure: ⚙ **Facilities:** ✳⬚⬚⬚ **Services:** ⊟⬚

→ ∪ ▶ ⊚ ⬚ ♫ ⬚ ⬚

DEVON

ASHBURTON   Map 03 SX77

▶ ▶ ▶ ▶ **Ashburton Caravan Park (SX753723)**
Waterleat TQ13 7HU ☎ 01364 652552
*Dir: In village right at T-junct for Buckland on the Moor
on unclass rd. Right fork at river bridge, site 1.5m on left*
★ ⊞ £7.50-£10 ▲ £7.50-£10
Open Etr-Sep Booking advisable bank hols & Jul-
Aug Last arrival 22.30hrs Last departure noon
*This well-maintained and attractive park is in a
sheltered south-facing valley alongside the River
Ashburton, and bordered by mature trees and
shrubs. Catering only for tents and motorhomes, it
is set in a very rural location within the Dartmoor
National Park. An ideal base for exploring the
moors and coast. A 2-acre site with 35 touring
pitches and 40 statics.*

Facilities: ⬚⊙♝✳⬚⬚⬚ **Services:** ⊟⬚⬚⬚

→ ∪ ▶ ♫ ⬚

▶ ▶ ▶ ▶ **Parkers Farm Holidays (SX779713)**
Higher Mead Farm TQ13 7LJ ☎ 01364 652598
*Dir: From A38 take 2nd left after the Plymouth 26m sign
at Alston signed Woodland-Debury*
★ ⊞ £5-£10 ⊞ £5-£10 ▲ £5-£10
Open Etr-end Oct Booking advisable Whitsun &
school hols Last departure 10.00hrs
*A well-developed site terraced into rising ground,
with maturing shrubs. This friendly park is part of a
working farm, and offers quality facilities which are
beautifully maintained. Large family rooms with
two shower cubicles, a large sink and a toilet are
especially appreciated by families with small
children. There are regular farm walks when all the
family can meet and feed the various animals, and
the park is located at the foot of Dartmoor National
Park. An 8-acre site with 60 touring pitches and 25
statics.*

Leisure: ♦ ⚙ **Facilities:** ⬚⊙✳⬚⬚⬚⬚⬚

Services: ⊟⬚♀⬚⬚⊓✕♨

→ ∪ ▶ ♫ ⬚ ⬚ ⬚ ⬚

▶ ▶ ▶ ▶ **River Dart Country Park (SX734700)**
Holne Park TQ13 7NP ☎ 01364 652511
*Dir: From M5 take A38 towards Plymouth, turn off at
Peartree Cross junc (between Ashburton and
Buckfastleigh) onto unclass rd towards Holne*
★ ⊞ £9.50-£13 ⊞ £9.50-£13 ▲ £9.50-£13
Open May-Aug (rs Apr/Sep no evening facilities ie
bar) Booking advisable Spring Bank Hol & Jul-Aug
Last arrival 21.00hrs Last departure 11.00hrs

THE RIVER DART COUNTRY PARK
Ashburton, South Devon

A magnificent 90 acre Park, once part of a Victorian Country Estate. The camping area is set along the fringes of woodland in gently sloping parkland with the River Dart running along one boundary. Being situated on the southern slopes of Dartmoor makes us an ideal site for exploring Dartmoor and the South Devon Coast.

• ETC • Outdoor heated swimming pool • 2 woodland adventure playgrounds • Tennis courts • heated toilet/shower block

The River Dart Country Park – (01364) 652511
Holne Park, Ashburton, TQ13 7NP.

Set in 90 acres of magnificent parkland that was once part of a Victorian estate, with many specimen and exotic trees, and in spring a blaze of colour from the many azaleas and rhododendrons. There are numerous outdoor activities, and high quality, well-maintained facilities. The open moorland of Dartmoor National Park is only a few minutes away. A 7-acre site with 170 touring pitches.

Leisure: ⚛ ⚲ 🛶 ⚙ ☐ **Facilities:** ➡ 🔥 ⊙ 🍴 ☀ ⚬ 📞
🔥 ⊞ 🎾 ★ **Services:** 🔌 🔟 ☂ 🖊 ⊞ ☐ ✖ 🍴 ➡
→ ○ ▶ 🛒 💳 💳 💳 💳 🔁

AXMINSTER　　　　　　　　　Map 03 SY29

▶ ▶ ▶ ▶ ▶ **Andrewshayes Caravan Park (SY248088)**
Dalwood EX13 7DY ☎ 01404 831225
Dir: On A35 3m from Axminster. Turn N at Taunton Cross signed Stockton/Dalwood. Site 150mtrs on right
🚐 £7.20-£9.50 🚐 £7.20-£9.50 ▲ £7.20-£8
Open Mar-Jan (rs Apr-21 May & Oct shop hours restricted, pool closed) Booking advisable Spring bank hol & Jul-Aug Last arrival 22.00hrs Last departure noon
A slightly sloping park in an ideal touring location within easy reach of Lyme Regis, Seaton, Branscombe and Sidmouth. The park boasts an attractive bistro beside the swimming pool. A 4-acre site with 90 touring pitches and 80 statics.
Licenced Bistro May-Sep.
Leisure: ⚛ 🛶 ⚙ ☐ **Facilities:** 🔥 ⊙ 🍴 ☀ ⚬ 📞 🔥 ⊞ ★
Services: 🔌 🔟 ☂ 🖊 ⊞ ✖ 🍴
→ ○ 🛒 💳 💳 💳 💳 🔁

Services: ☐ Toilet Fluid ✖ Café/ Restaurant 🍴 Fast Food/Takeaway ➡ Baby Care 🔌 Electric Hook Up 🔟 Launderette ☂ Licensed Bar 🖊 Calor Gaz ⚬ Camping Gaz ⊞ Battery Charging

BARNSTAPLE — Map 02 SS53

► ► **Midland Holiday Park (SS533346)**
Braunton Rd, Ashford EX31 4AU ☎ 01271 343691
Dir: 2m NW of Barnstaple off A361
★ ⬛ £8-£10
Open Mar-Nov Booking advisable all year Last
arrival 22.00hrs Last departure noon
*A gently sloping grassy park divided into paddocks,
being upgraded by new owners, close to the Tarka
Trail cycle route. Extensive leisure facilities are
available including indoor amusements, crazy golf,
licensed club, family bar, live entertainment and
aviary and pets' corner.The site is about 5 miles
from the sandy beaches of Saunton Sands and
Croyde Bay. An 8-acre site with 35 touring pitches
and 61 statics.*
Bouncy castle

Leisure: ✦ ⋀ Facilities: ⋔ ⊙ ✳ ⚊ ⛺ ⭑
Services: ⬛ ⬛ ⬛ ⬛ ⬛
→ ∪ ⮞ ◎ ⬛ ⬛ ⬛ ⬛ ⬛ ⬛ ⬛ ⬛ ⬛

BERRYNARBOR — Map 02 SS54

► ► ► ► **Napps Camping Site (SS561477)**
Old Coast Rd EX34 9SW ☎ 01271 882557 & 882778
*Dir: From A361 South Molton take A399 to Combe
Martin. Site signposted 1.5m W on A399*
★ ⬛ £5-£11 ⬛ £5-£10 ▲ £5-£10
Open Etr-Oct (rs Etr-Whit & Sep-Nov shop closed)
Booking advisable always for caravans Last arrival
22.00hrs Last departure noon

*Seclusion is guaranteed at this cliff top site adjacent
to Combe Martin. Spectacular views of the bay
below can be enjoyed through the perimeter trees
from its lofty position, and the coastal path to
Combe Martin is popular with walkers. A sandy
beach below the site is a delightful spot for old and
young alike. An 11-acre site with 250 touring pitches
and 2 statics.*
Childrens paddling pool & slide.

Leisure: ⟍ ✦ ✦ ⋀ ▱ Facilities: ⋔ ⊙ ✦ ✳ ⚊ ⛺ ⭑
Services: ⬛ ⬛ ⬛ ⬛ ⬛ ⬛ ⬛ ✕ ⬛
→ ∪ ⮞ ◎ ⬛ ⬛ ⬛ ⬛ ⬛ ⬛ ⬛

BICKINGTON (Near Ashburton) — Map 03 SX87

► ► ► ► *The Dartmoor Halfway Caravan Park
(SX804719)*
TQ12 6JW ☎ 01626 821270
*Dir: Direct access from A383, 1m from A38 Exeter-
Plymouth road*
⬛ ⬛

Open all year Booking advisable high season &
bank hols Last departure 10.00hrs
*A well-developed park tucked away on the edge of
Dartmoor, beside the River Lemon and adjacent to
the Halfway Inn. The neat and compact park has a
small toilet block with immaculate facilities, and
pitches separated by mature shrubs. An extensive
menu at the inn offers reasonably-priced food all
day and evening. A 2-acre site with 22 touring
pitches.*

Leisure: ⋀ Facilities: ⋔ ⊙ ✳ ⚊ ⚊ ⛺ ⭑
Services: ⬛ ⬛ ⬛ ✕
→ ∪ ⮞ ◎ ⬛ ⬛ ⬛ ⬛ ⬛ ⬛ ⬛ ⬛ ⬛ ⬛

► ► ► ► **Lemonford Caravan Park (SX793723)**
TQ12 6JR ☎ 01626 821242 & 821263
*Dir: From Exeter A38 take A382 turn, then 3rd exit on
rdbt and follow Bickington signs.*
⬛ £5-£9 ⬛ £5-£9 ▲ £5-£9
Open 16 Mar-Oct Booking advisable School
Holidays Last arrival 22.00hrs Last departure
11.00hrs
*Small, secluded and well-maintained park with a
good mixture of attractively laid out pitches. The
friendly owners pay a great deal of attention to
detail, and the toilets in particular are kept
spotlessly clean. The River Lemon runs along one
side of the park, offering fishing and a pleasant
riverside walk into the village. There is plenty here
to keep all of the family happy. A 7-acre site with 96
touring pitches and 18 statics.*
Clothes drying area.

See advertisement under NEWTON ABBOT

Leisure: ⋀ Facilities: ➡ ⋔ ⊙ ⚟ ✳ ⚊ ⛺ ⚊ ▱ ⭑
Services: ⬛ ⬛ ⬛ ⬛ ⬛ ⬛
→ ∪ ⮞ ◎ ⬛ ⬛

BRATTON FLEMING — Map 03 SS63

► ► ► **Greenacres Farm Touring Caravan Park
(SS658414)**
EX31 4SG ☎ 01598 763334
*Dir: From A361 Tiverton-Barnstaple take B3226 at 2nd
rdbt, signed Blackmoor Gate. Left at Stowfall X-rds, site
on left. Ignore Bratton Fleming signs*
★ ⬛ £3.50-£7.50 ⬛ £3.50-£7.50
Open Apr-Oct Booking advisable all times Last
arrival 23.00hrs Last departure 11.00hrs
*A very good, small site with well-appointed facilities
and enthusiastic owners. On farmland, with good
views over North Devon. A 4-acre site with 30
touring pitches.*

Leisure: ⋀ Facilities: ⋔ ⊙ ⚟ ✳ ⚊ ⛺ ▱ ⭑
Services: ⬛ ⬛ ⬛
→ ∪ ⬛ ⬛

BRAUNTON — Map 02 SS43

► ► ► **Lobb Fields Caravan & Camping Park
(SS475378)**
Saunton Rd EX33 1EB ☎ 01271 812090
*Dir: At X-rds in Braunton take B3231 to Croyde. Site
signed on right leaving Braunton*
★ ⬛ £7-£13 ⬛ £6-£10.50 ▲ £6-£10.50

Open 28 Mar-Oct Booking advisable Jul-Aug Last arrival 21.00hrs Last departure 10.30hrs
Gently sloping grassy site on outskirts of Braunton, with good wide entrance. A 14-acre site with 180 touring pitches.
Leisure: ⚲ Facilities: ⬤⊙⬤✳⬤⬤⬤
Services: ⬤⬤⬤⬤⬤
→ ∪ ⬤⬤⬤⬤

BRIDESTOWE   Map 02 SX58
► ► ► **Bridestowe Caravan Park (SX519893)**
EX20 4ER ☎ 01837 861261
Dir: Leave A30 at Sourton Down junct with A386, follow B3278 signed Bridestowe, and turn left in 5m. In village centre, left down unclass road for 1m
🚐 £6.60-£7.60 🚐 £6.60-£7.60 ⛺ £6.60-£7.60
Open Mar-Dec Booking advisable summer Last arrival 22.30hrs Last departure noon

A small, well-established mainly static park in a rural setting close to Dartmoor National Park. A 1-acre site with 13 touring pitches and 40 statics.
Leisure: ⚲ ⚲ Facilities: ⬤⊙⬤✳⬤⬤
Services: ⬤⬤⬤⬤⬤
→ ∪ ⬤

BRIDGERULE   Map 02 SS20
► ► ► **Hedleywood Caravan & Camping Park (SS262013)**
EX22 7ED ☎ 01288 381404
Dir: From B3254 take Widemouth road (unclass) at the Devon/Cornwall border
★ 🚐 £6-£8 🚐 £6-£8 ⛺ £6-£8
Open all year Booking advisable public hols & Jul-Aug Last arrival anytime Last departure anytime
An isolated site in a good location, with level pitches in a landscaped area of terraced woodland. A 16.5-acre site with 120 touring pitches and 16 statics.
Dog kennels, Nature Trail.
Leisure: ⚲ ⚲ ⬤ Facilities: ⬤⊙⬤✳⬤⬤⬤⬤⬤⬤
Services: ⬤⬤⬤⬤⬤⬤⬤⬤✗⬤
→ ∪ ⬤⬤⬤

BRIXHAM   Map 03 SX95
► ► ► **Galmpton Touring Park (SX885558)**
Greenway Rd TQ5 0EP ☎ 01803 842066
Dir: Signed off A3022 Torbay/Brixham road at Churston
★ 🚐 £6.20-£10 🚐 £6.20-£10 ⛺ £6.20-£10
Open Apr-Sep (rs Low season shop closed) Booking advisable Jul-Aug & bank hols Last arrival 22.00hrs Last departure 11.00hrs

An excellent location on high ground overlooking the River Dart, with outstanding views of the river and anchorage. A 10-acre site with 120 touring pitches.
Leisure: ⚲ Facilities: ⬤⊙⬤✳⬤⬤⬤⬤
Services: ⬤⬤⬤⬤⬤⬤
→ ⬤⊙⬤⬤⬤⬤⬤ ⬤⬤⬤⬤⬤

► ► ► **Hillhead Holiday Camp (SX903535)**
TQ5 0HH ☎ 01803 853204 & 842336
Dir: On B3205 between Brixham and Kingswear
🚐 🚐 ⛺
Open Etr-Oct Booking advisable Whit-Aug Last arrival 21.00hrs Last departure 10.30hrs
Attractive, well laid out site with screening and landscaping to each pitch. Good views all around of
contd.

countryside and sea. Amenities block well screened from touring park. A 12.5-acre site with 330 touring pitches.

Childrens clubroom & teenage disco room.

Leisure: ⊰ ◀ /▲ ▱ Facilities: ⋔ ⊙ ✳ ⊾ ⊑ ♞
Services: ⊕ 🔋 ⬗ 🔋 ⋔ ⬛ 🗓 ✕ ⬛
→ ⊳ ⌂ ⌄ ⌡

BRIXTON · Map 02 SX55

▶ ▶ **Brixton Caravan & Camping Park** (SX550520)
Venn Farm PL8 2AX ☎ 01752 880378
★ 🚐 £5.50-£7 🚐 £5.50-£7 ⚑ £5.50-£7
Dir: On A379, 4m from Plymouth.
Open 15 Mar-14 Oct (rs 15 Mar-Jun & Sep-14 Oct no warden) Booking advisable Jul-Aug Last arrival 23.00hrs Last departure noon
A small grassy site adjacent to a farm in the village. A 2-acre site with 43 touring pitches.
Facilities: ⬰ ⋔ ⊙ ✳ ⊾ ⬛ Services: ⊕
→ ∪ ⊳ ⌄ ⬗ ⌡

BUCKFASTLEIGH · Map 03 SX76

▶ **Beara Farm Caravan & Camping Site** (SX751645)
Colston Rd TQ11 0LW ☎ 01364 642234
Dir: Leave Exeter and follow signs for South Devon railway. 1st left into Old Totnes Rd. Right after 0.5m at brick cottages. Site signed from junction
★ 🚐 £6-£7 🚐 fr £6 ⚑ fr £6
Open all year Booking advisable peak periods Jul-Aug Last arrival anytime Last departure anytime
A very good farm park with clean unisex facilities and very keen and friendly owners. A well-trimmed camping field offers peace and quiet. Close to the River Dart and the Dart Valley steam railway line, within easy reach of sea and moors. Approach is narrow with passing places and needs care. A 3.75-acre site with 30 touring pitches.
River Dart adjoining site
Facilities: ⋔ ⊙ ✳ ♞ Services: ⬛
→ ⌡ 🔋 ⊾

▶ *Churchill Farm Campsite* (SX743664)
TQ11 0EZ ☎ 01364 642844
Dir: A38 Dart Bridge exit for Buckfastleigh/Totnes head towards Buckfast Abbey. Left at mini-rdbt, left at X-roads to site opposite Holy Trinity church
🚐 🚐 ⚑
Open Mar-Nov Booking advisable Jul & Aug Last arrival 22.30hrs

A working family farm in a relaxed and peaceful setting with panoramic views. A 3-acre site with 25 touring pitches.
Facilities: ⋔ ⊙ ✳ Services: ⊕ ⬛
→ ⊾

BUDLEIGH SALTERTON

See **Ladram Bay**

CHIVENOR · Map 02 SS53

▶ ▶ ▶ **Chivenor Caravan Park** (SS501351)
EX31 4BN ☎ 01271 812217 & 07071 228478
Dir: On rdbt at Chivenor Cross. Adjacent to RAF Chivenor
★ 🚐 £6-£8 🚐 £6-£8 ⚑ £5-£6.50
Open Mar-Nov Booking advisable Jul & Aug
Nicely laid out and well-maintained level site with good facilities. A 3-acre site with 34 touring pitches and 10 statics.
Leisure: /▲ Facilities: ⋔ ⊙ ✳ ⊾ ⊑ ♞
Services: ⊕ ⬛ ⬗ ⬛ 🗓
→ ∪ ⊳ ⬗ ⌡ ⬛ ⬛ ⬛

CHUDLEIGH · Map 03 SX87

Finlake Holiday Park (SX855786)
TQ13 0EJ ☎ 01626 853833
Dir: Signposted off A38 at Chudleigh exit
🚐 🚐 ⚑
Open Etr-Oct (rs Nov-Mar shop, tennis, golf, entertainment closed) Booking advisable bank hols & Jul-Aug Last arrival 22.00hrs Last departure 11.00hrs
A very well-appointed holiday centre situated in a wooded valley surrounded by 110 acres of wooded parkland. A wide range of leisure facilities and entertainment for adults and children is available, and the park has its own golf course and fishing lake. Tourers can choose between a quiet lakeside location and one nearer the lively complex, and there are three tenting areas. A 130-acre site with 410 touring pitches and 30 statics.
Fishing, horseriding, golf & fitness suite.
See advertisement under NEWTON ABBOT
Leisure: ⊰ ◀◀ /▲ Facilities: ⬰ ⋔ ⊙ ✳ ⊾ ⊾
⊑ ⋔ ♞ Services: ⊕ ⬛ ⬗ 🔋 ⬛ 🗓 ✕ ⬛
→ ∪ ⊳ ⌡ ⬛ ⬛ ⬛ ⬛ ⬛

▶ ▶ ▶ **Holmans Wood Tourist Park** (SX881812)
Harcombe Cross TQ13 0DZ
☎ 01626 853785
Dir: Follow M5 past Exeter onto A38 after racecourse at top of Haldon Hill. Left in 0.5m signed Chudleigh, park at end of short slip road on left
🚐 🚐 ⚑
Open mid Mar-Oct Booking advisable bank hols & Jul-Aug Last arrival 22.00hrs Last departure 11.00hrs
Delightful small, personally-managed touring site, set back in secluded wooded area off A38.

Convenient location for touring South Devon and Dartmoor National Park. A 20-acre site with 144 touring pitches.
Caravan storage facilities.

Leisure: ⚑ **Facilities:** ☈⊙☜⚹♿♿⚓☲☶☴
Services: ☎▣🛢🅐⊘⊞Ⓣ
→⋃▷↗ ☕☰▨◪

A very attractive location in a deep wooded valley in the Dartmoor National Park. The approach roads are narrow and steep in parts, and care is needed in towing large units. A 6-acre site with 65 touring pitches and 5 statics.
Fly fishing on site.

Leisure: ⚑🔦⚑ **Facilities:** ☈⊙☜⚹⚓☲☴
Services: ☎▣🛢🅐⊘⊞Ⓣ
→⋃▷↗

CLIFFORD BRIDGE   Map 03 SX78

▶ ▶ ▶ **Clifford Bridge Park** (SX782897)
EX6 6QE ☎ 01647 24226
Dir: From Cheriton Bishop follow signs and turn near Old Thatch Inn for 2m. Right at X-rds signed Clifford Bridge and continue over junct and bridge
★ ☎ £7.40-£11.50 ☎ £6.60-£10.70 ▲ £6.60-£11.50
Open Etr-Sep Booking advisable school & bank hols Last arrival 22.00hrs Last departure 11.00hrs

COLYTON   Map 03 SY29

▶ ▶ ▶ ▶ **Leacroft Touring Park** (SY217925)
Colyton Hill EX24 6HY ☎ 01297 552823
Dir: 1m from Stafford Cross on A3052 towards Colyton
☎ £9-£14 ☎ £9-£14 ▲ £9-£14
Open Etr-Oct Booking advisable Jul-Aug & Spring bank hol Last arrival 22.00hrs Last departure noon
Set outside the little town of Colyton, this park stands on a hill in a rural area with open views over the countryside to the south, and backed by woods which offer it some shelter. The park slopes slightly, but is well planted with shrubs, trees and flower beds. Amply-spaced pitches make it a very comfortable place to stay, and the good sanitary facilities are well maintained by enthusiastic owners. A 10-acre site with 138 touring pitches.
Off-licence.

Leisure: 🔦⚑ **Facilities:** ☈⊙☜⚹♿⚓☲▥☴
Services: ☎▣🛢🅐⊘⊞Ⓣ
→⋃▷⊙⚴☇↗

COMBE MARTIN   Map 02 SS54

PREMIER PARK

▶ ▶ ▶ ▶ ▶ **Stowford Farm Meadows** (SS560427)
Berry Down EX34 0PW ☎ 01271 882476
Dir: From A339 turn left onto B3343 to T-junct. Turn left, then right to site in 0.5m
★ ☎ £4.10-£9.60 ☎ £4.10-£9.60 ▲ £4.10-£9.60
Open Apr-Oct (rs Etr-Spring bank hol & Oct some amenities may be available ltd hrs)
Booking advisable bank hols & Jul-Aug Last arrival 20.00hrs Last departure 10.00hrs
Very gently sloping, grassy, sheltered and south-facing site approached down a wide, well-kept driveway. This large farm park is set in 500 acres, and offers many quality amenities, including a large swimming pool, horseriding and crazy golf. A 60-acre wooded nature trail is an added attraction, as is the mini zoo with its

contd.

stock of friendly animals. A 100-acre site with 570 touring pitches.
Horse rides, fun golf, mini zoo, snooker, cycle hire.

Leisure: 🎣 🚣 ⚙ 🖵 **Facilities:** 🛁 🍴 ☉ 🖤 ✳ ♿
⚲ ⚡ 🐕 Services: ☎ 🖃 🖳 🅿 🖉 🗄 Ⓣ ✕ 🖤
→ ∪ 🍴 ☉ 🍴 🍴 🚰 🐾 🗺

See advert under Ilfracombe

CROCKERNWELL   Map 03 SX79

▶ ▶ ▶ **Barley Meadow Caravan & Camping Park** (SX757925)
EX6 6NR ☎ 01647 281629
Dir: From M5 take A30, then exit for Tedburn. Turn left through Cheriton Bishop and Crockernwell and site on left
★ 🚐 £7.50-£8.50 🚐 £7.50-£8.50 Å £3.50-£7.50
Open 15 Mar-15 Nov Booking advisable bank hols & Jul-Aug Last arrival 23.30hrs Last departure noon
A small, very well-maintained site set on high ground in the National Park with easy access. Off the old A30, now bypassed, and isolated. A 4-acre site with 40 touring pitches.
Picnic tables.
Leisure: ⚙ 🖵 **Facilities:** 🍴 ☉ 🖤 ✳ ♿ ⚲ 🐕 **🐾**
Services: ☎ 🖃 🖳 🅿 🖉 🗄 Ⓣ → ∪ 🍴 🍴 🍴

DARTMOUTH   Map 03 SX85

▶ ▶ ▶ ▶ **Little Cotton Caravan Park** (SX858508)
Little Cotton TQ6 0LB ☎ 01803 832558
Dir: Exit A38 at Buckfastleigh, A384 to Totnes, A381 to Halwell, then A3122 Dartmouth Rd, park is on the right at entrance to the town.
★ 🚐 £5.75-£9.50 🚐 £5.75-£9.50 Å £5.75-£9.50
Open 15 Mar-Oct Booking advisable Jul & Aug Last arrival 22.00hrs Last departure noon
A very good grassy touring park set on high ground above Dartmouth, with quality facilities, and 'park and ride' to the town from the gate. The toilet blocks are heated, and superbly maintained. The friendly owners are happy to offer advice on touring in this pretty area. A 7.5-acre site with 95 touring pitches.
Facilities: 🍴 ☉ 🖤 ✳ ♿ ⚲ 🐕 **🐾 Services:** ☎ 🖃 🖳 🅿 🖉 🗄 Ⓣ
→ 🍴 ☉ ♿ ✕ 🍴 🍴 🍴 🚰 🐾 🗺

▶ ▶ ▶ ▶ *Woodlands Leisure Park* (SX813522)
Blackawton TQ9 7DQ ☎ 01803 712598
Dir: Signposted off A381 at Halwell
🚐 🚐 Å

Open 15 Mar-15 Nov Booking advisable anytime Last departure 11.00hrs 🚫
An extensive woodland park with a terraced grass camping area, and quality facilities which are maintained to a very high standard. The park caters for all the family in a relaxed atmosphere under the supervision of the owner's family. There is a large games room , and a wildlife park is attached, with entry free to campers who stay two nights. An 8-acre site with 225 touring pitches.
60 acre leisure park with animal farm complex.
Leisure: 🎣 ⚙ 🖵 **Facilities:** 🛁 🍴 ☉ 🖤 ✳ ♿ ⚲ 🐕 🖽 🏕
Services: ☎ 🖃 🖳 🅿 🖉 🗄 Ⓣ ✕ 🖤
→ ∪ 🍴 ✕ 🍴 🍴 🍴 🚰 🗺

▶ ▶ ▶ **Deer Park Holiday Estate** (SX864493)
Stoke Fleming TQ6 0RF ☎ 01803 770253
Dir: Direct access from A379 from Dartmouth before Stoke Fleming
🚐 £7-£10 🚐 £7-£10 Å £7-£10
Open 15 Mar-Oct Booking advisable Jul-Aug Last arrival anytime Last departure 11.00hrs
An open, mainly level grass site on high ground overlooking Start Bay, with good family facilities. A 6-acre site with 160 touring pitches.
Leisure: 🎣 ⚙ **Facilities:** 🍴 ☉ ✳ ♿ ⚲
Services: ☎ 🖃 🖳 🅿 🖉 Ⓣ ✕ 🖤
→ ∪ 🍴 ♿ ✕ 🍴 🍴 🍴 🍴 🚰 🗺

Facilities: 🛁 Bath 🍴 Shower ☉ Electric Shaver 🖤 Hairdryer ✳ Ice Pack Facility ♿ Disabled Facilities ⚲ Public Telephone ⚡ Shop on Site or within 200yds 🖃 Mobile Shop (calls at least 5 days a week) 🖽 BBQ Area 🍴 Picnic Area 🐕 Dog Exercise Area

England

DAWLISH　　　　　　Map 03 SX97

Golden Sands Holiday Park
(SX968784)
Week Ln EX7 0LZ ☎ 01626 863099
Dir: Signed off A379 Exeter/Dawlish road. 1m from Dawlish
★ ⊞ £5.50-£13.50 ⊞ £5.50-£13.50
Open Etr-Oct Booking advisable May-Sep Last arrival 22.00hrs Last departure 10.00hrs ⊛
A mainly static park with a small touring area set amongst trees, offering full family entertainment. A 2.5-acre site with 60 touring pitches and 188 statics.

Leisure: ⚲ ⚲ ⚑ ⚐　**Facilities:** ⚹ ⊙ ⚹ ⚹ ⚹
Services: ⚹⚹⚹⚹⚹⚹⚹
→⚹⚹⚹ ⚹ ⚹ ⚹

See advert on page 102

Lady's Mile Touring & Caravan Park
(SX968784)
EX7 0LX ☎ 01626 863411
Dir: 1m N of Dawlish on A379
⊞⊞Å
Open 17 Mar-27 Oct Booking advisable bank hols & Jul-Aug Last arrival 20.00hrs Last departure 11.00hrs
A well-ordered, clean and tidy site, with all grass pitches, offering indoor and outdoor pools with chutes, and other holiday activities. Fairly central for the surrounding beaches. A 16-acre site with 286 touring pitches and 1 static.

Leisure: ⚲ ⚲ ⚲ ⚑ ⚐　**Facilities:** ⚹ ⊙ ⚹ ⚹ ⚹
Services: ⚹⚹⚹⚹⚹⚹⚹
→⚹⚹⚹ ⚹ ⚹ ⚹

▶ ▶ ▶ ▶ **Cofton Country Holiday Park**
(SX967801)
Starcross EX6 8RP ☎ 01626 890111
Dir: On A379 Exeter/Dawlish road 3m from Dawlish
★ ⊞ £6.50-£11 ⊞ £6.50-£11 Å £6.50-£11

Open Etr-Oct (rs Etr-Spring bank hol & mid Sep-Oct swimming pool closed) Booking advisable bank hols & Jul-Aug Last arrival 20.00hrs Last departure noon
Set in a rural location surrounded by spacious open grassland, with plenty of well-kept flower beds throughout the park. Most pitches overlook either the swimming pool complex or the fishing lakes and woodlands. An on-site pub serves drinks, and meals or snacks, for all the family, and a mini- contd.

Facilities: ⚹ Bath　⚹ Shower　⊙ Electric Shaver　⚹ Hairdryer　⚹ Ice Pack Facility　⚹ Disabled Facilities　⚹ Public Telephone
⚹ Shop on Site or within 200yds　⚹ Mobile Shop (calls at least 5 days a week)　⚹ BBQ Area　⚹ Picnic Area　⚹ Dog Exercise Area

market caters for most shopping needs. A 16-acre site with 450 touring pitches and 62 statics. Coarse fishing, pub with family room.

Leisure: ⅂ ⚓ ⚲ **Facilities:** ♈ ⊙ ⚑ ✳ ⚿ ⚘ ⚙ ⚓ ⚒ 🐕

Services: 🖭 🖫 ♈ 🗑 ⊞ 🅣 ✕ ⚒

→ ⚑ ⊙ ⚲ ↙ ⚷ 🏧 ◻ 🔄 💳 🔄

▶ ▶ ▶ ▶ **Peppermint Park (SX978788)**
Warren Rd EX7 0PQ ☎ 01626 863436
Dir: From A379 at Dawlish follow signs for Dawlish Warren. Site 1m on left
★ 🚐 £5.50-£11 🚐 £5.50-£11 ▲ £5.50-£11
Open Etr-Oct Booking advisable Spring bank hol & Jul-Aug Last arrival 20.00hrs Last departure 10.00hrs

THE NEAREST TOURING & CAMPING PARK TO THE BEACH AT DAWLISH WARREN

Well-managed attractive park close to the coast, with excellent facilities including club and bar which are well away from pitches. Nestling close to sandy beaches, the park offers individually marked pitches

on level terraces in pleasant, sheltered grassland. The many amenities include a heated swimming pool and water chute, coarse fishing and launderette. A 26-acre site with 250 touring pitches and 35 statics.
Licensed club & free entertainment.

Leisure: ⅂ ⚓ ⚲ **Facilities:** ♈ ⊙ ✳ ⚘ ⚙ ⚓ ⚒ 🐕

Services: 🖭 🖫 ♈ 🗑 🅣

→ ⚑ ⊙ ⚲ ↙ ⚷ 🏧 ◻ 🔄 💳 🔄 ◻

▶ ▶ ▶ *Leadstone Camping (SX974782)*
Warren Rd EX7 0NG
☎ 01626 864411 & 872239 (Oct-May)
Dir: From M5 junct 30 take A379 to Dawlish. Before village turn left on brow of hill, signed Dawlish Warren. Site 0.5m on right
🚐 ▲
Open Jun-Sep Booking advisable 18 Jul-31 Aug Last departure noon
A traditional, mainly level grassy camping park approx 0.5m walk from sands and dunes at Dawlish Warren, an Area of Outstanding Natural Beauty. This mainly tented park has been run by the same friendly family for many years, and is an ideal base for touring south Devon. A regular bus service from outside the gate takes in a wide area. An 8-acre site with 160 touring pitches.

Leisure: ⚲ **Facilities:** ♈ ⊙ ⚑ ✳ ⚙ ⚓

Services: 🖭 🖫 ♈ 🗑

→ ⚑ ⊙ ⚐ ↙

Facilities: ⚒ Bath ♈ Shower ⊙ Electric Shaver ⚑ Hairdryer ✳ Ice Pack Facility ⚘ Disabled Facilities ⚓ Public Telephone ⚒ Shop on Site or within 200yds 🔄 Mobile Shop (calls at least 5 days a week) 🍴 BBQ Area ⚞ Picnic Area 🐕 Dog Exercise Area

England

DOLTON — Map 02 SS51

▶ ▶ ▶ *Dolton Caravan Park (SS573122)*
Acorn Farm House, The Square EX19 8QF
☎ 01805 804536
Dir: Take B3217 S at junct with B3220 at Dolton Beacon. Site signed from Dolton
⚏ ⚏ Å
Open Etr-15 Nov Booking advisable Jul-Aug Last arrival 22.00hrs Last departure noon
A well-maintained, landscaped paddock with wide countryside views, at the rear of the Royal Oak Inn in the centre of Dolton. A 2-acre site with 25 touring pitches.
Leisure: ⚒ Facilities: ⌕ ⊙ ✳ 🌣 Services: 🔌 🖾 🅘 ⌀ 🔲
→ ∪ ▶ 🎣

DREWSTEIGNTON — Map 03 SX79

▶ ▶ *Woodland Springs Touring Park (SX695912)*
Venton EX6 6PG ☎ 01647 231695
Dir: Leave A30 at Merrymeet rdbt, turn left onto A382 towards Moretonhampstead. Site 2m on left
⚏ ⚏ Å
Open all year Booking advisable Last arrival 22.30hrs Last departure 11.00hrs ⚘
An attractive site in a rural area within Dartmoor National Park. A 4-acre site with 85 touring pitches.
Facilities: ⌕ ⊙ ✳ 🌣 ᵶ 🏛 ⼌ Services: 🔌 🅘 ⌀
→ ∪ ▶ 🎣 🎀

EAST WORLINGTON — Map 03 SS71

▶ ▶ ▶ ▶ *Yeatheridge Farm Caravan Park (SS768110)*
EX17 4TN ☎ 01884 860330
Dir: On B3042 1.5m W of Thelbridge Arms Inn. Site is NOT in East Worlington village which is unsuitable for caravans
⚏ ⚏ Å
Open Etr-Sep Booking advisable Etr, Spring bank hol & school hols Last arrival 22.00hrs Last departure 22.00hrs
Gently sloping grass site with young trees set in meadowland in rural Devon. This very rural park offers good views of distant Dartmoor, and is of great appeal to families with its farm animals, horse riding and indoor swimming pool with flume. There are many attractive villages in this area. A 9-acre site with 85 touring pitches and 4 statics.
Horse riding, fishing & pool table.
See advertisement under TIVERTON

Leisure: ⚒ 🏊 🎱 🧩 □ Facilities: ⌕ ⊙ ⍾ ✳ 🌣 ᵶ 🌴
Services: 🔌 🖾 🅘 ⌀ ⌀ 🔲 🅣
→ ∪ 🎣 🍺 🚆

EXETER — See Kennford

EXMOUTH — Map 03 SY08

▶ ▶ ▶ *Webbers Farm Caravan Park (SY018874)*
Castle Ln, Woodbury EX5 1EA ☎ 01395 232276
Dir: 4m from junct 30 of the M5. Take A376, then B3179 to Woodbury village. Site is 500yds E of village
★ ⚏ £7.50-£10.50 ⚏ £7.50-£10.50 Å £7.50-£10.50
Open Etr-Sep Booking advisable all times Last arrival 20.00hrs Last departure 11.00hrs
Unspoilt farm site in two parts, with a fine view over River Exe towards Dartmoor. An 8-acre site with 115 touring pitches.
Pets corner, caravan storage facilities.
Leisure: ⚒ Facilities: ➡ ⌕ ⊙ ⍾ ✳ 🌣 ⼌ ᵶ 🌴
Services: 🔌 🖾 🅘 ⌀ 🔲 🅣
→ ∪ ▶ 🎣 🍺 🚆 🚌 🗘

HAWKCHURCH — Map 03 ST30

▶ ▶ ▶ *Hunters Moon Park (SY345988)*
EX13 5UL ☎ 01297 678402
Dir: From Charmouth take A35 W to B3165. Site 1.5m on left
★ ⚏ £4.50-£10 ⚏ £4.50-£10 Å £4.50-£10
Open 15 Mar-14 Nov Booking advisable Whit & Jul-Aug Last arrival 23.00hrs Last departure noon
An attractive site in wooded area with panoramic country views. A 12-acre site with 150 touring pitches.
Putting green & boules pitch.
Leisure: ⚒ 🏊 Facilities: ⌕ ⊙ ⍾ ✳ 🌣 ⼌ ᵶ 🌴
Services: 🔌 🖾 🅘 ⌀ 🔲 🅣 🅧 🚻
→ ∪ ▶ 🍽 🚌 🎣 🍺 🚆 ⓘ 🚌 🚌 🗘

HONITON — Map 03 ST10

See also Kentisbeare
▶ ▶ ▶ *Camping & Caravanning Club Site (ST176015)*
Otter Valley Park, Northcote EX14 8ST
☎ 01404 44546
Dir: Leave 1st exit to Honiton from A30. Keep left off slip road & keep left
★ ⚏ £10.60-£13.90 ⚏ £10.60-£13.90 Å £10.60-£13.90

contd.

International Caravan & Camping Park

FOREST GLADE HOLIDAY PARK, CULLOMPTON, DEVON EX15 2DT

A small country estate surrounded by forest in which deer roam.
Situated in an area of outstanding natural beauty.
Large, flat, sheltered camping/touring pitches
Modern facilities building, luxury 2/6 berth full service
holiday homes, also self contained flat for 2 persons.

COUNTRY HOLIDAY PARK
FREE COLOUR BROCHURE
Tel: (01404) 841381 (Evgs to 8pm) Fax: (01404) 841593
www.forestglade.mcmail.com email: forestglade@cwcom.net

Open 07 Apr-26 Sep Booking advisable bank hols &
Jul-Aug Last arrival 21.00hrs Last departure noon
A well run site just a short walk from the town.
Please see the advertisement on page 14 for details
of Club Members' benefits. A 56-acre site with 90
touring pitches.

Facilities: ⊓⊙☀⛄ **Services:** 🔌🗑🛢⟋
→ ▶ 🛒 💳 💳

ILFRACOMBE　　　　　　　　**Map 02 SS54**

▶ ▶ ▶ ▶ *Watermouth Cove Holiday Park*
(SS558477)
Berrynarbor EX34 9SJ
☎ 01271 862504
Dir: On A399 from Combe Martin, past Berrynarbor
🚐 🚐 Å

Open Etr-Oct (rs Etr-Whit & Sep-Nov pool,
takeaway, club & shop) Booking advisable Whit &
Jul-Aug Last arrival anytime Last departure
11.00hrs

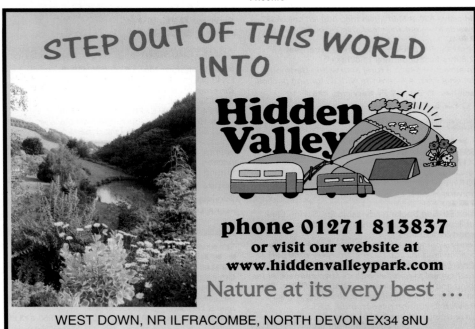

STEP OUT OF THIS WORLD INTO

Hidden Valley

phone 01271 813837
or visit our website at
www.hiddenvalleypark.com

Nature at its very best ...

WEST DOWN, NR ILFRACOMBE, NORTH DEVON EX34 8NU

Facilities: 🛁 Bath 🚿 Shower ⊙ Electric Shaver ⛉ Hairdryer ☀ Ice Pack Facility ♿ Disabled Facilities ☎ Public Telephone
🛒 Shop on Site or within 200yds ⊡ Mobile Shop (calls at least 5 days a week) 🍖 BBQ Area ⛱ Picnic Area 🐕 Dog Exercise Area

WELCOME TO
STOWFORD
Farm Meadows

Where Fun meets the countryside

Touring Caravan & Camping Park

Berry Down, Combe Martin. North Devon EX34 0PW
Telephone 01271 882476   Fax 01271 883053

- 500 acres of Glorious Devon Countryside
- Superb choice of 5 local beaches
- Renowned as a high quality park offering outstanding value
- Caravan storage available

Great Facilities

Shop · Take - Away & Carvery · Bars · Swimming Pool ·
Pitch & Putt · Snooker · Games Room · Crazy Golf ·
Horse Riding · Kiddies Kars · Mini - Zoo Petorama ·
Sports Field · Nature Walks in mature Woodland ·

Phone for a FREE Colour Brochure

e mail: enquiries@stowford.co.uk   Internet: www.stowford.co.uk

---

A popular site in very attractive surroundings, set amidst trees and bushes in meadowland with access to sea, beach and main road. This beautiful cove has a private sandy beach, and offers launching for boats and other water craft, as well as swimming. The site is two miles from both Combe Martin and Ilfracombe. A 6-acre site with 90 touring pitches.
Coastal headland fishing.

Leisure: ⚡ ⚓ ⚙ ☐ Facilities: ⚫☉♨☀⚫🏪🎣⚹
Services: ⚙🔲♈🔥⚱◐⊞Ⓣ✕⚒
➔ ∪ ▶ ⊚ ♨ ✦ ▦ ▧ ⊠

► ► ► Mullacott Cross Caravan Park (SS511446)
Mullacott Cross EX34 8NB ☎ 01271 862212
Dir: Located adjacent to A361 Braunton-Ilfracombe road
🚐 🚐 ⚱
Open Etr-Sep (rs Etr-Whit & Oct) Booking advisable Whit & Jul-Aug Last arrival 21.00hrs Last departure noon
This meadowland site is on gentle grass slopes with views over the Atlantic coastline, 2m S of Ilfracombe and 3m E of the sandy beach at Woolacombe. An 8-acre site with 115 touring pitches and 160 statics.
Caravan accessory shop.
Leisure: ⚙ Facilities: ⚫☉♨☀⚫⚒
Services: ⚙🔲♈🔥⚱◐⊞Ⓣ✕
➔ ∪ ▶ ✦ ♈ ✦ ▦ ▧ ⊠ ⊠

KENNFORD Map 03 SX98

► ► ► Kennford International Caravan Park (SX912857)
EX6 7YN ☎ 01392 833046
Dir: At end of M5, take A38, site signed at Kennford slip road
🚐 🚐 ⚱
Open all year Booking advisable public hols & Jul-Aug Last arrival mdnt Last departure 11.00hrs
A touring site on the A38, with mature landscaping, a convenient stopover for touring the West Country. An 8-acre site with 120 touring pitches and 6 statics.
Leisure: ⚫ ⚙ Facilities: ➔⚫☉♨☀⚫⚒
Services: ⚙🔲♈🔥⚱◐⊞Ⓣ✕⚒
➔ ∪ ▶ ✦ ♈ ✦ ▧ ⊠ ⊠ ⊠ ⊠

KENTISBEARE Map 03 ST00

► ► ► ► Forest Glade Holiday Park (ST100075)
Cullompton EX15 2DT ☎ 01404 841381
Dir: Tent traffic from A373, signed Keepers Cottage Inn, 2.5m E of M5 junct 28. Touring caravans via Honiton/Dunkeswell road
🚐 🚐 ⚱
Open 2 wks before Etr-Oct (rs low season) Booking advisable school hols Last arrival 21.00hrs
A quiet, attractive park in a forest clearing with well-kept gardens and beech hedge screening, on top of the Black Down Hills. One of its main attractions is the ability to step outside its environs straight into the forest which offers magnificent walks on this hillside, with surprising views over the valleys. *contd.*

Services: Ⓣ Toilet Fluid ✕ Café/ Restaurant ⚒ Fast Food/Takeaway ♈ Baby Care ⚙ Electric Hook Up
◐ Launderette ♈ Licensed Bar ⚱ Calor Gaz ⊘ Camping Gaz ⊞ Battery Charging

England

Please telephone for route details. There is no need to enter Kentisbeare Village. A 15-acre site with 80 touring pitches and 57 statics.
Adventure play area & childrens paddling pool.

See advertisement under HONITON

Leisure: ₹ ◨ ◣ ⋒ Facilities: ⋒ ⊙ ⅋ ✳ ⅋ ⅋ ⅋ ⅋
Services: ◨ ⊟ ⅋ ⅋ ⊟ ⬚ ⅋
→ ∪ ⅃ ◨ ▦ ▩ ▦ ⅋

LADRAM BAY   Map 03 SY08

▶ ▶ ▶ **Ladram Bay Holiday Centre (SY096853)**
EX9 7BX ☎ 01395 568398
★ ⅋ £6-£12 ▲ £5-£12
Open Spring bank hol-Sep (rs Etr-Spring Bank Hol no boat hire & entertainment) Booking advisable for caravans, school & Spring bank hols Last arrival 18.00hrs Last departure 10.00hrs

A large caravan site with many static vans and a separate camping area, set on terraced ground in wooded surroundings, overlooking rocky, shingle beach. A 50-acre site with 469 statics.
Boat & canoe hire, crazy golf.
Leisure: ₹ ◣ ⋒ Facilities: ⋒ ⊙ ✳ ⅋ ⅋ ⅋ ⋒ ⅋
Services: ◨ ⊟ ⅋ ⅋ ⅋ ⬚ ✗ ⅋
→ ∪ ▶ ✦ ⅋ ⅃ ◨ ▦ ▩ ▦ ⅋

LYDFORD   Map 02 SX58

▶ ▶ ▶ **Camping & Caravanning Club Site (SX512853)**
EX20 4BE ☎ 01822 820275
Dir: *From A30 take A386. Continue until reaching a filling station on the right. Turn right to Lydford. At War Memorial right. Site signed 200yds*
★ ⅋ £10.60-£13.90 ⅋ £10.60-£13.90 ▲ £10.60-£13.90
Open 20 Mar-1 Nov Booking advisable bank hols & peak periods Last arrival 21.00hrs Last departure noon
Site on mainly level ground looking towards the western slopes of Dartmoor at the edge of the village, near the spectacular gorge. Please see advertisement on page 14 for details of Club Members' benefits. A 7.5-acre site with 70 touring pitches.
Facilities: ⋒ ⊙ ⅋ ✳ ⅋ ⅋ ⅋ Services: ◨ ⊟ ⅋ ⅋ ⊟
→ ∪ ▶ ⅋ ✦ ⅃ ◨ ▦

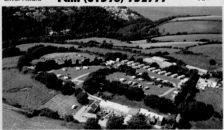
LYNTON   Map 03 SS74

▶ ▶ ▶ ▶ **Channel View Caravan Park (SS724482)**
Manor Farm EX35 6LD ☎ 01598 753349
Dir: *From Lynton take A39 E for 0.5m. Site signed on left*
★ ⅋ £7.50-£10 ⅋ £7.50-£10 ▲ £3.50-£9
Open Etr-mid Oct Booking advisable Jul-Aug Last arrival 22.00hrs Last departure noon
On the top of the cliffs overlooking the Bristol Channel, this delightful well-maintained park is on the edge of Exmoor, and close to both Lynton and Lynmouth. Pitches can be selected with panoramic views over Lynton and the Channel, or from a hidden area in the hedged perimeter field. The owner is accommodating and helpful, and there is a decent pub next door serving meals. A 6-acre site with 76 touring pitches and 36 statics.
Parent & Baby room
Leisure: ⋒ Facilities: ⋒ ⊙ ⅋ ✳ ⅋ ⅋ ⅋ ⅋
Services: ◨ ⊟ ⅋ ⅋ ⊟ ⬚
→ ∪ ⊙ ⅋ ⅋ ⅃ ◨ ▦ ▩ ▦ ⅋

▶ ▶ ▶ **Camping & Caravanning Club Site (SS700484)**
Caffyns Cross EX35 6JS ☎ 01598 752379
Dir: *From M5 take A361 to Barnstable. Right at Blackmoor Gate signed Lynmouth/Lynton. Follow for 5m to Caffyns Cross. Left at junct, then 1st right to site*
★ ⅋ £10.60-£13.90 ⅋ £10.60-£13.90 ▲ £10.60-£13.90
Open 20 Mar-1 Nov Booking advisable bank hols & peak periods Last arrival 21.00hrs Last departure noon

---

Facilities: ⇥ Bath ⋒ Shower ⊙ Electric Shaver ⅋ Hairdryer ✳ Ice Pack Facility ⅋ Disabled Facilities ⅋ Public Telephone ⅋ Shop on Site or within 200yds ◨ Mobile Shop (calls at least 5 days a week) ⬚ BBQ Area ▦ Picnic Area ⅋ Dog Exercise Area

WOOLACOMBE BAY
The Cream of Coastal Camping
www.woolacombe.co.uk

A level grassy site, with bushes, set below hill in well-wooded countryside. Please see the advertisement on page 14 for details of Club Members' benefits. A 5.5-acre site with 105 touring pitches.
Leisure: ⚏ **Facilities:** ⬥⊙⬟☀⬤ **Services:** ⬤⬒⬢⬡
→⬡⬥⬤⬢⬦⬟⬞⬢⬤ ⬤⬛⬛

▶ ▶ ▶ Sunny Lyn Holiday Park (SS719486)
Lynbridge EX35 6NS ☎ 01598 753384
Dir: Located on B3234
★ ⬤ £9.50-£10.50 ⬤ £9.50-£10.50 ⬤ £9.50-£10.50

Open Mar-Nov Booking advisable Etr, spring bank hol & mid Jul-Aug Last arrival 20.00hrs Last departure 11.00hrs
Part-level, part-sloping site, bordering trout stream, in a wooded combe within 1m of sea. A 4.5-acre site with 37 touring pitches and 31 statics.
Pool table & table tennis, trout fishing on site.
Leisure: ⚏ **Facilities:** ⬥⊙⬟☀⬤⬛⬦
Services: ⬤⬒⬡⬢⬡⬟⨯⬦
→⬡⊙⬟⬞⬢⬦

MODBURY	Map 03 SX65

▶ ▶ ▶ Camping & Caravanning Club Site (SX705530)
California Cross PL21 0SG ☎ 01548 821297
Dir: On A38 take A3121, continue to X-roads. Straight across onto B3196. Turn left after Calafornia Cross sign before petrol station. Site on right
★ ⬤ £10.60-£13.90 ⬤ £10.60-£13.90 ⬤ £10.60-£13.90
Open 07 Apr-Oct Booking advisable Spring bank hol & Jul-Aug Last arrival 21.00hrs Last departure noon
A well-ordered site sloping gently and partially terraced in rural surroundings, protected by high hedges. Please see advertisement on page 14 for details of Club Members' benefits. A 3.75-acre site with 80 touring pitches.

Leisure: ⚏ **Facilities:** ⬥⊙⬟☀⬤
Services: ⬤⬒⬢⬡⬡⬦⬤
→⬡⬥⬤⬦ ⬤⬛⬛

▶ ▶ ▶ Moor View Touring Park (SX705533)
California Cross PL21 0SG ☎ 01548 821485
Dir: Leave A38 at Wrangaton Cross & turn left at top of slip road. Follow signs to park
★ ⬤ £8-£10 ⬤ £8-£10 ⬤ £7-£10

Open Etr-Oct Booking advisable bank hols & mid Jul-Aug Last arrival 21.00hrs Last departure noon
A compact terraced site in picturesque South Hams, with wide views of Dartmoor. A 6-acre site with 68 touring pitches and 1 static.
Leisure: ⬥⚏⬚ **Facilities:** ⬥⊙⬟☀⬤⬛⬞⬦
Services: ⬤⬒⬢⬡⬦⬟⬞⬦
→⬡⬥⬦ ⬤⬛⬛⬛⬦

▶ ▶ ▶ Pennymoor Camping & Caravan Park (SX685516)
PL21 0SB ☎ 01548 830269 & 830542
Dir: Leave A38 at Wrangaton Cross. Turn left & straight over X-roads. Continue for 4m, pass petrol station & take 2nd left. Site 1m on right
★ ⬤ £5.50-£9 ⬤ £4.50-£8 ⬤ £5.50-£9
Open 15 Mar-15 Nov (rs 15 Mar-mid May 1 toilet & shower block only open) Booking advisable Jul-Aug Last arrival 22.30hrs Last departure noon
A well-established rural grassy site on gently sloping ground with good views. A 12.5-acre site with 154 touring pitches and 70 statics.
Leisure: ⚏ **Facilities:** ⬥⊙⬟☀⬤⬤⬦⬞
Services: ⬤⬒⬢⬡⬦⬟⬞
→⬡⬦

See advert on page 112

contd.

Services: ⬟ Toilet Fluid ✗ Café/ Restaurant ⬛ Fast Food/Takeaway ⬦ Baby Care ⬤ Electric Hook Up
⬡ Launderette ⬢ Licensed Bar ⬤ Calor Gaz ⬦ Camping Gaz ⬞ Battery Charging

England

Pennymoor

Camping & Caravan Park
Modbury South Devon PL21 0SB
Tel: Modbury (01548) 830269 & 830542
AA 3 Pennant Site
Proprietors: R.A. & M. Blackler

Immaculately maintained, well-drained, peaceful rural site, with panoramic views. Central for beaches, moors and towns. Ideal for touring caravans and tents. Luxury caravans for hire, with all services, colour TV.
Super, luxury toilet/shower block; fully tiled walls and floors; laundry room, dishwashing room, disabled facilities. Children's equipped playground. Shop. Gas. Public telephone.
Leave A38 at Wrangton Cross. 1 mile to crossroads. Go straight across. After approx. 4 miles take 2nd left after petrol station. Site 1½ miles.

►►► ***Southleigh Caravan & Camping Park (SX682515)***
PL21 0SB ☎ 01548 830346
Dir: *From A38 at Wrangaton take B3210 signed Modbury. After California Cross 2nd fork left signed Aveton/Gifford/Bigbury. Site 2nd on right*
Open 15 May-20 Sep (rs 19 Mar-14 May & 20 Sep-Oct limited facilities) Booking advisable mid Jul-Aug Last arrival 23.00hrs Last departure noon
A rural site with a good variety of amenities and entertainment for all the family. A 4-acre site with 100 touring pitches and 100 statics.
Family room with shower & toilet, entertainment.
Leisure: **Facilities:**
Services:
→

MORTEHOE — Map 02 SS44

►►► **Easewell Farm Coastal Holiday Park (SS465455)**
EX34 7EH ☎ 01271 870225
Dir: *From Mullacott Cross take B3343 to Mortehoe. Turn right at unclass road & site is 2m on the right*
★ £7-£11 £6.50-£9 £6.50-£9
Open Etr-Sep (rs Etr no shop) Booking advisable Jul-Aug Last arrival 22.00hrs Last departure 10.00hrs
A clifftop site of varying terrain, well-run and maintained, and with a friendly atmosphere. A 17-acre site with 250 touring pitches.
9 hole golf on site.
See advertisement under WOOLACOMBE
Leisure: **Facilities:**
Services:
→

►►► **Twitchen Parc (SS465447)**
EX34 7ES ☎ 01271 870343
Dir: *From Mullacott Cross rdbt take B3343 Woolacombe Rd to Turnpike Cross junct. Take the right fork & site is 1.5m on the left*
£11.50-£33 £11.50-£33 £8-£22
Open Mar-Oct Booking advisable May bank hol & Jul-Aug Last arrival 23.30hrs Last departure 10.00hrs
A part-sloping grass site with trees and bushes, set in downland and wooded meadowland. A 45-acre site with 250 touring pitches and 274 statics.
Table tennis, snooker, sauna, bus to beach, kids club
See advertisement under WOOLACOMBE
Leisure: **Facilities:**
Services:
→

►►► ***Warcombe Farm Camping Park (SS478445)***
Station Rd EX34 7EJ ☎ 01271 870690 & 0374 428770
Dir: *N towards Mortehoe from Mullacot Cross rdbt at A361 junct with B3343. Site 2m on right*
Open 15 Mar-Oct Booking advisable July/August
An open site extending to the cliffs, with views over the Bristol Channel, and an attractive fishing lake. A 19-acre site with 95 touring pitches.
Private fishing.
Leisure: **Facilities:**
Services:
→

NEWTON ABBOT — Map 03 SX87

PREMIER PARK

►►►►► ***Ross Park (SX845671)***
Park Hill Farm, Ipplepen TQ12 5TT
☎ 01803 812983
Dir: *Off A381, 3m from Newton Abbot towards Totnes, signed opposite Jet garage towards 'Woodland'*
(rs Nov-Feb & 1st 3wks of Mar Rest & Bar closed except Xmas & New Yr) Booking advisable Last arrival 21.00hrs Last departure 10.00hrs
A top-class park in every way, with large pitches, secluded areas, high quality facilities and lovely floral displays throughout. Helen and Mark Lowe have filled their 26 acres with an impressive display of flowers, and the beautiful tropical conservatory also offers a breathtaking show of colour. This very rural park enjoys superb views of Dartmoor, and good quality meals to suit all tastes and pockets are served in the restaurant.

Facilities: Bath · Shower · Electric Shaver · Hairdryer · Ice Pack Facility · Disabled Facilities · Public Telephone · Shop on Site or within 200yds · Mobile Shop (calls at least 5 days a week) · BBQ Area · Picnic Area · Dog Exercise Area

Winner of the Best Campsite of the Year for 2000. A 26-acre site with 110 touring pitches. Snooker, table tennis, bowling green, croquet.

Leisure: ♠ ⋒ ▢ **Facilities:** ⋔ ☉ ☜ ✳ ☘ 𝓔 🦺 ⌂ ⍭

Services: ▣ ◉ ♈ 🛢 ⌀ ⊞ 🅃 ✕ ➥

→ ⏵

► ► ► ► *Dornafield (SX838683)*
Dornafield Farm, Two Mile Oak TQ12 6DD
☎ 01803 812732

Dir: Take A381 (Newton Abbot-Totnes) for 2m. At Two Mile Oak Inn turn right, then left at X-roads in 0.5m to site on right

🚐 🚐 Å

Open Mar-Oct Booking advisable bank hols & Jul-Aug Last arrival 22.30hrs Last departure 11.00hrs
A quiet, very attractive and well-laid out site in a secluded wooded valley setting. A lovely old farmhouse sits at the entrance, and reception and
contd.

Services: 🅃 Toilet Fluid ✕ Café/ Restaurant 🍴 Fast Food/Takeaway ➥ Baby Care ▣ Electric Hook Up
▣ Launderette ♈ Licensed Bar 🛢 Calor Gaz ⌀ Camping Gaz ⊞ Battery Charging

the shop are housed in converted barns in a courtyard. The park is divided into three areas each with its own excellent modern heated toilet block. This family-run park sets and maintains very high standards, and guarantees a comfortable stay. A 30-acre site with 135 touring pitches. Wet weather room.

Leisure: ♦ ◀ ⚘ Facilities: ⋔ ⊙ ♖ ✳ ♿ ℓ ⌷ ⊞ ⋒
Services: ☎ 🖻 🅟 ⌀ ⊞ ⊤ ⚙ ↦
→ ∪ ▸ 🐾 🗐 ⨀ 🍽 ▭ ▒ ⧉ ⬚

▶ ▶ ▶ **Twelve Oaks Farm Caravan Park (SX852737)**
Teigngrace TQ12 6QT ☎ 01626 352769
Dir: Direct access form A38, signed 'Teigngrace only' SW towards Plymouth
⊞ ⊟ ⚠
Open all year Booking advisable Last departure 11.00hrs

An attractive small park with very good facilities, on a working farm. Close to River Teign and Templar Way walking route, with tidy pitches located amongst trees and shrubs. A 2-acre site with 35 touring pitches.

Leisure: ⚘ Facilities: ⋔ ♖ ✳ ♿ ℓ ⌷
Services: ☎ 🅟
→ ∪ ▸ ⨀ 🗐

OKEHAMPTON   Map 02 SX59

See also **Whiddon Down**
▶ ▶ ▶ **Yertiz Caravan & Camping Park (SX602954)**
Exeter Rd EX20 1QF ☎ 01837 52281
Dir: On left of B3260 50yds beyond Moorcroft Inn
⊞ ⊟ ⚠
Open all year Booking advisable bank holidays & Aug Last arrival 23.59hrs
Small friendly park with lovely views of Dartmoor, and pleasant local walks. A 3.5-acre site with 30 touring pitches and 5 statics.

Leisure: ⚘ Facilities: ⋔ ⊙ ♖ ✳ ♿ ℓ ⊞ ▭ ⋒
Services: 🅟 ⌀ ⊞
→ ∪ 🐾 🗐 ⌷

PAIGNTON   Map 03 SX86

Beverley Parks Caravan & Camping Park (SX886582)
Goodrington Rd TQ4 7JE
☎ 01803 843887
Dir: Along A380/A3022, 2m S of Paignton turn left into Goodrington Road
★ ⊞ £9-£22 ⊟ £9-£22 ⚠ £7-£18
Open Feb-Nov Booking advisable Jun-Sep Last arrival 22.00hrs Last departure 10.00hrs ⌁
A high quality family-run park with extensive views of the bay, and plenty of on-site amenities. The park boasts indoor and outdoor heated swimming pools, and the toilet facilities are very modern and clean. The park complex is attractively laid out. A 12-acre site with 194 touring pitches and 197 statics.
Table tennis, pool, spa bath, crazy golf, sauna, fitness room

Leisure: ♖ ⚮ ♦ ⚘ Facilities: ↦ ⋔ ⊙ ♖ ✳ ♿ ℓ ⌷ ▭ Services: ☎ 🅟 ⚙ ⌷ ⌀ ⊤ ✗ ⚱
→ ∪ ▸ ⨀ ⚶ ↟ 🐾 ⨀ 🍽 ▒ ⧉ ▒ ⬚

Grange Court Holiday Centre (SX888588)
Grange Rd TQ4 7JP ☎ 01803 558010
Dir: S on A380 past junct A385, left at traffic lights into Goodrington Road, 0.75m turn left into Grange Road, site in 500yds
⊞ £10-£25 ⊟ £10-£25
Open 23 May-19 Sep (rs 15 Feb-22 May & 20 Sep-15 Jan club closed) Booking advisable public hols & Jul-Aug Last arrival 22.00hrs Last departure 10.00hrs ⌁
Large grassy site situated amidst woodland near to sea, very well-equipped and maintained, and with lots of on-site amenities. A 10-acre site with 157 touring pitches and 520 statics.
Crazy golf, sauna, steam room, snooker
See advertisement under Preliminary Section

Leisure: ♖ ⚮ ♦ ⚘ Facilities: ↦ ⋔ ⊙ ♖ ✳ ℓ ⌷
Services: ☎ 🅟 ⚙ ⌷ ⌀ ⊤ ✗ ⚱
→ ∪ ▸ ⨀ ⚶ ↟ 🐾 ⨀ 🍽 ▒ ⧉ ▒ ⬚

▶ ▶ ▶ ▶ **Widend Camping Park (SX852619)**
Berry Pomeroy Rd, Marldon TQ3 1RT
☎ 01803 550116
Dir: Signed off the Torbay ring road
★ ⊞ £5.50-£10 ⊟ £5.50-£10 ⚠ £5.50-£10
Open Apr-Oct (rs Apr-mid May & mid Sep-Oct swimming pool, Club house May-Oct) Booking advisable Jul-Aug & Whit Last arrival 21.00hrs Last departure 10.00hrs
A terraced grass park paddocked and screened on high ground overlooking Torbay with views of Dartmoor. This attractive park is well laid out, divided up by mature trees and bushes but with plenty of open grassy areas. Facilities are of a high standard and well maintained, and offers a heated outdoor swimming pool with sunbathing area, a small lounge bar, and a well-stocked shop. A 22-acre site with 207 touring pitches.

contd.

▶ ▶ ▶

BYSLADES
•INTERNATIONAL•

Totnes Road, PAIGNTON, South Devon TQ4 7PY
Tel or Fax: (01803) 555072

This friendly award winning family park is set in 23 acres of rolling Devon countryside in the centre of the English Riviera. Ideally situated for visiting safe sandy beaches, Dartmoor National Park, the picturesque South Hams or the historic town of Totnes.

The level terrace pitches overlook a beautiful valley and the spacious leisure area includes a tennis court, badminton, crazy golf, children's adventure playground, an ornamental lake and an enclosure with sheep.

★ Some Super Pitches available ★ Coarse Fishing nearby
★ Heated Outdoor Swimming Pool with children's area
★ Licensed Clubhouse ★ Large Games Room ★ Refurbished Toilet & Shower Blocks ★ Dishwashing Facilities ★ Automatic Laundry ★ Electric Hook-ups ★ Separate Facilities for Disabled ★ Late Night Arrivals.

EXCELLENT

RECOMMENDED

Leisure: ⚲ ⚓ 🏔 **Facilities:** ↑ ⊙ ✳ ⭄ ⚲ ⛽ ↟
Services: 🔌 🗄 🍸 ⚕ 🔋 ⊟ ⊤ ⛟
→ ∪ ⅂ ⊚ △ ⅄ ⚎ ⚙ ✦ ▦ ▦ ▦ ▦ ▨

▶ ▶ ▶ **Byslades International Touring & Camping Park (SX853603)**
Totnes Rd TQ4 7PY ☎ 01803 555072
Dir: 2m W on A385. Signposted at entry to town
🚐 🚗 🅰

Open Jun-Oct (rs Mar-May & Oct bar & swimming pool closed) Booking advisable Jul-Aug Last arrival 22.00hrs Last departure 10.00hrs
A well-kept terraced site set in beautiful countryside only 2 miles from Paignton. A 23-acre site with 170 touring pitches.
Ornamental lake, crazy golf.

Leisure: ⚲ ⚓ ⚓ 🏔 ⊡ **Facilities:** ↑ ⊙ ✳ ⭄ ⚲ ⛽ ↟
Services: 🔌 🗄 🍸 ⚕ 🔋 ⊟ ⊤ ✕ ⛟
→ ∪ ⅂ ⊚ △ ⅄ ⚎ ⚙ ✦ ▦ ▦ ▦ ▦ ▨

▶ ▶ ▶ **Marine Park Holiday Centre (SX886587)**
Grange Rd TQ4 7JR ☎ 01803 843887
Dir: 2m S. Signposted from A3022 and B3198
★ 🚐 £9-£17 🚗 £9-£17

Open Etr-Oct Booking advisable Jul-Aug Last arrival 22.00hrs Last departure 10.00hrs ⚘
A mainly static site catering for those who prefer peace and quiet. Next door to sister site Beverley Park whose amenities are available. A 2-acre site with 23 touring pitches and 66 statics.

Leisure: 🏔 **Facilities:** ↪ ↑ ⊙ ✳ ⚲ ⛽ ↟
Services: 🔌 🗄 ⚕ ⊤
→ ∪ ⅂ ⊚ △ ⅄ ⚎ ⚙ ✦ ▦ ▦ ▦ ▨

PLYMOUTH   Map 02 SX45

▶ ▶ ▶ ▶ ▶ *Riverside Caravan Park (SX515575)*
Longbridge Rd, Marsh Mills, Plympton PL6 8LD
☎ 01752 344122
Dir: Access via Longbridge Road, E of Marsh Mills rdbt
🚐 🚗 🅰

Open Etr-Sep (rs Oct-Etr Bar, Restaurant & Take-away closed) Booking advisable Jun-Aug Last arrival 22.00hrs Last departure 10.00hrs
A well-groomed site on the outskirts of Plymouth on the banks of the River Plym, in a quiet location surrounded by woodland, and offering a good mix of grass and hard pitches. An 11-acre site with 293 touring pitches.

Leisure: ⚲ ⚓ 🏔 ⊡ **Facilities:** ↑ ⊙ ✳ ⭄ ⚲ ⛽ ↟
Services: 🔌 🗄 🍸 ⚕ 🔋 ⊟ ⊤ ✕ ⛟
→ ∪ ⅂ ⊚ △ ⅄ ⚎ ⚙ ✦ ▦ ▦ ▦ ▨

SALCOMBE   Map 03 SX73

▶ ▶ ▶ **Higher Rew Caravan & Camping Park (SX714383)**
Higher Rew, Malborough TQ7 3DW
☎ 01548 842681 & 843681
Dir: Follow A381 to Salcombe. Turn right at Townsend Cross & follow signs to Soar for 1m. Left at Rew Cross
★ 🚐 £6-£9 🚗 £6-£9 🅰 £6-£9

RIVERSIDE
CARAVAN PARK
Longbridge Road, Marsh Mills, Plymouth
Telephone: Plymouth (01752) 344122

"The award-winning touring park that'll stop you touring!"

"Riverside" the conveniently situated, secluded, countryside park has all the amenities, scenery, and relaxed atmosphere that will make you want to stay for the rest of your holiday. Surrounded by woodlands, and bordered by the River Plym, this pleasant site has the luxury of permanent facilities without losing the country charm.

Within a short distance you can also reach the freedom of Dartmoor, the shops and history of Plymouth, and the fun of many beaches and coves. The numerous sports, activities and attractions of the whole area mean "Riverside" can be the centre of a complete holiday experience. Ring or write for details.

★ Bar, Restaurant and Takeaway ★ Heated swimming pool ★ Games room ★ TV room and play areas ★ Shop and Telephone ★ Coffee bar ★ Off licence ★ Level pitches ★ Electricity ★ Tarmac roads ★ Street lights ★ Toilet and shower blocks ★ Laundry and dishwashing facilities ★ Special over 50's rates.

Facilities: ↪ Bath   ↑ Shower   ⊙ Electric Shaver   ⚲ Hairdryer   ✳ Ice Pack Facility   ⭄ Disabled Facilities   ⚲ Public Telephone
⛽ Shop on Site or within 200yds   ⊡ Mobile Shop (calls at least 5 days a week)   ▦ BBQ Area   ⊼ Picnic Area   ↟ Dog Exercise Area

England

Open Mar-Nov Booking advisable Spring bank hol & mid Jul-Aug Last arrival 22.00hrs Last departure noon
A long-established park in a remote location in sight of the sea. A 5-acre site with 75 touring pitches.
Play Barn
Leisure: ♦ **Facilities:** ℝ ☉ ۹ ※ ╚ ☎ ⊁
Services: ◘ 🗐 🛢 ⌀ ⊞
→ ♨ ⊹ 🗲

►►► Bolberry House Farm Caravan & Camping Park (SX687395)
Bolberry TQ7 3DY ☎ 01548 561251 & 560926
Dir: At Malborough on A381 turn right signed Hope Cove & Bolberry. Take left fork after village signed Soar & Bolberry. Site signed in 0.5m
★ 🚐 £7.50-£10 🚐 £7.50-£10 ▲ £6-£9
Open Etr-Oct Booking advisable Jul & Aug Last arrival 20.00hrs Last departure 11.00hrs

A level, well maintained family-run park in a peaceful setting on a coastal farm with sea views, fine cliff walks and nearby beaches. Discount in low season for senior citizens. A 6-acre site with 70 touring pitches and 10 statics.
Childrens play area & play barn.
Leisure: ⋀ **Facilities:** ℝ ☉ ۹ ※ ╚ ☎ ⊁
Services: ◘ 🗐 🛢 ⌀ ⊞
→ ∪ ▶ ◎ ⊹ 🛁 🗲

►►► *Karrageen Caravan & Camping Park (SX686395)*
Malborough TQ7 3EN ☎ 01548 561230
Dir: At Malborough on A381, turn sharp right through village, follow Bolberry signs for 0.5m. Turn right to Bolberry and park 1m on right
🚐 🚐 ▲
Open 15 Mar-15 Nov Booking advisable bank & school hols Last arrival 23.30hrs Last departure 11.30hrs

A small, friendly, family-run park with terraced grassy pitches giving extensive sea and country views. One mile from the beach in the pretty hamlet of Hope Cove. A 7.5-acre site with 75 touring pitches and 20 statics.
Baby room, licensed shop, 2 play areas, family shower
Facilities: ℝ ☉ ۹ ※ ⅋ ╚ ☎ 🕀 **Services:** ◘ 🗐 🛢 ⌀ ⊞ 🅃 ♨
→ ∪ ♨ ⊹ 🗲

►►► Sun Park Caravan & Camping Site (SX707379)
Soar Mill Cove TQ7 3DS ☎ 01548 561378
Dir: On entering village of Marlborough on A381, turn sharp right signed Soar. Follow signs on this road to Soar Mill Cove. Site situated 1.5m on right
🚐 £6-£9 ▲ £6-£9
Open Etr-Oct Booking advisable Jul-Aug Last arrival 20.00hrs Last departure 11.00hrs

A level grassy park in a peaceful rural location, approx 0.75m from a safe sandy beach at Soar Mill Cove. A 2.5-acre site with 65 touring pitches and 34 statics.
Leisure: ♦ ⋀ ▱ **Facilities:** ℝ ☉ ۹ ※ ╚
Services: ◘ 🛢 ⌀ ⊞
→ ♨ ⊹ 🗲 ☎

SAMPFORD PEVERELL   Map 03 ST01

►►► *Minnows Caravan Park (SS042148)*
Holbrook Ln EX16 7EN ☎ 01884 821770
Dir: From M5 junct 22 take A361 signed Tiverton and Barnstaple. Site signed on left almost immediately at 1st slip road
🚐 🚐
Open 6 Mar-13 Nov Booking advisable Bank Hols, Jun-Sep inc. Last departure 11.30hrs
Attractive park bounded by Grand Western Canal, with good facilities and well positioned as a holiday base. A 5.5-acre site with 45 touring pitches.
Tourist Info Centre, Full service pitches
Leisure: ⋀ **Facilities:** ℝ ☉ ۹ ※ ⅋ ╚ ☶ ⊁
Services: ◘ 🛢 ⌀ ⊞ ♨
→ ▶ 🗲 🗐 ╚ 💳 💳 💳 🎴 🔲

SEATON

See **Colyton**

Services: 🅃 Toilet Fluid ✖ Café/ Restaurant 🕍 Fast Food/Takeaway 🍼 Baby Care ◘ Electric Hook Up
🗐 Launderette ♀ Licensed Bar 🛢 Calor Gaz ⌀ Camping Gaz ⊞ Battery Charging

England

SIDMOUTH　　　　　　　　Map 03 SY18

▶ ▶ ▶ ▶ Oakdown Touring & Holiday Home Park (SY168901)

Weston EX10 0PH ☎ 01297 680387
Dir: Off A3052, 2.5m E of junct with A375
★ ⊞ £7.75-£11.65 ⊞ £7.75-£11.65 ▲ £7.75-£11.65
Open Apr-Oct Booking advisable Spring bank hol &
Jul-Aug Last arrival 22.00hrs Last departure
10.30hrs
Friendly, well-maintained, level park with good
landscaping by trees which are beginning to mature
attractively. Pitches are not regimented, but
grouped in areas surrounded by shrubs, and the
park is well screened from the A3502. Walks within
the park are conservation areas full of natural fauna
and flora, and there is a hide by the lagoon for both
casual and dedicated bird watchers. A 13-acre site
with 120 touring pitches and 46 statics.
6 Dishwashing sinks.

Leisure: ⚙🖵 Facilities: ➡🅡☉🔦❋👜🐕🌴
Services: 🔌🅱🛢🗑🗃🚽➡
➡☋🍴◎♨🛠🌐🏷 ⊞ 🎪 🔗 💳 🛒

▶ ▶ ▶ Kings Down Tail Caravan & Camping Park (SY173907)

Salcombe Regis EX10 0PD ☎ 01297 680313
Dir: Off A3052 3m E of junct with A375
⊞ £7.50-£9.50 ⊞ £7.50-£9.50 ▲ £7.50-£9.50
Open 15 Mar-15 Nov Booking advisable Whit, bank
hols & mid Jul-Sep Last arrival 22.00hrs Last
departure noon

Facilities: ➡ Bath 🅡 Shower ☉ Electric Shaver 🍃 Hairdryer ❋ Ice Pack Facility 🦽 Disabled Facilities 📞 Public Telephone
🛒 Shop on Site or within 200yds ▣ Mobile Shop (calls at least 5 days a week) 🍖 BBQ Area 🌲 Picnic Area 🐕 Dog Exercise Area

A well-kept site on level ground on east side of Sid Valley in tree-sheltered position. A 5-acre site with 100 touring pitches and 2 statics.
Off licence.
Leisure: ◄ ⚠ Facilities: 🖍⊙🕯✳ ⚓ ⛺ 🐾
Services: 🔌 🖊 ⊘ ➕ 🔲 Ⓣ
→ ∪ ▶ ◎ ✚ ⚓ ➕ 🍴 ⤴ 🖊 🔲 🎽

▶ ▶ ▶ **Salcombe Regis Caravan & Camping Park** (SY153892)
Salcombe Regis EX10 0JH ☎ 01395 514303
Dir: Off A3052 3m E of junct with A375
★ 🚐 £6.75-£9.75 🚛 £6.75-£9.75 ▲ £6.75-£9.75
Open Etr-Oct Booking advisable bank hols & Jul-Aug Last arrival 20.00hrs Last departure 10.00hrs
Spacious level park with well-maintained facilities, on the coastal path. A 16-acre site with 100 touring pitches and 10 statics.
Off licence, bike hire, putting & barbecue hire.
Leisure: ⚠ Facilities: ➡ 🖍⊙🕯✳ ⚓ ⛺ 🐾
Services: 🔌 🖊 ⊘ ⊘ Ⓣ
→ ∪ ▶ ◎ ⚓ ✚ ⤴ 🍴 🖊 💳 🔲 🎽

SLAPTON   Map 03 SX84

▶ ▶ ▶ **Camping & Caravanning Club Site** (SX825450)
Middle Grounds TQ7 1QW ☎ 01548 580538
Dir: On A379 from Kingsbridge, site entrance is 0.25m from A379, beyond brow of hill approaching Slapton Village
★ 🚐 £11.80-£14.90 🚛 £11.80-£14.90 ▲ £11.80-£14.90
Open 20 Mar-1 Nov Booking advisable bank hols & Jul-Aug Last arrival 21.00hrs
A very attractive location and well-run site open to non-members. The site overlooks Start Bay within a few minutes' walk of the beach. Please see the advertisement on page 14 for details of Club Members' benefits. A 5.5-acre site with 115 touring pitches.
Leisure: ⚠ Facilities: 🖍⊙🕯✳ ⚓ ⛺ 🐾
Services: 🔌 🖊 ⊘ ⊘ ➕ ➡
→ ∪ ▶ ⚓ 🖊 🐾 💳 🔲

SOURTON CROSS   Map 02 SX59

▶ ▶ ▶ **Bundu Camping & Caravan Park** (SX546916)
EX20 4HT ☎ 01837 861611
Dir: W on A30, past Okehampton. Take A861 to Tavistock. Take 1st left and left again
★ 🚐 fr £7 🚛 fr £7 ▲ £5-£7
Open 15 Mar-15 Nov Booking advisable Jul & Aug Last arrival 23.00hrs Last departure 14.00hrs
A level grassy site in an ideal location, on the border of the Dartmoor National Park and offering fine views. A 4-acre site with 38 touring pitches.
Leisure: ⚠ Facilities: 🖍⊙🕯✳ ⚓ ⛺ 🐾 ⛺ 🐾
Services: 🔌 🖊 ⊘ ⊘ ➕
→ ∪ ▶ 🐾

SOUTH BRENT   Map 03 SX66

▶ ▶ **Webland Farm Holiday Park** (SX715594)
Avonwick TQ10 9EX ☎ 01364 73273
Dir: Leave A38 at junct with A385 signed Marley Head. Site in 1m on unclass single track road
Open Etr-15 Nov Booking advisable school hols Last arrival 22.00hrs Last departure noon
A very rural park with extensive views, surrounded by farmland, with sloping pitches mainly for tents. For towed caravans, access can be awkward. A 5-acre site with 35 touring pitches and 50 statics.
Leisure: ⚠ Facilities: 🖍⊙✳🕯 ⚓ 🐾 Services: 🔌 🖊 ⊘
→ ∪ ▶ 🖊 🐾

STARCROSS

See **Dawlish**

STICKLEPATH   Map 03 SX69

▶ ▶ ▶ **Olditch Caravan & Camping Park** (SX645935)
EX20 2NT ☎ 01837 840734
Dir: Leave A30 at Merrymeet rdbt onto unclass road signed Sticklepath. Park on left at entry to village
🚐 £7-£9 🚛 £7-£9 ▲ £5-£9
Open 14 Mar-14 Nov Booking advisable bank hols & Jul-Aug Last arrival 22.00hrs Last departure 16.00hrs
A mainly sloping grassy park with some tiered level pitches, on outskirts of this now by-passed village. A 3-acre site with 32 touring pitches and 20 statics. Small tourist information area
Leisure: ◄ ⚠ 🏓 Facilities: 🖍⊙🕯✳ ⚓ 🏠 🏛
Services: 🔌 🖊 ⊘ Ⓣ ✖
→ ∪ ▶ 🐾 🖊 🔲 🐾 💳 🔲 🎽

STOKE GABRIEL   Map 03 SX85

▶ ▶ ▶ ▶ **Ramslade Touring Park** (SX861592)
Stoke Rd TQ9 6QB ☎ 01803 782575
Dir: Follow A380 towards Torquay. Turn right onto Paignton Ring Road. At junction with A385 turn right towards Totnes. Turn 2nd left to Stoke Gabriel
★ 🚐 £8.80-£13.80 🚛 £8.80-£13.80 ▲ £8.80-£13.80

Open end Mar-Oct Booking advisable Jul-Aug also Etr & Spring bank hol Last arrival 20.00hrs Last departure 11.00hrs
A high quality park in a rural setting next to the Dart Valley. Ramslade is surrounded by open countryside, and its landscaped grounds look out over the rolling Devon hills, and the River Dart. The

contd.

Services: Ⓣ Toilet Fluid ✖ Café/ Restaurant 🍴 Fast Food/Takeaway ➡ Baby Care 🔌 Electric Hook Up
⊘ Launderette ⚓ Licensed Bar 🔋 Calor Gaz ⊘ Camping Gaz ⊞ Battery Charging

park is quiet and well looked after, and is handy for both Paignton with its beaches and the picturesque village of Stoke Gabriel. Two special pitches with full facilities are designed to accommodate extra-long American-style motor homes. There is a good mix of grass and hard pitches, and a heated toilet block. An 8-acre site with 135 touring pitches.
Paddling pool.

Leisure: ♣ ⚠ ⬜ **Facilities:** ➡ ⟨ ⊙ ⟨ ✳ ⅙ ⟨ ⟨ ⟨ ⟨ ⟨ ⟨ ⟨
Services: ⟨ ⟨ ⟨ ⟨ ⟨ ⟨ ⟨ ⟨ ➡
➡ ⟨ ⟨ ⟨ ⟨ ⟨ ⟨ ⟨ ⟨ ⟨ ⟨ ⟨ ⟨

STOKENHAM   Map 03 SX84

► ► ► Old Cotmore Farm (SX804417)
TQ7 2LR ☎ 01548 580240 581252
Dir: Leave Kingsbridge on A379 Dartmouth Rd, passing through Frogmore and Chillington to mini rdbt at Stokenham. Right towards Beesands & site 1m on right
★ ⟨ £8-£9 ⟨ £8-£9 ⟨ £6.50
Open 15 Mar-15 Nov Booking advisable Jul & Aug Last arrival 22.00hrs Last departure 11.00hrs
A quiet park with some gentle slopes and mainly flat pitches set in an Area of Outstanding Natural Beauty. The family-run park enjoys fine views of the picturesque countryside of the South Hams. Facilities are modern and well maintained, and within walking distance are pebble and sandy beaches with cliff walks through woods and fields. A 3-acre site with 30 touring pitches.
Mountain bike hire

Leisure: ♣ ⚠ **Facilities:** ⟨ ⊙ ⟨ ✳ ⅙ ⟨ ⟨ ⟨ ⟨ ⟨
Services: ⟨ ⟨ ⟨ ⟨ ⟨ ⟨
➡ ⟨ ⟨ ⟨ ⟨ ⟨ ⟨ ⟨ ⟨ ⟨ ⟨

TAVISTOCK   Map 02 SX47

► ► ► ► Higher Longford Farm Caravan Site (SX520747)
Moorshop PL19 9LQ ☎ 01822 613360
Dir: Adjacent to B3357 between Ashburton & Tavistock in the Dartmoor National Park
★ ⟨ £7.50-£9 ⟨ £7.50-£9 ⟨ £7.50-£9
Open all year Booking advisable Jun-Aug Last arrival 22.30hrs Last departure noon

A very pleasant small park in Dartmoor National Park, with panoramic views of the moors. The mainly grassy pitches are sheltered, and some are secluded for extra peace and quiet. Higher Longford is surrounded by moorland parks, lanes and pretty rivers, yet Tavistock is only 2.5m away. The park is open all year round, and is well served with a bar, restaurant and shop. A 6-acre site with 52 touring pitches and 24 statics.

Leisure: ⚠ **Facilities:** ⟨ ⊙ ⟨ ✳ ⟨ ⟨ ⟨ ⟨ ⟨ ⟨
Services: ⟨ ⟨ ⟨ ⟨ ⟨ ⟨ ⟨ ⟨
➡ ⟨ ⟨ ⟨ ⟨ ⟨ ⟨

Leisure: ⚠ **Facilities:** ⟨ ⊙ ⟨ ✳ ⟨ ⟨ ⟨ ⟨ ⟨
Services: ⟨ ⟨ ⟨ ⟨ ⟨ ⟨ ⟨ ⟨ × ⟨
➡ ⟨ ⟨ ⟨

► ► ► Harford Bridge Holiday Park (SX504767)
Peter Tavy PL19 9LS ☎ 01822 810349
Dir: 2m N of Tavistock, off A386 Okehampton road. Take Petertavy turn 200yds on right
⟨ £6-£10.50 ⟨ £6-£10.50 ⟨ £6-£10.50
Open all year (rs end Mar-mid Nov holiday lets only) Booking advisable Aug Last arrival 21.00hrs Last departure noon
Level, grassy site with mature trees, set in Dartmoor National Park, beside the River Tavy. A 10-acre site with 120 touring pitches and 80 statics.
Fly fishing.

Leisure: ⟨ ♣ ⚠ ⬜ **Facilities:** ⟨ ⊙ ⟨ ✳ ⟨ ⟨ ⟨ ⟨ ⟨
Services: ⟨ ⟨ ⟨ ⟨ ⟨
➡ ⟨ ⟨ ⟨ ⟨ ⟨ ⟨ ⟨ ⟨ ⟨ ⟨ ⟨ ⟨ ⟨

► ► ► Langstone Manor Camping & Caravan Park (SX524738)
Moortown PL19 9JZ ☎ 01822 613371
Dir: 1.5m W off B3357
★ ⟨ £7-£9 ⟨ £7-£9 ⟨ £7-£9

Open 15 Mar-15 Nov Booking advisable bank hols & Jul-Aug Last arrival 23.00hrs Last departure 11.00hrs
A secluded site set in the well-maintained grounds of a manor house, within the National Park. A 5.5-acre site with 40 touring pitches and 25 statics.

Leisure: ♣ ⚠ **Facilities:** ⟨ ⊙ ⟨ ✳ ⟨ ⟨ ⟨ ⟨
Services: ⟨ ⟨ ⟨ ⟨ ⟨ ⟨ ×
➡ ⟨ ⟨ ⟨ ⟨

► ► ► Woodovis Park (SX432744)
Gulworthy PL19 8NY ☎ 01822 832968
Dir: From Tavistock take A390 signposted to Liskeard. At top of hill turn right at X-roads signed Lamerton. Park is 1m on left.
⟨ £8.50-£12.50 ⟨ £8.50-£12.50 ⟨ £8.50-£12.50
Open Apr-Nov Booking advisable Jun-Aug Last arrival 22.00hrs Last departure noon
A well-kept small park in a remote woodland setting. A 14.5-acre site with 50 touring pitches and 34 statics.
Mini-golf, sauna, jacuzzi,

Leisure: ⟨ ♣ ⚠ **Facilities:** ➡ ⟨ ⊙ ⟨ ✳ ⅙ ⟨ ⟨ ⟨ ⟨
Services: ⟨ ⟨ ⟨ ⟨ ⟨ ⟨
➡ ⟨ ⟨ ⟨ ⟨ ⟨ ⟨ ⟨ ⟨ ⟨ ⟨ ⟨

Facilities: ➡ Bath ⟨ Shower ⊙ Electric Shaver ⟨ Hairdryer ✳ Ice Pack Facility ⅙ Disabled Facilities ⟨ Public Telephone ⟨ Shop on Site or within 200yds ⟨ Mobile Shop (calls at least 5 days a week) ⟨ BBQ Area ⟨ Picnic Area ⟨ Dog Exercise Area

TEDBURN ST MARY   Map 03 SX89

▶ ▶ ▶ **Springfield Holiday Park (SX788935)**
Tedburn Rd EX6 6EW ☎ 01647 24242
Dir: From M5 junct 31 onto A30. Take 3rd exit. Right over bridge at rdbt. Follow signs to park
★ 🚐 £8-£10 🚐 £8-£10 ▲ £5-£9

Open 15 Mar-15 Nov Booking advisable Jul-Aug
Last arrival 22.00hrs Last departure 14.00hrs
This terraced site offers panoramic views of the surrounding countryside, a tranquil atmosphere and useful facilities. A 9-acre site with 80 touring pitches and 20 statics.
Licensed shop.
Leisure: ⚡ ♨ ⚑ Facilities: ➡ ⋔ ⊙ ☜ ✳ ⛲ ⛗ ⛤ ⛁ ☰ ⋔
Services: ♨ ⎙ ⛿ ⛿ ⚙ ⊞ ⦿ ✗ ⛟
→ ∪ ▶ ⚂ ● ▦ ▨ ⚘

TIVERTON

See **East Worlington**

Yeatheridge Farm
Caravan & Camping Park
E. WORLINGTON, CREDITON, DEVON EX17 4TN
Telephone Tiverton (01884) 860 330
www.yeatheridge.co.uk
OFF THE A377 AND B3137 ON THE B3042

AA ▷

WHY ARE WE DIFFERENT? We are a small Central Park with panoramic views on a genuine working farm with plenty of animals to see and some to touch! We also offer peace and space with freedom to roam the farm with its 2½ miles of woodland and river bank walks, coarse fishing lakes, 2 indoor heated swimming pools with 200 ft water flume, TV lounge, children's play area, hot and cold showers, wash cubicles – ALL FREE. Other amenities include horse riding from the park, electric hook-up points, campers' dish washing, laundry room, shop with frozen foods, fresh dairy products, ice pack service, a welcome for dogs ★ Summer parking in our storage area to save towing ★ Ideally situated for touring coast, Exmoor and Dartmoor. Golf and Tennis locally.
ALSO 4 CARAVANS TO LET –
PROPRIETORS/OWNERS – GEOFFREY & ELIZABETH HOSEGOOD
WRITE OR PHONE FOR FREE COLOUR BROCHURE

TORQUAY   Map 03 SX96

See also **Newton Abbot**
▶ ▶ ▶ ▶ **Widdicombe Farm Tourist Park (SX880650)**
Compton TQ3 1ST ☎ 01803 558325
Dir: On A380 dual carriageway, midway between two rdbts on N-bound lane from Compton Castle, and signed
🚐 🚐 ▲
Open mid Mar-mid Nov Booking advisable Whit & Jul-Aug Last arrival 21.30hrs Last departure 11.00hrs
A friendly family-owned and run park on a working farm, with good quality facilities and extensive views. The level pitches are terraced to take advantage of the views towards the coast and Dartmoor. A happy but quiet atmosphere pervades this park, encouraged by a large children's play area. Other amenities include a well-stocked shop, a restaurant, and a lounge bar. An 8-acre site with 200 touring pitches and 3 statics.
Leisure: ⚡ ♨ ⚑ Facilities: ⋔ ⊙ ☜ ✳ ⛲ ⛗ ⛤ ⛁ ☰ ⋔
Services: ♨ ⎙ ⛿ ⛿ ⚙ ⊞ ⦿ ✗ ⛟ ➡
→ ∪ ▶ ⊚ ⛟ ⚂ ● ▦ ▨ ▦ ⚘

TOTNES   Map 03 SX86

▶ ▶ ▶ **Edeswell Farm Country Caravan Park (SX731606)**
Edeswell Farm TQ10 9LN ☎ 01364 72177
Dir: Leave A38 Devon expressway at Marley Head junct onto the A385 to Paignton. Park is 0.5m on right
★ 🚐 £7-£10 🚐 £7-£10 ▲ £7-£10
Open all year (rs Nov-Mar Static hire only) Booking advisable school & bank hols Last arrival 20.30hrs Last departure noon
Gently sloping, terraced grass site with mature trees. The individual level pitches make the most of the hilly country near the river in this scenically attractive area. A 22-acre site with 46 touring pitches and 22 statics.
Badminton, table tennis, adventure playground.
Leisure: ⚡ ♨ ⚑ Facilities: ⋔ ⊙ ☜ ✳ ⛲ ⛗ ⛤ ⛁ ☰ ⋔
Services: ♨ ⎙ ⛿ ⛿ ⚙ ⊞ ⦿ ✗ ➡ ➡
→ ∪ ▶ ⚂ ● ▦ ▨ ✗ ▦ ⚘

UMBERLEIGH   Map 02 SS62

▶ ▶ ▶ **Camping & Caravanning Club Site (SS606242)**
Over Weir EX37 9DU ☎ 01769 560009
Dir: On A377 from Barnstaple turn right at 'Umberleigh' sign
★ 🚐 £10.60-£13.90 🚐 £10.60-£13.90 ▲ £10.60-£13.90
Open 07 Apr-27 Sep Booking advisable bank hols & Jul-Aug Last arrival 21.00hrs Last departure noon
🚫
A compact site on high ground, with fine country views, adjacent to a wooded area. Approached by metalled road, with wide entrance. Please see the advertisement on page 14 for details of Club Members' benefits. A 3-acre site with 60 touring pitches.
Fishing

contd.

Services: ⊤ Toilet Fluid ✗ Café/ Restaurant ⛟ Fast Food/Takeaway ➡ Baby Care ● Electric Hook Up ⎙ Launderette ⛿ Licensed Bar ⛁ Calor Gaz ⚙ Camping Gaz ⊞ Battery Charging

Leisure: ⊕ ♣ ⚲ ☐   Facilities: ⋔ ⊙ ⊕ ☀ ⓦ ☎ ☒ 🛋 🐕
Services: ☎ 🖫 🅑 🔓 ⚡ 🗒
→ ► ♣ ♪   ◑ ▦ ═

WEST DOWN   Map 02 SS54

PREMIER PARK

► ► ► ► ► **Hidden Valley Coast & Country Park** (SS499408)
EX34 8NU ☎ 01271 813837
Dir: On A361
⊞ £3.50-£13 ⊞ £3.50-£13 ▲ £3.50-£13
Open all year (rs 15 Nov-15 Mar All weather pitches only) Booking advisable high season
Last arrival 21.30hrs Last departure 11.00hrs
A delightful, well-appointed family site set in a wooded valley, with superb facilities and a restaurant. The park is set in a very rural, natural position not far from the beautiful coastline around Ilfracombe. A 25-acre site with 135 touring pitches.
Lounge/bar.
       See advertisement under ILFRACOMBE
Leisure: ♣ ⚲   Facilities: ⋔ ⊙ ⊕ ☀ & ⓦ ☎ ☒ 🛋 🐕
Services: ☎ 🖫 🅑 ⓟ 🔓 ⚡ 🗒 ⓣ ✕ ⓦ ⇆
→ ↻ ► ⅄ ⚒ ♪   ◑ ═ Ⓓ ▨ ▧ 🟡

WHIDDON DOWN   Map 03 SX69

► ► ► **Dartmoor View Holiday Park** (SX685928)
EX20 2QL ☎ 01647 231545
Dir: From M5 junct 31, take A30 towards Okehampton. Turn left at 1st rdbt towards Whiddon. Site is 1m on right
★ ⊞ £6.75-£9.50 ⊞ £6.75-£9.50 ▲ £6.75-£9.50
Open Mar-Oct Booking advisable Etr, Whitsun & Jul-Aug Last arrival 22.30hrs Last departure 10-12.00hrs

A pleasant, informal site with modern facilities on high ground within the National Park. A 5-acre site with 75 touring pitches and 40 statics.
Off licence, cycle/hire service, games room, putting.
Leisure: ₹ ♣ ⚲ ☐   Facilities: ⋔ ⊙ ⊕ ☀ ⓦ ☎ 🐕
Services: ☎ 🖫 ⓟ 🅑 🔓 ⚡ 🗒 ⓣ
→ ↻ ♪   ◑ ═ ▨ 🟡

WOODBURY SALTERTON   Map 03 SY08

► ► ► **Browns Farm Caravan Park** (SY016885)
Browns Farm EX5 1PS ☎ 01395 232895
Dir: From M5 junct 30 take A3052 for 3.7m. Right at White Horse Inn to Woodbury Salterton & site on right. Caravan must use this approach
★ ⊞ £4.50-£7 ⊞ £4.50-£7 ▲ £4.50-£7
Open all year Booking advisable All times
A small farm park adjoining a 14th-century thatched farmhouse, and located at the edge of a quiet village. Pitches all back onto hedgerows, and there are plenty of attractive trees. A pets' corner is popular with children. A 2.5-acre site with 20 touring pitches.
Caravan storage, hardstandings for winter period
Leisure: ♣   Facilities: ⋔ ⊙ ⊕ ☀ & ⓦ ☒   Services: ☎ 🗒
→ ↻ ► ♪ 🐕

WOOLACOMBE   Map 02 SS44

► ► ► **Golden Coast Holiday Village** (SS482436)
Station Rd EX34 7HW ☎ 01271 870343
Dir: Follow road to Woolacombe Bay from Mullacott & site is 1.5m on left
⊞ £11.50-£33 ⊞ £11.50-£33 ▲ £8-£22
Open Etr-Nov Booking advisable Whitsun & mid Jul-end Aug Last arrival 23.30hrs Last departure 10.00hrs ⌒
This holiday village includes villas and static caravans as well as the camping site. Woolacombe is surrounded by National Trust land. A 10-acre site with 53 touring pitches.   *contd.*

Facilities: 🛁 Bath   ⋔ Shower   ⊙ Electric Shaver   ⊕ Hairdryer   ☀ Ice Pack Facility   & Disabled Facilities   ☎ Public Telephone
🛒 Shop on Site or within 200yds   ◔ Mobile Shop (calls at least 5 days a week)   ▦ BBQ Area   ⚵ Picnic Area   🐕 Dog Exercise Area

Sauna, solarium, jacuzzi, tennis, entertainment.
Leisure: ⌇ ⌇ ⌇ ⌇ ⌇ 🏊 **Facilities:** ⌇ ⌇ ⌇ ⌇ ⌇ ⌇ ⌇ ⌇
Services: ⌇ ⌇ ⌇ ⌇ ⌇ ⌇ ⌇ ⌇ ⌇ ⌇
→ ∪ ⌇ ◎ △ ⌇ ⌇ ⌇ ⌇ ⌇ ⌇ ⌇ ⌇ ⌇

► ► ► Woolacombe Sands Holiday Park (SS471434)
Beach Rd EX34 7AF ☎ 01271 870569
Dir: From M5 junct 27 take A361 to Barnstaple. Follow signs to Ilfracombe, then onto Mullacot Cross. Turn left onto B3343 to Woolacombe. Site on left
★ 🚐 £5-£27.50 🚐 £5-£27.50 ▲ £5-£27.50
Open Apr-Oct Booking advisable 18 Jul-30 Aug & 23-30 May Last arrival 22.00hrs Last departure 10.00hrs
A terraced site with level pitches and good facilities. A 20-acre site with 200 touring pitches and 80 statics.
Leisure: ⌇ ⌇ 🏊 **Facilities:** ⌇ ⌇ ⌇ ⌇ ⌇ ⌇ ⌇
Services: ⌇ ⌇ ⌇ ⌇ ⌇ ⌇ ⌇
→ ∪ ⌇ ◎ ⌇ ⌇ ⌇ ⌇ ⌇ ⌇ ⌇

See advert on page 122

YELVERTON   Map 02 SX56
► ► ► Dartmoor Caravan Park (SX499676)
Abbey Ln, Crapstone PL20 7PG ☎ 01822 854509
Dir: Follow any sign to Buckland Abbey from A386 Plymouth to Tavistock. Site 300yds from village of Crapstone
🚐
Open all year Booking advisable

Superbly designed park in the attractive gardens of owner's home, with individual pitches divided by mature hedges. A 3-acre site with 20 touring pitches.
Facilities: ⌇ **Services:** ⌇ ⌇ ⌇
→ ⌇ ⌇ ⌇

DORSET

BERE REGIS   Map 03 SY89
► ► ► ► Rowlands Wait Touring Park (SY842933)
Rye Hill BH20 7LP ☎ 01929 472727
Dir: Approaching Bere Regis follow signs to Bovington Tank Museum. At top of Rye Hill, 0.75m from village turn right for 200yds to site
★ 🚐 £6.10-£9.10 🚐 £6.10-£9.10 ▲ £6.10-£9.10

Facilities: 🚿 Bath ⌇ Shower ⊙ Electric Shaver ⌇ Hairdryer ☀ Ice Pack Facility ⌇ Disabled Facilities ☎ Public Telephone ⌇ Shop on Site or within 200yds ⌇ Mobile Shop (calls at least 5 days a week) ⌇ BBQ Area ⌇ Picnic Area ⌇ Dog Exercise Area

Open Mar-Oct (winter by arrangement) Booking advisable bank hols & Jul-Aug Last arrival 21.30hrs Last departure noon
This park lies in a really attractive setting overlooking Bere and the Dorset countryside, set amongst undulating areas of trees and shrubs. Within a few miles of the Tank Musuem, and the mock tank battles are an attraction of the area. An 8-acre site with 71 touring pitches.

Leisure: ♦ ⚠ Facilities: ⌐ ⊙ ❄ ☆ ⌐ ☂ ⚷ 戸 ♈
Services: ⌐ ⊙ ┃ ∅ ⊞ ⊤
→ ∪ ⌐ ⊚ ✎ ▥ ▭ ▰ ▥ ⑤

BLANDFORD FORUM   Map 03 ST80

► ► ► ► **The Inside Park (ST869046)**
Down House Estate DT11 9AD ☎ 01258 453719
Dir: From town cross River Stour and follow signs for Winterbourne Stickland. Site in 1.5m
★ ⌐ £8-£13 ⌐ £8-£13 ▲ £8-£13
Open Etr-Oct Booking advisable bank hols & Jul-Aug Last arrival 22.00hrs Last departure noon
An attractive, well-sheltered and quiet site with some level pitches, one of the most beautiful parks in Dorset. A half-mile avenue off a country lane leads to a secluded dell with gentle slopes and a valley with three magnificent cedars. The choice of pitches ranges from wooded high points to the lush green slopes and valley floor of this spacious area. The whole park is surrounded by woodland, and the toilet facilities are very smart and well kept. A 12-acre site with 125 touring pitches.
Farm trips (main season). Kennels for hire.

Leisure: ♦ ⚠ Facilities: ⌐ ⊙ ❄ ☆ ⚷ ☂ ♈
Services: ⌐ ⊙ ┃ ∅ ⊞ ⊤ ➔
→ ∪ ⌐ ✎ ▥ ▭ ▰ ▥ ⑤

BRIDPORT   Map 03 SY49

PREMIER PARK

► ► ► ► ► **Highlands End Farm Holiday Park (SY454913)**
Eype DT6 6AR ☎ 01308 422139
Dir: 1m W of Bridport turn south for the village of Eype. Park signposted
⌐ £8-£12.50 ⌐ £8-£12.50 ▲ £8-£12.50
Open mid Mar-mid Nov Booking advisable public hols & Jul-Aug Last arrival 22.00hrs Last departure 11.00hrs
A well-screened site with magnificent clifftop views over Channel and Dorset coast, adjacent to National Trust land and overlooking Lyme Bay. Pitches are mostly sheltered by hedging and well spaced on hardstandings. There is a mixture of statics and tourers, but the tourers enjoy the best clifftop positions. A 9-acre site with 195 touring pitches and 160 statics.
Solarium, gym, steam room & sauna, pitch&putt
Leisure: ⏉ ⚷ ♦ ⚠ Facilities: ⌐ ⊙ ❄ ☆ ⚷ ☂ ♈
Services: ⌐ ⊙ ▣ ┃ ∅ ⊞ ⊤ ✕ ⚏ ➔
→ ∪ ⌐ ✕ ▥ ✎ ▭ ▰ ⑤

► ► ► ► **Binghams Farm Touring Caravan Park (SY478963)**
Melplash DT6 3TT ☎ 01308 488234
Dir: From Bridport take A3066 signposted Beaminster. After 0.5m turn left into private road to the farm
★ ⌐ £8-£12 ⌐ £8-£12 ▲ £8-£12
Open all year Booking advisable bank hols Last arrival 22.00hrs Last departure 11.00hrs
A very good adults-only site with quality buildings, fittings and services, in a lovely rural setting. The park is secluded down a steep drive, and offers great views over the hilly, unspoilt countryside. The terrain is slightly sloping, with shrub beds and ornamental trees, and pitches tastefully arranged around the park. Six super pitches are available, along with several hardstandings. The park is run by friendly owners. A 5-acre site with 60 touring pitches.
Leisure: ♦ Facilities: ⌐ ⊙ ❄ ⚷ ☂ 戸 ♈
Services: ⌐ ⊙ ▣ ┃ ∅
→ ∪ ⌐ ⊚ ⚏ ✕ ⚏ ✎ ☂

► ► ► ► **Freshwater Beach Holiday Park (SY493892)**
Burton Bradstock DT6 4PT ☎ 01308 897317
Dir: Take B3157 from Bridport towards Burton Bradstock. Located 1.5m on right from Crown rdbt
★ ⌐ £8.50-£19 ⌐ £8.50-£19 ▲ £8.50-£19
Open 15 Mar-10 Nov Booking advisable Jul-Aug Last arrival 23.30hrs Last departure 10.00hrs
A well-maintained family holiday park set behind the cliffs of the adjoining beach, and close to the

contd.

Services: ⊤ Toilet Fluid   ✕ Café/ Restaurant   ⚏ Fast Food/Takeaway   ➔ Baby Care   ⊙ Electric Hook Up
⊚ Launderette   ⚷ Licensed Bar   ┃ Calor Gaz   ∅ Camping Gaz   ⊞ Battery Charging

sea. To the north there are hills stretching east and west, and the park is located at one end of the Weymouth/Bridport coast with its spectacular views of Chesil Beach. There is a very good purpose-built toilet block. A 40-acre site with 400 touring pitches and 250 statics.

Leisure: ⚅ ⚓ ⚠ **Facilities:** ⚐ ⊙ ⚑ ✳ ⚒ ⚓ ⚌ ⚐
Services: ⚐ ⚑ ⚒ ⚓ ⚐ ⊞ ⚐ ✕ ⚐
→ ∪ ⚐ ◎ ⚐ ⚐ ⚐ ⚐ ⚐ ⚐ ⚐ ⚐

CERNE ABBAS   Map 03 ST60

▶ ▶ **Giant's Head Caravan & Camping Park** (ST675029)
Giants Head Farm, Old Sherborne Rd DT2 7TR
☎ 01300 341242
Dir: From Dorchester take Sherborne road to garage on right. Then left onto A352, after 1m fork right unclass rd to site 6m on right

★ ⚐ £6.50-£8 ⚐ £6.50-£8 ▲ £6.50-£8
Open Etr-Oct (rs Etr shop & bar closed) Booking advisable Aug Last arrival anytime Last departure 13.00hrs
A pleasant park set in Dorset downland near the famous Cerne Giant (a figure cut into the chalk) with stunning views. A good stopover site ideal for tenters and back-packers on the Ridgeway route. A 4-acre site with 50 touring pitches.
Two holiday chalets.
Leisure: ⚐ **Facilities:** ⚐ ⊙ ⚑ ✳ ⚌ ⚐ ⚐
Services: ⚐ ⚑ ⚒ ⚐ ⊞
→ ∪ ⚐ ◎ ⚐ ⚐

CHARMOUTH   Map 03 SY39

▶ ▶ ▶ ▶ **Monkton Wylde Farm Caravan Park** (SY336964)
DT6 6DB ☎ 01297 34525 & 631131 (May-Sep)
Dir: Leave A35 3m NW of Charmouth and take B3165 signed Marshwood. Site 0.25m on left
⚐ £6.50-£11.50 ⚐ £6.50-£11.50 ▲ £6.50-£11.50
Open Etr-Oct Booking advisable after Xmas Last arrival 22.00hrs Last departure 11.00hrs
A pleasant family park in a secluded location yet central for Charmouth, Lyme and the coast. Owned and run by working farmers, it has been tastefully designed with maturing landscaping. The slightly sloping pitches face south, and trees bordering the perimeter shield them from the lane. Opposite the entrance is the mainly sheep farm which children enjoy visiting. A 6-acre site with 60 touring pitches.

Facilities: ⛟ Bath ⚐ Shower ⊙ Electric Shaver ⚑ Hairdryer ✳ Ice Pack Facility ⚐ Disabled Facilities ⚐ Public Telephone
⚐ Shop on Site or within 200yds ⚐ Mobile Shop (calls at least 5 days a week) ⚐ BBQ Area ⚐ Picnic Area ⚐ Dog Exercise Area

Family shower room.
Leisure: ⚠ Facilities: ♄⊙🎱❋🐾♿🅿 Services: 🔌🖱🚻♨⊞
→∪🏴◎♨🔥🛁🧺♨

▶ ▶ ▶ ▶ **Wood Farm Caravan & Camping Park (SY356940)**
Axminster Rd DT6 6BT ☎ 01297 560697
Dir: From village centre travel W to A35 rdbt, and site entrance signed from here
★ 🚐 £7.50-£13.50 🚐 £7.50-£13.50 ▲ £7.50-£13.50
Open Etr-Oct Booking advisable school hols Last arrival 19.00hrs Last departure noon
A pleasant, well-established and mature park overlooking Charmouth, the sea and the Dorset hills and valleys. It stands on a high spot, and the four camping fields are terraced, each with its own toilet block. Convenient for Lyme Regis, Axminster, and this famous fossil coastline. A 13-acre site with 216 touring pitches and 83 statics.
Coarse fishing lake.
Leisure: 🎣 🎱 ⚠ Facilities: ♄⊙🎱❋♿🅿🐾
Services: 🔌🖱♨🚻⊞♨ → ∪🏴◎♨🔥🛁🧺♨ 💳 📠 🛒 🏧

▶ ▶ ▶ **Newlands Caravan & Camping Park (SY374935)**
DT6 6RB ☎ 01297 560259
Dir: 4m W of Bridport on A35
★ 🚐 £8-£17 🚐 £8-£17 ▲ £8-£17
Open all year (rs Nov-Mar Rest & shop closed)
Booking advisable school hols Last arrival 22.30hrs
Last departure 10.00hrs

Gently sloping, grass and gravel site in hilly country near the sea. A 23-acre site with 240 touring pitches and 86 statics.
Leisure: 🎣 🎱 ⚠ 🅿 Facilities: ♄⊙🎱❋♿🅿🐾 Services: 🔌🖱♨🚻⊞♨
→∪🏴🛁🧺♨ 💳 📠 🛒 🏧

CHIDEOCK — Map 03 SY49

▶ ▶ ▶ ▶ **Golden Cap Caravan Park (SY422919)**
Seatown DT6 6JX ☎ 01297 489341 & 01308 422139
Dir: On A35, in village of Chideock turn south for Seatown
🚐 £8-£12.50 🚐 £8-£12.50 ▲ £8-£12.50
Open mid Mar-early Nov Booking advisable public hols & Jul-Aug Last arrival 22.00hrs Last departure 11.00hrs
A grassy site, well-situated overlooking sea and beach and surrounded by National Trust parkland. This uniquely-placed park slopes down to the sea, although pitches are generally level. A slight dip hides the beach view from the back of the park, but this area benefits from having trees, scrub and meadows, unlike the more open areas closer to the sea. Ideal base for touring Dorset and Devon. An 11-acre site with 108 touring pitches.
Leisure: ⚠ Facilities: ♄⊙🎱❋♿🅿🐾 Services: 🔌🖱♨🚻⊞♨♨
→∪🏴🛁🧺♨ 💳 🛒 🏧

CHRISTCHURCH — Map 04 SZ19

PREMIER PARK

▶ ▶ ▶ ▶ ▶ **Hoburne Park (SZ194936)**
Hoburne Ln, Highcliffe-on-Sea BH23 4HU
☎ 01425 273379
Dir: Signed on A337 E of Christchurch
★ 🚐 £10.50-£27 🚐 £10.50-£27
Open Mar-Oct Booking advisable May BH & Jul-Aug 🐾
A large park with excellent facilities for family holidays, and over 20 super pitches. A 24-acre site with 229 touring pitches and 229 statics.
See advertisement under Preliminary Section
Leisure: 🎣 🎱 ⚠ Facilities: ♄🎱❋♿🅿 Services: 🖱♨♨🚻♨
→∪🏴♨🔥🛁🧺♨ 💳 📠 🛒 🏧

Services: ⊞ Toilet Fluid ✗ Café/ Restaurant ♨ Fast Food/Takeaway ♨ Baby Care 🔌 Electric Hook Up
🖱 Launderette ♨ Licensed Bar ♨ Calor Gaz ♨ Camping Gaz ⊞ Battery Charging

England

► ► ► **Grove Farm Meadow Holiday Caravan Park (SZ136946)**
Stour Way BH23 2PQ ☎ 01202 483597
Dir: Take Christchurch/Airport exit off A338, turn left for Christchurch and follow signs. W from Christchurch on A35, then right just before ford bridge.
★ ⌑ £6-£19 ⌑ £6-£19
Open Mar-Oct Booking advisable peak periods Last arrival 21.00hrs Last departure noon ⌀
A well-maintained site in rural surroundings on the banks of the River Stour, 1.5m from Christchurch and 3m from Bournemouth. A 2-acre site with 41 touring pitches and 180 statics.
Fishing on site, 21 Fully serviced pitches
Leisure: ◆ ⚠ **Facilities:** ➡ ℝ ⊙ ⛁ ᕈ ℄ ⚏ 🏢 ⊼
Services: ⬚ ⬚ ⬚ ⬚ ⊞ ⊤
→ ∪ ► ◎ △ ❄ ⚑ ⟟ ⬛ ⬛ ⬛ ⬛ ⬛

DORCHESTER
See **Cerne Abbas**

HOLTON HEATH   Map 03 SY99

► ► ► ► **Sandford Holiday Park (SY939916)**
BH16 6JZ ☎ 01202 631600 & 622513
Dir: From Wareham East on A351 turn left after 2m at traffic lights, and site on left
⌑ ⌑ ⅄
Open May-Oct (rs Nov-Apr) Booking advisable Jul-Aug & bank hols Last arrival 22.00hrs Last departure 11.00hrs ⌀

Good family site for those wanting entertainment, set in wooded meadowland with direct access to A351 Poole-Wareham road. A 60-acre site with 481 touring pitches and 268 statics.
Hairdressers, entertainment, dancing, crazy golf.
See advertisement under POOLE
Leisure: ⌇ ⚲ ◆ ⚠ ⬚ **Facilities:** ➡ ℝ ⊙ ᕈ ❄ ℄ ℄
⚏ 🏢 ⊼ ℩ **Services:** ⬚ ⬚ ⬚ ⬚ ⬚ ⊤ ✕ ⬚
→ ∪ ► ◎ ❄ ❄ ⚑ ⬛ ⬛ ⬛ ⬛ ⬛

HORTON   Map 04 SU00

► ► ► **Meadow View Touring Caravan Park (SU045070)**
Wigbeth BH21 7JH ☎ 01258 840536
Dir: Follow unclass road from Horton to site 0.5m from Druscilla pub
⌑ ⌑
Open all year Booking advisable Jul-Aug Last arrival 21.00hrs Last departure 11.00hrs
A small, comfortable site in a secluded rural setting, with level and gently sloping pitches. A 1.5-acre site with 15 touring pitches.
Coarse fishing, pitch & putt
Leisure: ⌇ ⚠ **Facilities:** ℝ ⊙ ᕈ ❄ 🏢 ⊼
Services: ⬚ ⬚ ⊞
→ ∪ ►

LYME REGIS
See **Hawkchurch (Devon)** & **Charmouth**

LYTCHETT MINSTER   Map 03 SY99

▶ ▶ ▶ **South Lytchett Manor Caravan Park**
(SY954926)
The Lodge, Dorchester Rd BH16 6JB
☎ 01202 622577
Dir: On B3067, off A35, 1m E of Lytchett Minster
🚐 £8.40-£10.50 🚐 £8.40-£10.50 ▲ £8.40-£10.50
Open Mar-Oct Booking advisable bank hols & mid
Jul-Aug Last arrival 22.00hrs Last departure 11.00hrs
A small, well-maintained site with mature trees set
in meadowland. An 11-acre site with 50 touring
pitches.
Pool table & table tennis
Leisure: ⚄ ▢ **Facilities:** ⎘ ⊙ ⌇ ✳ ⅋ ⌁ ⚏
Services: ⚙ ⓖ ⬥ ⊘ ⊞ Ⓣ ⬛

→ ∪ ▶ ☷ ♩ ⬤ ⚏ CONNECT ⬛ ⬛

MORETON   Map 03 SY88

▶ ▶ ▶ **Camping & Caravanning Club Site**
(SY782892)
Station Rd DT2 8BB ☎ 01305 853801
Dir: From Poole on A35, continue past Bere Regis, turn
left onto B3390 signposted Alfpuddle. After approx 2m
site on left before Moreton Station
★ 🚐 £11.80-£14.90 🚐 £11.80-£14.90 ▲ £11.80-£14.90
Open 20 Mar-29 Nov Booking advisable bank hols &
peak periods Last arrival 21.00hrs Last departure
noon
Modern purpose-built site on level ground with
good amenities. This tidy, well-maintained park
offers electric hook-ups to most pitches, and there
is a first class play area for children. Please see the
advertisement on page 14 for details of Club
Members' benefits. A 7-acre site with 130 touring
pitches.
Leisure: ⚄ **Facilities:** ⎘ ⊙ ⌇ ✳ ⅋ ⌁ ⚏ ⍭
Services: ⚙ ⓖ ⬥ ⊘ ⊞ Ⓣ

→ ∪ ▶ ⚠ ☷ ♩ ⬤ ⬛

ORGANFORD   Map 03 SY99

▶ ▶ ▶ ▶ **Pear Tree Touring Park (SY938915)**
Organford Rd, Holton Heath BH16 6LA
☎ 01202 622434
Dir: 6m W of Poole off A351 at Holton Heath
🚐 £7-£10 🚐 £7-£10 ▲ £7-£10
Open Etr & Apr-Oct Booking advisable Etr, Spring
bank hol & end Jul-Aug Last arrival 21.00hrs Last
departure 11.00hrs
An attractive park on fairly level grass. A 7.5-acre
site with 125 touring pitches.
Leisure: ⚄ **Facilities:** ⎘ ⊙ ⌇ ✳ ⅋ ⌁ ⚏ ⍰ ⍭
Services: ⚙ ⓖ ⬥ ⊘ ⊞ Ⓣ ⬥

→ ∪ ▶ ⚠ ✛ ☷ ♩ ⬤ ⬛ CONNECT ⬛ ⬛

▶ ▶ *Organford Manor (SY943926)*
BH16 6ES ☎ 01202 622202 & 623278
Dir: First on left off A35 after Lytchett rdbt at junct of
A35/A351. Site entrance on right
🚐 🚐 ▲
Open 15 Mar-Oct Booking advisable peak periods
Last arrival 22.00hrs Last departure noon

A quiet, secluded site in the grounds of the manor
house, with level grassy areas with trees and
shrubs. An 8-acre site with 75 touring pitches and
45 statics.
Leisure: ⚄ **Facilities:** ⎘ ⊙ ⌇ ✳ ⌁
Services: ⚙ ⓖ ⬥ ⊘ ⊞

→ ∪ ▶ ♩ ⬛

OWERMOIGNE   Map 03 SY78

▶ ▶ ▶ **Sandyholme Caravan Park (SY768863)**
Moreton Rd DT2 8HZ ☎ 01305 852677
Dir: 1m outside the village of Owermoigne
★ 🚐 £6.50-£12 🚐 £6.50-£12 ▲ £6.50-£12
Open Apr-Oct Booking advisable peak periods Last
arrival 21.30hrs Last departure noon

contd.

Pear Tree Caravan Park

England

Level, grass site with trees and bushes set in woodland near the coast at Lulworth Cove. A 5-acre site with 57 touring pitches and 48 statics. Restaurant/takeaway in peak season.

Leisure: ♦ ⋀ **Facilities:** ↿ ⊙ ¶ ✳ ⌞ ⅀ ㅈ
Services: ♥ 🖃 ♀ ⓘ ∅ 🔡 Ⓣ ✕ 👍
→ ⌡ 🚍 ⥂ 🚐 ◨

POOLE   Map 03 SZ09

► ► ► ► Beacon Hill Touring Park (SY977945)
Blandford Rd North BH16 6AB ☎ 01202 631631
Dir: On A350, 0.25m N of junct with A35, 4m N of Poole
★ ⊞ £9-£17 ⊞ £8.50-£17 ▲ £8.50-£17
Open Etr-Sep (rs low & mid season bar/take-away/coffee shop, swimming pool) Booking advisable Etr, Whit & Jul-Aug Last arrival 23.00hrs Last departure 11.00hrs
Set in attractive, wooded area with conservation very much in mind. Two large ponds are within the grounds and the terraced pitches offer some fine views. A 30-acre site with 170 touring pitches. Fishing & view point.

Leisure: ¬ ⚲ ♦ ⋀ ▢ **Facilities:** ↿ ⊙ ¶ ✳ ⅋ ⌞ ⅀ ⼗
Services: ♥ 🖃 ♀ ⓘ ∅ 🔡 Ⓣ ✕ 👍
→ ∪ ▸ ⌂ ✛ ⅏ ⌡

► ► ► Rockley Park (SY982909)
Hamworthy BH15 4LZ ☎ 01202 679393
Dir: Take A31 off M27 to Poole centre, then follow signs to park
★ ⊞ £13-£23 ⊞ £13-£23 ▲   *contd.*

Facilities: 🛁 Bath 🚿 Shower ⊙ Electric Shaver ¶ Hairdryer ✳ Ice Pack Facility ⅋ Disabled Facilities ⌞ Public Telephone ⅀ Shop on Site or within 200yds 🔡 Mobile Shop (calls at least 5 days a week) 🜨 BBQ Area ㅈ Picnic Area ⼗ Dog Exercise Area

Open Mar-Oct Booking advisable Jul-Aug & bank hols Last arrival 20.00hrs Last departure noon
A touring park within a static site, with all the advantages of a holiday centre. A 4.25-acre site with 98 touring pitches and 1077 statics.

Leisure: ⚓ ⚓ ⚓ ⚓ 🅰 **Facilities:** 🅿 ☺ ☜ ☀ ♿ ⚰ 🐕 📧
Services: 🚐 🚽 🛒 ✕ 🛁
→ 🏐 ◎ ♨ ⛏ ♨ ⚓ 💳 🚂 ⚡ 📶 🏴

ST LEONARDS   Map 04 SU10

▶ ▶ ▶ **Camping International Holiday Park (SU104024)**
Athol Lodge, 229 Ringwood Rd BH24 2SD
☎ 01202 872817 & 872742
Dir: On A31 between Ringwood and Wimborne, 3m W of Ringwood
★ 🚐 £8.30-£12.50 🚐 £8.30-£12.50 🛖 £8.30-£12.50

Open Mar-Oct (rs Mar-May & Sep-Oct (ex bank hols) restaurant/take-away available on demand) Booking advisable school & bank hols Last arrival 22.30hrs Last departure 10.30hrs
A well-equipped, level camping site surrounded by trees. Pitches are mainly on a lawned area with plenty of decorative trees and shrubs, and for children there is an adventure area and a paddling pool, as well as a swimming pool. An 8-acre site with 200 touring pitches.
Football, basketball park, Tots Play Area
Leisure: ⚓ ⚓ ⚓ 🅰 🎾 **Facilities:** 🅿 ☺ ☜ ☀ ⚰ 🛖 🐕 🏑
Services: 🚐 🚽 🛒 ⊘ 🛁 🅃 ✕ 🛁 ♨
→ ◎ 🏐 ♨ 💳 🚂 ⚡ 📶 🏴

▶ ▶ ▶ **Oakdene Forest Park (SZ095023)**
BH24 2RZ ☎ 01590 648331
Dir: 3m W of Ringwood off A31, turn left after foot bridge over A31
★ 🚐 £5.10-£23 🚐 £5.10-£23 🛖 £5.10-£23
Open Feb-5 Jan Booking advisable all times Last arrival 22.00hrs Last departure 10.00hrs
An open site surrounded by forest, with good on-site facilities. A 55-acre site with 150 touring pitches and 207 statics.
Woodland walks, mini bowling/crazy golf, bike hire
Leisure: ⚓ ⚓ ⚓ 🅰 **Facilities:** 🅿 ☺ ☀ ⚰ 🐕 🏑
Services: 🚐 🚽 🚽 🛒 ⊘ 🅃 ✕ 🛁
→ ◎ ♨ 💳 🚂 ⚡ 📶 🏴

See advert on page 143

▶ ▶ ▶ **Shamba Holiday Park (SU105029)**
230 Ringwood Rd BH24 2SB ☎ 01202 873302
Dir: 3m W of Ringwood off A31
★ 🚐 £8.50-£12.50 🚐 £6.50-£12.50 🛖 £6.50-£12.50
Open Mar-Oct Booking advisable bank hols & Jul-Aug Last arrival 23.30hrs Last departure 11.00hrs
Level grassy site in hilly wooded country. A 7-acre site with 150 touring pitches.
Leisure: ⚓ ⚓ 🅰 **Facilities:** 🅿 ☺ ☜ ☀ ⚰ 🛖
Services: 🚐 🚽 🚽 🛒 ⊘ ◎ 🅃 ✕ 🛁
→ ◎ 🏐 ♨ ♨ 💳 🚂 ⚡ 📶 🏴

SHAFTESBURY   Map 03 ST82

▶ ▶ ▶ *Blackmore Vale Caravan & Camping Park (ST835233)*
Sherborne Causeway SP7 9PX
☎ 01747 851523 & 852573
Dir: From Shaftesbury's Ivy Cross rdbt take A30 signed Sherborne. Site 2m on right
Open all year Booking advisable BHs
A good touring park with well-maintained facilities. A 3-acre site with 20 touring pitches and 12 statics.
Cycle hire
Facilities: 🅿 ☺ ☀ 🛖 ⚰ 📧 🏑 🐕 **Services:** 🚐 ⊘ 🅃 🅃
→ ◎ 🏐 ♨ 🛒 💳 🚂 ⚡ 📶 🏴

SIXPENNY HANDLEY   Map 03 ST91

▶ ▶ *Church Farm Caravan & Camping Park (ST994173)*
The Bungalow, Church Farm High St SP5 5ND
☎ 01725 552563
Dir: Between Salisbury and Blandford, turn off towards Sixpenny Handley, and site at top of village
🚐 🚐 🛖
Open all year
An open spacious site in rural area, with well-maintained facilities. A 5-acre site with 20 touring pitches and 1 static.
Facilities: 🅿 ♿ 🏑 **Services:** ◎ ⊘

SWANAGE   Map 03 SZ07

▶ ▶ ▶ **Ulwell Cottage Caravan Park (SZ019809)**
Ulwell Cottage, Ulwell BH19 3DG ☎ 01929 422823
Dir: From Swanage travel N for 3m on unclass road towards Studland
★ 🚐 £10-£21 🚐 £10-£21 🛖 £10-£21
Open Mar-7 Jan (rs Mar-spring bank hol & mid Sep-early Jan takeaway closed, shop open variable hours) Booking advisable bank hols & Jul-Aug Last arrival 23.00hrs Last departure 11.00hrs
Nestling under the Purbeck Hills surrounded by scenic walks and only 2m away from the beach. A 13-acre site with 77 touring pitches and 140 statics.
Leisure: ⚓ 🅰 **Facilities:** 🅿 ☺ ☀ ⚰ ♿ ⚰ 🛖 🏑
Services: 🚐 🚽 🚽 🛒 ⊘ 🅃 ✕ 🛁
→ ◎ 🏐 ◎ ♨ ⛏ ♨ 💳 🚂 🚂 📶 🏴

Facilities: 🛁 Bath 🅿 Shower ☺ Electric Shaver ☜ Hairdryer ☀ Ice Pack Facility ♿ Disabled Facilities ☎ Public Telephone
🛒 Shop on Site or within 200yds 📧 Mobile Shop (calls at least 5 days a week) 🛖 BBQ Area 🏕 Picnic Area 🐕 Dog Exercise Area

England

VERWOOD — Map 04 SU00

► ► ► **Camping & Caravanning Club Site (SU069098)**
Sutton Hill, Woodlands BH21 6LF ☎ 01202 822763
Dir: Turn left on A354 13m from Salisbury onto B3081, site is 1.5m W of Verwood
★ ⌷ £11.80-£14.90 ⌷ £11.80-£14.90 ▲ £11.80-£14.90
Open 20 Mar-1 Nov Booking advisable Jul-Aug & bank hols Last arrival 21.00hrs Last departure noon
A popular site with pleasant wardens and staff. Please see the advertisement on page 14 for details of Club Members' benefits. A 12.75-acre site with 150 touring pitches.
Recreation room, pool table, table tennis.
Leisure: ◣ ⚊ Facilities: ⌐ ⊙ ⌐ ✳ ⌂ ⌐ ⌐ Services:
⌂ ⊡ ⌂ ⌀ ↠
→ ∪ ▶ ⌂ ⌗ ⌐ ⌐ ⌐

WAREHAM — Map 03 SY98

► ► ► *Birchwood Tourist Park (SY917883)*
Bere Rd, North Trigon BH20 7PA ☎ 01929 554763
Dir: 3m N of Wareham on road linking A351 at Wareham and Bere Regis
⌐ ⌐ ▲
Open Mar-Oct Booking advisable bank hols & Jul-Aug Last arrival 22.00hrs Last departure noon
A well-maintained site which is maturing into a very attractive park. A 25-acre site with 175 touring pitches.
Riding stable, bike hire, pitch & putt, paddling pool

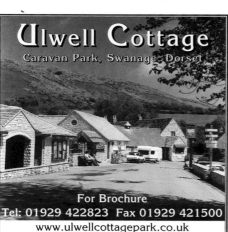

Leisure: ⚊ ◣ ⚊ Facilities: ⌐ ⊙ ⌐ ✳ ⌂ ⌐ ⌐ ⌐ ⌐
Services: ⌂ ⊡ ⌂ ⌀ ⊟ ⊤ ✕ ⌐
→ ∪ ▶ ⌐ ⌐ ⌐ ● ▬ ▬ ▬ ⌐

► ► ► **Lookout Holiday Park (SY927858)**
Stoborough BH20 5AZ ☎ 01929 552546
Dir: On B3075 1m S
★ ⌷ £9.50-£13 ⌷ £9.50-£13 ▲ £9.50-£13

Open Mar-Oct (rs Feb & Nov Static only) Booking advisable bank hols & Jul-Aug Last arrival 22.00hrs Last departure noon ⌀
Ideal family touring site on main road to Swanage. The touring pitches are set well back from the road. 150 touring pitches and 90 statics.
Leisure: ◣ ⚊ Facilities: ⌐ ⊙ ⌐ ✳ ⌂ ⌐
Services: ⌂ ⊡ ⌂ ⌀ ⊟ ⊤ ⌐
→ ∪ ▶ ⌐ ⌐ ⌐ ● ▬ ▬ ⌐

▶ ▶ ▶ *Manor Farm Caravan Park (SY872866)*
1 Manor Farm Cottage, East Stoke BH20 6AW
☎ 01929 462870
Dir: From Wareham follow A352 for 2m towards
Dorchester, then left onto B3070. At 1st X-roads turn
right, at next X-roads right and site on left
Open Etr-Sep Booking advisable school hols Last
arrival 22.00hrs Last departure 11.00hrs
*An attractive, mainly touring site in a quiet rural
setting. A 2.5-acre site with 50 touring pitches.*
Leisure: ⚲ **Facilities:** ℝ☉🔍✳✿⬤🏇🛖
Services: 🖳🔋🍴🚻

→ ⛽ ▶ 🍴 ♨ ⏀ 🔋🛒

▶ ▶ ▶ *Ridge Farm Camping & Caravan Park*
(SY936868)
Barnhill Rd, Ridge BH20 5BG
☎ 01929 556444
Dir: From Wareham take A351 towards Corfe Castle,
cross river to Stodborough, then left to Ridge and
follow site signs for 1.5m
🚐🚐🏕
Open Mar-Oct Booking advisable Jul/Aug Last
arrival 21.00hrs Last departure noon 🐕
*Quiet rural site with very pleasant owners.
A 3.5-acre site with 60 touring pitches.*
Facilities: ℝ☉🔍✳✿🛖 **Services:** 🖳🔋🍴🚻⏀

→ ⛽ ▶ 🔺♨ 🔋 ♨

WARMWELL	**Map 03 SY78**

▶ ▶ ▶ ▶ *Warmwell Country Touring Park*
(SY764878)
DT2 8JD ☎ 01305 852313
Dir: Take B3390 1m N of Warmwell
🚐🚐🏕
Open all year Booking advisable Etr-Sep & Xmas
Last arrival 22.00hrs Last departure 11.00hrs
*An attractive wooded park built in an old quarry, with
landscaped terraced pitches, 5m from the Lulworth
beaches. A 15-acre site with 190 touring pitches.*
Leisure: ⚲⚲ **Facilities:** ℝ☉🔍✳✿⬤🏇🛖
Services: 🖳🔋🍴🍴🚻⏀🛒

→ ⛽ ▶ ☺ 🔺♨ ♨ 💳 💳 📶 ♨

WEYMOUTH	**Map 03 SY67**

▶ ▶ ▶ *Bagwell Farm Touring Park (SY627816)*
Chickerell DT3 4EA ☎ 01305 782575
Dir: 4m W of Weymouth on B3157 (Abbotsbury-
Bridport), 500yds past Victoria Inn pub
🚐 £6.50-£11.50 🚐 £6.50-£11.50 🏕 £6-£10.50

Open all year Booking advisable Jul-Aug Last
arrival 21.30hrs Last departure 11.00hrs
*Attractive terraced site set in hillside and valley
leading to sea, with good views of Dorset
downland. A 14-acre site with 320 touring pitches.
Wet suit shower, campers shelter.*
Leisure: ⚲⚲ **Facilities:** ➡ℝ☉🔍✳✿⬤🏇🛖
Services: 🖳🔋🍴🍴🚻⏀✖🚿

→ ⛽ ▶ 🔺♨ ♨ ⬤ 💳 ♨

▶ ▶ ▶ *Pebble Bank Caravan Park (SY659775)*
Camp Rd, Wyke Regis DT4 9HF ☎ 01305 774844
Dir: From Weymouth take the Portland road. At the last
rdbt turn right, then 1st left to Army Tent Camp. Site
opposite
★ 🚐 £7.50-£14.50 🚐 £7-£14.50 🏕 £6-£11.50

Open Etr-mid Oct bar open high season & wknds
only Booking advisable peak times Last arrival
21.00hrs Last departure 11.00hrs
*A sloping, mainly static site overlooking Lyme Bay
and Chesil Beach. A 4-acre site with 40 touring
pitches and 80 statics.*
Leisure: ⚲ **Facilities:** ℝ☉🔍✳✿🛖
Services: 🖳🔋🍴🍴🚻⏀

→ ⛽ ▶ ☺ 🔺♨ ♨ ♨

▶ ▶ ▶ *Waterside Holiday Park (SY702822)*
Bowleaze Cove DT3 6PP ☎ 01305 833103
Dir: From Weymouth take A353 E for 2m, then right fork
to park in 0.5m
🚐🚐🏕
Open Mar-Oct Booking advisable Last departure
10.00hrs
*A well-established holiday park with good facilities
and plenty of on-site amenities. A 4-acre site with
120 touring pitches and 475 statics.*
Leisure: 🎣 🏊⚲⚲ **Facilities:** ℝ☉🔍✳✿⬤🏇🛖⏀🏇🛖
Services: 🖳🔋🍴🍴✖🚿

→ ⛽ ▶ ☺ 🔺♨ ♨ ⬤ 💳 📶 ♨

WIMBORNE MINSTER	**Map 03 SZ09**

PREMIER PARK

▶ ▶ ▶ ▶ ▶ *Merley Court Touring Park*
(SZ008984)
Merley BH21 3AA ☎ 01202 881488
Dir: From Wimborne take B3073 to rdbt, turn left to
next rdbt with A31, turn right & site is signed
★ 🚐 £7-£12 🚐 £7-£12 🏕 £7-£12

Facilities: ➡ Bath ℝ Shower ☉ Electric Shaver 🔍 Hairdryer ✳ Ice Pack Facility ⬤ Disabled Facilities ✿ Public Telephone
🛖 Shop on Site or within 200yds 🔲 Mobile Shop (calls at least 5 days a week) 🏇 BBQ Area 🟥 Picnic Area 🏇 Dog Exercise Area

Open Mar-7 Jan (rs low season pool closed & bar/shop open limited hrs) Booking advisable bank hols & Jun-Sep Last arrival 22.00hrs Last departure 11.00hrs
A superb site in a quiet, rural position on the edge of Wimborne, with woodland on two sides and good access roads. A 20-acre site with 160 touring pitches.
Badminton, mini football, table tennis, crazy golf.
Leisure: ⊰ ९ ✎ ⁄△ **Facilities:** ➡ 𝄐⊙᷆ 🍴 ⚖ 🛆 ℄
🐾 ⌂ 🛉 **Services:** 🖭 𝄐 🔋 ⍾ ⌀ 🆚 🕻 ✕ 🍴
→ ∪ 🏇 ⊚ ⌕ 🐶 ♨ ⌁ 🎦 🚏 🍴 ⊠ 🎇 ⍾

▶ ▶ ▶ ▶ ▶ **Wilksworth Farm Caravan Park (SU004018)**
Cranborne Rd BH21 4HW
☎ 01202 885467
Dir: 1m N of Wimborne on the B3078
★ 🚐 £6-£14 🚐 £6-£14 ⅄ £6-£14
Open Mar-30 Oct (rs Mar no shop/coffee shop) Booking advisable Spring bank hol & Jul-Aug Last arrival 21.00hrs Last departure 11.00hrs
This popular and attractive site lies in the heart of Dorset. It is well-maintained with good facilities. An 11-acre site with 85 touring pitches and 77 statics.
Paddling pool, volley ball, mini football pitch.
Leisure: ⊰ ९ ✎ ⁄△ **Facilities:** 𝄐⊙᷆ 🍴 ⚖ 🛆 ℄ 🐾 ⎕ 🛉
Services: 🖭 𝄐 🔋 ⍾ ⌀ 🆚 🕻 ✕ 🍴
→ ∪ 🏇 ⊚ ♨ ⌁

WILKSWORTH FARM CARAVAN PARK

Cranborne Road, ▶▶▶▶▶
Wimborne BH21 4HW
Telephone: (01202) 885467

AA Best Campsite for South of England 1994

A family run park for families. A high standard awaits you at our peaceful secluded park, close to Kingston Lacy, Poole and Bournemouth. An attractively laid out touring and camping park, with heated outdoor swimming pool and tennis court. No statics to hire.
Completely re-furbished toilet block with family bathroom and disabled shower room.
New coffee shop and takeaway.

▶ ▶ ▶ **Springfield Touring Park (SY987989)**
Candys Ln, Corfe Mullen BH21 3EF ☎ 01202 881719
Dir: Turn left off A31 at rdbt at W end of Wimborne bypass signed Corfe Mullen. Within 0.25m turn right into Candys Lane & entrance 300yds past farm
🚐 £7.50-£8.50 🚐 £7.50-£8.50 ⅄ £6-£8.50
Open mid Mar-Oct Booking advisable bank hols & Jul-Aug Last arrival 22.00hrs Last departure 11.00hrs
A small touring site with good facilities and hardworking owners in a quiet position overlooking the Stour Valley. A 3.5-acre site with 45 touring pitches.
Leisure: ⁄△ **Facilities:** 𝄐⊙᷆ 🍴 ⚖ 🛆 ℄ 🐾
Services: 🖭 𝄐 ⍾ ⌀ 🆚 ➡
→ ∪ 🏇 ♨

WOOL   Map 03 SY88

▶ ▶ ▶ **Whitemead Caravan Park (SY841869)**
East Burton Rd BH20 6HG ☎ 01929 462241
Dir: 300yds W of the A352
★ 🚐 £6.25-£10.25 🚐 £6.25-£10.25 ⅄ £6.25-£10.25

Open mid Mar-Oct Booking advisable public hols & mid Jul-Aug Last arrival 22.00hrs Last departure noon
Well laid-out level site in valley of River Frome. A 5-acre site with 95 touring pitches.
Leisure: ⁄△ **Facilities:** 𝄐⊙᷆ 🍴 ⚖ 🕻 🐾 🛉
Services: 🖭 𝄐 🔋 ⍾ ⌀ 🆚 🍴
→ ∪ 🏇

CO DURHAM

BARNARD CASTLE   Map 12 NZ01

▶ ▶ ▶ ▶ **Camping & Caravanning Club Site (NZ025168)**
Dockenflatts Ln, Lartington DL12 9DG
☎ 01833 630228
Dir: Take B6277 to Middleton in Teesdale. After 1m take left turn signed Raygill Riding Stables. Site 500mtrs on left
★ 🚐 £11.80-£14.90 🚐 £11.80-£14.90 ⅄ £11.80-£14.90
Open 20 Mar-1 Nov Booking advisable Jan-Mar Last arrival 21.00hrs Last departure noon
A peaceful site surrounded by mature woodland and meadowland, with first class facilities. This immaculately-maintained park is set in the heart of the countryside, with an open aspect over farmland. Pitches are well laid out and generous, on mainly

contd.

England

England

level grass with some hardstandings. Close to the historic market town of Barnard Castle. Please see the advertisment on page 14 for details of Club Members' benefits. A 10-acre site with 92 touring pitches.

Leisure: ⚐ Facilities: ⬆☉☽✳&⛊☛
Services: ⊠🅐
→∪▶△🐌 🐽 🏧

▶ ▶ Pecknell Farm Caravan Park (NZ028178)
Lartington DL12 9DF ☎ 01833 638357
Dir: 1.5m from Barnard Castle. From A66 take B6277. Site on right 1.5m from junct with A67
★ ⚐ £5-£6.50 ⚐ £5-£6.50 Å £5-£6.50
Open Mar-Oct Booking advisable Jul, Aug & Bank hols
A small well laid out site on a working farm in beautiful rural meadowland, with spacious marked pitches on level ground. A 1.5-acre site with 10 touring pitches.

Facilities: ⬆☉☽✳&⛊ Services: ⊠🔋
→∪▶☉🔧🐌

| **BEAMISH** | **Map 12 NZ25** |

▶ ▶ ▶ Bobby Shafto Caravan Park (NZ232545)
Cranberry Plantation DH9 0RY ☎ 0191 370 1776
Dir: From A1693 signed Beamish to sign for Beamish Museum. Take approach road and turn right immediately before museum, left at pub to site 1m on right
⚐⚐Å
Open Mar-Oct Booking advisable school hols Last arrival 23.00hrs Last departure 11.00hrs
A tranquil rural site surrounded by mature trees, with well-organised facilities. A 9-acre site with 20 touring pitches and 35 statics.

Leisure: ♣⚐⬜ Facilities: ⬆☉☽✳⛊🐌
Services: ⊠🔋🔋🅐🅔🅣
→∪▶🔧💺🔧🅐 🐽 🏧

| **CASTLESIDE** | **Map 12 NZ04** |

▶ ▶ ▶ Allensford Caravan & Camping Park (NZ083505)
DH8 9BA ☎ 01207 505572
Dir: 2m SW of Consett, N on A68 for 1m, then right at Allensford Bridge
★ ⚐ £7.50-£10.50 ⚐ £7.50-£10.50 Å fr £5
Open Mar-Oct Booking advisable Whit wknd, Etr, Aug bank hol Last arrival 22.00hrs Last departure noon
Level parkland with mature trees, in hilly moor and woodland country near the urban area adjacent to River Derwent and A68. A 2-acre site with 40 touring pitches and 50 statics.
Tourist information centre.

Leisure: ⚐ Facilities: ⬆☉☽✳&⛊🐌🅐
Services: ⊠🅐🔋🅐
→▶💺🔧 🐽 ▇ 🏧 ▨ ▨ 🅓

| **WINSTON** | **Map 12 NZ11** |

▶ ▶ ▶ Winston Caravan Park (NZ139168)
The Old Forge DL2 3RH ☎ 01325 730228
Dir: Leave A67 Darlington/Barnard Castle into village centre and follow signposts
⚐⚐Å
Open Mar-Oct Booking advisable bank hols
Attractive tree-lined park with level sheltered pitches, ideally located for exploring surrounding countryside. A 2.5-acre site with 20 touring pitches and 11 statics.

Facilities: ⬆☽✳&🐌🅐 Services: ⊠🅐🔋🅔
→∪🔧

| **WYCLIFFE (Near Barnard Castle)** | **Map 12 NZ11** |

▶ ▶ ▶ Thorpe Hall (NZ105141)
DL12 9TW ☎ 01833 627230
Dir: From A66 1m SE of Greta Bridge take unclass road signed Wycliffe
⚐⚐
Open Mar-Oct Booking advisable bank hols & Jul-Aug Last arrival 22.30hrs Last departure 13.00hrs
A very pleasant site with good facilities in the grounds of a large country house. Lies South of the River Tees and 5m from Barnard Castle. A 2-acre site with 12 touring pitches and 16 statics.

Leisure: ⚐ Facilities: ⬆☉✳⛊☛ Services: ⊠🅐🔋🅔
→🔧🔋

ESSEX

| **BRENTWOOD** | **Map 05 TQ59** |

▶ ▶ ▶ Camping & Caravanning Club Site (TQ577976)
Warren Ln, Frog St, Kelvedon Hatch CM15 0JG
☎ 01277 372773
Dir: M25 junct 28. Brentwood 2m left on A128 signposted Ongar. After 3m turn right
★ ⚐ £10.60-£13.90 ⚐ £10.60-£13.90 Å £10.60-£13.90
Open 22 Mar-1 Nov Booking advisable bank hols & Jul-Aug Last arrival 21.00hrs Last departure noon
A very pretty rural site with many separate areas amongst the trees, and a secluded field for campers. Please see the advertisement on page 14 for details of Club Members' benefits A 12-acre site with 90 touring pitches.

Leisure: ⚐ Facilities: ⬆☉☽✳&⛊☛
Services: ⊠🅐🔋🅐🅔
→▶🔧🔋 🐽 🏧

| **CANEWDON** | **Map 05 TQ99** |

▶ ▶ ▶ Riverside Village Holiday Park (TQ929951)
Creeksea Ferry Rd, Wallasea Island SS4 2EY
☎ 01702 258297
Dir: Signed from A127 near Southend. Approach from Rochford, not Canewden village
★ ⚐ £9-£11 ⚐ £9-£11 Å £4-£6
Open Mar-Oct Booking advisable public hols Last arrival 22.00hrs Last departure 17.00hrs
A pleasant and popular riverside site, well laid out

and very neat. A 24-acre site with 60 touring pitches
and 180 statics.
Boule pitch.

Leisure: 🛝 Facilities: ⬛☉🐾❄✦✦🛒🎣🐎
Services: ⊕🗑🛢☒✗
→∪▶⚠♨

COLCHESTER   Map 05 TL92

► ► ► ► **Colchester Camping Caravan Park**
(TL971252)
Cymbeline Way, Lexden CO3 4AG ☎ 01206 545551
*Dir: Follow tourist signs from A12, then A133 Colchester
Central slip road*
🚐 £11-£15.25 🚍 £11-£15.25 ⚑ £9.25-£12.75
Open all year Booking advisable public hols Last
arrival 20.00hrs Last departure noon
*A well-designed campsite on level grassland, on the
west side of Colchester near the town centre. Close
to main routes to London (A12) and east coast.
There is good provision for hardstandings, and the
owner's attention to detail is reflected in the neatly
trimmed grass and well-cut hedges. Toilet facilities
are housed in a smart main block and in two older
buildings which are also well equipped. A 12-acre
site with 168 touring pitches.*
Badminton court & putting green on site.

Leisure: 🛝 Facilities: ⬛☉🐾❄✦✦🛒🎣🐎
Services: ⊕🗑🛢⊘☒🇹
→∪▶⚠♨☒ 🚐 ▤ 🏧 ❾

MERSEA ISLAND   Map 05 TM01

 Waldegraves Holiday Park
(TM033133)
West Mersea, Mersea Island CO5 8SE
☎ 01206 382898
*Dir: B1025 to Mersea Island across the Strood. Left
to East Mersea, 2nd turn on right, follow tourist
signs to park*
🚐 £9-£14 🚍 £9-£14 ⚑ £9-£14
Open Mar-Nov Booking advisable bank hols Last
arrival 22.00hrs Last departure noon
*A spacious and pleasant site, located between
farmland and its own private beach on the
Blackwater Estuary. Facilities include two
freshwater fishing lakes, heated swimming pool,
club, amusements, café and golf, and there is
generally good provision for families. A 25-acre
site with 60 touring pitches and 205 statics.*
Boating and fishing on site.

Leisure: ≋ ♦ 🛝 ▭ Facilities: ⬛☉🐾❄✦✦🛒🎣
🛒🎣🐎 **Services:** ⊕🗑🛢⊘☒🇹✗🏧
→∪◎⚠♨☒🐾🇹 🚐 ▤ 🏧 ❾

ROYDON   Map 05 TL41

► ► ► **Roydon Mill Leisure Park (TL403104)**
CM19 5EJ ☎ 01279 792777
*Dir: From A414 between Harlow & A10, follow tourist
signs to park. Situated at the N end of the High Street
adjacent to Railway station*
🚐 £9.50-£11 🚍 £9.50-£11 ⚑ £9.50-£11
Open all year Booking advisable bank hols Last
arrival 22.00hrs Last departure 22.00hrs ♽
*A busy complex with caravan sales and water
sports. The attractive camping field is behind an old
mill in a hedged meadow, and the caravan pitches
have hardstandings. An 11-acre site with 120
touring pitches and 149 statics.*
Large lake, clay pigeon shooting, water-ski school.

Leisure: ♦ 🛝 **Facilities:** ⬛☉❄✦✦🛒🎣🐎
Services: ⊕🗑🛢⊘☒🇹✗🏧
→∪▶⚠✦♨☒ 🚐 ▤ 🏧 ❾

SOUTHMINSTER   Map 05 TQ99

► ► ► *Beacon Hill Leisure Park (TL959055)*
St Lawrence Bay CM0 7LP ☎ 01621 779248
*Dir: Signed off B1010 at Letchingdon, between Maldon
and Bradwell-on-Sea*
🚐 🚍 ⚑
Open mid Mar-Oct Booking advisable Bank &
School Holidays Last arrival 22.00hrs Last departure
17.00hrs
*Small well-kept touring section of a large leisure
park, on the banks of the River Blackwater, and
offering swimming pool and clubhouse facilities. A
45-acre site with 130 touring pitches and 330 statics.*
Boating lake, jacuzzi, children's pool, sports field.

Leisure: ≋ ♦ 🛝 Facilities: ⬛☉🐾❄✦🛒🎣🐎
Services: ⊕🗑🛢⊘☒🇹✗🏧
→⚠✦♨☒ 🚐 ▤ ❾

GLOUCESTERSHIRE

CHELTENHAM   Map 03 SO92

▶ ▶ ▶ ▶ *Briarfields (SO899215)*
Gloucester Rd GL51 0SX ☎ 01242 235324 & 274440
*Dir: From Cheltenham take A40 to Golden Valley rdbt,
then 3rd turning left and follow signs*

🚐 🚐 🛆

Open all year Booking advisable Last arrival mdnt
Last departure 14.00hrs
*A well-designed, comfortable park, with a
hotel/restaurant on site. There is some spectacular
country around the area, and the park is well-
positioned between Cheltenham and Gloucester. A
6-acre site with 87 touring pitches.*

Facilities: ♠ ⊙ ◖ ※ ୧ 🚿 🎢 ⅋   **Services:** 🚱 ⧉ ⓘ ⌀ ⊞
→ ∪ ▶ ♧ ♃ ♨ ♪ ♣   ⬤ ▤ ▦ ⚡ 🔯

▶ ▶ ▶ *Freedom Camping & RV Park (SO901217)*
Bamfurlong Ln GL51 6SL
☎ 01452 712705 & 855511
*Dir: M5 junct 11, A40 towards Cheltenham for 1m. Turn
left at rdbt (B4063), after 50yds turn left, right at sharp
bend, 100yds on left*

🚐

Open all year Booking advisable bank hols

*Ideal site for motorhomes, particularly large
American vehicles. Good access from M5 junct 11.
A 2-acre site with 40 touring pitches.*
Liquid Propane Gas available

Facilities: ♠ ⊙ ◖ ⅋   **Services:** 🚱 ⧉ ⓘ ⌀ ⊞ ⊤
→ ∪ ▶ ⊚ ♨ ♪ ♣   ⬤ ▪ ▦ ⓞ 🔯 🔯

CHRISTCHURCH   Map 03 SO51

▶ ▶ *Bracelands Caravan & Camping Site
(SO575129)*
Bracelands GL16 7NN ☎ 01594 833376
*Dir: Approach from A4136 junct with unclass road at the
Pike House Inn, Berry Hill, 1m N of Coleford. Take Grove
Road for 0.5m, then left Bracelands Drive*

🚐 🚐 🛆

Open Mar-Oct Booking advisable bank hols & peak
season Last arrival 22.00hrs Last departure noon
*A peaceful Forestry Commission park in lovely
wooded surroundings, on the edge of the Forest of
Dean. A 30-acre site with 520 touring pitches.*

Leisure: ⚠   **Facilities:** ♠ ⏚ ◖ 🚿 🎢
Services: 🚱 ⧉ ⓘ ⊞ ⊤
→ ∪ ♨   ⬤ ▤ ▦ 🔯 🔯

CIRENCESTER   Map 04 SP00

▶ ▶ ▶ *Mayfield Touring Park (SP020055)*
Cheltenham Rd, Perrott's Brook GL7 7BH
☎ 01285 831301
Dir: Off A35, 2m from Cirencester
🚐 £7.50-£10 🚐 £6.70-£10 🛆 £6.20-£10
Open all year Booking advisable public hols & Jun-
Aug Last arrival 22.30hrs Last departure noon ⌖
*Part-level, part-sloping grass site, in hilly
meadowland in the Cotswolds, an Area of
Outstanding Natural Beauty. A 4-acre site with 72
touring pitches.*

Facilities: ♠ ⊙ ◖ ※ ◖ ୧ 🚿 🎢   **Services:** 🚱 ⧉ ⓘ ⌀ ⊞ ⊤
→ ▶ ♨   ⬤ ▤ ▦ 🔯 🔯

COLEFORD   Map 03 SO51

▶ ▶ ▶ *Christchurch Caravan & Camping Site
(SO575129)*
Bracelands Dr GL16 7NN
☎ 01594 833376 (in season) & 0131 314 6505
Dir: 2m N of Coleford, off A1436
★ 🚐 £5.60-£10.80 🚐 £5.60-£10.80 🛆 £5.60-£10.80
Open Apr-Dec Booking advisable all times Last
arrival 22.00hrs Last departure noon ⌖
*A well-appointed site in open forest with good
amenities. A good base for walking. A 20-acre site
with 280 touring pitches.*

Leisure: ◣ ⚠   **Facilities:** ♠ ⊙ ※ ⏚ ◖ ୧ 🚿 🎢
Services: 🚱 ⧉ ⓘ ⌀ ⊤
→ ∪ ▶ ♨ ♪   ⬤ ▤ ▦ 🔯 🔯

Facilities: ➡ Bath   ♠ Shower   ⊙ Electric Shaver   ◖ Hairdryer   ※ Ice Pack Facility   ⏚ Disabled Facilities   ◖ Public Telephone
୧ Shop on Site or within 200yds   ▦ Mobile Shop (calls at least 5 days a week)   🚿 BBQ Area   🎢 Picnic Area   ⅋ Dog Exercise Area

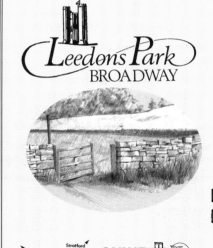

GLOUCESTER — Map 03 SO81

► ► ► **Red Lion Camping & Caravan Park** (SO849258)
Wainlode Hill, Norton GL2 9LW ☎ 01452 730251
Dir: Turn off A38 at Norton and follow road to river
🚐 £8 🚐 £8 ▲ £8
Open all year Booking advisable spring bank hol
Last arrival 22.00hrs Last departure 11.00hrs
An attractive meadowland site opposite River Severn. Ideal fishing centre and touring base. A 13-acre site with 60 touring pitches and 20 statics. Bar snacks, hot & cold food.
Facilities: 🏪 ⊙ ↖ ☀ 🔌 🐾 Å ★ **Services:** 🚱 🍴 🛢 ⊘ ✗
→ ∪ ► 🔧

SLIMBRIDGE — Map 03 SO70

► ► ► ► **Tudor Caravan & Camping** (SO728040)
Shepherds Patch GL2 7BP
☎ 01453 890483 & 0402 989940

Dir: From M5 junct 13 follow signs for Wildfowl Trust. Site at rear of Tudor Arms pub
★ 🚐 £7.50-£7.75 🚐 £7.50-£7.75 ▲ £5-£7.75
Open all year Booking advisable bank & school hols
Last arrival 21.00hrs Last departure 18.00hrs
An orchard-style park, with level grass and gravel pitches, and mature trees and bushes, set in meadow by canal. Nearby is the Slimbridge Wildlife Trust, and there is much scope locally for birdwatching. An 8-acre site with 75 touring pitches.
Facilities: 🏪 ⊙ ↖ ☀ 🔌 🐾 Å ★
Services: 🚱 🍴 🛢 ⊘ ⊕ T ✗
→ ∪ 🔧 🔋

SOUTH CERNEY — Map 04 SU09

 Cotswold Hoburne (SU055958)
Broadway Ln GL7 5UQ
☎ 01285 860216
Dir: From Cirencester take A419 for 3m. Turn right at sign and right again in 1m. Site on left
★ 🚐 £10.50-£23 🚐 £10.50-£23 ▲ £10.50-£23
Open Good Fri-Oct Booking advisable public hols & high season Last arrival 21.00hrs Last departure 10.00hrs 🐾
A large holiday centre on flat grassy ground and adjoining the Cotswold Water Park. This well-equipped park is sited close to several lakes, each one adapted for either sailing, water-skiing, fishing or nature reserve. There is also a lake on site with a good stock of tench for anglers to enjoy. A 70-acre site with 302 touring pitches and 211 statics. *contd.*

Services: T Toilet Fluid ✗ Café/ Restaurant 🍴 Fast Food/Takeaway 🍼 Baby Care 🔌 Electric Hook Up 🔋 Launderette 🍷 Licensed Bar 🛢 Calor Gaz ⊘ Camping Gaz 🔋 Battery Charging

Crazy golf, fishing & pedal-boat hire.
See advertisement under Preliminary Section
Leisure: ↘ ↘ ♦ ♦ /⚠ ☐ **Facilities:** ♪ ☉ ✳ ⚹ ℃ ℠
Services: ▣ ⬚ ♀ ⬚ ⌀ ✕ ⏚
→ ∪ ▶ ▲ ⚓ ♨ ✎ ● ▤ ▨ ⬚

WINCHCOMBE   Map 04 SP02

▶ ▶ ▶ **Camping & Caravanning Club Site**
(SP007324)
Brooklands Farm, Alderton GL20 8NX
☎ 01242 620259
*Dir: On A46 from Tewkesbury keep straight on at rdbt &
take B4077 to Stow-on-the-Wold. Site 3m on right*
★ ⚘ £11.80-£14.90 ⚘ £11.80-£14.90 ▲ £11.80-£14.90
Open 16 Mar-16 Jan Booking advisable
*A pleasant site on B4077, with immaculate facilities
and pitches spaced around an attractive lake. Ideal
for touring this historic area between Cheltenham
and Tewkesbury. Please see the advertisement on
page 14 for details of Club Members' benefits.
A 20-acre site with 80 touring pitches.*
Fishing, pool table, table tennis
Leisure: ♦ /⚠ **Facilities:** ♪ ☉ ℘ ✳ ℩
Services: ▣ ⬚ ♀ ⌀ ⏚
→ ▶ ✎ ℠ ● ▤

GREATER MANCHESTER

LITTLEBOROUGH   Map 07 SD91

▶ ▶ ▶ *Hollingworth Lake Caravan Park*
(SD943146)
Round House Farm, Rakewood Rd, Rakewood
OL15 0AT ☎ 01706 378661 & 373919
*Dir: From Littleborough or Milnrow (M62 junct 21),
follow 'Hollingworth Lake Country Park' signs to
Fishermans Inn. Take 'No Through Road' to Rakewood*
⚘ ⚘ ▲
Open all year Booking advisable bank hols Last
arrival 20.00hrs Last departure 14.00hrs
*A popular park adjacent to Hollingworth Lake, at the
foot of the Pennines, within easy reach of many
local attractions. Backpackers walking the Pennine
Way are welcome at this family-run park, and there
are also large rally fields. A 5-acre site with 50
touring pitches and 53 statics.*
Pony Trekking.
Facilities: ♪ ☉ ✳ ⚹ ℃ ℠ ⚏ **Services:** ▣ ⬚ ♀ ⌀
→ ▶ ♨ ✎

ROCHDALE   Map 07 SD81

▶ ▶ ▶ **Gelder Wood Country Park (SD852127)**
Ashworth Rd, Heywood OL11 5UP
☎ 01706 364858 & 620300
*Dir: Signed off B6222 midway between Bury &
Rochdale. Approached into Ashworth Rd at Hooley
Bridge.*
★ ⚘ £8-£9 ⚘ £8-£9 ▲ £8-£9
Open Mar-Oct Booking advisable Etr Last departure
22.00hrs

*A very rural site in a peaceful private country park
with excellent facilities. All pitches have extensive
views of the moor. This park is now adults only, and
children are not permitted to visit. A 10-acre site
with 34 touring pitches.*
Facilities: ♪ ☉ ⚹ ℩ **Services:** ▣ ♀ ⌀ ⬚
→ ∪ ✎ ⬚ ℠

HAMPSHIRE

NEW FOREST The New Forest covers 144 square
miles and is composed of broadleaf and coniferous
woodland, open commonland and heath. This
unique area was originally a royal hunting forest
and there are long established rights of access.
Facilities for visitors are maintained by the Forestry
Commission; these include caravan and camp sites,
picnic sites, car parks, way-marked walks and an
ornamental drive. The camp sites are open from the
Friday before Easter until the end of September
(two sites remain open in October). Information and
camping leaflet available from the Forestry
Commission, 231 Corstorphine Road, Edinburgh
EH12 7AT. Telephone 0131 334 0066. Information
also available from the Tourist Information Centre
at Lyndhurst Car Park. Telephone Lyndhurst 023
80282269. See Ashurst, Bransgore, Brokenhurst,
Fritham, and Lyndhurst for AA pennant classified
sites.

ASHURST   Map 04 SU31

▶ ▶ ▶ **Ashurst Caravan & Camping Site**
(SU332099)
Lyndhurst Rd SO4 2AA ☎ 0131 314 6505
Dir: 5m SW of Southampton on A35
★ ⚘ £6.20-£12 ⚘ £6.20-£12 ▲ £6.20-£12
Open Etr-Sep Booking advisable all times Last
arrival 23.30hrs Last departure noon ⚹
*This quiet, secluded Forestry Commission site is set
amongst woodlands and heathland on the fringe of
the New Forest. See under 'Forestry Commission'
for further information. A 23-acre site with 280
touring pitches.*
Facilities: ♪ ☉ ℘ ✳ ⚹ ℃ ☴
→ ∪ ▶ ● ▤ ▨ ▦ ⬚

BRANSGORE   Map 04 SZ19

▶ ▶ ▶ ▶ **Harrow Wood Farm Caravan Park**
(SZ194978)
Harrow Wood Farm, Poplar Ln BH23 8JE
☎ 01425 672487
*Dir: Leave village from S and take last turning on left
past shops. Site at top of lane*
⚘ £9.50-£13.25 ⚘ £9.50-£13.25
Open Mar-6 Jan Booking advisable bank & school
hols Last arrival 22.00hrs Last departure noon ⚹
*A very well laid out site in a pleasant rural position
with adjoining woodland and fields. A 6-acre site
with 60 touring pitches.*
See advertisement under CHRISTCHURCH
Facilities: ♪ ☉ ℘ ✳ ℃ **Services:** ▣ ⬚ ♀ ⌀ ⬚
→ ✎ ℠ ● ▤ ▨ ⬚

Facilities: ⏚ Bath ♪ Shower ☉ Electric Shaver ℘ Hairdryer ✳ Ice Pack Facility ⚹ Disabled Facilities ℃ Public Telephone
℠ Shop on Site or within 200yds ⬚ Mobile Shop (calls at least 5 days a week) ⚏ BBQ Area ☴ Picnic Area ℩ Dog Exercise Area

England

▶ ▶ ▶ **Holmsley Caravan & Camping Site**
(SZ215991)
Forest Rd, Holmsley BH23 7EQ ☎ 0131 314 6505
Dir: Located off A35 Lyndhurst-Christchurch road, 8m SW of Lyndhurst
★ 🚐 £6.20-£11.30 🚐 £6.20-£11.30 ▲ £6.20-£11.30
Open Etr-Nov Booking advisable all times Last arrival 23.30hrs Last departure noon
A large site in rural surroundings on the fringe of the New Forest. See under Forestry Commission for further information. An 89-acre site with 700 touring pitches.
Leisure: 🛝 **Facilities:** ⬛⊙🍴✳⬛💧⬛🎋
Services: 🔌🔧🛢Ⓣ⛟
➔ ∪ ▶ 💳 ▧ ▧ ▧ 🎵

BROCKENHURST   Map 04 SU30

▶ ▶ ▶ **Hollands Wood Caravan & Camping Site**
(SU303034)
Lyndhurst Rd SO42 7QH ☎ 0131 314 6505
Dir: Located just off A337 Lyndhurst-Brockenhurst road, 3m S of Lyndhurst
★ 🚐 £7-£12.70 🚐 £7-£12.70 ▲ £7-£12.70
Open Etr-Sep Booking advisable all times Last arrival 23.30hrs Last departure noon
Large and very popular secluded site, set amongst oak and woodland, within the New Forest adjoining Balmer Lawn. See under 'Forestry Commission' for further information. A 168-acre site with 600 touring pitches.
Facilities: ⬛⊙🍴✳⬛💧🎋
➔ ∪ ▶ 💳 ▧ ▧ ▧ 🎵

▶ ▶ **Roundhill Caravan & Camping Site**
(SU332021)
Beaulieu Rd SO42 7QL ☎ 0131 314 6505
Dir: Off B3055 Brockenhurst to Beaulieu road, 2m E of Brockenhurst
★ 🚐 £5.80-£10.30 🚐 £5.80-£10.30 ▲ £5.80-£10.30
Open Etr-Sep Booking advisable all times Last arrival 23.30hrs Last departure noon
Large secluded Forestry Commission site amongst gorse and birch within the New Forest, offering a separate area for motorcyclists and also a lightweight camping area. A 156-acre site with 500 touring pitches.
Separate motorcycle field.
Facilities: ⊙🍴✳⬛💧⬛🎋 **Services:** Ⓔ
➔ ∪ ▶ 🔧 💳 ▧ ▧ ▧ 🎵

FORDINGBRIDGE   Map 04 SU11

  Sandy Balls Holiday Centre
(SU167148)
Sandy Balls Estate Ltd,
Godshill SP6 2JY ☎ 01425 653042
Dir: Take B3078 for Cadnam, 1.25m E
🚐 £12.75-£24 🚐 £12.75-£24 ▲ £11.25-£24
Open all year Booking advisable public & school hols Last arrival 20.00hrs Last departure 11.00hrs
A mostly wooded New Forest site with open fields, river walks and fishing. Facilities and amenities constantly improving. A 30-acre site with 256 touring pitches and 294 statics.
Jacuzzi, steam room, sauna, sunbeds, gym, fitness suite

contd.

Services: Ⓣ Toilet Fluid ✗ Café/ Restaurant 🍴 Fast Food/Takeaway 🍼 Baby Care 🔌 Electric Hook Up
🔲 Launderette ⚲ Licensed Bar 🛢 Calor Gas ∅ Camping Gaz 🔋 Battery Charging

Leisure: ヽ ┐ ◀ ⚠ Facilities: ⇥ ⚑ ⊙ ♁ ✳ ♿ ☎
🛒 🏧 �🅿 🎋 Services: ♨ 🅶 🅇 🛒 🔌 🗓 ✕ ♨ ⚑
→ ◑ △ ⤴ ⚫ ▦ ▧ ☷ 🦆

FRITHAM   Map 04 SU21

► ► **Ocknell Caravan & Camping Site (SU251119)**
SO43 7HH ☎ 0131 314 6505
Dir: Take B3079 off A31 at Cadnam through Brook and Fritham
★ 🚐 £5.80-£9.70 🚐 £5.80-£9.70 ▲ £5.80-£9.70
Open Etr-Sep Booking advisable bank hols Last arrival 23.30hrs Last departure noon
An open Forestry Commission site amid trees, shrubs and open heath. A 28-acre site with 300 touring pitches.
Facilities: ⊙ ✳ ♿ ☎ �🅿 Services: 🅇
→ ◑ ► ⤴ ⚫ ▦ ▧ ☷ 🦆

► **Longbeech Caravan & Camping Site (SU251119)**
SO43 7HH ☎ 4358 314 6505
Dir: Take B3079 off A31 at Cadnam through Brook and Fritham
★ 🚐 £5.80-£9.70 🚐 £5.80-£9.70 ▲ £5.80-£9.70
Open Etr-Sep Booking advisable bank hols Last arrival 23.30hrs Last departure noon
Large Forestry Commission site set attractively amongst trees and close to a disued airfield bordering the New Forest. Own sanitary facilities essential. A 20-acre site with 180 touring pitches.
Facilities: ✳ ☎ 🏧 ⅂🅿
→ ◑ ► ⤴ ⚫ ▦ ▧ ☷ 🦆

RIVERSIDE
TOURING & HOLIDAY
PARK

ROSE AWARD
BRITISH GRADED HOLIDAY PARKS ★★★★
CARAVAN HOLIDAY PARK 2001

Set midway between Portsmouth, New Forest & Winchester
Just 2 miles off Junc. 8 M27
www.riversideholidays.co.uk

⚓ Beautiful views over the marina and River Hamble
⚓ Serviced touring pitches
⚓ Free showers
⚓ Excellent sailing, walking, fishing and horse riding nearby
⚓ Luxurious self catering accommodation
⚓ Launderette
⚓ Lodges available all year including Xmas breaks

Satchell Lane, Hamble, Hants SO31 4HR
Ring now for your free colour brochure
FREEPHONE: 0500 575959
enquiries@riversideholidays.co.uk

HAMBLE   Map 04 SU40

► ► ► **Riverside Park (SU481081)**
Satchell Ln SO31 4HR ☎ 023 80453220
Dir: M27 junct 8, follow signs to Hamble B3397. Turn left into Satchell Lane, 1m down lane on the left
🚐 £8-£12 🚐 £8-£12 ▲ £6-£12
Open Mar-Oct (rs Nov-Feb open wknds & bank hols for statics only) Booking advisable bank hols & peak season Last arrival 22.00hrs Last departure 11.00hrs
A slightly sloping, pleasant and peaceful site adjacent to marina. A 6-acre site with 60 touring pitches and 57 statics.
Bike hire.
Facilities: ⚑ ⊙ ♁ ✳ ☎ Services: ♨ 🅶 🅇 🖬
→ ◑ ► △ ↳ ⤴ 🎋 ⚫ ▦ ▧ ☷ 🦆

LYNDHURST   Map 04 SU30

► **Denny Wood Caravan & Camping Site (SU334069)**
Beaulieu Rd SO43 7FZ ☎ 0131 314 6505
Dir: Take B3056 from Lyndhurst. The site is 2.5m on right
★ 🚐 £5.30-£7.20 🚐 £5.30-£7.20 ▲ £5.30-£7.20
Open Etr-Sep Booking advisable bank hols Last arrival 23.30hrs Last departure noon ⚘
Quiet Forestry Commission site in pleasant surroundings of mixed woodland, grass and gravel surface. Own sanitary facilities essential. A 20-acre site with 170 touring pitches.
Facilities: ☎ Services:
→ ◑ ⚫ ▦ ▧ ☷ 🦆

► **Matley Wood Caravan & Camping Site (SU332076)**
Beaulieu Rd SO43 7FZ ☎ 0131 314 6505
Dir: Take B3056 from Lyndhurst. The site is 1.5m on left
★ 🚐 £5.30-£7.20 🚐 £5.30-£7.20 ▲ £5.30-£7.20
Open Etr-Sep Booking advisable bank hols Last arrival 23.30hrs Last departure noon
A Forestry Commission park made up of clearings in pleasant partially wooded area. Own sanitary facilities essential. An 8-acre site with 70 touring pitches.
→ ◑ ⚫ ▦ ▧ ☷ 🦆

MILFORD ON SEA   Map 04 SZ29

► ► ► ► **Lytton Lawn Touring Park (SZ293937)**
Lymore Ln, Everton SO41 0TX ☎ 01590 648331
Dir: From Lymington take A337 towards Christchurch for 2.5m. Turn left onto B3058 towards Milford-on-Sea. After 0.25m turn left onto Lymore Lane
★ 🚐 £5.10-£23 🚐 £5.10-£23 ▲ £5.10-£23
Open Feb-5 Jan Booking advisable at all times Last arrival 22.00hrs Last departure 10.00hrs
An ideal family site with refurbished facilities and plans for future improvements. A 5-acre site with 126 touring pitches.
Leisure: ◀ ⚠ Facilities: ⚑ ⊙ ♁ ✳ ♿ ☎ 🛒 🐎
Services: ♨ 🅶 🅇 🔌 🅇
→ ◑ ► △ ⤴ ⚫ ▦ ▧ ☷ 🦆

South Coast & New Forest

With two high quality destinations to choose from, Shorefield Country Parks offers you the best of both worlds in touring locations

LYTTON LAWN

Set in beautiful natural parkland close to Milford beach and the historic New Forest with views to the Isle of Wight. Peaceful, unspoilt and relaxing. Electricity hook-up, showers, laundrette, shop, 'Premier Pitches' and a children's area. Optional Leisure Club facilities 2¹/₂ miles away.

OAKDENE
FOREST PARK

Over 55 acres of beautiful parkland giving direct access to the Avon Forest, and only 9 miles from Bournemouth's sandy beaches. New indoor and outdoor pools, sauna, steam room, spa bath, flume, gym, riding stables, adventure playground, club with entertainment, cafeteria, takeaway, general store and launderette.

SHOREFIELD
HOLIDAYS LIMITED

RALLIES WELCOME AT BOTH SITES

1999 DAVID BELLAMY CONSERVATION AWARD GOLD

For further details telephone
01590 648331 Ref. AA

ENGLAND FOR EXCELLENCE
THE ENGLISH TOURIST BOARD
AWARDS FOR TOURISM

Oakdene Forest Park, St. Leonards, Ringwood, Hants BH24 2RZ
Lytton Lawn, Lymore Lane, Milford on Sea, Hants SO41 0TX
e-mail: holidays@shorefield.co.uk **www.shorefield.co.uk**

England

NEW MILTON — Map 04 SZ29

PREMIER PARK

▶ ▶ ▶ ▶ ▶ **Bashley Park (SZ245972)**
Sway Rd BH25 5QR ☎ 01425 612340
Dir: 1m N of New Milton on B3055
★ ⊞ £10.50-£30 ⊞ £10.50-£30
Open Mar-Oct Booking advisable Last arrival
22.00hrs Last departure 10.00hrs
*A large, well-organised site in reasonably flat
open fields with new all weather pitches,
bordered by woodland and shrubbery.
A 100-acre site with 420 touring pitches and
380 statics.*
Leisure: ⌇ ⌇ ⌇ /Ⓐ **Facilities:** 🅝⊙🅆占📞💺🐕
Services: 🔤🔤🅨👤🖉🔤
→ ∪ ▶ ⊙ ↘ ✍ ⊞ ⊞ 🔤 🔤

▶ **Setthorns Caravan & Camping Site (SU262003)**
Wootton BH25 5UA ☎ 0131 314 6505
*Dir: Signposted from A35 Lyndhurst-Christchurch Road,
7m SW of Lyndhurst*
★ ⊞ £5.40-£8.70 ⊞ £5.40-£8.70 ▲ £5.40-£8.70
Open all year Booking advisable all times Last
arrival 23.30hrs Last departure noon
*Pleasant level Forestry Commission site in
woodland with no sanitary facilities but 120 electric
hook-ups. A 60-acre site with 320 touring pitches.*
Facilities: 📞🚿🎋 **Services:** 🔤
→ ∪ ▶ 🔤 🔤 🔤 🔤 🔤

WOOLSBRIDGE MANOR FARM CARAVAN PARK
THREE LEGGED CROSS WIMBORNE, DORSET BH21 6RA
Tel: (01202) 826369

Situated approx. 3½ miles from the New Forest
Market town of Ringwood – easy access to the
South Coast. 7 acres of level, semi sheltered, well
drained spacious pitches. Quiet country location
on a working farm – ideal and safe for families.
Childrens play area on site. Fishing, Moors Valley
Country Park, Golf Course, Pub/Restaurant all
close by. AA 3 pennant grading

OWER — Map 04 SU31

▶ ▶ ▶ **Green Pastures Farm (SU321158)**
SO51 6AJ ☎ 023 80814444
*Dir: From M27 junct 2, follow Salisbury signs for 0.5m.
Then follow signs to farm. Aslo signposted from A36 &
A3090 at Ower*
⊞ £9 ⊞ £9 ▲ £9
Open 15 Mar-Oct Booking advisable bank hols &
peak periods Last departure noon
*A working farm with hardworking owners, with
modern, well-equipped toilet facilities. The park is
set in rural surroundings on the edge of New
Forest, with open level grassy pitches. A 5-acre site
with 45 touring pitches.*
Facilities: 🅝⊙🅆占📞💺🐕 **Services:** 🔤👤🖉⊞
→ ▶ ✍

RINGWOOD — Map 04 SU10

▶ ▶ ▶ *Woolsbridge Manor Farm Caravan Park
(SZ103050)*
Three Legged Cross BH21 6RA ☎ 01202 826369
*Dir: 2m off A31, 3m W of Ringwood. From Three
Legged Cross continue S to Woolsbridge.
Site 1.75m on left*
⊞ ⊞ ▲
Open Etr-Oct Booking advisable bank hols & Aug
Last arrival 22.00hrs Last departure 13.00hrs
*A flat quiet site with a very low density and clean,
well-maintained toilets. A 6.75-acre site with 60
touring pitches.*
Leisure: /Ⓐ **Facilities:** 🅝⊙🅆✳占📞💺🎋🐕
Services: 🔤👤🖉⊞🅣
→ ∪ ▶ ✍🔤

ROMSEY — Map 04 SU32

▶ ▶ ▶ **Hill Farm Caravan Park (SU287238)**
Branches Ln, Sherfield English SO51 6FH
☎ 01794 340402
*Dir: Signed off A27 Salisbury to Romsey road. 4m NW
of Romsey and M27 junct 2*
⊞ ⊞
Open Mar-Oct Booking advisable Last arrival
22.00hrs Last departure noon
*A small, well sheltered site, peacefully located
amidst mature trees and fields. Enthusiastic new
owners are gradually improving standards, and
facilities are well maintained. A 10.5-acre site with
45 touring pitches and 7 statics.
9 hole pitch 'n' putt.*
Leisure: /Ⓐ **Facilities:** 🅝⊙🅆✳📞💺🎋🐕
Services: 🔤🅨👤🖉🅣
→ ▶ ⛾ ✍

WARSASH — Map 04 SU40

▶ ▶ ▶ **Dibles Park (SU505060)**
Dibles Rd SO31 9SA ☎ 01489 575232
*Dir: From M27 junct 8, turn left onto A27 to Fareham.
Turn right at top of Sarisbury Hill into Barnes Lane, then
follow caravan signs to park*
★ ⊞ £7 ⊞ £7 ▲ £6
Open all year Booking advisable bank hols & Jul-
Aug Last arrival 20.30hrs Last departure 13.00hrs

A small, level grass park adjacent to a private park, within easy reach of the River Hamble and the Solent. A 0.75-acre site with 14 touring pitches and 46 statics.

Facilities: ⊪ ⊙ ⊕ ⚹ ⚘ ⊞ **Services:** ⊡ ⊡ ⊞ ⊺
→ ∪ ✈ ⬚ ⚊

HEREFORDSHIRE

LITTLE TARRINGTON   Map 03 SO64

▶ ▶ ▶ *The Millpond (SO625410)*
The Gables HR1 4JD ☎ 01432 890243
Dir: 300yds off A438 on Ledbury side of Tarrington village
⊟ ⊟ Å
Open Mar-Oct Booking advisable peak periods Last arrival 23.00hrs Last departure 11.00hrs
A spacious open camping field beside a fishing lake in a peaceful location, with good toilet facilities. A 0.5-acre site with 18 touring pitches.
Fishing.

Facilities: ⊪ ⊙ ⚭ ⚘ ☇ **Services:** ⊡ ⊞
→ ✈ ⚊

PETERCHURCH   Map 03 SO33

▶ ▶ ▶ ▶ **Poston Mill Caravan & Camping Park (SO355373)**
HR2 OSF ☎ 01981 550225 & 01584 711280
Dir: 11m W of Hereford on B4348
Open all year (rs Nov-Mar Limited toilet facilities) Booking advisable bank & summer hols Last departure noon
Set in the Golden Valley and surrounded by hills, with beautiful views and a peaceful riverside position. This park has excellent facilities and sporting amenities, and there is also an adjoining restaurant and bar. Close to the River Dore. A 33-acre site with 83 touring pitches and 83 statics.

Leisure: ⚲ ⚯ ⚏ ⊡ **Facilities:** ⊪ ⊙ ⚹ ⚹ ⚭ ☇
⚊ ⊟ ⊞ ⊓ ☇ **Services:** ⊡ ⊡ ⊔ ⊟ ⊞ ⊞ ⊞ ✕ ⬚ ⭲
→ ∪ ▸ ⊚ ✈ ⬤ ⬛ ⬛ ⬛ ⬛

STANFORD BISHOP   Map 03 SO65

▶ ▶ ▶ **Boyce Caravan Park (SO692528)**
WR6 5UB ☎ 01885 483439
Dir: From B4220 Malvern road take sharp turn opposite Herefordshire House pub, then right after 0.25m
★ ⊟ fr £7.50 ⊟ fr £7.50 Å fr £7.50

Open Mar-Oct Booking advisable bank hols & Jun-Aug Last arrival 18.00hrs Last departure noon
A pleasant site on an Elizabethan farm with good facilities. A 10-acre site with 25 touring pitches and 80 statics.
Course fishing available.

Leisure: ⚏ **Facilities:** ⊪ ⊙ ⚹ ⚹ ⚭ ☇
Services: ⊡ ⊟ ⊞ ⊟ ⊞ → ✈ ⚊

SYMONDS YAT (West)   Map 03 SO51

▶ ▶ ▶ **Doward Park Camp Site (SO539167)**
Great Doward HR9 6BP ☎ 01600 890438
Dir: 2m from A40 between Ross-on-Wye and Monmouth take turn to Crockers Ash & follow site signs
⊟ £8 ⊟ £8 Å £6-£8
Open Mar-Oct Booking advisable weekends, Jul & Aug Last arrival 21.00hrs Last departure noon
A very, attractive site in woodland on the hillside above the River Wye, run by friendly owners. The timber-built toilet block is well appointed. Light refreshments are available on site. A 1.5-acre site .

Facilities: ⊪ ⊙ ⚹ ⚭ ☇ ☇ **Services:** ⊡ → ▸ ⚹ ✈ ⊟

HERTFORDSHIRE

HERTFORD   Map 04 TL31

▶ ▶ ▶ ▶ **Camping & Caravanning Club Site (TL334113)**
Mangrove Ln SG13 8QF ☎ 01992 586696
Dir: Follow A414 Hertford signs, straight over rdbt. After 200yds left signed Balls Park. Left at T-junct into Mangrove Rd. Site on left
★ ⊟ £11.80-£14.90 ⊟ £11.80-£14.90 Å £11.80-£14.90
Open 20 Mar-1 Nov Booking advisable Last arrival 21.00hrs Last departure noon
A spacious, well-landscaped club site in a rural setting one mile south of Hertford, with immaculate modern toilet facilities. There are several hedged areas with good provision of hardstandings, and a cosy camping

contd.

England

section in an old orchard. All kinds of wildlife flourish around the lake. Please see the advertisement on page 14 for details of Club Members' benefits. A 32-acre site with 247 touring pitches.

Leisure: ⚑ **Facilities:** ↖ ☺ ☜ ✳ ♿ ☎ ⌂
Services: 🚽 📧 🛢 ⊘ ⊞ 🄣
→ ∪ 🅿 ✂ ✈ 🛒 ● ▦

HODDESDON   Map 05 TL30

► ► ► **Lee Valley Caravan Park (TL383082)**
Dobbs Weir, Essex Rd EN11 0AS ☎ 01992 462090
Dir: Leave A10 at Hoddesdon junct and follow signs for Dobbs Weir. Park 1m on right
🚐 £10.66 🚙 £10.66 ▲ £10.66
Open Etr-Oct Booking advisable public hols Last arrival 21.30hrs Last departure noon
Neat, well kept site in a peaceful field surrounded by hedges and tall trees, with a good play area and local walks. An 8-acre site with 100 touring pitches and 100 statics.
Fishing.
Leisure: ⚑ **Facilities:** ↖ ☺ ☜ ✳ ♿ ☎ ⌂
Services: 🚽 📧 🛢 ⊘ 🄣
→ ✂ 🐾 ✈ ● ▦ 🯄 🄖

WALTHAM CROSS   Map 05 TL30

► ► **Camping & Caravanning Club Site (TL344005)**
Theobalds Park, Bulls Cross Ride EN7 5HS
☎ 01992 620604
Dir: M25 junct 25. A10 towards London, keep in right lane. Right at 1st lights. Right at T-junct, right behind dog kennels. Site towards top of lane on right
★ 🚐 £9.80-£12.40 🚙 £9.80-£12.40 ▲ £9.80-£12.40
Open 20 Mar-1 Nov Booking advisable Last arrival 21.00hrs Last departure noon
Lovely open site surrounded by mature trees, and set in parkland at Theobalds Hall. Please see the advertisement on page 14 for details of Club Members' benefits. A 14-acre site with 90 touring pitches.
Table tennis
Leisure: ⚫ ⚑ **Facilities:** ↖ ☺ ✳ ☎ ⌂
Services: 🚽 📧 🛢 ⊘ ⊞
→ ∪ 🅿 △ ✈ 🛒 ● ▦

KENT

ASHFORD   Map 05 TR04

► ► ► **Broad Hembury Holiday Park (TR009387)**
Steeds Ln, Kingsnorth TN26 1NQ ☎ 01233 620859
Dir: From M20 junct 10 take A2070 for 3m. Left at 2nd rdbt signed Kingsnorth, then left at 2nd X-roads in village
★ 🚐 £10-£12 🚙 £10-£12 ▲ £10-£12
Open all year Booking advisable Jul-Aug Last arrival 23.00hrs Last departure noon
Well-run and maintained small family site surrounded by open pasture, with pitches sheltered by mature hedges, and all neatly landscaped. Six super pitches have proved a popular addition to the park, and there is a well-equipped campers' kitchen. A 5-acre site with 60 touring pitches and 25 statics.

Sports field with football & volley ball.
Leisure: ⚫ ⚑ ▭ **Facilities:** ↖ ☺ ☜ ✳ ☎ ⌂
Services: 🚽 📧 🛢 ⊘ 🄣
→ ∪ 🅿 ☺ 🐾 ✈ ● ▦ 🄖

► ► *Dunn Street Farm (TR992480)*
Westwell ☎ 01233 712537
🚐 🚙 ▲
Open all year ⊘
Peaceful, partly-sloping grassy site situated behind the farm and beside the Pilgrims Way on top of the North Downs, just north of Westwell. Simple, clean sanitary facilities housed in a converted farm building. Well placed for visting Canterbury and the Weald of Kent. 30 touring pitches.
Facilities: ↖ ☺ **Services:** 🚽

BIDDENDEN   Map 05 TQ83

► ► ► **Woodlands Park (TQ867372)**
Tenterden Rd TN27 8BT ☎ 01580 291216
Dir: Turn off A28 onto A262. Site 1.5m on right
★ 🚐 £8.50-£10 🚙 £8.50-£10 ▲ £8.50-£10

Open Mar-Oct (rs Mar-Apr weather permitting)
Booking advisable bank hols & Jul-Aug Last arrival anytime Last departure anytime
A site of level grassland bordered by hedges and trees, with two ponds and a smart and well-maintained modern toilet block. Ideal centre for Kent, Sussex and Channel ports. A 9-acre site with 100 touring pitches and 205 statics.
Camping accessory sales. Small site shop.
Leisure: ⚑ **Facilities:** ↖ ☺ ☜ ✳ ♿ ☎ ▦ ☖
Services: 🚽 📧 ☕ 🛢 ⊘ ⊞ 🄣
→ ∪ 🅿 ☺ ✈

BIRCHINGTON   Map 05 TR36

► ► ► **Quex Caravan Park (TR321685)**
Park Rd CT7 0BL ☎ 01843 841273
Dir: From Birchington (A28) turn SE into Park Road to site in 1m
★ 🚐 £9-£12 🚙 £9-£12
Open Mar-Nov Booking advisable bank hols Last arrival anytime Last departure noon
Small parkland site, quiet and secluded, with very good sanitary facilities. An 11-acre site with 88 touring pitches and 120 statics.
Leisure: ⚑ **Facilities:** ↖ ☺ ☜ ✳ ☎ ▦
Services: 🚽 📧 🛢 ⊘ ⊞ 🄣
→ ∪ 🅿 ☺ △ ✂ ☺ ✈

► ► ► **Two Chimneys Caravan Park (TR320684)**
Shottendane Rd CT7 0HD ☎ 01843 810689 & 843157
*Dir: From A28 in Birchington turn right by church along
Park Lane (B2048). Left at Manston Road along
Shottendane Road to site on right*
★ ⚍ £9-£15.50 ⚍ £9-£15.50 ▲ £9-£15.50
Open Mar-Oct (rs Mar-May & Sep-Oct
shop/bar/pool/takeaway restricted) Booking
advisable bank & school hols Last arrival 23.00hrs
Last departure noon
*A good, well-managed site with a swimming pool
and well-tended grounds. A 9-acre site with 75
touring pitches and 65 statics.*
Sauna, spa bath, solarium, amusement arcade.
Leisure: 🏊 🎱 🎣 🎮 **Facilities:** 🖭 ⊙ 🗣 ☀ 🔥 🗑 ⚍
Services: 🔌 🗑 🏪 ⌀ ⚡ 🖭 🖭 🛒
→ ∪ ► ◎ 🍴 ⚡ 👶 ♨ 🛒 🚮 🖭 🖭 🖭 🖭 🔋

CANTERBURY — Map 05 TR15

See also **Petham**
► ► ► **Camping & Caravanning Club Site
(TR172577)**
Bekesbourne Ln CT3 4AB ☎ 01227 463216
*Dir: From Canterbury follow A257 signs (Sandwich),
turn right opposite golf course*
★ ⚍ £11.80-£14.90 ⚍ £11.80-£14.90 ▲ £11.80-£14.90
Open all year Booking advisable bank hols & peak
periods Last arrival 21.00hrs Last departure noon
*An attractive tree-screened site in pleasant rural
surroundings yet within walking distance of the city
centre. The park is well landscaped, and offers very
smart toilet facilities in one block, with another
older but well-kept building housing further
facilities. Please see the advertisement on page 14
for details of Club Members' benefits. A 20-acre site
with 207 touring pitches.*
Leisure: 🎮 **Facilities:** 🖭 ⊙ 🗣 ☀ 🔥 🗑 🏪 🛒
Services: 🔌 🗑 🏪 ⌀ 🖭 🖭
→ ∪ ► ♨ 🛒 🖭

► ► ► *Yew Tree Caravan Park (TR137507)*
Stone St CT4 5PL ☎ 01227 700306
Dir: 4m S of Canterbury on B2068
🔌 ⚍ ▲
Open Mar-Oct Booking advisable Jul, Aug & Bank
Hols Last arrival 21.00hrs Last departure noon ⊘
*Very attractive park set in rolling countryside with
beautiful views over Chartham Downs. A 4.5-acre
site with 45 touring pitches and 13 statics.*
Leisure: 🏊 🎮 **Facilities:** 🖭 ⊙ 🗣 ☀ 🔥 🗑 🏪 **Services:**
🔌 🗑 🏪 ⌀ 🛒 🖭 🖭 🔋

CHATHAM — Map 05 TQ76

► ► **Woolmans Wood Caravan Park (TQ746638)**
Bridgewood ME5 9SB
☎ 01634 867685 & 07957 765839
*Dir: From M2 junct 3 take A229 and B2097 for 0.75m
and site 3.25m S of Rochester*
★ ⚍ £9.50-£11 ⚍ £9.50-£11 ▲ fr £8
Open all year Booking advisable Last arrival
22.00hrs Last departure 14.00hrs
Small site alongside the city airport and close to the

London-Dover road with clean and well maintained
facilities, and a refurbished toilet block. A 5-acre site
with 60 touring pitches.
Caravan servicing, washing & valeting.
Facilities: 🖭 ⊙ 🗣 ☀ 🔥 🗑 🏪 🔥 🏪 **Services:** 🔌 🗑 🏪 ⌀ 🖭 🖭
→ ∪ ► ✈ 👶 🛒

DOVER

See **Martin Mill**

FAVERSHAM — Map 05 TR06

► ► **Painters Farm Caravan & Camping Site
(TQ990591)**
Painters Forstal ME13 0EG ☎ 01795 532995
*Dir: Leave A2 at Faversham, signs to Painters Forstal
and Eastling. 1.5 m down 'No through road' at Forstal*
★ ⚍ £6.80-£8.80 ⚍ £6.80-£8.80 ▲ £6.80-£8.80
Open Mar-Oct Booking advisable bank hols Last
arrival 23.59hrs
*Delightful simple farm site in immaculately kept
cherry orchard, with spotless toilets in converted
farm buildings. A 3-acre site with 50 touring pitches.*
Facilities: 🖭 ⊙ ☀ 🔥 🏪 🔥 **Services:** 🔌 🏪 ⌀ 🖭 🖭
→ ∪ ► 👶

FOLKESTONE — Map 05 TR23

► ► ► **Little Satmar Holiday Park (TR260390)**
Winehouse Ln, Capel Le Ferne CT18 7JF
☎ 01303 251188
Dir: Signposted off B2011
★ ⚍ £9-£12 ⚍ £9-£12 ▲ £9-£12
Open Mar-Oct Booking advisable bank hols & Jul-
Aug Last arrival 23.00hrs Last departure 14.00hrs
*A quiet, well-screened site well away from the road,
with improving facilities. A useful base for touring
Dover/Folkestone area. A 5-acre site with 46 touring
pitches and 80 statics.*
Leisure: 🎣 🎮 **Facilities:** 🖭 ⊙ 🗣 ☀ 🗑 🏪 🔥
Services: 🔌 🗑 🏪 ⌀ 🖭 🖭
→ ∪ ► 👶 🛒 🖭 🖭 🔋

► ► **Camping & Caravanning Club Site (TR246376)**
The Warren CT19 6PT ☎ 01303 255093
*Dir: Approaching on A260, left at island into Folkestone,
Hill Road. Over X-roads into Wear Bay Rd & 2nd left
past Martello Tower. Site 0.5m on right*
★ ⚍ £9.80-£12.40 ▲ £9.80-£12.40
Open 7 Apr-25 Sep Booking advisable bank hols &
peak periods Last arrival 21.00hrs Last departure
noon
*This site commands marvellous views across the
Strait of Dover and is well located for the channel
ports. It nestles on the side of the cliff and is tiered
in some areas. Please see the advertisement on
page 14 for details of Club Members' benefits.
A 4-acre site with 82 touring pitches.*
Facilities: 🖭 ⊙ ☀ 🗑 🏪
→ 🛒 🖭 🖭

Services: 🖭 Toilet Fluid ✗ Café/ Restaurant 🍴 Fast Food/Takeaway ✈ Baby Care 🔌 Electric Hook Up
🗑 Launderette 🍷 Licensed Bar 🏪 Calor Gaz ⌀ Camping Gaz 🖭 Battery Charging

England

▶ ▶ **Little Switzerland Camping & Caravan Site** (TR248380)
Wear Bay Rd CT19 6PS ☎ 01303 252168
Dir: Signposted from A20 E of Folkestone
★ ⊞ £8-£10 ⊞ £8-£10 ▲ £4.50
Open Mar-Oct Booking advisable from Mar Last arrival mdnt Last departure noon
A small site perched on the cliffs overlooking the Dover Straits, with cosy, sheltered pitches. A 4-acre site with 18 touring pitches and 12 statics.
Facilities: ⬅⊙❋✆⬛⊡⌸★ Services: ▣⬛❓▮⌀✕⬛
→ ∪ ▶⊙⬛⬛◢

HARRIETSHAM   Map 05 TQ85

▶ ▶ ▶ **Hogbarn Caravan Park** (TQ885550)
Hogbarn Ln, Stede Hill ME17 1NZ ☎ 01622 859648
Dir: Signed in village off A20 between Ashford & Maidstone
⊞ ⊞ ▲
Open Apr-Oct (rs Oct-Mar rallies only) Booking advisable bank hols & Jul-Aug Last arrival 22.00hrs Last departure noon
A peaceful rural park tucked away along lanes on top of the North Downs, with improving super pitches, first-class toilets, and a secluded touring area well screened from the static site. Attractive low walls and much planting enhance the bar and swimming pool area. A 5-acre site with 60 touring pitches and 70 statics.
Coffee bar & Sauna.
Leisure: 🏊 🎣 ⚠ ▢ Facilities: ⬅⊙🔲❋✆⬛⚄⌸★
Services: ▣⬛❓▮⌀⊡⬅
→ ∪ ▶⬛⬛◢ ⬛ ⬛⬛ ⬛

HOATH   Map 05 TR26

▶ ▶ ▶ **South View** (TR205648)
Maypole Ln CT3 4LL ☎ 01227 860280
Dir: Off A291 & A28
★ ⊞ £10 ⊞ £10 ▲ £10
Open Mar-Oct Booking advisable bank hols Last arrival 23.00hrs Last departure 22.00hrs
A small, peaceful and well-secluded site with level pitches and good toilets. A quiet base from which to explore Canterbury and the north Kent coast. A 3-acre site with 45 touring pitches.
Leisure: ⚠ Facilities: ⬅⊙🔲❋⚄⌸▢
Services: ▣⬛❓▮⌀⊡
→ ∪ ▶⬛◢⬛⬛◢⬛

MAIDSTONE   Map 05 TQ75

▶ ▶ ▶ ▶ **Pine Lodge Touring Park** (TQ815549)
Ashford Rd, Bearsted, Hollingbourne ME17 1XH
☎ 01622 730018
Dir: On A20, 0.5m from M20 junct 8, 3m E of Maidstone
★ ⊞ £9-£11 ⊞ £9-£11 ▲ £8-£11
Open all year Booking advisable bank hols Last arrival 22.00hrs Last departure 14.00hrs ⚘
A very well run park with good landscaping resulting from the far-sighted planting of trees. The toilet facilities are impeccably maintained, and offer high quality comfortable fittings in a centrally heated block. There is provision for large motorhomes on the park, which is close to Leeds Castle and well placed for the Channel ports and the M20. A 7-acre site with 100 touring pitches. Waste disposal points.
Leisure: ⚠ Facilities: ⬅⊙🔲❋⚄✆⬛
Services: ▣⬛▮⌀⊡
→ ∪ ▶⬛◢ ⬛ ⬛⬛ ⬛⬛ ⬛

MANSTON   Map 05 TR36

▶ ▶ ▶ **Manston Caravan & Camping Park** (TR348662)
Manston Court Rd CT12 5AU ☎ 01843 823442
Dir: Follow signs to London/Manston (Kent Int Airport). After passing entrance turn left into Manston Court Rd. Entrance 400yds on right
★ ⊞ £9-£12 ⊞ £10-£12 ▲ £6.50-£12
Open Etr-Oct (rs Apr shop open weekends only (off-peak)) Booking advisable bank hols & Jul-Aug Last arrival 23.55hrs Last departure 11.00hrs
A level grassy site with mature trees situated near Manston Airport and convenient for the seaside resorts on the Isle of Thanet. A 5-acre site with 100 touring pitches and 46 statics.
Leisure: ⚠ Facilities: ⬅⊙❋✆⬛⚄★
Services: ▣⬛▮⌀⊡
→ ∪ ▶⬛◢⬛✚⬛◢⬛ ⬛⬛ ⬛⬛ ⬛

MARTIN MILL   Map 05 TR34

▶ ▶ ▶ ▶ **Hawthorn Farm Caravan Park** (TR342464)
Station Rd CT15 5LA ☎ 01304 852658 & 852914
Dir: Signed from A258
★ ⊞ £9-£12 ⊞ £9-£12 ▲ £9-£12
Open Mar-mid Dec (rs winter (water off if weather cold)) Booking advisable bank hols & Jul-Aug Last arrival anytime Last departure noon

Facilities: ⬅ Bath 🔲 Shower ⊙ Electric Shaver 🔲 Hairdryer ❋ Ice Pack Facility ⚄ Disabled Facilities ✆ Public Telephone
⬛ Shop on Site or within 200yds ⊡ Mobile Shop (calls at least 5 days a week) ⬛ BBQ Area ⌸ Picnic Area ★ Dog Exercise Area

This pleasant rural site is screened by young trees and hedgerows, in grounds which include a rose garden and woods. A 15-acre site with 250 touring pitches and 176 statics.

Facilities: ⬤☉⬤☀⬤⬤⬤ **Services:** ⬤⬤⬤⬤⬤⬤✗
→⬤⬤⬤⬤⬤⬤⬤⬤ ⬤⬤⬤⬤ ⬤

PETHAM   Map 05 TR15

▶ ▶ *Ashfield Farm (TR138508)*
Waddenhall CT4 5PX ☎ 01227 700624
Dir: Signed off B2068
⬤⬤⬤

Open Apr-Oct Booking advisable Jul & Aug Last arrival anytime Last departure noon
Small rural site with new toilet block and well-drained pitches, located south of Canterbury. A 4.5-acre site with 20 touring pitches and 1 static.
Mini golf, short term kennelling.

Facilities: ⬤☉☀⬤⬤⬤⬤ **Services:** ⬤⬤⬤⬤⬤
→⬤⬤▶⬤

SANDWICH   Map 05 TR35

▶ ▶ ▶ **Sandwich Leisure Park (TR326581)**
Woodnesborough Rd CT13 0AA
☎ 01304 612681 & 01227 771777
Dir: Towards Sandwich town centre, then follow tourist signs
★ ⬤ £6.80-£10.20 ⬤ £6.80-£10.20 ⬤ £4.50-£10.20
Open Mar-Oct Booking advisable Etr, Spring bank hol & Jul-Aug Last arrival 20.00hrs Last dep 11.00hrs
A useful touring site on the edge of Sandwich, with well laid out pitches, and new, smart modern toilet facilities. A 19-acre site with 140 touring pitches and 103 statics.

Leisure: ⬤ **Facilities:** ⬤☉⬤☀⬤⬤⬤
Services: ⬤⬤⬤⬤
→⬤⬤▶⬤⬤⬤⬤

SEVENOAKS   Map 05 TQ55

▶ ▶ ▶ **Camping & Caravanning Club Site (TQ577564)**
Styants Bottom Rd, Styants Bottom, Seal TN15 0ET
☎ 01732 762728
Dir: Take A25 from Sevenoaks towards Borough Green. Left just after Crown Point Inn, on right, down narrow lane to Staynts Bottom. Site on left
★ ⬤ £10.60-£13.90 ⬤ £10.60-£13.90 ⬤ £10.60-£13.90
Open 20 Mar-1 Nov Booking advisable bank hols & peak periods Last arrival 21.00hrs Last departure noon
A quiet park in the centre of NT woodlands, with buildings blending well into the surroundings. Please see the advertisement on page 22 for details of Club Members' benefits. A 6-acre site with 60 touring pitches.

Leisure: ⬤ **Facilities:** ⬤☉⬤☀⬤⬤⬤
Services: ⬤⬤⬤
→⬤⬤▶ ⬤⬤

WESTENHANGER   Map 05 TR13

▶ ▶ *Caravan Club Site (TR128371)*
Folkestone Racecourse, Stone St CT21 4HX
☎ 01303 261761 & 266407
Dir: From M20 junct 11 onto A261 at rdbt with A20, signed Sellinge
⬤⬤⬤
Open late Mar-mid Sep Booking advisable Jul-Aug Last arrival 20.00hrs Last departure noon
Situated in rural surroundings 7m west of Folkestone and 3m from nearest beach. Conveniently positioned for Channel ports. A 4-acre site with 55 touring pitches.

Facilities: ⬤☉☀⬤⬤⬤ **Services:** ⬤⬤⬤⬤
→⬤⬤▶⬤⬤⬤⬤ ⬤⬤⬤⬤ ⬤

WHITSTABLE   Map 05 TR16

▶ ▶ ▶ **Seaview Caravan Park (TR145675)**
St John's Rd CT5 2RY ☎ 01227 792246
Dir: Signed off A229, 0.5m E of Whitstable
★ ⬤ £9.50-£11.50 ⬤ £9.50-£11.50 ⬤ fr £9.50
(rs Feb & Nov Limited facilities) Booking advisable all times Last arrival 21.30hrs Last departure noon
Pleasant open site on the edge of Whitstable, set well away from the static site with a smart, modern toilet block. A 12-acre site with 20 touring pitches and 452 statics.
Amusements in games room & adventure trail.

Leisure: ⬤⬤⬤ **Facilities:** ⬤☉⬤☀⬤⬤⬤⬤⬤
Services: ⬤⬤⬤⬤⬤⬤✗⬤
→⬤⬤▶⬤⬤⬤⬤ ⬤⬤⬤⬤ ⬤⬤ ⬤

Services: ⬤ Toilet Fluid ✗ Café/ Restaurant ⬤ Fast Food/Takeaway ⬤ Baby Care ⬤ Electric Hook Up ⬤ Launderette ⬤ Licensed Bar ⬤ Calor Gaz ⬤ Camping Gaz ⬤ Battery Charging

WROTHAM HEATH   Map 05 TQ65

► ► ► *Gate House Wood Touring Park (TQ635585)*
Ford Ln TN15 7SD ☎ 01732 843062
Dir: On A20 at Wrotham Heath, 0.5m E of M20/M26 junct 2A
🏕🏕⚠

Open all year Booking advisable Last arrival 22.00hrs Last departure noon ♨
A maturing site in a disused sand quarry, well sheltered by tall trees and banks, and with smart new facilities. A 3.5-acre site with 55 touring pitches.

Leisure: ⚠ Facilities: 🅿⊙🍴✳🅱🔌🛒🏓
Services: 🖵🛢🚿⚡🚰🚽
→ ∪ ►

LANCASHIRE

See also sites under **Greater Manchester & Merseyside**

BLACKPOOL   Map 07 SD33

Marton Mere Holiday Village (SD347349)
Mythop Rd FY4 4XN ☎ 01253 760771
Dir: Leave M55 at junct 4 onto A583 towards Blackpool. Turn right past windmill at 1st traffic lights into Mythop Road. Park 150yds on left
★ 🏕 £14-£21 🏕 £14-£21
Open Mar-Oct Booking advisable Last arrival 22.00hrs Last departure noon
A large holiday centre with plenty of on-site entertainment directed at all ages, and a regular bus service into Blackpool. The separate touring area on this extensive park has all hardstanding and electric pitches. This area is on the edge of the mere, where plenty of birdlife is to be spotted. A 30-acre site with 431 touring pitches and 921 statics.

Leisure: ⚓ ⚓ ⚓ ⚠ ☐ Facilities: 🅿⊙🍴✳🔌
🛒🏓🐕 Services: 🖵🛢🚿⚡🚰🚽🔧✕🚮
→ ∪ ►⊙✚🚌🚲♨ 🍴🍴🍴🍴🍴🍴

► ► ► ► *Pipers Height Caravan Park (SD355327)*
Peel Rd, Peel FY4 5JT ☎ 01253 763767
Dir: Leave M55 at junct with A583 towards Preston. Turn right at 1st traffic lights, then sharp left to site 200yds on right
🏕🏕⚠

Open Mar-Nov (rs Nov Weekends only) Booking advisable School holidays Last arrival 22.00hrs
Family owned and run park in a rural area, yet within 4m of the extensive beaches and entertainment of Blackpool and Lytham St Annes. Attractive and cheerful buildings house the reception, shop, bar and restaurant, and there is some family entertainment in the school holidays and at weekends. A 9-acre site with 137 touring pitches.

Leisure: ⚓ ⚠ Facilities: 🅿⊙✳🔌🛒🏓🐕
Services: 🖵🛢🚿⚡🚰✕
→ ∪ ►⊙✚🚌♨

► ► Mariclough Hampsfield Camping Site (SD356329)
Preston New Rd, Peel Corner FY4 5JR
☎ 01253 761034
Dir: On A583 0.5m S of M55 junct 4
★ 🏕 £6-£7 🏕 £6-£7 ⚠ £6-£7
Open Etr-Oct Booking advisable high season bank hols (for caravans) Last arrival 22.30hrs Last departure noon
A small, tidy, family camping site located on A583 and on the outskirts of Blackpool, set in open countryside. A 2-acre site with 50 touring pitches and 2 statics.

Leisure: ⚠ Facilities: 🅿⊙✳🔌 Services: 🖵⚡🚰🚽🚿
→ ∪ ►🚮🚌♨🛒

BOLTON-LE-SANDS   Map 07 SD46

► ► ► Sandside Caravan & Camping Park (SD472681)
The Shore LA5 8JS ☎ 01524 822311
Dir: From M6 junct 35 follow A6 through Carnforth, turn right at Little Chef in Bolton-le-Sands, and over level crossing to site
★ 🏕 £9.25-£11.50 🏕 £9.25-£11.50 ⚠ £6.50-£8
Open Mar-Oct Booking advisable bank hols & Jul-Aug Last arrival 22.00hrs
A well-maintained site on pleasant sloping ground overlooking Morecambe Bay, with distant views of the Lake District. A 13-acre site with 92 touring pitches and 35 statics.

Facilities: 🅿⊙🍴✳🔌🛒🏓🐕 Services: 🖵🛢⚡🚰
→ ∪ ►⊙⚡✚♨🚲 🍴🍴🍴🍴🍴🍴

► ► Bolton Holmes Farm (SD481693)
Mill Ln LA5 8ES ☎ 01524 732854
Dir: Turn down Mill Lane on West side of A6 in Bolton-Le-Sands. Over railway bridge onto Shore Front. Road to left of White House
★ 🏕 fr £5 🏕 fr £5 ⚠ fr £5.50
Open Apr-Sep Booking advisable peak periods
A gently sloping site forming part of a farm complex, offering good views across Morecambe Bay and to the hills of the Lake District. The friendly owners keep the field well trimmed and neat, and the toilet facilities are very clean. Site is signed off A6 between Morecambe and Carnforth. A 5-acre site with 30 touring pitches and 45 statics.

Facilities: 🅿⊙✳🔌 Services: 🖵⚡🚰
→ ∪✚♨🚲🛒

Facilities: ➡ Bath 🅿 Shower ⊙ Electric Shaver 🍴 Hairdryer ✳ Ice Pack Facility 🔌 Disabled Facilities 🔌 Public Telephone
🛒 Shop on Site or within 200yds 🖵 Mobile Shop (calls at least 5 days a week) 🏓 BBQ Area 🏓 Picnic Area 🐕 Dog Exercise Area

England

► ► **Detron Gate Farm (SD478683)**
LA5 9TN ☎ 01524 732842 & 733617 (night)
🚐 🚐 ⚠
Open Mar-Oct (rs Mar-May shop hours restricted)
Booking advisable bank hols Last arrival 22.00hrs
Last departure 18.00hrs
*Rural grassy site overlooking Morecambe Bay off
A6. A popular site on sloping ground with a small
farm adjacent. A 10-acre site with 100 touring
pitches and 42 statics.*
Leisure: ♦ ⚠ ▢ Facilities: ℕ ☉ ※ ⚴ ☎
Services: ⚡ ▢ ▮ ⌀ ⊞ ▢
→ ∪ ▶ ◎ ◬ ✦ ☙ ↲

► ► ► **Old Hall Caravan Park (SD533716)**
LA6 1AD ☎ 01524 733276 & 735996
*Dir: M6 junct 35 follow signs to Over Kellet, left onto
B6254, left at village green signed Capernwray. Site
1.5m on right*
🚐 £12-£14 🚐 £12-£14
Open Mar-10 Jan Booking advisable bank hols &
Jul-Aug
*Set in a clearing in lovely secluded woods in a
natural setting with marked walks. A 3-acre site with
38 touring pitches and 160 statics.*
Leisure: ⚠ Facilities: ℕ ☉ ⚰ ⚴ ⚴ ➤
Services: ⚡ ▢ ▮ ⌀ ⊞
→ ∪ ◬ ✦ ↲ ☎

► ► ► **Camping & Caravanning Club Site
(SD727413)**
Edisford Bridge, Edisford Rd BB7 3LA
☎ 01200 425294
*Dir: A671 to Clitheroe. Left at Longridge sign. Turn into
Greenacre Rd. Left at Edisford Rd T-junct. Sports Centre
on right. Site 50mtrs on left*
★ 🚐 £9.80-£12.40 🚐 £9.80-£12.40 ⚠ £9.80-£12.40
Open 20 Mar-1 Nov Booking advisable bank hols &
peak periods Last arrival 21.00hrs Last departure
noon
*Set on the banks of the River Ribble, this site is
ideal for fishing and walking as well as enjoying the
adjacent park. Please see the advertisement on
page 14 for details of Club Members' benefits.
A 6-acre site with 80 touring pitches.*
Facilities: ℕ ☉ ⚰ ※ ⚴ ☎ Services: ⚡ ▢ ▮ ⌀ ⊞
→ ∪ ▶ ☙ ↲ ▦ ▦

*Cockerham Sands Country Park
(SD435529)*
LA2 0BB ☎ 01524 751387
*Dir: Leave Lancaster on A588 towards Cockerham,
turn right at sign to Glasson Dock, and after 1.5m,
turn left following signs for Cockerham Sands*
🚐 🚐
Open Mar-11 Dec Booking advisable Last
departure 10.00hrs
A small touring area close to all the amenities of

*a large holiday complex on the estuary of the
River Lune. The emphasis is on entertainment
for all the family on site. A 7-acre site with 9
touring pitches and 260 statics.*
Leisure: ⚴ ♦ ⚠ Facilities: ℕ ☉ ⚰ ☎ ☎
Services: ⚡ ▢ ▢ ♀ ▮ ⊞ ⚱
→ ∪ ↲

► ► ► **Mosswood Caravan Park (SD456497)**
Crimbles Ln LA2 0ES ☎ 01524 791041
*Dir: Situated approx 4m from A6/M6 junct 33, 1m W of
Cockerham on A588*
🚐 🚐 ⚠
Open Mar-Oct Booking advisable bank hols & Jul-
Sep Last arrival 20.00hrs Last departure 16.00hrs
*A tree-lined grassy park with sheltered, level
pitches, located on peaceful Cockerham Moss. The
modern toilet block is attractively clad in stained
wood, and the facilities include cubicled washing
facilities and a launderette. A 3-acre site with 25
touring pitches and 143 statics.*
Leisure: ⚠ Facilities: ℕ ☉ ⚰ ※ ⚴ ☎ ⚴ ➤
Services: ⚡ ▢ ▮ ⌀ ⊞
→ ∪ ▶ ↲ ☙ ▬ ▦ ▦ ▢

► ► ► **Royal Umpire Touring Park (SD504190)**
Southport Rd PR5 7JB ☎ 01772 600257
Dir: Signed off A581 from Chorley
🚐 🚐 ⚠
Open all year (rs 7 Nov-21 Dec only serviced pitches
available) Booking advisable bank hols & peak
season Last arrival 22.00hrs Last departure noon
*A pleasant, level site with good facilities and high
standard of maintenance, set in open countryside.
A 10-acre site with 200 touring pitches.
Assault course, five-a-side football pitch.*
Leisure: ♦ ⚠ Facilities: ℕ ☉ ⚰ ※ ⚴ ☎ ⚴ ➤
Services: ⚡ ▢ ▮ ⌀ ⊞ ⚱ ⚱ ⚴
→ ∪ ▶ ↲ ☙ ▬ ▦ ▦ ▢

► ► ► ► **Claylands Caravan Park (SD496485)**
Cabus PR3 1AJ ☎ 01524 791242
*Dir: Signposted off A6 down private road on Lancaster
side of Garstang*
★ 🚐 £9.50-£11.55 🚐 £9.50-£11.50 ⚠ £9.50-£11.50
Open Mar-4 Jan (rs Jan & Feb Holiday park only)
Booking advisable bank hols & Jul-Aug Last arrival
23.00hrs Last departure 14.00hrs
*A well-maintained site with lovely river and
woodland walks and good views over the River
Wyre towards the village of Scorton. This friendly
park is set in delightful countryside, and guests can
enjoy fishing in a very relaxed atmosphere. The
quality facilities and amenities are of a high
standard, and everything is immaculately
maintained. Convenient for A6 and M6 between
junctions 32 and 33. A 14-acre site with 40 touring
pitches and 60 statics.
Fishing.*

contd.

Services: ⊤ Toilet Fluid ✗ Café/ Restaurant ⚱ Fast Food/Takeaway ⚴ Baby Care ⚡ Electric Hook Up
▢ Launderette ♀ Licensed Bar ▮ Calor Gaz ⌀ Camping Gaz ⊞ Battery Charging

Leisure: ◆ ⚠ Facilities: ⋒☉⚬✳⚐⬙⚑⬚⊞ ⋔
Services: ⊙⊟♀⬙⧉⊞⚑✕⛟ ⟿
⇥ ∪ ▸ ✦ ⬙ ⬛⬚⬛ ⊠ ⬙

▶ ▶ ▶ *Bridge House Marina & Caravan Park* *(SD483457)*
Nateby Crossing Ln, Nateby PR3 0JJ
☎ 01995 603207
Dir: Off A6 on unclass road signed Knott End
⚐ ⚑
Open Mar-4 Jan Booking advisable bank hols Last arrival 22.00hrs Last departure 13.00hrs
A well-maintained site in attractive countryside by the Lancaster Canal, with good views towards the Trough of Bowland. A 4-acre site with 50 touring pitches and 20 statics.
Leisure: ⚠ Facilities: ⋒☉⚑✳⚑⬙⚐⋔
Services: ⊙⊟♀⧉⊞⊤
⇥ ▸ ⚘ ✦ ⬙ ⬚⬛ ⬚⬛ ⊠ ⬙

GISBURN · Map 07 SD84

▶ ▶ ▶ **Rimington Caravan Park (SD825469)**
Hardacre Ln, Rimington BB7 4EE
☎ 01200 445355 & 447235
Dir: Off A682 1m S of Gisburn
★ ⚑ £12 ⚑ £12 ⚑ £10
Open Apr-Oct (rs Mar hardstanding available only) Booking advisable bank hols & Jul-3 Sep Last arrival 20.00hrs Last departure noon no cars by caravans no cars by tents
A well-cared for site set in an attractive rural valley close to the Pendle Hills. An 11-acre site with 30 touring pitches and 150 statics.
Leisure: ◆ Facilities: ⋒☉⚑✳⚑⬙⚐
Services: ⊙⊟♀⬙⧉⊞⊤
⇥ ∪ ✦

GLASSON · Map 07 SD45

▶ ▶ ▶ *Marina Caravan Park (SD450561)*
Conder Green Rd LA2 0BP ☎ 01524 751787
Dir: Off A588 at Condor Green; follow unclass road towards Glasson Dock. Park on left before entering village
⚐ ⚑
Open Mar-Jan Booking advisable Last arrival 22.00hrs Last departure noon
Level touring pitches on hardstandings in a pleasant rurally-situated park. A short stroll to the waterside village of Glasson Dock, with its lock between Lancaster Canal and the sea. A 2-acre site with 15 touring pitches and 123 statics.
Pool table Video games
Leisure: ⚓◆ Facilities: ⋒⚑✳⚑⬙⚐⚑
Services: ⊙⊟♀⬙⧉⚑
⇥ ▸ ⚐ ⚘ ✦ ⚑ ⬙ ⬚⬛ ⬚⬛ ⊠ ⬙

HEYSHAM · Map 07 SD46

Ocean Edge Caravan Park (SD407591)
Moneyclose Ln LA3 2XA
☎ 01524 855657
Dir: From junct 34 on M6, follow A683 to Heysham. Site signed at Heysham before ferry pont
⚐ ⚑ ⚑
Open Mar-Oct
A newly developed touring area of a large holiday complex adjacent to the sea. A 10-acre site with 100 touring pitches and 629 statics.
Leisure: ⚓ ⚠ Facilities: ⚑ ⚑ Services: ⊟♀✕⧉

KIRKBY LONSDALE

See **Cumbria**

LANCASTER · Map 07 SD46

▶ ▶ ▶ *New Parkside Farm Caravan Park* *(SD507633)*
Denny Beck, Caton Rd LA2 9HH
☎ 01524 770723 & 770337
Dir: Leave M6 at junct 34 onto A683 in direction of Kirkby Lonsdale (east). Park 0.75m on right
⚐ ⚑ ⚑
Open Mar-Oct Booking advisable bank hols
Peaceful, friendly grassy park on a working farm with extensive views of Lune Valley and Ingleborough. A 3-acre site with 40 touring pitches and 10 statics.
Facilities: ⋒☉⚑⬙⚑ Services: ⊙⬙⧉
⇥ ∪ ▸ ⚘ ⚐ ⬙ ⊟

LONGRIDGE · Map 07 SD63

▶ ▶ ▶ *Beacon Fell View Caravan Park (SD618382)*
110 Higher Rd PR3 2TF ☎ 01772 785434
Dir: Leave A6 at Broughton on B5269 into Longbridge & follow B6243 out of the town centre. Then take left fork signed Jeffrey Hill. Site 0.75m on right
★ ⚑ £7.50-£15.50 ⚑ £7.50-£15.50 ⚑ £7.50-£15.50
Open 8 Apr-28 Oct (rs after Etr-end May entertainment weekends only) Booking advisable bank & school hols & weekends Last arrival 21.00hrs Last departure 18.00hrs
An elevated park with views over Beacon Fell. This tiered park with level pitches has an indoor swimming pool, and an extensive free evening entertainment programme in the clubhouse. A 7-acre site with 90 touring pitches and 397 statics.
Free evening entertainment, pool tables, darts.
Leisure: ⚓ ◆ ⚠ Facilities: ⋒☉⚑⬙⚑⚐⋔
Services: ⊙⊟♀⬙⧉
⇥ ∪ ▸ ✦ ⬙ ⬚⬛ ⬚⬛ ⊠ ⬙

LYTHAM ST ANNES · Map 07 SD32

▶ ▶ ▶ *Bank Lane Caravan Park (SD335427)*
Warton PR4 1TB ☎ 01772 633513
Dir: On unclass road, off A584 at Warton, 3m from Lytham
⚐
Open Mar-Oct Booking advisable

England

A grassy touring area with open aspect at edge of a mainly static park, situated close to British Aerospace aerodrome, and handy for beaches. A 2-acre site with 50 touring pitches and 180 statics.

Leisure: ⚠ Facilities: 🏧 🍴 🛁 🚿 ☂ Services: 🖿 🖩 🔋 ∅
→ ∪ ▶ ⊙ ⚙ ⤴ ☎ ⚓

▶ ▶ ▶ **Eastham Hall Caravan Site (SD379291)**
Saltcotes Rd FY8 4LS ☎ 01253 737907
Dir: Leave M55 at junct 3. Straight over 3 rdbts onto B5259. Through Wrea Green & Moss Side, park 1m after level crossing
★ 🚐 £10-£11.50 🚗 £10-£11.50
Open Mar-Oct Booking advisable bank hols & Jul Last arrival 21.00hrs Last departure 16.00hrs
A level, secluded site with trees and hedgerows, in rural surroundings. A 15-acre site with 200 touring pitches and 200 statics.
Leisure: ⚠ Facilities: 🏧 ⊙ 🍴 🚿 🛁 ☂
Services: 🖿 🖩 🔋 ∅ 🅃
→ ∪ ▶ ⚓ ⚙ 🍴 🍔 🔋 ⚓

MERE BROW   Map 07 SD41

▶ ▶ ▶ **Leisure Lakes (SD408176)**
PR4 6JX ☎ 01772 813446 & 814502
Dir: From Southport, take A565 for 3.5m, right turn on B5246 to site
★ 🚐 £6-£10 🚗 £6-£10
Open all year Booking advisable bank hols, Jun-Aug & wknds Last arrival 21.00hrs Last departure 16.30hrs
A level grassy site in spacious parkland with ample amenities including watersports, fishing and walking. A 30-acre site with 90 touring pitches. Windsurfing, canoe, golf range, Horse, golf
Leisure: ⚓ ⚠ Facilities: 🏧 ⊙ 🚿 🛁 ☂ 🎡 ☂
Services: 🖿 🖩 ⚐ ∅ 🔋 ✕ 🍴
→ ∪ ▶ ⚓ ⚙ 🔋 🍔 🍔 📛 🔋

MIDDLETON (Near Morecambe)   Map 07 SD45

▶ ▶ ▶ **Melbreak Caravan Park (SD415584)**
Carr Ln LA3 3LH ☎ 01524 852430
Dir: M6 junct 34 onto A683. After 6m turn left at rdbt, pass Middleton and turn right into village. Site 0.5m out
🚐 £7.25 🚗 £7.25 ▲ £6.75
Open Mar-Oct Booking advisable Jul-Aug Last arrival 22.00hrs Last departure noon
Small, well run, tidy site in open countryside south of Morecambe. A 2-acre site with 20 touring pitches and 30 statics.
Facilities: 🏧 ⊙ 🍴 🚿 🛁 Services: 🖿 🖩 🔋 ∅ 🔋 ⚓
→ ∪ ▶ ⚓

MORECAMBE   Map 07 SD46

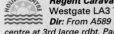 *Regent Caravan Park (SD431629)*
Westgate LA3 7DB ☎ 01524 413940
Dir: From A589 turn left towards town centre at 3rd large rdbt. Park 1.5m on left
🚐 🚗
Open Mar-1 Jan Booking advisable Last arrival 21.00hrs Last departure noon

A full entertainment complex for all ages, in a first class holiday centre, close to town and promenade. Amenities include extensive bars with snooker tables, pool tables, darts and wide-screen TV. A 2-acre site with 24 touring pitches and 330 statics.
Leisure: ⚡ ⚠ Facilities: 🏧 🍴 🛁 ☂
Services: 🖩 ⚐ ✕ ⚓
→ ∪ ▶ ⊙ 🍔 ⚓

▶ ▶ ▶ **Riverside Caravan Park (SD448615)**
Snatchems LA3 3ER ☎ 01524 844193
Dir: On unclass road off B5273 near Heaton
★ 🚐 £6-£7 🚗 £6-£7 ▲ fr £6

Open Mar-Oct Booking advisable public hols & high season Last arrival 22.00hrs Last departure noon
A nice level grassy site with views over River Lune and Morecambe Bay. A 2-acre site with 50 touring pitches.
Leisure: ⚠ Facilities: 🏧 ⊙ 🍴 🚿 🛁 🏧 ☂
Services: 🖿 🔋 🔋 🅃
→ ∪ ▶ ⚓ 🍔 ⚙ 🖩 🔋

▶ ▶ ▶ **Venture Caravan Park (SD436633)**
Langridge Way, Westgate LA4 4TQ ☎ 01524 412986
Dir: M6 junct 34. Take A683 to Lancaster. Follow signs to Morecambe. Straight over 2 rdbt, then left at 3rd. 0.75m right into Langridge Way
★ 🚐 £9-£11 🚗 £9-£11 ▲ £9-£11
Open all year (rs 6 Jan - 22 Feb touring vans only, one toilet block open) Booking advisable bank hols & peak periods Last arrival 22.00hrs Last departure noon
A large park which has been recently upgraded, with modern toilet facilities and a licensed clubhouse. Close to the centre of town, and with many statics. A 17.5-acre site with 56 touring pitches and 304 statics.
Amusement arcade & off licence.
Leisure: ⚡ ⚠ 🎯 Facilities: ⤴ 🏧 ⊙ 🍴 🚿 🛁 ☂
Services: 🖿 🖩 ⚐ 🔋 ∅ 🔋 🅃 ⚓
→ ▶ 🍔 ⚓

ORMSKIRK   Map 07 SD40

▶ ▶ ▶ ▶ **Abbey Farm Caravan Park (SD434098)**
Dark Ln L40 5TX ☎ 01695 572686
Dir: M6 junct 27 onto A5209 to Burscough. 4m left onto B5204 then immediately right into Hobcross Lane. Park 1.5m on right
★ 🚐 £8-£12.50 🚗 £8-£12.50 ▲ £4-£9.50   *contd.*

Services: 🅃 Toilet Fluid   ✕ Café/ Restaurant   🔋 Fast Food/Takeaway   ⚓ Baby Care   ⚡ Electric Hook Up
🖩 Launderette   ⚐ Licensed Bar   🔋 Calor Gaz   ∅ Camping Gaz   🔋 Battery Charging

Open all year Booking advisable public hols & Jul-Aug Last arrival 22.00hrs Last departure 13.00hrs
A well-maintained rural park in the grounds of the 12th-century Burscough Abbey, just 1.5m from the old market town of Ormskirk. The level grassy pitches are sheltered by mature trees and shrubs, and divided into paddocks. The park is connected by footpath to a local inn where food is available. A 6-acre site with 56 touring pitches and 44 statics. Off-licence.

Leisure: ◣ ⋀ Facilities: ➡ ⋔ ⊙ ◲ ✳ � ᒪ ᰔ ⊞ 戸 ⋔
Services: ◲ 回 🔋 🚽 ⊞ ⊤
→ ∪ ► ♪ ● 🚋 🔣 🔀 🔄

► ► ► *Shaw Hall Caravan Park (SD397119)*
Smithy Ln, Scarisbrick L40 8HJ ☎ 01704 840298
Dir: 200yds S of canal bridge at Scarisbrick, 0.25m off A570 at Smithy Lane
🚐 🚐 ▲
Open Mar-7 Jan Booking advisable bank hols & peak periods
A quiet, family run park with direct access to the Leeds-Liverpool Canal, offering good quality facilities. It has a clubhouse with a large concert room where weekend live entertainment is staged. A 26-acre site with 43 touring pitches and 300 statics.

Leisure: ⋀ 🔲 Facilities: ⋔ ◲ ✳ ᗔ ᒪ ᰔ 戸 ⋔
Services: ◲ 回 🔋 🔋 ⊞ 🏺
→ ∪ ► ♪ ● 🚋 🔣 🔀 🔄

ROCHDALE

See **Greater Manchester**

SILVERDALE   Map 07 SD47
PREMIER PARK

► ► ► ► ► Holgate's Caravan Park
(SD455762)
Middlebarrow Plain, Cove Rd LA5 0SH
☎ 01524 701508
Dir: Junct 35 of M6. 5m NW of Carnforth. From Carnforth centre take unclass Silverdale road & follow tourist signs after Warton
★ 🚐 £17.75-£19.50 🚐 £17.75-£19.50 ▲ £17.75-£19.50
Open mid Feb-5 Nov (rs 22 Dec-mid Feb pool, shop, cafe, bar) Booking advisable school & public hols & wknds Last arrival 22.00hrs Last departure 14.00hrs

A superb family holiday park set in wooded countryside adjacent to the sea. This park demonstrates high quality in all areas, and offers a wide range of leisure amenities. Its relaxing position overlooking Morecambe Bay combined with excellent touring facilities mark this park out as special. A 10-acre site with 70 touring pitches and 350 statics.
Sauna, spa bath, steam room & mini-golf.

Leisure: ⋐ ◣ ⋀ Facilities: ⋔ ⊙ ◲ ✳ ᗔ ᒪ ᰔ ⋔
Services: ◲ 回 🔋 🔋 🚽 ⊞ ⊤ ✕ 🏺
→ ∪ ► ♪ ● 🚋 🔣 🔀 🔄

SOUTHPORT

See **Merseyside**

THORNTON CLEVELEYS   Map 07 SD34

► ► ► ► Kneps Farm Holiday Park (SD353429)
River Rd, Stanah FY5 5LR ☎ 01253 823632
Dir: Leave A585 at rdbt onto B5412 to Little Thornton. Turn right after school onto Stanah Rd, leading to River Rd
🚐 £10-£12.50 🚐 £10-£12.50 ▲ £10-£12.50
Open Mar-mid Nov Booking advisable at all times Last arrival 20.00hrs Last departure noon

A quality park with a mixture of hard and grass pitches, adjacent to the River Wyre, and the Wyre Estuary Country Park. This family-run park boasts a luxurious toilet block, and these facilities are always immaculate. The park is in a quiet location, yet handily placed for the attractions of Blackpool and the Fylde Coast. A 10-acre site with 70 touring pitches and 80 statics.

Leisure: ⋀ Facilities: ➡ ⋔ ⊙ ◲ ✳ ᗔ ᒪ ᰔ ⋔
Services: ◲ 回 🔋 🚽 ⊞ ⊤ ➡
→ ► ◉ ♦ ♪ ● ■ 🚋 ⊙ 🔀 🔄

Facilities: ➡ Bath ⋔ Shower ⊙ Electric Shaver ◲ Hairdryer ✳ Ice Pack Facility ᗔ Disabled Facilities ᒪ Public Telephone
ᰔ Shop on Site or within 200yds 🔲 Mobile Shop (calls at least 5 days a week) 戸 BBQ Area 戸 Picnic Area ⋔ Dog Exercise Area

LEICESTERSHIRE

CASTLE DONINGTON   Map 08 SK42

▶ ▶ **Donington Park Farmhouse Hotel (SK414254)**
Melbourne Rd, Isley Walton DE74 2RN
☎ 01332 862409
Dir: M1 junct 24, pass airport to Isley Walton, right towards Melbourne. Park 0.5m on right
🚐 £9-£11 🚎 £9-£11 ▲ £9-£11
Open Mar-Dec (rs winter months hardstanding only) Booking advisable summer season Last arrival 20.00hrs Last departure noon
A developing site at rear of hotel beside Donington Park racecourse. Booking essential on race days, but a quiet rural site at other times. A 6-acre site with 60 touring pitches.
Leisure: ⚠ Facilities: ⌂☉♿❧ Services: 🔌♀🛢✕
→ ↻ ♪ ⊚ 🕳 🔳 🛢 🚐 ■ ☎ 🔵 📦 🔌 🗑

ULLESTHORPE   Map 04 SP58

▶ ▶ *Ullesthorpe Garden Centre (SP515872)*
Lutterworth Rd LE17 5DR ☎ 01455 202144
Dir: From M1 junct 20 take A4303 through Lutterworth, then B577 for 2m, and site just SE of Ullesthorpe village
🚐
Open Mar-Oct Booking advisable Bank Hols & Wknds Last arrival anytime Last departure anytime
A pleasant site next to the garden centre, ideal for the self-contained caravanner, with nature walk and fishing on site. A 7-acre site with 16 touring pitches.
Facilities: ❄ ❧ Services: 🔌🖺🗑✕🍺
→ ↻ ▶ 🛢 ♪ 🛢 🚐 ■ 🔵 📦 🔌 🗑

LINCOLNSHIRE

ANCASTER   Map 08 SK94

▶ ▶ ▶ *Woodland Waters (SK979435)*
Willoughby Rd NG32 3RT ☎ 01400 230888
Dir: On A153 W of X-roads with B6403
🚐
Open all year
A newly-established park built around an attractive lakeside fishing park, in woodland surroundings. Facilities include a brand new toilet block, and a pub/clubhouse with restaurant. A 5-acre site with 62 touring pitches and 4 statics.

ANDERBY   Map 09 TF57

▶ ▶ ▶ *Manor Farm Caravan Park (TF533761)*
Sea Rd PE24 5YB ☎ 01507 490372
Dir: On unclass road off A52 Skegness-Mablethorpe
🚐 🚎 ▲
Open Mar-Nov Booking advisable bank hols
A pleasant farm site in peaceful rural surroundings with newly-equipped toilet facilities. A 3-acre site with 30 touring pitches.
Leisure: ⚠ Facilities: ➡⌂☉🍴❄♿❧🎠❧
Services: 🔌🖺🗑
→ ▶ 🚐 🔵 📦 🔌 🗑

BARTON-UPON-HUMBER   Map 08 TA02

▶ ▶ ▶ **Silver Birches Tourist Park (TA028232)**
Waterside Rd DN18 5BA ☎ 01652 632509
Dir: Follow Bridge Viewing Point signs to Waterside rd, site just past Sloop pub
🚐 fr £6.50 🚎 fr £6.50 ▲ £4.50-£6.50
Open Apr-Oct Booking advisable bank hols Last arrival 23.00hrs Last departure 20.00hrs
A very pleasant, well-screened site, convenient for Humber Bridge as well as Humberside and Lincolnshire. A 2-acre site with 24 touring pitches. Putting green.
Leisure: ⚠ Facilities: ⌂☉❄♿❧🛢🎠
Services: 🔌🛢∅🗑
→ ↻ ♪

BOSTON   Map 08 TF34

▶ ▶ ▶ ▶ *Pilgrims Way (TF358434)*
Church Green Rd, Fishtoft PE21 0QY
☎ 01205 366646
Dir: From Boston travel N on A16(T), turn right onto A52 and right again at Ball House pub to Fishtoft 1m on left
🚐 🚎 ▲
Open Etr & Apr-Sep Booking advisable Bank Holidays Last arrival 20.00hrs Last departure noon
A very attractive site in the gardens of the Grange, with individually screened pitches and purpose-built toilet facilities. This park is ideal for those seeking peace and tranquillity, and is well-placed for touring around the Boston area, and visiting the Pilgrim Fathers' Memorial. A 1-acre site with 22 touring pitches.
Facilities: ⌂☉❄♿❧🛢🎠 Services: 🔌🖺🛢∅🗑
→ ↻ ▶ 🛢♿🚐♪

▶ ▶ ▶ *Midville Caravan Park (TF386578)*
Stickney PE22 8HW ☎ 01205 270316
Dir: From A16(T) at Stickney travel E to Midville. Turn left at bridge (Hobhole Drain), site clearly signed
🚐 🚎 ▲
Open Mar-Nov Booking advisable bank & school hols Last arrival 22.00hrs
A pleasant touring site in a quiet area. A 3-acre site with 24 touring pitches and 40 statics.
Leisure: ⚠ Facilities: ⌂☉❧🚿 Services: 🔌🖺🛢
→ ♪ 🛢

CLEETHORPES   Map 08 TA30

 Thorpe Park Holiday Centre (TA321035)
DN35 0PW ☎ 01472 813395
Dir: Take unclass road off A180 at Cleethorpes, signed Humberstone and Holiday Park
★ 🚐 £11-£20 🚎 £11-£20 ▲
Open Mar-Oct Booking advisable bank hols & school hols Last departure noon
A large static site with new touring facilities, including fully-serviced pitches, adjacent to the beach. This holiday centre offers excellent recreational and leisure activities, including an indoor pool with bar, bowling greens, crazy golf, tennis courts, and a games area. Parts of the site

contd.

Services: 🖺 Toilet Fluid   ✕ Café/ Restaurant   🍺 Fast Food/Takeaway   ♿ Baby Care   🔌 Electric Hook Up   🔵 Launderette   ♀ Licensed Bar   🛢 Calor Gaz   ∅ Camping Gaz   🗑 Battery Charging

overlook the sea. A 100-acre site with 95 touring pitches and 2500 statics.
Crazy golf & pets corner.

Leisure: ≈ ⊛ ⚓ ⚑ **Facilities:** ⋔⚘ ⚒ & ⚓ ⛏ ⊞ ⛆ ⊓

Services: ⚙ ⚏ ⚑ ⓘ ⌀ ⊞ ✕ ⛟

→ ⋃ ⌖ ⊙ ⚒ ⚎ ⚐ ⚑ ⟁ ⊞ ⟠ ⟿ ⊡

FLEET HARGATE   Map 09 TF32

▶ ▶ ▶ **Delph Bank Touring Caravan & Camping Park (TF388248)**
Old Main Rd PE12 8LL ☎ 01406 422910
Dir: Turn off A17 (King's Lynn-Sleaford) into Fleet Hargate and follow signs
★ ⚲ £6.50-£7.50 ⚲ £6.50-£7.50 ▲ £6.50-£7.50
Open Mar-Nov Booking advisable 1-10 May Last arrival 22.30hrs Last departure noon
A quiet, well-screen park with much improved facilities. This attractive grassy site now has new access roads and flower beds, and upgraded electric hook-ups. A 3-acre site with 45 touring pitches.

Facilities: ⋔⊙⚒⚘ & ⚓ ⛏ **Services:** ⚙⚏ⓘ⌀⊞⊓

→ ⚐

MABLETHORPE   Map 09 TF58

▶ ▶ ▶ **Golden Sands Holiday Park (TF501861)**
Quebec Rd LN12 1QJ ☎ 01507 477871
Dir: 1m W of town off A1031 Cleethorpes road
★ ⚲ £9-£23.50 ⚲ £9-£23.50 ▲ £7-£16.50
Open Apr-Oct Booking advisable May/spring bank hol & Jul-Sep Last arrival 20.00hrs Last departure 10.00hrs
A large, well-equipped seaside holiday park with separate touring facilities on two sites, including fully modernised toilets. The first floor entertainment rooms are only accessible via stairs (no lifts). A 127-acre site with 350 touring pitches and 1300 statics.
Mini bowling alley, snooker/pool, indoor fun palace.

Leisure: ≈ ⚓ ⚓ ⚑ **Facilities:** ⋔⚘ & ⚓ ⛏ ⊓

Services: ⚙⚏⚑ⓘ⌀⊓✕⛟

→ ⌖ ⚒ ⚐ ⚑ ⟁ ⊞ ⟿ ⊡

▶ ▶ ▶ **Camping & Caravanning Club Site (TF499839)**
Highfield, Church Ln LN12 2NU ☎ 01507 472374
Dir: On the outskirts of Mablethorpe, on A1104, just after the 'Welcome to Mablethorpe' sign. Continue 800yds to end of lane. Site on right
★ ⚲ £9.80-£12.40 ⚲ £9.80-£12.40 ▲ £9.80-£12.40
Open 20 Mar-27 Sep Booking advisable bank hol & peak periods Last arrival 21.00hrs Last departure noon
Level, mainly grassy site off main road about 1m from sea, with a brand new toilet block. Please see the advertisement on page 14 for details of Club Members' benefits. A 6-acre site with 105 touring pitches.

Leisure: ⚑ **Facilities:** ⋔⊙⚒⚘ & ⚓

Services: ⚙ⓘ⌀⊞⊓

→ ⋃ ⌖ ⚒ ⚐ ⚑ ⟁ ⊞

▶ ▶ ▶ **Kirkstead Holiday Park (TF509835)**
North Rd, Trusthorpe LN12 2QD ☎ 01507 441483
Dir: Situated 1m out of Mablethorpe towards Sutton-on-sea, signed Kirkstead off Alford Rd
★ ⚲ £8.50-£13 ⚲ £8.50-£13 ▲ £7-£13

Open Mar-Nov Booking advisable bank hols & Jul-Aug Last arrival mdnt Last departure 15.00hrs
A pleasant family-run site with a good quality toilet block. A 6-acre site with 60 touring pitches and 70 statics.
Snooker room, childrens room, evening bar meals.

Leisure: ⚓ ⚑ ⊡ **Facilities:** ⋔⊙⚒⚘ & ⚓ ⛏ ⛆ ⊓ ⛏

Services: ⚙⚏⚑ⓘ⌀⊞⛟

→ ⋃ ⌖ ⊙ ⚎ ⚐ ⚑ ⊞ ⟿ ⊟ ⊡ ⟠ ⟿ ⊡

MARKET RASEN   Map 08 TF18

▶ ▶ ▶ **Racecourse Caravan Park (TF123883)**
Legsby Rd LN8 3EA ☎ 01673 842307 & 843434
Dir: Eastern side of Market Rasen on A631, turn right 300yds after lights onto Legsby Rd, site racecourse entrance is 0.75m on left
★ ⚲ £5-£6.20 ⚲ £5-£6.20 ▲ £5.50-£6.70
Open Apr-8 Oct Booking advisable bank hols & race days Last arrival 22.00hrs Last departure 15.00hrs
Well-run, mainly level, grass site on racecourse. A 3-acre site with 55 touring pitches.
Reduced rate for racing & golf

Leisure: ⚓ ⚑ **Facilities:** ⋔⊙⚒ & ⚓ ⛏

Services: ⚙ⓘ⌀⊞⊓

→ ⋃ ⌖ ⚏ ⟿ ⊟ ⟿

▶ ▶ ▶ **Walesby Woodlands Caravan Park (TF117906)**
Walesby Rd LN8 3UN ☎ 01673 843285
Dir: B1203 from Market Rasen to Tealby. After 0.75m, turn left onto the road to Walesby. After 0.25m take lane on left. Site is 150yds on right
★ ⚲ £8-£10 ⚲ £8-£10 ▲ £8-£10
Open Mar-Oct Booking advisable public hols Last arrival 22.00hrs Last departure 17.00hrs
A thoroughly well-planned, immaculate site. A 3-acre site with 60 touring pitches.

Leisure: ⚑ **Facilities:** ⋔⊙⚒ & ⚓

Services: ⚙⚏ⓘ⌀⊞⊓

→ ⋃ ⌖ ⚐ ⟿ ⊟

Facilities: ⚊ Bath ⋔ Shower ⊙ Electric Shaver ⚒ Hairdryer ⚘ Ice Pack Facility & Disabled Facilities ⚓ Public Telephone
⚓ Shop on Site or within 200yds ⊞ Mobile Shop (calls at least 5 days a week) ⛏ BBQ Area ⊓ Picnic Area ⛏ Dog Exercise Area

OLD LEAKE Map 09 TF45

▶ ▶ ▶ **White Cat Park (TF415498)**
Shaw Ln PE22 9LQ ☎ 01205 870121
Dir: Just off A52, 7m NE of Boston
★ ⬛ £6-£7 ⬛ £6-£7 ▲ £6-£7
Open mid Mar-mid Nov Booking advisable bank
hols Last arrival 22.00hrs Last departure 14.00hrs
*An efficient and pleasant site in quiet rural
surroundings. A 2.5-acre site with 40 touring pitches
and 4 statics.*
Leisure: 🅰 Facilities: 🏕⊙☀✆🌄
Services: 🔌🔋⊘🔲🅣
→ ♪

ORBY Map 09 TF46

▶ ▶ ▶ **Heron's Mead Fishing Lake & Touring Park
(TF508673)**
Marsh Ln PE24 5JA ☎ 01754 873357
*Dir: From A158 Lincoln to Skegness road turn left at
rdbt and continue through Orby village for 0.5m*
⬛ ▲
Open Etr-Oct Booking advisable bank hols/school
hols Last arrival 21.00hrs Last departure noon
*A pleasant fishing and touring park with coarse
fishing and an 8-acre woodland walk. Quiet couples
and elderly visitors are particularly welcome. A 4-
acre site with 30 touring pitches.*
Facilities: 🏕⊙🔳☀✆🌄 Services: 🔌🍴
→▶◎🔋♪🔲🌄

SUTTON ST EDMUND Map 08 TF31

▶ ▶ ▶ **Orchard View Caravan & Camping Park
(TF365108)**
Broadgate PE12 0LT ☎ 01945 700482
*Dir: A47 Peterborough to Wisbech road. Turn towards
Wisbech St Mary & Murrow. Through Murrow, over
Double Bridge, then 2nd right. Site 0.5m on right*
★ ⬛ £5.50-£8 ⬛ £5.50-£8 ▲ £5-£8
Open 31 Mar-Oct Booking advisable bank hols &
Spalding Flower Festival Last arrival anytime Last
departure anytime
*A small, family-run park in level meadowland. It is
well screened with maturing trees and has its own
clubhouse. It is continually being improved. A 6-
acre site with 35 touring pitches and 2 statics.
Pets corner & rally field.*
Leisure: 🅰🔲 Facilities: 🏕⊙🔳☀✆🌄🔲🌄
Services: 🔌🔲🅈🔋🔲
→∪▶◎☀♪

SUTTON ST JAMES Map 09 TF31

▶ ▶ ▶ **Foremans Bridge Caravan Park (TF409197)**
PE12 0HU ☎ 01945 440346
Dir: 2m from A17 on B1390
★ ⬛ fr £6 ⬛ fr £6 ▲ fr £6
Open Mar-Nov Booking advisable Last arrival
21.00hrs

*A nicely-kept, trim site with good sanitary
facilities. Good fishing available from the site. A 2.5-
acre site with 40 touring pitches and 7 statics.*
Facilities: 🏕⊙🔳☀✆🌄🔲🌄 Services: 🔌🔲🔋⊘🔲
→▶♪

WOODHALL SPA Map 08 TF16

Bainland Country Park (TF215640)
Horncastle Rd LN10 6UX
☎ 01526 352903 & 353572
Dir: 1.5m from town, on B1191
⬛ £9-£30 ⬛ £9-£30 ▲ £7-£30
Open all year Booking advisable all year Last
arrival 20.00hrs Last departure 11.30hrs
*More a country club than a purely touring park,
this is one of the best equipped parks in the
country with an impressive array of leisure
facilities, combined with high standards of
maintenance. The touring pitches are all
screened by shrubs and trees, with many being
block paved and fully serviced. Children are well
catered for with an outdoor adventure
playground and an indoor soft playroom, and
there is an indoor swimming pool. A 12-acre site
with 100 touring pitches and 10 statics.
Jacuzzi, solarium, sauna, par 3 golf, putting,
boule.*
Leisure: 🎾 ⚲ ⚓ 🅰 🔲 Facilities: ➡🏕⊙🔳☀✆
🌄🔲🌄 Services: 🔌🅈🔋⊘🔲🅣✕🍴➡
→∪▶◎🔋🔲♪ 🔲🔲🔲🔲

*Horncastle Road, Woodhall Spa, Lincolnshire, LN10 6UX
Tel: Woodhall Spa (01526) 352903*

OPEN ALL YEAR

Services: 🅣 Toilet Fluid ✕ Café/ Restaurant 🍴 Fast Food/Takeaway ➡ Baby Care 🔌 Electric Hook Up
🔲 Launderette 🅈 Licensed Bar 🔋 Calor Gaz ⊘ Camping Gaz 🔲 Battery Charging

England

▶ ▶ ▶ **Camping & Caravanning Club Site**
(TF225633)
Wellsyke Ln, Kirkby-on-Bain LN10 6YU
☎ 01526 352911
Dir: From Sleaford or Horncastle take A153 to Haltham.
At garage turn onto side road. Over bridge. Left towards
Kirkby-on-Bain. 1st turn right, signed
★ 🏕 £11.80-£14.90 🚐 £11.80-£14.90 ⛺ £11.80-£14.90
Open 20 Mar-1 Nov Booking advisable bank hols &
Jul-Aug Last arrival 21.00hrs Last departure noon
A pleasant site in silver birch wood and moorland,
with pitches laid out around a central lake. Please
see the advertisement on page 14 for details of Club
Members' benefits. A 6-acre site with 99 touring
pitches.
Facilities: 🏕⊙🔫✳&ᶜ🐾 **Services:** 🔌🛢🖊🚰🗑🚮
→ ᴜ ᴘ🛒♨♨🚮⚡ 🍴🚬

LONDON

E4 CHINGFORD   Map 05 TQ39

▶ ▶ ▶ *Lee Valley Campsite (TQ381970)*
Sewardstone Rd E4 7RA ☎ 020 8529 5689
Dir: From M25 junct 26 to A112 and signed
🚐🚐⛺
Open Apr-Oct Booking advisable bank hols & Jul-
Aug Last arrival 22.00hrs Last departure noon
Well-run useful North London site with excellent
modern facilities and a peaceful atmosphere, with
easy access to town. Overlooking King George's
reservoir and close to Epping Forest. A 12-acre site
with 200 touring pitches.
Leisure: ⚲ **Facilities:** 🏕⊙🔫✳&ᶜ🐾🐾
Services: 🔌🛢🖊🚰🗑Ⓣ
→ ᴜ ᴘ🛒⚡🚮 🍴🚬🚬🚬🚬🍴

N9 EDMONTON   Map 05 TQ39

▶ ▶ ▶ *Lee Valley Leisure Centre Camping &*
Caravan (TQ360945)
Meridian Way N9 0AS ☎ 020 8803 6900 & 8345 6666
Dir: from M25/J25, A10 South, first left, approx 5m to
Leisure Centre. From A406 (North Circular), N on A1010,
left after 0.25m, right (Pickets Lock Lne)
🚐🚐⛺
Booking advisable Jul-Aug Last arrival 22.00hrs Last
departure noon
A pleasant open site tucked away behind a large
sporting complex with use of swimming pool, roller
skating and golf driving range. Very good toilet
facilities, and handy for London. A 4.5-acre site with
160 touring pitches.
Membership of adjacent sports complex.
Leisure: ⚲ ♠ ⚲ **Facilities:** 🏕⊙🔫✳&ᶜ🐾
Services: 🔌🛢🖊🗑🖊Ⓣ✕🛁🚮
→ ᴘ🛒🔧♨🚮⚡ 🍴🚬🚬🚬🚬🍴

The Perfect Place to Stay

There are 4 camping and caravan sites to
choose from in Lee Valley Regional Park

Lee Valley Leisure
Centre Campsite -
North London
On the doorstep of a
large leisure centre and
only 34 minutes from
the West End.
Tel: 020 8803 6900

Lee Valley Caravan Park -
Herts
Enjoy the peace and
tranquillity with some
angling, walking or
cycling nearby.
Tel: 01992 462090

Lee Valley Campsite -
Chingford, London
Easily accessible from the
M25 and just 45 minutes
from central London.
Tel: 020 8529 5689

Lee Valley Cycle Circuit -
Leyon, East London
4 miles from the Tower
of London and set in 40
acres of parkland
Tel: 020 8534 6085

Lee Valley Park

For more information call our Information Centre
on **01992 702200** or find us
on the web at: **www.leevalleypark.org.uk**

MERSEYSIDE

SOUTHPORT   Map 07 SD31

▶ ▶ ▶ *Hurlston Hall Country Caravan Park*
(SD398107)
Southport Rd L40 8HB ☎ 01704 841064
Dir: On A570, 3m from Ormskirk towards Southport
🚐🚐⛺
Open Etr-Oct Booking advisable bank hols Last
arrival 21.00hrs Last departure 17.00hrs ⚹
A peaceful tree-lined touring park next to a static
site in attractive countryside about a 10-minute
drive from Southport. This caravan park is maturing
well, with growing trees and coarse fishing lakes on
site. The well-maintained facilities are a credit to the
enthusiastic owners. A 5-acre site with 60 touring
pitches and 68 statics.
Coarse fishing
Leisure: ⚲ **Facilities:** 🏕🔫&ᶜ **Services:** 🔌🛢🖊🖊
→ ᴘ🚮

▶ ▶ ▶ *Willowbank Holiday Home & Touring Park*
(SD305110)
Coastal Rd, Ainsdale PR8 3ST ☎ 01704 571566
Dir: Leave A56(T) at traffic lights onto coastal road to
Southport. Site 300mtrs from lights on left before
railway bridge
🚐🚐⛺
Booking advisable bank hols Last arrival 22.00hrs
Last departure 16.00hrs

Facilities: 🚮 Bath 🏕 Shower ⊙ Electric Shaver 🔫 Hairdryer ✳ Ice Pack Facility & Disabled Facilities ᶜ Public Telephone
🚮 Shop on Site or within 200yds 🗑 Mobile Shop (calls at least 5 days a week) 🍴 BBQ Area 🌲 Picnic Area 🐾 Dog Exercise Area

Set in a wooded clearing on a nature reserve, this site is just off the coastal road to Southport. A 6-acre site with 64 touring pitches and 102 statics.

Leisure: 🅐 **Facilities:** 🏵⊙🔾♿🕭🎠🏕

Services: 🔌🗄🛢

→ ∪ ► ⛽ 🛒 🍴 🏪 ● 🚬 ▦ 🏧 🗐

NORFOLK

BARNEY   Map 09 TF93

► ► ► ► **The Old Brick Kilns (TG007328)**
Little Barney Ln, Barney NR21 0NL ☎ 01328 878305
Dir: Follow brown tourist signs from A148 (Fakenham-Cromer) to Barney, then Little Barney
🚐 £9.25-£11.75 🚍 £9.25-£11.75 🛆 £9.25-£11.75
Open 20 Feb-6 Jan (rs low season bar food/takeaway selected nights only) Booking advisable bank hols & Jul-Aug Last arrival 22.00hrs Last departure noon
A secluded and peaceful park approached via a quiet leafy country lane. The park is on two levels with its own boating and fishing pool and many mature trees. Excellent, well-planned toilet facilities can be found in two blocks, and a short dog walk. A 6.5-acre site with 60 touring pitches.
Boules, outdoor draughts/chess, family games area.

Leisure: ♠🅐🎱 **Facilities:** 🏵⊙🔾✳♿🕭🏪🍴🎠🏕

Services: 🔌🗄🍽🛢∅🗄🔲✖🚼

→ 🍴 ● 🚬 ▣ 🏧 🗐

BELTON   Map 05 TG40

► ► ► **Rose Farm Touring & Camping Park (TG488033)**
Stepshort NR31 9JS ☎ 01493 780896
Dir: Follow signs to Belton off A143, right at lane called Stepshort, site 1st on right
★ 🚐 £5-£7 🚍 £5-£7 🛆 £5-£7
Open all year Booking advisable Jul-Aug
A very neat site with a good toilet block and tidy facilities. A 6-acre site with 80 touring pitches.

Leisure: ♠🅐🎱 **Facilities:** 🏵⊙✳♿🏪🕭

Services: 🔌🗄🛢∅🗄

→ ∪ ► 🔾 🍴

► ► ► **Wild Duck Holiday Park (TG475028)**
Howards Common NR31 9NE ☎ 01493 780268
Dir: Signed from A143
★ 🚐 £10-£20 🚍 £8-£17 🛆
Open Mar-Oct (rs Off peak Restricted times of certain venues) Booking advisable Jun-Aug & school holidays Last arrival 23.00hrs Last departure noon
This is a large holiday complex with facilities for all ages indoors and out. Level grassy site in forest with small cleared areas for tourers and well laid out facilities. A 60-acre site with 240 touring pitches and 370 statics.
Sauna, jacuzzi

Leisure: 🏊🎿🎱♠🅐 **Facilities:** 🏵⊙🔾✳🕭🏪🎠

Services: 🔌🗄🍽🛢∅🔲✖🍴

→ ∪ ► 🔾 ⛽ 🛒 🍴 ● 🚬 ▦ 🏧 🗐

CAISTER-ON-SEA   Map 09 TG51

► ► ► **Grasmere Caravan Park (TG521115)**
9 Bultitude's Loke, Yarmouth Rd NR30 5DH
☎ 01493 720382
Dir: From A149 at Stadium rdbt after 0.5m sharp left turn just past petrol station
★ 🚐 £5.75-£7.95 🚍 £5.75-£7.95
Open Apr-Oct Booking advisable school & bank hols Last arrival 22.00hrs Last departure 11.00hrs ✍
Mainly level grass and gravel site with mature trees. Set in meadowland in an urban area with access to A149. A 2-acre site with 46 touring pitches and 62 statics.

Leisure: 🅐 **Facilities:** 🏵⊙✳♿🔾🏪

Services: 🔌🗄🛢∅🗄

→ ∪ ► 🔾 🏪 🍴 ● 🚬 🏧 🗐

► ► ► **Old Hall Leisure Park (TG521122)**
High St NR30 5JL ☎ 01493 720400
Dir: Opposite church
★ 🚐 £8-£13 🚍 £8-£13
Open Spring bank hol wk & 22 Jun-1 Sep (rs Apr-21 Jun pool closed, bar/rest limited opening) Booking advisable Spring bank hol & Jul-Aug Last arrival mdnt Last departure 10.00hrs ✍
A small site at rear of hotel on main street (B1159) with a neat and attractive layout. Convenient for shops and beach. A 2-acre site with 35 touring pitches and 38 statics.

Leisure: 🎿🅐 **Facilities:** 🏵⊙🔾✳🔾

Services: 🔌🗄🍽🛢🗄✖

→ ∪ ► ⊚ ⛽ 🔾 🏪 🍴 🛒 ● 🚬 ▦ 🏧 🗐

CAWSTON   Map 09 TG12

► ► ► **Haveringland Hall Park (TG153213)**
NR10 4PN ☎ 01603 981302
Dir: Turn off A140 onto B1149 towards Holt. Continue through Horsford then left and follow signs for 4m then right through lodge gates
★ 🚐 £7.50-£8 🚍 fr £7.50 🛆 fr £6.50
Open Mar-Oct Booking advisable public hol wks & Jul-Aug Last arrival 21.00hrs Last departure noon
A very pleasant park set in 110 acres of woodland and meadowland with direct access to its own 14-acre fishing lake. Spacious, well-drained and level pitches are located in different areas, with interesting mature trees and some hardstandings. A 110-acre site with 40 touring pitches and 50 statics. 14 acre fishing lake.

Facilities: 🏵⊙✳🔾🕭🎠🏕 **Services:** 🔌🗄🛢∅🗄

→ ∪ ► ⛽ 🍴 🏪 ● 🚬 🗐

CLIPPESBY   Map 09 TG41

► ► ► **Clippesby Holidays (TG423147)**
Clippesby Hall NR29 3BL ☎ 01493 367800
Dir: From A47 follow tourist signs for The Broads. At Acle rdbt take A1064, after 2m left onto B1152, 0.5m turn left opposite village sign, 400yds on right
★ 🚐 £8.60-£15.75 🚍 £8.60-£15.75 🛆 £8.60-£15.75
Open Etr wk, 5 May-23 Sep (rs Mayday wknd-24 May some facilities may close) Booking advisable school hols Last arrival 17.30hrs Last departure 11.00hrs
contd.

A lovely country house estate with vans hidden among trees and a friendly welcome. A new café and crazy family golf. A 30-acre site with 100 touring pitches.
Putting, bicycle hire & tea room.

Leisure: ⚲ ⚲ ● ⚠ **Facilities:** ſ ☉ ⚲ ☀ ♿ ⚲ ᵇ ⚲ ⛳
Services: ⚲ ⚲ ⚲ ⚲ ⚲ ⚲ ⚲ ✗
→ ∪ ☉ ⚲ ⚲ ⚲ ⚲ 📷 📷 📷 📷 ⚲

CROMER   Map 09 TG24

► ► ► ► **Seacroft Camping Park (TG206424)**
Runton Rd NR27 9NJ ☎ 01263 511722
Dir: 1m W of cromer on A149 coast road
⚲ ⚲ ▲
Open Mar-Oct Booking advisable school hols, 22-31 May & 4 Sep Last arrival 23.00hrs Last departure noon

A very good touring site, well laid out and landscaped. Touring pitches are well screened for privacy, and there is a separate large playing field with children's play equipment. Toilets and showers in the sanitary buildings are tiled and spotless. There is a heated swimming pool and bar/restaurant. A 5-acre site with 120 touring pitches.
Baby change.

Leisure: ⚲ ● ⚠ ▢ **Facilities:** ſ ☉ ⚲ ☀ ♿ ⚲ ᵇ ⚲ 📷 ⛳
Services: ⚲ ⚲ ⚲ ⚲ ⚲ ⚲ ⚲ ✗ ⚲
→ ∪ ☉ ⚲ ⚲ ⚲ ⚲ 📷 📷 📷 📷 ⚲

► ► ► **Forest Park Caravan Site (TG233405)**
Northrepps Rd NR27 OJR ☎ 01263 513290
Dir: A140 from Norwich, left at T-junc signed Cromer, right signed Northrepps, right then immediate left, left at T-junc and park is on right
⚲ £8.50-£12.50 ⚲ £8.50-£12.50 ▲ £8.50-£12.50

Open Apr-Oct Booking advisable Etr, Spring bank hol & Jul-Aug Last arrival 22.00hrs Last departure 14.00hrs
Surrounded by forest, this gently sloping parkland offers a wide choice of pitches. An 85-acre site with 344 touring pitches and 372 statics.
BMX track.

Leisure: ⚲ ● ⚠ **Facilities:** ſ ☉ ⚲ ☀ ⚲ ᵇ 📷
Services: ⚲ ⚲ ⚲ ⚲ ⚲ ⚲ ⚲ ✗
→ ∪ ☉ ⚲ ⚲ ⚲ ⚲ 📷 📷 📷 📷 ⚲

DISS

See **Scole**

ERPINGHAM   Map 09 TG13

► ► ► **Little Haven Caravan & Camping Park (TG204323)**
The Street NR11 7QD ☎ 01263 768959
Dir: From A140 6m S of Cromer turn by the Horseshoes public house signed Erpingham. Site 200yds on right
⚲ £7.50-£9 ⚲ £7.50-£9 ▲ £7.50-£9
Open Mar-Oct Booking advisable Bank holidays Last arrival 21.00hrs Last departure 14.00hrs
A delightful small family-run park surrounded by hawthorn hedges and trees, with good facilities. The large pitches are arranged around a central grass area with flower beds and pergola with

---

Facilities: ⚲ Bath ſ Shower ☉ Electric Shaver ⚲ Hairdryer ☀ Ice Pack Facility ♿ Disabled Facilities ⚲ Public Telephone
⚲ Shop on Site or within 200yds ⚲ Mobile Shop (calls at least 5 days a week) ᵇ BBQ Area 📷 Picnic Area ⛳ Dog Exercise Area

seating. An ideal park for relaxing, and for this reason children are not accepted. A 3-acre site with 25 touring pitches.
Lending library, tourist info, milk, papers
Facilities: **Services:**

FAKENHAM — Map 09 TF92

Caravan Club M.V.C. Site (TF926288)
Fakenham Racecourse NR21 7NY ☎ 01328 862388
Dir: *0.75m SW of Fakenham off A1065 Swaffham road*
Open all year (rs race days) Booking advisable Etr & May-Aug Last arrival anytime Last departure noon
A level grassy site with mature trees. Tourers move on race days to centre of course, and have free racing. An 11.5-acre site with 120 touring pitches.
TV aerial hook-ups
Leisure: **Facilities:**
Services:

FREE with YOUR HOLIDAY

★ FREE ★ Five Star Studded Entertainment
★ FREE ★ Indoor Tropical Waterworld
★ FREE ★ Sport and Fitness Fun
★ FREE ★ Kid's Club and Nursery
Plus much, much more!

Tops for Tourers
OVER 250 ALL ELECTRIC SITES
AWNINGS FREE
GRASS & HARD STANDINGS
MODERN SHOWER & TOILET BLOCKS
FREE CAR PARKING
GAS CYLINDER REFILLS ON SITE
NEW SUPER PITCH
Full mains service pitch with hedged, landscaped and awning areas

ROSE AWARD 2001

CALL FOR A FREE BROCHURE QUOTING REF:4,
TEL: 01493 857231
4 Acle New Road Great Yarmouth Norfolk NR30 1TB

GREAT YARMOUTH — Map 05 TG50

See also **Caister-on-Sea**

Vauxhall Holiday Park (TG520083)
4 Acle New Rd NR30 1TB
☎ 01493 857231
Dir: *Close to A47*
★ £13-£24 £13-£24 £13-£24
Open Etr then mid May-Sep Booking advisable mid Jul-Aug Last arrival 21.00hrs Last departure 10.00hrs
A very large holiday complex with plenty of entertainment and access to beach, river, estuary, lake and main A47. The touring pitches are laid out in four separate areas, each with its own amenity block, and all arranged around the main entertainment. A 40-acre site with 256 touring pitches and 421 statics.
Childrens pool, Sauna, Solarium, Fitness centre.
Leisure: **Facilities:**
Services:

FAKENHAM RACECOURSE

Caravan & Camping Site
The ideal choice for your Norfolk holiday
A country Site. Near the sea.

Set in beautiful countryside and sheltered by tall conifers, the grounds and modern facilities are excellently maintained. Pitches accommodating touring caravans, motorvans and tents. Ideally located for visiting Norfolk's coastal resorts, stately homes, wildlife and bird sanctuaries and many other attractions.
From £8.50 to £11.00 for 2 adults per night
★★★ TOURING PARK English Tourism Council
Fakenham Racecourse Caravan and Camping Site
The Racecourse, Fakenham, Norfolk NR21 7NY
Tel: 01328 862388 Fax: 01328 855908

HUNSTANTON — Map 09 TF64

Searles of Hunstanton (TF671400)
South Beach PE36 5BB
☎ 01485 534211 & 532342 ext 100
Dir: *A149 from King's Lynn to Hunstanton. At rdbt follow signs for South Beach. At 2nd rdbt go straight on. Searles is on left*
★ £9-£22 £10-£25 £7-£18
Open Etr/Mar-Nov (rs Mar-May & Oct-Nov outdoor pool closed) Booking advisable bank

contd.

hols & Jul-Aug Last arrival 20.45hrs Last departure 11.00hrs

A large seaside holiday complex with well-managed facilities, adjacent to sea and beach. The tourers have their own areas, including two excellent toilet blocks, and pitches are individually lined with small maturing shrubs for privacy. A 50-acre site with 350 touring pitches and 450 statics.

Stables, entertainment programme & hire shop.

Leisure: ≷ ⋟ ◖ ◣ ⚲ 瓜 **Facilities:** ➡ ⋔ ☉ ℚ ✳ ⅍ ℄ 🏪 🛒 🗂 🐾 **Services:** 🗪 🗒 ♈ ⅊ ⌀ ☐ ⊤ ✕ ♨ → ∪ ⌖ ◉ ♿ ⚓ ⅏ ♨ 🚐 ▨▨ 🗂

KING'S LYNN

See **Narborough & Stanhoe**

MUNDESLEY   Map 09 TG33

▶ ▶ *Links Caravan Site (TG305365)*
Links Rd NR11 8AE ☎ 01263 720665
Dir: From B1159 at Mundesley turn into Church Road
🚐 🚐 Å
Open Etr-1st wk Oct Booking advisable bank hols & peak season Last arrival 22.00hrs Last departure noon
A pleasant site on a south-facing slope with level pitches, offering distant rural views. Adjacent to golf club. A 2-acre site with 32 touring pitches.
Leisure: 瓜 **Facilities:** ⋔ ☉ ✳ **Services:** 🗪 → ∪ ⌖ ◉ ♿ 🗂 🏪

NARBOROUGH   Map 09 TF71

▶ ▶ ▶ **Pentney Park (TF742141)**
Gayton Rd, Pentney PE32 1HU
☎ 01760 337479 & 709120
Dir: Adjacent to A47 Swaffham-King's Lynn road
🚐 🚐 Å
Open all year (rs Nov-Feb outdoor swimming pool closed) Booking advisable bank hols Last arrival 22.30hrs Last departure 11.00hrs
A large family touring site set in woods and meadowland. A 16-acre site with 200 touring pitches.
Leisure: ≷ ⋟ ◖ 瓜 **Facilities:** ⋔ ☉ ℚ ✳ ⅍ ℄ 🏪 🐾 **Services:** 🗪 🗒 ⅊ ⌀ ☐ ⊤ ✕ ♨ ➡ → ♿ 🚐 ▨▨ 🗂

NORTH WALSHAM   Map 09 TG23

▶ ▶ ▶ ▶ **Two Mills Touring Park (TG291286)**
Yarmouth Rd NR28 9NA ☎ 01692 405829
Dir: 1m S of North Walsham on Old Yarmouth Road past police station and hospital on left
★ 🚐 £7.50-£10.50 🚐 £7.50-£10.50 Å £7.50-£10.50
Booking advisable Jul & Aug Last arrival 20.30hrs Last departure noon
Situated in superb countryside, in an ideally peaceful spot which is also convenient for touring. Some fully serviced pitches have panoramic views over the site, and the layout of pitches and facilities is excellent. This park is particularly attractive to the mature caravanner since it does not accept children.

Facilities: ➡ Bath ⋔ Shower ☉ Electric Shaver ℚ Hairdryer ✳ Ice Pack Facility ⅍ Disabled Facilities ℄ Public Telephone 🏪 Shop on Site or within 200yds 🛒 Mobile Shop (calls at least 5 days a week) 🗂 BBQ Area 🗂 Picnic Area 🐾 Dog Exercise Area

The very friendly and helpful owners keep the park in immaculate condition. A 5-acre site with 50 touring pitches.

Leisure: ▢ Facilities: ♠⊙🐾⚒⚓🏕🛖
Services: ⚡🖥🍴🏮⛽⊞🔩 ●● 🚐 ▦ ▧ 🔧

NORWICH — Map 05 TG20

▶ ▶ **Camping & Caravanning Club Site (TG237063)**
Martineau Ln NR1 2HX ☎ 01603 620060
Dir: From A47 join A146 towards City Centre. Left at lights to next set of lights, under low bridge to Cock Public House, turn left. Site 150yds on right
★ 🚐 £10.60-£13.90 🚐 £10.60-£13.90 ▲ £10.60-£13.90
Open 20 Mar-1 Sep Booking advisable bank hols & Jul-Aug Last arrival 21.00hrs Last departure noon
A small site on the outskirts of Norwich close to a river and screened by trees from the city. Please see the advertisement on page 14 for details of Club Members' benefits. A 2.5-acre site with 50 touring pitches.
Fishing

Facilities: ♠⊙🐾🌸⚒🛒🏕🛖 Services: ⚡🖥🔩⊞
→ ▶♠☀️🐕🍴 ●● 🚐

SADDLE BOW — Map 09 TF61

▶ ▶ ▶ **Bank Farm Caravan Park (TF593157)**
Fallow Pipe Rd PE34 3AS ☎ 01553 617305
Dir: Leave A47 at signs for Saddlebow. In the village cross over river bridge. After 1m turn right into Fallow Pipe Road. Farm is at end of road
★ 🚐 £5-£6.50 🚐 £5-£6.50
Open Mar-Oct Booking advisable Bank holidays Last arrival 23.00hrs Last departure 11.00hrs
A very pleasant, quiet park on a working farm on the banks of the River Ouse. Pitches are well laid out among mature trees, and facilities are housed in converted farm buildings. A 1.5-acre site with 15 touring pitches.
Putting green

Leisure: ♣ Facilities: ♠⊙🐾🌸⚒🛒🔩
Services: ⚡🔩⊞🔲
→ 🍴

ST JOHN'S FEN END — Map 09 TF51

▶ ▶ **Virginia Lake Caravan Park (TF538113)**
Sneeth Rd, Marshland PE14 8JF
☎ 01945 430332 & 430676
Dir: From A47 E of Wisbech follow Tourist Board signs to Terrington St John. Park situated on the left
★ 🚐 £6.50-£8.50 🚐 £6.50-£8.50 ▲ £6.50-£8.50
Open all year Booking advisable
A well-established park beside a 2-acre fishing lake with good facilities for both anglers and tourers. A clubhouse serves a selection of meals and offers weekend entertainment. A good base for touring west Norfolk. A 5-acre site with 50 touring pitches and 4 statics.
Fishing

Leisure: ♨ Facilities: ⊙🐾⚒🛒🔩🏕🛖
Services: ⚡🖥🍴🔩✕🍴
→ ○▶⊚🎱

SANDRINGHAM — Map 09 TF62

▶ ▶ ▶ ▶ **Camping & Caravanning Club Site (TF683274)**
The Sandringham Estate, Double Lodges PE35 6EA
☎ 01485 542555
Dir: From A148 turn left onto B1440 signposted West Newton. Follow signs to site. Or take A149 turning left and following signs to site
★ 🚐 £13.90-£14.90 🚐 £13.90-£14.90 ▲ £13.90-£14.90
Open 21 Feb-29 Nov Booking advisable bank hols & high season Last arrival 21.00hrs Last departure noon
A prestige park, very well landscaped and laid out in mature woodland, with toilets and other buildings blending in with the scenery. There are plenty of walks from the site, and this is a good touring base for the rest of Norfolk. Please see the advertisement on page 14 for details of Club Members' benefits. A 28-acre site with 262 touring pitches.

Leisure: ⛰ Facilities: ♠⊙🐾🌸⚒🛒🔩🛖
Services: ⚡🖥🔩⚓🔧
→ ○▶⊚♨🍴 ●● 🚐

SCOLE — Map 05 TM17

▶ ▶ ▶ *Willows Camping & Caravan Park (TM146789)*
Diss Rd IP21 4DH ☎ 01379 740271
Dir: At Scole rdbt on A140 turn onto A1066, site 150yds on left
🚐 🚐 ▲

Open May-Sep Booking advisable Spring bank hol & school hols Last arrival 23.00hrs Last departure noon
A quiet garden on the banks of the River Waveney, bordered by willow trees. The new owners are planning many improvements. A 4-acre site with 32 touring pitches.

Leisure: ⛰ Facilities: ♠⊙🌸 Services: ⚡🔩⚓⊞🔲
→ ▶🍴⊚🛒

SCRATBY — Map 09 TG51

▶ ▶ ▶ **Scratby Hall Caravan Park (TG501155)**
NR29 3PH ☎ 01493 730283
Dir: Signed off B1159
★ 🚐 £4.95-£10.50 🚐 £4.95-£10.50 ▲ £4.95-£10.50
Open Spring bank hol-mid Sep (rs Etr-Spring bank hol & mid Sep-Oct reduced hours & shop closed) Booking advisable Spring bank hol wk & Jul-Aug

contd.

England

Scratby Hall Caravan Park
Last arrival 22.00hrs Last departure noon
An immaculate grass site with very tidy toilet block and new children's play area, close to beach and the Norfolk Broads. A 5-acre site with 108 touring pitches.
Washing-up & food preparation room.
Leisure: ♦ ⚠ **Facilities:** ⋒ ⊙ ☜ ✳ ⚲ ⚭ ☎
Services: 🚱 📧 ⓘ ∅ 🔲 ⓣ
→ ∪ ▶ ✕ ♪

SNETTISHAM　　　　Map 09 TF63

► ► ► **Diglea Caravan & Camping Park (TF656336)**
Beach Rd PE31 7RB ☎ 01485 541367
Dir: Turn left at Snettisham beach sign. Site on left 1.5m from turning
★ 🚐 £6.50-£10 🚐 £6.50-£10 ▲ £6.50-£10
Open Apr-Oct Booking advisable bank hols & mid Jul-Aug Last arrival 22.30hrs Last departure noon
A mainly grassy site with mature trees and shrubs - rural yet close to the beach. A 15-acre site with 200 touring pitches and 150 statics.
Leisure: ♦ ⚠ **Facilities:** ⋒ ⊙ ✳ ⚭ ☎ 🏠 ★
Services: 🚱 📧 ⓧ ⓘ ∅ 🔲 ⓣ ⇶
→ ∪ ♨ ♪

STANHOE　　　　Map 09 TF83

► ► ► **The Rickels Caravan & Camping Park (TF794355)**
Bircham Rd PE31 8PU ☎ 01485 518671
Dir: From King's Lynn take A148 to Hillington, then B1153 to Great Bircham. Pick up B1155 to X-roads, straight over, site is 100yds on left
★ 🚐 £7-£8.50 🚐 £7-£8.50 ▲ £7-£8.50
Open all year Booking advisable Bank holidays Last arrival 21.00hrs Last departure 11.00hrs
Set in three acres of grassland, with good open views and a pleasant, relaxing atmosphere. The land is slightly sloping with some level areas and sheltering for tents. Children using the play equipment can be safely watched from all pitches. A 3-acre site with 30 touring pitches.
Leisure: ⚠ ❑ **Facilities:** ⋒ ⊙ ✳ ☎ ★
Services: 🚱 ⓘ ∅ 🔲

SYDERSTONE　　　　Map 09 TF83

► ► ► ***The Garden Caravan Site (TF812337)***
Barmer Hall Farm PE31 8SR ☎ 01485 578220
Dir: Signed off B1454 at Barmer between A148 and Dorking, 1m NW of Syderstone
🚐 🚐 ▲
Open Mar-Nov Booking advisable Last dep noon
In the tranquil setting of a former walled garden beside a large farmhouse, with mature trees and shrubs, and surrounded by woodland, a secluded site. A 3.5-acre site with 30 touring pitches.
Facilities: ⋒ ⊙ ☜ ✳ ⚭ ☎ 🏠 ★ **Services:** 🚱 ⓘ 🔲
→ ∪ ▶ ⚭

TRIMINGHAM　　　　Map 09 TG23

► ► ► **Woodlands Caravan Park (TG274388)**
NR11 8AL ☎ 01263 579208
Dir: 4m SE on B1159 coast road
★ 🚐 £7.95-£10.95 🚐 £7.95-£10.95
Open Apr-Oct Booking advisable public hols & Jul-Aug Last arrival 23.00hrs Last departure noon

A pleasant woodland site close to the sea but well sheltered from winds. Pitches in open areas among the trees, and good clubhouse with bowling green. A 10-acre site with 85 touring pitches and 179 statics.
Leisure: ♦ ⚠ **Facilities:** ⋒ ⊙ ☜ ✳ ⚭ ☎ 🏠 ☐
Services: 🚱 ⓧ ⓘ 🔲 ⓧ ⇶
→ ∪ ▶ ⚭ ♪ 🍺 ☰ ⚏ 🛒 ⓖ

WEST RUNTON　　　　Map 09 TG14

► ► ► **Camping & Caravanning Club Site (TG189419)**
Holgate Ln NR27 9NW ☎ 01263 837544
Dir: On A148 from King's Lynn, approaching West Runton turn left at Roman Camp Inn. Site entry track 0.5m long is right at crest of hill
★ 🚐 £13.90-£14.90 🚐 £13.90-£14.90 ▲ £13.90-£14.90
Open 20 Mar-1 Nov Booking advisable bank hols & peak periods Last arrival 21.00hrs Last departure noon
A lovely, well-kept site with some gently sloping pitches on pleasantly undulating ground. Surrounded by woodland. Please see the advertisement on page 14 for details of Club Members' benefits. A 15-acre site with 225 touring pitches.
Leisure: ⚠ **Facilities:** ⋒ ⊙ ☜ ✳ ⚭ ☎ ★
Services: 🚱 📧 🔲 ⓣ ⇶
→ ∪ ▶ ♨ 🍺 ♪ 🍺 ☰

Facilities: ⇶ Bath ⋒ Shower ⊙ Electric Shaver ☜ Hairdryer ✳ Ice Pack Facility ⚭ Disabled Facilities ☎ Public Telephone ⚭ Shop on Site or within 200yds ⚏ Mobile Shop (calls at least 5 days a week) 🏠 BBQ Area ☐ Picnic Area ★ Dog Exercise Area

WORTWELL   Map 05 TM28

► ► ► ► **Little Lakeland Caravan Park**
(TM279849)
IP20 0EL ☎ 01986 788646
Dir: From W leave A143 at sign for Wortwell. In village turn right 300yds past garage. From E on A143, left onto B1062, then right. After 0.25m turn left
⊞ £7.80-£9.80 ⊞ £7.80-£9.80
Open Mar-Oct (rs Mar-Etr restricted laundry facilities) Booking advisable bank hols & peak periods Last arrival 22.00hrs Last departure noon
A well-kept and pretty site built round a fishing lake, and accessed by a lake-lined drive. The individual pitches are sited in hedged enclosures for complete privacy, and the purpose-built toilet facilities are excellent. A 4.5-acre site with 40 touring pitches and 16 statics.
Library & fishing on site.
Leisure: ⚠ **Facilities:** ฿ ☉ ℚ ☀ ⚅ ☎
Services: ◖ ▮ ⌀ ⊞ ▯
→ ∪ ▶ ⤳ ✔

NORTHAMPTONSHIRE

THRAPSTON   Map 04 SP97

► ► **Mill Marina (SP994781)**
Midland Rd NN14 4JR ☎ 01832 732850
Dir: Take Thrapston exit from A14 or A605. Site signposted
★ ⊞ £9.80-£10.80 ⊞ £8.80-£9.80 ▲ £7.80-£8.80
Open Apr-Dec (rs Jan-Mar) Booking advisable public hols & summer wknds Last arrival 21.00hrs Last departure 18.00hrs
Level riverside site with mature trees and bushes, with pleasure trips by boat from site. An 8-acre site with 45 touring pitches and 6 statics.
Slipway for boats & canoes, coarse fishing on site
Facilities: ฿ ☉ ℚ ☀ ⚅ ⊞ ⌂ ✗ **Services:** ◖ ▯ ⌛ ▮ ⌀ ⊞ ▯
→ ∪ ⚄ ✔ ☎

NORTHUMBERLAND

ALWINTON   Map 12 NT90

► ► ► *Clennell Hall (NT928072)*
Clennell NE65 7BG ☎ 01669 650341
Dir: From B6341 take unclass road signed Alwinton and caravan signs
⊞ ⊞ ▲
Open Mar-Jan (rs Feb by arrangement only)
Booking advisable summer & bank hols Last arrival 23.00hrs Last departure 16.00hrs
A tranquil rural site on the fringe of the National Park NW of Rothbury. A 14.5-acre site with 50 touring pitches and 18 statics.
Leisure: ⤳ ⚠ ☐ **Facilities:** ฿ ☉ ☀ ⚅ ⌛ ☎ ⌂
Services: ◖ ▯ ⌛ ▮ ⌀ ✗ ☎
→ ∪ ✔

BAMBURGH   Map 12 NU13

► ► ► *Glororum Caravan Park (NU166334)*
Glororum Farm NE69 7AW ☎ 01668 214457
Dir: Leave A1 at junct B1341 (Purdy's Lodge), in 3.5m turn left onto unclass rd. Site 300yds on left
⊞ £8-£10 ⊞ £8-£10 ▲ £8-£10
Open Apr-Oct Booking advisable school hols Last arrival 22.00hrs Last departure 11.00hrs
A well-run site with good facilities, pleasantly situated off B1341, 1m W of Bamburgh. The open countryside setting gives views of Bamburgh Castle and surrounding farmland. A 6-acre site with 100 touring pitches and 150 statics.
Leisure: ⚠ **Facilities:** ฿ ☉ ℚ ☀ ⚅ ☎ ⌂ ☂
Services: ◖ ▯ ▮ ⌀ ⊞
→ ∪ ▶ ☉ ⚄ ⤳ ✔

► ► ► *Waren Caravan Park (NU155343)*
Waren Mill NE70 7EE ☎ 01668 214366
Dir: 2m E of town on B1342. From A1 turn onto B1342 signed Bamburgh and take unclass road past Waren Mill, signed Budle
⊞ ⊞ ▲
Open Apr-Oct Booking advisable Spring bank hol & Jul-Aug Last arrival 20.00hrs Last departure noon
Attractive seaside site close to beach, surrounded by a slightly sloping grassy embankment affording shelter for caravans. Immaculate sanitary facilities. A 4-acre site with 120 touring pitches and 300 statics.
100 acres of private heathland.
Leisure: ⤳ ◣ ⚠ **Facilities:** ฿ ☉ ℚ ☀ ⚅ ⌛ ☎ ⌂ ☂
Services: ◖ ▯ ⌛ ▮ ⌀ ⊞ ▯ ✗ ☎
→ ∪ ▶ ☉ ✔ 🅿 ▆ ▆ ▆ ▆ ◻

BEADNELL   Map 12 NU22

► ► **Camping & Caravanning Club Site (NU231297)**
NE67 5BX ☎ 01665 720586
Dir: Leave A1 & follow B1430 signed Seahouses. At Beadnell ignore signs for Beadnell Village. Site on left after village, just beyond the left bend
★ ⊞ £10.60-£13.90 ▲ £10.60-£13.90
Open 7 Apr-25 Sep Booking advisable bank hols & Jul-Aug Last arrival 21.00hrs Last departure noon
Level, grassy site set in coastal area with access to sea, beach and main road. No caravans are accepted. Please see the advertisement on page 14 for details of Club Members' benefits. A 14-acre site with 150 touring pitches.
Facilities: ฿ ☉ ℚ ☀ ⚅ ☎ **Services:** ▯ ▮ ⌀
→ ∪ ▶ ⚄ ⤳ ✔ ▆ ▆

BELLINGHAM   Map 12 NY88

► ► ► ► **Brown Rigg Caravan & Camping Park (NY835826)**
NE48 2JY ☎ 01434 220175
Dir: On B6320 0.5m S of Bellingham
★ ⊞ £7.50-£8.50 ⊞ £7.50-£8.50 ▲ £7.50-£8.50
Open wk before Etr-Oct Booking advisable bank & school hols Last arrival 20.30hrs Last departure noon

contd.

Brown Rigg Caravan & Camping Park

Set in a pleasant rural location, this quiet park is surrounded by trees on one side but affords extensive views across the countryside on the other boundary. The camping area is flat and grassy, with marked pitches for caravans. Sanitary facilities are modern and first class, with spacious showers and toilets. The park is central to the various attractions of Northumberland, set as it is between Keilder Water and Hadrian's Wall. A 5.5-acre site with 60 touring pitches.

Leisure: ◣ ⋀ ▢ Facilities: ⋔ ⊙ ℚ ✳ ᶜ ℞ 龠 ⋔
Services: ⊟ ⊠ ⓘ ⌀ ⛝ ⓣ → ⟆ ⌡

BERWICK-UPON-TWEED   Map 12 NT95

Haggerston Castle (NU041435)
Beal TD15 2PA
☎ 01289 381333 & 381200
Dir: On A1, 5.5m S of Berwick-upon-Tweed and signed
★ ⊞ £13-£23 ⊞ £13-£23
Open Mar-Oct Booking advisable Last arrival 21.00hrs Last departure 10.00hrs
A large holiday centre with a very well equipped touring park, offering comprehensive holiday activities. A 7-acre site with 156 touring pitches and 1200 statics.

Leisure: ♢ ⋨ ◣ ⋀ ▢ Facilities: ⋔ ⊙ ℚ ✳ ᶜ
℞ 龠 ⋒ ⋔ Services: ⊟ ⊠ ℚ ⓘ ⛝ ♨
→ ∪ ⟆ ⊚ ◬ ⅃ ● ⬛ ▦ ▨ ▧

caravanning spares as well as clothing and equipment. A 42-acre site with 79 touring pitches and 200 statics.
Crazy golf, table-tennis, 6-hole pitch&putt.

Leisure: ⋀ Facilities: ➜ ⋔ ⊙ ℚ ✳ & ᶜ ℞ ⋔
Services: ⊟ ⊠ ℚ ⓘ ⌀ ⓣ ⛝ ➜
→ ⟆ ⊚ ◬ ⍩ ⅃ ● ⬛ ▦ ▨ ♨

CRASTER   Map 12 NU21

▶ ▶ ▶ **Dunstan Hill Camping & Caravanning Club Site (NU236214)**
Dunstan Hill NE66 3TQ ☎ 01665 576310
Dir: From A1 take B1340 signed Seahouses. Right at T-junct at Christon Bank. Next right signed Embleton. Right at X-roads then 1st left signed Craster
★ ⊞ £11.80-£14.90 ⊞ £11.80-£14.90 ▲ £11.80-£14.90
Open 20 Mar-1 Nov Booking advisable Spring bank hol & Jul-Aug Last arrival 21.00hrs Last departure noon
An immaculately maintained site with pleasant landscaping close to the beach and historic town of Alnwick, but in a countryside setting. Please see the advertisement on page 14 for details of Club Members' benefits. A 10-acre site with 150 touring pitches.

Facilities: ⋔ ⊙ ℚ ✳ & ᶜ ⋔ Services: ⊟ ⊠ ⓘ ⌀ ➜
→ ∪ ⟆ ◬ ⅃ ℞ ● ⬛

HALTWHISTLE   Map 12 NY76

▶ ▶ ▶ **Camping & Caravanning Club Site (NY685621)**
Burnfoot, Park Village NE49 OJP ☎ 01434 320106
Dir: Follow sign posts from Bypass
★ ⚌ £9.80-£12.40 ⚌ £9.80-£12.40 ▲ £9.80-£12.40
Open 20 Mar-1 Nov Booking advisable bank hols &
high season Last arrival 21.00hrs Last departure
noon
*An attractive site on the banks of the River South
Tyne, amid mature trees, on the Bellister Castle
Estate. Please see the advertisement on page 14 for
details of Club Members' benefits. A 3-acre site with
62 touring pitches.*
Fishing.
Facilities: ⬓⊙⬔⬍⬊⬕ Services: ⬛⬓⬍⬕
→ ⬓⬍⬓ ⬛⬛⬛

HEXHAM   Map 12 NY96

▶ ▶ ▶ *Causey Hill Caravan Park (NY925625)*
Benson's Fell Farm NE46 2JN ☎ 01434 604647
*Dir: To avoid steep hill out of Hexham, follow B6305,
signed Allendale/Alston. Left in 3m onto unclass road,
left 300yds past racecourse. Site 100yds*
⚌⚌▲
Open Apr-Oct Booking advisable public hols & Jul-
Sep Last arrival 22.00hrs Last departure noon
*A well-maintained site on very sloping ground with
some level pitches. Attractively screened by trees.
A 2-acre site with 30 touring pitches and 105 statics.*
Off Licence.
Leisure: ⬔ ⬓ Facilities: ⬓⊙⬍⬊⬕ Services: ⬛⬓⬕
→ ⬓ ⬍⬓⬕⬓⬊ ⬓

▶ ▶ ▶ **Hexham Racecourse Caravan Site (NY919623)**
Hexham Racecourse NE46 3NN
☎ 01434 606847 & 606881
*Dir: From Hexham take B6305 signed Allendale/Alston,
turn left in 3m signed to Racecourse. Site 1.5m on right*
⚌ £7.50-£9 ⚌ £7.50-£9 ▲ fr £3
Open May-Sep Booking advisable wknds & bank
hols for electric hook-up Last arrival 20.00hrs Last
departure noon
*A part-level and part-sloping grassy site on
racecourse overlooking Hexhamshire Moors. The
facilities are functional but well-maintained.
A 4-acre site with 40 touring pitches.*
Leisure: ⬓ ⬔ Facilities: ⬓⊙⬍⬊⬕⬕
Services: ⬛⬓⬓⬕⬕
→ ⬓ ⬍⊙⬕⬕⬓⬊⬓

KIELDER   Map 12 NY69

▶ ▶ ▶ **Kielder Caravan & Camping Site (NY626938)**
NE48 1EJ ☎ 01434 250291 (in season) 0131 314 6505
*Dir: The site is 500yds N of Kielder village on the right
side of the road*
★ ⚌ £6.80-£9.20 ⚌ £6.80-£9.20 ▲ £6.80-£9.20
Open Etr-Sep Booking advisable bank hols & Jul-
Aug Last arrival 22.00hrs Last departure noon

*Forestry Commission site set in riverside fields with
Kielder Water a few minutes' drive away. A 10-acre
site with 70 touring pitches.*
Leisure: ⬔ Facilities: ⬓⊙⬍⬊⬕⬓⬕
Services: ⬛
→ ⬓⬍⬓⬍ ⬛⬛⬛⬛⬛⬕

ROTHBURY   Map 12 NU00

▶ ▶ ▶ **Coquetdale Caravan Park (NU055007)**
Whitton NE65 7RU ☎ 01669 620549
*Dir: From B6341 in Rothbury turn onto B6342. After
crossing river bridge turn right onto unclass road
signed Newtown. Site 0.75m on left*
★ ⚌ £8-£13 ⚌ £8-£13 ▲ £8-£10
Open mid Mar/Etr-Oct Booking advisable bank hol
wknds Last arrival anytime Last departure evening
*Partly level and sloping grass site in hilly country
adjacent to River Coquet, and overlooked by
Simonside Hills and moorland. An 11-acre site with
50 touring pitches and 180 statics.*
Adventure playground for Older Children/Adults
Leisure: ⬔ Facilities: ⬓⊙⬍⬊⬕⬓⬕
Services: ⬛⬓⬕
→ ⬓ ⬍⬓⬊

NOTTINGHAMSHIRE

CLUMBER PARK   Map 08 SK67

▶ ▶ **Camping & Caravanning Club Site (SK626748)**
The Walled Garden S80 3BD ☎ 01909 482303
*Dir: From A1 turn onto A614 southbound, take first
entrance into Clumber Park and follow signs*
★ ⚌ £9.80-£12.40 ▲ £9.80-£12.40
Open 20 Mar-1 Nov Booking advisable bank hols &
Jul-Aug Last arrival 21.00hrs Last departure noon
*Pleasant and peaceful site, well-maintained and
situated in the splendid wooded surroundings of
Clumber Park. Members only caravans. Please see
the advertisement on page 14 for details of Club
Members' benefits. A 2.5-acre site with 55 touring
pitches.*
Facilities: ⬓⊙⬔⬍⬊⬕ Services: ⬛⬓⬕⬓⬕
→ ⬓ ⬍⬓ ⬛⬛

MANSFIELD WOODHOUSE   Map 08 SK56

▶ ▶ ▶ *Redbrick House Hotel (SK568654)*
Peafield Ln NG20 0EW ☎ 01623 846499
Dir: Off A6075, 1m NE of Mansfield Woodhouse
⚌ ⚌
Open all year
*A park in the secluded grounds of an
hotel/restaurant, but with separate facilities. Set in
the heart of Sherwood Forest. There are no toilets,
so own toilet facilities essential. A 5-acre site with
30 touring pitches.*

NEWARK

See **Southwell & Wellow**

NOTTINGHAM

See **Radcliffe on Trent**

Services: ⓣ Toilet Fluid ✖ Café/ Restaurant ⬓ Fast Food/Takeaway ⬓ Baby Care ⬓ Electric Hook Up
⬓ Launderette ⬓ Licensed Bar ⬓ Calor Gaz ⬓ Camping Gaz ⬓ Battery Charging

Thorntons Holt
Camping Park ▶▶▶

**Stragglethorpe, Radcliffe-on-Trent,
Nottingham NG12 2JZ**
Tel: 0115 9332125   Fax: 0115 9333318
www.thorntons-holt.co.uk

Situated off the A52, Nottingham to Grantham Road
**Where the peace of the countryside meets the
culture and entertainment of Nottingham**
13 acres of sheltered, landscaped, level grassland and
orchards for approximately 100 caravans or tents.
Open 1st April to 1st November with full facilities
2nd November to 31st March with limited facilites
★ 83 pitches with electric hook-ups ★
★ Pub and restaurants 10min away ★
★ Good toilet/shower/laundry ★
★ Indoor heated swimming pool ★
★ Shop and information centre ★
★ Play area and games room ★
★ Rallies catered for ★

RADCLIFFE ON TRENT   Map 08 SK63

▶ ▶ ▶ **Thornton's Holt Camping Park (SK638377)**
Stragglethorpe Rd, Stragglethorpe NG12 2JZ
☎ 0115 9332125 & 9334204
*Dir: Take A52, 3m E of Nottingham. Turn S at lights
towards Cropwell Bishop, Park 0.5m on left. Or A46 SE
of Nottingham, N at lights, Park 2.5m on right*
★ 🚐 £7.50-£8.50 🚐 £7.50-£8.50 ⚑ £7.50-£8.50
Open Apr-1 Nov (rs 2 Nov-Mar limited facilities)
Booking advisable bank hols & wknds mid May-Oct
Last arrival 21.00hrs Last departure 13.00hrs
*A level grass site with young trees and bushes, set
in meadowland. A 13-acre site with 84 touring
pitches.*
Leisure: 🏊 🎱 🎪 🖵 Facilities: 🌂⊙🅡⚹🖰🌡🛒🏋
Services: 🚻🖭🛈🖉🔲🔟✕
➔ 🖒 🏲 ⚒ ⚰️ ⚒ 🍴

SOUTHWELL   Map 08 SK65

▶ ▶ **Robin Hood View Caravan Park (SK668593)**
Middle Plantation Farm, Belle Eau Park, Kirklington
☎ 01623 870361
*Dir: From A617/A614 r/about, travel east 1.5 miles and
follow tourist signs to site.*
★ 🚐 £6-£8 🚐 £6-£8 ⚑ £5-£8
Open 31 Mar-14 Nov Booking advisable Peak
season & Bank hols Last arrival 20.00hrs Last
departure 14.00hrs

---

*A pleasant, family-run site in a peaceful rural
location with many mature trees and shrubs, and
good views over open country. Not a suitable site
for school-age children. A 5-acre site with 30
touring pitches and 1 static.*
Leisure: 🏊 Facilities: ⊙⚹🏋 Services: 🚻
➔ 🖒 🏲 🖭 ⚒ 🍴 🔲 🔟

TEVERSAL   Map 08 SK46

▶ ▶ ▶ **Shardaroba Caravan Park (SK472615)**
Silverhill Ln NG17 3JJ
☎ 01623 551838 & 07940 936712
*Dir: 3m NW of Sutton-in-Ashfield off B6028, signed
300yds past Carnarvon Arms on left*
🚐 fr £8 🚐 fr £8 ⚑ fr £8
Open all year Booking advisable Peak season Last
arrival 22.30hrs Last departure 12.00hrs
*A newly-established park with good purpose-built
facilities. Ideally situated for touring Sherwood
Forest and Peak District areas. A 6-acre site with 100
touring pitches.*
Tourist information & book-lending room
Facilities: 🌂⊙🅡⚹🖰🌡🛒🎋🏋 Services: 🚻🖭🛈🔲
➔ 🖒 🏲 ⚒ 🍴 🍴

TUXFORD   Map 08 SK77

▶ ▶ ▶ **Orchard Park Touring Caravan & Camping
Park (SK754708)**
Marnham Rd NG22 0PY
☎ 01777 870228 & 870320
*Dir: Turn off A1 at Tuxford via slip road onto A6075.
After 0.5m turn right into Marnham Road & site is
0.75m on right*
★ 🚐 £7-£8 🚐 £7-£8 ⚑ £7-£8
Open mid Mar-Oct Booking advisable bank hols &
Jul-Aug Last arrival mdnt
*A very pleasant developing site with newly-built
toilet block. A 7-acre site with 60 touring pitches.
Family shower room.*
Leisure: 🏊 Facilities: 🌂⊙⚹🖰🌡🛒🏋
Services: 🚻🛈🖉🔲🔟
➔ 🖒 🍴 🖭 ⚒ 🚫🚫 🚫🚫 🔄

WELLOW   Map 08 SK66

▶ ▶ ▶ **The Shannon Caravan & Camping Park
(SK665666)**
Wellow Rd NG22 9AP
☎ 01636 703820 & 07979018565
Dir: On A616 between Wellow and Ollerton
Open all year
*A newly-developed park with good facilities
including a new toilet block, and hardstandings and
electricity throughout. There is a separate tenting
area, and the park is 0.5 miles from Ollerton on the
edge of the village of Wellow, which is famous for
its maypole celebrations and local hostelries. A 4-
acre site with 37 touring pitches.*
Facilities: 🌂⊙⚹🖰🏋 Services: 🚻

OXFORDSHIRE

BANBURY   Map 04 SP44

▶ ▶ ▶ ▶ **Barnstones Caravan & Camping Site (SP455454)**
Great Bourton OX17 1QU ☎ 01295 750289
Dir: 3m N of M40 junct 11. Leave Banbury on A423 signed Southam. After 3m turn right signed Gt Burton/Cropredy and site 100yds on right
⊞ £5.50 ⊞ £5.50 ▲ £3.50-£5.50
Open all year Booking advisable public hols
Popular, neatly laid-out site with plenty of hardstandings, some fully serviced pitches, and a smart, newly-refurbished toilet block. Well run by personable owner. A 3-acre site with 49 touring pitches.
Leisure: ⚠ Facilities: ⬚⊙✳☒⚹⬚⬚⬚
Services: ⬚⬚⬚⬚⬚⬚
→ ⊙ ▶ ⊙ ⬚⬚⬚⬚⬚

▶ ▶ ▶ ▶ *Bo Peep Farm Caravan Park (SP481348)*
Bo Peep Farm, Aynho Rd, Adderbury OX17 3NP
☎ 01295 810605
Dir: 1m E of Adderbury and A4260, on B4100 Aynho road
⊞ ⊞ ▲
Open Apr-Oct Booking advisable Bank Holidays, British Grand Prix Last arrival 20.00hrs Last departure noon
A delightful park enjoying a lofty position with good views. Four well laid out camping areas, including a paddock with hardstandings, that are all planted with maturing shrubs and trees to provide good shelter and screening. The facility buildings are made from attractive Cotswold stone, and include spotless toilets. The park occupies a peaceful spot bedside the owner's farmhouse at the end of a long drive. A 13-acre site with 88 touring pitches.
Facilities: ⬚⊙⬚✳⬚⬚⬚⬚ Services: ⬚⬚⬚⬚⬚
→ ▶ ⬚

▶ ▶ ▶ *Mollington Touring Caravan Park (SP443477)*
The Yews, Mollington OX17 1AZ
☎ 01295 750731 & 0966 171959
Dir: Leave M40 at junct 11 onto A422 signed Banbury. Take A423 signed Southam and site 3.5m on left
⊞ ⊞ ▲

Open Feb-Dec Booking advisable banks hols Last arrival 22.00hrs
A neat, well-run small farm site with brick-built toilet facilities. On the edge of the village, adjacent to A423. A 2-acre site with 24 touring pitches. Field play area.
Facilities: ⬚⊙⬚✳⬚⬚ Services: ⬚
→ ⊙⊙⬚⬚

BENSON   Map 04 SU69

▶ ▶ **Benson Waterfront Riverside Park (SU613917)**
Benson Waterfront OX10 6SJ
☎ 01491 838304
Dir: Signed from A4074 in Benson
★ ⊞ £14 ⊞ £14 ▲ £10
Open Apr-Oct Booking advisable bank hols & Jul-Aug Last arrival 19.00hrs Last departure noon
An attractive riverside site close to a busy road. A 1-acre site with 22 touring pitches and 25 statics.
Facilities: ⬚⊙⬚✳⬚⬚⬚⬚⬚⬚
Services: ⬚⬚⬚⬚⬚✗⬚
→ ⊙▶⬚⬚⬚⬚⬚ ⬚ ⬚

BLETCHINGDON   Map 04 SP51

▶ ▶ ▶ **Diamond Farm Caravan & Camping Park (SP513170)**
Islip Rd OX5 3DR ☎ 01869 350909
Dir: From M40 junct 9 onto A34 S for 3m, then B4027 to Bletchingdon. Site 1m on left
⊞ £7-£10 ⊞ £7-£10 ▲ £7-£10
Open all year (rs Oct-Mar shop, bar & swimming pool closed) Booking advisable bank hols & Jul-Sep Last arrival 22.00hrs Last departure noon

A well-run, quiet rural site in good level surroundings, and ideal for touring the Cotswolds. Situated 7m north of Oxford in the heart of the Thames Valley. This popular park is well planted, and offers a heated outdoor swimming pool and a games room for children. A 3-acre site with 37 touring pitches.
Leisure: ⬚⬚⚠ Facilities: ⬚⬚⊙⬚✳⬚⬚
Services: ⬚⬚⬚⬚⬚⬚⬚
→ ▶⬚

CASSINGTON   Map 04 SP41

▶ ▶ ▶ **Cassington Mill Caravan Park (SP451099)**
Eynsham Rd OX8 1DB ☎ 01865 881081
Dir: First turn left, 2.5m W of Oxford, on A40 to Witney
★ ⊞ £8.50-£10.50 ⊞ £8.50-£10.50 ▲ £8.50-£10.50
contd.

Open Apr-Oct Booking advisable bank hols & Jun-Aug Last arrival 21.00hrs Last departure noon
Secluded pretty site on the banks of the River Evenlode. Well placed for visiting Oxford, the park benefits from a new laundry, and facilities are always clean and well-maintained. A 4-acre site with 83 touring pitches and 50 statics.

See advertisement under OXFORD

Leisure: ⚑ Facilities: ♠ ⊙ ✳ ♿ ℂ ☎ ⚓
Services: 🖵 🖩 🛢 ⊘ ⊞ 🆃
→ ⚓ ♨ 🍽 🏧 ☎ ⊙ 🔫 🅑

CHARLBURY — Map 04 SP31

▶ ▶ ▶ ▶ **Cotswold View Caravan & Camping Site**
(SP365210)
Enstone Rd OX7 3JH ☎ 01608 810314
Dir: Signed from A44 on to B4022
🚐 £8-£11 🚐 £8-£11 ⚑ £8-£11

Open Etr or Apr-Oct Booking advisable bank hols Last arrival 21.00hrs Last departure noon
A really first class Cotswold site, well-screened with attractive views. The well-managed park offers fully-equipped family rooms and bathrooms, and spacious, sheltered pitches. A 10-acre site with 125 touring pitches.
Off-licence, cycle hire, skittle alley.

Leisure: ♒ ⚑ Facilities: ☕ ♠ ⊙ 🔫 ✳ ♿ ℂ ☎ ⚓
Services: 🖵 🖩 🛢 ⊘ ⊞ 🆃 ☕
→ ♨ 🏧 🅑

CHIPPING NORTON — Map 04 SP32

▶ ▶ ▶ **Camping & Caravanning Club Site**
(SP315244)
Chipping Norton Rd OX7 3PE ☎ 01608 641993
Dir: Take A44 to Chipping Norton. Then A361 Burford road. Turn left at X-roads. Site 150yds
★ 🚐 £11.80-£14.90 🚐 £11.80-£14.90 ⚑ £11.80-£14.90
Open 20 Mar-1 Nov Booking advisable bank hols & Jul-Aug Last arrival 21.00hrs Last departure noon
A hilltop site surrounded by trees but close to a busy main road. Toilets very clean. Please see the advertisement on page 14 for details of Club Members' benefits. A 4-acre site with 105 touring pitches.

Leisure: ⚑ Facilities: ♠ ⊙ 🔫 ✳ ♿ ℂ ☎
Services: 🖵 🖩 🛢 ⊘ ⊞
→ ⚓ ♨ 🍽 ♨ ☎ 🍽 🏧

▶ ▶ ▶ *Churchill Heath Touring Caravan & Camp Site*
Kingham OX7 6UJ ☎ 01608 658317
Dir: On B4450 between Churchill and Kingham, 3m SW of Chipping Norton
🚐 🚐 ⚑

Open all year Booking advisable bank hols & school hols Last arrival 22.00hrs Last departure noon
An improving, peaceful little site on the Cotswold Way, with good views and sheltered pitches. A 7.5-acre site with 50 touring pitches.

Leisure: ⚑ Facilities: ♠ ⊙ 🔫 ✳ ℂ ☎ 🏮 ➤ ☎
Services: 🖵 🖩 🛢 ⊘ 🆃
→ ♨ ▶ ♨

HENLEY-ON-THAMES — Map 04 SU78

▶ ▶ ▶ *Swiss Farm International Camping*
(SU759837)
Marlow Rd RG9 2HY ☎ 01491 573419
Dir: On A4155
🚐 🚐 ⚑

Open Mar-Oct Booking advisable Bank Hols Last arrival 22.00hrs
Pleasantly screened rural site just outside Henley. A 6-acre site with 165 touring pitches and 6 statics.
Football pitch & fishing lake.

Leisure: ♒ ♦ ⚑ Facilities: ☕ ♠ ⊙ 🔫 ✳ ♿ ℂ ☎ 🏮 ☎
Services: 🖵 🖩 🍽 🛢 ⊘ ✕ 🖩
→ ♨ ▶ 🍽 🐾 ♨

OXFORD — Map 04 SP50

▶ ▶ ▶ **Camping & Caravanning Club Site**
(SP518041)
426 Abingdon Rd OX1 4XN ☎ 01865 244088
Dir: From M40 leave A34 at A423, turn left immediately after junct into Abingdon Road. Site on left behind Touchwood Sports
★ 🚐 £11.80-£14.90 🚐 £11.80-£14.90 ⚑ £11.80-£14.90
Open all year Booking advisable bank hols & Jul-Aug Last arrival 22.00hrs Last departure noon
A very busy town site with handy park-and-ride into Oxford. See advertisement on page 14 for details of Club Members' benefits. A 5-acre site with 84 touring pitches.

Facilities: ♠ ⊙ 🔫 ✳ ♿ ℂ ☎ ⚓ Services: 🖵 🛢 ⊘ 🆃
→ ⚓ 🍽 ♨ 🖩 🍽 🏧 ☎ ⊙ 🔫 🅑

Facilities: 🛁 Bath ♠ Shower ⊙ Electric Shaver 🔫 Hairdryer ✳ Ice Pack Facility ♿ Disabled Facilities ℂ Public Telephone
🛒 Shop on Site or within 200yds 🚌 Mobile Shop (calls at least 5 days a week) 🏮 BBQ Area ➤ Picnic Area 🐾 Dog Exercise Area

STANDLAKE Map 04 SP30

PREMIER PARK

▶ ▶ ▶ ▶ ▶ **Lincoln Farm Park** (SP395028)
High St OX8 7RH ☎ 01865 300239
Dir: Located on A415
★ ⊞ £5.50-£12.95 ⊞ £5.50-£12.95 ▲ £5.50-£12.95
Open Feb-Nov Booking advisable bank hols, Jul-Aug & most wknds Last arrival 21.00hrs Last departure noon
An attractively landscaped park, in a quiet village setting, with superb facilities and excellent maintenance. Family rooms, super pitches, two indoor swimming pools and a fully-equipped gym are part of the comprehensive amenities here. A 9-acre site with 90 touring pitches and 19 statics.
Indoor leisure centre, putting green.

Leisure: ⚄ ⚐ Facilities: ➤ ⎔ ⊙ ⚘ ✳ ⚲ ⚑ ⚏ ⊓ ⚹
Services: ⚡ ⊟ 🅐 ⚗ ⊞ ⊤
→ ∪ ▶ ▲ ⚒ ⚄ 🚐

▶ ▶ ▶ **Hardwick Parks** (SP388047)
Downs Rd OX8 7PZ ☎ 01865 300501
Dir: 4.5m S of Witney. Signed from A415 at Standlake
★ ⊞ £8-£10 ⊞ £8-£10 ▲ £8-£10
Open Apr-Oct Booking advisable bank hols Last arrival 21.00hrs Last departure 17.00hrs
A level riverside site with views across the lake and its own water activities. A 20-acre site with 250 touring pitches and 116 statics.
Fishing, windsurfing, boating, jet ski, water skiing.

Leisure: ⚐ Facilities: ⎔ ⊙ ⚘ ✳ ⚲ ⚑ ⚏ ⊓ ⚹
Services: ⚡ ⊟ ⚥ 🅐 ⚗ ⊞ ⊤ ✗ ⚖
→ ∪ ⚒ 🚐

SHROPSHIRE

BRIDGNORTH Map 07 SO79

▶ ▶ ▶ ▶ **Stanmore Hall Touring Park** (SO742923)
Stourbridge Rd WV15 6DT ☎ 01746 761761
Dir: 2m E of Bridgnorth on A458
★ ⊞ £10.60-£14.60 ⊞ £10.60-£14.60 ▲ fr £10.60

Open all year Booking advisable bank hols & Jul-Aug Last arrival 20.00hrs Last departure noon
An excellent park in peaceful surroundings offering outstanding facilities. The pitches, many of them fully-serviced, are arranged around the lake in Stanmore Hall, home of the Midland Motor Museum. A 12.5-acre site with 131 touring pitches.

Leisure: ⚐ Facilities: ⎔ ⊙ ⚘ ✳ ⚲ ⚑ ⚏ ⊓ ⚹
Services: ⚡ ⊟ 🅐 ⚗ ⊞ ⊤ ➤
→ ▶ ⚥ ⚒ 🚐

Services: ⊤ Toilet Fluid ✗ Café/ Restaurant ⚖ Fast Food/Takeaway ➤ Baby Care ⚡ Electric Hook Up
🅐 Launderette ⚥ Licensed Bar ⚓ Calor Gaz ⚗ Camping Gaz ⊞ Battery Charging

England

BROOME   Map 07 SO48

▶ ▶ *Engine & Tender Inn (SO399812)*
SY7 ONT ☎ 01588 660275
Dir: W from Craven Arms on B4368, fork left to B4367, site in village, 2m on right
🏕🚐⚠

Open all year Booking advisable bank hols Last departure 14.00hrs
A pleasant country pub site with gently sloping ground, in a rural setting with a good set of facilities. A 2-acre site with 30 touring pitches and 2 statics.
Leisure: ⚓ **Facilities:** 🚿⊙☀🔌🖤
Services: 🕹♀⊞✗⚱
→♨️▶🔧🛢🛒 💳 🛒 🍱

ELLESMERE

See **Lyneal**

HAUGHTON   Map 07 SJ51

▶ ▶ *Camping & Caravanning Club Site (SJ546164)*
Ebury Hill, Telford TF6 6BU ☎ 01743 709334
Dir: 2.5m through Shrewsbury on A53. Turn left signed Haughton & Upton Magna. Continue 1.5m site on right
★ 🚐 £8.60-£9.60 🚐 £8.60-£9.60 ⚠ £8.60-£9.60
Open 20 Mar-1 Nov Booking advisable bank hols & high season Last arrival 21.00hrs Last departure noon
A wooded hill fort with a central lake overlooking the Shropshire countryside. Well-screened by very mature trees. Own sanitary facilities essential. Please see the advertisement on page 14 for details of Club Members' benefits. An 18-acre site with 104 touring pitches.
Fishing.
Leisure: ⚠ **Facilities:** ☀🔌🖤 **Services:** 🕹
→▶ 💳 🛒

HUGHLEY   Map 07 SO59

▶ ▶ ▶ *Mill Farm Holiday Park (SO564979)*
SY5 6NT ☎ 01746 785208 & 785255
🏕🚐⚠

Open Mar-Oct Booking advisable peak periods Last arrival 20.00hrs Last departure noon
A well-established farm site set in meadowland adjacent to river, with mature trees and bushes providing screening, situated below Wenlock Edge. A 7-acre site with 55 touring pitches and 85 statics. Fishing & horse riding.
Facilities: 🚿⊙✑☀🔌🖤📏🖤 **Services:** 🕹♀🔩⌀⊞
→♨️🔧

LYNEAL (Near Ellesmere)   Map 07 SJ43

▶ ▶ ▶ ▶ *Fernwood Caravan Park (SJ445346)*
SY12 0QF ☎ 01948 710221
Dir: From A495 in village of Welshampton take B5063, over canal bridge, turn right
★ 🚐 £10-£14 🚐 £10-£14
Open Mar-Nov Booking advisable bank hols Last arrival 21.00hrs Last departure 17.00hrs

A peaceful park set in wooded countryside, with a screened, tree-lined touring area and fishing lake. The approach is past flower beds, and the static area which is tastefully arranged around an attractive children's playing area. There is a small child-free touring area for those wanting complete relaxation, and the park has 20 acres of woodland walks. A 26-acre site with 60 touring pitches and 165 statics.
Lake for coarse fishing on site.
Leisure: ⚠ **Facilities:** 🚿⊙✑☀🔌🖤🛒🖤
Services: 🕹⊞🔩Ⓣ
→☀🔧 💳 🛒 🍱 🛒 🍱

MINSTERLEY   Map 07 SJ30

▶ ▶ *The Old School Caravan Park (SO322977)*
Shelve SY5 0JQ ☎ 01588 650410 & 0797 4135659
Dir: 5m SW on A488
🚐 £8 🚐 £8 ⚠ £8

Open Mar-Nov Booking advisable bank hols Last departure 10.30hrs
A well-designed site in a beautiful setting. A 1-acre site with 12 touring pitches.
Dish washing with hot water. CCTV over park.
Facilities: 🚿⊙☀🔌🛒🖤 **Services:** 🕹⊞
→♨️🔧🔩

SHREWSBURY   Map 07 SJ41

PREMIER PARK

▶ ▶ ▶ ▶ ▶ *Beaconsfield Farm Caravan Park (SJ522189)*
Battlefield SY4 4AA ☎ 01939 210370 & 210399
Dir: Take A49 at Hadnall, signed Astley. Site 2m N of Shrewsbury
🏕🚐

Open all year Booking advisable bank hols & Aug Last arrival 19.00hrs Last departure 12.00hrs
A purpose-built family-run park on a working farm in open parkland, designed to take full advantage of the countryside. Facilities include a heated indoor swimming pool, and superior toilets, and fly and coarse fishing are available from the park's own fishing lake. Handily placed for visiting the Medieval Quest, including Brother Caedfel's workshop. An 8-acre site with 50 touring pitches and 35 statics.
Fly fishing.
Leisure: 🐟 **Facilities:** ➡🚿⊙✑☀🔌🖤📏🖤
Services: 🕹♀🔩✗
→▶◎🍱🔩🔩

Facilities: ➡ Bath 🚿 Shower ⊙ Electric Shaver ✑ Hairdryer ☀ Ice Pack Facility 🔌 Disabled Facilities 🖤 Public Telephone
🛒 Shop on Site or within 200yds 🔳 Mobile Shop (calls at least 5 days a week) 🛒 BBQ Area 📏 Picnic Area 🖤 Dog Exercise Area

▶ ▶ ▶ ▶ *Oxon Touring Park (SJ455138)*
Welshpool Rd SY3 5FB ☎ 01743 340868
Dir: Leave A5 ring road at junct with A584. Park shares entrance with 'Oxon Park & Ride'
🚐 🚐 🛆

Open all year Booking advisable high season Last arrival 21.00hrs
An excellent park with quality facilities, offering grass and fully serviced pitches. A small adult-only area has proved very popular with those wanting a peaceful holiday, and a restful patio area overlooks a small lake, next to the reception and shop. Ideally located for Shrewsbury and the surrounding countryside. A 15-acre site with 130 touring pitches.
Leisure: 🇦 Facilities: 🛈⊙🕾🔥🐾🛝🐕 Services: 🔌🗑🛢⌀🔋🚼
→ ▶ 🍴 🧺 🍴 💳 ▆▆ ▆▆ ▆▆ 🔵

TELFORD   Map 07 SJ60

▶ ▶ ▶ *Severn Gorge Caravan Site (SJ705051)*
Bridgnorth Rd, Tweedale TF7 4JB ☎ 01952 684789
Dir: From junct 4, M54 take Queensway road A464, then A442 signed Tweedale. From A5 take Shifnal road A4169, then A442 to site
🚐 🚐 🛆

Open all year Booking advisable bank hols Last arrival 23.00hrs
A very pleasant wooded site in the heart of Telford, well screened and immaculately maintained. A 16-acre site with 110 touring pitches and 1 static.
Bike hire, 3 hole golf, lake & fishing.
Leisure: 🇦 Facilities: 🛈⊙🕾☀🔥🐾🛝🐕
Services: 🔌🗑🛢⌀🔋🚼
→ ▶ ⊙ 🛢 🧺 🍴 💳 ▆▆ ▆▆ 🔵

WEM   Map 07 SJ52

▶ ▶ ▶ *Lower Lacon Caravan Park (SJ534304)*
SY4 5RP ☎ 01939 232376
Dir: Take A49 to B5065. Site 3m on the right
🚐 £10.50-£15 🚐 £10.50-£15 🛆 £10.50-£11

Open all year (rs Nov-Mar club wknds only, toilets closed if frost) Booking advisable public hols & Jul-Aug Last arrival 20.00hrs Last departure 18.00hrs
Level grass site set in meadowland with good sanitary facilities. A 48-acre site with 270 touring pitches and 50 statics.
Pony rides & crazy golf.
Leisure: 🎣 🐟 🇦 🖵 Facilities: 🚽🛈⊙🕾☀🔥🐾🐕
Services: 🔌🗑🛢⌀🔋🔋✗🚼
→ ▶ 🍴 🧺 ▆▆ ▆▆ 💳 ▆▆ 🔵

WENTNOR   Map 07 SO39

▶ ▶ ▶ *The Green Caravan Park (SO380932)*
SY9 5EF ☎ 01588 650605
Dir: 1m NE of Bishop's Castle to Lydham Heath on A489. Turn right & site signed
★ 🚐 fr £6.50 🚐 fr £6.50 🛆 fr £6.50
Open Etr-Oct Booking advisable bank hols Last arrival 21.00hrs Last departure 15.00hrs
A very pleasant spot with many recent improvements and more planned. Mostly level, grassy pitches. A 15-acre site with 140 touring pitches and 20 statics.
Leisure: 🇦 Facilities: 🛈⊙🕾☀🔥🐕
Services: 🔌🗑🛢⌀🔋✗
→ ∪ 🍴 💳 ▆▆ 💳 🔵

SOMERSET

BATH   Map 03 ST76

▶ ▶ ▶ ▶ *Bath Marina & Caravan Park (ST719655)*
Brassmill Ln BA1 3JT ☎ 01225 428778 & 424301
Dir: From Bath centre head for suburb of Newbridge. Site signed off A4 1.5m W towards Bristol/Wells
🚐 £12-£13 🚐 £12-£13
Open all year Booking advisable bank hols & Jun-Sep Last departure noon
A very pleasant site on the edge of Bath in park-like grounds among maturing trees and shrubs. A 4-acre site with 88 touring pitches.
Leisure: 🇦 Facilities: 🛈⊙🕾☀🔥🐾🛝🐕
Services: 🔌🗑🛢⌀🔋
→ ∪ ▶ ⊙ ☀ 🧺 🍴 💳 ▆▆ ▆▆ 💳 🔵

▶ ▶ ▶ ▶ **Newton Mill Caravan and Camping Park** (ST715649)
Newton Rd BA2 9JF ☎ 01225 333909
Dir: From Bath travel W on A4 to A39 rdbt, take immediate left and site 1m on left
★ ⊞ £10.95-£13.95 ⊞ £10.95-£12.95 ▲ £9.95-£11.95
Open all year Booking advisable public hols & Jul-Aug Last arrival 21.00hrs Last departure noon
Tranquil terraced site with excellent facilities by trout stream and partially bordered by woodland. Set in a secluded valley, this attractive park is environmentally interesting with plenty of attractions. Situated within easy reach of main routes. A 42-acre site with 180 touring pitches. Satellite TV hook ups.
Leisure: ♠ /Ⓜ Facilities: ℝ⊙☜⚲⚓⛄⛁⛀⚶
Services: 🖵🖴🏧🛈⌔🖽🕔✕♨
➔ ↻ ▶ ⚡ ♨ ⚙ 🅙 💳 ▦ 💳

BAWDRIP   Map 03 ST33

▶ ▶ ▶ ▶ **Fairways International Touring Caravan & Camp** (ST349402)
Woolavington Corner, Bath Rd TA7 8PP
☎ 01278 685569
Dir: 3.5m E of Bridgwater, 100yds off A39 on B3141
★ ⊞ £8-£10 ⊞ £8-£10 ▲ £8-£10
Open Mar-15 Nov Booking advisable Spring bank hol & Jul-Aug Last departure noon
A well-planned site offering good quality facilities. This quiet park is nevertheless family-orientated, and it makes an ideal base for touring the north Somerset coast, Glastonbury and the Quantocks. A 5.5-acre site with 200 touring pitches. Off-licence.
See advertisement under BRIDGWATER
Leisure: ♠ /Ⓜ ☐ Facilities: ℝ⊙☜⚲⚓⛄⛁⚶⚶⌱⚶
Services: 🖵🖴🛈⌔🖽🕔
➔ ↻ ⚫ ⚡ ♨ ♨

BISHOP SUTTON   Map 03 ST55

▶ ▶ ▶ ▶ *Chew Valley Caravan Park* (ST583603)
Ham Ln BS39 5TZ ☎ 01275 332127
Dir: From Bath take A4 W to rdbt with A38 to Bishop Sutton. Turn right opposite Red Lion pub and park 400yds on left
⊞ ⊞ ▲
Open all year Booking advisable Last arrival 18.00hrs Last departure noon no cars by caravans
A garden site with large pitches divided by flower beds, in an Area of Outstanding Natural Beauty. This strictly 'adults only' park is a very tidy encampment, and the ornate garden and rockery displays make attractive designs around the pitches. Close by the lovely Chew Valley Lake, in a spectacularly scenic part of Somerset. A 2.75-acre site with 31 touring pitches.
Facilities: ℝ⊙☜⚲⚓⛀⚶ Services: 🖵🖴🛈⌔🖽🕔
➔ ↻ ▶ ⚫ ⚡ ♨ ♨ ⚙ ⛁

BLUE ANCHOR   Map 03 ST04

▶ ▶ ▶ ▶ **Blue Anchor Park** (ST025434)
TA24 6JT ☎ 01643 821360
Dir: 0.25m E of West Somerset Railway Station on B3191
★ ⊞ £8-£16 ⊞ £8-£16
Open Mar-Oct (rs Mar & Oct shop & swimming pool limited) Booking advisable bank hols & Jul-Aug Last arrival 22.00hrs Last departure 10.00hrs ⚲
Large coastal site, partly wooded on level ground overlooking bay with individual areas screened. A 29-acre site with 103 touring pitches and 300 statics. Crazy golf.
See advertisement under Preliminary Section
Leisure: ⚲ /Ⓜ Facilities: ℝ⊙☜⚲⚓⛄⛁⚶
Services: 🖵🖴🛈⌔🖽🕔✕♨
➔ ↻ ⚫ ⚡ ♨ 🅙 💳 ▦ 💳 💳

BREAN   Map 03 ST25

▶ ▶ ▶ **Northam Farm Camping & Caravan Park** (ST299556)
TA8 2SE ☎ 01278 751244 & 751222
Dir: Take road to Brean, and site on left in 500yds
★ ⊞ fr £4 ⊞ fr £4 ▲ fr £4
Open Etr-Sep (rs Oct shop & takeaway closed) Booking advisable bank & school hols Last arrival 22.00hrs Last departure 10.30hrs
An attractive site a short walk from the sea with game, coarse and sea fishing close by. A 30-acre site with 350 touring pitches and 112 statics. Pond fishing.

Facilities: ➡ Bath ℝ Shower ⊙ Electric Shaver ☜ Hairdryer ✳ Ice Pack Facility ⛄ Disabled Facilities ♨ Public Telephone
⛁ Shop on Site or within 200yds ⌔ Mobile Shop (calls at least 5 days a week) ⚶ BBQ Area ⚶ Picnic Area ⚶ Dog Exercise Area

Leisure: ⚘ **Facilities:** ➡ ⋔ ⊙ ⬚ ❋ ♿ ⛄ ☎ ⚑
Services: 🔌 🔲 ⬛ ⬛ ⬚ 🔲 ✖ ⬛
➔ ∪ ▶ ⚓ 💳 ⬛ ⬛ ⬛ ⬛

BRIDGETOWN   Map 03 SS93

▶ ▶ ▶ *Exe Valley Camping Site (SS921332)*
TA22 9JR ☎ 01643 851432
Dir: On A396 between Dunster and Dulverton
🚐 🚐 Å
Open Mar-Oct Booking advisable
A pleasant site alongside River Exe, with fly fishing, and good walks. No facilities for children, and dangerous water mill and stream. A 2.5-acre site with 30 touring pitches.
Facilities: ⋔ ⊙ ⬚ ❋ ♿ ☎ ⛄ ⬛ ⚑ **Services:** 🔲 ⬛ ⬚

BRIDGWATER   Map 03 ST23

▶ ▶ ▶ ▶ *Mill Farm Caravan & Camping Park (ST219410)*
Fiddington TA5 1JQ ☎ 01278 732286
Dir: From Bridgwater take A39 W, turn left at Cannington rdbt for 2m, then right just beyond Apple Inn towards Fiddington and follow camping signs
🚐 🚐 Å

Open all year Booking advisable peak periods Last arrival 23.00hrs Last departure 10.00hrs
Established, mature site with helpful owners, and plenty of interests for all the family. A waterfall, stream and safe boating pool with ducks are always popular features, and there is a swimming pool, games room, and pony and horse riding school. A 6-acre site with 125 touring pitches.
Canoes for hire, pool table, trampolines.
Leisure: ⚒ ❀ ⚘ ☐ **Facilities:** ➡ ⋔ ⊙ ⬚ ❋ ☎ ⛄ ⬛ ⚑
Services: 🔌 🔲 ⚲ ⬛ ⬚ 🔲 ⬚ ⬛
➔ ▶ ◎ ⚓

BRUTON   Map 03 ST63

▶ ▶ ▶ Batcombe Vale Caravan & Camping Park (ST681379)
Batcombe Vale BA4 6BW ☎ 01749 830246
Dir: Off B3081 between Evercreech & Bruton
★ 🚐 £9 🚐 £9 Å £9
Open May-Sep Booking advisable bank hols & Jul-Aug Last arrival 22.00hrs Last departure noon
A small, attractive and very quiet site in a secluded valley close to three lakes. Standards of maintenance remain high. A 4-acre site with 30 touring pitches. Coarse fishing, free boats for use.
Leisure: ⚘ **Facilities:** ⋔ ⊙ ❋ ☎ ⛄ ⬛ ⚑
Services: 🔌 ⬛ ⬛ ⬚
➔ ∪ ⬛ ❋ ⚓ ⛄

BURTLE   Map 03 ST34

▶ *Ye Olde Burtle Inn (ST397434)*
Catcott Rd TA7 8NG ☎ 01278 722269 & 722123
Dir: Beside the pub in the centre of the village
🚐 🚐 Å
Open all year Booking advisable Jul-Aug Last arrival anytime
Tenting only site in a cider apple orchard. A 0.75-acre site with 30 touring pitches.
Leisure: ❀ ⚘ **Facilities:** ⊙ ❋ ☎ ⛄ ⬛ **Services:** ⚲ ✖ ⬛
➔ ∪ ⚓ 💳 💳 ⬛ ⬛ ⬛ ⬛ ⬛

CHARD   Map 03 ST30

▶ ▶ ▶ ▶ South Somerset Holiday Park (ST279098)
Howley TA20 3EA ☎ 01460 62221 & 66036
Dir: 3m W of Chard on A30
★ 🚐 £7.30-£8 🚐 £7.30-£8 Å £7.30-£8
Open all year Booking advisable bank hols & High Season Last arrival 23.00hrs Last departure noon
An immaculate site with impressive facilities and levels of maintenance. A 7-acre site with 110 touring pitches and 42 statics.
Leisure: ⚘ **Facilities:** ⋔ ⊙ ⬚ ❋ ♿ ☎ ⬛ ⚑
Services: 🔌 🔲 ⚲ ⬛ ⬚ 🔲 ✖ ⬛
➔ ⚓

▶ ▶ ▶ *Alpine Grove Touring Park (SY342071)*
Forton TA20 4HD ☎ 01460 63479
Dir: Turn off A30 between Chard and Crewkerne towards Cricket St Thomas and follow signs. Park 2m on right
🚐 🚐 Å

contd.

Services: Ⓣ Toilet Fluid   ✖ Café/ Restaurant   ⬛ Fast Food/Takeaway   ➡ Baby Care   🔌 Electric Hook Up
🔲 Launderette   ⚲ Licensed Bar   ⬛ Calor Gaz   ⬚ Camping Gaz   ⬛ Battery Charging

Open Apr-1 Oct Booking advisable bank hols & Jul-Aug Last arrival 23.00hrs
An attractive, quiet wooded site, close to Cricket St Thomas Park. A 7.5-acre site with 40 touring pitches and 1 static.

Leisure: 〜 瓜 Facilities: 📵 ⊙ 🦘 🔆 📞 🐾 🍖 🗛 🐕
Services: 🖨 🗒 🔋 ⏏ Ⓣ
→ ∪ ▶ ♪

CHEDDAR   Map 03 ST45

PREMIER PARK

▶ ▶ ▶ ▶ ▶ **Broadway House Holiday Caravan & Camping Park (ST448547)**
Axbridge Rd BS27 3DB ☎ 01934 742610
Dir: From M5 junct 22 follow signs to Chedder Gorge and Caves (8m). Site midway between Chedder and Axbridge on A371
★ 🚐 £5-£13.50 🚐 £5-£10.50 Å £5-£13.50
Open Mar-Mid Nov (rs Mar-end May & Oct-Nov no bar & pool open, limited shop hours)
Booking advisable bank hols & end Jul-Aug Last departure noon
A well-equipped family park on the slopes of the Mendips with exceptional adventure areas for children, plus a jacuzzi and sun bed. The accent is on activity, and adults and children can try anything from archery to walking the nature trails. An ideal park for the active and adventurous family. The pitches are terraced and south-facing, backing onto the Mendips. A 30-acre site with 200 touring pitches and 35 statics.
Sunbed, table tennis, crazy golf
Leisure: 〜 ♦ 瓜 ▢ Facilities: ➡ 📵 ⊙ 🦘 🔆 ♿ 📞 🐾 🍖 🗛 🐕 Services: 🖨 🗒 🔋 ⏏ 🔌 Ⓔ Ⓣ ✕ 🛆
→ ∪ ▶ ⊙ 🛆 ♪ 🍴 🍴 ━ ⓪ ━ 🔩 🗑

▶ ▶ ▶ *Froglands Farm Caravan & Camping Park (ST462529)*
BS27 3RH ☎ 01934 742058 & 743304
Dir: On A371, 150yds past Cheddar church
🚐 🚐 Å
Open Etr or Apr-30 Oct Booking advisable Whitsun, Jul-Aug & school hols Last arrival 23.00hrs Last departure 13.00hrs
Farmland site on undulating ground with trees and shrubs, located on A371 Weston-Super-Mare to Wells road on SE outskirts of Cheddar. A 3-acre site with 68 touring pitches.
Facilities: 📵 ⊙ 🔆 📞 🐾 🐕 Services: 🖨 🗒 🔋 ⏏ Ⓔ
→ ∪ ▶ ⊙ ♪

CROWCOMBE   Map 03 ST13

▶ ▶ ▶ ▶ *Quantock Orchard Caravan Park (ST138357)*
TA4 4AW ☎ 01984 618618
Dir: Set back from the A358
★ 🚐 £7-£10.45 🚐 £7-£10.45 Å £3.50-£10.45
Open all year Booking advisable bank hols & Jul-Aug Last arrival 22.00hrs Last departure noon
An attractive, quiet site sitting at the western foot of the Quantocks midway between Taunton and

Minehead, and offering good views. The park is well laid out in an old orchard setting with pretty flower beds. A new fitness complex is next to the swimming pool, complete with jacuzzi, sauna and exercise machines. A 3.5-acre site with 75 touring pitches.
Gym & leisure suite, off-licence on site
Leisure: 〜 ♦ 瓜 ▢ Facilities: ➡ 📵 ⊙ 🦘 🔆 ♿ 📞 🐾 🍖
Services: 🖨 🗒 🔋 ⏏ Ⓔ Ⓣ
→ ∪ ▶ ♪ 🍴 ━ 🔩 🗑

EMBOROUGH   Map 03 ST65

▶ ▶ ▶ **Old Down Touring Park (ST628513)**
Old Down BA3 4SA ☎ 01761 232355
Dir: Follow A37 from Farrington Gurney through Ston Easton. After 2m left onto B3139 to Emborough. Site opposite Old Down Inn on right
★ 🚐 £7-£10.50 🚐 £7-£10.50 Å £7-£10.50
Open Mar-Nov Booking advisable Bank holidays & Jul-Aug Last arrival 22.00hrs Last departure 11.00hrs
An attractive park set in open parkland. Children are welcome, but the park is used mainly by retired caravanners. A 4-acre site with 30 touring pitches and 1 static.
Leisure: 瓜 Facilities: 📵 ⊙ 🦘 🔆 📞 🐾 🗛
Services: 🔋 ⏏ Ⓔ Ⓣ
→ ∪ ▶ ♪ 🗒

EXFORD   Map 03 SS83

► ► **Westermill Farm (SS825398)**
TA24 7NJ ☎ 01643 831238 & 831216
*Dir: Leave Exford on Porlock road. After 0.25m fork left,
pass another campsite until 'Westermill' sign on tree.
Take left fork*
★ ⊟ fr £8 ▲ fr £8

Open all year (rs Nov-MarMay larger toilet block &
shop closed) Booking advisable Spring bank hol &
Jul-Aug
*An idyllic site for peace and quiet, in sheltered
valley in the heart of Exmoor, which has won
awards for conservation. Four waymarked walks
over 500-acre working farm. Approach not suitable
for caravans. A 6-acre site with 60 touring pitches.
Shallow river for fishing/bathing Marked walks*
Facilities: ℝ ⊙ ℝ ☀ 🕻 🔓 ⁂ **Services:** 🗑 🛢 ⌀
→ ∪ ♪

FROME   Map 03 ST74

► ► ► *Seven Acres Caravan & Camping Site
(ST777444)*
Seven Acres, West Woodlands BA11 5EQ
☎ 01373 464222
*Dir: On B3092 approx 0.75m from rdbt with A361 Frome
bypass*
⊟ ⊟ ▲
Open Mar-Oct Booking advisable
*A level meadowland site beside the shallow River
Frome, ideal for families. Fresh farm produce
available on site. A 3-acre site with 22 touring
pitches.*
Facilities: ℝ ℝ 🔓 ⁂ **Services:** 🖵
→ ♨ ♪ 🗑 🔓

GLASTONBURY   Map 03 ST53

PREMIER PARK

► ► ► ► ► **Old Oaks Touring Park
(ST521394)**
Wick Farm, Wick BA6 8JS ☎ 01458 831437
*Dir: Take A361 towards Shepton Mallet in 1.75m
turn left at sign Wick, site on left in 1m*
⊟ £7.50-£10 ⊟ £7.50-£10 ▲ £7.50-£10
Open Mar-Oct Booking advisable bank hols &
main season Last arrival 21.00hrs Last departure
11.00hrs
*An ideal family park on a working farm on the
east side of Glastonbury Tor with panoramic
views towards the Mendip Hills. Glastonbury's
two famous 1,000 year old oaks - Gog and*

*Magog - are on site, hence the name. An
outstanding toilet block offers en-suite facilities,
plus four super pitches. This remarkable park
retains its farm environment while offering
highly sophisticated services. An adult-only area
is available.There is no play area or games
room. A 2.5-acre site with 40 touring pitches.
Fishing & off-licence on site.*
Facilities: ⇥ ℝ ⊙ ℝ ☀ 🔓 🕻 🔓 ⁂
Services: 🖵 🗑 🛢 ⌀ ⊞ 🔲 ⇥
→ ♪ 📞 ▦ ▦ 🔧

► ► ► ► **Isle of Avalon Touring Caravan Park
(ST494397)**
Godney Rd BA6 9AF ☎ 01458 833618
*Dir: M5 junct 23, A39 to outskirts of Glastonbury, 2nd
exit signed Wells at B & Q rbt, straight over next rbt, 1st
exit at 3rd rbt (B3151), 200yds right*
★ ⊟ £9-£10 ⊟ £9-£10 ▲ £9-£10
Open all year Booking advisable mid Jul-mid Aug
Last arrival 21.00hrs Last departure 11.00hrs
*An excellent, expanding and developing site of a
very high standard set below this historic town, and
an ideal touring centre. The level park offers a quiet
and restful environment in which to unwind. Owners
Sharon and Michael Webb are very warm and
welcoming. An 8-acre site with 120 touring pitches.
Cycle hire.*
Leisure: ⚲ **Facilities:** ℝ ⊙ ℝ ☀ 🔓 🕻 🔓
Services: 🖵 🗑 🛢 ⌀ ⊞ 🔲
→ ∪ ♨ ♪

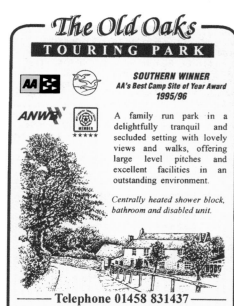
Services: 🔲 Toilet Fluid ✗ Café/ Restaurant 🖮 Fast Food/Takeaway ➡ Baby Care 🖵 Electric Hook Up
🗑 Launderette ♀ Licensed Bar 🛢 Calor Gaz ⌀ Camping Gaz ⊞ Battery Charging

England

NEW HOUSE FARM
►►►

Mark Road, Highbridge, Somerset TA9 4RA
Telephone: 01278 782218

TOURING CARAVAN & CAMPING PARK
An ideal site for peace and tranquillity,
level with easy access, no noisy club or bar
but a lovely country pub within ⅓ mile.
Course fishing within 2 miles. Luxury toilet
block with free showers. Small laundry
and dish washing area.
Children's play area.
Dogs welcome but must be
kept on a lead at all times.

HIGHBRIDGE   Map 03 ST34

► ► ► ► *New House Farm Caravan & Camping Park (ST338469)*
Walrow TA9 4RA ☎ 01278 782218 & 783277
⊞ ⊞ Å
Open Mar-Oct Booking advisable Jul & Aug Last arrival 23.30hrs Last departure 18.30hrs
A very neat, quiet farm site with well-maintained facilities, sheltered by boundary hedging and trees. The grass is cropped close around the pitches, and there are friendly and helpful wardens. Not far from the famous Brean Beaches, and Burnham-on-Sea, but far enough to escape from crowds. A 4-acre site with 30 touring pitches.
Leisure: ⚠ Facilities: ⋒ ⊙ ✳ ⅃ ⍩ Services: ⊡ ⓘ ⓘ ⊡
→ ∪ ► ⌂ ⍨ ⅃

► ► ► *Edithmead Leisure & Park Homes (ST337459)*
TA9 4HE ☎ 01278 783475
Dir: From Highcliffe follow signs to M5 rdbt and site on right
⊞ ⊞ Å
Open 9 Feb-11 Jan Booking advisable bank hols & Jul-Sep Last arrival mdnt Last departure noon
Level, compact site adjacent to M5. A 15-acre site with 250 touring pitches and 65 statics. Amusement arcade.
Leisure: ⚠ Facilities: ⋒ ⊙ ✳ ⅃ ⍰ ⍩ ⍩
Services: ⊡ ⓘ ⓘ ⍰ ⌀ ⓣ ⍓
→ ∪ ⊙ ⌂ ⍨ ⅃

LANGPORT   Map 03 ST42

► ► ► *Thorney Lakes Caravan Park (ST430237)*
Thorney West Farm, Muchelney TA10 0DW
☎ 01458 250811
Dir: From Langport take Mucheley road. Site 3m on left
⊞ fr £8 ⊞ fr £8 Å fr £8
Open 16 Mar-Oct Booking advisable
A small basic but very attractive site. A 6-acre site with 16 touring pitches.
Coarse fishing on site.
Facilities: ⋒ ⊙ ⅆ Services: ⊡
→ ► ⅃ ⍨

MARTOCK   Map 03 ST41

► ► ► ► *Southfork Caravan Park (ST448188)*
Parrett Works TA12 6AE ☎ 01935 825661
Dir: Located 1.5m from centre of Martock. From South Petherton follow road N for 2m
★ ⊞ £6-£9 ⊞ £6-£9 Å £6-£9
Open all year Booking advisable bank hols & Jul-Aug Last arrival 23.00hrs Last departure noon
An excellent park in deepest rural Somerset, tastefully surrounded by stone walls. This park is popular with country lovers, and offers very neat pitches on level ground on parkland. There are excellent amenities, but this is not a typical holiday park with entertainment. A 2-acre site with 30 touring pitches and 3 statics.
Caravan service/repair centre & accessories shop.
Leisure: ⚠ Facilities: ⋒ ⊙ ⍰ ✳ ⅃ ⍩ ⍩
Services: ⊡ ⓘ ⓘ ⌀ ⊡ ⓣ
→ ∪ ► ⅃ ⍰ ⍰ ⍰ ⍓

MINEHEAD   Map 03 SS94

► ► ► *Camping & Caravanning Club Site (SS958471)*
Hill Rd, North Hill TA24 5LB ☎ 01643 704138
Dir: From A39 head towards town centre. On main street turn into Blenheim Rd & then left into Martlet Rd. Campsite signed from here
★ ⊞ £9.80-£12.40 Å £9.80-£12.40
Open 20 Mar-27 Sep Booking advisable bank hols & Jul-Aug Last arrival 21.00hrs Last departure noon
A secluded site offering glorious views of the Bristol Channel and Quantocks. The approach road is narrow with sharp bends, and no caravans are allowed on the park. Please see the advertisement on page 14 for details of Club Members' benefits. A 3.75-acre site with 60 touring pitches.
Facilities: ⋒ ⊙ ⍰ ✳ ⅃ Services: ⓘ ⌀ ⊡
→ ∪ ► ⌂ ⍨ ⍨ ⅃ ⍰ ⍰ ⍰ ⍰

► ► ► *Minehead & Exmoor Caravan Site (SS950457)*
Minehead & Exmoor Caravan Park,
Porlock Rd TA24 8SN ☎ 01643 703074
Dir: 1m W adjacent to A39
★ ⊞ £8 ⊞ £8 Å £8
Open Mar-22 Oct Booking advisable bank hols & Jul-Aug Last arrival 23.00hrs Last departure noon
Small, terraced, grassy site near the town with many young trees and plants, on the edge of Exmoor. A 2.5-acre site with 50 touring pitches.

Facilities: ➳ Bath ⋒ Shower ⊙ Electric Shaver ⍰ Hairdryer ✳ Ice Pack Facility ⅆ Disabled Facilities ⅃ Public Telephone ⍩ Shop on Site or within 200yds ⊡ Mobile Shop (calls at least 5 days a week) ⍰ BBQ Area ⍱ Picnic Area ⍩ Dog Exercise Area

Leisure: 🏔 Facilities: 📶⊙🔍✳️🚰🍴 Services: 🔌🛢🔋⌀➕🔲

→ ∪ ▶ 🛆 🔦 🎪 🍴 ▦

NORTH WOOTTON — Map 03 ST54

▶ ▶ **Greenacres Camping (ST553416)**
Barrow Ln BA4 4HL ☎ 01749 890497
*Dir: A361 to Glastonbury. Turn at Steanbow Farm &
follow campsite signs*
★ 🅰 fr £9
Open Apr-Oct Booking advisable school hols Last
arrival 21.00hrs Last departure noon ✖
*An immaculately maintained site peacefully set
within sight of Glastonbury Tor. Mainly family
orientated with many thoughtful extra facilities
provided. A 4.5-acre site with 30 touring pitches.*
Leisure: 🏔 Facilities: 📶⊙🔍✳️ Services: 🔋⌀➕

→ ∪ ▶ 🛆 🎪 🍴 🛢 🚰

PORLOCK — Map 03 SS84

▶ ▶ ▶ **Burrowhayes Farm Caravan & Camping
Site (SS897460)**
West Luccombe TA24 8HT ☎ 01643 862463
*Dir: Take A39 through Porlock. After 4.5m turn left
towards Horner and West Luccombe. Site 0.25m on right*
★ 🚐 £6-£8 🚐 £6-£8 🅰 £6-£8

Open 15 Mar-Oct Booking advisable Etr, Spring
bank hol & Jun-Aug Last arrival 20.00hrs Last
departure noon
*A delightful site on the edge of Exmoor, on slope to
the river, and ideal for exploring surrounding area.
An 8-acre site with 140 touring pitches and 20
statics.*
Pony-treking available, riding stables
Facilities: 📶⊙✳️🚰🍴 Services: 🔌🛢🔋⌀➕🔲

→ ▶ ⊙ 🔦 🍴 🎪 ▦ ▦ 🔲 ▦ 🛢

▶ ▶ ▶ **Porlock Caravan Park (SS882469)**
TA24 8ND ☎ 01643 862269
Dir: Located in village by west car park
★ 🚐 fr £8 🚐 fr £7 🅰 fr £8
Open 15 Mar-Oct Booking advisable Etr, Whitsun &
Jul-Aug Last arrival 23.00hrs Last departure noon
*A well-planned site, in valley with shrubs and trees,
and an ideal touring centre for Exmoor. A 3-acre
site with 40 touring pitches and 56 statics.*
Facilities: 📶⊙🔍✳️🚰🍴 Services: 🔌🛢🔋⌀➕🔲

→ ∪ ▶ 🔦 🎪 🍴

PRIDDY — Map 03 ST55

▶ ▶ ▶ **Mendip Heights Camping & Caravan Park
(ST522519)**
Townsend BA5 3BP ☎ 01749 870241
*Dir: Take A39 N from Wells. After 3m turn left at lights
along B3135 to Cheddar. After 4.5m turn left. Campsite
200yds on right.*
★ 🚐 £7-£7.95 🚐 £7-£7.95 🅰 £7-£7.95
Open Mar-15 Nov Booking advisable bank & school
hols Last arrival 22.00hrs
*Quiet family park on the Mendip Hills above
Cheddar Gorge. The enthusiastic owners organise
walks, and badger and deer watches. A 4.5-acre site
with 90 touring pitches and 1 static.*
Archery, canoeing, abseiling, caving, table tennis.
Leisure: 🏔 Facilities: 📶⊙🔍✳️🚰🍴
Services: 🔌🛢🔋⌀➕🔲

→ ∪

REDHILL — Map 03 ST46

▶ ▶ ▶ **Brook Lodge Farm Camping & Caravan
Park (ST486620)**
Cowslip Green BS40 5RD ☎ 01934 862311
*Dir: 1.5m S of Redhill on A38. From M5 junct 18 follow
signs for Bristol Airport, and site 3m on left*
★ 🚐 £8.70-£12.50 🚐 £8.70-£12.50 🅰 £8.50-£11.50
Open Mar-Oct (rs Nov-Feb) Booking advisable 22
May-4 Sep & bank hols Last arrival 20.30hrs Last
departure noon

contd.

Brook Lodge Farm Camping & Caravan Park
A naturally sheltered country touring park nestling in a valley of the Mendip Hills, surrounded by trees and a historic walled garden. Country walks and trout fishing can be enjoyed in the park. A 3-acre site with 29 touring pitches.

Leisure: ⚲ **Facilities:** ⬚⊙⌇✳↻⬚⛴⍓
Services: ⬚⊞⛨
→ ∪ ▶ ⊿ ⬚

RODNEY STOKE   Map 03 ST44

▶ ▶ ▶ ▶ **Bucklegrove Caravan & Camping Park (ST487502)**
Wells Rd BS27 3UZ ☎ 01749 870261
Dir: On A371 midway between Cheddar & Wells
⚑ £5-£11 ⚑ £5-£11 ▲ £5-£11
Open Mar-Jan Booking advisable bank hols & peak periods Last arrival 22.00hrs Last departure noon ⚒
A well-sheltered site on the southern slopes of the Mendip Hills providing superb views of Somerset. This popular park offers sophisticated facilities, and amenities including an indoor swimming pool and café. An ideal touring base, it backs onto the Mendips, facing south over the Somerset Flats, and is a pleasant sun trap. A 7.5-acre site with 125 touring pitches and 35 statics.
Large tourist information room.

Leisure: ⚑ ⚭ ⚲⬚ **Facilities:** ➧⬚⊙⌇✳↻↻⬚⛴
Services: ⬚⬚⚏⚓⬚⊞⛨✕⬚
→ ∪ ▶ ⊙⚏⊿ ⬚⬚⬚ ⬚⬚⬚

SPARKFORD   Map 03 ST62

▶ ▶ ▶ **Long Hazel International Caravan & Camping (ST602262)**
High St BA22 7JH ☎ 01963 440002
⚑ ⚑ ▲
Open Mar-Dec Booking advisable Last arrival 23.00hrs Last departure noon
A very neat, smart site, situated next to the Sparkford Inn in the village High Street. A 3.5-acre site with 75 touring pitches and 3 statics.
Badminton & Croquet, 9-Hole Putting Green

Leisure: ⚲ **Facilities:** ⬚⊙⌇✳↻⬚⬚⍓
Services: ⬚⚓⬚⊞⛨
→ ∪ ▶ ⊙⊿⛴

TAUNTON   Map 03 ST22

▶ ▶ ▶ **Ashe Farm Camping & Caravan Site (ST279229)**
Thornfalcon TA3 5NW ☎ 01823 442567
Dir: Leave M5 at junct 25, take A358 eastwards for 2.5m. Turn right at Nags Head Pub. Site 0.25m on the right
⚑ £6.50-£8 ⚑ £6.50-£8 ▲ £6.50-£8

Open Apr-Oct Booking advisable Jul-Aug
Attractive, well-screened farm site with clean facilities. A 7-acre site with 30 touring pitches and 2 statics.

Leisure: ⚲⚭⚲ **Facilities:** ⬚⊙⌇✳↻⬚⍓
Services: ⬚⬚⚓⬚⊞⛨
→ ∪ ▶ ⚏⊿

▶ ▶ ▶ **Holly Bush Park (ST220162)**
Culmhead TA3 7EA ☎ 01823 421515
Dir: M5 junct 25. Turn left at 1st lights for B3170 to Corfe. 3.5m from Corfe turn right at X-roads to Wellington. Right at T-junct. Site 150yds on left
⚑ £6-£7.50 ⚑ £6-£7.50 ▲ £6-£7.50

Open all year Booking advisable bank hols & high season Last arrival 22.00hrs Last departure noon
An immaculate small park set in an orchard in attractive countryside with easy access to Wellington and Taunton. A 2-acre site with 40 touring pitches.

Facilities: ⬚⊙✳↻⬚⬚⍓ **Services:** ⬚⬚⚓⬚⊞⛨
→ ∪ ▶ ⊿

▶ ▶ ▶ **Waterrow Touring Park (ST053251)**
Wiveliscombe TA4 2AZ ☎ 01984 623464 624280
Dir: In Waterrow, site on left after the Rock Pub
★ ⚑ £7-£8 ⚑ £7-£8 ▲ £6.50-£8.50
Open all year Booking advisable Last arrival 22.30hrs Last departure none

---

Facilities: ➧ Bath ⬚ Shower ⊙ Electric Shaver ⌇ Hairdryer ✳ Ice Pack Facility ↻ Disabled Facilities ↻ Public Telephone ⛴ Shop on Site or within 200yds ⊞ Mobile Shop (calls at least 5 days a week) ⬚ BBQ Area ⍓ Picnic Area ⍓ Dog Exercise Area

A beautiful, brand new site in very attractive valley on River Tone. A 6-acre site with 90 touring pitches and 1 static.

Facilities: ⬤⊙🔦✳🔌🏕🚿🚻🚽 **Services:** 🔌🗑🚿⌀
➜∪🅿🔽🚿🧺🚂

WATCHET   Map 03 ST04

▶ ▶ ▶ **Doniford Bay Holiday Park (ST095433)**
TA23 OTJ ☎ 01984 632423
Dir: E of Watchet off A39
★ 🚐 £16-£22.50
Open Etr-end Oct Booking advisable Jul-Aug & Whitsun Last arrival 20.00hrs Last departure 10.00hrs
A level site with some hardstanding pitches for caravans and surfaced internal roadways, overlooking the sea (Minehead Bay). A 3-acre site with 46 touring pitches.
Free evening entertainment, amusements, Go-Karts.
Leisure: 🐠 🎣🎱🚣📽 **Facilities:** ⬤⊙🔦🚻🌡🐕
Services: 🔌🗑🍺🔋🍴✗🍔
➜🚿 🚐📧🏧💳🗑

WELLINGTON   Map 03 ST12

▶ ▶ ▶ **Gamlins Farm Caravan Park (ST083195)**
Gamlins Farm, Greenham TA21 0LZ
☎ 01823 672596
Dir: Situated off A38 on the Greenham road
🚐£7-£8 🚐£7-£8 ▲ £6-£8
Open Etr-Sep Booking advisable bank hols Last arrival 20.00hrs Last departure noon
A well-planned site in a secluded position with panoramic views. A 3-acre site with 25 touring pitches.
Leisure: 🎣 **Facilities:** ⬤⊙🔦✳🌡🐕 **Services:** 🔌🗑
➜∪🅿🍔🧺🚿

WELLS   Map 03 ST54

See also **Priddy**
▶ ▶ ▶ **Homestead Caravan & Camping Park (ST532474)**
Wookey Hole BA5 1BW ☎ 01749 673022
Dir: 0.5m NW off A371 Wells to Cheddar road
★ 🚐 £9 🚐 £8.50 ▲ £9
Open Etr-Oct Booking advisable Bank holidays Last arrival 20.00hrs Last departure noon
Attractive small site by stream with mature trees. Set in hilly woods and meadowland with access to river and Wookey Hole. A 2-acre site with 50 touring pitches and 28 statics.

Childrens fishing.
Facilities: ➜⬤⊙🔦✳🔌🚿 **Services:** 🔌🗑⌀🔋
➜∪🅿🍔🧺🚿🗑

WESTON-SUPER-MARE   Map 03 ST36

▶ ▶ ▶ *Country View Caravan Park (ST335647)*
Sand Rd, Sand Bay BS22 9UJ ☎ 01934 627595
Dir: From Weston-super-Mare travel E to A370/M5 rdbt, turn left to Kewstroke/Sandy Bay and follow signs. First caravan park on right. 3m N of town
🚐🚐▲
Open Mar-Oct Booking advisable bank hols & peak periods Last arrival 21.00hrs Last departure noon
A pleasant, flat, open site in a country area not far from the coast. An 8-acre site with 120 touring pitches and 65 statics.
Leisure: 🎣🎱⚲ **Facilities:** ⬤⊙🔦✳🌡🔌🚿🏕
Services: 🔌🗑🍺⌀🔋
➜∪🅿🔽🧺🚿 🚐🏧

▶ ▶ ▶ *Purn International Holiday Park (ST332568)*
Bridgwater Rd, Bleadon BS24 0AN ☎ 01934 812342
Dir: Take A370 from Weston-super-Mare towards Edithmead and site on right by The Anchor Inn, about 1m from 1st rdbt
🚐🚐▲
Open Mar-7 Nov (rs Mar-Apr & Oct Club only open at weekends) Booking advisable Jul & Aug Last arrival mdnt Last departure 10.30hrs
A good flat site in a handy position for touring the Somerset coast. An 11-acre site with 168 touring pitches and 120 statics.
River with fishing.
Leisure: 🎣🚣⚲📺 **Facilities:** ⬤⊙🔦✳🔌🚿🏕🌡🐕
Services: 🔌🗑🍺⌀🔋🍴🚿
➜∪🅿⊙🔽🧺🚿

▶ ▶ ▶ *Rose Tree Caravan Park (ST348639)*
Lower Norton Ln, Kewstoke BS22 9YR
☎ 01934 620351 & 07747 692167
Dir: From Weston-super-Mare turn E on A370 to rdbt at West Wick. Turn left into unclass road and over 3 more rdbts. Site on right in Lower Norton Lane
🚐▲
Open Apr-Sep (rs Mar & Oct) Booking advisable Last arrival 23.00hrs Last departure noon
An attractive little park with very well maintained facilities, 2m from a sandy bay. A 5-acre site with 20 touring pitches.
Facilities: ⬤⊙✳🐕 **Services:** 🔌🔋
➜🅿🧺🚿🗑🚿

▶ ▶ ▶ **West End Farm Caravan & Camping Park (ST354600)**
Locking BS24 8RH ☎ 01934 822529
Dir: Leave M5 at junct 21 onto A370. Follow signs for International Helicopter Museum. Turn right at rdbt & follow signs to site
★ 🚐 £8.50-£11 🚐 £8.50-£11 ▲ £8.50-£11
Open all year Booking advisable peak periods Last arrival 22.00hrs Last departure noon

contd.

A flat, hedge-bordered site by helicopter museum with good clean facilities and landscaping. Good access to Weston-super-Mare and the Mendips. A 10-acre site with 75 touring pitches and 20 statics.

Leisure: ♣ ⚠ **Facilities:** ↿⊙🔍❋☆ᐤ🐾

Services: ⌺🖃🛈∅🅣

→◡▶◉♨↡💈↲ 🔌 ▬ ▤ ▨ ▦ 🔲

▶ ▶ ▶ **Weston Gateway Caravan Site (ST370621)**
West Wick BS24 7TF ☎ 01934 510344
Dir: Close to A370 & junct 21 of M5
★ 🚐 £6.50-£9.50 🚐 £6.50-£9.50 ⚠ £6.50-£9.50
Open Apr-Oct Booking advisable Jul-Aug Last arrival 23.00hrs Last departure noon
A pleasant site set among trees and shrubs. Plenty of entertainment but basic toilet block. A 15-acre site with 175 touring pitches.
Leisure: ♣ ⚠ **Facilities:** ↿⊙🔍❋☆ᐤ🐾

Services: ⌺🖃♨🛈∅🅗🅣

→◡▶💈↲

WINSFORD   **Map 03 SS93**

▶ ▶ ▶ **Halse Farm Caravan & Camping Park (SS894344)**
TA24 7JL ☎ 01643 851259
Dir: From Minehead take A396, turn right just before Bridgetown towards Winsford, then left by pub up narrow winding lane to top. Entrance over cattle grid
🚐 🚐 ⚠

Open 22 Mar-Oct Booking advisable bank hols & mid Jul-Aug Last arrival 22.00hrs Last departure noon
An Exmoor site overlooking a typical wooded valley with glorious views. Midway between Minehead and Tiverton. A 3-acre site with 44 touring pitches.
Leisure: ⚠ **Facilities:** ↿⊙🔍❋☆ᐤ🐾

Services: ⌺🖃🛈∅↩

→↲💈

STAFFORDSHIRE

CANNOCK CHASE   **Map 07 SJ91**

▶ ▶ ▶ **Camping & Caravanning Club Site (SK039145)**
Old Youth Hostel, Wandon WS15 1QW
☎ 01889 582166
Dir: On A460 to Hednesford turn right at signpost for Rawnsley, Hazelslade. Then take 1st left. Site 0.5m past golf club

★ 🚐 £10.60-£13.90 🚐 £10.60-£13.90 ⚠ £10.60-£13.90
Open 20 Mar-1 Nov Booking advisable bank hols & Jul-Aug Last arrival 21.00hrs Last departure noon
Very popular site in an excellent location in the heart of the Chase. A gently sloping site with timber-built facility blocks. Please see the advertisement on page 14 for details of Club Members' benefits. A 5-acre site with 60 touring pitches.
Facilities: ↿⊙🔍❋☆ᐤ🐾 **Services:** ⌺🖃↩

→◡▶↲💈 🔌 ▤

CHEADLE   **Map 07 SK04**

▶ ▶ ▶ *Quarry Walk Park (SK045405)*
Coppice Ln, Croxden Common, Freehay ST10 1RQ
☎ 01538 723495
Dir: 1m from A522 Cheadle-Uttoxeter road at Freehay
🚐 🚐 ⚠
Open all year Booking advisable bank hols Last arrival 23.00hrs Last departure noon
A pleasant park in an old quarry, well-screened with mature trees and shrubs. A 14-acre site with 40 touring pitches.
Off site pub owned by campsite used as clubhouse.
Leisure: ⚠ **Facilities:** ↿⊙❋ᐤᚷ🏮
Services: ⌺🖃🛈∅🅗

→◡↲💈

LEEK   **Map 07 SJ95**

▶ ▶ ▶ **Camping & Caravanning Club Site (SK008599)**
Blackshaw Grange, Blackshaw Moor ST13 8TL
☎ 01538 300285
Dir: 2m from Leek on main Leek to Buxton road. Site 200yds past the sign for 'Blackshaw Moor' on left
★ 🚐 £11.80-£14.90 🚐 £11.80-£14.90 ⚠ £11.80-£14.90
Open all year Booking advisable Jan-Mar Last arrival 21.00hrs Last departure noon
A beautifully located club site, with well-screened pitches. The facilities have been completely refurbished, with an extra new toilet block. Please see the advertisement on page 14 for details of Club Members' benefits. A 6-acre site with 90 touring pitches.
Leisure: ⚠ **Facilities:** ↿⊙🔍❋☆ᐤᐤ🐾
Services: ⌺🖃🛈∅🅣

→▶↡↲ 🔌 ▤

LONGNOR   **Map 07 SK06**

▶ ▶ ▶ **Longnor Wood Caravan Park (SK072640)**
SK17 ONG ☎ 01298 83648 01538 398081
Dir: From centre of Longnor turn off B5053 signed Leek and Royal Cottage. Site on left after 800yds, and immediately right.
🚐 £8.10-£9 🚐 £8.10-£9 ⚠ £8.10-£9
Open Apr-Oct Booking advisable Bank hols, Jul-Aug Last arrival 22.00hrs Last departure 14.00hrs

---

Facilities: ↩ Bath ↿ Shower ⊙ Electric Shaver 🔍 Hairdryer ❋ Ice Pack Facility ☆ Disabled Facilities ᐤ Public Telephone
💈 Shop on Site or within 200yds 🖃 Mobile Shop (calls at least 5 days a week) 🏮 BBQ Area 🥘 Picnic Area 🐾 Dog Exercise Area

A delightful woodland park in a beautiful Peak District location, a good walking base and ideal for visiting Leek and Buxton. This park is for adults only, and does not accept children. A 5-acre site with 33 touring pitches and 14 statics.
Off licence
Facilities: ◈ ⊙ ◥ ✳ ◟ 🐾 ⊞ 戸 ⊩
Services: 🔌 ⊡ ⓘ ⌀ ⊞ Ⓣ

OAKAMOOR Map 07 SK04

▶ ▶ ▶ **Star Caravan & Camping Park (SK066456)**
Cotton ST10 3BN ☎ 01538 702256 & 702219
Dir: 1.25m N of Oakamoor off B5417, 1.5m S of A52
🚐 £8 🚍 £8 ▲ £8

Open Mar-Oct Booking advisable anytime Last arrival 23.30hrs Last departure 19.00hrs
A pleasant, well screened park with much improved facilities, situated within one mile of Alton Towers. A 20-acre site with 120 touring pitches and 58 statics.
Leisure: 🛝 **Facilities:** ◈ ⊙ ◥ ✳ ◟ 🐾 戸 ⊩
Services: 🔌 ⊡ ⓘ ⌀ Ⓣ
→ ∪ ▶ ↗

UTTOXETER Map 07 SK03

▶ ▶ ▶ **Racecourse Site (SK099334)**
Uttoxeter Racecourse ST14 8BD
☎ 01889 564172 & 562561
Dir: Located off B5017
★ 🚐 £5.20-£6.50 🚍 £5.20-£6.50 ▲ fr £7
Open Apr-Oct (rs Mar & Nov limited opening)
Booking advisable bank hols & race meeting dates Last arrival 20.00hrs Last departure noon
Situated on SE edge of small market town, mainly level site in hilly country. Ideal for Alton Towers and Peak District (5m). A 3-acre site with 83 touring pitches.
Facilities: ◈ ⊙ ✳ ◟ 戸 ⊩ **Services:** 🔌 ⓘ ⌀ Ⓣ
→ ∪ ▶ ⛽ ↗ ⊡ 🝙 🍴 🍟 🧺 🔋 🧷 🗲

SUFFOLK

BECCLES Map 05 TM48

▶ ▶ ▶ **Beulah Hall Caravan Park (TM478892)**
Dairy Ln, Mutford NR34 7QJ ☎ 01502 476609
Dir: 0.5m from A146, mid-way between Beccles and Lowestoft
🚐 £6-£8 🚍 £6-£8 ▲ £6-£8
Open Apr-Oct Booking advisable Jul-Aug
Small secluded site in well kept grounds with mature trees and hedging. Neat pitches and pleasant tent area beneath large trees opposite the swimming pool. Clean and well maintained portaloo toilets. A peaceful spot for those wishing to visit the Broads and the Suffolk coast. A 2.5-acre site with 30 touring pitches.
Leisure: ◥ **Facilities:** ◈ ⊙ ✳ ⊩ **Services:** 🔌 ⓘ ⌀ ⊞
→ ∪ ▶ ▲ ✚ 🝙 ↗ ⊡ 🝙

BUNGAY Map 05 TM38

▶ ▶ ▶ **Outney Meadow Caravan Park (TM333905)**
Outney Meadow NR35 1HG ☎ 01986 892338
Dir: Park is signposted from rdbt junction of A143 and A144 at Bungay
🚐 £7-£12 🚍 £7-£12 ▲ £7-£12

Open Mar-Oct Booking advisable public hols Last arrival 22.00hrs Last departure 21.00hrs
Pleasant park beside the River Waveney with mature trees and hedging, and three neatly kept level fields. The main toilet block houses improved sanitary facilities. A 6-acre site with 45 touring pitches and 30 statics.
Fishing Boat, canoe and bike hire.
Facilities: ◈ ⊙ ◥ ✳ ◟ 🐾 ⊩ **Services:** 🔌 ⊡ ⓘ ⌀ ⊞ Ⓣ
→ ∪ ▶ ▲ ✚ ↗

BURY ST EDMUNDS Map 05 TL86

▶ ▶ ▶ **The Dell Touring & Caravan Park (TL928640)**
Beyton Rd, Thurston IP31 3RB ☎ 01359 270121
Dir: Signed off A14 at Beyton/Thurston, 4m E of Bury St Edmunds
🚐 🚍 ▲
Open all year Booking advisable bank hols Last arrival anytime Last departure anytime

contd.

The Dell Touring & Caravan Park

A small developing site with enthusiastic owners, making an ideal stopover or base for exploring picturesque area. A 6-acre site with 60 touring pitches.

Leisure: ⚊ Facilities: ⬤⬤⬤⬤⬤⬤ Services: ⬤⬤⬤
→ ⬤

BUTLEY   Map 05 TM35

► ► ► **Forest Camping (TM355485)**
Rendalsham Forest IP12 3NF ☎ 01394 450707
Dir: From junct of A12 with A1152, follow tourist signs to Rendlesham Forest Centre on B1084

★ ⬤ £8-£10 ⬤ £8-£10 ⬤ £8-£10
Open Apr-Oct Booking advisable bank & school hols Last arrival 22.00hrs Last departure noon
Good, quiet, level grass site, situated on the edge of a deep forest with attractive walks. A 7-acre site with 90 touring pitches.
Leisure: ⚊ Facilities: ⬤⬤⬤⬤⬤⬤
Services: ⬤⬤⬤⬤⬤⬤
→ ⬤⬤ ⬤⬤⬤⬤⬤

DUNWICH   Map 05 TM47

► ► ► **Cliff House (TM475692)**
Minsmere Rd IP17 3DQ
☎ 01728 648282
Dir: From A12, follow sign to Dunwich Heath and Minsmere RSPB Reserve
★ ⬤ £10-£15 ⬤ £10-£15
Open Etr or Apr-Oct Booking advisable all year Last arrival 21.00hrs Last departure 11.00hrs
A delightful woodland park on the cliffs near Minsmere Bird Reserve. At its centre is a large house with a walled garden. A 30-acre site with 87 touring pitches and 93 statics.
Campers wash room, pool
Leisure: ⬤⚊ Facilities: ⬤⬤⬤⬤⬤⬤⬤
Services: ⬤⬤⬤⬤⬤⬤⬤⬤
→ ⬤ ⬤⬤⬤⬤⬤⬤

Facilities: ⬤ Bath ⬤ Shower ⬤ Electric Shaver ⬤ Hairdryer ⬤ Ice Pack Facility ⬤ Disabled Facilities ⬤ Public Telephone ⬤ Shop on Site or within 200yds ⬤ Mobile Shop (calls at least 5 days a week) ⬤ BBQ Area ⬤ Picnic Area ⬤ Dog Exercise Area

EAST BERGHOLT — Map 05 TM03

PREMIER PARK

▶ ▶ ▶ ▶ ▶ *Grange Country Park (TM098353)*
The Grange CO7 6UX ☎ 01206 298567 & 298912
Dir: 3m off A12 between Colchester and Ipswich
🚐 🚐 Å

Open 31 Mar-Oct (rs Oct-Mar) Booking advisable for stays of 1 wk or more Last arrival 22.00hrs Last departure 18.00hrs

Set in gently rolling countryside close to Flatford Mill in the heart of Constable country, a first class park sheltered by mature trees and bushes. The well-laid out grassy site offers plenty of screened super pitches, and the toilet facilities are of a superb standard. An attractive poolside area with a café is a new additon to this very popular holiday location. An 8-acre site with 120 touring pitches and 55 statics.

Leisure: ☀ ◀ 🅰 ⬜ **Facilities:** 🅁⊙🅀✳⬥🝔🅴🎢🎯
Services: 🕽🗑🍸🛢🧴🆃✕⚱
→ ∪⬥✚🍴

FELIXSTOWE — Map 05 TM33

▶ ▶ ▶ *Peewit Caravan Park (TM290338)*
Walton Av IP11 8HB ☎ 01394 284511 & 670217
Dir: Signed from A14 in Felixstowe
🚐 🚐 Å

Open Apr or Etr-Oct (rs early & late season shop closed) Booking advisable school & bank hols Last arrival 21.00hrs Last departure 11.00hrs
A useful town site, not overlooked by houses. The site is neat and tidy with clean toilets, and the beach is a few minutes away by car. A 3-acre site with 65 touring pitches and 220 statics.
Bowling green.

Leisure: 🅰 **Facilities:** 🅁⊙🅀✳⬥🝔
Services: 🕽🗑🛢🧴🆃
→ 🍴🍴

GISLEHAM — Map 05 TM58

▶ ▶ *Chestnut Farm Touring Park (TM510876)*
NR33 8EE ☎ 01502 740227
Dir: At S rdbt of Kessingland bypass take W exit signed Rushmere, Mutford and Gisleham. Site 2nd on left
🚐 🚐 Å

Open Apr-Oct Booking advisable bank hols Last arrival mdnt

A nice little farm site with old but well-maintained toilets in a peaceful setting. A 3-acre site with 20 touring pitches.
Fishing on site.

Facilities: 🅁⊙🎢 **Services:** 🕽
→ ∪🍴⊙⬥✚🍴🍴

IPSWICH — Map 05 TM14

▶ ▶ ▶ **Low House Touring Caravan Centre (TM227425)**
Bucklesham Rd, Foxhall IP10 0AU
☎ 01473 659437 & 0402 612219
Dir: From A45 south ring road take slip road to A1156 signed East Ipswich. Right in 1m and right again in 0.5m. Site on left
🚐 £6.50-£8.50 🚐 £6.50-£8.50 Å £4.25-£6.50
Open all year Booking advisable Last arrival anytime Last departure anytime
An appealing, secluded site with immaculate facilities and a very caring owner. A beautifully kept garden contains ornamental trees and plants, and there are unusual breeds of rabbits, bantams and guinea fowl. Tents accepted only if room available. A 3.5-acre site with 30 touring pitches. Temporary membership of sports centre opposite.

Leisure: 🅰 **Facilities:** 🅁⊙🅀✳🝔🎢
Services: 🕽🛢🧴🆃
→ ∪🍴⊙🍴🍴🗑

▶ ▶ ▶ **Priory Park (TM198409)**
IP10 0JT ☎ 01473 727393 & 726373
Dir: Leave A14 at Ipswich Southern Bypass and head for town centre. After 300mtrs left towards Priory Park. Follow the single carriageway into park
★ 🚐 £14-£15 🚐 £14-£15 Å £14-£15
Open Apr-Oct (rs Apr-May & Sep-Oct limited number of sites, club/pool closed) Booking advisable bank & school hols Last arrival 21.00hrs Last departure noon
Well-screened south-facing site with panoramic views overlooking Orwell. Convenient for Ipswich southern bypass. A 100-acre site with 75 touring pitches and 260 statics.
9 hole golf, small boat launching, table tennis.

Leisure: ☀ ◀ 🅰 **Facilities:** ⬅🅁⊙🅀✳🝔🎢🎢
Services: 🕽🗑🍸🛢🧴🆃✕
→ ∪🍴⬥🍴🍴🍴

See advert on page 186

KESSINGLAND — Map 05 TM58

▶ ▶ ▶ ▶ **Heathland Beach Caravan Park (TM533877)**
London Rd NR33 7PJ ☎ 01502 740337
★ 🚐 £10.50-£14 🚐 £10.50-£14 Å £6-£14
Open Apr-Oct Booking advisable peak periods Last arrival 22.00hrs Last departure noon
A well-run and maintained park offering superb toilet facilities. The park is set in meadowland, with level grass pitches, and mature trees and bushes. There is direct access to the sea and beach, and good provisions for families on site with a heated swimming pool and three play areas. An 11-acre site with 106 touring pitches and 200 statics. contd.

Freshwater/sea fishing.
Leisure: ᕯ ᖾ /ᴧ **Facilities:** ⋒⊙ঀ☀᳭⅃ᗺ☶╫
Services: ⊟⏍Ⴖᛘ∥⊡✕➜
→ ∪ ▶ ᐃ ⚡ ♨ ♪ ⬮⬮ ▦ ◨

▶ ▶ ▶ **Camping & Caravanning Club Site**
(TM520860)
Suffolk Wildlife Park, Whites Ln NR33 7SL
☎ 01502 742040
Dir: On A12 from Lowestoft at Kessingland rdbt, follow
Wildlife Park signs, turn right through park entrance
★ ⚘ £10.60-£13.90 ⚘ £10.60-£13.90 ᴀ £10.60-£13.90
Open 20 Mar-1 Nov Booking advisable bank hols &
Jul-Aug Last arrival 21.00hrs Last departure noon
An open site next to a wildlife park, with beaches
close by. Very tidy and well maintained.
Concessions to wildlife park. Please see the
advertisement on page 14 for details of Club
Members' benefits. A 6.5-acre site with 90 touring
pitches.
Leisure: /ᴧ **Facilities:** ⋒⊙ঀ☀᳭☶╫
Services: ⊟⏍Ⴖ∥⊡⏍ⓣ
→ ∪ ▶ ⊚ ⚡ ♨ ♪ ᗺ ⬮⬮ ▦

LEISTON   **Map 05 TM46**
▶ ▶ ▶ **Cakes & Ale (TM432637)**
Abbey Ln, Theberton IP16 4TE
☎ 01728 831655 & 01473 736650
Dir: E on B1119 from Saxmundham, after 3m follow
minor rd over level crossing, turn right, after 0.5m
straight on at X-roads, entrance 0.5m on left

⚘ £15-£16 ⚘ £15-£16 ᴀ £15-£16
Open Apr-Oct (rs low season club, shop/reception
open limited hours) Booking advisable public &
school hols Last arrival 21.00hrs Last departure
16.00hrs
A large, well spread out site with many trees and
bushes on a former Second World War airfield. The
spacious touring area includes plenty of
hardstandings and super pitches, and there is a
good bar and a well-maintained toilet block. A 5-
acre site with 50 touring pitches and 200 statics.
Tennis, 5-acre recreation ground, Driving Range &
Net
Leisure: ᖾ /ᴧ **Facilities:** ╫⋒⊙ঀ☀᳭ᗺ╫
Services: ⊟⏍Ⴖᛘ∥
→ ∪ ♨ ♪ ⬮⬮ ▦

LOWESTOFT
See **Kessingland**

NEWMARKET   **Map 05 TL66**
▶ ▶ **Camping & Caravanning Club Site (TL622625)**
Rowley Mile Racecourse CB8 8JL ☎ 01638 663235
Dir: From A1304 follow signs to racecourse. Drive down
the Rowley Mile which is signposted to site keeping
grandstand on the left
★ ⚘ £9.80-£12.40 ⚘ £9.80-£12.40 ᴀ £9.80-£12.40
Open 7 Apr-15 Sep Booking advisable Last arrival
21.00hrs Last departure noon
A level grassy site on Newmarket Heath with
panoramic country views. Please see the

Facilities: ╫ Bath ⋒ Shower ⊙ Electric Shaver ঀ Hairdryer ☀ Ice Pack Facility ᳭ Disabled Facilities ☎ Public Telephone
ᗺ Shop on Site or within 200yds ⊡ Mobile Shop (calls at least 5 days a week) ▦ BBQ Area ⅃ Picnic Area ╫ Dog Exercise Area

advertisement on page 14 for details of Club Members' benefits. A 10-acre site with 90 touring pitches.
Recreation room with TV, horse racing
Leisure: ⚠ **Facilities:** ⚱ ☀ ✆ **Services:** ♨ 🗑 🛢 🄀
→ ∪ ⚏ ● ▥

POLSTEAD   Map 05 TL93

▶ ▶ ▶ **Polstead Touring Park (TL986480)**
Holt Rd CO6 5BZ ☎ 01787 211969
Dir: 150yds off A1071 between Boxford and Hadleigh
★ 🚐 £7.50-£9 🚐 £7.50-£9 ▲ £5-£8
Open Mar-Oct (rs Feb & Nov) Booking advisable Jul & Aug Last arrival 22.30hrs Last departure noon
Brand new small site in the heart of the Suffolk countryside, close to Lavenham and Sudbury. Well-equipped, purpose built toilet block, and sheltered pitches attractively laid out. A 2.5-acre site with 30 touring pitches.
Leisure: ⚠ **Facilities:** ⚱ ☉ ⚒ ☀ ⚴ ⚲ ⚱ ⚏ ⚞ ⚓
Services: ♨ 🛢 🄀 ⊞
→ ∪ ▶ 🄍 🗑

SAXMUNDHAM   Map 05 TM36

▶ ▶ ▶ **Lonely Farm Camping & Caravaning Park (TM105878)**
Carlton IP17 2QP ☎ 01728 663416 & 07778 643419
★
Open Etr-1 Oct Booking advisable
Small, well-maintained farm site occupying three sheltered fields close to the owner's house. Good, level pitches in a peaceful, rural location. A good base for exploring the Heritage coast and Suffolk attractions. An adults-only site. A 3.5-acre site with 25 touring pitches.
Facilities: ⚱ ☉ ⚴ ⚓ **Services:** ♨ ⊞
→ 🄍

▶ ▶ ▶ **Whitearch Touring Caravan Park (TM379610)**
Main Rd, Benhall IP17 1NA
☎ 01728 604646 & 603773
Dir: On the junct of A12 & B1121
★ 🚐 fr £10.50 🚐 fr £10.50 ▲ fr £8.50
Open Apr-Oct Booking advisable bank hols Last arrival 20.45hrs
A small maturing park set around an attractive coarse-fishing lake, with clean toilet facilities and secluded pitches tucked away among mature trees and shrubs. Adjacent to A1 so can be noisy. A 14.5-acre site with 40 touring pitches.
Fishing lake
Leisure: ⚲ ⚠ **Facilities:** ⚱ ☉ ☀ ⚴ ⚲ ⚱ ⚏ ⚓
Services: ♨ 🗑 🛢 🄀
→ 🄍

▶ ▶ **Marsh Farm Caravan Site (TM385608)**
Sternfield IP171HW ☎ 01728 602168
Dir: Take Aldeburgh road from A12, at Snape X-roads turn left signed Sternfield and follow signs to farm
🚐 🚐

Open all year Booking advisable Jun-Aug Last arrival 22.30hrs Last departure 22.30hrs
Very attractive site with adjoining lakes offering coarse fishing. No showers. A 6-acre site with 30 touring pitches.
Leisure: ⚠ **Facilities:** ⚞ ⚱ ⚞ ⚓ **Services:** ♨ ⊞
→ ∪ ▶ ⚏ 🄍 🗑

SHOTTISHAM   Map 05 TM34

▶ **St Margaret's House (TM323447)**
Hollesley Rd IP12 3HD ☎ 01394 411247
Dir: Turn off B1083 at village. Site in 0.25m SE of church
🚐 🚐 ▲
Open Apr or Etr-Oct Booking advisable bank hols & Jul-Aug Last arrival 22.00hrs Last departure noon
A pleasant little family-run site in attractive village setting. A 3-acre site with 30 touring pitches.
Milk & newspapers to order.
Facilities: ⚱ ☉ ☀ **Services:** ♨ 🛢 🄀 ⊞ 🄣
→ ∪ ▶ ⚏ 🄍 ⚏

SUDBURY   Map 05 TL84

▶ ▶ ▶ **Willowmere Caravan Park (TL886388)**
Bures Rd, Little Cornard CO10 0NN ☎ 01787 375559
Dir: 1.5m S of Sudbury on B1508 Bures road
🚐
Open Etr-Sep
A pleasant little site in a quiet location tucked away beyond a tiny residential static area, offering spotless facilities. A 3-acre site with 40 touring pitches and 9 statics.

WOODBRIDGE   Map 05 TM24

PREMIER PARK

▶ ▶ ▶ ▶ ▶ **Moon & Sixpence (TM263454)**
Newbourn Rd, Waldringfield IP12 4PP
☎ 01473 736650
Dir: Follow caravan signs from A12 Ipswich East Bypass. Turn left at X-roads 1.5m from A12
🚐 £12-£18 🚐 £12-£18 ▲ £12-£18
Open Apr-Oct (rs low season club/shop/reception open limited hours) Booking advisable school & bank hols Last arrival 20.00hrs Last departure noon
A splendid, well-planned site, with tourers occupying a sheltered valley position around an attractive boating lake with a sandy beach. Toilet facilities are housed in a smart Norwegian cabin, and there is a laundry and immaculate dishwashing area. Leisure facilities include two tennis courts, a magnificent bowling green, fishing, boating and games room. This landscaped park includes 45 super pitches and an adult-only area, and there is a strict 'no groups and no noise after 9pm' policy. A 5-acre site with 65 touring pitches and 175 statics.
Lake, Woodland cycle trail,10 acre Sports & Rec area
Leisure: ⚲ ⚓ ⚠ **Facilities:** ➡ ⚱ ☉ ⚒ ☀ ✆ ⚲ ⚱ ⚓
Services: ♨ 🗑 🄎 🛢 🄀 ⊞ ✕
→ ∪ ▶ ⚑ ⚏ 🄍 ● ▥

See advert on page 188

Services: 🄣 Toilet Fluid ✕ Café/ Restaurant ⚒ Fast Food/Takeaway ➡ Baby Care ♨ Electric Hook Up 🗑 Launderette 🄎 Licensed Bar 🛢 Calor Gaz 🄍 Camping Gaz ⊞ Battery Charging

SURREY

CHERTSEY — Map 04 TQ06

► ► ► **Camping & Caravanning Club Site** (TQ052667)
Bridge Rd KT16 8JX ☎ 01932 562405
Dir: M25 junct 11, follow A317 to Chertsey. At rdbt take 1st exit to lights. Straight over next set. Turn right 400yds, then turn left into site
★ 🚐 £13.90-£14.90 🚐 £13.90-£14.90 Å £13.90-£14.90
Open all year Booking advisable Jul-Aug & bank hols Last arrival 21.00hrs Last departure noon
A pretty riverside site with many trees, shrubs, and well-looked after grounds. Fishing and boating allowed on the River Thames. Please see the advertisement on page 14 for details of Club Members' benefits. A 12-acre site with 196 touring pitches.
Table tennis, fishing.
Leisure: ⚏ ▢ **Facilities:** ⌐ ⊙ ⚛ ✳ ঌ ৳ ⚞ ⠇
Services: ⚲ ▣ ⓘ ⊘ ☰ ⊤
→ ⠇ ⌂ ⚐ 🗲 ⚄ ▨

EAST HORSLEY — Map 04 TQ05

► ► ► ► **Camping & Caravanning Club Site** (TQ083552)
Ockham Rd North KT24 6PE ☎ 01483 283273
Dir: S from M25 & take 1st major turning signed Ockham, Send & Ripley. Take left turn site is on right
★ 🚐 £11.80-£14.90 🚐 £11.80-£14.90 Å £11.80-£14.90

Open 20 Mar-1 Nov Booking advisable bank hols & Jul-Aug Last arrival 21.00hrs Last departure noon
Beautiful lakeside site with plenty of trees and shrubs, and separate camping fields, providing a tranquil base within easy reach of London. The park is well organised and immaculate, and the number of electric hook-ups has been increased recently. Please see the advertisement on page 14 for details of Club Members' benefits. A 12-acre site with 135 touring pitches.
Table tennis, fishing, dartboard.
Leisure: ⚘ ⊙ ▢ **Facilities:** ⌐ ⊙ ⚛ ✳ ঌ ৳ ⚞ ⠇
Services: ⚲ ▣ ⓘ ⊘ ⠇
→ ∪ ⠇ 🗲 ⚄ ▨

LINGFIELD — Map 05 TQ34

► ► ► **Long Acres Caravan & Camping Park** (TQ368425)
Newchapel Rd RH7 6LE ☎ 01342 833205
Dir: From A22 turn E into Newchapel Rd. Site signed from here
🚐 £9.50 🚐 £9.50 Å £9.50
Open all year Booking advisable bank hols & for electric hook ups Last arrival 22.30hrs Last departure noon
A pleasant ex-farm site, well-screened and well-maintained, with heated toilet facilities. Under Gatwick flight path. A 7-acre site with 60 touring pitches.
Free fishing, bike tracks
Leisure: ⚏ **Facilities:** ⌐ ⊙ ✳ ঌ ৳ 🍴 ⊼ ⠇
Services: ⚲ ▣ ⓘ ⊘ ☰ ⊤
→ ∪ ⠇ ⚬ ⚐

SUSSEX, EAST

BATTLE   Map 05 TQ71

▶ ▶ ▶ **Crazy Lane Touring Park (TQ782169)**
Whydown Farm, Crazy Ln, Sedlescombe TN33 0QT
☎ 01424 870147
*Dir: 100yds past B2244, off A21 travelling S, opposite
Black Brooks Garden Centre*
🚐 £8-£9.50 🚐 £8-£9.50 ▲ £8-£9.50
Open Mar-Oct Booking advisable bank hols
*A very good site on two levels amid attractive
scenery and overlooking cider orchards. A 3.5-acre
site with 36 touring pitches.*
Facilities: 🅵⊙🔄※🔥🔧🔋 **Services:** 🔌🔲🔋🔧🔋🔳🔲
➔ ∪ ▶ 🔧

▶ ▶ **Brakes Coppice Park (TQ765134)**
Forewood Ln TN33 9AB ☎ 01424 830322
*Dir: From Battle on A2100 towards Hastings. After 2m
turn right for Crowhurst. Site 1m on the left*
★ 🚐 £6-£7 🚐 £6-£7 ▲ £6-£7

Open Mar-Oct Booking advisable public hols & Jul-
Aug Last arrival 21.00hrs Last departure noon
*Secluded farm site in meadow surrounded by
woodland with small stream and fishing lake.
Pitches are neatly laid out on a terrace, and tents
are pitched on grass edged by woodland. A 3-acre
site with 30 touring pitches.*
Fishing.
Leisure: ⚠ **Facilities:** 🅵⊙🔄※🔥🔋🔳🔲🔧🔳
Services: 🔌🔲🔋🔧🔋🔳
➔ ∪ ▶ 🔧

CROWBOROUGH   Map 05 TQ53

▶ ▶ ▶ ▶ **Camping & Caravanning Club Site**
(TQ520315)
Goldsmith Recreation Ground TN6 2TN
☎ 01892 664827
*Dir: From N turn right & from S left off A26 into the
entrance to Goldsmiths Ground, signed Leisure Centre.
At top of road right onto site lane*
★ 🚐 £11.80-£14.90 🚐 £11.80-£14.90 ▲ £11.80-£14.90
Open Feb-19 Dec Booking advisable bank hols &
peak periods Last arrival 21.00hrs Last departure
noon
*A spacious terraced site with stunning views across
the Weald to the North Downs in Kent. This good
quality site has clean, modern toilets, a new kitchen
and eating area for campers, and good provision of
hardstandings. An excellent leisure centre is
adjacent to the park. Please see the advertisement
on page 14 for details of Club Members' benefits.
A 13-acre site with 90 touring pitches.*
Leisure: ⚠ **Facilities:** 🅵⊙🔄※🔥🔋🔋
Services: 🔌🔲🔧
➔ ∪ ▶ ※🔋🔧 🔋🔳

FURNER'S GREEN   Map 05 TQ42

▶ ▶ **Heaven Farm (TQ403264)**
TN22 3RG ☎ 01825 790226
*Dir: On A275 between Lewes and East Grinstead,
1m N of Sheffield Park Gardens*
🚐 🚐 ▲
Open Apr-Oct Booking advisable Last arrival
21.00hrs Last departure noon

contd.

▶ ▶ **Senlac Park Caravan & Camping Site**
(TQ722153)
Main Rd, Catsfield TN33 9DU
☎ 01424 773969 & 752590
*Dir: From Battle take A271, then left on B2204 signed
Bexhill*
🚐 🚐 ▲
Open Mar-Oct Booking advisable bank hols Last
arrival 20.30hrs Last departure noon
*A pretty woodland site with many secluded bays,
well landscaped and attractively laid out. A 5-acre
site with 32 touring pitches.*
Facilities: 🅵⊙※🔥🔋🔧 **Services:** 🔌🔋🔳🔲
➔ ∪ ▶ 🔧🔋 🔋🔳

Services: 🔲 Toilet Fluid ✗ Café/Restaurant 🏭 Fast Food/Takeaway 🍼 Baby Care 🔌 Electric Hook Up
🔳 Launderette 🍺 Licensed Bar 🔋 Calor Gaz 🔧 Camping Gaz 🔳 Battery Charging

England

Delightful small rural site on a popular farm complex incorporating a farm museum, craft shop, tea room and nature trail. Good clean facilities in well-converted outbuildings. A 1.5-acre site with 25 touring pitches.

Facilities: ⬅☺✳⬇️♿💧🛒🎏🐾 Services: 🔌✕
➔ ∪ ▶ ⏏

HASTINGS & ST LEONARDS Map 05 TQ80

► ► ► Shearbarn Holiday Park (TQ842112)

Barley Ln TN35 5DX ☎ 01424 423583 & 716474
Dir: From A259 to Rye-Folkestone, right at Stables Theatre into Harrow Rd, right into Gurth Rd, left at end into Barley Lane. Site signed
★ 🚐 £7.50-£17.25 🚐 £6.50-£17.25 ⚑ £5.50-£17.25
Open Mar-15 Jan (rs Mar-Etr, early May & mid Sep-15 Jan facilities may be closed or reduced) Booking advisable bank hols & Jul-Aug Last arrival 22.00hrs Last departure 10.00hrs
A large touring area set away from the statics and clubhouse on a high hill above Hastings with good sea views. Pitches are spacious, and good planting provides shade and shelter. A 16-acre site with 450 touring pitches and 250 statics.
Entertainment & amusements on site.

Leisure: ♦ ⚑ Facilities: ⬅☺✳⬇️♿💧🛒
Services: 🔌🗄💷🥛🔧📶🎫🅃✕🧹
➔ ∪ ▶ 🍴 ✕ 🅙 💳 🚮 📶 ⛽

HEATHFIELD   Map 05 TQ52

► ► Greenview Caravan Park (TQ605223)

Broad Oak TN21 8RT ☎ 01435 863531
Dir: Drive through Heathfield on A265 for 1m. Site on left after Broad Oak sign.
★ 🚐 fr £6.50 🚐 fr £6.50 ⚑ fr £6
Open Apr-Dec (rs Mar-Apr & Oct-Dec bookings only) Booking advisable Jul-Aug Last arrival 22.00hrs Last departure 10.30hrs 🐾
Small, attractive site with older-style facilities, adjoining residential park and main A265 at Broad Oak 1m E of Heathfield. A 3-acre site with 10 touring pitches and 51 statics.

Facilities: ⬅☺✳💧 Services: 🔌🗄💷🥛🔧🔧

HORAM   Map 05 TQ51

► ► ► Horam Manor Touring Park (TQ579170)

TN21 0YD ☎ 01435 813662
Dir: On A267, 3m S of Heathfield and 10m N of Eastbourne
★ 🚐 fr £11.85 🚐 fr £11.85 ⚑ fr £11.85

Open Mar-Oct Booking advisable peak periods
A well landscaped park in a peaceful location on former estate land, set in gently-sloping grassland surrounded by woods, nature trails and fishing lakes. A 7-acre site with 90 touring pitches.
Parent and toddler room

Facilities: ⬅☺✳⬇️♿💧🎏🐾 Services: 🔌🗄💷🔧📶🅃
➔ ∪ ▶ 🅙🚮

PETT   Map 05 TQ81

► ► Carters Farm (TQ887145)

Elm Ln TN35 4JD ☎ 01424 813206 & 812244
Dir: From A259 from Hastings turn right after Guestling, signed Pett
★ 🚐 £7-£8.50 🚐 £7-£8.50 ⚑ £7-£8.50
Open Mar-Oct Last arrival 21.00hrs Last departure noon
A very secluded, long-established working farm site in partly sloping meadow. A 12-acre site with 100 touring pitches and 85 statics.

Facilities: ⬅☺✳💧🚮 Services: 🔌💷🔧📶🅃🅃
➔ 🅙

PEVENSEY   Map 05 TQ60

► ► ► Camping & Caravanning Club Site (TQ682055)

Normans Bay BN24 6PP ☎ 01323 761190
Dir: From rdbt at junct of A27/A259 follow A259 signed Eastbourne. In Pevensey Bay village 1st left signed Beachlands only. After 1.25m site on left
★ 🚐 £11.80-£14.90 🚐 £11.80-£14.90 ⚑ £11.80-£14.90
Open 20 Mar-1 Nov Booking advisable bank hols & peak periods Last arrival 21.00hrs Last departure noon
A well-kept site with immaculate toilet block, right beside the sea. This popular family park enjoys good rural views towards Rye and Pevensey. Please see the advertisement on page 14 for details of Club Members' benefits. A 3-acre site with 200 touring pitches.
Recreation hall

Leisure: 🎾♦⚑ Facilities: ⬅☺🍳✳⬇️♿💧🐾🎏
Services: 🔌🗄💷🔧📶🅃
➔ ∪ ▶ 🅰🅙 💳 🚮

PEVENSEY BAY   Map 05 TQ60

► ► ► Bayview Caravan and Camping Park (TQ648028)

Old Martello Rd BN24 6DX ☎ 01323 768688
Dir: Signed off A259. On sea side of A259 along private road towards beach
🚐 £8.90-£9.95 🚐 £8.90-£9.95 ⚑ £8.50-£9.20
Open Mar-Oct Booking advisable bank & school hols Last arrival 22.00hrs Last departure noon
A pleasant well-run site just yards from the beach, in an area east of the town centre known as 'The Crumbles'. The level grassy site is very well maintained. A 3.5-acre site with 49 touring pitches and 5 statics.

Leisure: ⚑ Facilities: ⬅☺🍳✳💧🛒
Services: 🔌🗄💷🔧📶🅃
➔ ▶ 🅙🅰🍴 🅙

Facilities: ⬅ Bath 🍴 Shower ☺ Electric Shaver 🧖 Hairdryer ✳ Ice Pack Facility ♿ Disabled Facilities 💧 Public Telephone
🛒 Shop on Site or within 200yds 🖥 Mobile Shop (calls at least 5 days a week) 🚻 BBQ Area 🎏 Picnic Area 🐾 Dog Exercise Area

credit with many items ava[...]
38 weeks interest-free. Plus, [...]
for up to 150 weeks interest-free
credit on selected items!

FREE 14-day Approval
Try before you buy and if
you're not completely
satisfied, return it FREE!

SEAFORD — Map 05 TV49

►►► ***Buckle Caravan & Camping Park (TV469960)***
Marine Pde BN25 2QR ☎ 01323 897801
Dir: *Signed off A259 on W side of Seaford towards Newhaven*

Open Mar-2 Jan Booking advisable bank hols & Jul-Aug Last arrival 21.00hrs Last departure noon
A friendly, well-maintained site set alongside the sea wall.The main area is for adults only, with grassy pitches, low fencing and selective planting, while a second area with relaxed pitches is for families. A 9-acre site with 110 touring pitches.
Leisure: **Facilities:**
Services:
→

SUSSEX, WEST

BOGNOR REGIS — Map 04 SZ99

►► ***Lillies Nursery & Caravan Park (SU964040)***
Yapton Rd, Barnham PO22 0AY ☎ 01243 552081
Dir: *On B2233 in Barnham, 2m off A27 & 6m from Bognor Regis*

Open Mar-Oct Booking advisable Jul-Sep Last departure 11.00hrs

A friendly little site tucked behind the owner's nursery, with gradually improving facilities in secluded peaceful countryside. A 3-acre site with 36 touring pitches and 6 statics.
Play area for ball games.
Facilities: **Services:**
→

CHICHESTER

See advert below and entry p.193

DIAL POST — Map 04 TQ11

►►►► **Honeybridge Park (TQ152183)**
Honeybridge Ln RH13 8NX ☎ 01403 710923
Dir: *10m S of Horsham on A24. Turn left 1m past Dial Post at Old Barn Nurseries, continue 300yds, park on right*
★ £7.50-£11.50 £7.50-£11.50 £7.50-£11.50

contd.

Services: Toilet Fluid · Café/ Restaurant · Fast Food/Takeaway · Baby Care · Electric Hook Up · Launderette · Licensed Bar · Calor Gaz · Camping Gaz · Battery Charging

Open all year Booking advisable bank hols & high
season Last arrival 22.00hrs Last departure 20.00hrs
Gently sloping and part level site surrounded by
hedgerows and mature trees.The hardworking and
enthusiastic young owners keep the sanitary
facilities immaculate, and there are plenty of
hardstandings and electric hook-ups. An excellent
children's play area includes an aerial runway and
adventure equipment. A 15-acre site with 100
touring pitches.
Leisure: ♣ ⚠ Facilities: ♦ ⊙ ⬛ ✳ ♿ ☎ ⚡ ⬛ 🎋 ➤
Services: ⬛ ⬛ ⬛ ⬛ ⬛ ⬛
➜ ∪ ▶ ⬛ ♪ ⬛ ⬛ ⬛ ⬛

GOODWOOD   Map 04 SU81

▶ ▶ ▶ **Goodwood Racecourse Caravan Park**
(SU885111)
Goodwood Racecourse PO18 0PS
☎ 01243 755033 & 755022
Dir: Off A285, Petworth/Chicester road or A286
Midhurst/Chichester road. 5m N of Chichester
⬛ ⬛ Å
Open Etr-Sep (rs during race meetings site is
closed) Booking advisable public hols & Jul-Aug
Last arrival 20.00hrs Last departure noon
A neat and tidy level grassy site on Goodwood
Racecourse. Closed when race meetings are held.
A 3-acre site with 62 touring pitches.
Leisure: ⚠ Facilities: ♦ ⊙ ♿ ☎ 🎋 Services: ⬛ ⬛ ⬛
➜ ∪ ▶ ⬛ ⬛ ⬛ ⬛

GRAFFHAM   Map 04 SU91

▶ ▶ ▶ **Camping & Caravanning Club Site**
(SU941187)
Great Bury GU28 0QJ ☎ 01798 867476
Dir: From Petworth on A285 pass Badgers Pub on left
and BP garage on right. Take next right signposted
Selham Graffham. Follow camping sign to the site
★ ⬛ £11.80-£14.90 ⬛ £11.80-£14.90 Å £11.80-£14.90
Open 20 Mar-1 Nov Booking advisable bank hols &
peak periods Last arrival 21.00hrs Last dep noon
A superb wooded site, with each pitch occupying its
own private, well-screened area. Please see the
advertisement on page 14 for details of Club
Members' benefits. A 20-acre site with 90 touring
pitches.
Facilities: ♦ ⊙ ⬛ ✳ ♿ ☎ ⬛ 🎋 ➤
Services: ⬛ ⬛ ⬛ ⬛ ⬛ ⬛ ↩
➜ ∪ ♪ ⬛ ⬛

HENFIELD   Map 04 TQ21

▶ **Harwoods Farm (TQ196153)**
West End Ln BN5 9RF ☎ 01273 492820
Dir: From Henfield High Street, turn into Church St,
continue for 2m to end of Farm Lane, site on right at the
end
⬛ £6 Å £6
Open Etr-Oct Booking advisable bank hols Last
arrival mdnt Last departure evening
A really unspoilt site with earth closets and drinking
water taps down a rough, narrow lane in good
walking area. A 1.75-acre site with 35 touring
pitches.
♿ Services:
➜ ⬛

LITTLEHAMPTON   Map 04 TQ00

▶ ▶ ▶ ***White Rose Touring Park (TQ029039)***
Mill Ln, Wick BN17 7PH ☎ 01903 716176
Dir: From A284 turn left into Mill Lane
⬛ ⬛ Å
Open 15 Mar-15 Jan Booking advisable bank hols &
Jul-Aug Last departure noon

A well-maintained family-run site providing level,
well-drained ground surrounded by farmland.
Located close to Arundel and Littlehampton which
provide good local facilities. A 7-acre site with 127
touring pitches and 14 statics.
Leisure: ⚠ Facilities: ♦ ⊙ ⬛ ✳ ♿ ☎ ⬛ 🎋
Services: ⬛ ⬛ ⬛ ⬛ ⬛
➜ ∪ ▶ ⬛ ⬛ ♪ ⬛ ⬛ ⬛ ⬛

SELSEY   Map 04 SZ89

Warner Farm Touring Park (SZ845939)
Warner Ln, Selsey PO20 9EL
☎ 01243 604121 & 604499
Dir: Turn right onto School Lane & follow signs
★ ⊕ £10-£25 ⊕ £10-£25 ▲ £10-£25
Open Mar-Oct Booking advisable 3 wks prior to
arrival Last arrival 20.00hrs Last departure
10.00hrs
*A well-screened touring site adjoining three
static sites under same ownership. A courtesy
bus runs around the complex to entertainment
and supermarkets. The park backs onto open
grassland, but the new leisure facilities with bar,
amusements and bowling alley, and the
swimming pool/sauna complex are also
accessible. A 10-acre site with 200 touring
pitches and 1500 statics.*
See advertisement under CHICHESTER

Leisure: ⚡ ⚡ ⚡ ⚡ ⚑ 🛆 □ **Facilities:** 🏕️ ☉ ✻ ⚓ ℂ
🐾 ✿ 🎋 🐾 **Services:** ⚡ 🅑 ⚡ ⚓ ⚓ 🖽 🗓 ✕ 🖤
→ ∪ ▶ ⊚ ♪ 🍴 ▦ ⚋⚋ ▨▨▨ ▨▨ 🗐

SLINDON   Map 04 SU90

▶ **Camping & Caravanning Club Site (SU958084)**
Slindon Park BN18 0RG ☎ 01243 814387
*Dir: From A27 Fontwell to Chichester turn right at sign
for Britten's Lane & 2nd right to Slindon. Site on this
road*
★ ⊕ £8.60-£9.60 ⊕ £8.60-£9.60 ▲ £8.60-£9.60
Open 20 Mar-27 Sep Booking advisable bank hols &
peak periods Last arrival 21.00hrs Last departure
noon
*Beautiful former orchard, completely screened by
NT trees and very quiet. Own sanitary facilities
essential. Please see the advertisement on page 14
for details of Club Members' benefits. A 2-acre site
with 40 touring pitches.*
Facilities: ✻ ℂ 🐾 **Services:** ⚡ 🛈
→ ▶ ♪ 🍴 ▨▨▨

SOUTHBOURNE   Map 04 SU70

▶ ▶ ▶ **Camping & Caravanning Club Site
(SU774056)**
343 Main Rd PO10 8JH ☎ 01243 373202
*Dir: From Chichester take A259 to Southampton, site on
right past Inlands Rd*
★ ⊕ £13.90-£14.90 ⊕ £13.90-£14.90 ▲ £13.90-£14.90
Open all year Booking advisable bank hols, wknds
& mid Jun-mid Sep Last arrival 22.00hrs Last
departure 14.00hrs
*Situated in open meadow and orchard, a very
pleasant, popular site with well looked after, clean
facilities. Well placed for Chichester, South Downs
and the ferry ports. Please see the advertisement on
page 14 for details of Club Members' benefits. A 3-
acre site with 58 touring pitches.*
Facilities: 🏕️ ☉ ⚡ ✻ ⚓ **Services:** ⚡ 🅑
→ ∪ ▶ 🛆 ♪ 🐾 🍴 ▨▨▨

SOUTHWATER   Map 04 TQ12

▶ ▶ ▶ **Raylands Park (TQ170265)**
Jackrells Ln RH13 7DH ☎ 01403 730218 & 731822
Dir: Signposted from A24 in Southwater
★ ⊕ fr £9 ⊕ fr £9 ▲ £6-£9

Open Mar-Oct Booking advisable bank hols & high
season Last arrival 20.00hrs Last departure 14.00hrs
*A very well run site in an excellent setting.
Reasonably level ground, superb modern toilet
blocks, a clubhouse and children's play area. Well
maintained access roads. A 6-acre site with 40
touring pitches and 60 statics.*
Leisure: ⚡ ⚡ ⚑ 🛆 □ **Facilities:** 🏕️ ☉ ✻ ⚓ ℂ 🎋
Services: ⚡ 🅑 ⚡ 🛈 ⚓ 🖽 ✕ 🖤
→ ∪ ▶ 🛆 🐾 ♪ 🐾 🍴 ▦ ⚋⚋ ▨▨ ▨▨ 🗐

WEST WITTERING   Map 04 SZ79

▶ ▶ ▶ **Wicks Farm Holiday Park (SZ796995)**
Redlands Ln PO20 8QD ☎ 01243 513116
*Dir: From Chichester take A286/B2179 to West Wittering.
Follow road for 6m, then 2nd right after Lamb Inn.*
⊕ ▲
Open 14 Mar-Oct Booking advisable peak periods
Last arrival 21.00hrs Last departure noon
*A pleasant rural site, well-screened by trees with
good walks nearby and 2m from coast. A 14-acre
site with 40 touring pitches.*
Bicycle hire.
Leisure: ⚡ ⚑ **Facilities:** 🏕️ ☉ ⚡ ✻ ℂ 🐾 🎋
Services: ⚡ 🅑 🛈 ⚓ 🖽
→ ▶ ⊚ 🛆 ♪ 🍴 ▨▨▨ ▨▨ 🗐

TYNE & WEAR

ROWLANDS GILL   Map 12 NZ15

▶ ▶ ▶ *Derwent Park Caravan Site (NZ168586)*
NE39 1LG ☎ 01207 543383
Dir: On edge of Rowlands Gill at junct of A694 and B6314
⊕ ⊕ ▲
Open Apr-Sep Booking advisable public hols & Jul-
Aug Last arrival 23.30hrs Last departure noon
*A very pleasant and well-maintained municipal site.
A 3-acre site with 47 touring pitches and 25 statics.*
Fishing, crazy golf, giant draughts & chess, bowling.
Leisure: ⚡ ⚑ **Facilities:** 🏕️ ☉ ⚡ ✻ ⚓ ℂ 🐾 ✿ 🎋 🐾
Services: ⚡ 🅑 🛈 ⚓ 🖽 🖤 ⇛
→ ∪ ▶ ⊚ 🐾 ♪ 🍴 ▨▨▨ ▨▨ 🗐

Services: 🖽 Toilet Fluid ✕ Café/ Restaurant 🖤 Fast Food/Takeaway ⇛ Baby Care ⚡ Electric Hook Up
🅑 Launderette ⚡ Licensed Bar 🛆 Calor Gaz ⊘ Camping Gaz ⚓ Battery Charging

SOUTH SHIELDS   Map 12 NZ36

► ► ► **Lizard Lane Caravan & Camping Site** (NZ399648)
Lizard Ln NE34 7AB
☎ 0191 454 4982 & 0191 455 7411
Dir: 2m S of town centre on A183 Sunderland road
★ ⊞ £7.20-£9.60 ⊞ £7.20-£9.60 ▲ £6.30-£7.20
Open Mar-Oct Booking advisable for complete wks Jul-5 Sep Last arrival anytime Last dep 11.00hrs
Sloping, grass site near beach, well-kept and maintained. A 2-acre site with 45 touring pitches and 70 statics.
9 hole Putting Green
Leisure: ⚠ Facilities: ⋒⊙ℚ❋❋♥ℤ🎋
Services: ⊡ ⅰ ∅ ⊞
→ ∪ ▶ ⚌ ⅍ ⚌ ♩ ▤ ▦

────────────────────

► ► ► **Sandhaven Caravan & Camping Park** (NZ376672)
Bents Park Rd NE33 2NL
☎ 0191 454 5594 & 0191 455 7411
Dir: Situated on A183, 0.5m from the town centre with an entrance on Bents Park Road
★ ⊞ £9.30-£10.50 ⊞ £9.30-£10.50 ▲ £8.30-£9.50
Open Mar-Oct Booking advisable for complete wks Jul-5 Sep Last arrival anytime Last departure 11.00hrs
A spacious site adjoining the seafront, set in a well-screened and fenced area next to a public park. A 3.5-acre site with 52 touring pitches and 46 statics.
Facilities: ⋒⊙ℚ❋❋♥ℤ🎋 Services: ⊡ⅰ∅
→ ∪ ▶ ⅍ ⚌ ♩ ▤

WARWICKSHIRE

ASTON CANTLOW   Map 04 SP16

► ► ► ► **Island Meadow Caravan Park** (SP137596)
The Mill House B95 6JP ☎ 01789 488273
Dir: 0.25m W of Aston Cantlow on Alcester road
⊞ fr £10.50 ⊞ fr £10.50 ▲ £4-£12
Open Mar-Oct Booking advisable peak periods Last arrival 21.00hrs Last departure noon
A small well-kept site bordered by the River Alne on one side and its mill stream on the other. Mature willows line the banks, and this is a very pleasant place to relax and unwind. A 7-acre site with 24 touring pitches and 56 statics.
Free fishing for guests.
Facilities: ⋒⊙❋❋♥ℤ🎋🐕 Services: ⊡ⅰ∅⊞Ⓣ
→ ∪ ▶ ◎ ♩

KINGSBURY   Map 04 SP29

► ► ► **Camping & Caravanning Club Site** (SP202968)
Kingsbury Water Park, Bodymoor Heath B76 0DY
☎ 01827 874101
Dir: Junct 9 off M42 take B4097 Kingsbury Rd. At rdbt left, proceed past main entrance to water park, over motorway, next right, follow for 0.5m to site
★ ⊞ £9.80-£12.40 ⊞ £9.80-£12.40 ▲ £9.80-£12.40

Open 20 Mar-1 Nov Booking advisable bank hols & Jul-Aug Last arrival 21.00hrs Last departure noon
A former gravel pit, now reclaimed and landscaped, the site is part of a level complex of lakes, canals, woods and marshland with good access roads. Please see the advertisement on page 14 for details of Club Members' benefits. An 18-acre site with 120 touring pitches.
Facilities: ⋒⊙ℚ♥⅃ Services: ⊡⊞ⅰ∅⊞Ⓣ
→ ⚌ ⅍ ♩ ℤ ⚌ ● ▦

────────────────────

► **Tame View Caravan Site** (SP209979)
Cliff B78 2DR ☎ 01827 873853
Dir: 400yds off A51 Tamworth-Kingsbury road, 1m N of Kingsbury opposite restaurant. Signed 'No through road'
⊞ ⊞ ▲
Open all year Booking advisable 1 month in advance Last arrival 23.00hrs Last departure 23.00hrs
Enclosed level meadow on high bank overlooking River Tame, with minimal sanitary facilities. A 5-acre site with 55 touring pitches.
Fishing.
Facilities: ❋ℤ🎋🐕 Services: Ⓣ
→ ∪ ▶ ◎ ⚌ ⅍ ⚌ ♩ ▤

WOLVEY   Map 04 SP48

► ► ► **Wolvey Villa Farm Caravan & Camping Site** (SP428869)
LE10 3HF ☎ 01455 220493 & 220630
Dir: M6 junct 2 follow Wolvey signs on B4065, or M69 junct 1, again follow Wolvey signs
⊞ £6-£6.20 ⊞ £6-£6.20 ▲ £6-£6.20
Booking advisable Spring bank hol-mid Aug Last arrival 22.00hrs Last departure noon

Level, grass site with mature trees and bushes set in meadowland. About 1m S of Wolvey. Ideally located to explore the Midlands area. A 7-acre site with 110 touring pitches.
Fishing, putting green, off licence.
Leisure: ☐ Facilities: ⋒⊙❋♥ℤ🎋🐕
Services: ⊡⊞ⅰ∅⊞Ⓣ
→ ∪ ▶ ♩

WIGHT, ISLE OF

BEMBRIDGE
See **Whitecliff Bay**

FRESHWATER   Map 04 SZ38

▶ ▶ ▶ *Heathfield Farm Camping (SZ335879)*
Heathfield Rd PO40 9SH ☎ 01983 756756 & 752480
Dir: Signed off A3054 in Freshwater. 2m S of Yarmouth
🚐 🚐 Å

Open all year Booking advisable bank hols & Jul-Aug Last arrival 22.30hrs Last departure 22.30hrs
Level grassy park enjoying sea views across the Solent to Hurst Castle. Well-maintained, with plenty of electric hook-ups and spotless portaloo sanitary facilities. A 4-acre site with 60 touring pitches.
Facilities: ↿ ⊙ ℜ ⚹ ⚸ ☍ **Services:** 🖭 ⊘
➜ ∪ ▶ ⚹ ⤳ 🗓 🖳

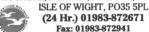
NEWBRIDGE   Map 04 SZ48

PREMIER PARK

▶ ▶ ▶ ▶ ▶ **Orchards Holiday Caravan Park** (SZ411881)
PO41 0TS ☎ 01983 531331 & 531350
Dir: From A1 turn E onto A698 to Berwick & site is 1m on the right. Entrance opposite Post Office
🚐 £7.95-£11.55 🚐 £7.95-£11.55 Å £7.95-£11.55
Open 17 Feb-2 Jan (rs Etr-Apr & late Sep-Oct)
Booking advisable Etr, Spring bank hol & late Jun-Aug Last arrival 23.00hrs Last departure 11.00hrs
An excellent, well-managed park set in a peaceful village location amid downs and meadowland, with glorious downland views. Pitches are terraced, and offer a good provision of hardstandings, including super pitches. The toilet facilities are immaculate, and the park benefits from both indoor and outdoor swimming pools. There is excellent provision for families, and disabled access to all facilities on site, plus disabled toilets. An 8-acre site with 175 touring pitches and 65 statics.
Coarse fishing, petanque.
Leisure: ⌇ ⌇ ♦ ⁄△☐ **Facilities:** ➡↿⊙ℜ⚹
⏁⛾🖳👪 **Services:** 🖭🛢🗑⊞☐✕♨
➜∪⤳ 🍴 ▤▦ ▦ 🖳

See advert on page 196

NEWCHURCH   Map 04 SZ58

PREMIER PARK

▶ ▶ ▶ ▶ ▶ **Southland Camping Park** (SZ557847)
PO36 0LZ ☎ 01983 865385
Dir: Take A3056 to Sandown. Turn down the 2nd road on the left after Fighting Cocks pub towards Newchurch. Site 1m on left
🚐 £7.25-£11 🚐 £7.25-£11 Å £7.25-£11
Open Etr-Sep Booking advisable Jul-Aug Last arrival 21.30hrs Last departure 11.00hrs

Beautifully maintained site, peacefully located and impressively laid out, on the outskirts of the village in the Arreton Valley. Spotless, newly extended sanitary facilities, including spacious family rooms, enhance the park. Pitches are well screened by lovely trees and shrubs, and everything is under the personal supervision of the hard-working owners. A 7-acre site with 120 touring pitches.

contd.

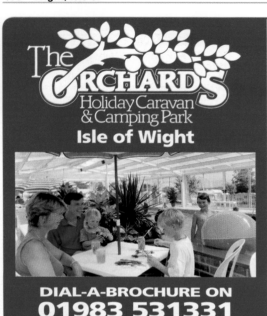

12 volt transformers available.

Leisure: ⚠ **Facilities:** ➡ ⚓ ☉ ⛱ ✳ ⛵ ♨ ⊞ 🔥 ☎ **Services:** ⚙ 🗑 ⬆ ⌀ ⊞ 🅣 ➡
→ ∪ ▶ ◉ ⛷ ✚ 🏕 ⚗ 💳 🚂 📶 🔁

PONDWELL   Map 04 SZ69

▶ ▶ ▶ **Pondwell Camp Site (SZ622911)**
PO34 5AQ ☎ 01983 612330
Dir: From Ryde take A3055 turning left along B3350 to Seaview. Site is next to Wishing Well pub
🚐 £6-£8 🚍 £6-£8 ▲ £6-£8
Open May-26 Sep Booking advisable Aug Last arrival 23.00hrs Last departure 11.00hrs ⚘
A secluded site in quiet rural surroundings close to the sea, slightly sloping with some level areas. Signed from Ryde. A 9-acre site with 250 touring pitches.
Leisure: ⚓ ⚠ ⛱ **Facilities:** ➡ ⚓ ☉ ⛱ ✳ ⛵ ♨ 🔥
Services: ⚙ 🗑 ⬆ ⌀ ⊞ → ▶ ◉ ✚ 🏕 ⚗ 💳 🚂 🔁

SANDOWN   Map 04 SZ58

PREMIER PARK

▶ ▶ ▶ ▶ ▶ *Adgestone Camping Park (SZ590855)*
Lower Adgestone Rd PO36 0HL
☎ 01983 403432 & 403989
Dir: 2m NW of Sandown. Take A3055 to Lake, at Old Manor pub, take The Fairway, follow signs
🚐 🚍 ▲

Open Etr/mid Mar-Sep (rs Off peak limited opening of takeaway) Booking advisable high season Last arrival dusk Last departure 11.00hrs
A popular, well-managed park in a quiet, rural location not far from Sandown. The level pitches are imaginatively laid out, and surrounded by beautiful flower beds and trees set close to a small river. This planting offers good screening as well as enhancing the appearance of the park. Spotless sanitary facilities include two family rooms. Excellent provision for families. A 17.5-acre site with 200 touring pitches. River fishing, football pitch, petanque, volleyball.
Leisure: 🎣 ⚠ **Facilities:** ⚓ ☉ ⛱ ✳ ⛵ ♨ 🔥
Services: ⚙ 🗑 ⬆ ⌀ ⊞ 🅣 🧹 ➡
→ ∪ ▶ ◉ ⛷ ✚ 🏕 ⚗ 💳 🚂 📶 🔁

▶ ▶ ▶ **Old Barn Touring Park (SZ573833)**
Cheverton Farm, Newport Rd, Apse Heath PO36 9PJ
☎ 01983 866414
Dir: On A3056 from Newport, site on left after Apse Heath
★ £11.80-£14.90 🚍 £11.80-£14.90 ▲ £11.80-£14.90
Open 20 Mar-27 Nov Booking advisable bank hols & peak periods Last arrival 21.00hrs Last dep noon
A terraced site with good quality facilities, bordering on open farmland. Please see the advertisement on page 14 for details of Club Members' benefits. A 4-acre site with 50 touring pitches.

Leisure: ◖ ▭ Facilities: ⋒⊙℥⋇⅋⚮⊾ ⼞
Services: ◙⬚⊟ 𝄄 ⌀⊞
→ ∪ ▶ ◮⛬⛢⌙⛴ ⛟ ▤

▶ ▶ **Cheverton Copse Holiday Park (SZ570833)**
Scotchells Brook Ln PO36 0JP ☎ 01983 403161
Dir: 400yds from A3056 towards Newport,
1m from Lake
⛺
Open Apr-Oct
New owners are gradually improving facilities at
this small park situated on the edge of open
farmland close to the resort attractions of Sandown
and Shanklin. Part-sloping touring field with some
terraced pitches and simple, clean toilet facilities.
A 1-acre site with 26 touring pitches.

▶ **Queen Bower Dairy Caravan Park (SZ567846)**
Alverstone Rd, Queen Bower PO36 0NZ
☎ 01983 403840 & 407392
Dir: 3m N of Sandown off A3056 towards Cowes.
Between Heath and Alverstone
★ ⛟ £4-£6 ⛟ £4-£6 ⚠ £4-£6
Open May-Oct Booking advisable Jul & Aug Last
arrival anytime Last departure anytime
A site with basic amenities, run by an enthusiastic
owner, that will appeal to campers keen to escape
the crowds and the busy, larger sites. Situated three
miles north of Sandown. A 2.5-acre site with 20
touring pitches.
Facilities: ⛴ Services: ◙ ⊞
→ ▶ ◉ ◮ ⛢ ⛟ ⛟ ▥

SHANKLIN   Map 04 SZ58

▶ ▶ ▶ **Landguard Camping Park (SZ577825)**
Landguard Manor Rd PO37 7PH
☎ 01983 867028
Dir: Take A3056 to Sandown, turn right after passing
"Safeways" at Lake into Whitecross Lane.
Follow signs to site
★ ⛟ £6.80-£11 ⛟ £6.80-£11 ⚠ £6.80-£11

Open Etr-Sep Booking advisable school hols Last
arrival 22.00hrs Last departure noon ⚷
Part of a holiday complex, the touring area is
secluded and surrounded by trees, in a rural setting.
A 7-acre site with 150 touring pitches.
Horse riding.
Leisure: ⟋ ⟋ ⋔ Facilities: ⋒⊙℥⋇⅋⊾⛴
Services: ◙⬚⚲𝄄⌀⊞⊞⤬⯊⤙
→ ∪ ▶ ◉ ◮⛬⛢⛟ ⛟ ▤ ▤ ▥

▶ ▶ ▶ **Ninham Country Holidays (SZ573825)**
Ninham Farm PO37 7PL ☎ 01983 864243 866040
Dir: Signposted off A3056 Newport to Sandown road
★ ⛟ £7.50-£10.50 ⛟ £7.50-£10.50 ⚠ £7.50-£10.50
Open Est-Sep Booking advisable Jun-Sep
Enjoying a lofty rural position with fine country
views, this delightful, spacious park occupies two
separate well-maintained areas in a country park
setting near the sea and beach. An 8-acre site with
88 touring pitches.
Coarse fishing.
Leisure: ⟋ ⼭ Facilities: ⋒⊙℥⋇⛴⚮⛴⼞
Services: ◙⬚𝄄⌀⊞⊞⤬⤙
→ ∪ ▶ ◉ ◮⛬⛢⛟ ⛟ ▤ ▨ ▥

TOTLAND BAY   Map 04 SZ38

▶ ▶ *Stoats Farm Camping (SZ324620)*
PO39 0HE ☎ 01983 755258 & 753461
⛺
Open Mar-Oct

A friendly, personally run site in a quiet country
setting close to Alum Bay, Tennyson Down and The
Needles. It has good laundry and shower facilities,
and the shop, though small, is well stocked. Popular
with families, walkers and cyclists. A 10-acre site
with 100 touring pitches.
Facilities: ⋒

WHITECLIFF BAY   Map 04 SZ68

 Whitecliff Bay Holiday Park
(SZ637862)
Hillway Rd, Bembridge PO35 5PL
☎ 01983 872671
Dir: 1m S of Bembridge, signed off B3395 in village
★ ⛟ £6.80-£12 ⛟ £6.80-£12 ⚠ £6.80-£12
Open May-Oct (rs Mar-Apr limited
entertainments) Booking advisable Jul-Aug
A large seaside complex on two sites, with
tourers and tents on one and tourers and statics
on the other. Toilets of a very high standard.
Many entertainments and easy access to beach.
A 49-acre site with 400 touring pitches and 227
statics.
Leisure centre with fun pool, spa bath & sauna.
Leisure: ⟋ ⟋ ◖ ⼭ Facilities: ⤙⋒⊙℥⋇⅋⊾⛴
Services: ◙⬚⚲𝄄⌀⊞⊞⤬⯊
→ ∪ ▶ ⛢ ⛟ ⛟ ▤ ▥

See advert on page 195

Services: ⊞ Toilet Fluid   ⤬ Café/ Restaurant   ⯊ Fast Food/Takeaway   ⤙ Baby Care   ◙ Electric Hook Up
⬚ Launderette   ⚲ Licensed Bar   𝄄 Calor Gaz   ⌀ Camping Gaz   ⊞ Battery Charging

England

WOOTTON BRIDGE   Map 04 SZ59

► ► ► *Kite Hill Farm Caravan Park (SZ549206)*
Firestone Copse Rd PO33 4LE
☎ 01983 882543 & 883261
Dir: Signposted off A3054 at Wootton Bridge, between Ryde and Newport
⊡
Open all year
The park, on a gently sloping field, is tucked away behind the owners' farm, just a short walk from the village and attractive river estuary. Facilities are well maintained and the atmosphere pleasantly relaxing. A 12.5-acre site with 50 touring pitches.

WROXALL   Map 04 SZ57

► ► ► Appuldurcombe Gardens Caravan & Camping Park (SZ546804)
Appuldurcombe Rd PO38 3EP ☎ 01983 852597
Dir: From Newport take A3020, turning off towards Shanklin, through Godshill. Turn right at Whitely Bank rdbt towards Wroxhall
⊞ £7-£11 ⊞ £7-£11 Å £7-£11
Open Spring bank hol-Oct (rs Mar-Spring bank hol & Aug bank hol-Oct pool & bar closed, shop restricted hrs) Booking advisable Jul-Aug Last arrival 23.00hrs Last departure noon
An attractive secluded site with a small stream running through it. A 12-acre site with 110 touring pitches and 42 statics.
Crazy golf & putting.
Leisure: ⤙ ⚠ Facilities: ♠⊙⚲※�ᕟᏞ
Services: ⊞⊟♀⬥⊘⊞①
→⛯▸⊚⬦⚡⬜⤸ ⬤⬛⬛⬛⬟

YARMOUTH

See **Newbridge**

WILTSHIRE

CALNE   Map 03 ST97

► ► ► ► *Blackland Lakes Holiday & Leisure Centre (ST973687)*
Stockley Ln SN11 0NQ ☎ 01249 813672
Dir: From Calne take A4 E for 1.5m, turn right at camp sign & site on left in 1m
⊞ ⊞ Å
Open all year (rs Nov-mid Mar bookings only)
Booking advisable all year Last arrival 23.00hrs Last departure noon
A level, well-kept site in a rural area surrounded by Colstowe, and the North and West Downs. There are good outdoor facilities on site, including an indoor heated swimming pool and a well-equipped health centre. The park boasts two carp fisheries which are kept well stocked for the enthusiast. Some excellent walks are close by, and the interesting market town of Devizes is a few miles away. A 17-acre site with 180 touring pitches.
Wildfowl sanctuary, fishing facilities
Leisure: ⤙ ⚠ Facilities: ♠⊙⚲※ᕟᏞ⬥⊞⊟♠
Services: ⊞⊟♠⊘⊞①⬥
→⛯▸⤸

DEVIZES   Map 03 SU06

► ► ► Camping & Caravanning Club Site (ST950621)
Scout Ln, Nr. Seend, Melksham SN12 6RN
☎ 01380 828839
Dir: On A361 from Devizes turn right onto A365, over canal and next left down lane beside '3 Magpies' Public House. Site is on the right
★ ⊞ £13.90-£14.90 ⊞ £13.90-£14.90 Å £13.90-£14.90
Open all year
A popular, well-designed park beside the Kennet and Avon canal, with a gate to the towpath and fishing available in the canal. Well situated for exploring Salisbury Plain and the Marlborough Downs. See advertisement on p.14 for Club Members' benefits. 90 touring pitches.
Leisure: ⚠ Facilities: ♠⊙⚲⬥Ꮮ Services: ⊟
→ ⤸

LACOCK   Map 03 ST96

► ► ► Piccadilly Caravan Site (ST913683)
Folly Ln West SN15 2LP ☎ 01249 730260
Dir: 4m S of Chippenham. From Melksham on A350 towards Lacock for 3m. Turn left at sign marked Gastard & site is 200yds on the left
⊞ £8.50-£10 ⊞ £8.50-£10 Å £8.50-£10
Open Apr-Oct Booking advisable school & bank hols Last arrival 22.00hrs Last departure noon
A good family site, well-established and overlooking Lacock village. A 2.5-acre site with 41 touring pitches.
Leisure: ⚠ Facilities: ♠⊙⚲※ᏞᏞ
Services: ⊞⊟♠⊘⊞
→⛯▸⬛⤸Ᏼ

MARSTON MEYSEY   Map 04 SU19

► ► ► Second Chance Caravan Park (SU140960)
SN6 6SZ ☎ 01285 810675 & 810909
Dir: Midway between Swindon & Cirencester on A419 exit at the Fairford signpost. Follow brown tourist caravan park signs
⊞ £7 ⊞ £7 Å £7
Open Mar-Nov Booking advisable peak periods Last arrival 21.00hrs Last departure 13.30hrs ⊗
A quiet and beautiful site with good toilet facilities, attractively situated near the source of the Thames. A 1.75-acre site with 22 touring pitches and 4 statics.
Fishing on site, canoeing.
Facilities: ♠⊙⚲Ᏺ Services: ⊞♠⊘
→▸⬥⤸Ᏼ

SALISBURY   Map 04 SU12

► ► ► ► Coombe Touring Park (SU099282)
Race Plain, Netherhampton SP2 8PN
☎ 01722 328451
Dir: 2m SW off A3094
★ ⊞ £7-£9 ⊞ £7-£9 Å £7-£9
Open all year (rs Sep-Etr gas only, shop) Booking advisable bank hols (by letter only) Last arrival 21.00hrs Last departure noon

---

Facilities: ➡ Bath ♠ Shower ⊙ Electric Shaver ⚲ Hairdryer ※ Ice Pack Facility ⬥ Disabled Facilities ♠ Public Telephone
⬛ Shop on Site or within 200yds ⊞ Mobile Shop (calls at least 5 days a week) ⬥ BBQ Area Ᏺ Picnic Area Ᏼ Dog Exercise Area

Coombe Touring Park
*A very neat and attractive site adjacent to the
racecourse with views over the downs, and
outstanding flower beds. The park is well landscaped
with shrubs and maturing trees, and the very
colourful beds are stocked from the owner's
greenhouse. A comfortable park with a superb luxury
toilet block. A 3-acre site with 50 touring pitches.*
Leisure: ⚙ **Facilities:** ⬤⊙🔍❄⬤⬤⬤
Services: ⬤⬤⬤⬤🔍⬤⬤ → ⬤ ⬤

▶ ▶ ▶ **Alderbury Caravan & Camping Park**
(SU197259)
Southampton Rd, Whaddon SP5 3HB
☎ 01722 710125
Dir: *Located just off A36, 3m from Salisbury*
⬤⬤⬤
Open all year Booking advisable anytime Last
arrival 22.00hrs Last departure 13.00hrs
*A pleasant, attractive park set in a village of
Whaddon not far from Salisbury. The small site is
well maintained by friendly owners. A 1.5-acre site
with 39 touring pitches.*
Washing-up room.
Leisure: ⚙ **Facilities:** ⬤⊙⬤⬤⬤ **Services:** ⬤
→ ⬤ ⬤ ⬤ ⬤ ⬤ ⬤ ⬤

▶ ▶ ▶ **Camping & Caravanning Club Site**
(SU140320)
Hudsons Field, Castle Rd SP1 3RR
☎ 01722 320713
Dir: *1.5m from Salisbury on A345. Large open field next
to Old Sarum*
★ ⬤ £11.80-£14.90 ⬤ £11.80-£14.90 ⬤ £11.80-£14.90
Open 20 Mar-1 Nov Booking advisable bank hols &
peak periods Last arrival 21.00hrs Last departure
noon
*A well-kept site with friendly and helpful wardens.
Please see the advertisement on page 14 for details
of Club Members' benefits. A 4.5-acre site with 148
touring pitches.*
Facilities: ⬤⊙⬤❄⬤ **Services:** ⬤⬤⬤⬤
→ ⬤ ⬤ ⬤ ⬤ ⬤

▶ ▶ ▶ **Stonehenge Touring Park (SU061456)**
Orcheston SP3 4SH ☎ 01980 620304 620902
Dir: *Turn right off A360*
⬤ £6-£10 ⬤ £6-£10 ⬤ £6-£10
Open all year Booking advisable bank hols & Jul-
Aug Last arrival 21.00hrs Last departure 11.00hrs

---

*A quiet site adjacent to the small village of
Orcheston near the centre of Salisbury Plain and
4m from Stonehenge. Site maturing and popular.
A 2-acre site with 30 touring pitches and 6 statics.*
Leisure: ⚙ **Facilities:** ⬤⊙⬤❄⬤⬤⬤⬤
Services: ⬤⬤⬤⬤🔍⬤⬤⬤
→ ⬤

▶ ▶ **Brades Acre (SU035477)**
SP3 4RX ☎ 01980 620402
Dir: *From Tilshead turn S on A360 to end of village &
site is on the right*
⬤⬤⬤
Open all year Booking advisable public hols Last
arrival 21.00hrs Last departure 11.00hrs
*A small, pleasantly situated country site set among
trees and shrubs in the heart of Salisbury Plain.
A 2-acre site with 25 touring pitches.*
Facilities: ⬤⊙❄⬤⬤⬤ **Services:** ⬤⬤⬤⬤
→ ⬤

▶ ▶ ▶ **Brokerswood Country Park (ST836523)**
Brokerswood BA13 4EH ☎ 01373 822238 & 823880
Dir: *From M4 travel S on A350. Right at Yarnbrook to
Rising Sun pub at North Bradley, then left onto site.
Other approaches difficult for caravans*
★ ⬤ £8-£12 ⬤ £8-£12 ⬤ £8-£12
Open all year Booking advisable Peak season Last
arrival 21.00hrs Last departure 13.00hrs
*A pleasant park with nature trails and a fishing lake
set in 80 acres of woodland. An adventure
playground offers plenty of fun for all ages, and
there is also an indoor play centre. The park boasts
its own miniature railway of one-third of a mile. A 6-
acre site .*
Facilities: ⬤⊙🔍❄⬤⬤⬤⬤⬤⬤
Services: ⬤⬤⬤🔍⬤⬤
→ ⬤ ⬤ ⬤ ⬤

WORCESTERSHIRE

▶ ▶ ▶ ▶ **Leedon's Park (SP080384)**
Childswickham Rd WR12 7HB ☎ 01386 852423
Dir: *From A44 Evesham-Oxford take B4632. Park 6m SE
of Evesham*
★ ⬤ £5-£11 ⬤ £5-£11 ⬤ £5-£11
Open all year Booking advisable peak periods Last
arrival 20.00hrs Last departure 11.00hrs
*A large site on the edge of the Vale of Evesham, 1m
from the historical village of Broadway; an ideal
base from which to tour the Cotswolds. The park
enjoys 40 acres of lawns and gardens, with duck
ponds proving popular with children. Pet and pet-
free areas cater to all needs, and there is a large
play fort complex. A 16-acre site with 450 touring
pitches and 86 statics.*
See advertisement under GLOUCESTER

contd.

Leisure: ⚸ ⚲ ⚛ ⚠ 🖵 Facilities: ➤ ↑ ☉ ℚ ✳ �\ ॰ 🐾
Services: 🖵 🗊 ⓐ ⚙ ⚡ 🔲 ✕ 🕯
→ ∪ ► 🚾 🚮 🚷 🎴 🔲

CLENT HILLS

See **Romsley**

HANLEY SWAN   Map 03 SO84

► ► ► **Camping & Caravanning Club Site**
(SO812440)
WR8 0EE ☎ 01684 310280
Dir: A38 to Upton upon Severn. Turn N over River
Bridge. Take 2nd left, then 1st left signed Hanley Swan.
Site is on right after 1m
★ 🚐 £13.90-£14.90 🚐 £13.90-£14.90 ▲ £13.90-£14.90
Open 03 Apr-Dec Booking advisable Jan-Mar Last
arrival 21.00hrs Last departure noon
Well-established wooded park, ideally located for
exploring the Malvern Hills and Worcester. Two
new toilet blocks have considerably improved the
facilities. Please see the advertisement on page 14
for details of Club Members' benefits. A 12-acre site
with 200 touring pitches.
Pool table, table tennis, recreation hall
Leisure: ⚛ ⚠ Facilities: ↑ ☉ ℚ �\ ⚲ 🐾
Services: 🖵 🗊 ⓐ
→ ∪ ► △ ✙ ⚷ ⚡ 🚾 🚮

★ RANCH
CARAVAN PARK
HOLIDAY CENTRE ✚

● **Established family-run park**
● **Located in the vale of Evesham**
● **Tourers welcome**
● **Electric hook-ups available**
● **multi-service hook-ups**
● **Licensed club serving meals**
● **Heated outdoor swimming pool**
● **Shop**
● **Laundry**

HONEYBOURNE
EVESHAM
WORCS
WR11 5QG

AA ►◄

Tel: Evesham (01386) 830744

HONEYBOURNE   Map 04 SP14

► ► ► ► **Ranch Caravan Park (SP113444)**
Station Rd WR11 5QG ☎ 01386 830744
Dir: Through village crossroads towards Bidford,
entrance 400m on left side
★ 🚐 £10-£15 🚐 £10-£15
Open Mar-Nov (rs Mar-May & Sep-Nov swimming
pool closed, shorter club hours) Booking advisable
school hols Last arrival 20.00hrs Last departure
noon
An attractive and well-run park set amidst farmland
in the Vale of Evesham, but landscaped with trees
and bushes to break it up into different areas.
Tourers (but not tents) have their own excellent
facilities in two locations, and the use of an outdoor
heated swimming pool in peak season. There is
also a licensed club serving meals. Tents not
accepted. A 12-acre site with 120 touring pitches
and 180 statics.
Leisure: ⚸ ⚛ ⚠ 🖵 Facilities: ↑ ☉ ℚ ✳ �\ ⚲ 🐾
Services: 🖵 🗊 ⚡ ⓐ ⚙ 🔲 ✕ 🕯
→ ∪ ⚷ 🚾 🚮 🎴 🔲

MALVERN   Map 03 SO74

► ► ► **Riverside Caravan Park (SO833463)**
Little Clevelode WR13 6PE ☎ 01684 310475
Dir: From A449 signed onto B4424
★ 🚐 fr £6 🚐 fr £6 ▲ fr £6
Open Mar-Dec (rs Nov, Dec & Mar water supply
depends on weather) Booking advisable bank hols
& end Jun-Aug Last arrival 20.00hrs Last departure
noon
An open field site with some sloping pitches and a
large play area. A 25-acre site with 70 touring
pitches and 130 statics.
Slipway for boats, fishing on river.
Leisure: ⚲ ⚛ ⚠ 🖵 Facilities: ↑ ☉ ✳ �\ ⚲ 🐾
Services: 🖵 🗊 ⚡ ⓐ ⚙ 🔲
→ ∪ ► ✙ ⚷

ROMSLEY   Map 07 SO98

► ► ► ► **Camping & Caravanning Club Site**
(SO955795)
Fieldhouse Ln B62 0NH ☎ 01562 710015
Dir: Leave M5 at junct 3, take A456 then left on B4551 to
Romsley, turn right past Sun Hotel, take 5th left turn
from 'Sun' junct & next left for site
★ 🚐 £11.80-£14.90 🚐 £11.80-£14.90 ▲ £11.80-£14.90
Open 20 Mar-1 Nov Booking advisable bank hols &
peak periods Last arrival 21.00hrs Last departure
noon
A very pretty, well tended park surrounded by
wooded hills. The site offers excellent facilities,
including new hard stands to provide flat pitches for
motorhomes. Lovely views of the Clent Hills can be
enjoyed from this park, and there are plenty of local
scenic walks. Please see the advertisement on page
14 for details of Club Members' benefits. A 7.5-acre
site with 118 touring pitches.
Leisure: ⚛ ⚠ Facilities: ↑ ☉ ℚ ✳ �\ ⚲ 🐾
Services: 🖵 🗊 ⓐ ⚙ ➤
→ ∪ △ ✙ ⚷ ⚡ 🚾 🚮

Facilities: ➤ Bath ↑ Shower ☉ Electric Shaver ℚ Hairdryer ✳ Ice Pack Facility �\ Disabled Facilities ⚲ Public Telephone
⚡ Shop on Site or within 200yds 🔲 Mobile Shop (calls at least 5 days a week) 🔥 BBQ Area 🏕 Picnic Area 🐾 Dog Exercise Area

England

WOLVERLEY   Map 07 SO87

► ► ► **Camping & Caravanning Club Site (SO833792)**
Brown Westhead Park DY10 3PX ☎ 01562 850909
Dir: From Kidderminster A449 to Wolverhampton, turn left at lights onto B4189 signed Wolverley. Follow brown camping signs, turn right. Site on left
★ 🚐 £10.60-£13.90 🚐 £10.60-£13.90 ▲ £10.60-£13.90
Open 20 Mar-1 Nov Booking advisable bank hols & Jul-Aug Last arrival 21.00hrs Last departure noon
Very pleasant grassy site on edge of the village, with good access to nearby motorways. Please see the advertisement on page 14 for details of Club Members' benefits. A 12-acre site with 120 touring pitches.
Table tennis, darts.
Leisure: ♠ ⚠ ☐   Facilities: �📶 ⊙ 🗑 & ↳ 🐾 �
Services: 🔌 🗑 🛢 ⌀ ⬚
→ ∪ ▶ 🛆 ↳ 🛥 ⚓   🍴 ⚒

YORKSHIRE, EAST RIDING OF

BRANDESBURTON   Map 08 TA14

► ► ► **Dacre Lakeside Park (TA118468)**
YO25 8RT ☎ 01964 543704 & 542372
Dir: Off A165 bypass, midway between Beverley and Hornsea
★ 🚐 £7.50-£8 🚐 £7.50-£8 ▲ £7.50-£8
Open Mar-Oct Booking advisable bank hols Last arrival 21.00hrs Last departure noon

Brandesburton, Driffield, East Yorks
Tel: (01964) 543704 (Site Office)
(01964) 542372 (Admin)
Fax: (01964) 543851
www.dacrepark.co.uk

Excellent landscaped park set around an 8 acre lake for windsurfing, sailing, canoeing etc. Club house and games room plus full facilities for 120 caravans, motor caravans or tents. Ideally situated for East Coast resorts and historic towns of York and Beverley. Tennis, golf, bowling and jet skiing. Nearby is attractive village with pubs, Chinese restaurant and shops.

A pleasant, level grassy site beside a lake with good adjacent sports facilities. A new clubhouse is now available, offering additional amenities. An 8-acre site with 120 touring pitches.
Windsurfing, fishing, tennis & bowling green.
Leisure: ⚙ ♠   Facilities: 📶 ⊙ 🗑 ☀ & ↳ 🐾 🐎
Services: 🔌 🗑 ♀ 🛢 ⌀ ⬚ 🔋
→ ∪ ▶ 🛆 ↳ 🛥

BRIDLINGTON   Map 08 TA16

See also **Rudston**
► ► ► **Fir Tree Caravan Park (TA195702)**
Jewison Ln, Sewerby YO16 6YG ☎ 01262 676442
Dir: 1.5m from centre of Bridlington. Turn left off B1255 at Marton Corner & site is 600yds on left
★ 🚐 £7-£11
Open Mar-Nov Booking advisable Jul/Aug & bank hols Last arrival 21.00hrs Last departure noon
Separate facilities provided for touring units at this mainly static park in a rural setting. A 22-acre site with 50 touring pitches and 400 statics.
See advertisement under FILEY
Leisure: ≈ ♠ ⚠   Facilities: 📶 ☀ & ↳ 🐎
Services: 🔌 🗑 ♀ 🛢 ⬚ 🔋 ⬚ 🍴
→ ∪ ▶ ⊙ 🛆 ↳ 🛥 ⚓

FANGFOSS   Map 08 SE75

► ► ► **Fangfoss Old Station Caravan Park (SE747527)**
Old Station House YO41 5QB ☎ 01759 380491
Dir: Turn off A1079 at Wilberfoss, follow signpost in centre of Wilberfoss, 1.5m in the direction of Fangfoss
★ 🚐 £7.70-£9.70 🚐 £7.70-£9.70 ▲ £6-£12.50
Open Mar-Oct Booking advisable bank hols Last arrival 19.30hrs Last departure noon
A well-maintained site in a pleasant rural area. The track and sidings of the old railway station are grassed over and provide excellent hardstanding with a level landscaped field adjacent. A 4.5-acre site with 75 touring pitches.
Tennis, horse riding, fishing
Leisure: ⚠   Facilities: 📶 ⊙ 🗑 ☀ & ↳ 🐎 🏓 ㄇ 🐾
Services: 🔌 🗑 🛢 ⌀ ⬚ 🔋
→ ∪ ⚓   ⚒

HULL

See **Sproatley**

RUDSTON   Map 08 TA06

► ► ► **Thorpe Hall Caravan & Camping Site (TA108677)**
Thorpe Hall YO25 4JE ☎ 01262 420393 & 420574
Dir: 5m from Bridlington on B1253
★ 🚐 £5.80-£10.90 🚐 £5.80-£10.90 ▲ £4.80-£9.80
Open Mar-Oct Booking advisable bank hols & peak periods Last arrival 22.00hrs Last departure noon
A very attractive and well-ordered site in the walled garden of a large estate on edge of village. A 4.5-acre site with 90 touring pitches.

contd.

Services: ⬚ Toilet Fluid   ✗ Café/ Restaurant   🍴 Fast Food/Takeaway   🍼 Baby Care   🔌 Electric Hook Up
🗑 Launderette   ♀ Licensed Bar   🛢 Calor Gaz   ⌀ Camping Gaz   🔋 Battery Charging

THORPE HALL

EAST YORKSHIRE'S QUALITY SITE

Quiet, sheltered within kitchen garden walls. Centrally heated toilet block. Toilet and bathroom for disabled persons. Dogs welcome. Own Coarse Fishery.

Thorpe Hall Caravan and Camping Site,
Rudston, Driffield, East Yorkshire YO25 4JE
Tel: 01262 420393 Fax: 01262 420588
Manager Mrs Jayne Chatterton
Residence: 01262 420574
E-mail: caravansite@thorpehall.co.uk

Leisure: ● 🎠 📺 **Facilities:** 🛁 🚿 ⊙ 💨 ✳ ♿ 📞 🏪 ⊓ 🐕
Services: ☺ ▣ ▮ 🍃 ⊞ Ⓣ
→ ∪ 🐟

Far Grange Caravan Park

★ LOOKING FOR MORE THAN A HOLIDAY – TAKE A LOOK AT FAR GRANGE PARK ★

Full facilities for tourers, tents and motor homes, including all weather premium pitches, now available for weekend use OUT OF SEASON

Luxury fully centrally heated and double glazed holiday accommodation available from March to November plus Winter Weekends

A wide range of New and Pre-owned Holiday Homes for sale

Please telephone or write for a brochure to:
Far Grange Caravan Park Limited,
Skipsea, Driffield, East Yorkshire YO25 8SY
Tel: 01262 468293/469248
E-mail: enquiries@fargrangepark.co.uk
Web: www.fargrangepark.co.uk

SKIPSEA — Map 08 TA15

Far Grange Park (TA181530)
Hornsea Rd YO25 8SY
☎ 01262 468248 & 468293
***Dir:** On B1242, 2m S of village on seaward side next to golf course*
★ 🚐 £11-£18 🚙 £11-£18 ▲ £11-£18
Open Mar-Oct (rs Nov-Feb Superpitch's only available) Booking advisable bank & school hols
Last arrival 21.00hrs Last departure 11.00hrs
A very smart holiday centre with pleasing public buildings and nicely laid out grounds of shrubs, hedges and trees. The park is next to a private sandy beach on a fairly quiet part of the coast, and a 60-acre country park and fishing lake are part of the complex. An arboretum has recently been added, with nature walks and an information centre. Winner of Campsite of the Year for Northern England 2000. A 30-acre site with 130 touring pitches and 500 statics.
Fishing, snooker, gym, sauna, solarium.
Leisure: 🏊 🎾 ● 🎠 **Facilities:** 🛁 🚿 ⊙ ✳ ♿ 📞 🏪 ⊓ 🐕 **Services:** ☺ ▣ 🍷 ▮ 🍃 Ⓣ 🍴 🧺
→ ⚑ 🐟 [MasterCard] [Visa] [Delta] [Switch]

PREMIER PARK

▶ ▶ ▶ ▶ ▶ **Low Skirlington Leisure Park (TA188528)**
YO25 8SY ☎ 01262 468213 & 468466
***Dir:** From M62 head for Beverley then Hornsea. Follow tourist signs onto B1242 to Skirlington*
★ 🚐 £10-£13.50 🚙 £10-£13.50 ▲ £10-£13.50
Open Mar-Oct Booking advisable Jul-Aug
A large seaside park on partly sloping grass with young trees and shrubs, set in meadowland close by the beach. This continually improving family-run site has five toilet blocks, and a new supermarket and amusement arcade. The wide range of family amenities include an indoor heated swimming pool complex with sauna, jacuzzi and sunbeds. Outdoors there is a well-stocked fishing lake, pitch and putt, and a large new children's play area. A 24-acre site with 285 touring pitches and 450 statics.
Sauna, sunbed, jacuzzi & bowls.
Leisure: 🏊 ● 🎠 📺 **Facilities:** 🛁 🚿 ⊙ 💨 ✳ ♿ 📞 🏪 ⊓ 🐕 **Services:** ☺ ▣ 🍷 ▮ 🍃 ⊞ 🍴 🧺
→ ∪ ⚑ ◎ ⛵ 🏄 🐟 [MasterCard] [Visa] [Barclays Connect] [Switch]

SPROATLEY — Map 08 TA13

▶ ▶ ▶ **Burton Constable Country Park (TA186357)**
Old Lodges HU11 4LN ☎ 01964 562508 & 562316
***Dir:** Off A165 onto B1238 to Sproatley. Follow signs to park*
★ 🚐 fr £8.50 🚙 fr £8.50 ▲ fr £7.50

Facilities: 🛁 Bath 🚿 Shower ⊙ Electric Shaver 💨 Hairdryer ✳ Ice Pack Facility ♿ Disabled Facilities 📞 Public Telephone 🏪 Shop on Site or within 200yds 📦 Mobile Shop (calls at least 5 days a week) ⊞ BBQ Area ⊓ Picnic Area 🐕 Dog Exercise Area

LOW SKIRLINGTON LEISURE PARK

Pleasantly situated between the villages of Skipsea and Atwick on the East Yorkshire Coast (on the B1242), we are a family run business with a reputation for high standards throughout, and offer a wide range of facilities and activities for the whole family, including a heated indoor swimming pool, sauna, jacuzzi and sunbed, well stocked fishing lake, pitch and putt course, amusement arcade, supermarket, and new outdoor childrens play area.

The Towbar Inn offers a variety of entertainment and a choice between restaurant or bar meals, and our own Fish and Chip shop.

There is a wealth of things to do and places to visit in the area, including a popular Sunday Market which is held adjacent to the park, and local market towns such as Beverley and Driffield. We are also within minutes drive of the seaside resorts of Hornsea and Bridlington. We have a large number of touring pitches available, and super deals on both new and used holiday homes.

Our facilities are also open to non residents.

Low Skirlington Leisure Park, Skipsea, Driffield, East Yorkshire YO25 8SY
Tel: (01262) 468213 Fax: (01262) 468105
E-mail: enquiries@skirlington.com
Website: www.skirlington.com

Open Mar-Oct Booking advisable bank hols Last arrival 23.00hrs Last departure 16.00hrs
A beautiful site close to boating and fishing lakes in the grounds of Burton Constable Hall, with a brand-new toilet block and all-electric touring pitches. A 20-acre site with 179 touring pitches and 180 statics.
Leisure: ⚙ Facilities: ♿⊙🏊✳&🗜❓🛱🐾
Services: 🔌🖨⚲🔋🖍⊞
➔ ☋ ▶ ⚲

STAMFORD BRIDGE   Map 08 SE75

▶ ▶ ▶ **Weir Caravan Park (SE713557)**
YO41 1AN ☎ 01759 371377
Dir: Located off A166 Bridlington road
★ 🚐 £8.50-£11 🚐 £8.50-£11 ▲ £8.50-£11
Open Mar-Oct Booking advisable bank hols & Jul-Aug Last arrival 21.30hrs Last departure noon
Slightly sloping grass site near urban area and River Derwent. An 8-acre site with 50 touring pitches and 125 statics.
Fishing & boating on site.
Leisure: ♦ ⚙ Facilities: ♿♿⊙❓&🗜
Services: 🔌🖨🔋🖍⊞
➔ ☋ ▶ ✚ ⚲

YORKSHIRE, NORTH

ACASTER MALBIS   Map 08 SE54

▶ ▶ ▶ *Chestnut Farm Caravan Park (SE589456)*
YO2 1UQ ☎ 01904 704676
Dir: Leave A64 at Copmanthorpe, turning S signed Acaster Malbis. Site on unclass road in 2m
🚐 🚐 ▲
Open Apr-Oct Booking advisable public hols & Jul-Aug Last arrival 23.00hrs Last departure noon
Level, grassy site with assorted trees and shrubs, adjacent to river. A 5-acre site with 25 touring pitches and 56 statics.
Facilities: ♿♿⊙❓✳&🗜🛱 Services: 🔌🖨🔋🖍⊞🗂
➔ ☋ ▶ ✚ 🛱 ⚲

▶ **Moor End Farm (SE589457)**
YO23 2UQ ☎ 01904 706727 & 0860 405872
Dir: Follow signs to Acaster Malbis from A64/A1237 junction at Copmanthorpe
🚐 £8.50-£11 🚐 £8-£10 ▲ £8-£11
Open Etr or Apr-Oct Booking advisable bank hols & end Jul-early Aug Last arrival 22.00hrs Last departure 14.00hrs
Level, grassy site with hedges, well-drained and maintained. Set in meadowland adjacent to road. A 1-acre site with 10 touring pitches and 53 statics.
Use of fridge/freezer & microwave
Leisure: ⚙ Facilities: ♿⊙❓✳🗜 Services: 🔌⊞
➔ ▶ ✚ 🛱 ⚲ 🖨

ALLERSTON   Map 08 SE88

▶ ▶ ▶ ▶ *Vale of Pickering Caravan Park (SE879808)*
Carr House Farm YO18 7PQ ☎ 01723 859280
Dir: On B1415, 1.75m off main Pickering-Scarborough road
🚐 🚐 ▲
Open Apr-Oct (rs Mar) Booking advisable anytime Last departure noon
An attractively maintained park with high quality facilities, and surrounded by mature hedges with lots of colourful landscaping. Set in open countryside within the North Yorkshire Moors National Park. An 8-acre site with 120 touring pitches and 1 static.
Leisure: ⚙ Facilities: ♿♿⊙❓✳&🗜🐾 Services: 🔌🖨🔋🖍⊞🗂
➔ ☋ ▶ 🖍 ⚲

ALLERTON PARK   Map 08 SE45

▶ ▶ ▶ ▶ *Allerton Park Caravan Site (SE417576)*
Allerton Mauleverer HG5 0SE
☎ 01423 330569 & 01759 371377
Dir: Off A59, 400yds E of junct with A1(M)
★ 🚐 £8.50-£11 🚐 £8.50-£11 ▲ £8.50-£11
Open Feb-3 Jan Booking advisable bank hols Last arrival 21.00hrs Last departure 17.00hrs
An immaculately maintained site set in parkland surrounded by mature trees, and offering peace and quiet. An ideal stopover site for those travelling to
contd.

and from Scotland and the North, or well-positioned for touring the Dales, and York. Several modern cubicle suites in the sanitary block contain various combinations of toilet/washbasins/showers or baths. A 12-acre site with 30 touring pitches and 90 statics.

Leisure: ⚠ **Facilities:** ➡ ☂ ⊙ ◖ ✳ ⛵ ⛄ ⛏ 🎪 🛖 ✝
Services: ⛽ 🖲 ⓘ ⌁ ⊞ ⊤
→ ∪ ► ✦

ARNCLIFFE   Map 07 SD97

► ► ► ► *Hawkswick Cote Caravan Park (SD947703)*
Hawkswick Cote BD23 5PX ☎ 01756 770226
Dir: *From B6160 1m N of Kilnsey, take unclass road signed Arncliffe. Site 1.5m on left*
⛺ 🚐 ⛏
Open Mar-14 Nov Booking advisable bank hols & Jul-Aug Last arrival 22.00hrs Last departure noon
A spacious site in the Dales, with mature landscaping and views of the surrounding fells. Various camping areas are divided by traditional dry stone walling, which complement the stone park buildings, some of which have been converted from farm buildings. The park blends in with the towering fells on both sides of Littondale, and there are pleasant views in all directions. Also convenient for Skipton and surrounding area. A 3-acre site with 50 touring pitches and 90 statics.

Leisure: ⚠ **Facilities:** ☂ ⊙ ◖ ✳ ⛵ ⛄ ⛏ 🛖 🎪 ✝
Services: ⛽ 🖲 ⓘ ⌁ ⊤
→ ∪ ✦

AYSGARTH   Map 07 SE08

► ► ► ► *Westholme Caravan & Camping Park (SE016882)*
DL8 3SP ☎ 01969 663268
Dir: *1m E of Aysgarth off A684*
★ 🚐 £7-£9.70 🚐 £7-£9.70 ⛏ £7-£9.70
Open Mar-Oct Booking advisable bank hols & Jul-Aug Last arrival 22.00hrs Last departure noon

A beckside site with level grassy pitches in various paddocks set into the hillside. The modern sanitary facilities and other amenities are maintained to a consistently high standard. There is a well-equipped children's playground, a well-stocked shop, and a licensed bar and club room where meals are served every weekend throughout the season, and daily during the peak months. The famous Aysgarth Falls is nearby. A 4-acre site with 70 touring pitches and 44 statics.

Fishing free on site.
Leisure: ◣ ⚠ ▢ **Facilities:** ☂ ⊙ ◖ ✳ ⛵ ⛄ ⛏
Services: ⛽ 🖲 ⓘ ⓘ ⌁ ⊞ ⊤ ✕
→ ✦

BISHOP MONKTON   Map 08 SE36

► ► ► **Church Farm Caravan Park (SE286658)**
Knaresborough Rd HG3 3QQ ☎ 01765 677668
Dir: *From A61, 3m S of Ripon, take unclass rd to Bishop Monkton. At X-rds in 1m right towards Knaresborough, site 500mtrs on right*
★ 🚐 fr £6 🚐 £6-£7.50 ⛏ fr £6
Open Apr-Oct Booking advisable peak periods
A meadowland park set in a delightful secluded rural environment, with first-class sanitary facilities. New owners have lavished considerable care on refurbishing the park to a very high standard. A 5-acre site with 30 touring pitches and 3 statics.

Facilities: ☂ ⊙ ✳ ⛵ ⛄ 🛖 ✝ **Services:** ⛽ ⓘ ⌁ ⊞
→ ∪ ► ⛵ ✦

BOROUGHBRIDGE   Map 08 SE36

► ► ► ► **Camping & Caravanning Club Site (SE384662)**
Bar Ln, Roecliffe YO51 9LS ☎ 01423 322683
Dir: *From A48/A1(M) North & Southbound slip roads follow signs for Bar Lane Ind Est & Roecliffe Village. Site entrance 0.25m from rdbt*
★ 🚐 £11.80-£14.90 🚐 £11.80-£14.90 ⛏ £11.80-£14.90
Open all year Booking advisable bank hols & Jul & Aug Last arrival 21.00hrs Last departure noon
A quiet, riverside site completely upgraded recently and offering very upmarket facilities. There is direct access onto the River Ure, with fishing and boating available. The natural features of the park are complemented by landscaping and planting to provide a pleasant, relaxing rural environment. Close to the dales and the market town of Boroughbridge. Please see the advertisement on page 14 for details of Club Members' benefits. A 6-acre site with 73 touring pitches. Fishing.

Leisure: ◣ ⚠ **Facilities:** ☂ ⊙ ◖ ✳ ⛵ ⛄
Services: ⛽ 🖲 ⓘ ⌁
→ ∪ ► ✦ ✦ 📧 ▨

CAWOOD   Map 08 SE53

► ► ► ► **Cawood Holiday Park (SE563385)**
Ryther Rd YO8 3TT ☎ 01757 268450
Dir: *From A1 take B1222, turn at Cawood lights signed Tadcaster onto B1223 for 1m, park is on left*
★ 🚐 £8.50-£12 🚐 £8.50-£12 ⛏ £8.50-£12
Open Mar-Jan Booking advisable bank hols & Jul-Aug Last arrival 23.00hrs Last departure 11.00hrs
A peaceful park in a rural area with its own fishing lake, which the camping area overlooks. The 10-acre site is bordered by hedges and mature trees, and is well away from the road. Amenities are modern and consistently maintained to a high standard. The club house with a comfortable bar is

sited on one side of the lake, and there is occasional entertainment here. Coarse fishing is available. An 8-acre site with 60 touring pitches and 10 statics. Coarse fishing.

Leisure: ♦ ◀ /Ⅶ ☐ **Facilities:** ⋒⊙ℚ※も⛓⛲⊞☴☂

Services: ⊟⑤♀⋒∂⊞Ⓣ✕♨

→∪▶⚠♪ ●◼◉▨☳

CONEYSTHORPE (Near Malton)   Map 08 SE77

▶ ▶ ▶ **Castle Howard Caravan & Camping Site (SE705710)**
YO60 7DD ☎ 01653 648316
Dir: Well signposted from A64 & B1257. Caravans prohibited on A170 at Sutton Bank between Thirsk and Helmsley.
🚐 £8.50 🚐 £8.50 ▲ £8.50
Open Mar-Oct Booking advisable public hols Last arrival 21.00hrs Last departure 14.00hrs
A sheltered, peaceful park adjacent to the great lake of Castle Howard, which is well stocked with record catches. Situated in the village of Coneysthorpe, it is within walking distance of the magnificent castle, and 15 miles from York. A 13-acre site with 70 touring pitches and 120 statics.

Facilities: ⋒⊙ℚ※も⛓⛲☂ **Services:** ⊟⑤⋒∂Ⓣ

→∪♪

CONSTABLE BURTON   Map 07 SE19

▶ ▶ ▶ ▶ **Constable Burton Hall Caravan Park (SE158907)**
DL8 5LJ ☎ 01677 450428
Dir: Located off A684
🚐 £8.50-£11 🚐 £8.50-£11 ▲ £8.50-£11
Open Apr-Oct Booking advisable public hols Last arrival 22.00hrs Last departure noon
A pretty site in the former deer park of the adjoining Constable Burton Hall, screened from the road by the deer park walls and surrounded by mature trees in a quiet rural location. The large campable area is spacious and comfortable, and most park buildings are made from natural stone in the local style. The laundry, however, is housed in a converted 18th-century deer barn. A 10-acre site with 120 touring pitches and 80 statics.

Facilities: ⋒⊙ℚ※も☂ **Services:** ⊟⋒∂⊞Ⓣ✕

→∪▶♨♪⛓

CROCKEY HILL   Map 08 SE64

▶ **Swallow Hall Caravan Park (SE657463)**
YO1 4SG ☎ 01904 448219
Dir: From A19 at Crockey Hill turn E onto unclass rd, site 2m on left
★ 🚐 £7.50-£10.50 🚐 £7.50-£10.50 ▲ £7.50-£10.50
Open Etr/Mar-Oct Booking advisable Etr & Spring bank hol Last arrival 22.00hrs
A quiet site on meadowland at the edge of a forest within easy reach of the centre of York. Pitches are separated by mature trees. A 5-acre site with 30 touring pitches.
Golf driving range & 18-hole-course.

Leisure: ℚ /Ⅶ **Facilities:** ⋒⊙※も☂

Services: ⊟♀⋒⊞✕

→▶♪⛓

CROPTON   Map 08 SE78

▶ ▶ ▶ **Spiers House Campsite (SE756918)**
YO18 8ES ☎ 01751 417591 (in season) 0131 3146505
Dir: Approach through Cropton on A170. 1m N of Cropton on the Rosedale road. Turn right into the forest at the signpost
★ 🚐 £6.50-£9 🚐 £6.50-£9 ▲ £6.50-£9
Open Etr-2 Oct Booking advisable bank & school hols Last arrival 22.00hrs
Beautiful forest site in a clearing with good facilities and peaceful surroundings. Walks are marked by the Forestry Commission. This site is attractive for birdwatchers, who can listen to the nightjar in the adjoining woodland. A 15-acre site with 150 touring pitches.

Leisure: /Ⅶ **Facilities:** ⋒⊙ℚ※も⛓⛲☂

Services: ⊟⑤⋒∂Ⓣ

→∪♪ ●◼▨☳

EASINGWOLD   Map 08 SE56

▶ ▶ ▶ *Hollybrook Caravan Park (SE533686)*
Pennycar Ln, Off Stillington Rd YO61 3EU
☎ 01347 821906
Dir: From rdbt on A19 S of Easingwold take unclass road signed Easingwold. In 1m turn right signed Stillington, then right in 0.25m into signed lane
🚐 🚐 ▲
Open Mar-Dec
A flat, all grass site with spacious numbered pitches, in a quiet rural location 0.5m from the village. No children under 15. A 2-acre site with 30 touring pitches.

Facilities: も **Services:** ⑤

Services: Ⓣ Toilet Fluid ✕ Café/ Restaurant ⛲ Fast Food/Takeaway ♨ Baby Care ⊟ Electric Hook Up ⑤ Launderette ♀ Licensed Bar ⋒ Calor Gaz ∂ Camping Gaz ⊞ Battery Charging

England

FILEY   Map 08 TA18

See also **Lebberston**

Flower of May Holiday Park (TA085835)
Lebberston Cliff YO11 3NU
☎ 01723 584311
Dir: Signed off A165 on Scarborough side of Filey
★ 🚗 £7.75-£12 🚐 £7.75-£12 ▲ £7.75-£12
Open Etr-Oct (rs early & late season) Booking
advisable Spring bank hol wk & Jul-Aug Last
arrival 21.00hrs Last departure noon
*A delightful family site with level grassy pitches
and excellent facilities. This large landscaped
park offers a full range of recreational activities,
with plenty to occupy everyone. Grass or hard
pitches are available, all on level ground. A 13-
acre site with 270 touring pitches and 179
statics.*
Squash, bowling & 9-hole golf.
Leisure: 🏃 🎣 🛝 🎱 **Facilities:** 🌳☺🍴❄️&📞
🛒 🌲 **Services:** 🔌🔋🍴🛒🗑️🚽🔟✕🚿
→ ∪ 🅿️ ☺ ⚓ ❄️ 🐕 ♨️ 🎣

▶ ▶ ▶ ▶ *Crows Nest Caravan Park (TA094826)*
Gristhorpe YO14 9PS ☎ 01723 582206
Dir: On seaward side of A165, signed off rdbt
🚗 🚐
Open Mar-Oct Booking advisable Last departure
noon
*A beautifully situated park on the Yorkshire
Heritage coast between Scarborough and Filey,
family owned and run to a high standard. The large
and mainly static park offers lively entertainments
and two bars. A 2-acre site with 49 touring pitches
and 217 statics.*
Leisure: 🏃 🎣 🛝 **Facilities:** 🌳☺❄️📞🛒🐕
Services: 🔌🔋🍴🛒🗑️🔟🚿
→ ∪ 🅿️ ☺ ⚓ 🎣

▶ ▶ ▶ *Centenary Way Camping & Caravan Park
(TA115798)*
Muston Grange YO14 0HU
☎ 01723 516415 & 512313
*Dir: On A1039 near junct with A165 on Bridlington side
of Filey*
🚗 🚐 ▲
Open Mar-Oct Booking advisable bank hols & Jul-
Aug Last arrival 21.00hrs Last departure noon

*A family-owned park, mainly for tents, with
footpath access to nearby beach. Close to the
seaside resort of Filey. A 3-acre site with 100
touring pitches.*
Phone 25m from site
Leisure: 🛝 **Facilities:** 🌳☺❄️🛒🐕
Services: 🔌🔋🗑️🔟
→ ∪ 🅿️ ☺ ❄️ 🎣 🚿

▶ ▶ ▶ **Filey Brigg Touring Caravan & Country
Park (TA115812)**
North Filey YO14 9ET ☎ 01723 513852
*Dir: Located 0.5m from Filey town centre on the coast
road from Scarborough, A165*
🚗 £5.50-£10 🚐 £5.50-£10 ▲ £3-£10
Open Etr/Apr-Oct Booking advisable bank hols &
Jul-Aug Last arrival 18.00hrs Last departure noon
*A municipal park overlooking Filey Brigg with
splendid views along the coast, and set in a country
park. The beach is just a short walk away, as is the
resort of Filey. Level grassy park with some mature
trees, near sea and beach. A 9-acre site with 158
touring pitches.*
Leisure: 🛝 **Facilities:** 🌳❄️&📞🛒🌲🐕
Services: 🔌🔋🗑️🔟✕🚿
→ ∪ 🅿️ ☺ ❄️ 🎣 🚌 🚉 🏧 🛒

▶ ▶ ▶ *Muston Grange Caravan Park (TA113797)*
Muston Rd YO14 0HU
☎ 01723 512167 & 01947 810415 winter
*Dir: On A1039 near junct with A165 on Bridlington side
of Filey*
🚗 🚐
Open Etr/Apr-20 Oct Booking advisable bank hols &
Jul-Aug Last arrival 22.00hrs Last departure noon
*A large touring park with views over the Yorkshire
Wolds, with a footpath to Filey town and beach.
A 10-acre site with 220 touring pitches.*
Leisure: 🛝 **Facilities:** 🌳☺❄️🛒 **Services:** 🔌🔋🛒🔟
→ ∪ 🅿️ ☺ 🎣

FYLINGDALES ('Flask' Inn)   Map 08 NZ90

▶ ▶ ▶ **Grouse Hill Caravan Park (NZ928002)**
Flask Bungalow Farm YO22 4QH
☎ 01947 880543 & 880560
*Dir: Off A171 (Whitby-Scarborough rd), entered via a
loop rd, at the Flask Inn.*
🚗 £7-£8.50 🚐 £7-£8.50 ▲ £7-£8.50
Open Spring bank hol-Sep (rs Etr-May shop &
reception restricted) Booking advisable public hols
Last arrival 22.00hrs Last departure noon
*Set in the midst of spectacular scenery in North
Yorkshire Moors National Park, this family-run park
is surrounded by rugged moorland and woodland,
an ideal base for walking and touring. A 14-acre site
with 175 touring pitches.*
Leisure: 🎣 🛝 **Facilities:** 🌳☺❄️&📞🛒🐕
Services: 🔌🔋🍴🗑️🔟
→ ∪ 🅿️

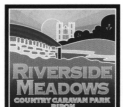

England

WOOD NOOK
NEAR GRASSINGTON

Small secluded park in the heart of the
YORKSHIRE DALES
Tel/Fax: (01756) 752412
Caravan Holiday Homes for Hire
TOURING CARAVANS AND TENTS
TOILETS, SHOWERS, ELECTRIC HOOK-UPS,
SHOP, CHILDRENS PLAY AREA

AA ▶▶▶▶

ROSE
AWARD
CARAVAN
HOLIDAY
PARK

Stamp for brochure to:
Mrs Thompson,
Wood Nook Caravan Park,
Skirethorns, Threshfield, Skipton,
N. Yorks BD23 5NU
Enquiries@wood-nook.demon.co.uk
www.ukparks.co.uk/woodnook

---

lovingly maintain their high-quality facilities,
and there is a heated swimming pool and sauna,
a games room, and a covered play room for
small children. An 18-acre site with 100 touring
pitches and 10 statics.
Nursery playroom, sauna, football.
Leisure: ⌇ ◣ /𝔸 **Facilities:** ⋔⊙🕾⚙❄ & ℄ 🐾 🛉
Services: 🔌🖥️🛢❢⊘⊞Ⓣ
→ ∪ ▶ ◎ ⚒ ♨ ⚓

▶ ▶ ▶ ▶ ▶ **Rudding Holiday Park (SE333531)**
Follifoot HG3 1JH ☎ 01423 870439
*Dir: From A1 take A59 to A658, turn S signed
Bradford. Continue for 4.5m then right and follow
signs*
★ 🚐 £9.50-£21 🚐 £9.50-£21 ▲ £7-£13
Open Apr-Oct (rs 1-21 Mar no hot water no
shop) Booking advisable bank hols Last arrival
22.30hrs Last departure 14.00hrs
*A spacious park set in the stunning 200-acres of
mature parkland and walled gardens of Rudding
Park. The natural setting has been tastefully
enhanced by landscaping which has resulted in
terraced pitches and dry-stone walls. A separate
area houses super pitches where all services are
supplied including picnic table and TV
connection. The toilet blocks have been
upgraded to provide first class facilities. The
park enjoys its own 18-hole golf course, and
there is a heated outdoor swimming pool, the*

GRASSINGTON

See **Threshfield**

GUISBOROUGH   Map 08 NZ61

▶ ▶ ▶ **Tockett's Mill Caravan Park (NZ626182)**
Skelton Rd TS14 6QA ☎ 01287 610182
Dir: 1.5m W of Guisborough on A173
★ 🚐 £7-£9 🚐 £7-£9
Open Mar-Oct Booking advisable bank hols & high
season Last arrival 21.00hrs Last departure noon
*Situated in a private wooded valley alongside a
stream, the site is centred around a preserved
watermill. A 7-acre site with 30 touring pitches and
75 statics.*
Leisure: /𝔸 **Facilities:** ⋔⊙🕾 & ℄
Services: 🔌🖥️🍴❢ 👜
→ ∪ 🐾

HARROGATE   Map 08 SE35

▶ ▶ ▶ ▶ ▶ **Ripley Caravan Park (SE289610)**
Knaresborough Rd, Ripley HG3 3AU
☎ 01423 770050
Dir: Access on B6165, 0.75m S of Ripley
★ 🚐 £6.95-£8.50 🚐 £6.95-£8.50 ▲ £6.95-£8.50
Open Etr-Oct Booking advisable bank hols Last
arrival 21.00hrs Last departure noon
*A superb, well-run rural site in attractive
meadowland which has been landscaped with
mature tree plantings. The resident owners*

Ripley Caravan Park

where the country and enjoyment comes naturally ...
*This luxury touring caravan park in the beautiful North
Yorkshire countryside, is within easy reach of Ripley Castle
and village, and only ten minutes north of Harrogate. First
class facilities include indoor heated swimming pool, sauna,
games room, nursery playroom, childrens playground and play
area. There is a shop, laundry, telephone, electric hook-up
points and amenities for the disabled.*

For further information:
Peter & Valerie House, Ripley Caravan Park,
Ripley, Harrogate, HG3 3AU.
Tel: (01423) 770050

David Bellamy Silver Award

TOURING CARAVANS
and family camping

Award winning holiday park, situated in the North Yorkshire Dales 3 miles south of Harrogate, offering superb facilities for touring caravans and tents. Set in beautiful parkland with lovely gardens and magnificent views; facilities include heated swimming pool, licensed bar serving meals, children's playground, games room and bicycle hire. Excellent amenities include centrally heated toilet blocks with free showers, electrical hook-up points, launderette, public telephones, park lighting and well stocked shop.

Supersites: Individual pitches, hard standing for tourers, 16amp electricity, water, direct drainage, TV and satellite connections and picnic tables.

18 hole Golf Course available on a daily fee basis plus covered driving range

ROSE AWARD 1999

Please send for free brochure.

RUDDING
holiday PARK

Follifoot, Harrogate, HG3 1JH. Tel:(01423) 870439.

Deer House bar and restaurant, and a children's play area. Winner of Best Campsite of the Year 2001, and Best Campsite for England. A 55-acre site with 141 touring pitches and 95 statics. Golf course, driving range & cycle hire.

Leisure: ⌇ ♦ ⚠ **Facilities:** ➥ ⋔ ⊙ ⚅ ⋇ ⊹ ⟁ ⚘ ⚑ ⊞ ⅂
Services: ⊡ ⌷ ⚲ ⊜ ⊞ ⊺ ✕ ⊯
→ ∪ ⌤ ⅄ ≌ ⨿ ⊜ ⊞ ⊠ ⊠ ⅁

▶ ▶ ▶ ▶ **High Moor Farm Park (SE242560)**
Skipton Rd HG3 2LT ☎ 01423 563637 & 564955
Dir: On A59 Harrogate-Skipton road
⚘ £10-£12 ⚘ £10-£12 Å £10-£12
Open Apr-Oct Booking advisable public hols Last arrival 23.30hrs Last departure 15.00hrs
An excellent site with first class facilities, set beside a small wood and surrounded by thorn hedges. The numerous touring pitches are located in meadowland fields, each area with its own toilet block. A large heated indoor swimming pool and a games room are very popular, and there is a large fishing lake, a golf course, and a full-sized crown bowling green. A 15-acre site with 320 touring pitches and 180 statics.
Course fishing, 9-hole golf course.

Leisure: ⌇ ♦ ⚠ **Facilities:** ➥ ⋔ ⊙ ⚅ ⟁ ⚘ ⊞ ⟍
Services: ⊡ ⌷ ⚲ ⚲ ⊞ ⊺ ✕ ⊯
→ ∪ ⌤ ≌ ⨿ ⊜ ⊞ ⊠ ⊠ ⅁

▶ ▶ ▶ **Shaws Trailer Park (SE325557)**
Knaresborough Rd HG2 7NE ☎ 01423 884432
Dir: On A59 1m from town centre. 0.5m N of Starbeck railway crossing, alongside Johnsons Dry Cleaners
★ ⚘ £8.50 ⚘ £8.50 Å £5-£9
Open all year Booking advisable public hols Last arrival 21.00hrs Last departure noon
A level, grassy site with mature trees and hardstandings. An 11-acre site with 43 touring pitches and 146 statics.

Facilities: ➥ ⋔ ⊙ ⚲ ⚘ **Services:** ⊡ ⊞ ⚶
→ ∪ ⌤ ⅄ ≌ ⨿

HAWES   Map 07 SD88

▶ ▶ **Bainbridge Ings Caravan & Camping Site (SD879895)**
DL8 3NU ☎ 01969 667354
Dir: Approaching Hawes from Bainbridge on A684, turn left at signpost marked Gayle, 300yds on left
⚘ £7.50 ⚘ £7 Å £7
Open Apr-Oct Booking advisable school hols Last arrival 22.00hrs Last departure 14.00hrs
A family run site in open countryside, close to Hawes in the heart of Upper Wensleydale. A 5-acre site with 55 touring pitches and 14 statics.

Facilities: ⋔ ⊙ ⋇ **Services:** ⊡ ⚶ ⊘ ⊞
→ ⨿ ⚘

HELMSLEY   Map 08 SE68

▶ ▶ ▶ ▶ **Golden Square Touring Caravan Park (SE604797)**
Oswaldkirk YO62 5YQ ☎ 01439 788269
Dir: 1m from Ampleforth towards Helmsley on Caravan route
★ ⚘ £6.50-£9.50 ⚘ £6.50-£9.50 Å £6.50-£9.50
Open Mar-Oct Booking advisable bank hols Last arrival 22.00hrs Last departure noon

An all-round excellent site with manicured grounds and first class toilets. This friendly park is set in a quiet rural situation with lovely views over the N Yorks Moors. The park is terraced on three levels surrounded by trees, and caters particularly for families. Country walks and mountain bike trails start here, and the market town of Helmsley is just 2.5 miles away. Caravans are prohibited from the A170 at Sutton Bank between Thirsk and Helmsley. A 12-acre site with 129 touring pitches.
Microwave oven.

Leisure: ♦ ⚠ **Facilities:** ➥ ⋔ ⊙ ⚅ ⋇ ⟁ ⚘ ⊞ ⟍
Services: ⊡ ⊞ ⚶ ⊘ ⊞ ⊺ ➥
→ ∪ ⌤ ⊙ ⚘

Services: ⊞ Toilet Fluid ✕ Café/ Restaurant ⊯ Fast Food/Takeaway ➥ Baby Care ⊡ Electric Hook Up
⊜ Launderette ⚲ Licensed Bar ⚘ Calor Gaz ⊘ Camping Gaz ⊞ Battery Charging

FOXHOLME ►►► CARAVAN PARK

Campsite of the Year North Region Winner 1986
60 Touring Vans, Motor Caravans & Tents

English Tourist Council
★★★★★

Ryedale, North Yorkshire, (4 miles from Helmsley and the North York Moors National Park). A quiet site suitable for exploring North Yorkshire.
60 pitches set in individual clearings in the woodland. Luxury toilet blocks, AA graded Excellent for environment, wc's, hot water, showers, wash basins in cubicles and shaver points.
Reception, late arrival park, shop and mains hook-up points. Some pitches for tents.
Caravan Club approved. Camping Club listed.
For brochure, please send stamp to:

FOXHOLME CARAVAN PARK
(AA), Harome, Helmsley, York YO62 5JG
Tel. (01439) 771241 Fax: (01439) 771744

►►► **Foxholme Caravan Park (SE658828)**
Harome YO62 5JG ☎ 01439 770416 & 771241
Dir: Follow A170 from Helmsley in direction of Scarborough, turn right signposted Harome
★ ⊞ £7-£7.50 ⊞ £7-£7.50 Å £7-£7.50
Open Etr-Oct Booking advisable bank & school hols Last arrival 23.00hrs Last departure noon
A quiet park set in secluded wooded countryside, with pitches in individual clearings divided by mature trees. The facilities are well maintained, and the site is ideal as a touring base or a place to relax. Caravans are prohibited on the A170 at Sutton Bank between Thirsk and Helmsley. A 6-acre site with 60 touring pitches.
Facilities: ♠⊙🏳⚡✳🔥⚓🐕 **Services:** ♨🗑🔌🚻🆃
→ ∪ ▶ ♫

►►► **Wrens of Ryedale Touring Park (SE656840)**
Gale Ln, Nawton YO62 7SD ☎ 01439 771260
Dir: On A170 3m E of Helmsley, turn right in villages of Nawton/Beadlam into Gate Lane. Park 400m on right
★ ⊞ £6-£7.25 ⊞ £6-£7.25 Å £6-£7.25
Open Apr-16 Oct Booking advisable bank & school hols Last arrival 22.00hrs Last departure noon
A small family-owned park divided into three areas by mature trees and shrubs. The sheltered grass pitches are ideal for those seeking a quiet and relaxing holiday. Caravans are prohibited on the A170 at Sutton Bank between Thirsk and Helmsley. A 2.5-acre site with 30 touring pitches.

Bike hire.
Leisure: ⚠ **Facilities:** ♠⊙🏳✳🔥⚓🐕
Services: ♨🗑🔌🚻🆃
→ ∪ ▶ ♫

HIGH BENTHAM   Map 07 SD66

►►► **Riverside Caravan Park (SD665688)**
LA2 7HS ☎ 01524 261272 & 262163
Dir: Off B6480, signed from town centre
⊞ ⊞ Å
Open Mar-Oct Booking advisable bank hols Last arrival 20.00hrs Last departure 13.00hrs
This site is set on the banks of the River Wenning, in delightful countryside and screened by trees. A 12-acre site with 30 touring pitches and 170 statics. Free fishing.
Leisure: ♠⚠ **Facilities:** ♠⊙🏳✳🔥⚓🐕
Services: ♨🗑🔌🚻🆃
→ ∪ ▶ ♫

HUNMANBY   Map 08 TA07

►►►► **Orchard Farm Holiday Village (TA105779)**
Stonegate YO14 0PU ☎ 01723 891582
Dir: Signed from A1039
★ ⊞ £7-£12 ⊞ £7-£12 Å £7-£12
Open all year (rs Nov-Mar not all facilities) Booking advisable bank hols & peak season Last arrival 23.00hrs Last departure 11.00hrs

Facilities: ♨ Bath 🏳 Shower ⊙ Electric Shaver 🏳 Hairdryer ✳ Ice Pack Facility 🚻 Disabled Facilities ♜ Public Telephone
⚓ Shop on Site or within 200yds 🔌 Mobile Shop (calls at least 5 days a week) 🔥 BBQ Area 🏳 Picnic Area 🐕 Dog Exercise Area

A level grassy site with pitches ranged around a large coarse fishing lake, and with its own small gauge miniature railway. This all-round high quality park is run by keen and friendly owners, and offers a wide range of amenities including an indoor heated swimming pool and two licensed bars. A 14-acre site with 91 touring pitches and 26 statics.
Veg prep area, boating lake, fishing.

Leisure: ⚓ ⚓ 🎠 ▢ **Facilities:** 🅿️⊙🔍✳️⚹✆🛒▣🛁🚻
🐕 **Services:** 🕹️▣🍺🚰⚿🔌▣🚰🚿
→ ∪ ⏩ ◎ ♨ ↯ 🎵

Facilities: 🅿️⊙🔍✳️⚹✆🛒🚻🐕
Services: 🕹️▣🍺🚰⚿🔌▣
→ ⏩ ◎ ♨ ↯ ⚽ 🎵 🚌 🚌 🚎 ⓓ 🚐 🚋 🚲

▶ ▶ ▶ **Kingfisher Caravan Park** (SE343603)
Low Moor Ln, Farnham HG5 9DQ ☎ 01423 869411
Dir: From Knaresborough take A6055. After 1m turn left towards Farnham & left again in village signed Scotton. Site 1m on left
🚐 🚐 ⚊

Open mid Mar/Etr-Oct Booking advisable bank hols & 15 Jul-1 Sep Last arrival 23.00hrs Last departure 16.00hrs
A large grassy site with open spaces set in wooded area in rural countryside. A 4-acre site with 35 touring pitches and 30 statics.
Leisure: 🎠 **Facilities:** 🅿️⊙🔍✳️⚹✆🛒🚻🐕
Services: 🕹️▣🍺⚿▣
→ ∪ ♨ ⚽ 🎵

▶ ▶ ▶ **Lebberston Touring Caravan Park** (TA077824)
Filey Rd YO11 3PE ☎ 01723 585723
Dir: Off A165 Filey to Scarborough road. Site signposted from road
★ 🚐 £6-£10 🚐 £6-£10
Open Mar-Oct Booking advisable bank hols
A peaceful family park in a gently-sloping rural area. The quality facilities are maintained to a high standard of cleanliness. The keen owners are friendly and helpful, and create a relaxing atmosphere. A 7.5-acre site with 125 touring pitches.
Facilities: ➡️🅿️⊙🔍✳️⚹✆🛒🐕 **Services:** 🕹️🍺⚿▣
→ ∪ ⏩ ◎ ♨ ↯ ⚽ 🎵 🚰▣

▶ ▶ ▶ *Naburn Lock Caravan & Camping Park* (SE596446)
YO19 4RU ☎ 01904 728697
Dir: From A64 N on A19, turn left signed Naburn, and site on right 0.5m past village
🚐 🚐 ⚊
Open Mar-6 Nov Booking advisable anytime Last arrival 22.00hrs
A meadowland site close to river in a rural area south of York. Mainly level pitches divided by mature hedges. A 7-acre site with 100 touring pitches.

▶ ▶ ▶ **Sleningford Water Mill Caravan Camping Park** (SE280783)
HG4 3HQ ☎ 01765 635201
Dir: Adjacent to A6108. 4m N of Ripon & 1m N of North Stainley
★ 🚐 £7.50-£11 🚐 £7.50-£11 ⚊ £7.50-£11
Open Etr & Apr-Oct Booking advisable bank hols & school holidays Last arrival 22.00hrs Last departure 12.30hrs
Level, grassy site with mature trees set in woods and meadowland adjacent to River Ure. A 14-acre site with 80 touring pitches.
Off-licence, canoe access, fly fishing.
Leisure: ⚓ 🎠 **Facilities:** 🅿️⊙✳️⚹✆🛒🚻🐕
Services: 🕹️▣🍺⚿▣
→ ⏩ ♨ 🎵

▶ ▶ ▶ **Cote Ghyll Caravan Park** (SE461983)
North End DL6 3AH ☎ 01609 883425
Dir: From junct of A1/A684 take unclass road signed Osmotherley. In village turn left at T-junct and site is 0.5m on the right
★ 🚐 fr £6.50 🚐 fr £6 ⚊ fr £5.75
Open Apr-Oct Booking advisable bank hols & Jul-Aug Last arrival 21.00hrs Last departure noon
Quiet, peaceful site in pleasant valley on edge of moors, close to village. A 4-acre site with 77 touring pitches and 17 statics.
Facilities: 🅿️⊙✳️🐕 **Services:** 🕹️▣🍺⚿▣
→ 🛒

▶ ▶ ▶ *Upper Carr Touring Park* (SE804816)
Upper Carr Ln, Malton Rd YO18 7JP
☎ 01751 473115
Dir: Off A169 Malton-Pickering road, approx 1.5m from Pickering; signed opposite Black Bull pub
🚐 🚐 ⚊
Open Mar-Oct
Attractive and well-maintained rural touring park set amongst mature trees and hedges, with animal corner and adjacent 9-hole golf course. The park has a family history library, with internet research

contd.

England

facilities. A nature trail leads to the quaint village of Thornton-le-Dale, with streams running through the centre. A 4-acre site with 80 touring pitches. Off-licence.

Leisure: 🅰 **Facilities:** 🏪⊙🔌&📞🐕 **Services:** 🔌🗑🛈

→🅿

► ► ► Wayside Caravan Park (SE764859)
Wrelton YO18 8PG ☎ 01751 472608
Dir: 2.5m W of Pickering on A170, follow signs at Wrelton
🚐 £8.50-£9 🚐 £8-£8.50 Å £7.50-£8
Open Etr-early Oct Booking advisable Etr, Spring bank hol & Jul-Aug Last arrival 23.00hrs Last departure noon

Located in the village of Wrelton, this well-maintained park is divided into small paddocks by mature hedging. Caravans are prohibited from using the A170 at Sutton Bank between Thirsk and Helmsley. A 10-acre site with 75 touring pitches and 80 statics.
Facilities: 🏪⊙🔌&📞🐕 **Services:** 🔌🗑🛈📧🗑
→🚰🅿🍴🗑 🔌🔧🌐🗑

RICHMOND　　　　　　　Map 07 NZ10
► ► ► ► Brompton-on-Swale Caravan & Camping Park (NZ199002)
Brompton-on-Swale DL10 7EZ ☎ 01748 824629
Dir: Take B1263 off A1 signed Richmond and site is 1m on the left
★ 🚐 £8.30-£12.50 🚐 £8.30-£12.50 Å £3.70-£8.30
Open Etr or Mar-Oct Booking advisable school & bank hols Last arrival 21.00hrs Last departure 12.00hrs
A peaceful riverside site on former meadowland with mature trees and other natural features. Resident owners maintain the first class facilities to

a very high standard. There is a choice of bankside pitches or fully-serviced pitches on level higher ground overlooking the park. Fishing is available on the River Swale which flows through the park, and there is a good playground to keep the children amused. A 10.5-acre site with 177 touring pitches and 22 statics.
Fishing on site

Leisure: 🅰 **Facilities:** 🏪⊙🔌❄&📞🐕🏕🐕
Services: 🔌🗑🛈🗑🗑🗑
→🚰🅿🔺🗑🗑 🔌🗑🗑🗑 🔌🗑

► Swale View Caravan Site (NZ134013)
Reeth Rd DL10 4SF ☎ 01748 823106
Dir: 3m W of Richmond on A6108
🚐 fr £5.70 🚐 fr £5.70 Å fr £5.70
Open Mar-Oct Booking advisable bank hols & summer hols Last arrival 21.00hrs Last departure noon
A level, grassy site shaded by trees, lying on the banks of the River Swale in picturesque country. A 4-acre site with 60 touring pitches and 100 statics.
Leisure: 🍴🅰 **Facilities:** 🏪⊙❄📞🐕🐕
Services: 🔌🗑🛈🗑🗑
→🅿🗑🗑

RIPON　　　　　　　　Map 08 SE37
► ► ► Riverside Meadows Country Caravan Park (SE317726)
Ure Bank Top HG4 1JD ☎ 01765 602964
Dir: Leave A1 at junct with A61 signed Ripon. At bypass rdbt turn right onto unclass road, then at the 2nd rdbt take the 2nd left
★ 🚐 £7-£11 🚐 £7-£11 Å £7-£11
Open Etr-Oct (rs Mar-Apr bar open wknds only) Booking advisable bank hols & high season Last arrival 22.00hrs Last departure noon
This pleasant and well-maintained site stands on high ground overlooking the River Ure, 1 mile from town centre. There is no access to the river from the site. A 28-acre site with 200 touring pitches and 200 statics.

See advertisement under FILEY

Leisure: 🍴🅰🗑 **Facilities:** 🏪⊙❄&📞🐕🐕
Services: 🔌🗑🗑🛈🗑🗑🗑
→🚰🅿🔺❄🗑🗑

ROSEDALE ABBEY　　　　Map 08 SE79
► ► ► Rosedale Caravan & Camping Park (SE725858)
YO18 8SA ☎ 01751 417272
Dir: From Pickering turn left onto A170 for 2.25m. Turn right at Wrelton for Cropton & Rosedale on unclass road for 7m. Park on left in village
🚐 🚐 Å
Open Mar-Oct Booking advisable
Set in a sheltered valley in the centre of the North Yorkshire Moors National Park, and divided into separate areas for tents, tourers and statics. A very popular park, with well-tended grounds, and close to the pretty village of Rosedale Abbey. A 10-acre site with 100 touring pitches and 37 statics.

Leisure: ♣ ⚲ Facilities: ⊙ ⬟ ⚼ ⚦ 🏛 ⛱ ⊬
Services: 🔌 🔲 🛢 ⌀ ⊞ Ⓣ
→ ∪ ▸ ◎ ⤳ 🔋

SCARBOROUGH   **Map 08 TA08**

▶ ▶ ▶ ▶ Spring Willows Touring Caravan Park
(TA026794)
Main Rd, Staxton Roundabout YO12 4SB
☎ 01723 891505
Dir: A64 to Scarborough, then take A1039 to Filey.
Entrance on right
★ 🚐 £7-£16.50 🚐 £7-£16.50 ▲ £7-£16.50
Open Mar-Oct (rs Mar & Oct bar/pool/take-
away/restaurant restricted) Booking advisable bank
hols, Etr, Jul & Aug Last arrival 18.00hrs Last
departure 11.00hrs

See full entry under STAXTON, page 216

Services: Ⓣ Toilet Fluid   ✗ Café/ Restaurant   🏛 Fast Food/Takeaway   ➹ Baby Care   🔌 Electric Hook Up
🔲 Launderette   ⵚ Licensed Bar   🛢 Calor Gaz   ⌀ Camping Gaz   ⊞ Battery Charging

▶ ▶ ▶ **Arosa Caravan & Camping Park (TA011830)**
Ratten Row, Seamer YO12 4QB
☎ 01723 862166
Dir: 4m from Scarborough. From junct with unclass road & A64 S of Seamer, travel N into village. Site 250yds along Ratten Row
★ 🚐 £10.50-£15 🚐 £7.50-£9.50 ▲ £6.50-£15
Open Mar-4 Jan Booking advisable bank hols & Aug Last arrival anytime Last departure anytime
A very well laid out site with screening from mature trees. Emphasis at this family-owned park is placed on the friendly clubhouse which offers occasional entertainment. A 3.5-acre site with 105 touring pitches.
Leisure: ◆ ⚙ Facilities: ⟦⊙🕯※♿℃🛍⊞🗊🎠🐾
Services: 🖃⊡♀🍴⊘⊞🗊🖕
➝ ∪ ▶ ☖ ⚡ ♨ ✂

See advert on page 213

▶ ▶ ▶ **Jacobs Mount Caravan Park (TA021868)**
Jacobs Mount, Stepney Rd YO12 5NL
☎ 01723 361178
Dir: Direct access from A170
★ 🚐 £7.50-£9.50 🚐 £7.50-£9.50 ▲ £7.50-£9.50
Open Mar-Oct (rs Mar-May & Oct limited hours at shop/bar) Booking advisable bank hols & late Jun-early Sep Last arrival 21.00hrs Last departure noon
A sheltered family-run park surrounded by woodland and open countryside on the edge of Forge Valley National Park area. There are many all-weather full-

facility touring pitches in a separate area, and the park is only two miles from Scarborough. An 18-acre site with 156 touring pitches and 44 statics.
Leisure: ◆ ⚙🕮 Facilities: ⟦⊙🕯※℃🐾🐾
Services: 🖃⊡♀⊘⊞🗊✕🖕
➝ ∪ ▶ ⊙☖⚡♨✂

▶ ▶ ▶ *Killerby Old Hall (TA063829)*
Killerby YO11 3TW ☎ 01723 583799
Dir: Direct access via B1261 at Killerby, near Cayton
🚐🚐
Open Etr-Oct Booking advisable
A small secluded park well sheltered by mature trees and shrubs, located on the lawn at the rear of old hall. A 1-acre site with 10 touring pitches.
Leisure: ⥀ ◆ ⚙ Facilities: ⟦⊙※℃🔲🐾🐾
Services: 🖃⊡⊞
➝ ∪ ▶ ⊙☖✂🛍

▶ ▶ ▶ **Scalby Close Park (TA020925)**
Burniston Rd YO13 0DA ☎ 01723 365908
Dir: 2m N of Scarborough on A615 coast road, 1m from junct with A171
🚐 £6-£10 🚐 £6-£10 ▲ £6-£10
Open Mar-Oct Booking advisable bank hols & high season Last arrival 22.00hrs Last departure noon
An attractive small park with upgraded facilities and enthusiastic owners. Only two miles from Scarborough, and handy for exploring both coast and countryside. . A 3-acre site with 42 touring pitches and 5 statics.
Facilities: ⟦⊙※℃🐾🐾 Services: 🖃⊡⊘⊞🗊
➝ ∪ ▶ ⚡♨✂ 💳 💳

▶ ▶ ▶ **Scalby Manor Caravan & Camping Park (TA025911)**
Field Ln, Station Rd, Scalby YO13 0DA
☎ 01723 366212
Dir: 2m N of Scarborough town centre on the A165 to Whitby
🚐 £5.50-£10 🚐 £5.50-£10 ▲ £3-£10
Open Etr-Oct Booking advisable bank hols Jul & Aug Last arrival 18.00hrs Last departure noon
Slightly undulating, grassy site in rural surroundings. This large park has plenty of strategically placed facilities, and the grass is well trimmed. A 22-acre site with 300 touring pitches.

Off-licence.
Leisure: ⚙ Facilities: ⟦♿℃🔲🐾🐾
Services: 🖃⊡⊘⊞
➝ ∪ ▶ ⚡♨✂🖃🛍 💳 💳 💳 💳 💳

England

SCOTCH CORNER   Map 08 NZ20

▶ ▶ ▶ **Scotch Corner Caravan Park** (NZ210054)
DL10 6NS ☎ 01748 822530 & 822961 (winter)
*Dir: From Scotch Corner junct of A1 & A66 take A6108
towards Richmond. Proceed 250mtrs then cross central
reservation and return 200mtrs to site entrance*
★ ⊞ £8.20-£9.50 ⊞ £8.20-£9.50 ▲ £8.20-£9.50

Open Etr-mid Oct Booking advisable public hols &
Jul-Aug Last arrival 22.30hrs Last departure noon
*A well-maintained site with excellent facilities.
A 7-acre site with 96 touring pitches.*
Leisure: ⚙ **Facilities:** ⬕⊙℟✳&⛄⚘⭐
Services: ⬙⬕⚲🛒⬕⊞⊤✕
→ ∪ ▶ ⚙ 🔵⬛⬛⬛ 🔵

SHERIFF HUTTON   Map 08 SE66

▶ ▶ ▶ **Camping & Caravanning Club Site**
(SE638652)
Bracken Hill YO60 6QG ☎ 01347 878660
*Dir: From York take 'Earswick/Strensall' signs. Keep left
at filling station and Ship Inn. Site 2nd on the left*
★ ⊞ £11.80-£14.90 ⊞ £11.80-£14.90 ▲ £11.80-£14.90
Open 20 Mar-1 Nov Booking advisable bank hols &
peak periods Last arrival 21.00hrs Last departure
noon
*A quiet rural site in open meadowland within easy
reach of York. Please see the advertisement on
page 14 for details of Club Members' benefits. A 10-
acre site with 96 touring pitches.*
Leisure: ⚙ **Facilities:** ⬕⊙℟✳&⛄⭐
Services: ⬙⬕⚲⬕⊞
→ ∪ ▶ ⚘⚙⛄ 🔵⬛

SLINGSBY   Map 08 SE67

▶ ▶ ▶ **Camping & Caravanning Club Site**
(SE699755)
Railway St YO6 7AA ☎ 01653 628335
*Dir: From A64 left for Castle Howard. Straight through
estate until reaching Malton-Helmsly Rd. Into Slingsby
and through village 0.25m to site*
★ ⊞ £11.80-£14.90 ⊞ £11.80-£14.90 ▲ £11.80-£14.90
Open 20 Mar-1 Nov Booking advisable bank hols &
peak periods Last arrival 21.00hrs Last dep noon
*A well cared for park in a traditional North Yorkshire
village with a maypole on the village green. Pitches
are a mixture of grass and hardstanding, and the very
modern toilet block is clean and bright. Caravans are
prohibited on the A170 at Sutton Bank between
Thirsk and Helmsley. Please see advertisement on
page 14 for details of Club Members' benefits.
A 3-acre site with 60 touring pitches.*
Facilities: ℟⊙℟✳&⛄⚘ **Services:** ⬙⬕⚲🛒⬕⊞⊤
→ ∪ ▶ ⚙ ⚘⬛

▶ ▶ ▶ **Robin Hood Caravan & Camping Park**
(SE701748)
Green Dyke Ln YO62 4AP ☎ 01653 628391
*Dir: Situated on the edge of the village of Slingsby with
access of the B1257 Malton to Helmsley Road*
★ ⊞ £9-£15 ⊞ £9-£11 ▲ £9-£11
Open Mar-Oct Booking advisable bank hols & 15
Jul-1 Sep Last arrival 18.00hrs Last departure noon
*A pleasant, well-maintained grassy site, well-
situated for touring the Yorkshire Dales. A 2-acre
site with 39 touring pitches and 13 statics.*
Caravan hire. Off-license.
Leisure: ⚙ **Facilities:** ℟⊙℟✳&⛄⚘⭐⭐
Services: ⬙⬕⚲⬕⊞⊤
→ ∪ ⚙

SNAINTON   Map 08 SE98

▶ ▶ ▶ **Jasmine Caravan Park** (SE928813)
Cross Ln YO13 9BE ☎ 01723 859240
*Dir: Turn S off A170 in Snainton village. Then follow
signposts*
★ ⊞ £6.50-£9.50 ⊞ £6.50-£9.50 ▲ £6.50-£9.50

Open Mar-Dec Booking advisable 3 wks in advance
for bank hols Last arrival 22.00hrs Last departure
noon
*A well-screened rural site on edge of this peaceful
village, sheltered by high hedges. Midway between
Pickering and Scarborough, on the edge of the*

contd.

Services: ⊤ Toilet Fluid ✕ Café/ Restaurant ⬛ Fast Food/Takeaway ⬙ Baby Care ⬙ Electric Hook Up
⬕ Launderette ⚲ Licensed Bar ⬕ Calor Gaz ⚘ Camping Gaz ⊞ Battery Charging

North Yorkshire Moors National Park. A 5-acre site with 90 touring pitches and 11 statics.

Facilities: ➔ ♠ ⊙ ❄ ✳ ᚼ ᚼ ♿ ❧ ⚓ **Services:** 🖳 ⛽ ᛜ ⏀ ∅ ⊞ Ⓣ
→ ∪ ┣ ᛜ 🍴 ●₩ ⊞⊞ ▤▤ ᛜ▨ ⛽

STAINFORTH   Map 07 SD86

► ► ► **Knight Stainforth Hall Caravan & Campsite (SD816672)**
BD24 0DP ☎ 01729 822200
Dir: Approach only possible from B6479 at Giggleswick. Leave A65 for Settle on B6480. Turn into road signed Little Stainforth opposite school. Site 2.5m
★ 🚐 fr £8.75 🚐 fr £8.75 ▲ fr £8.75
Open May-Oct Booking advisable bank hols & Jul-Aug Last arrival 22.00hrs Last departure noon
A very well-maintained site located near the River Ribble in the Yorkshire Dales National Park. A 6-acre site with 100 touring pitches and 60 statics. Fishing on site.
Leisure: ♦ ⚘ ▢ **Facilities:** ♠ ⊙ ❄ ✳ ❧ ⚓ ᚼ ᚼ
Services: 🖳 ⛽ ᛜ ⏀ ∅ ⊞ Ⓣ
→ ∪ ┣ ᛜ 🍴 ●₩ ⊞⊞ ▤▤ ᛜ▨ ⛽

STAXTON   Map 08 TA07

► ► ► ► **Spring Willows Touring Caravan Park (TA026794)**
Main Rd, Staxton Roundabout YO12 4SB
☎ 01723 891505
Dir: A64 to Scarborough, then take A1039 to Filey. Entrance on right
★ 🚐 £7-£16.50 🚐 £7-£16.50 ▲ £7-£16.50
Open Mar-Oct (rs Mar & Oct bar/pool/take-away/restaurant restricted) Booking advisable bank hols, Etr, Jul & Aug Last arrival 18.00hrs Last departure 11.00hrs
A lively park offering a full evening entertainment programme, and a restaurant serving food throughout the day and evening. Other amenities include a Mexican themed bar, and a popular children's club. The pitches are divided by shrubs and bushes, and sheltered by high sand dunes, with a natural spring running through the park. A 16-acre site with 184 touring pitches.
Sauna, solarium, coffee lounge
See advertisement under SCARBOROUGH
Leisure: ❅ ♦ ⚘ ▢ **Facilities:** ♠ ⊙ ❄ ✳ ♿ ❧ ⚓ 🖳 ᚼ ᚼ
Services: 🖳 ⛽ ▥ ⏀ ∅ ⊞ Ⓣ ✕ 🛒 ➔
→ ∪ ┣ ●₩ ⊞⊞ ᛜ▨ ⛽

STILLINGFLEET   Map 08 SE54

► ► ► *Home Farm Caravan & Camping (SE575427)*
Moreby YO19 6HN ☎ 01904 728263
Dir: 6m from York on B1222, 1.5m N of Stillingfleet village
🚐
Open Feb-Dec Booking advisable bank hols Last arrival 22.30hrs

A meadowland site on a working farm bordered by parkland and the River Ouse. A 5-acre site with 25 touring pitches.
Facilities: ♠ ⊙ ❄ ✳ ❧ ᚼ **Services:** 🖳 ⛽ ∅ ⊞ Ⓣ
→ ∪ ᛜ ⚓

SUTTON-ON-THE-FOREST   Map 08 SE56

► ► ► ► **Goosewood Caravan Park (SE595636)**
YO61 1ET ☎ 01347 810829
Dir: From A1237 take B1363. After 1.5m take unclass road signed Eastmoor & turn right in 0.25m. Take right turn after 0.5m & site on right
🚐 £8.50-£10.50 🚐 £8.50-£10.50

Open 2wks before Etr-Oct Booking advisable bank hols Last arrival 20.00hrs Last departure noon
An immaculately maintained park with its own lake and seasonal fishing, set in attractive woodland within the Vale of York. The park caters exclusively for touring caravans, and all pitches include hardstandings and flagged patios. There is a well-stocked fishing lake on site, and extensive woodland walks. In addition to the usual children's play equipment there is a woodland assault course. Sanitary facilities are first class, and include a family room with bath. A 12-acre site with 75 touring pitches.
Fishing lake.
Leisure: ⚘ **Facilities:** ➔ ♠ ⊙ ❄ ✳ ❧ ⚓ ᚼ ᚼ
Services: 🖳 ⛽ ᛜ ∅ ⊞ Ⓣ
→ ∪ ┣ ⚓ ᛜ

THIRSK   Map 08 SE48

► ► ► **Sowerby Caravan Park (SE437801)**
Sowerby YO7 3AG ☎ 01845 522753
Dir: 0.5m S of Sowerby on unclass road to Dalton
★ 🚐 £6.75-£7.25 🚐 £6.75-£7.25
Open Mar-Oct Booking advisable bank hols Last arrival 22.00hrs no cars by tents
A level grassy site, with a tree-lined river bank. A 1-acre site with 25 touring pitches and 85 statics.
Leisure: ♦ ⚘ **Facilities:** ♠ ⊙ ❄ ♿ ❧ ⚓
Services: 🖳 ⛽ ᛜ ∅ ⊞ Ⓣ
→ ∪ ⚓ ᛜ

THRESHFIELD — Map 07 SD96

► ► ► ► **Wood Nook Caravan Park (SD974641)**
Skirethorns BD23 5NU ☎ 01756 752412
*Dir: From Skipton take B6265 to Threshfield, then B6160
for 50yds. Turn left into Skirethorns Lane, then follow
signposts to park*
★ ⊞ £8-£10.80 ⊞ £8-£10.80 ▲ £8-£9.80
Open Mar-Oct Booking advisable bank hols & peak
periods Last arrival 22.00hrs Last departure noon
*Gently sloping site in a rural setting, completely
hidden by natural features of surrounding hills and
woodland. The first class facilities are housed in
converted farm buildings within the courtyard of
the farmhouse. Pitches are all on firm, well-drained
ground or hardstandings. A separate tenting field
accommodates tents and non-electric caravans. A 2-
acre site with 48 touring pitches and 11 statics.*
                See advertisement under GRASSINGTON
Leisure: ⚲ **Facilities:** ⛌⊙⚲☀╰╘☂
Services: ⚍⊡⬝⊘⊞Ⓣ
→∪⬥⚲⌿ ⊞ ⎯ ▨ ⎙

UGTHORPE — Map 08 NZ71

► ► ► **Burnt House Holiday Park (NZ784112)**
YO21 2BG ☎ 01947 840448
*Dir: 9m W of Whitby off A171 Teeside road. Signed onto
unclass rd to Ugthorpe.*
★ ⊞ fr £8.50 ⊞ fr £8.50 ▲ fr £8.50
Open Mar-Oct Booking advisable bank hols & Jul-
Aug Last arrival 21.00hrs Last departure noon
*A sheltered park with mature trees and bushes, set
in moorland as part of the North Yorkshire Moors
National Park. There is a long sandy beach at the
pretty seaside village of Sandsend, 4.5m away. A
7.5-acre site with 99 touring pitches and 41 statics.*
Leisure: ⚲ ⚲ **Facilities:** ⛌⊙⚲☀╰⊟
Services: ⚍⊡⬝⊘⊞
→▸⬥⚲

WHITBY — Map 08 NZ81

See also **Ugthorpe**
► ► ► ► **Northcliffe Holiday Park (NZ930076)**
YO22 4LL ☎ 01947 880477
*Dir: 3m S of Whitby on A171, turn left onto B1447
signed High Hawsker & Robin Hood's Bay. Park signed
on left through Hawsker village*
⊞ £6-£11 ⊞ £6-£11 ▲ £6-£11
Open Etr or end Mar-Oct Booking advisable school
& bank hols & Jul-Aug Last arrival 21.00hrs Last
departure 11.00hrs ⚒

*A lovely park in a peaceful position on the outskirts
of Whitby, with clifftop views and country walks.
There are excellent all-round facilities and
amenities, and everything is maintained to a very
high standard. The Cleveland Way footpath, and the
Trailway cycle route both pass beside this park. A 2-
acre site with 30 touring pitches and 171 statics.
Off-licence.*
Leisure: ⚓ ⚲ **Facilities:** ⛌⊙⚲☀╰╘
Services: ⚍⊡⬝⊘Ⓣ✗⬚
→◎⚲⌿ ⊞ ⎯ ▨ ⎙

► ► ► *Ladycross Plantation Caravan Park
(NZ821080)*
Egton YO21 1UA ☎ 01947 895502
*Dir: Signed and situated on unclass road off A171
Whitby-Teeside road, 6m from Whitby centre*
⊞ ⊞
Open Etr-Oct Booking advisable Bank hols & Aug
Last arrival 20.30hrs Last departure noon
*A sheltered and screened woodland park set on
high ground with level, mainly grassy pitches with
some hardstandings set out in bays giving a degree
of privacy. At the end of the North Yorkshire Moors
railway line to Pickering, in Eskdale about 3m from
Grosmont. A 12-acre site with 116 touring pitches.*
Facilities: ⛌⊙⚲☀╰╘☂ **Services:** ⚍⊡⬝⊘⊞Ⓣ
→⌿ ⊞ ⎯

► ► ► *Middlewood Farm Holiday Park
(NZ945045)*
Middlewood Ln, Fylingthorpe YO22 4UF
☎ 01947 880414
*Dir: Leave A171 towards Robin Hood's Bay, into
Fylingthorpe village and turn into Middlewood Lane to
park*
⊞ ⊞ ▲

                                                    contd.

*LADYCROSS PLANTATION
TOURING CARAVAN PARK*

Services: Ⓣ Toilet Fluid ✗ Café/ Restaurant ⬚ Fast Food/Takeaway ⬝ Baby Care ⚍ Electric Hook Up
⊡ Launderette ⚲ Licensed Bar ⬝ Calor Gaz ⊘ Camping Gaz ⊞ Battery Charging

Open Etr-Oct Booking advisable Bank & School Holidays Last arrival 22.00hrs Last departure noon
A peaceful, friendly family park enjoying panoramic views, on a working farm, close to Robin Hood's Bay in a picturesque fishing village. A 7-acre site with 140 touring pitches and 30 statics.
Leisure: ⚐ **Facilities:** ↑⊙⊙※↖✠
Services: ◻◻◻⦿◻◻
→ ∪ ⊢ ↖ ↲ ↖ ◻◻◻◻◻

▶ ▶ ▶ **Rigg Farm Caravan Park (NZ915061)**
Stainsacre YO22 4LP
☎ 01947 880430
Dir: From A171 Scarborough road left onto B1416 signed Ruswarp. In 3.25m right unclass road signed Hawsker. In 1.25m left. Site in 0.5m
★ ⊞ £7.50-£8.50 ⊞ £7.50-£8.50 ▲ £7.50-£8.50
Open Mar-Oct Booking advisable bank hols & Jul-Aug Last arrival 22.00hrs Last departure noon
A neat rural site with distant views of the coast and Whitby Abbey. Set in peaceful surroundings, a former farm with reception and shop housed in a traditional Yorkshire farmhouse. A 3-acre site with 14 touring pitches and 15 statics.
Leisure: ◆ ⚐ **Facilities:** ↑⊙※↖✠
Services: ◻◻◻◻◻
→ ∪ ⊢ ⊙ ↖ ↲

▶ ▶ ▶ *Sandfield House Farm Caravan Park (NZ875115)*
Sandsend Rd YO21 3SR
☎ 01947 602660
Dir: On A174, 1m N of Whitby
⊞ ⊞
Open mid Mar-Oct Booking advisable school & bank hols Last arrival 21.00hrs Last departure 11.00hrs
Fine sea views can be enjoyed from this park, set in undulating countryside close to Whitby Golf Club. A short stroll leads to the centre of a long sandy beach, with good walks to Whitby in one direction, and Sandsend in the other. A 12-acre site with 50 touring pitches and 150 statics.
Leisure: ⚘ **Facilities:** ↑⊙⊙※↖✠
Services: ◻◻◻◻
→ ⊢ ⊙ ◻ ↲ ↲ ⚒

▶ ▶ ▶ **York House Caravan Park (NZ926071)**
YO22 4LW ☎ 01947 880354
Dir: 3.5m S, off A171
★ ⊞ £6.50-£7.50 ⊞ £6.50-£7.50 ▲ £6.50-£7.50
Open Mar-Oct Booking advisable Spring bank hol & mid Jul-Aug Last arrival 22.00hrs Last departure noon
On the edge of the North Yorkshire Moors National Park this is a very well-kept site in an undulating position located south of Whitby. Ideal for touring coast or moors. A 4-acre site with 59 touring pitches and 41 statics.
Open area for games.
Leisure: ⚐ **Facilities:** ↑⊙⊙※↖☜⚞✠ **Services:** ◻◻◻◻◻
→ ∪ ⊢ ⊙ △ ↲ ⚒ ↲

▶ ▶ ▶ **Woodhouse Farm & Country Park (SE241715)**
HG4 3PG ☎ 01765 658309
Dir: Situated 6m W of Ripon off B6265 Pateley Bridge road, 2.5m from Fountains Abbey, signed Grantley
⊞ £8-£12.50 ⊞ £8-£12.50 ▲ £7.50-£8.50

Open Mar-Oct Booking advisable bank hols & mid Jul-Aug Last arrival 21.00hrs Last departure noon
An attractive rural site on a former working farm, with existing hedges used to screen pitches, and meadowland and mature woods surrounding. Friendly, knowledgable owners. A 16-acre site with 140 touring pitches and 62 statics.
Coarse fishing lake.
Leisure: ◆ ⚐ ⊡ **Facilities:** ↑⊙⊙※↖☜⚞✠
Services: ◻◻◻◻◻
→ ∪ ↲ ⦿ ◻ ◻

▶ ▶ ▶ ▶ *St Helens Caravan Park (SE967836)*
St Helens in the Park YO13 9QD ☎ 01723 862771
Dir: On A170 in village, 150yds on left beyond Downe Arms Hotel towards Scarborough
⊞ ⊞ ▲
Open Mar-Oct (rs Nov-Jan shop/laundry closed) Booking advisable bank hols & Jul-Aug Last arrival 22.00hrs Last departure 17.00hrs
Set on the edge of the North York Moors National Park this delightfully landscaped park is extremely well-maintained and thoughtfully laid out with strategically placed, top quality facilities. The site is divided into terraces with tree-screening creating

---

Facilities: ⊷ Bath ↑ Shower ⊙ Electric Shaver ⊙ Hairdryer ※ Ice Pack Facility ⚒ Disabled Facilities ↖ Public Telephone
☜ Shop on Site or within 200yds ◫ Mobile Shop (calls at least 5 days a week) ⚞ BBQ Area ✠ Picnic Area ✠ Dog Exercise Area

smaller areas, including an 'adult zone'. A cycle
route leads through the surrounding Wykeham
estate, and there is a short pathway to the adjoining
Downe Arms country pub. A 25-acre site with 250
touring pitches.
Caravan storage.

Leisure: ♣ ⚏ **Facilities:** ➡ ⋔ ⊙ ⚑ ✳ ↖ ＆ ☎ 🛒 ☂ ⟟
Services: ⊡ 🗐 🔋 ⌀ ⊞ Ⓣ ✗ 🍴 ➡
➡ ∪ ⌘ ⦿ ⚙ ♨ ✈ ✔ ☒ 🚐 ▤ 🗑 ▦ 📶 🗐

YORK   Map 08 SE65

See also **Acaster Malbis**
► ► ► ► **Rawcliffe Manor Caravan Site**
(SE583553)
Manor Ln, Shipton Rd YO3 5TZ ☎ 01904 624422
*Dir: From A1273 York ring road, turn towards York at
junct with A19. Take 1st left & site located after 0.5m*
🚐 Å
Open all year Booking advisable all times Last
arrival 20.00hrs Last departure noon
*A level site divided into hedged paddocks, with
immaculate landscaping incorporating an
outstanding display of rose trees. Although situated
within a built-up area, the tree-planting ensures that
there is the pleasant feel of camping in a large
garden. The two sanitary blocks provide a very high
standard of facilities including full disabled
provision, and there is a restaurant attached to a
large licensed clubhouse serving bar meals. A 4.5-
acre site with 120 touring pitches.*
Petanque pitches & satellite TV.

Leisure: ♣ ⚏ ▭ **Facilities:** ➡ ⋔ ⊙ ⚑ ✳ ＆ ↖ ☎ 🛒 ⟟
Services: ⊡ 🗐 🔋 ⌀ ⊞ ✗ 🍴
➡ ∪ ⌘ ⦿ ✔ 🐾 ✈ 🚐 ▤ 🗑 ▦ 📶 🗐

► ► ► **Riverside Caravan & Camping Park**
(SE598477)
Ferry Ln, Bishopthorpe YO2 1SB
☎ 01904 705812 & 704442
*Dir: From A64 take A1036. Right at lights signed
Bishopthorpe & left into main street at T-junct. At end of
road right into Ancaster Lane & left in 150yds*
★
Open Apr-Oct Booking advisable Jul-Sep Last
arrival 22.00hrs Last departure noon
*A small level grassy park in a hedged field on the
banks of the River Ouse, in a village setting on the
outskirts of York. A 1-acre site with 25 touring
pitches.*

Leisure: ⚏ **Facilities:** ⋔ ⊙ ⚑ ✳ ↖ ☎ ⟟
Services: ⊡ ⚌ 🔋 ⌀ ⊞ Ⓣ ✗
➡ ∪ ⌘ ✔ 🐾 ✈ 🗑 🚐 📶 🗐

YORKSHIRE, SOUTH

DONCASTER

See **Hatfield**

HATFIELD   Map 08 SE60

► ► ► **Hatfield Waterpark (SE670098)**
Old Thorne Rd DN7 6EQ ☎ 01302 841572 & 737343
Dir: Signposted from Hatfield off A18
🚐 🚐 Å
Open all year (rs Nov-Mar (phone 01302 737343))
Booking advisable bank hols Last arrival 17.30hrs
Last departure noon
*A clean, well-run site with fishing and good
supervised marina facilities, including windsurfing,
sailing and canoeing equipment for hire.
Bunkhouse accommodation for up to 32, handy for
tenters in very wet weather. A 10-acre site with 75
touring pitches.*
Canoeing, rowing, sailing, windsurfing & fishing.

Leisure: ⚏ **Facilities:** ⋔ ⊙ ✳ ＆ ↖ ☎ ⟟
Services: ⊡ ➡
➡ ∪ ⌘ ✔ 🐾 ✈ ✔ 🚐

SHEFFIELD

See **Worsbrough**

WORSBROUGH   Map 08 SE30

► ► ► **Greensprings Touring Park (SE330020)**
Rockley Abbey Farm, Rockley Ln S75 3DS
☎ 01226 288298
*Dir: From M1 junct 36 take A61 to Barnsley. Turn left
after 0.25m onto road signed to Pilley. Site entrance 1m
at the bottom of the hill*
★ 🚐 fr £6.50 🚐 fr £6.50 Å fr £4.50
Open Apr-Oct Booking advisable when hook up is
required Last arrival 21.00hrs Last departure noon
*Part-level, part-sloping, grass site with young trees
and bushes, set in woods and meadowland with
access to river. A 4-acre site with 65 touring pitches.*
Cycle hire. TV hook up.

Facilities: ⋔ ⊙ ⚑ ✳ ⟟ **Services:** ⊡ 🔋 ⌀
➡ ∪ ⌘ 🐾 ✈ 🗑 🚐

YORKSHIRE, WEST

BARDSEY   Map 08 SE34

► ► ► *Glenfield Caravan Park (SE351421)*
Blackmoor Ln LS17 9DZ ☎ 01937 574657
*Dir: From A58 at Bardsey turn into Church Lane,
continue into Blackmoor Lane. Site 0.5m on right*
🚐 🚐 Å
Open all year Booking advisable   *contd.*

England

A rural site in a hedge-lined meadow with level pitches. A 4-acre site with 30 touring pitches and 1 static.

Leisure: ⚠ Facilities: 🌧⊙✳🐾📞🐕

Services: 🚮📖🛒🔌

→ ∪ ▶ 🎪 🍴 🛒

▶ ▶ ▶ **Moor Lodge Park (SE352423)**
Blackmoor Ln LS17 9DZ
☎ 01937 572424
Dir: Turn right after Bracken Fox pub (Ling Lane) then right at X-roads, site 0.5m on right
🚐 £8 🚐 £8
Open all year Booking advisable all times Last arrival 23.00hrs Last departure 23.00hrs
A neat, well-kept site in a peaceful and pleasant rural location convenient to surrounding areas of interest. The touring area is for adults only. A 7-acre site with 12 touring pitches and 60 statics.
Leisure: ⚠ Facilities: 🌧⊙🍴✳📞🛁🎍🐕
Services: 🚮📖🛒🔌🔧🔌

→ ∪ ▶ 🍴 🛒

LEEDS   Map 08 SE23

See also **Bardsey**
▶ ▶ **Roundhay Park Site (SE339376)**
Roundhay Park, Elmete Ln, Wetherby Rd LS8 2LG
☎ 0113 2652354 (in season) & 2661850
Dir: Situated 6m N of Leeds city centre, off the A58 Wetherby Rd at Oakwood. Site is signposted
★ 🚐 £8.25-£8.65 🚐 £8.25-£8.65 ⚐ £8.20
Open 16 Mar-Oct Booking advisable Spring bank hol & Jul-Aug Last arrival 21.00hrs Last departure noon
On a south-facing hillside. A very well-maintained municipal site. An 8-acre site with 60 touring pitches.
Leisure: ⚠ Facilities: 🌧⊙🍴✳🛁📞🛁🎍🐕
Services: 🚮🛒🔧

→ ▶ 🎪 🍴 🔌🛒

SILSDEN   Map 07 SE04

▶ ▶ *Dales Bank Holiday Park (SE036483)*
Low Ln BD20 9JH
☎ 01535 653321 & 656523
Dir: From A6034 in town centre turn N, take left then right into Bradley Road. After 1m turn right. Site in 500yds
🚐🚐⚐
Open Apr-Oct (rs Mar) Booking advisable public hols Last arrival 22.00hrs Last departure 16.00hrs
A pleasant farm site with very good facilities in open countryside of typical Dales scenery. A 3-acre site with 40 touring pitches and 12 statics.
Leisure: ⚓⚠ Facilities: 🌧⊙🍴✳📞🛒
Services: 🚮📖🛒🔧🔌🔧✖

→ ∪ ▶ 🎪 🔌🛒 🍴🔧

CHANNEL ISLANDS
GUERNSEY

CATEL (CASTEL)   Map 16

▶ ▶ ▶ **Fauxquets Valley Farm**
GY5 7QA ☎ 01481 255460
Dir: Off pier. 2nd exit off rdbt. Top of hill left onto Queens Rd. Continue for 2m. Turn right onto Candie Rd. Opposite sign for German Occupation Museum
⚐ £9-£10.40
Open Mid Jun-Aug (rs May-mid Jun & 1-15 Sep Haybarn restaurant and Bar closed) Booking advisable last 2 wks Jul-1st 3 wks Aug
Beautiful, quiet farm site in a hidden valley yet close to the sea. Friendly, helpful owners who understand campers' needs offer good quality facilities and amenities, including an outdoor swimming pool, bar/restaurant, nature trail and sports areas. This park is the winner of a special Campsite of the Year Award for the Channel Islands for 2001. A 3-acre site with 90 touring pitches.
Nature trail & bird watching.
Leisure: 💧⚓⚠ Facilities: 🌧⊙🍴✳📞🛒🎍🐕
Services: 🚮📖🛒🔌🔧🔌✖🛁

→ ∪ ▶ ☕ ♨ 🎪 🍴 🍺 🚬 💳 🔌

ST SAMPSON   Map 16

▶ ▶ ▶ *Le Vaugrat Camp Site*
Route de Vaugrat GY2 4TA
☎ 01481 257468
Dir: From the main coast road at NW of island, site is signed at Port Grat Bay into Route de Vaugrat, near Peninsula Hotel
⚐
Open May-mid Sep Booking advisable all year 🐕
Overlooking the sea and set within the grounds of a lovely 17th-century house, this level grassy park is backed by woodland, and close to lovely sandy beaches. A 6-acre site with 150 touring pitches.
Leisure: ⚓⚠🚩 Facilities: 🌧🍴✳📞🛒🛁🎍
Services: 🔌🔧🔌

VALE   Map 16

▶ ▶ ▶ **La Bailloterie Camping & Leisure**
Bailloterie Ln GY3 5HA
☎ 01481 243636 & 07781 103420
Dir: 3m N of St Peter Port, take Vale road to Crossways & turn right into Rue du Braye. Site 1st left at sign
★ ⚐ £8.40-£10
Open 15 May-15 Sep Booking advisable All times Last arrival 23.00hrs
Pretty little site with one large touring field and a few small, well-screened paddocks, on a working freesia farm. An 8-acre site with 100 touring pitches.
Volleyball net & boules pitch.
Leisure: ⚓⚠🚩 Facilities: 🌧⊙🍴✳📞🛒🛁🎍🐕
Services: 🚮📖🛒🔌🔧🔌✖🛁🚽

→ ∪ ▶ ☕ ♨ 🎪 🍴

England

HERM

HERM   Map 16

▶ ▶ ▶ *Seagull Campsite*
GY1 3HR ☎ 01481 722377
🚐
Open May-Sep

*An away-from-it-all location on the tiny island of
Herm, which is a 20-minute boat-ride from St Peter
Port, Guernsey. The grassy site is well maintained,
and all pitches are level, some in individually
terraced bays. Herm is traffic-free, so parking must
be arranged at St Peter Port. Contact Travel Trident
on 01481 721379 or ask when booking at the park.
50 touring pitches.*

JERSEY

ST BRELADE   Map 16

▶ ▶ ▶ ▶ *Rose Farm*
Route Des Genets JE3 8DE ☎ 01534 741231
*Dir: 1m W of St Aubin's village on A13. At junct with
A57 turn right into Rose Farm Lane*
Å £9-£16
Open May-Sep Booking advisable as early as
possible Last arrival 21.00hrs Last departure
10.00hrs
*An attractive site set in a valley close to St Aubins,
with friendly owners and secluded pitches. Facilities
are of a very good standard. A 5-acre site with 150
touring pitches.*
Leisure: ⚓ ◣ ⚠ ⊡ **Facilities:** ⬟ ☉ ♜ ⚹ ⟐ ⚲ ☲
Services: ⚑ ▣ ⚎ ⬚ ⌀ ✕ ⬛
→ ∪ ▶ ◎ ⚄ ⚓ ⤙ ♪ 🍴 💳 🔌 ⬙

ST MARTIN   Map 16

▶ ▶ ▶ ▶ *Beuvelande Camp Site*
Beuvelande JE3 6EZ ☎ 01534 853575 & 852223
*Dir: Take A6 from St Helier to St Martin & follow signs
to campsite*
Å
Open May-15 Sep Booking advisable Last arrival
anytime
*An old established site with refurbished facilities, in
peaceful countryside close to St Martin. A 6-acre
site with 150 touring pitches.*   *contd.*

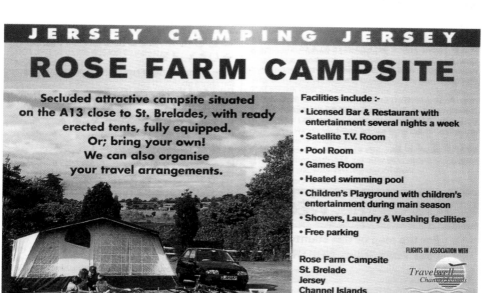
Services: Ⓣ Toilet Fluid ✕ Café/ Restaurant ⬛ Fast Food/Takeaway 🍼 Baby Care ⚑ Electric Hook Up
ⓞ Launderette ⚎ Licensed Bar ⬚ Calor Gaz ⌀ Camping Gaz ⬙ Battery Charging

Leisure: 飞 🏊 🎣 🔲 Facilities: 🍴 ⊙ 🦺 ❄ 🖕 🚻 🛒
Services: 🅿 🎱 🛒 🛈 🗑 🔲 ✕
→ ∪ 🐾 🔱 🎣

► ► ► ► Rozel Camping Park
Summerville Farm JE3 6AX
☎ 01534 856797 & 851656
Dir: From St Helier follow A6 Bagatelle Road or A7 Saviour's Road then B38
★ 🚲 £13.20
Open May-mid Sep (rs May, June & Sep snack bar closed) Booking advisable Jul-Aug Last departure noon ✂
An attractive and well-maintained secluded holiday site offering excellent amenities in a lovely farm location. Last arrival and departure time as soon as possible after car ferry docks. A 4-acre site with 70 touring pitches and 20 statics.
Leisure: 飞 🏊 🎣 🔲 Facilities: 🍴 ⊙ 🦺 ❄ 🖕 🚻 🛒 🏢
Services: 🅿 🎱 🛈 🗑 🔲 🛈
→ ∪ 🐾 🔱 🎣 🚌 🚉 🚗 🗑

SARK

SARK	**Map 16**

► ► ► *Pomme de Chien Campsite*
GY9 0SB ☎ 01481 832316
Dir: Tractor from ferry to top of Harbour Hill, then on foot to X-rds. Left at Nat West bank, then 1st lane on right to site in third of mile
🚲
Open all year Booking advisable ✂ no cars by caravans no cars by tents
Sheltered level grassy park in centre of island, close to shops and beaches, in peaceful countryside. Take tractor. A 1-acre site with 8 statics.
Facilities: 🍴 ❄

► ► ► *La Valette*
La Valette GY9 0SE ☎ 01481 832066 & 832202
Dir: Tractor from ferry to top of Harbour Hill, then on foot and right at Nat West bank. 1st right past Aladdin's Cave shop to farm in 300yds
Open all year Booking advisable no cars by caravans no cars by tents
🚲
On an elevated position with panoramic views towards Jersey and French coast, this park is on a working farm with direct access to coastal path near the lighthouse.
Facilities: 🍴 ⊙ ❄
→ 🎣 🛒

ISLE OF MAN

Caravans are not allowed on the Island.

GREEBA	**Map 06 SC38**

► ► Cronk-Dhoo Farm (SC303810)
☎ 01624 851327
Dir: A1 road from Douglas to Peel. 6m from Douglas, 3m from Peel. Private drive 100yds
★ 🚲 £7.90 🚲 £7.90 🚲
Open Apr-Nov Booking advisable Last arrival 22.00hrs Last departure 22.00hrs
Set on a 50-acre farm with good facilities in converted farm buildings which include dog kenelling if needed. This is an ideal TT site, with direct access to the course. A 14-acre site with 120 touring pitches.
Leisure: 🎣 🔲 Facilities: 🍴 ⊙ 🦺 ❄ 🖕 🚻 🏖
Services: 🅿 🗑 🔲 👕 → ∪ 🐾 🔱 🎣 🗑 🛒

KIRK MICHAEL	**Map 06 SC39**

► ► ► Glen Wyllin Campsite (SC302901)
IM6 1AL ☎ 01624 878231 & 878836
Dir: From Douglas follow A1 road to Ballacraine, right at lights & follow A3 to Kirk Michael. Turn left onto A4 signed Peel. Site entrance 100yds on right
★ 🚲 fr £7 🚲 fr £7
Open mid May-mid Sep Booking advisable end May-mid Jun Last departure noon
This tree-lined glen is divided by a tarmac road leading down to the beach. One side is for touring and the other offers tents for rental. A 9-acre site with 90 touring pitches.
Sweet shop
Leisure: 🎣 🔲 Facilities: 🍴 ⊙ 🦺 ❄ 🖕 🚻 🛒 🏖
Services: 🅿 🎱 🛈 🗑 🔲
→ ∪ 🐾 🎣

► ► Cronk Aashen Farm (SC321880)
Barregarroo IM6 1HQ ☎ 01624 878305
Dir: 1.5m S of Kirk Michael on B10 Sartfield road
★ 🚲 £7 🚲 £7
Open all year Booking advisable
A pleasant, small family-run site with good facilities in converted farm buildings and with its own wooded glen. Good views of the sea and convenient base for walking. A 3-acre site with 25 touring pitches.
Facilities: 🍴 ⊙ ❄ 🏢 🏖 Services: 🅿 🔲
→ ∪ 🎣 🛒

LAXEY	**Map 06 SC48**

► ► *Laxey Commissioners Campsite (SC438841)*
Quarry Rd, Minorca Hill ☎ 01624 861241
🚲 🚲
Open Apr-Sep Booking advisable Apr-May Last arrival anytime
A level grass park with open views over Laxey Glen, with easy foot access to the village and trams to Douglas and Ramsey. A 2-acre site with 50 touring pitches.
Facilities: 🍴 ⊙ 🛒
→ 🔱 🎣 🗑

PEEL   Map 06 SC28

▶ ▶ **Peel Camping Park (SC252839)**
Derby Rd IM5 1RG ☎ 01624 842341 & 843667
Dir: On A20, 0.25m from Peel, past Clothmaker's School
★ 🚐 £9 ▲ £7

Open mid Apr-Sep Booking advisable 1st & 2nd
week Jun ⌀
A pleasant grass site on the edge of town
surrounded by hedges, with good toilet facilities
and handy for beach and town. A 4-acre site .
Leisure: ⊡ **Facilities:** 🖍⊙🍳✳⚓🛟🛒🎋
Services: 🔌
→🡒 🔧 ▣

Services: Ⓣ Toilet Fluid ✕ Café/ Restaurant 🍴 Fast Food/Takeaway 🍼 Baby Care 🔌 Electric Hook Up
▣ Launderette ⏲ Licensed Bar 🛢 Calor Gaz ⊘ Camping Gaz ⊞ Battery Charging

Scotland

SCOTLAND

ABERDEENSHIRE

ABOYNE Map 15 NO59

▶ ▶ ▶ ▶ *Aboyne Loch Caravan Park (NO538998)*
AB34 5BR ☎ 013398 86244 & 01330 811351
Dir: Located on A93, 1m E of Aboyne
🚐 🚐 Δ
Open 31 Mar-Oct Booking advisable Jul-Aug Last
arrival 20.00hrs Last departure 11.00hrs
*Attractively-sited caravan park set amidst woodland
on the shores of the lovely Aboyne Loch in scenic
Deeside. All pitches enjoy hardstandings and
electric hook-ups, and many also come with a good
view of the loch. The facilities are modern and
immaculately maintained, and amenities include
boat launching, boating and fishing. An ideally-
located park for touring Royal Deeside and the
Aberdeenshire uplands. A 6-acre site with 55
touring pitches and 40 statics.*
Coarse fishing.
Leisure: ♠ ∅ Facilities: 🏕 ⊙ ♦ ☀ ⅃ 🕍 🛒 ♔
Services: 🚱 🗑 🏧 🚿 🝙
→ ∪ ▶ ♣ ⚚ ⚡

CUMINESTOWN Map 15 NJ85

▶ *East Balthangie Caravan Park (NJ841516)*
East Balthangie AB53 5XY
☎ 01888 544261 & 544921
*Dir: From N leave A98 to head S on A9027 to New Byth,
then unclass road signed New Deer to junct with farm
road in 2.25m*
🚐 🚐 Δ
Open Mar-Oct Booking advisable Jul & Aug Last
arrival 22.00hrs Last departure noon
*A small farm site with level pitches, sheltered by
trees to the north and with extensive views to the
south. A remote rural setting. A 2-acre site with 12
touring pitches and 1 static.*
Facilities: 🏕 ⊙ ♦ ☀ ⅃ 🕍 🛒 ♔ Services: 🚱 🝙
→ ∪ ▶ ♣ ⚚ 🚿

FORDOUN Map 15 NO77

▶ ▶ *Brownmuir Caravan Park (NO740772)*
AB30 1SL ☎ 01561 320786
*Dir: From N on the A90 take B966 signed Fettercain & site
1.5m on left. From S take unclass road signed Fordoun*
🚐 🚐
Open Apr-Oct Booking advisable Last departure
noon
*A mainly static site set in a rural location with level
pitches and good touring facilities. A 2-acre site
with 15 touring pitches and 45 statics.*
Leisure: ∅ Facilities: 🏕 ⊙ ☀ ⅃ 🕍 🗂 Services: 🚱 🗑 🏧
→ ▶ ⚚ 🚿

KINTORE Map 15 NJ71

▶ ▶ ▶ Hillhead Caravan Park (NJ777163)
AB51 0YX ☎ 01467 632809
*Dir: Located 1m from the village & A96 Aberdeen to
Inverness road. Follow caravan signs from A96 to park,
following B994 & taking unclass road to site*
🚐 £7.50-£9.40 🚐 £7.50-£9.40 Δ £5.90-£8.20
Open all year Booking advisable at all times Last
arrival 22.00hrs Last departure 13.00hrs
*An attractive, peaceful site in the River Don Valley.
A 1.5-acre site with 24 touring pitches and 5 statics.*
Caravan storage
Leisure: ∅ Facilities: 🏕 ⊙ ♦ ☀ ⅃ 🕍 🛒 🗂 ♔
Services: 🚱 🗑 🏧 🚿 🝙 🏧 🝙
→ ▶ ⚚ 🝙 ▦ ▦ ▦ 🝙

MACDUFF Map 15 NJ76

▶ *Wester Bonnyton Farm Site (NJ741638)*
Gamrie AB45 3EP ☎ 01261 832470
*Dir: From A98 1m S of Macduff join B9031 signed
Rosehearty & site on right in 1.25m*
🚐 🚐 Δ
Open Mar-Oct Booking advisable
*A farm site in a screened meadow, with level
touring pitches enjoying views across Moray Firth.
A 1-acre site with 10 touring pitches and 18 statics.*
Leisure: ∅ Facilities: 🏕 ⊙ ⅃ Services: 🗑

NORTH WATER BRIDGE Map 15 NO66

▶ ▶ ▶ Dovecot Caravan Park (NO648663)
AB30 1QL ☎ 01674 840630
*Dir: Take A90, 5m S of Laurencekirk. At RAF Edzell sign
turn left. Site 500yds on the left*
🚐 £7-£8 🚐 £7-£8 Δ £6-£7
contd.

Services: Ⅲ Toilet Fluid ✗ Café/ Restaurant 🍔 Fast Food/Takeaway 🍼 Baby Care ⚡ Electric Hook Up
🗑 Launderette ⅃ Licensed Bar 🛢 Calor Gaz ⊘ Camping Gaz 🝙 Battery Charging

Open Apr-Oct Booking advisable Jul & Aug for hook up Last arrival 20.00hrs Last departure noon
A level grassy site in a country area close to the A90, with mature trees screening one side and the River North Esk on the other. A handy overnight stop in a good touring area. A 6-acre site with 25 touring pitches and 44 statics.

Leisure: ◣ /▲ ☐ **Facilities:** ⋔ ☺ ⅗ ☀ ↻ ↺ ⅗ ⌦
Services: ⊟ ⅰ ☉

ST CYRUS   Map 15 NO76

► ► ► ► **East Bowstrips Caravan Park**
(NO745654)
DD10 0DE ☎ 01674 850328
Dir: *From S on A92 coast rd enter St Cyrus. Pass hotel on left. Take 1st left and then 2nd right. Site signposted*
★ ⊞ £7-£8 ⊟ £7-£8 ⅄ £6.50-£8
Open Etr or Apr-Oct Booking advisable Jun-Aug Last arrival 22.00hrs Last departure noon
A quiet, rural site close to seaside village, with thoughtfully modernised facilities and a particular welcome for the disabled. The park is surrounded by farmland on the edge of a village, and there are extensive views to be enjoyed. Touring pitches are sited on rising ground amongst attractive landscaping with ornamental trees and shrubs, and flowers. A 4-acre site with 30 touring pitches and 18 statics.

Leisure: /▲ **Facilities:** ⋔ ☺ ⅗ ☀ ↻ ↺ ⅗ ⌦
Services: ⊟ ⅟ ⅰ ☉
→ ⅃

STONEHAVEN   Map 15 NO88

► ► ► *Queen Elizabeth Caravan Site (NO875866)*
AB39 2NH ☎ 01569 764041(in season) & 762001
Dir: *Leave A90 N of Stonehaven at junct with B979. Site on left after joining A957 at N end of Stonehaven*
⊞ ⊟
Open Apr-mid Oct Booking advisable anytime Last arrival 20.00hrs Last departure 10.00hrs
A gently sloping grass site with hardstandings offering a good range of recreational facilities, situated between a main road and seafront adjoining a public park. A 4.5-acre site with 35 touring pitches and 76 statics.
Site adjacent to Leisure Centre & outdoor pool.
Facilities: ⋔ ☺ ⅗ **Services:** ⊟ ⅟ ⅰ ⌀ ☉ ☉
→ ↻ ⌦ ⅍ ⅃ ⅗

TARLAND   Map 15 NJ40

► ► ► **Camping & Caravanning Club Site**
(NJ477044)
Drummie Hill AB34 4UP
☎ 01339 881388
Dir: *On A93 from Aberdeen, turn right in Aboyne at Struan Hotel onto B9094. After 6m take next right & then fork left before bridge, continue for 600yds*
★ ⊞ £10.60-£13.90 ⊟ £10.60-£13.90 ⅄ £10.60-£13.90
Open 20 Mar-1 Nov Booking advisable Jul-Aug Last arrival 23.00hrs Last departure noon
A level, sheltered site screened by mature trees. See advertisement on page 14 for details of Club Members' benefits. An 8-acre site with 40 touring pitches.

Leisure: ◣ /▲ **Facilities:** ⋔ ☺ ☀ ↻ ⅗ ⌦ ⌦
Services: ⊟ ⅰ ⌀ ☉
→ ↻ ⌦ ⅃ ⊞ ▦

ANGUS

CARNOUSTIE   Map 12 NO53

► ► ► **Woodlands Caravan Park (NO560350)**
Newton Rd DD7 6HR ☎ 01241 854430 & 853246
Dir: *From A92 follow signs to Carnoustie. Enter Carnoustie main street & follow signs to site*
★ ⊞ £6.50-£9.50 ⊟ £6.50-£9.50 ⅄ £3.50-£5.80
Open mid Mar-mid Oct Booking advisable Jul-mid Aug Last arrival 20.00hrs Last departure by arrangement
An excellent, well-maintained site with good facilities. Set in a quiet area of town. A 4.5-acre site with 106 touring pitches and 14 statics.
Leisure: ☐ **Facilities:** ⋔ ☺ ⅗ ↻ ⅗ ⌦ **Services:** ⊟ ⅰ
→ ↻ ⌦ ⅍ ⅃ ⊞ ⅗

EDZELL   Map 15 NO66

► ► ► *Glenesk Caravan Park (NO602717)*
DD9 7YP ☎ 01356 648565 & 648523
Dir: *Situated on unclass road to Glen Esk, 1m N of the B966*
⊞ ⊟ ⅄
Open Apr-Oct Booking advisable public hols & mid Jun-Aug Last arrival 22.00hrs Last departure 16.00hrs
A carefully maintained woodland site surrounding a small fishing lake. An 8-acre site with 45 touring pitches and 10 statics.
Leisure: ◣ /▲ ☐ **Facilities:** ⋔ ☺ ⅗ ☀ ↻ ⅗ ⊞ ▦ ⌦
Services: ⊟ ⅟ ⅰ ⌀ ☉ ☉
→ ↻ ⌦ ⅍ ⅃ ⅗

FORFAR   Map 15 NO45

► ► ► ► *Lochside Caravan Park (NO450505)*
Forfar Loch Country Park DD8 1BT
☎ 01307 464201 & 468917
Dir: *Well signed off A94 ring road*
⊞ ⊟ ⅄
Open late Mar-early Oct Booking advisable mid Jun-Aug Last arrival 21.00hrs Last departure noon
A pleasant, well laid out park on the shore of Forfar Loch, within the Forfar Loch Country Park and adjacent to the leisure centre. The generously-spaced pitches are on a firm, level grassy base, and the modern facilities are immaculately kept by careful and knowledgeable resident staff. Pitch and putt, crazy golf and swimming are available locally. A 4.75-acre site with 74 touring pitches.
Leisure: ⅗ /▲ **Facilities:** ⋔ ☺ ↻ ⅗ ⌦ ⌦ **Services:** ⊟
→ ⌦ ◎ ⅃

Facilities: ⊶ Bath ⋔ Shower ☺ Electric Shaver ⅗ Hairdryer ☀ Ice Pack Facility ↻ Disabled Facilities ↺ Public Telephone ⅗ Shop on Site or within 200yds ☉ Mobile Shop (calls at least 5 days a week) ▦ BBQ Area ⌦ Picnic Area ⌦ Dog Exercise Area

KIRRIEMUIR   Map 15 NO35

▶ ▶ ▶ ▶ **Drumshademuir Caravan Park (NO381509)**
Roundyhill DD8 1QT ☎ 01575 573284
Dir: 2.5m S of Kirriemuir on A928
★ ⚲ £8.75-£9.75 ⚲ £8.75-£9.75 ⚑ £7-£8
Open all year Booking advisable public hols & Jun-Aug Last arrival 23.00hrs Last departure 16.00hrs
Set amidst farmland between the town of Kirriemuir and Glamis Castle, with lovely views across the Strathmore Valley. The park offers first class, immaculately maintained toilet facilities, and heating in winter ensures visitors' comfort. All pitches have wheel runs or hardstandings so that caravans are always level on the slightly sloping site. Some generously-proportioned pitches are also available, fenced off from the rest. A small bar and restaurant serve drinks, lunches and evening meals, and there is a very good children's play area. A 15-acre site with 80 touring pitches and 34 statics.
Bar food & putting, Woodland walk, Caravan storage

Leisure: ⚏ Facilities: ⚑⊙⚲☀⚐⚑⚐⚐⚑⚑
Services: ⚑⚑⚑⚑⚑⚑⚑⚑✗⚐
→ ∪ ▶ ⚑ ⚑

MONIFIETH   Map 12 NO43

▶ ▶ ▶ **Riverview Caravan Park (NO502322)**
Marine Rd DD5 4NN ☎ 01382 535471
Dir: Signed in both directions from A930 in centre of Monifieth
⚲ £9.50-£11.50 ⚲ £9.50-£11.50 ⚑ £7-£11.50
Open Apr-Oct Booking advisable Jul-Aug Last arrival 22.00hrs Last departure 12.30hrs
A well-landscaped seaside site with individual hedged pitches, and direct access to the beach, close to town centre and amenities. Set on the shores of the Firth of Tay with views of the estuary and the distant hills of Fife. The modernised toilet block has first class facilities which are immaculately maintained. An 8-acre site with 60 touring pitches and 25 statics.
Multi-gym, sauna, steam bath

Leisure: ⚫ ⚏ Facilities: ⚑⊙⚲☀⚐⚑⚑⚐⚑⚑
Services: ⚑⚑⚑⚑⚑⚑⚑
→ ∪ ▶ ⊙ ⚑ ⚑ ⚑ ⚑ ⚑ ⚑ ⚑ ⚑ ⚑ ⚑ ⚑ ⚑ ⚑

MONTROSE   Map 15 NO75

▶ ▶ ▶ *South Links Caravan Park (NO725575)*
Traill Dr DD10 8EJ ☎ 01674 72026 & 72105
Dir: From A92 follow signs to golf course
⚲ ⚲ ⚑
Open late Mar-early Oct Booking advisable mid Jun-Aug Last arrival 21.00hrs Last departure noon
A well-maintained site with good facilities, partly overlooked by a processing plant but close to the shore. A 10.75-acre site with 172 touring pitches.
Leisure: ⚏ Facilities: ⚑⊙⚐⚑⚑⚑ Services: ⚑
→ ▶ ⚑ ⚑

ARGYLL & BUTE

ARDGARTAN   Map 10 NN20

▶ ▶ ▶ **Ardgartan Caravan & Camping Site (NN275030)**
G83 7AL
☎ 01301 702293 (in season) & 0131 314 6505
Dir: 2m W of Arrochar on A83 Glasgow to Inverary road
★ ⚲ £5.80-£8.20 ⚲ £5.80-£8.20 ⚑ £5.80-£8.20
Open Etr-Oct Booking advisable public hols & Jul-Aug Last arrival 22.30hrs Last departure noon
Situated on a small promontory alongside Loch Long with access to shingle beach; a grassy Forestry Commission site on two levels. A 17-acre site with 160 touring pitches.
Slip-way for launching small boats.

Leisure: ⚏ Facilities: ⚑⊙⚲⚐⚑⚑⚑⚑⚑
Services: ⚑⚑⚑⚑
→ ∪ ⚑ ⚑ ⚑ ⚑ ⚑ ⚑ ⚑

ARDUAINE   Map 10 NM71

▶ ▶ *Arduaine Caravan & Camping Park (NM800101)*
PA34 4XA ☎ 01852 200331
Dir: Access is from A816
⚲ ⚲ ⚑
Open Mar-Oct Booking advisable Spring bank hol & Jul-Aug Last arrival 22.00hrs Last departure noon
Gently sloping grass site pleasantly situated by the seashore beside a small jetty with views of Shuna, Scarba, Jura and Luing. A 5-acre site with 40 touring pitches.
Free dinghy launching into sea.

Facilities: ⚑⊙⚲☀⚑ Services: ⚑⚑
→ ∪ ⚑ ⚑ ⚑ ⚑ ⚑

BARCALDINE   Map 10 NM94

▶ ▶ ▶ ▶ **Camping & Caravanning Club Site (NM966420)**
PA37 1SG ☎ 01631 720348
Dir: N on A828, 7m from the Connel Bridge turn into site at the Camping Club Sign on the right
★ ⚲ £10.60-£13.90 ⚲ £10.60-£13.90 ⚑ £10.60-£13.90
Open 20 Mar-1 Nov Booking advisable bank hols & Jul-Aug Last arrival 21.00hrs Last departure noon
A sheltered site within a walled garden, bordered by Barcaldine Forest, close to Loch Creran. Tourers are arranged against the old garden walls, with some located outside in quiet grassed areas. There are pleasant woodland walks from the park, including the Sutherland Memorial Woods close by. Please see the advertisement on page 14 for details of Club Members' benefits. A 4.5-acre site with 86 touring pitches.
Leisure: ⚫ ⚏ ⚑ Facilities: ⚑⊙⚲☀⚐⚑⚑
Services: ⚑⚑⚑⚑⚑⚑⚑✗
→ ∪ ▶ ⚑ ⚑ ⚑ ⚑ ⚑

Scotland

CARRADALE   Map 10 NR83

▶ ▶ ▶ **Carradale Bay Caravan Park (NR815385)**
PA28 6QG ☎ 01583 431665
Dir: Approach via Tarbert, leaving by A83 Campbeltown
road. After 5m turn onto B8001, then B842 Carradale
road. In Carradale head for pier. Site is in 0.5m
★ 🚐 £7.50-£12.80 🚐 £7.50-£12.80 ▲ £7.50-£12.80
Open Etr-Sep Booking advisable bank hols & Jul-
Aug Last arrival 22.00hrs Last departure noon
*A beautiful, natural site on the sea's edge with
superb views over Kilbrannan Sound to Isle of
Arran. An 8-acre site with 75 touring pitches and 3
statics.*
Canoe use.
Facilities: 🆁⊙🔍☀🅲🆂🅴🠗 Services: 🚱🅴
➔▶♻♨♪

GLENDARUEL   Map 10 NR98

▶ ▶ ▶ **Glendaruel Caravan Park (NR005865)**
PA22 3AB ☎ 01369 820267
Dir: Situated off A866
🚐 £8.50-£10.50 🚐 £8.50-£10.50 ▲ £8.50-£10.50
Open Apr-Oct Booking advisable Spring bank hol &
mid Jul-Aug Last arrival 22.00hrs Last departure
noon
*Attractive, grassy, level site in 23 acres of wooded
parkland in a valley surrounded by mountains, with
many rare species of trees on site. A 3-acre site with
45 touring pitches and 30 statics.*
Bicycles for hire, fishing sea trout & salmon.
Leisure: ◣ ⋀ Facilities: 🆁⊙🔍☀🅲🆂🅴🠗
Services: 🚱🅴🅸⌀🅷🆃
➔ ♪ 💳 📧

INVERARAY   Map 10 NN00

▶ ▶ ▶ ▶ *Argyll Caravan Park (NN075055)*
PA32 8XT ☎ 01499 302285
Dir: 2.5m S of Inveraray on A83
🚐 ▲
Open Apr-Oct Last arrival anytime Last departure
noon
*An attractive touring park on the shores of Loch
Fyne, part of a large site with vans on
hardstandings with fully-serviced pitches, and two
large grass areas for other tourers and tents. There
are ample on-site facilities including a large indoor
sports hall. A 6-acre site with 100 touring pitches
and 187 statics.*
Indoor sports hall
Leisure: ◣ ⋀ Facilities: 🆁⊙🔍☀♿🅲🆂🠗
Services: 🚱🅴🅀🅸⌀🅃✕♨
➔♨▶♻♨♪ 💳 📧 ♻

INVERUGLAS   Map 10 NN30

▶ ▶ ▶ ▶ **Loch Lomond Holiday Park (NN320092)**
G83 7DW ☎ 01301 704224
Dir: Situated on A82, 3.5m N of Tarbet
★ 🚐 £8-£13 🚐 £8-£13
Open Mar-Oct (rs Dec-Jan main amenity building
restricted hours) Booking advisable May-Aug Last
arrival 21.00hrs Last departure 11.45hrs

*A lovely setting on the shores of Loch Lomond with
views of forests and mountains, and boat hire
available. The small touring area is beautifully
situated overlooking the loch, and handily placed
for the toilets and clubhouse. A 6-acre site with 18
touring pitches and 72 statics.*
Satellite TV, pool tables, boat hire.
Leisure: ◣ ⋀ ▢ Facilities: 🆁⊙🔍☀♿🅲🆂🅴🆁🠗
Services: 🚱🅴🅸⌀🅃♥
➔♨♻♨♪ 💳 📧 ▤ ♻

LOCHGILPHEAD   Map 10 NR88

▶ ▶ ▶ *Lochgilphead Caravan Site (NR859881)*
PA31 8NX ☎ 01546 602003
Dir: Situated beside A83
🚐 🚐 ▲
Open Apr-Oct Booking advisable Jul-Aug
*Mainly level, grassy site close to the shore of Loch
Gilp, an inlet of Loch Fyne. Convenient to the town
centre facilities. Fishing and sailing available on the
Loch. A 7-acre site with 70 touring pitches and 30
statics.*
Mountain bike hire.
Leisure: ◣ ⋀ Facilities: 🆁⊙🔍☀🅲🆂🅴🆁🠗
Services: 🚱🅴🅸⌀🅃🆃
➔♨▶♪ 💳 📧 ♻

LUSS   Map 10 NS39

▶ ▶ ▶ ▶ **Camping & Caravanning Club Site
(NS360936)**
G83 8NT ☎ 01436 860658
Dir: Take A82 from Erkside Bridge heading N towards
Tarbet. Take right turn signed Lodge of Loch Lomond &
International Camping Sign
★ 🚐 £11.80-£14.90 🚐 £11.80-£14.90 ▲ £11.80-£14.90
Open 20 Mar-1 Nov Booking advisable bank hols &
Jul-Aug Last arrival 21.00hrs Last departure noon
*Lovely grass tenting site on west shore of Loch
Lomond. Motorvans and caravans of Club Members
only permitted. The site has two excellent newly-
built toilet blocks, with a delightful parent and child
facility, and a good laundry. Please see the
advertisement on page 14 for details of Club
Members' benefits. A 12-acre site with 90 touring
pitches.*
Fishing, watersports
Leisure: ⋀ Facilities: 🆁⊙🔍☀♿🅲🆂🠗
Services: 🚱🅴⌀
➔♨▶♻♨♪ 💳 📧

MACHRIHANISH   Map 10 NR62

▶ ▶ ▶ **Camping & Caravanning Club Site
(NR647208)**
East Trodigal PA28 6PT ☎ 01586 810366
Dir: On A83 from Inveraray take B843 to Machrihanish,
site entrance on right, 200yds past chimney
★ 🚐 £9.80-£12.40 🚐 £9.80-£12.40 ▲ £9.80-£12.40
Open 7 Apr-25 Sep Booking advisable bank hols &
high season Last arrival 21.00hrs Last departure
noon

A very open site with superb sea views, situated adjacent to the golf course. Please see the advertisement on page 14 for details of Club Members' benefits. An 8-acre site with 90 touring pitches.

Facilities: ⚑☺✳ & ⛄ ⟊   **Services:** ⚑ ⓐ ∅
→ ▶ ◬ ⤴ 🍴 ⊖ ▭

OBAN   Map 10 NM82

▶ ▶ ▶ *Oban Caravan & Camping Park (NM831277)*
Gallanachmore Farm, Gallanach Rd PA34 4QH
☎ 01631 562425
Dir: From Oban centre follow signs for Mull Ferry, then take turning past terminal signed Gallanach, for 2m to site
⚑ ⚑ A

Open Etr/Apr-Oct Last arrival 23.00hrs Last departure noon
A well-equipped tourist park in an attractive location close to sea and ferries. This family park is an ideal boating centre, and offers two large rally areas in addition to the touring pitches, one with hardstandings and some electrics. A 15-acre site with 140 touring pitches and 12 statics.

Leisure: ◕ /⚠ **Facilities:** ⚑☺✳ ⛄ 🍴 ⟊
Services: ⚑ ⓐ ⓘ ∅ ⊞ Ⓣ
→ ∪ ▶ ◬ ✚ ⛄ ⤴

For Ayrshire See East Ayrshire & South Ayrshire

CITY OF EDINBURGH

EDINBURGH   Map 11 NT27

▶ ▶ ▶ ▶ *Mortonhall Caravan Park (NT265680)*
38 Mortonhall Gate, Frogston Rd East EH16 6TJ
☎ 0131 664 1533
Dir: Take the new city by-pass to junct with A702 & follow signs to Mortonhall
⚑ ⚑ A

Open mid Mar-Oct Booking advisable Jul-Aug Last arrival 22.00hrs Last departure noon
This park is set in the 200-acre Mortonhall country estate to the south of Edinburgh, and provides a spacious camping area with grass-based and hard pitches, some with full service. The lovely park is bordered by mature trees, and is extensively planted to give a deceptively rural aspect to the park. The excellent facilities are kept spotlessly cleaned and well cared for. A 22-acre site with 250 touring pitches and 19 statics.

Leisure: ◕ /⚠ ▢ **Facilities:** ⚑☺ ⓠ✳ & ⛄ 🍴
Services: ⚑ ⓐ Ⓠ ⓘ ∅ ⊞ Ⓣ ✗
→ ∪ ▶ ⛄ ⊖ ▭ ▨ ⊡

DRUM MOHR CARAVAN PARK
Near Edinburgh

East Lothian's premier touring park for caravanners and campers. A secluded, well landscaped site on the edge of East Lothian's beautiful countryside, yet only 20 minutes from Princes Street, Edinburgh. Facilities are of an exceptionally high standard, and the toilet blocks include showers, laundry room, dishwashing area and chemical waste disposal. 120 pitches (most with electric hook-up and a few fully serviced), children's play area, well stocked shop, plus tourist information at reception.

Send for brochure to: Drum Mohr Caravan Park
Levenhall, Musselburgh, Nr Edinburgh EH21 8JS
Tel: 0131-665 6867 Fax: 0131-653 6859
E-mail: bookings@drummohr.org
Web: www.drummohr.org

Best of British
CAMPSITE OF THE YEAR
AA
SCOTLAND 1993

DUMFRIES & GALLOWAY

ANNAN   Map 11 NY16

▶ ▶ *Galabank Caravan & Camping Site (NY192676)*
North St DG12 5BQ ☎ 01556 503806
Dir: Follow B721 into town centre, turn right at traffic lights into Lady Street & site 500yds on left
★ ⚑ £6.65 ⚑ £6.65 A £6.65
Open May-early Sep Last departure noon
A tidy, well-maintained grassy little park close to the centre of town but with pleasant rural views, and skirted by the River Annan. A 1-acre site with 30 touring pitches.

Facilities: ⚑ ⓠ 🍴 **Services:** ⚑
→ ▶ ⛄ ⤴

AUCHENMALG   Map 10 NX25

▶ ▶ ▶ *Cock Inn Caravan Park (NX238518)*
DG8 0JT ☎ 01581 500227
Dir: Take A75 Glenluce by-pass, turn onto A747 Port William Road, 5m to Auchenmalg
⚑ £7-£12.50 ⚑ £7-£12.50 A £6-£8.70
Open Mar-Oct Booking advisable bank hols & Jul-Aug Last arrival 22.00hrs Last departure 11.00hrs
A grassy site in meadowland, close to sea, beach and main road. Overlooking Luce Bay, and ideal for boating and other water activities. A 2-acre site with 35 touring pitches and 70 statics.

contd.

Services: Ⓣ Toilet Fluid ✗ Café/ Restaurant 🍴 Fast Food/Takeaway ✚ Baby Care ⚑ Electric Hook Up
ⓐ Launderette Ⓠ Licensed Bar ⓘ Calor Gaz ∅ Camping Gaz ⊡ Battery Charging

Cock Inn Caravan Park

Leisure: ⚠ **Facilities:** ➡ 🏪 ⊙ ⅊ ✳ ⚲ ✆ 🐾 🛖
Services: 🔌 🚐 🛈 ⊘ ✚ 🛗 🔲 ✕
➡ ∪ ▶ ⊙ ✚ ♪

BALMINNOCH Map 10 NX26

► ► ► ► **Three Lochs Holiday Park (NX272655)**
DG8 OEP ☎ 01671 830304
Dir: Follow A75 W towards Stranraer. Approx 10km
from Newton Stewart rdbt turn right at small x-roads,
follow signs to site, 7m park on left
★ 🚐 £9-£10 🚐 £9-£10 ⚠ £6-£9
Open Mar-Oct Booking advisable bank hols & Jul-
Aug Last arrival 22.00hrs Last departure 11.00hrs
*A spacious, mainly grassy park set in moorland
with lochs and woodland nearby. A remote and
comfortable park in a peaceful location, with some
heardstanding pitches. A 45-acre site with 45
touring pitches and 90 statics.*

Games room & snooker.
Leisure: ⚲ ⚪ ⚠ **Facilities:** 🏪 ⊙ ⅊ ✳ ⚲ ✆ 🐾 🛖 🏕
Services: 🔌 🚐 🛈 ⊘ 🛗 🔲
➡ ✚ ♪

BRIGHOUSE BAY Map 11 NX64

PREMIER PARK

► ► ► ► ► **Brighouse Bay Holiday Park**
(NX628453)
DG6 4TS ☎ 01557 870267
Dir: Turn left off B727, 2m S of Kirkcudbright at
signpost to Brighouse Bay on unclass road
🚐 fr £9.95 🚐 fr £9.95 ⚠ fr £9.95
Open all year Booking advisable Etr, Spring
bank hol & Jul-Aug Last arrival 21.30hrs Last
departure 11.30hrs
*This grassy site enjoys a marvellous coastal
setting adjacent to the beach and with superb
sea views. Pitches have been imaginatively
sculpted into the meadowland with stone walls
and hedges blending in with the site's mature
trees. These features together with the large
range of leisure activities available make this an
excellent holiday centre. A 30-acre site with 190
touring pitches and 120 statics.*
Mini golf, riding, fishing, quad bikes,18-hole
golf.
Leisure: ⚲ ⚪ ⚠ **Facilities:** ➡ 🏪 ⊙ ⅊ ✳ ⚲ ✆
🐾 🏕 🛖 **Services:** 🔌 🚐 🛈 ⅊ ⊘ 🛗 🔲 ✕ 🛒 ➡
💳 🔲 📧 🅿

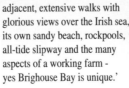

CAIRNRYAN Map 10 NX06

► ► ► *Cairnryan Caravan & Chalet Park (NX075673)*
DG9 8QX ☎ 01581 200231
Dir: Located 5m N of Stranraer on A77
🚐 🚐 Å
Open Etr/Mar-Oct (rs Apr-21 May restricted pub hours) Booking advisable Jul-Aug Last arrival 23.00hrs Last departure noon
A well run park, with keen family owners, in a lovely location overlooking Loch Ryan. Opposite ferry terminal for Northern Ireland (Larne), 4m from Stranraer. A 7.5-acre site with 15 touring pitches and 83 statics.
Snooker & pool tables.
Leisure: ⥃ ♦ /ᐱ Facilities: ╠ ⊙ ♊ ✳ ℓ
Services: 🔌 🔟 ♈ 🛢 ⊞ 🕂
→ Ụ ► ✒ 🏋

CASTLE DOUGLAS Map 11 NX76

► ► ► Lochside Caravan & Camping Site (NX766618)
Lochside Park DG7 1EZ ☎ 01556 502949 & 503806
Dir: Off A75 to Castle Douglas by Carlingwark Loch
★ 🚐 £7.95-£9.30 🚐 £7.95-£9.30 Å £7.95-£9.30
Open Etr-mid Oct Last departure noon
Municipal touring site incorporating park with recreational facilities, on southern edge of town in attractive setting adjacent to Carlingwark Loch. A 5.5-acre site with 161 touring pitches.
Putting, rowing boats (wknds & high season)
Leisure: ⥃ /ᐱ Facilities: ╠ ⊙ ✳ ⚿ ℓ 🏋 🎋
Services: 🔌 🔟
→ ► ✚ ✒

CREETOWN Map 11 NX45

► ► ► ► ► *Castle Cary Holiday Park (NX475576)*
DG8 7DQ ☎ 01671 820264
Dir: Signed with direct access off A75, 0.5m S of village
🚐 🚐 Å
Open all year (rs Oct-Mar reception/shop, no heated outdoor pool) Booking advisable Bank hols & Jul-Aug Last arrival anytime Last departure noon
This attractive site in the grounds of Cassencarie House is sheltered by woodlands, and faces south towards Wigtown Bay. The park is in a secluded location with beautiful landscaping and excellent facilities. The bar/restaurant is housed in part of an old castle, and enjoys extensive views over the River Cree estuary. A 6-acre site with 50 touring pitches and 26 statics.
Mountain bike hire, crazy golf & snooker.
See advertisement under Preliminary Section
Leisure: ⥃ ⥃ ♦ /ᐱ ⎕ Facilities: ➡ ╠ ⊙ ♊ ⚿ ℓ
🏋 🏓 🎋 ⸙ Services: 🔌 🔟 ♈ 🛢 ⊘ ⊞ 🕂 ✕ 🧹 ⛽
→ ► ◎ ✒

► ► ► *Creetown Caravan Park (NX474586)*
Silver St DG8 7HU ☎ 01671 820377
Dir: Off A75 into village of Creetown, turn between clock tower & hotel, then turn left along Silver Street
🚐 🚐 Å

Open Mar-Oct Booking advisable Jul & Aug Last arrival 22.30hrs Last departure 14.00hrs
Neat and well-maintained park set in village centre with views across the estuary. In an attractive setting beside the Minipool Burn on the River Cree. A 2-acre site with 15 touring pitches and 50 statics.
Leisure: ⥃ ♦ /ᐱ Facilities: ╠ ⊙ ♊ ℓ
Services: 🔌 🔟 🛢 ⊞
→ ✒ 🏋

CROCKETFORD   Map 11 NX87

▶ ▶ ▶ ▶ *Park of Brandedleys (NX830725)*

DG2 8RG ☎ 01556 690250

Dir: Situated in the village on A75, on left in Dumfries to Stranraer direction

🚐 🚉 Å

Open all year (rs Early or Late season Shop, bar, Restaurant hours may be restricted) Booking advisable public hols & Jul-Aug Last arrival 22.00hrs Last departure noon

A well-maintained site in an elevated position off the A75, with fine views of Auchenreoch Loch and beyond. This comfortable park offers a wide range of amenities, and is well placed for enjoying walking, fishing, sailing and golf, or exploring the fine scenery or local historic castles. A 9-acre site with 80 touring pitches and 27 statics.

Putting, badminton court & outdoor draughts.

Leisure: 🎾 🎣 🚣 ♨ 🎱 **Facilities:** 🚾 🚻 ⊙ 🍴 🔆 👶 📞

🛒 🍖 🍱 🐾 **Services:** 🔌 🔃 🍽 🥛 🛢 🗓 🚻 ✗ 🛒 🗑

🗑 ⊙ 🚿 🍺 🔁 📶 🎲

See advert on page 231

DALBEATTIE   Map 11 NX86

▶ ▶ ▶ *Glenearly Caravan Park (NX838628)*

Park Farm DG5 4NE ☎ 01556 611393

Dir: From Dumfries take A711 towards Dalbeattie. Park entrance is past Edingham Farm on the right, 200yds before boundary sign

🚐 🚉 Å

Open all year Booking advisable

An excellent small park set in open countryside with panoramic views of Long Fell, Maidenpap and Dalbeattie Forest. The park is located in 84 beautiful acres of farmland which visitors are invited to enjoy. A 3-acre site with 50 statics.

Leisure: 🎣 ♨ **Facilities:** 🚻 ⊙ 🍴 🔆 👶 📞 🐾

Services: 🔌 🔃 🍽 🗓

🗑 🅿️ ⊙ 🍺 🔁 🎲 🛒

▶ ▶ **Islecroft Caravan & Camping Site (NX837615)**

Colliston Park, Mill St DG5 4HE

☎ 01556 610012 & 503806

Dir: From A710 in town centre. Access via Mill St. Adjacent to Colliston Park

★ 🚐 £6.15-£7.30 🚉 £6.15-£7.30 Å £6.15-£7.30

Open Etr-Sep Last departure noon

A neat site in two sections tucked away to the rear of town. The park overlooks the well-landscaped town park, where there is a variety of activities, and a river running through. A 3.5-acre site with 74 touring pitches.

Leisure: ♨ **Facilities:** 🚻 ⊙ 📞 🛒 🍱 **Services:** 🔌

🗑 🅿️ ✗ 🎲

ECCLEFECHAN   Map 11 NY17

PREMIER PARK

▶ ▶ ▶ ▶ ▶ **Hoddom Castle Caravan Park (NY154729)**

Hoddom DG11 1AS ☎ 01576 300251

Dir: From M74 junct 19, follow signposts to site

★ 🚐 £6-£11.50 🚉 £6-£11.50 Å £5-£8.50

Open Etr or Apr-Oct (rs early season cafeteria closed) Booking advisable bank hols & Jul-Aug Last arrival 21.00hrs Last departure 14.00hrs

The peaceful, well-equipped park on the banks of the River Annan, that offers a good mix of grassy and hard pitches. Careful landscaping has resulted in pitches blending with the beauty of the surrounding countryside, and there are signed nature trails which are maintained by the park's countryside ranger. There is also a 9-hole golf course, and trout and salmon fishing, and plenty of activity ideas for children. A 12-acre site with 170 touring pitches and 29 statics.

Nature trails, visitor centre & 9-hole golf course.

See advertisement under LOCKERBIE

Leisure: 🎣 ♣ ♨ **Facilities:** 🚻 ⊙ 🍴 🔆 👶 📞 🛒 🍖 🍱 🐾

Services: 🔌 🔃 🍽 🥛 🛢 🗓 🚻 ✗ 🛒 🗑

🗑 🅿️ ⊙ 🍺 🔁 📶 🎲

▶ ▶ ▶ ▶ **Cressfield Caravan Park (NY196744)**

Park House DG11 3DR ☎ 01576 300702

Dir: Leave A74(M) at junct 19 and follow B7076 for 0.5m to S side of village. 8m N of Gretna Green, 5m S of Lockerbie

★ 🚐 £6.50-£8.50 🚉 £6.50-£8.50 Å £6.50-£7

Open all year Booking advisable bank hols Last arrival 23.00hrs Last departure 13.00hrs

An open, spacious park with views to the hills, ideal as a stopover or for touring the area. The park is set in beautiful undulating countryside on the edge of the village, and facilities are always immaculately maintained by the friendly owner. There are level hardstandings, and a separate grass area for tents, while a large sports field caters for many activities. A 12-acre site with 65 touring pitches and 48 statics.

Sports enclosure, putting green, boule

Leisure: ♨ **Facilities:** 🚾 🚻 ⊙ 🍴 🔆 👶 📞 🐾

Services: 🔌 🔃 🍽

🗑 🅿️ ⊙ 🎲

GATEHOUSE OF FLEET   Map 11 NX55

Auchenlarie Holiday Park (NX536522)

DG7 2EX ☎ 01557 840251

Dir: Direct access off A75, 5m W of Gatehouse of Fleet

🚐 🚉 Å

Open Mar-Oct Booking advisable all year Last arrival midnight Last departure noon

A well-organised family park with good facilities, set on cliffs overlooking Wigtown Bay towards the Isle of Whithorn, and with its own sandy beach. A 5-acre site with 35 touring pitches and 202 statics.

Leisure: ♦ ⚅ Facilities: 🐾 ⊙ 🍴 ✳ ⚗ & 🏪 🍴 ⊞ 🐕 🌳
Services: 🔌 📖 ⚗ 🛢 🚿 🚻 ✕ 📇 ⚓
→ 🛒 ⊙ 🍴 ⚙ ✦ 💳 ▬ ▬ 💳 🅾 📶 🖻

▶ ▶ ▶ **Anwoth Caravan Site (NX595563)**
DG7 2JU ☎ 01557 814333 & 840251
Dir: Leave A75 into Gatehouse of Fleet, park on right towards Stranraer. Signposted from town centre
🚐 £5-£10.50 🚐 £5-£10.50
Open Mar-Oct Booking advisable Jul-Aug Last arrival 22.00hrs Last departure noon
A peaceful sheltered park within easy walking distance of the town, ideally placed for exploring the hills, valleys and coastline. A 2-acre site with 28 touring pitches and 38 statics.
Facilities: ➡ 🐾 ⊙ 🍴 ✳ & Services: 🔌 📖 🛢
→ 🛒 ⚙ 🛢 💳 ▬ 💳 📶 🖻

▶ ▶ ▶ *Mossyard Caravan & Camping Park (NX546518)*
Mossyard DG7 2ET ☎ 01557 840226
Dir: Located 0.75m off A75 on private tarmaced farm road, 4.5m W of Gatehouse of Fleet
🚐 🚐 ▲
Open Etr/Apr-Oct Booking advisable
A grassy park with its own beach, located on a working farm, and offering an air of peace and tranquillity. Stunning sea and coastal views from touring pitches, and the tenting field is almost on the beach. A 6.5-acre site with 35 touring pitches and 15 statics.
Facilities: 🐾 ⊙ 🍴 🥤 Services: 🔌 📖 🛢 🚿 ⊞
→ ⚙ 🛢

▶ ▶ ▶ *Sandgreen Caravan Park (NX578523)*
DG7 2DU ☎ 01557 814351
Dir: Site signed off A75 at Gatehouse of Fleet & situated at end of 3m unclass cul-de-sac to beach
Open Apr-Oct Booking advisable
A peaceful natural park in secluded unspoilt countryside close to beach, overlooking the picturesque Fleet Bay, and fenced off from other areas. 20 touring pitches and 180 statics.
Facilities: 🐾 🥤 🛢 Services: 🔌 🛢 🚿 ⊞ 🄣
→ 🛒 ⚓ ⚙

▶ ▶ ▶ **Glenluce Caravan & Camping Park (NX201576)**
DG8 0QR ☎ 01581 300412
Dir: Off A75 in centre of Glenluce, opposite Inglenook Bistro
★ 🚐 £7.70-£9.20 🚐 £7.70-£9.20 ▲ £5.50-£8.20
Open Mar-Oct Booking advisable Jul-Aug Last arrival 22.00hrs Last departure noon
A neat, well-maintained site situated beside a small river close to the village centre. The large camping area is secluded within a walled garden, and a heated swimming pool is the latest attraction at this personally-run park. A 5-acre site with 30 touring pitches and 30 statics.
Leisure: 🥤 ⚅ Facilities: 🐾 ⊙ 🍴 ✳ & 🥤 🏪 ⊞ 🐕
Services: 🔌 📖 🛢 🚿 ⊞
→ ⚓ 🛒 ⚙

▶ ▶ ▶ **Whitecairn Farm Caravan Park (NX300434)**
DG8 0NZ ☎ 01581 300267
Dir: Leave A75 in the centre of Glenluce village, & park is signed on unclassified road to Glassnock Bridge. 1.5m N of Glenluce village
🚐 £7-£9 🚐 £7-£9 ▲ £7-£9
Open Mar-Oct Booking advisable Last arrival 22.00hrs Last departure 11.00hrs
A well-maintained farmland site, in open countryside with extensive views of Luce Bay. The park is next to the owner's working farm along a quiet country road. A 3-acre site with 10 touring pitches and 40 statics.
Leisure: ⚅ Facilities: 🐾 ⊙ 🍴 ✳ 🥤 🏪 ⊞ 🐕
Services: 🔌 🛢 🚿
→ ⚓ 🛒

▶ ▶ ▶ **Caldons Caravan & Camping Site (NX400790)**
DG8 6SU
☎ 01671 840218 (in season) & 0131 314 6505
Dir: Take A714 Newton Stewart to Girvan Road. Turn right at Bargrennan, passing Glen Trool & follow signs
★ 🚐 £6-£7.60 🚐 £6-£7.60 ▲ £6-£7.60
Open Etr-Sep Booking advisable bank hol & Jul-Aug Last arrival 22.00hrs Last departure noon
Secluded Forestry Commission site amidst fine hill, loch and woodland scenery in Galloway Forest Park. Pitches are level despite the undulating countryside, and there are plenty of waymarked trails, forest walks and cycle routes. A 25-acre site with 160 touring pitches.
Leisure: ♦ ⚅ Facilities: 🐾 ⊙ ✳ & 🥤 🏪 🏪 ⊞
Services: 🔌 🛢 🚿
→ ⚙ 💳 ▬ 💳 📶 🖻

▶ ▶ ▶ **Glen Trool Holiday Park (NX400790)**
DG8 6RN ☎ 01671 840280
Dir: Leave Newton Stewart on A417, right at Bargrennan towards Glen Trool. Park on left before village.
⚏ £8-£9 ⚏ £8-£9 ▲ £7-£9
Open Mar-Oct Booking advisable Jul-Aug Last arrival 21.00hrs Last departure noon
A small family-owned park close to the village of Glen Trool and bordered by the Galloway National Park. An ideal base for walking and cycling. A 4-acre site with 18 touring pitches and 26 statics.
Trout pond for fly fishing
Leisure: ♦ ⚌ Facilities: ⋒⊙🏐⋇👍📞🛒
Services: 🖪💧⌀⊞
→ ⋃ 🍴 🍽 🔲 🎬 🐟

GRETNA   Map 11 NY36

▶ ▶ ▶ *The Old Toll Bar Caravan Park (NY325670)*
Sark Bridge Rd DG16 5JD ☎ 01461 337439
Open all year Booking advisable Last arrival 23.00hrs
A grassy park on the edge of the River Sark, and situated exactly on the England/Scotland border by the Sark Bridge. This is the first house in Scotland, and the park has its own licensed marriage room. Facilities are to a good standard, and the park is neat and well-trimmed. A 2.5-acre site with 40 touring pitches and 1 static.
Facilities: ⋒👍🛒🐕 Services: 🖪💧⌀✕🚿
→ ⋃ ▶ 🍴 🍽 🔲 🎬

▶ ▶ ▶ **Braids Caravan Park (NY313674)**
Annan Rd DG16 5DQ ☎ 01461 337409
Dir: Situated on B721. 0.5m from village on right, towards Annan
★ ⚏ £7.90 ⚏ £7.90 ▲ £5-£7

Open all year Booking advisable Jul-Sep Last arrival 24.00hrs Last departure noon
A well-maintained grassy site in centre of the village just inside Scotland. A good number of hard pitches further enhance this busy and popular park. A 6-acre site with 70 touring pitches and 5 statics.
Leisure: ⚌ Facilities: ⋒⊙🏐⋇👍📞🛒🐕
Services: 🖪💧⌀⊞Ⓣ
→ ▶ 🍴

IRONGRAY   Map 11 NX97

▶ ▶ *Barnsoul Farm (NX876778)*
DG2 9SQ ☎ 01387 730249
Dir: Leave A75 between Dumfries & Crocketford at site sign onto unclass road signed Shawhead at T-junct Turn right & immediate left. Site 1m on left
⚏ ⚏ ▲

Open Apr-Oct (rs Mar) Booking advisable Jul & Aug Last arrival anytime Last departure anytime
A scenic farm site set in 250 acres of woodland, parkland and ponds. A 4-acre site with 30 touring pitches and 6 statics.
Emergency food, milk, tinned meat, fish, fruit
Facilities: ⋒⊙🏐⋇👍🚿📷🐕 Services: 🖪⊠⊞
→ ⋃ 🍴 🛒

ISLE OF WHITHORN   Map 11 NX43

▶ ▶ ▶ *Burrowhead Holiday Village (NX450345)*
DG8 8JB ☎ 01988 500252
Dir: Leave A75 at Newton Stewart on A714, take A746 to Whithorn, then road to Isle of Whithorn. Turn right in village onto single track road
⚏ ⚏ ▲
Open Mar-Oct Booking advisable high season
An extensive holiday park in 100 acres of undulating ground overlooking the waters of Solway Firth and the Isle of Man. The park is geared around the swimming pool and bar complex. A 100-acre site with 100 touring pitches and 400 statics.
Sauna, jacuzzi, swimjet, spa, splash pool.
Leisure: ⌇ ⚌ Facilities: ⋒⊙🏐⋇👍📷🐕
Services: 🖪⊠💦💧⌀✕🚿
→ ◎ 🍴 🛒 🍽 🎫 🔲 🎬

KIPPFORD   Map 11 NX85

▶ ▶ ▶ **Kippford Holiday Park (NX844564)**
DG5 4LF ☎ 01556 620636
Dir: Direct access off A710
⚏ £9-£11 ⚏ £9-£11 ▲ £7-£11
Open all year (rs Nov-Feb Booking required, no shop) Booking advisable Last departure noon
Part-level, part-sloping grass site surrounded by trees and bushes, set in hilly country adjacent to Urr Water estuary and stony beach. Kippford is a sailing haven with the tidal estuary running into the Solway Firth. An 18-acre site with 45 touring pitches and 119 statics.
Children's adventure playground.
Leisure: ⚌ Facilities: ⋒⊙🏐⋇👍🛒📷🐕
Services: 🖪⊠💧⊞
→ ⋃ ▶ 🔺 🍴

KIRKCUDBRIGHT   Map 11 NX65

▶ ▶ ▶ ▶ **Seaward Caravan Park (NX662494)**
Dhoon Bay DG6 4TJ ☎ 01557 870267 & 331079
Dir: 2m SW off B727 Borgue Road
🚐 fr £8.65 🚐 fr £8.65 ▲ fr £8.65

Open Mar-Oct (rs Mar-mid May & mid Sep-Oct
swimming pool closed) Booking advisable Spring
bank hols & Jul-Aug Last arrival 21.30hrs Last
departure 11.30hrs
*This very attractive elevated site has outstanding
views over Kirkcudbright Bay which forms part of
the Dee estuary. Access to a sandy cove with rock
pools is just across the road. Facilities are well
organised and neatly kept, and the park offers a
peaceful location. The leisure facilities of the other
Gillespie leisure parks are available to guests. An 8-
acre site with 26 touring pitches and 30 statics.*
TV aerial hook-up, mini golf.
Leisure: ⚓ ◆ ⚲ ▢ **Facilities:** ➡ ↿ ☉ ⚲ ☀ & ⌧ ☕ ⊞ ☂
Services: ⚡ ▣ ⎚ ⌀ ⌀ ⊞
→ ∪ ▶ ⏣ ⏎

▶ ▶ ▶ **Silvercraigs Caravan & Camping Site
(NX686508)**
Silvercraigs Rd DG6 4BT
☎ 01557 330123 & 01556 503806
*Dir: Located in Kirkcudbright off Silvercraigs Rd,
overlooking the town. Access via A711, follow signs to
campsite*
★ 🚐 £7.95-£9.55 🚐 £7.95-£9.55 ▲ £7.95-£9.55
Open Etr-mid Oct Last departure noon
*A well-maintained municipal park in an elevated
position with extensive views overlooking the
picturesque, unspoilt town and harbour to the
countryside beyond. Toilet facilities are of a very
good standard, and the town centre is just a short
stroll away. A 6-acre site with 50 touring pitches.*
Leisure: ⚲ **Facilities:** ↿ ☉ ☀ & ☕ ☂ ⌧
Services: ⚡ ▣
→ ∪ ▶ ⏣ ⏎

KIRKGUNZEON   Map 11 NX86

▶ ▶ ▶ *Mossband Caravan Park (NX872665)*
DG2 8JP ☎ 01387 760208
*Dir: Adjacent to A711 to Dalbeattie, 1.5m E of
Kirkgunzeon*
🚐 🚐 ▲
Open Etr-Oct Booking advisable mid Jul-mid Aug
*Level park on site of old railway station, set in a
peaceful rural location. This family-run park has*

good views of the countryside, and comfortable
facilities. A 3-acre site with 25 touring pitches and
12 statics.
Leisure: ⚲ ⚲ **Facilities:** ↿ ☉ **Services:** ⚡ ⌀ ⊞
→ ∪ ▶ ⏎ ☕

LANGHOLM   Map 11 NY38

▶ ▶ ▶ *Ewes Water Caravan & Camping Park
(NY365855)*
Milntown DG13 0DH ☎ 013873 80386 80358
*Dir: Directly off A7 approx 0.5m N of Langholm.
Situated within Langholm Rugby Club*
🚐 🚐 ▲
Open Apr-Sep Last departure noon
*On the banks of the River Esk, this is a very
attractive park in sheltered wooded valley close to
unspoilt Borders town. A 2-acre site with 24 touring
pitches.*
Large Playing Area
Facilities: ↿ ☉ ☀ & ☕ ⌧ ☂ **Services:** ⚡ ⚡ ⌀ ⊞
→ ▶ ⏎ ☕

LOCHMABEN   Map 11 NY08

▶ ▶ ▶ **Halleaths Caravan Site (NY098818)**
DG11 1NA ☎ 01387 810630
*Dir: From M74 take A709 to Dumfries. 3m from
Lockerbie turn right. Signposted to site*
★ 🚐 £8.50 🚐 £8.50 ▲ £7-£8.50

Open Mar-Nov Booking advisable bank hols & Jul-
Aug Last arrival 23.30hrs Last departure noon
*Level, grassy site in a sheltered position with a
wood on one side and a high hedge on the other.
Close to the three lochs around this historic little
town, and the River Annan. An 8-acre site with 71
touring pitches and 17 statics.*
Fishing (charged). Wide range within 1mile
Leisure: ⚲ **Facilities:** ↿ ☉ ☀ ☕ ☂ 🎣 ⌧ ☂
Services: ⚡ ▣ ⌀ ⊞
→ ▶ ⌒ ⏎ ⏎

▶ ▶ **Kirkloch Caravan & Camping Site (NY082825)**
☎ 01556 503806
Dir: Located in Lochmaben – enter via Kirkloch Brae
★ 🚐 £6.45-£7.50 🚐 £6.45-£7.50 ▲ £6.45-£7.50
Open Etr-end Sept Last departure noon
*A grassy lochside site with superb views and well-
maintained facilities. Some hard pitches are
available at this municipal park, which is adjacent to*

contd.

a golf club, and close to three lochs. A 1.5-acre site with 30 touring pitches.

Leisure: ⚠ **Facilities:** ☎ ⊙ ⚑ ⚡ **Services:** ⊖
→ ⚑ ⚓

LOCHNAW   Map 10 NW96

▶ ▶ ▶ ▶ *Drumlochart Caravan Park (NW997634)*
DG9 0RN ☎ 01776 870232
Dir: From Stranraer take A718 to Leswalt, then left onto B7043 & park in on right in 1.5m
🚐 £8.50-£10 🚐 £8.50-£10
Open Mar-Oct Booking advisable bank hols & Jul-Aug Last arrival 22.00hrs Last departure noon
A peaceful rural site in hilly woodland, adjacent to Loch Ryan and Luce Bay, offering coarse fishing. This manicured park with sparkling toilet facilities is a credit to the friendly family owners. There are many woodland walks to be enjoyed in an area of outstanding natural beauty, and a heated swimming pool in a sheltered sunny position is very popular. A 9-acre site with 30 touring pitches and 96 statics.
10-acre Loch for coarse fishing & rowing boats.

Leisure: ⚓ ⚓ ⚠ **Facilities:** ☎ ⊙ ⚑ ⚡ ⚡
Services: ⊖ ⊡ ⚡ ⚑ ⓘ
→ ∪ ▶ ⚑ ⚓ ⚓ ⊞ ⊠ ⚑ ⊡

LOCKERBIE

See **Ecclefechan**

MOFFAT   Map 11 NT00

▶ ▶ ▶ **Camping & Caravanning Club Site**
(NT085050)
Hammerlands Farm DG10 9QL ☎ 01683 220436
Dir: Take Moffat sign from A74. After 1m turn right by the Bank of Scotland, right again in 200yds. Sign for site on right follow rd round to site
★ 🚐 £11.80-£14.90 🚐 £11.80-£14.90 ▲ £11.80-£14.90
Open 20 Mar-1 Nov Booking advisable Spring bank hol & peak periods Last arrival 21.00hrs Last departure noon
Well-maintained level grass touring site, with extensive views of the surrounding hilly countryside from many parts of the park. This busy stopover site is always well maintained, and looks bright and cheerful thanks to meticulous wardens. Please see the advertisement on page 14 for details of Club Members' benefits. A 10-acre site with 180 touring pitches.

Leisure: ⚠ **Facilities:** ☎ ⊙ ⚑ ✳ ⚓ ⚡ ✝
Services: ⊖ ⊡ ⓘ ⊘ ⊞
→ ∪ ▶ ⚑ ⚓ ⊞ ⊠

NEWTON STEWART   Map 10 NX46

▶ ▶ ▶ *Creebridge Caravan Park (NX415656)*
Minnigaff DG8 6AJ ☎ 01671 402324 & 402432
Dir: 0.25m E of Newton Stewart at Minnigaff on the bypass, signed off A75
🚐 🚐 ▲
Open Apr-Oct (rs Mar only one toilet block open) Booking advisable Jul-Aug Last arrival 20.00hrs Last departure noon
A level urban site a short walk from the amenities of town. A 5.5-acre site with 36 touring pitches and 50 statics.
Security street lighting.

Leisure: ⚓ ⚠ **Facilities:** ☎ ⊙ ⚑ ✳ ⚡ ⚡ ⚑
Services: ⊖ ⊡ ⓘ ⊘ ⊞
→ ∪ ▶ ⊚ ⚡ ⚓

PALNACKIE   Map 11 NX85

▶ ▶ ▶ **Barlochan Caravan Park (NX819572)**
DG7 1PF ☎ 01556 600256 & 870267
Dir: On A711 N of Palnackie village, signposted
🚐 fr £7.85 🚐 fr £7.85 ▲ fr £7.85
Open Apr-Oct (rs Apr-mid May & mid Sep-end Oct swimming pool) Booking advisable Spring bank hol & Jul-Aug Last arrival 21.30hrs Last departure 11.30hrs

A small terraced park with quiet landscaped pitches in a level area backed by rhododendron bushes. There are spectacular views over the River Urr estuary, and the park has its own coarse fishing loch nearby. A 9-acre site with 20 touring pitches and 40 statics.
Fishing, pitch & putt.
Leisure: ≒ ◀ ⚅ ▢ Facilities: ⋒ ☉ ⦶ ✳ ⟱ ⟍ ⚞ ⟱ ⌷ ⋔
Services: ⊞ ☶ ⦙ ⌀ ⊞ ⛢
→ ▶ ↲

PARTON Map 11 NX67

▶ ▶ ▶ **Loch Ken Holiday Park (NX687702)**
DG7 3NE ☎ 01644 470282
Dir: Located on A713, N of Parton village
★ ⊞ £8-£10 ⊞ £8-£10 ▲ £7-£9
Open mid Mar-mid Nov (rs Mar/Apr (ex Etr) & late Sep-Nov restricted shop hours) Booking advisable Etr, Spring bank hol & Jun-Aug Last arrival 20.00hrs Last departure noon

A busy and popular park with a natural water-borne emphasis, on the eastern shores of Loch Ken, with superb views. Family owned and run, it is in a peaceful and beautiful spot opposite the RSPB reserve, with direct access to the loch for boat launching. The park offers a variety of water sports, as well as farm visits and nature trails. A 7-acre site with 52 touring pitches and 33 statics.
Bike, boat & canoe hire, fishing on loch.
Leisure: ⚅ Facilities: ⋒ ☉ ⦶ ✳ ⟱ ⟍ ⚞ ⌲ ⌷ ⋔
Services: ⊞ ☶ ⦙ ⌀ ⊞ ⊡
→ ⛝ ↯ ↲

PENPONT Map 11 NX89

▶ ▶ ▶ **Penpont Caravan and Camping Park (NX852947)**
DG3 4BH ☎ 01848 330470
Dir: From Thornhill on the A702, site on left 0.5m before Penpont village
★ ⊞ £7.80 ⊞ £6.50-£7.80 ▲ £6.50-£7.80
Open Etr or Apr-Oct Booking advisable Jul-Aug Last arrival 22.00hrs Last departure 14.00hrs
Peaceful, grassy, slightly sloping site in a rural area, excellently situated for touring. A 1.5-acre site with 20 touring pitches and 20 statics.
Facilities: ⋒ ☉ ✳ ⟱ ⋔ Services: ⊞ ☶ ⦙ ⌀ ⊞
→ ▶ ↲

PORTPATRICK Map 10 NW95

▶ ▶ ▶ **Galloway Point Holiday Park (NX005537)**
Portree Farm DG9 9AA ☎ 01776 810561
Dir: Take A75 W from Dumfries or A77 S from Glasgow. 1st left after 30mph sign on entering Portpatrick. Park is 0.5m on right opposite The Barn Inn
⊞ £10-£12 ⊞ £9-£12 ▲ £4-£10
Open Etr-Oct (rs Apr & Oct) Booking advisable Mar, & May-Oct Last arrival 23.00hrs Last dep 14.00hrs
Strung out along gorse-clad downland, the holiday park looks out on the North Channel 1m south of town. An 18-acre site with 100 touring pitches and 60 statics.
Leisure: ⚅ Facilities: ⋒ ☉ ✳ ⟱ ⚞ ⌷ ⋔
Services: ⊞ ☶ ⟁ ⦙ ⌀ ⊞ ⊡ ✗ ⛢
→ ∪ ▶ ☺ ↯ ↲

▶ ▶ ▶ *Sunnymeade Caravan Park (NX005540)*
DG9 8LN ☎ 01776 810293
Dir: Approach on A77, then 1st unclass road on left after entering village. 1st caravan park on the left at the top of the hill
⊞ ⊞ ▲
Open mid Mar-Oct Booking advisable
Extensive views of the Irish Sea and coast can be enjoyed from this mainly grassy, family-run park. The picturesque village of Portpatrick with its small beach and busy harbour is just one mile away. An 8-acre site with 15 touring pitches and 75 statics. Private coarse fishing pond on site.
Facilities: ⋒ ☉ ✳ ⟱ Services: ⊞ ☶ ⦙ ⊞
→ ∪ ▶ ☺ ↯ ⚞

PORT WILLIAM Map 10 NX34

▶ ▶ ▶ *Kings Green Caravan Site (NX340430)*
South St DG8 9SG ☎ 01988 700536
Dir: Direct access from A747 at junct with B7085, towards Whithorn
⊞ ⊞
Open Etr-Oct
This newly developed level grassy park is near the sea shore of Luce Bay and is community owned and run. Adjacent to the unspoilt village with all its amenities and attractive harbour. Approached through The Marchars and coast road, this park has views as far as the Isle of Man. A 3-acre site with 30 touring pitches.
Facilities: ⋒ ☉ ⟱ ⟍ ⚞ Services: ⊞

POWFOOT Map 11 NY16

▶ ▶ ▶ *Queensberry Bay Caravan Park (NY135653)*
DG12 5PU ☎ 01461 700205
Dir: Follow signs to Powfoot off B724 & drive through village past golf club on single track road on shore edge to site in 0.75m
⊞ ⊞ ▲
Open Etr-Oct Booking advisable Jul-Aug Last arrival 20.00hrs Last departure noon
A flat, mainly grassy site in a quiet location on the shores of the Solway Firth with views across the estuary to Cumbrian hills. A 5-acre site with 100 touring pitches and 60 statics.
Facilities: ⋒ ☉ ⟱ ⚞ Services: ⊞ ☶ ⦙ ⌀ ⊞
→ ▶ ⚞ ↲

ROCKCLIFFE Map 11 NX85

► ► ► **Castle Point Caravan Park (NX851539)**
DG5 4QL ☎ 01556 630248
Dir: From Dalbeattie take A710. After approx 5m take signposted road to Rockcliffe. On entering village the site is signposted
★ ♨ £8-£10.50 ♨ £8-£10.50 ▲ £8-£10.50

Open Etr-Mid Oct (rs Mar-Etr & Late Oct limited supervision) Booking advisable Whit wk & Jul-Aug Last arrival 23.00hrs Last departure 11.00hrs
Set in an Area of Outstanding Natural Beauty, this level grass park is adjacent to a rocky shore, and has stunning views across the estuary and the surrounding hilly countryside. The park is noted for its flora and fauna, and has direct access to coastal walks and the attractive sandy beach. A 3-acre site with 22 touring pitches and 33 statics.
Facilities: ╚⊙╗☀⅊⊁ **Services:** ♨回⬧⊘⊞
→ ∪ ▶⊙⥂⅃⅋

SANDHEAD Map 10 NX04

► ► ► ► **Sands of Luce Caravan Park (NX103510)**
Sands of Luce D69 9JR ☎ 01776 830456
Dir: Turn left off A75 onto B7084 2m from Glenluce, signed Sandhead & Drummore. Site signed on left in 5m, after junct of A716 Stranraer rd
♨ £7.50-£9.50 ♨ £7-£9 ▲ £7.50-£9.50
Open Mar-Oct Booking advisable Jul-Aug Last arrival 22.00hrs Last departure noon
A friendly site on the grassy banks on the edge of a beautiful sandy beach, with lovely views across Luce Bay. Facilities are well-maintained and clean, and the area around the park is protected by the Nature Conservancy Council. A 12-acre site with 50 touring pitches and 40 statics.
Boat launching.
Leisure: ⅋ ╱╲ **Facilities:** ╚⊙╗☀⅊⅊ **Services:** ♨回⬧⊘⊞
→ ⅃

SANDYHILLS Map 11 NX85

► ► ► **Sandyhills Bay Leisure Park (NX892552)**
DG5 4NY ☎ 01557 870267 & 01387 780257
Dir: Located on A710 coast road, 7m from Dalbeattie, 6.5m from Kirkbean
♨ fr £7.85 ♨ fr £7.85 ▲ fr £7.85
Open Apr-Oct Booking advisable Spring bank hol & Jun-Aug Last arrival 21.30hrs Last departure 11.30hrs

A well-maintained park in a superb location beside a 'blue-flag' beach, and close to many attractive villages. The flat, grassy site offers access to south-facing Sandyhills Bay and beach, and is sheltered by woods and hills. A 6-acre site with 26 touring pitches and 34 statics.
Leisure: ╱╲ **Facilities:** ╚⊙╗☀⅊⅋⅊⊁
Services: ♨回⬧⊘⊞⊤⬧
→ ∪ ▶⅃

SANQUHAR Map 11 NS70

► ► ► **Castleview Caravan & Camping Park (NS787095)**
Townfoot DG4 6AX ☎ 01659 50291 & 50125
Dir: Located with direct access off A76 at S end of town
♨ ♨ ▲
Open Etr-Oct
A very good little park on edge of olde worlde village, with lovely views and close to Southern Upland Way coast to coast walk. A 2-acre site with 15 touring pitches.
Facilities: ╚⊙⅊ **Services:** ♨回⬧⊘⊞
→ ∪ ▶⅃ ⬤▮▭Ⓓ▤▥

SOUTHERNESS Map 11 NX95

 Southerness Holiday Village (NX976545)
DG2 8AZ ☎ 01387 880256 & 880281
Dir: From S take A75 from Gretna to Dumfries. From N take A74, exit at A701 to Dumfries. Take A710 coast road. Southerness approx 16m. Site easily seen
★ ♨ £8-£10 ♨ £8-£10 ▲ £8-£10
Open Mar-Oct Booking advisable Jul & Aug & bank holidays Last departure 16.00hrs
A continually improving holiday centre with the emphahsis on family entertainment. Recent upgrading has resulted in new all-weather pitches, with good shop, large laundry and better than ever leisure areas. Standards of maintainance and cleanliness remain high, and a sandy beach on the Solway Firth, near Southerness Point, is close by. An 8-acre site with 200 touring pitches and 350 statics. Amusement centre, disco, videos.
Leisure: ⅊ ⅋ ╱╲ **Facilities:** ╚⊙☀⅊⅊▥⊁
Services: ♨回⅊⬧⊘⊞⊤✕⬧
→ ▶⅃ ⬤▭Ⓓ▤▥

STRANRAER   Map 10 NX06

▶ ▶ ▶ ▶ **Aird Donald Caravan Park (NX075605)**
London Rd DG9 8RN ☎ 01776 702025
Dir: Turn left off A75 on entering Stranraer Town,
(signed). Opposite school, site 300yds
★ ⊞ £8-£8.50 ⊞ £8-£8.50 ▲ £3.90-£7.90
Open all year Booking advisable Last departure
16.00hrs
A spacious touring site, mainly grass but with
tarmac hard-standing area, with pitches large
enough to accommodate a car and caravan
overnight without unhitching. On the fringe of town
screened by mature shrubs and trees. Ideal
stopover en route to N.I. ferry ports. A 12-acre site
with 100 touring pitches.
Leisure: 🛝 Facilities: 🅿⊙🔞✿🔥🐃
Services: 🖪🅰⊘🎚 ➝∪▶🍴🚺🍴🖪

WHITHORN   Map 10 NX44

▶ ▶ **Castlewigg Caravan & Camping Park**
(NX432431)
DG8 8DP ☎ 01988 500616
Dir: From A714 at Wigtown take A746 through
Sorbie & park is on the right in approx 3m
★ ⊞ £8-£10 ⊞ £8-£10 ▲ £6-£8
Open all year Booking advisable
A small park set in a sheltered wall garden,
surrounded by beautiful countryside. The owners
are currently improving the toilet facilities, and the
grounds are well maintained. A 5-acre site with 20
touring pitches and 22 statics.
Leisure: 🛝 Facilities: 🅿⊙🔥🐃 Services: 🖪♀🅰⊘✗
➝∪🍴🖪

For Dunbartonshire see West Dunbartonshire.
For Edinburgh see City of Edinburgh.

EAST AYRSHIRE

KILMARNOCK   Map 10 NS43

▶ ▶ **Cunningham Head Estate Caravan Park**
(NS370418)
Cunningham Head, Irvine KA3 2PE
☎ 01294 850238
Dir: Located 3.5m NE of Irvine on B769. From Irvine take
A736 Glasgow road. At Stanecastle rdbt turn E onto
B769 Stewarton road. Park is 3m on the left
★ ⊞ £7.50-£8.50 ⊞ £7.50-£8.50 ▲ £7.50-£8.50

Open Apr-Sep Booking advisable Jul-Aug Last
arrival 22.00hrs Last departure noon
A rural site in the grounds of a farmland estate. A 7-
acre site with 50 touring pitches and 50 statics.
Leisure: 🛝 Facilities: 🅿⊙🔞 Services: 🖪🅰⊘🎚
➝🚺🍴🖪

EAST LOTHIAN

DUNBAR   Map 12 NT67

PREMIER PARK

▶ ▶ ▶ ▶ ▶ **Thurston Manor Holiday Home**
Park (NT712745)
Innerwick EH42 1SA ☎ 01368 840643 & 840688
Dir: 4m S of Dunbar, signposted off A1
★ ⊞ £10-£12 ⊞ £10-£12 ▲ £7-£12
Open Mar-Nov (rs 1-23 Dec Weekends only)
Booking advisable Etr, bank hols & high season
Last arrival 9.00hrs Last departure noon
A pleasant park set in 250 acres of unspoilt
countryside just a few minutes drive from the
many quiet bays on the coast. The touring and
static areas of this large park are in separate
areas which are spacious and well laid out, and
complemented by landscaping and mature
trees. The main touring area occupies an open,
level position, and the toilet facilities are modern
and exceptionally well maintained. The park
boasts a heated indoor swimming pool, steam
room, sauna, jacuzzi, mini-gym and fitness room
with qualified assistants. In high season there is
regular entertainment. The park has 100 acres of
private woodlands and a well-stocked fishing
loch. A 250-acre site with 100 touring pitches
and 400 statics.
Private lake, pony trekking, fitness room,
sauna/steam
Leisure: 🔥🏊🛝🖵 Facilities: 🅿⊙🔞✿🔥
🐃♨🐃 Services: 🖪🖪♀🅰⊘🎚🗓✗🧺➡
➝∪▶⊙♨🍴 🍴🚂🚂🖪

▶ ▶ ▶ **Camping & Caravanning Club Site**
(NT723773)
Barns Ness EH42 1QP ☎ 01368 863536
Dir: On A1, 6m S of Dunbar (near power station). Sign
for Barns Ness & Skateraw 1m down rd. Turn right at
camp site sign towards the lighthouse
★ ⊞ £9.80-£12.40 ⊞ £9.80-£12.40 ▲ £9.80-£12.40
contd.

Services: 🎚 Toilet Fluid ✗ Café/ Restaurant 🍴 Fast Food/Takeaway ➡ Baby Care 🖪 Electric Hook Up
🖪 Launderette ♀ Licensed Bar 🅰 Calor Gaz ⊘ Camping Gaz 🎚 Battery Charging

Open 20 Mar-1 Nov Booking advisable bank hols & high season Last arrival 21.00hrs Last departure noon
A grassy, landscaped site close to the foreshore and lighthouse on a coastline noted for its natural and geological history. Please see the advertisement on page 14 for details of Club Members' benefits. A 10-acre site with 80 touring pitches.
Bike hire

Leisure: ⚠ **Facilities:** ⬧⊙🔍☀🔌🐕
Services: 🔌🅱🛈⌀🖃Ⓣ
→ ∪ ⫠ ⤬ ↵ 🛒 🍴 🚐

LONGNIDDRY   Map 12 NT47

Seton Sands Holiday Village (NT420759)
EH32 0QF
☎ 01875 813333 & 0345 508508
Dir: Take A1 to Tranent slip road, then B6371 to Cockenzie & right onto B1348. Park 1m on left
★ 🚐 £12-£21 🚐 £12-£21
Open Mar-Oct Booking advisable Last arrival 23.00hrs Last departure noon
A large, mainly static park, with reasonable touring facilities on a grassy paddock near the road. A 1.75-acre site with 60 touring pitches and 120 statics.

Leisure: 🎣 🎣 ⚠ **Facilities:** ⬧⊙🔍🔌🛒🍴🌲🐕
Services: 🔌🅱🛈Ⓟ⌀🖃Ⓣ✕🛗
→ ∪ ⫠ ⊙ 🍴 ↵ 🛒 🚐 🚐 🚐

MUSSELBURGH   Map 11 NT37

▶ ▶ ▶ ▶ **Drum Mohr Caravan Park (NT373734)**
Levenhall EH21 8JS ☎ 0131 665 6867
Dir: Leave A1 at junct with A199 heading towards Musselburgh, at rdbt turn right onto unclass road signed Prestonpans, take 1st left & site in 400yds
🚐 £8-£10 🚐 £8-£10 Å £8-£10
Open Mar-Oct Booking advisable Jul-Aug Last arrival 22.00hrs Last departure noon
This attractive park is sheltered by mature trees on all sides, and carefully landscaped within. The park is divided into separate areas by mature hedging and planting of trees and ornamental shrubs. Pitches are generous in size, and there are a number of full-serviced pitches with water, waste, electricity and hardstanding. The first-class amenities are immaculately clean and maintained to a very high standard. From the north of the park there are views across the Firth of Forth to Fife. A 9-acre site with 120 touring pitches.
See advertisement under EDINBURGH

Leisure: ⚠ **Facilities:** ⬧⊙🔍☀🔌🛒
Services: 🔌🅱🛈⌀🖃Ⓣ
→ ⫠ 🍴 🛒 🚐 🚐 🚐

NORTH BERWICK   Map 12 NT58

▶ ▶ ▶ **Tantallon Caravan Park (NT570850)**
Dunbar Rd EH39 5NJ ☎ 01620 893348
Dir: Located off A198 Dunbar road
🚐 Å
Open Mar-Oct Booking advisable Jul-Aug Last arrival 20.00hrs Last departure noon

Level grass site in meadowland in urban area with direct access to sea and beach. A 10-acre site with 147 touring pitches and 60 statics.

Leisure: 🎣 ⚠ ⌗ **Facilities:** ⬧⊙🔍☀🔌🛒🐕
Services: 🔌🅱🛈⌀🖃
→ ∪ ⫠ ⊙ 🍴 💳 💳 💳 🚐 🚐

FIFE

ELIE   Map 12 NO40

▶ ▶ ▶ **Shell Bay Caravan Park (NO465005)**
Kincraig Hill KY9 1HB ☎ 01333 330283 & 330334
Dir: 1.5m NW of Elie off A917, signed off unclass road, with direct access to beach
★ 🚐 £12.50-£15.50 🚐 £12.50-£15.50 Å £8.50-£9.50
Open 21 Mar-Oct Booking advisable Jul-Aug Last arrival 21.00hrs Last departure noon
Large, mainly static holiday site utilizing natural coastal area of a secluded bay. A 5-acre site with 120 touring pitches and 250 statics.
Children's club

Leisure: 🎣 ⚠ ⌗ **Facilities:** ⬧⊙🔍☀🔌🛒🌲🍴
Services: 🔌🅱Ⓟ🛈⌀🖃✕🛗
→ ∪ ⫠ ⊙ 🔺 ↵ 🍴 💳 💳 🚐

KIRKCALDY   Map 11 NT29

▶ ▶ ▶ ▶ **Dunnikier Caravan Park (NT283940)**
Dunnikier Way KY1 3ND ☎ 01592 267563 & 266701
Dir: Exit M90 at junct 2a which is A92. Exit A92 at Kirkcaldy West. Follow road for Kirkcaldy. At 1st rdbt take 3rd exit & follow road for 1m. Park on left
★ 🚐 £7.50-£9.50 🚐 £7.50-£9.50 Å £5.60-£8
Open Mar-Jan Booking advisable peak periods Last arrival 19.00hrs Last departure noon
Set in mature parkland on the edge of Dunniker Park of which it once formed part, bordered with mature woods and planted with trees and shrubs. The generously-spaced pitches are on level, mainly grassy land, and every one has a hardstanding. The amenities here are first class and immaculately maintained, and the park offers a peaceful and pleasant environment in a country atmosphere yet within easy reach of the town. Dunniker Park Golf Club is a short walk away, and other Fife courses are within easy driving distance. An 8-acre site with 60 touring pitches and 24 statics.

Leisure: ⚠ **Facilities:** ⬧⊙🔍☀🔌🛒🌲🐕
Services: 🔌🅱🛈⌀🖃
→ ∪ ⫠ ⊙ 🔺 ↵ 👥 🍴

LUNDIN LINKS   Map 11 NO40

▶ ▶ ▶ **Woodland Gardens Caravan & Camping Site (NO418031)**
Blindwell Rd KY8 5QG ☎ 01333 360319
Dir: Located off A915 coast road at Largo. At E end of Lundin Links, turn left off A915, 0.5m signposted
★ 🚐 £7.50-£8.50 🚐 £7.50-£8.50 Å £7.50-£8.50
Open Apr-Oct Booking advisable Jul-Aug Last arrival 22.00hrs Last departure noon
A secluded and sheltered site. A 1-acre site with 20 touring pitches and 5 statics.

CRAIGTOUN MEADOWS HOLIDAY PARK
ADAC *St Andrews* ANWB
AA ▶▶▶▶▶

• 1.5 miles from St Andrews • Shop •
• Restaurant • Takeaway • Launderette •
• Games Room • Information Room •
• Children's Play Areas • Tennis Court •
• Mini Gym •
Craigtoun Meadows Holiday Park
Mount Melville, St Andrews Fife. KY16 8PQ.
Tel: +44 (0)1334 475959
Fax: +44 (0)1334 476424
email: craigtoun@aol.com
www.craigtounmeadows.co.uk

Leisure: ✎ ☐ **Facilities:** ↿ ⊙ ⚲ ※ ⚻ ☎ 🐾 ⅍
Services: 🖭 🛢 ⌀ 🔡
➔ ∪ ▶ △ ↵

ST ANDREWS — Map 12 NO51

PREMIER PARK

▶ ▶ ▶ ▶ ▶ **Craigtoun Meadows Holiday Park (NO482150)**
Mount Melville KY16 8PQ ☎ 01334 475959
Dir: From M90 N to junct 8 onto A91 for St Andrews. From St Andrews via Argyle Street & Hepburn Gardens, bearing left at fork
★ 🚐 £13.50-£21 🚐 £13.50-£21 ▲ £11.50-£14.50
Open Mar-Oct Booking advisable bank hols & Jun-Aug Last arrival 21.00hrs Last departure noon
An attractive site set unobtrusively in mature woodlands with large pitches in hedged paddocks. The park is beautifully maintained to a very high standard, with extensive landscaping including flowers, trees and shrubs. All pitches are generously sized, and offer hardstandings and electricity, plus individual water points and drainage. There are also a number of patio pitches which are equipped with paved area and a summerhouse with picnic table and chairs, divided by ornamental trees and shrubs. The modern toilet block offers cubicled wash basins and toilets in addition to spacious showers, baths, disabled facilities and baby changing. There is a licensed restaurant and coffee shop, takeaway, launderette and

shop, and indoor and outdoor games areas. Located 2m from sea and sandy beaches. A 32-acre site with 70 touring pitches and 143 statics. Adult mini-gymnasium.
Leisure: ✎ ✎ ⚲ **Facilities:** ↿ ↿ ⊙ ⚲ ※ ⚻ ☎
🐾 ☐ 🐾 **Services:** 🖭 🛢 ⌀ 🔡 🅃 ✗ ⚙
➔ ∪ ▶ ☎ ↵ 🚌 ▥ ⚙

▶ ▶ ▶ **Kinkell Braes Caravan Site (NO522156)**
KY16 8PX ☎ 01334 474250
Dir: On A917 1m S of St Andrews
★ 🚐 £9.50-£15.20 🚐 £9.50-£15.20
Open 21 Mar-Oct Booking advisable Jun-Aug Last departure noon no cars by tents
A mainly static site with touring area giving views across St Andrews and the Eden estuary. A 4-acre site with 100 touring pitches and 392 statics.
Leisure: ✎ ⚲ ☐ **Facilities:** ↿ ⊙ ※ ⚻ ☎ 🐾 ⅍
Services: 🖭 🛢 ⚲ ⌀ ✗ 🔡
➔ ▶ ☎ ↵ 🚌 ▥ ⚙

ST MONANS — Map 12 NO50

▶ ▶ ▶ *St Monans Caravan Park (NO529019)*
KY10 2DN ☎ 01333 730778 & 310185
Dir: Located on A917, 100yds E of St Monans
🚐 🚐
Open 21 Mar-Oct Booking advisable Jul-Aug Last arrival 22.00hrs Last departure noon
Mainly static site on fringe of coastal village adjacent to main road and public park. A 1-acre site with 18 touring pitches and 112 statics.
Leisure: ⚲ **Facilities:** ↿ ⊙ ⚻ 🐾 🔡 ⅍ **Services:** 🖭 🛢
➔ ∪ ▶ ◎ ☎ ↵ 🚌 ↵

HIGHLAND

APPLECROSS — Map 13 NG74

▶ ▶ ▶ *Applecross Campsite (NG714443)*
IV54 8ND ☎ 01520 744268 & 744284
Dir: Follow unclass road off A896, 300yds from village
🚐 🚐 ▲
Open Etr-Oct (rs Apr, May, Sep & Oct only 1 toilet block open) Last arrival 22.00hrs
A quiet site in a lovely remote area close to mountains, moorland and beach. This park has the benefit of a café approached through a flower tunnel. Caravans should approach via Shieldaig. A 6-acre site with 60 touring pitches and 4 statics. Bakery.
Facilities: ↿ ⊙ ※ 🐾 **Services:** 🖭 🛢 ⌀ 🔡 🅃 ✗
➔ ↵ 🚌

ARISAIG — Map 13 NM68

▶ ▶ ▶ ▶ *Camusdarach Campsite (NM664916)*
Camusdarach PH39 4NT ☎ 01687 450221
Dir: Located on A830, 4m N of Arisaig village
🚐 🚐 ▲
Open 15 Mar-15 Oct Booking advisable Jul-Aug Last arrival 22.00hrs Last departure 18.00hrs no cars by tents
contd.

Services: 🅃 Toilet Fluid ✗ Café/ Restaurant 🚌 Fast Food/Takeaway 🚼 Baby Care 🖭 Electric Hook Up
🛢 Launderette ⚲ Licensed Bar 🛢 Calor Gaz ⌀ Camping Gaz 🔡 Battery Charging

Scotland

Camusdarach Campsite

Very attractive, quiet and secluded park with new sanitary facilities, and access to silver sandy beach. The superb quality of both beaches and scenery has to be seen to be believed. This park is within easy walking distance of the Mallaig Ferry to the Isle of Skye. A 2.75-acre site with 42 touring pitches.

Facilities: 🏕 ⊙ 🍴 ⚒ ☂ ⚓ ℃ ▦ **Services:** 🅿 🅰 ▣
→ ⊩ ⚒ ◢ ⚘

▶ ▶ ▶ **Gorten Sands Caravan Site (NM640879)**
Gorten Farm PH39 4NS ☎ 01687 450283
Dir: A830 to Point, 2m W of Asisaig. Turn left at signpost 'Back of Keppoch'. Continue 0.75m to road across cattle grid
★ ⊞ fr £10 ⊞ £8.50-£10 ▲ £8-£10.50
Open Etr-Sep Booking advisable Jul-Aug Last arrival 23.00hrs Last departure 13.00hrs
A well-run site with mainly modern facilities, carefully maintained and peacefully located off the beaten track. A 6-acre site with 44 touring pitches and 1 static.
Facilities: 🏕 ⊙ 🍴 ⚒ ℃ ▦ 🐕 **Services:** 🅿 🅰 ◢ ▣
→ ⊩ ◢ ⚘

▶ ▶ ▶ **Portnadoran Caravan Site (NM651892)**
Bunacaimbe PH39 4NT ☎ 01687 450267
Dir: A830 Fort William to Mallaig road, 2m N of Arisaig village
★ ⊞ £7-£10 ⊞ £7-£9 ▲ £5-£8
Open Apr-Oct Booking advisable Jul-Aug Last arrival 23.00hrs Last departure noon
Small, level, grassy site situated close to sandy beach overlooking the Islands of Eigg, Rhum and Skye. Very welcoming. A 2-acre site with 55 touring pitches and 9 statics.
Leisure: ⌂ **Facilities:** 🏕 ⊙ ⚒ ℃ ▦ 🐕
Services: 🅿 🅰 ▣ → ⊩ ◢ ⚘

AVIEMORE   Map 14 NH81

▶ ▶ ▶ **Dalraddy Holiday Park (NH859083)**
PH22 1QB ☎ 01479 810330 & 01540 651255
Dir: 3.5m S of Aviemore. From A9, take Aviemore turn. Turn right onto B9152 towards Kincraig. Park 3m
★ ⊞ £7.50-£9.50 ⊞ £7.50-£9.50 ▲ £3.50-£7
Open all year (rs Nov open 9am-5pm) Booking advisable Jul-Aug Last arrival 20.00hrs Last departure noon
A secluded site set amidst heather and young birch trees with mountain views. A 25-acre site with 23 touring pitches and 99 statics.

DALRADDY HOLIDAY PARK ▶▶▶
Aviemore, Inverness-shire

Quiet family park in 25 acres of woodland with views of the Cairngorm Mountains, within walking distance of the River Spey. Tents, touring caravans and motor homes welcome, static caravans and log chalets for hire. Licensed craft/farm shop, launderette and play park. Nearby activities include fishing, pony trekking, walking, skiing, off-road driving. Dogs welcome – short breaks available.
For more information, phone (01479) 810330.
E-mail: dhp@alvie-estate.co.uk
Fax: (01479) 810330

Leisure: ⌂ **Facilities:** 🏕 ⊙ 🍴 ⚒ ☂ ℃ ⚘ ▦ 🐕
Services: 🅿 🅱 🅰 ◢ ▣ Ⓣ
→ ∪ ◎ ♨ ⚒ ◢ 🍴 🎱 🚽 📶 🅖

▶ ▶ ▶ **Glenmore Caravan & Camping Site (NH976097)**
Glenmore PH22 1QU
☎ 01479 861271 & 0131 314 6505
Dir: From A9 turn onto B9152 S of Aviemore. At Aviemore right onto B970, keeping right at Coylumbridge to site in 5m
★ ⊞ £7.70-£9.70 ⊞ £7.70-£9.70 ▲ £7.70-£9.70
Open Dec-Oct Booking advisable bank hols & Jul-Aug Last arrival 22.00hrs Last departure noon
An attractive Forestry Commission site with grassy areas, landscaped with mature trees, and close to the eastern end of Loch Morlich at the head of Glenmore. There are sandy beaches close by. A 17-acre site with 220 touring pitches.
Leisure: ⌂ **Facilities:** 🏕 ⊙ 🍴 ⚒ ☂ ℃ ⚘ ▦
Services: 🅿 Ⓣ
→ ♨ ⚒ ◢ 🍴 🎱 🚽 📶 🅖

▶ ▶ ▶ **Rothiemurchus Camping & Caravan Park (NH916108)**
Coylumbridge PH22 1QU ☎ 01479 812800
Dir: 1.5m E on A951
★ ⊞ £8-£12 ⊞ £8-£12 ▲ £7-£10
Open all year Booking advisable Jul-Aug Last arrival 22.00hrs Last departure 11.00hrs no cars by tents

---

Facilities: 🛁 Bath 🚿 Shower ⊙ Electric Shaver 🍴 Hairdryer ☂ Ice Pack Facility ⚓ Disabled Facilities ℃ Public Telephone ⚘ Shop on Site or within 200yds ▣ Mobile Shop (calls at least 5 days a week) ▦ BBQ Area ⚒ Picnic Area 🐕 Dog Exercise Area

A secluded site in tree-studded undulating ground off approach road to the Cairngorm Mountains. An attractive natural site offering very clean and well-maintained facilities. A 4-acre site with 39 touring pitches and 50 statics.

Facilities: ⬤⊙❄✕⬤⬤⬤➤ Services: ⬤⬤⬤⬤⬤⬤⬤
➤ ∪ ➤ ⊚ ⬤ ⬤ ⬤ ⬤ ⬤ ⬤ ⬤

BALMACARA   Map 14 NG82

▶ ▶ ▶ ▶ **Reraig Caravan Site (NG815272)**
IV40 8DH ☎ 01599 566215
Dir: On A87 at rear of Balmacara Hotel
★ ⬤ £7.50 ⬤ £7.50 ▲ £7.50
Open Etr-Sep Last arrival 22.00hrs Last departure noon
Set on level, grassy ground surrounded by trees, the site is located on the saltwater Sound of Sleet, and looks south towards Loch Alsh and Skye. Very nicely organised with a high standard of maintenance, and handy for the bridge crossing to the Isle of Skye. A pub, petrol station and mini-market are two minutes' walk. A 2-acre site with 45 touring pitches.

Facilities: ⬤⊙⬤⬤ Services: ⬤⬤ ⬤ ⬤ ⬤

▶ ▶ **Balmacara Caravan & Camping Site (NG803279)**
IV40 8DN
☎ 01599 566374 (in season) & 0131 314 6505
Dir: NE on A87 towards Kyle of Lochlash, take 2nd right after Reraig village signposted Balmacara Square
★ ⬤ £5.40-£6.30 ⬤ £5.40-£6.30 ▲ £5.40-£6.30
Open Etr-Sep Booking advisable Last arrival 22.00hrs Last departure noon
An attractive and sheltered Forestry Commission site. A 7-acre site with 60 touring pitches. Forest walks.

Facilities: ⬤⬤➤ Services: ⬤
➤ ∪ ➤ ⬤ ⬤ ⬤ ⬤ ⬤ ⬤ ⬤

BOAT OF GARTEN   Map 14 NH91

▶ ▶ ▶ *Campgrounds of Scotland (NH939191)*
PH24 3BN ☎ 01479 831652
Dir: Located off A95
⬤ ⬤ ▲
Open all year Booking advisable 26 Dec-2 Jan & 25 Jul-7 Aug Last arrival 22.00hrs Last departure 11.00hrs

Level, grass site with young trees and bushes set in mountainous woodland in the village itself, near the River Spey and Loch Garten. A 3.5-acre site with 37 touring pitches and 60 statics.
Leisure: ⬤ Facilities: ⬤⊙⬤❄⬤⬤⬤
Services: ⬤⬤⬤⬤⬤⬤⬤✕
➤ ➤ ⬤

CANNICH   Map 14 NH33

▶ ▶ ▶ *Cannich Caravan and Camping Park (NH345317)*
IV4 7LN ☎ 01456 415364 & 415263
Dir: Situated on A831, 200yds SE of Cannich Bridge
⬤ ⬤ ▲
Open Mar-Nov Booking advisable Jul & Aug Last arrival 23.00hrs Last departure noon
Quietly situated in Strath Glass, close to the River Glass and near Cannich village. This well-run park has attractive mountain views, and is set in ideal walking and naturalist country. A 12-acre site with 140 touring pitches and 9 statics.
Mountain bike hire & fishing.
Leisure: ⬤⬤▢ Facilities: ⬤⊙⬤❄⬤⬤⬤⬤
Services: ⬤⬤⬤⬤⬤⬤
➤ ∪ ➤ ⬤ ⬤ ⬤ ⬤

CORPACH   Map 14 NN07

PREMIER PARK

▶ ▶ ▶ ▶ ▶ **Linnhe Lockside Holidays (NN074771)**
PH33 7NL ☎ 01397 772376
Dir: On A830, 1m W of Corpach village, 5m from Fort William
⬤ £11.50-£13.50 ⬤ £11.50-£13.50 ▲ £8.50-£10.50
Open Etr-Oct (rs 15 Dec-Etr shop & main toilet block closed) Booking advisable school hols & peak periods Last arrival 21.00hrs Last departure 11.00hrs no cars by tents
An excellently maintained site in a beautiful setting on the shores of Loch Eil, with Ben Nevis to the east and the mountains and Sunart to the west. The owners have worked in harmony with nature to produce an idyllic environment, where they offer the highest standards of design and maintenance. A 5.5-acre site with 73 touring pitches and 100 statics.
Launching slipway, private beach, free fishing.
See advertisement under FORT WILLIAM
Leisure: ⬤ Facilities: ⬤⬤⊙⬤❄⬤⬤⬤⬤➤
Services: ⬤⬤⬤⬤⬤⬤
➤ ➤ ⬤ ⬤ ⬤ ⬤ ⬤ ⬤

DAVIOT   Map 14 NH73

▶ ▶ ▶ **Auchnahillin Caravan & Camping Centre (NH742386)**
IV2 5XQ ☎ 01463 772286
Dir: 4m S of Inverness off A9 on the B9154, Daviot-East & Moy road
⬤ £7.20-£9.20 ⬤ £7.20-£9.20 ▲ £5.70-£8.20
Open Etr-Oct Booking advisable Jun-Aug Last arrival 22.00hrs Last departure noon

contd.

Level grassy site with clean and spacious facilities, surrounded by hills and forest. A 10-acre site with 65 touring pitches and 35 statics.

Leisure: **Facilities:**

Services:

DINGWALL **Map 14 NH55**

►►►► **Camping & Caravanning Club Site (NH555588)**

Jubilee Park IV15 9QZ ☎ 01349 862236

Dir: *Follow A862 to Dingwall, take right turn down Hill Street, past filling station. Right into High Street & 1st left after railway bridge. Site ahead*

★ £11.80-£14.90 £11.80-£14.90 £11.80-£14.90

Open 20 Mar-1 Nov Booking advisable bank hols & Jul-Aug Last arrival 21.00hrs Last departure noon

A quiet park with attractive landscaping and very good facilities maintained to a high standard. A convenient touring centre close to the historic market town of Dingwall. Please see the advertisement on page 14 for details of Club Members' benefits. A 6.5-acre site with 85 touring pitches.

Facilities: **Services:**

DORNOCH **Map 14 NH78**

Grannie's Heilan Hame Holiday Park (NH818924)

Embo IV25 3QD

☎ 01862 810383 & 810753

Dir: *A949 to Dornoch, turn left in square & follow signs for Embo*

★ £7.50-£14.50 £7.50-£14.50 £7.50-£14.50

Open Mar-Oct (rs Mar Limited Facilities) Booking advisable Jul-Aug Last arrival 23.30hrs Last departure 14.00hrs

A holiday centre with a wide range of leisure facilities, including indoor swimming pool with sauna and solarium, separate play areas for under and over fives, putting green, tennis courts and very much more. The sanitary facilities are clean and well maintained, and the park is set on the beach yet handy for the Highlands. A 60-acre site with 300 touring pitches and 148 statics.

Spa bath, sauna, solarium & mini ten-pin bowling.

Leisure: **Facilities:**

Services:

►►►► ***Pitgrudy Caravan Park (NH795911)***

Poles Rd IV25 3HY ☎ 01862 821253

Dir: *On B9168, between A9 and A949*

Open May-Sep

A very high quality park in terms of design, environment, sanitary facilities and customer care. Many of the pitches are fully serviced, and all have their own water supplies. This very quiet park is close to the historic town of Dornoch in rural surroundings, and convenient for beaches, mountains and lochs. A 3.5-acre site with 50 touring pitches and 38 statics.

Facilities: **Services:**

Facilities: Bath, Shower, Electric Shaver, Hairdryer, Ice Pack Facility, Disabled Facilities, Public Telephone, Shop on Site or within 200yds, Mobile Shop (calls at least 5 days a week), BBQ Area, Picnic Area, Dog Exercise Area

FORT WILLIAM — Map 14 NN17

PREMIER PARK

► ► ► ► ► **Glen Nevis Caravan & Camping Park (NN124722)**
Glen Nevis PH33 6SX ☎ 01397 702191 & 705181
Dir: Follow A82 to mini-rdbt at northern outskirts of Fort William. Exit for Glen Nevis. Site 2.5m on right
★ 🚐 £7.80-£11.50 🚙 £7.60-£11.20 ▲ £6.10-£11.20
Open 15 Mar-Oct (rs Mar & mid-end Oct limited shop & restaurant facilities) Booking advisable Jul-Aug Last arrival 22.00hrs Last departure noon
A tasteful site with well-screened enclosures, at the foot of Ben Nevis, in the midst of some of the Highlands' most spectacular scenery – an ideal walking and touring area. The park boasts a restaurant which offers a high standard of cooking and provides good value for money. One of the best parks in Scotland. A 30-acre site with 380 touring pitches and 30 statics. Licensed club/bar adjacent to site.
Leisure: 🅰 **Facilities:** 🅜⊙🅠☀️🖑🅲🅻🅐☔🅣
Services: 🖃🅑🅘🖊🖃🅣🗙🖐
→🅟🚙🖊 🆑🆑🆑🆑🆓

GAIRLOCH — Map 14 NG87

► ► ► **Gairloch Caravan & Camping Park (NG798773)**
Strath IV21 2BX
☎ 01505 614343 & 01445 712373
Dir: From A832 take B8021 signed Melvaig, heading towards Strath. After 0.5m turn right, just after Millcroft Hotel. Immediately after hotel, right again
★ 🚐 £8.50-£9.50 🚙 £8.50-£9.50 ▲ £7.50-£8.50
Open Etr-Oct Booking advisable Last arrival 21.30hrs Last departure noon
A clean, well-maintained site on flat coastal grassland close to Loch Gairloch. A 6-acre site with 70 touring pitches and 3 statics. Adjacent café, restaurant, activity centre & bar.
Leisure: ◣ **Facilities:** 🅜⊙🅠☀️🅲🅻
Services: 🖃🅑🅘
→🅤🅟🛆🖊🗲 🆑🆑

► ► ► **Sands Holiday Centre (NG758784)**
IV21 2DL ☎ 01445 712152
Dir: 3m W of Gairloch on B8021
★ 🚐 £8.50-£9.50 🚙 £8.50-£8.90 ▲ £8.50-£9.50
Open 20 May-10 Sep (rs Apr-19 May & 11 Sep-mid Oct no shop, some toilets closed) Booking advisable Jul-Aug Last arrival 22.00hrs Last departure noon
Part-level site close to sandy beach with a panoramic outlook towards Skye. A 51-acre site with 360 touring pitches and 20 statics. Boat slipway.
Leisure: 🅰 **Facilities:** 🅜⊙🅠☀️🅲🅻🅐☔🅣
Services: 🖃🅑🅘🖊🖃🅣
→🅟⊙🛆🖊 🆑🆑🆑🆑🆓

GLENCOE — Map 14 NN15

► ► ► ► **Invercoe Caravan Site (NN098594)**
PH49 4HP ☎ 01855 811210
Dir: Turn right off A82 at Glencoe Hotel onto B863 for 0.25m
★ 🚐 fr £10 🚙 fr £10 ▲ £8-£10

Open Mar-Oct Booking advisable Jul-Aug for electric hook ups Last departure noon
Level, grass site set on the shore of Loch Lever with excellent mountain views. The area is ideal for both walking and climbing, and also offers a choice of several freshwater and saltwater lochs. Convenient for the good shopping at Fort William. A 5-acre site with 60 touring pitches and 5 statics.
Leisure: 🅰 **Facilities:** 🅜⊙🅠☀️🅲🅻🅐🅣
Services: 🖃🅑🅘🖃🅣
→🔆🖊

► ► ► **Glencoe Caravan & Campsite (NN111578)**
Carnoch PH49 4LA ☎ 01855 811397 & 811278
Dir: 1m SE from Glencoe village on A82
★ 🚐 £6-£8 🚙 £6-£8 ▲ £6
Open Etr/Apr-Oct Booking advisable Jul-Aug Last arrival 22.00hrs Last departure 17.00hrs
Part-level, part-sloping, grass, gravel and sand site with young trees and bushes in mountainous woodland. A 25-acre site with 64 touring pitches.
Facilities: 🅜⊙🅠☀️🅲🅻🅐☔🅣
Services: 🖃🅑🅘🖊🖃🅣
→🛆🔆🖊

GRANTOWN-ON-SPEY — Map 14 NJ02

PREMIER PARK

► ► ► ► ► **Grantown on Spey Caravan Park (NJ028283)**
Seafield Av PH26 3JQ ☎ 01479 872474
Dir: From town turn N at Bank of Scotland Park, straight ahead from 0.25m
★ 🚐 £7-£10.50 🚙 £7-£10.50 ▲ £6-£8
Open Mar-Oct Booking advisable Etr, May day, Spring BH & Jul-Aug Last arrival 22.00hrs
An attractive park in a mature setting near the river, amidst hills, mountains, moors and woodland. The planning and design of this park, and its landscaping are all excellent, and the day-to-day running and customer care are exemplary. The park is well sited for golf, fishing, moutaineering, walking, sailing and canoeing which are all nearby, and the area is

contd.

interesting for bird and nature enthusiasts. Table tennis and snooker available on site. A 15-acre site with 100 touring pitches and 45 statics. Football pitch

Leisure: ♠ ⚲ **Facilities:** ╟ ⊙ ⊠ ✳ ╲ 戸 ★
Services: ⊕ ⊠ ▮ ∅ ⊞ Ⓣ
→ ∪ ┌ ⊙ ┛ ⊾ ● ▤ ▦ ⊠ Ⓖ

INVERGARRY   Map 14 NH30

▶ ▶ ▶ *Faichemard Farm (NH288016)*
Faichemard Farm PH35 4HG ☎ 01809 501314
Dir: Situated 1m W of Invergarry off A87
⊞ ⊞ Å
Open Apr-Oct Booking advisable Last arrival 22.00hrs Last departure 11.30hrs
A quiet, very low density park with very attractive views. The mountains make a picturesque backdrop which blends with the park's rugged scenery. A 10-acre site with 40 touring pitches.
Every pitch has own picnic table
Facilities: ╟ ⊙ ⊠ ✳ ╲ 戸 ★ **Services:** ⊕ ⊠ ⊞
→ ∆ ↘ ┛ ⊾

▶ ▶ ▶ *Faichem Park (NH285023)*
Ardgarry Farm, Faichem PH35 4HG ☎ 01809 501226
Dir: Take A87 at Invergarry junct & continue W for 1m. Turn right at the 'Faichem' signpost & proceed up hill. Reception 1st on right at top of hill
⊞ £7-£7.50 ⊞ £7-£7.50 Å £7-£7.50
Open 16 Mar-16 Oct Booking advisable Jul-Aug Last arrival 22.00hrs Last departure noon

Small, quiet touring site with good, clean facilities and panoramic views. Customer care is given a high priority here, as is the attention to detail which is meticulous. An ideal location for walking, climbing, and for touring the Highlands. A 2-acre site with 30 touring pitches.

Facilities: ╟ ⊙ ⊠ ✳ ╲ 螶 ★ **Services:** ⊕ ▮ ∅ ⊞
→ ∆ ↘ ┛ ⊾

INVERNESS   Map 14 NH64

▶ ▶ ▶ ▶ ▶ *Torvean Caravan Park (NH654438)*
Glenurquhart Rd IV3 8JL ☎ 01463 220582
Dir: 1m W of Inverness on A82 at Tomnahuich Canal bridge
⊞ ⊞
Open Apr-Oct Booking advisable Jun-Aug Last arrival 21.00hrs Last departure 12.00hrs
Located on the Caledonian Canal, this park is quiet and well secluded yet close to Inverness town centre. Every feature of the park has been planned, constructed and maintained to the highest standard. The landscaped grounds are immaculate, and there is a good quality children's play area. Good shopping, leisure facilities and historic buildings in Inverness, and plenty to entertain children and adults. A 3-acre site with 50 touring pitches and 10 statics.
Leisure: ⚲ **Facilities:** ╟ ⊙ ⊠ ✳ ╲ 凵
Services: ⊠ ▮ ∅ ⊞ Ⓣ
→ ∪ ┌ ↘ ⊞ ┛ ⊾

JOHN O'GROATS   Map 15 ND37

▶ ▶ ▶ *John O'Groats Caravan Site (ND382733)*
KW1 4YS ☎ 01955 611329 & 07718 914161
Dir: Located at the end of A99
⊞ £7.50-£8.50 ⊞ £7.50-£8.50 Å £7.50-£8.50
Open Apr-Oct Booking advisable Last arrival 22.00hrs Last departure noon
Good clean and attractive site in open position above the seashore and looking out towards the Orkney Islands. Passenger ferry nearby. A 4-acre site with 90 touring pitches.
Facilities: ╟ ⊙ ⊠ ✳ ╲ ⊾ ⊾ **Services:** ⊕ ⊠ ▮ ∅ ⊞
→ ┛

LAIDE   Map 14 NG99

▶ ▶ ▶ *Gruinard Bay Caravan Park (NG903918)*
Laide IV22 2ND ☎ 01445 731225
Dir: Located on A832, 300yds N of village
⊞ ⊞ Å
Open Apr-Oct Booking advisable Jul-Aug Last arrival 22.00hrs Last departure 11.00hrs
Campers receive a warm welcome at this spotless, lovingly managed site on the outskirts of Laide. A

Scotland

3.25-acre site with 43 touring pitches and 14 statics. Laundry service.

Facilities: ➡️⊙❄❅☂🐾 **Services:** 🔌🛢️🛒⊞Ⓣ
➔☂🛢️🍴

LAIRG   Map 14 NC50

► ► ► **Dunroamin Caravan Park (NC585062)**
Main St IV27 4AR ☎ 01549 402447
Dir: Located 300mtrs from centre of Lairg on the S side of A839
🚐 £6.50-£10 🚐 £5.50-£10 ▲ £5-£10

Open Apr-Oct Booking advisable anytime Last arrival 23.00hrs Last departure noon
A small, attractive and well laid out site. A 10-acre site with 40 touring pitches and 9 statics.
Facilities: ➡️⊙❄❅☂🐾 **Services:** 🔌🛢️🛒⊞Ⓣ✗🍴
➔☂🛢️🍴 🚐🚙🚗

► ► ► **Woodend Caravan & Camping Site (NC551127)**
Achnairn IV27 4DN ☎ 01549 402248
Dir: 4m N of Lairg off A838, signed at Achnairn
★ 🚐 £7-£8 🚐 £7-£8 ▲ £6-£7
Open Apr-Sep Booking advisable Last arrival 23.00hrs

A clean, fresh site set in hilly moors and woodland with access to sea, beach, river and Loch Shin, offering a spacious camper's kitchen. The area is popular with fishing and boating enthusiasts, and there is a choice of golf courses within 30 miles. A 4-acre site with 60 touring pitches and 5 statics.
Leisure: Ⓜ **Facilities:** ➡️⊙❄❅☂🐾
Services: 🔌🛢️🛒⊞
➔☂🛢️

LOCHALINE   Map 13 NM64

► ► ► **Fiunary Camping & Caravanning Park (NM614467)**
Morvern PA34 5XX ☎ 01967 421225
Dir: Signed 5m W of Lochaline & ferry on Loch Shore at Fiunary

Open May-Oct (rs Apr hot water & showers not available) Booking advisable Last arrival 22.00hrs Last departure noon
A small, carefully maintained site with beautiful lochside views, quiet and secluded and in an area of great interest to naturalists. A 3.5-acre site with 25 touring pitches and 2 statics.
Facilities: ➡️⊙❄☂🐾 **Services:** 🔌⊞
➔☂🛢️🍴

NAIRN   Map 14 NH85

Nairn Lochloy Holiday Park (NH895574)
East Beach IV12 4PH
☎ 01667 453764 & 454646
Dir: On entering Nairn take the signpost for the harbour
★ 🚐 £10-£17.50 🚐 £10-£17.50 ▲ £8-£15.50
Open Mar-Oct Booking advisable Jun-Aug Last arrival 22.00hrs Last departure 10.00hrs
A busy holiday park with good facilities, bordered by the beach, the River Nairn and the golf course. Some of the many activities offered here include an adventure playground, indoor swimming pool, and pool table, and there is a lounge bar and a fish and chip shop. A 15-acre site with 45 touring pitches and 230 statics. Discount on adjacent golf course.
Leisure: 🎣🎱Ⓜ **Facilities:** ➡️⊙❄❅☂🐾
Services: 🔌🛢️🛒⊞Ⓣ✗🍴
➔∪🅿️⊙☂🛢️🍴 🚐🚙🚗

► ► ► ► **Spindrift Caravan & Camping Site (NH863537)**
Little Kildrummie IV12 5QU ☎ 01667 453992
Dir: Take B9090 S for 1.5m, turn right at sharp left hand bend signposted Little Kildrummie, site 400yds on left
🚐 £6.50-£9.50 🚐 £6.50-£9.50 ▲ £6.50-£9.50
Open Apr-Oct Booking advisable Jul-Aug Last arrival 22.00hrs Last departure noon
An informal site in attractive setting with good facilities and first class maintenance. Landscaping has been tastefully designed, and includes beautiful floral displays, and smart toilet buildings which blend in well with their surroundings. Within a two mile river walk or drive of Nairn, the beaches and

contd.

Services: Ⓣ Toilet Fluid ✗ Café/ Restaurant 🍴 Fast Food/Takeaway ➡️ Baby Care 🔌 Electric Hook Up
🛢️ Launderette 🍷 Licensed Bar 🛢️ Calor Gaz ⊘ Camping Gaz ⊞ Battery Charging

leisure facilities. Natural interest includes the varied birdlife and red squirrels. A 3-acre site with 40 touring pitches.
Fishing permits available from reception.
Facilities: ⬧⊙🝙✳❄ ⬩ **Services:** ⬛🖥🅸🔩⊞
→⊍▶◉♨⤵⬧

▶ ▶ ▶ **Camping & Caravanning Club Site (NH852552)**
Delnies Wood IV12 5NX ☎ 01667 455281
Dir: Off the main A96 Inverness to Aberdeen Rd. 2m W of the town of Nairn
★ 🚐 £9.80-£12.40 🚐 £9.80-£12.40 ▲ £9.80-£12.40
Open 20 Mar-Oct Booking advisable end Jun-early Aug Last arrival 22.00hrs Last departure noon
An attractive site amongst pine trees. Facilities have been much improved recently, and the park is close to Nairn with its beaches, shopping, golf and leisure activities. See advertisement on page 14 for details of Club Members' benefits. A 14-acre site with 90 touring pitches and 16 statics.
Leisure: ◀ ⚠ **Facilities:** ⬧⊙🝙✳❄⬩ ⬧🖧🎋🐾
Services: ⬛🖥🅸🔩⊞🆃
→⊍▶⤵ 🍴 🔄

POOLEWE   Map 14 NG88
▶ ▶ ▶ **Camping & Caravanning Club Site (NG862812)**
Inverewe Gardens IV22 2LF ☎ 01445 781249
Dir: On A832, N of Poolewe village
★ 🚐 £11.80-£14.90 🚐 £11.80-£14.90 ▲ £11.80-£14.90
Open 20 Mar-1 Nov Booking advisable bank hols & Jul-Aug Last arrival 21.00hrs Last departure noon
A well-run site located in Loch Ewe Bay, not far from Inverewe Gardens. Please see the advertisement on page 14 for details of Club Members' benefits. A 3-acre site with 55 touring pitches.
Facilities: ⬧⊙🝙✳❄⬩🐾 **Services:** ⬛🅸⌀
→▶⤵♨⬧ 🍴 🔄

RESIPOLE (Loch Sunart)   Map 13 NM76
▶ ▶ ▶ ▶ **Resipole Farm (NM725639)**
PH36 4HX ☎ 01967 431235
Dir: Take A861 after leaving Corran Ferry. Park 8m W of Strontian
★ 🚐 £8.50-£9.50 🚐 £8.50-£9.50 ▲ £8.50-£9.50
Open Apr-Oct Booking advisable bank hols Last arrival 22.00hrs Last departure 11.00hrs
A quiet, relaxing park in beautiful surroundings, with deer frequently sighted, and of great interest to naturalists. Situated on the saltwater Loch Sunart in the Ardnamurchan Peninsula, and offering a great deal of space and privacy. Hidden away within the park's woodland is a 9-hole golf course, and a restaurant and lounge bar. An 8-acre site with 45 touring pitches and 15 statics.
Private slipway, 9-hole golf.
Facilities: ⬧⊙🝙✳⬩❄⬧🎋🐾
Services: ⬛🖥🍴🅸⌀⊞🆃✖
→▶♨⤵⬧ 🍴 🔄 ▦ 🎞

ROSEMARKIE   Map 14 NH75
▶ ▶ **Camping & Caravanning Club Site (NH739569)**
IV10 8SE ☎ 01381 621117
Dir: Take A832. A9 at Tore rdbt. Through Avoch, Fortrose then right at Police house. Down Ness Rd. 1st left, small turning signed Golf & Caravan site
★ 🚐 £9.80-£12.40 🚐 £9.80-£12.40 ▲ £9.80-£12.40
Open 7 Apr-25 Sep Booking advisable bank hols & Jul-Aug Last arrival 21.00hrs Last departure noon
A very clean and well-maintained site, with pitches close to road. Please see the advertisement on page 14 for details of Club Members' benefits. A 4-acre site with 60 touring pitches.
Facilities: ⬧⊙🝙✳⬩🐾 **Services:** 🖥
→⬧⤵⬧ 🍴 🔄

SCOURIE   Map 14 NC14
▶ ▶ ▶ **Scourie Caravan & Camping Park (NC153446)**
Harbour Rd IV27 4TE ☎ 01971 502060 & 502061
Dir: Located in the centre of village off A894, Ullapool to Durness road
🚐 fr £8 🚐 fr £8 ▲ fr £8
Open Etr-Sep Last arrival 22.00hrs Last departure noon
An attractive and well-equipped site adjacent to beach and sea. A 4-acre site with 60 touring pitches.
Facilities: ⬧⊙🝙✳⬩❄⬩ **Services:** ⬛🖥🍴⊞✖🛒
→⤵⬧

TAIN   Map 14 NH78
▶ ▶ ▶ **Dornoch Firth Caravan Park (NH748844)**
IV19 1JX ☎ 01862 892292
Dir: Located on A9 N of Tain, at S end of Dornoch Firth Bridge
🚐 🚐 ▲
Open all year Booking advisable Jul-Aug Last arrival 22.00hrs Last departure noon
A pleasant family site with meticulously maintained facilities. A 2-acre site with 30 touring pitches and 15 statics.
Restaurant adjacent to site.
Leisure: ⚠ **Facilities:** ⬧⊙🝙✳⬩ **Services:** ⬛🖥⊞
→⊍▶⤵⬧

THURSO   Map 15 ND16
▶ ▶ ▶ **Thurso Caravan & Camping Site (ND111688)**
Smith Ter, Scrabster Rd KW14 7JY
☎ 01847 894631 & 01955 607776
Dir: Signed on A882 on W side of Thurso
★ 🚐 £7.80-£8.90 🚐 £7.80-£8.90 ▲ £5.50-£8.10
Open May-Sep Booking advisable 14 days in advance Last arrival 22.00hrs Last departure noon
Exposed grassy site, set high above the coast on the west side of town with panoramic views out to sea. A 4.5-acre site with 117 touring pitches and 10 statics.
Leisure: ⚠🏓 **Facilities:** ⬧⊙⬩⬧🐾
Services: ⬛🖥✖🛒
→▶♨⤵⬧

Broomfield ► Holiday Park ►

Ullapool, Ross & Cromarty
Telephone: (01854) 612020 & 612664
Fax: (01854) 613151
E-mail: sross@broomfieldhp.com

This is the only caravan and camping park in Ullapool

Situated on the sea front at the West End of Ullapool and extends to some 12 acres of level grass overlooking the Summer Isles, famous for marvellous sunsets. The site has 2 large toilet blocks with flush toilets and hot & cold wash basins, shaving points, hairdryers and hand dryers, hot & cold showers, coin operated, and coin operated washing machines and tumble dryers. Power hook-ups. Children's playground. Within 5 minutes walk from the park entrance are supermarkets, bars, restaurants, cafes, bus stops, post office, telephone and boat hire. Also 9-hole golf course, tennis courts, leisure centre and covered swimming pool.

ULLAPOOL   Map 14 NH19

► ► ► ► **Ardmair Point Camping & Caravan Park** (NH108983)
IV26 2TN ☎ 01854 612054
Dir: 3m N of Ullapool on A835
★ ⊞ £8.50-£10 ⊞ £8-£10 ▲ £8-£10
Open May-Sep Booking advisable Jul-Aug Last arrival 22.00hrs Last departure noon
An excellent touring site on small peninsula, with superb views of mountains and sea lochs, and an interesting children's play area. Pitches adjoin and overlook the beaches. A 7-acre site with 45 touring pitches.
Boats, fishing, canoes for hire.
Leisure: ⚊ Facilities: ⬧⊙⬧⬧⬧⬧⬧⬧
Services: ⬧⬧⬧⬧⬧⬧⬧ →⬧⬧⬧⬧⬧⬧ ⬧⬧⬧⬧

► ► ► **Broomfield Holiday Park** (NH123939)
West Shore St IV26 2UR
☎ 01854 612020 & 612664
Dir: Take the 2nd right past Harbour
★ ⊞ £11-£12 ⊞ £10-£11 ▲ £9-£11
Open Apr-Oct Booking advisable Last dep noon
A level grass site by the shore of Loch Broom close to the harbour and town centre. A 10-acre site with 140 touring pitches.
Leisure: ⚊ Facilities: ⬧⊙⬧⬧⬧⬧
Services: ⬧⬧⬧ →⬧⬧⬧⬧⬧

For Lanarkshire see North Lanarkshire & South Lanarkshire.
For Lothian see East Lothian & West Lothian.

MIDLOTHIAN

DALKEITH   Map 11 NT36

► ► ► **Fordel** (NT359668)
Lauder Rd EH22 2PH
☎ 0131 663 3046 & 0131 660 3921
Dir: On A68 1.5m S of Dalkeith
★ ⊞ £9-£13 ⊞ £9-£13 ▲ £7.50-£8.50

Open Apr-Sep Booking advisable Jul-Aug Last departure noon
A small, tree lined, grassy site, adjacent to a 24-hour service station. Ideal for longer or stop-over stay. A 3-acre site with 35 touring pitches.
Leisure: ⚊ Facilities: ⬧⊙⬧⬧⬧⬧⬧⬧⬧
Services: ⬧⬧⬧⬧⬧⬧⬧
→⬧⬧⬧⬧ ⬧⬧ ⬧⬧ ⬧⬧ ⬧⬧ ⬧

ROSLIN   Map 11 NT26

► ► ► ► *Slatebarns Caravan Club Site* (NT277632)
EH25 9PU ☎ 0131 440 2192
Dir: From A720 by-pass take A701, signed Penicuik & Peebles. Travel S to B7006, turn left signed Roslin Chapel & take unclass road at end of village
⊞ ⊞ ▲
Open Etr-Oct Booking advisable Jul & Aug Last arrival 20.00hrs Last departure noon
A good modern site with marked pitches, set in a rural landscape near to Roslin Glen and the historic 15th-century Rosslyn Chapel yet within easy access of Edinburgh. The site offers excellent amenities, and has been planted liberally with trees and shrubs to make for a pleasant and peaceful environment. A 2.5-acre site with 30 touring pitches.
Facilities: ⬧⊙⬧⬧⬧⬧⬧⬧ Services: ⬧⬧⬧⬧
→⬧⬧⬧⬧

MORAY

ABERLOUR   Map 15 NJ24

► ► ► ► **Aberlour Gardens Caravan Park** (NJ282434)
AB38 9LD ☎ 01340 871586
Dir: Midway between Aberlour & Craigellachie on A95. Turn onto unclass road. Site signposted. Vehicles over 10'6" use A941 to Dufftown
★ ⊞ £6.75-£9.25 ⊞ £6.75-£9.25 ▲ £6.50-£9.25

contd.

Services: Ⓣ Toilet Fluid ✗ Café/ Restaurant ⬧ Fast Food/Takeaway ⬧ Baby Care ⬧ Electric Hook Up
⬧ Launderette ⬧ Licensed Bar ⬧ Calor Gaz ⬧ Camping Gaz ⬧ Battery Charging

Open Apr-Oct, Xmas & New Year Booking advisable bank hols & Jul-Aug

Set in the quiet walled gardens of a former country house, this park enjoys a quiet, peaceful and relaxing atmosphere amongst the mature trees and other landscaping features. Campers have the choice of hard pitches set along the curving garden wall, or level grassy pitches. The superb facilities are kept in immaculate order by the resident owners. A 5-acre site with 35 touring pitches and 26 statics.

Leisure: 🏔 Facilities: 🖍☉🔧✳️♿📞🐕🏪
Services: 🕹🖥🛢🚿🚽🚻♿
→ ∪ ▶ ◎ ♪

ALVES   Map 15 NJ16

▶ ▶ ▶ **North Alves Caravan Park** (NJ122633)
IV30 3XD ☎ 01343 850223
Dir: 1m W of A96, halfway between Elgin & Forres. Site signed on right
★ 🚐 £7.50-£10.50 🚐 £7-£10 ⛺ £6-£10
Open Apr-Oct Booking advisable peak periods Last arrival 23.00hrs Last departure noon
A quiet rural site in attractive rolling countryside within three miles of a good beach. A 10-acre site with 45 touring pitches and 12 statics.

Leisure: ⚓ 🏔 ▢ Facilities: 🖍☉🔧✳️📞🐕
Services: 🕹🖥🛢🚿🚽🚻
→ ∪ ▶ ✖ 🐕 ♪

CRAIGELLACHIE   Map 15 NJ24

▶ ▶ ▶ **Camping & Caravanning Club Site** (NJ257449)
Elchies AB38 9SD ☎ 01340 810414
Dir: From S leave A9 at Carrbridge, follow A95 to Grantown-on-Spey, leaving Aberlour on A941. Take next left turn B9102 signed Archiestown. Site 3m on left
★ 🚐 £11.80-£14.90 🚐 £11.80-£14.90 ⛺ £11.80-£14.90
Open all year Booking advisable bank hols & Jul-Aug Last arrival 21.00hrs Last departure noon
A rural site with views across meadowland towards Speyside, and the usual high Club standards. Please see the advertisement on page 14 for details of Club Members' benefits. A 7-acre site with 75 touring pitches.

Leisure: 🏔 Facilities: 🖍☉🔧✳️♿📞🐕
Services: 🕹🖥✖
→ ∪ ▶ ⛽ ♪ 🍴 💳 💳

FOCHABERS   Map 15 NJ35

▶ ▶ ▶ **Burnside Caravan Site** (NJ350580)
Keith Rd IV32 7PF ☎ 01343 820511 & 820362
Dir: Located 0.5m E of town off A96
🚐 🚐 ⛺
Open Apr-Oct Booking advisable Jul-Aug Last departure noon
Attractive site in tree-lined sheltered valley with footpath to the village. A 5-acre site with 110 touring pitches and 60 statics.

Leisure: 🎣 ⚓ 🏔 ▢ Facilities: 🖍☉📞🐕
Services: 🕹
→ ∪ ▶ ♪

LOSSIEMOUTH   Map 15 NJ27

▶ ▶ ▶ ▶ **Silver Sands Leisure Park** (NJ205710)
Covesea, West Beach IV31 6SP ☎ 01343 813262
Dir: From Lossiemouth follow B9040 2m W to site
★ 🚐 £8-£17.70 🚐 £8-£17.70 ⛺ £8-£12.20
Open Apr-Oct (rs Apr, May & Oct shops & entertainment restricted) Booking advisable Jul-Aug Last arrival 22.00hrs Last departure noon
A large holiday park with entertainment for all during the peak season, set on the links between the coast road and the shore of the Moray Firth. Touring campers and caravans are catered for in three areas: one offers de-luxe facilities including water, drainage, electricity and hard and grassed area, while the other areas are either unserviced or include electric hook-ups and water. A well-stocked shop sells holiday gear, and there is a clubroom and bar plus takeaway food outlet. The large amenity block is modern and well appointed. A 7-acre site with 140 touring pitches and 200 statics. Children's entertainment.

Leisure: 🎣 ⚓ 🏔 ▢ Facilities: 🛁🖍☉🔧✳️📞🏪🏓🍴🐕
Services: 🕹🖥🛢🅿️🛢♿🚽🚻✖🚿
→ ∪ ▶ ◎ ⛽ ✖ ♪ 🍴 💳 🚐 💳

NORTH LANARKSHIRE

MOTHERWELL   Map 11 NS75

► ► ► **Strathclyde Country Park Caravan Site** (NS717585)
366 Hamilton Rd ML1 3ED ☎ 01698 266155
Dir: Direct access to park from junct 5 of the M74
★ 🚐 £8.20 🚐 £8.20 ▲ £3.70-£7.10
Open Apr-Oct Booking advisable Jun-Aug Last arrival 22.30hrs Last departure noon
A level grass site situated in a country park amidst woodland and meadowland with lots of attractions. A large area caters for 150 tents, while 100 well-screened pitches, with electrics and some hardstandings are also available. 250 touring pitches.
Leisure: 🏊 Facilities: 🏪⊙🌳🚻🚿 Services: 🔌🗑💧🧺✗
➜ ∪ ► 🛒 🛶 ⚽ 🍴

PERTH & KINROSS

ABERFELDY   Map 14 NN84

► ► ► **Aberfeldy Caravan Park** (NN858495)
Dunkeld Rd PH15 2AQ
☎ 01887 820662 & 01738 475211
Dir: Located off A827 on E edge of town
🚐 🚐 ▲

Open late Mar-late Oct Booking advisable Jul-Aug Last arrival 20.00hrs Last departure noon
A very well-run site, with good facilities and some landscaping, at the eastern end of the town and lying between main road and banks of the River Tay. Good views of surrounding hills. A 5-acre site with 92 touring pitches and 40 statics.
Leisure: 🏊 Facilities: 🏪⊙🌳🚻🚿🛒🚿🐾
Services: 🔌🗑
➜ ► ▲ 🛶 💳 💷 📶 📋

AUCHTERARDER   Map 11 NN91

► ► ► **Auchterarder Caravan Park** (NN964138)
Nether Coul PH3 1ET ☎ 01764 663119
Dir: Take A824 from A9, S onto B8062 signed Dunning. 0.75m E of Auchterarder. Site 50yds on left
🚐 £8-£9 🚐 £8-£9 ▲ £6-£9

Open all year Booking advisable Jul-Aug Last arrival 22.00hrs Last departure noon
A small, level touring site, well-run and well-maintained. A 4-acre site with 23 touring pitches. Private fishing.
Facilities: 🏪⊙🌳🚻🚿🛒🚿🐾 Services: 🔌🛒🗑📋
➜ ∪ ► 🛶

BIRNAM   Map 14 NO04

► ► ► ► **Erigmore House Holiday Park** (NO036416)
PH8 9XX ☎ 01350 727236 & 727677
Dir: Situated off A9 on B898
🚐 🚐

Open Mar-Oct Booking advisable
Situated in the grounds of 18th-centruy Erigmore House, with its many unusual trees. The site is well-secluded from the main road. An 18-acre site with 26 touring pitches and 189 statics.
Facilities: 🏪⊙🌳🚻🚿🛒🚿 Services: 🔌🗑🍺💧🧺✗🚽
➜ ► 🛶 💳 💷 📶 📋

BLAIR ATHOLL   Map 14 NN86

PREMIER PARK

► ► ► ► ► **River Tilt Caravan Park** (NN875653)
PH18 5TE ☎ 01796 481467 & 0378 149184
Dir: 7m N of Pitlochry on A9, take B8079 to Blair Atholl & site at rear of Tilt Hotel
🚐 🚐 ▲
Booking advisable Jul-Aug Last arrival 21.00hrs Last departure 11.00hrs
An attractive grass park with magnificent views of the surrounding mountains, and careful landscaping and layout. This park is idyllically set in hilly woodland country on the banks of the River Tilt, next to golf course. The sanitation block is of an extremely high standard, with cubicled facilities for both sexes. Fully-serviced pitches are available along with plain grass or hardstandings. The park boasts a bistro and AA 2-rosette Loft Restaurant, a leisure complex with heated indoor swimming pool, sun lounge area, spa pool and gym. Outdoors there is a short tennis court. This park was Scottish winner of the Best Campsite of the Year Award for 2000. A 2-acre site with 37 touring pitches and 92 statics. Multi-gym, sauna & solarium. Steam room, spa pool.
Leisure: 🏊 🏊 🏊 Facilities: 🏪⊙🌳🚻🛒🚿🐾
Services: 🔌🗑🍺💧🧺🚽✗
➜ ∪ ► 🔵 🛶 🍴 💳 💷 💷 🔴 📶 📋

PREMIER PARK

► ► ► ► ► **Blair Castle Caravan Park** (NN874656)
PH18 5SR ☎ 01796 481263
Dir: From A9/B8079 junct at Aldclune, to Blair Atholl. Site on right after bridge
★ 🚐 £8-£10 🚐 £8-£10 ▲ £6.50-£10
Open Apr-late Oct Booking advisable bank hols & Jul-Aug Last arrival 21.30hrs Last departure noon   *contd.*

Attractive site set in impressive seclusion within the impressive Atholl estate, surrounded by mature woodland and the River Tilt. Although a large park, the various groups of pitches are located throughout the extensive parkland, and each has its own sanitary block with all-cubicled facilities of a very high standard. There is a choice of grass pitches, hardstandings, or fully-serviced pitches. This park is particularly suitable for the larger type of motorhome. A 32-acre site with 283 touring pitches and 112 statics.

Leisure: ♦ ⚠ ▢   Facilities: ⇥ ↿ ⊙ ۹ ₵ ⅃ ⅄ 戸 ⅄
Services: ▢ ⓢ ⓘ ∅ ⊞ ⇥
→ ∪ ▸ ⌡ ⊜ ▦ ⛴ ▩ ⓢ

BRIDGE OF CALLY   Map 15 NO15

▶ ▶ ▶ ▶ *Corriefodly Holiday Park (NO134513)*
PH10 7JG ☎ 01250 886236
Dir: Situated 150yds N of Bridge of Cally on A924
🚗 🚐 ⅄

Open early Dec-early Nov Booking advisable bank hols & Jul-Aug Last arrival 22.00hrs Last departure noon
A secluded park on the banks of the River Ardle, surrounded by mature woodland on all sides. The caravan pitches are all on terraced hardstandings with electric hook-ups, while tents are accommodated in a separate level field. The park boasts a bowling green, and fishing is available in the river. Other amenities include a licensed bar with an indoor games room. A 17.5-acre site with 38 touring pitches and 72 statics.
Bowling green & fishing on site.
Leisure: ♦ ⚠   Facilities: ↿ ⊙ ۹ ✲ ₵ ⅃ ⅄ 戸 ⅄
Services: ▢ ⓢ ⓘ ⓨ ∅
→ ⌡

COMRIE   Map 11 NN72

▶ ▶ ▶ *Twenty Shilling Wood Caravan Park (NN750218)*
PH6 2JY ☎ 01764 670411
Dir: 0.5m W of Comrie on A85 opposite 'Farm Food Restaurant'
🚗 🚐

Open 19 Mar-25 Oct Booking advisable bank holidays, Jul & Aug Last arrival 21.00hrs Last departure noon
A secluded and sheltered south-facing park with level, individual pitches all with electric and TV hook-ups. Tents not accepted. A 10.5-acre site with 26 touring pitches and 42 statics.
Leisure: ♦ ⚠   Facilities: ↿ ⊙ ۹ ✲ ₵ ⅄
Services: ▢ ⓢ ⓘ ∅ ⊞ ⓣ
→ ∪ ▸ ⌡ ⊜ ▦ ▩

CRIEFF   Map 11 NN82

▶ ▶ ▶ *Crieff Holiday Village (NN857225)*
Turret Bank PH7 4JN ☎ 01764 653513
Dir: 1m W of Crieff on A85
★ 🚗 £7-£9 🚐 £7-£9 ⅄ £6-£8
Open all year Booking advisable Jul-Aug Last arrival mdnt

Blair Castle
Caravan Park
BLAIR ATHOLL, PERTHSHIRE PH18 5SR
Tel: 01796 481263 Fax: 01796 481587

● 32 acre Park set amidst spectacular mountain scenery
● Grass and hard-standing mains serviced pitches
● 'Roll-On, Roll-Off' pitches
● Heated amenity blocks
● Spacious park and recreation areas
● Extensive woodland, hill and riverside walks
● Caravan Holiday Homes for hire
● Indoor Games Room and Television Lounge
● Situated in the grounds of Blair Castle (open to the public)
● Voted 'Readers' Choice' for Scotland by Practical Caravan in 1995, 1996, 1997 and 1999
● Pony trekking, golf; fishing, bowling, mountain bikes all available from the village of Blair Atholl

PLEASE WRITE OR TELEPHONE FOR OUR FREE COLOUR BROCHURE

A level site by the riverside, with smart refurbished toilets. A 3-acre site with 40 touring pitches and 40 statics.
Leisure: ♦ ⚠ ▢   Facilities: ↿ ⊙ ۹ ✲ ₵ ⅄ 🖪 ⅄
Services: ▢ ⓢ ⓘ ∅ ⊞ ⓣ
→ ∪ ▸ ⊙ ✲ ⌡ ⊜ ▦

DUNKELD   Map 14 NO04

See also **Birnam**
▶ ▶ ▶ *Inver Mill Farm Caravan Park (NO015422)*
Inver PH8 0JR ☎ 01350 727477
Dir: Turn off A9 onto B822 then immediately right to Inver
★ 🚗 £8-£9
Open Apr-Oct Booking advisable Jul-Aug Last arrival 22.00hrs Last departure noon
A peaceful park on level former farmland, located on the banks of the River Braan and surrounded by mature trees and hills. The active resident owners keep the park in very good condition. A 5-acre site with 65 touring pitches.
Facilities: ↿ ⊙ ۹ ✲ ₵ ₵   Services: ⓢ ⓘ ∅ ⊞
→ ▸ ⅄

INCHTURE   Map 11 NO22

▶ *Inchmartine Caravan Park & Nurseries (NO263277)*
Dundee Rd PH14 9QQ ☎ 01821 670212 & 686251
Dir: Main A90 Dundee to Perth road
★ 🚗 £9.50 🚐 £9.50 ⅄ £9.50
Open Mar-Oct Last arrival 20.00hrs Last departure noon

A quiet site with excellent toilet facilities. An 8-acre site with 45 touring pitches.
Golf range

Facilities: � ⊙ ੧ **Services:** ⊡
→ ∪ ⚍

KENMORE   Map 14 NN74

► ► ► ► **Kenmore Caravan & Camping Park**
(NN772458)
PH15 2HN ☎ 01887 830226
*Dir: A9 to Balliuluig, then W on A827 to Aberfeldy.
Proceed 6m to Kenmore*
🚐 £10-£11 🚐 £10-£11 ▲ £9-£10

Open mid Mar-Oct Booking advisable mid Jul-mid
Aug Last arrival 22.00hrs Last departure 14.00hrs
*A pleasant riverside site with an air of spaciousness
and a very good licensed bar/restaurant. Set on the
banks of the River Tay, it has good views of the
surrounding mountains, as well as offering on-site
river fishing; fishing in a nearby loch is also
available. The modern facilities include a laundry,
family bathrooms, and two children's playgrounds.
There is a par 70 golf course in the park. A 14-acre
site with 160 touring pitches and 60 statics.*
Cycle hire, 9-hole golf, games & TV room, fishing.

Leisure: ⊶ ✎ ⚑ ❏ **Facilities:** ↑⊙੧☀ᕲᏨ⚍ᛟ♔
Services: ⊡◙♀◗⊘⊞⊤✗⊞➡
→ ∪ ▶ ⚐ ⅄ ✦ 💳 ▤▤ ▨

KINLOCH RANNOCH   Map 14 NN65

► **Kilvrecht Campsite (NN623567)**
PH8 0JR ☎ 01350 727284
*Dir: 3m along the S shore of Loch Rannoch. Approach
via unclass road along Loch Shore with Forestry
Commission signs*
★ 🚐 £6 🚐 £6 ▲ £3-£6
Open Etr-Oct Last arrival 22.00hrs Last departure
10.00hrs
*A basic site in a large clearing in the forest, about
0.75 mile from Loch Rannoch shore, with no hot
water. A 17-acre site with 60 touring pitches.*

Facilities: ⚲ ☷ ♔
→ ⅄ ✦

PERTH   Map 11 NO12

► ► ► ► *Cleeve Caravan Park (NO097227)*
Glasgow Rd PH2 0PH ☎ 01738 639521 & 475211
*Dir: Adjacent to the A93 Perth to Glasgow road, 2m W
of Perth*
🚐 ▲

Open late Mar-late Oct Booking advisable Jul-mid
Aug Last arrival 21.00hrs Last departure noon
*Mature woodland surrounds this park which is
situated in a residential area of the city, and
consequently it retains the atmosphere of a rural
garden. The buildings and modern sanitary facilities
are maintained to a very high standard. The marked
pitches are on terraced levels or in a walled garden,
and the whole area is attractively landscaped with
shrubs and flowers. A 5.5-acre site with 100 touring
pitches.*
Free use of microwave.

Leisure: ⚑ **Facilities:** ↑⊙੧☀ᕲᏨ⚍ᛟ⌑☷♔
Services: ⊡◙♀◗⊘⊤➡
→ ∪ ▶ ◉ ⚐ ⅄ ♨ ✦ 💳 ▤▤ ▨ ▨

► ► ► **Camping & Caravanning Club Site**
(NO108274)
Scone Racecourse, Scone PH2 6BB ☎ 01738 552323
*Dir: Follow signs for Scone Palace. Once through
continue for 2m. Left following site signs. After 1m left
into Racecourse Rd. Site entrance from car park*
★ 🚐 £10.60-£13.90 🚐 £10.60-£13.90 ▲ £10.60-£13.90
Open 20 Mar-1 Nov Booking advisable bank hols &
peak periods Last arrival 21.00hrs Last departure
noon
*A sheltered site in wooded area adjacent to a
racecourse. Please see the advertisement on page
14 for details of Club Members' benefits. A 16-acre
site with 150 touring pitches and 20 statics.*
Recreation room. Table tennis.

Leisure: ✎ ⚑ **Facilities:** ↑⊙੧☀ᕲᏨ⚍♔
Services: ⊡◙♀◗⊘⊞⊤
→ ∪ ▶ ♨ ✦ 💳 ▤▤

PITLOCHRY   Map 14 NN95

► ► ► ► *Faskally Caravan Park (NN916603)*
PH16 5LA ☎ 01796 472007
Dir: 1.5m N of Pitlochry on B8019
🚐 🚐 ▲

Open 15 Mar-Oct Booking advisable Jul-Aug Last
arrival 23.00hrs
*A large park attractively divided into various
sections by mature trees, occupying a rural position
in gently-sloping meadowland beside the tree-lined
River Garry. The excellent amenities include a
leisure complex with heated indoor swimming pool,
sauna and steam room, bar, restaurant and indoor
amusements. There are extensive views of the
surrounding countryside, and this park is well*

contd.

Services: ⊤ Toilet Fluid ✗ Café/ Restaurant ⊞ Fast Food/Takeaway ➡ Baby Care ⊡ Electric Hook Up
◙ Launderette ♀ Licensed Bar ◗ Calor Gaz ⊘ Camping Gaz ⊞ Battery Charging

placed as a centre for touring, being close to but unaffected by the A9. A 23-acre site with 255 touring pitches and 65 statics.
Steam room, spa, sauna & mini golf.

Leisure: ↑ ◀ ⚠ **Facilities:** ⚲ ⊙ ♉ ✳ & ℓ ☎

Services: ⊡ ⬚ ♀ ⅃ ⬚ ⒯ ✕

→ ∪ ▶ ⌐ ⌡ 👄 🔲

▶ ▶ ▶ ▶ **Milton of Fonab Caravan Site (NN945573)**
Bridge Rd PH16 5NA ☎ 01796 472882
Dir: Located 0.5m S of town off A924
★ 🚐 £9.50-£10 🚎 £9.50-£10 ▲ £9.50-£10
Open Apr-Oct Booking advisable Jul-Aug Last arrival 21.00hrs Last departure 13.00hrs
Set on the banks of the River Tummel, this park offers extensive views down the river valley and the surrounding mountains. The flat, mainly grassed park offers level pitches, and is close to the centre of Pitlochry, and adjacent to the Pitlochry Festival Theatre. The sanitary facilities are of an exceptionally high standard, with most contained in combined shower/wash basin and toilet cubicles. The owner personally supervises the park, and maintains immaculate conditions throughout. A 12-acre site with 154 touring pitches and 36 statics.
Mountain bike hire, free trout fishing.

Facilities: ⚲ ⌐ ⊙ ♉ ✳ & ℓ ☎ ⚶ ⊀

Services: ⊡ ⬚ ⅃ ⬚

→ ∪ ⌐ ⊙ ✕ ⌡

▶▶▶▶
🌲

Faskally
Caravan Park

Pitlochry, Perthshire PH16 5LA
Tel: (01796) 472007 & 473202
Fax: (01796) 473896

This park is situated outside the town and on the banks of the River Garry, which is bordered on one side by the main road. It is on gently sloping grassland dotted with trees and with splendid views. Indoor Leisure Pool with Spa Bath, Sauna and Steam Room. Turn off A9 Pitlochry by-pass ½ mile north of town then proceed 1 mile north on B8019.
Bar and Restaurant.

E-mail: ehay@easynet.co.uk
Web: www.faskally.co.uk

TUMMEL BRIDGE   Map 14 NN75

Tummel Valley Holiday Park (NN764592)
PH16 5SA ☎ 01882 634221
Dir: From Perth take A9 N to bypass Pitlochry. 3m after Pitlochry turn onto B8019 signed to Tummel Bridge. Park in 11m along this road on left
★ 🚐 £7.40-£19.40 🚎 £7.40-£19.40
Open Apr-Oct Booking advisable bank hols & Jun-Aug Last arrival 21.00hrs Last departure 10.00hrs
Well-developed site amongst mature forest in this attractive valley. A 55-acre site with 37 touring pitches and 153 statics.
Bicycle hire, crazy golf, fishing rod hire.

Leisure: ↑ ◀ ⚠ **Facilities:** ⚲ ⌐ ⊙ ♉ ✳ & ℓ

⚶ ⬚ ⌂ **Services:** ⊡ ⬚ ♀ ✕ ⬚

→ ⅃ 👄 🔲 🔲 🔲 🔲 🔳

SCOTTISH BORDERS

BONCHESTER BRIDGE   Map 12 NT51

▶ ▶ ▶ *Bonchester Bridge Caravan Park (NT586123)*
Fernbank TD9 8JN ☎ 01450 860676
Dir: On A6088 N of village centre
🚐 🚎 ▲
Open Apr-Oct Booking advisable Jul-Aug Last arrival 22.00hrs Last departure noon
Neat level country village site close to Bure Water. A 3-acre site with 25 touring pitches.

Facilities: ⌐ ⊙ ✳ ℓ ⚶ ⬚ ⌂ ⊀ **Services:** ⊡ ℓ ⬚ ⊞

→ ⅃

COLDINGHAM   Map 12 NT96

▶ ▶ ▶ *Scoutscroft Holiday Centre (NT906662)*
St Abbs Rd TD14 5NB ☎ 018907 71338
Dir: From A1 take B6438 signed Coldingham & St Abbs & site on edge of Coldingham village
🚐 🚎 ▲
Open Mar-Oct Booking advisable bank hols & Jul-Aug Last arrival mdnt Last departure noon
A large grassy site on edge of village. 0.75m from the sea. A 16-acre site with 70 touring pitches and 120 statics.
Sub Aqua Centre.

Leisure: ◀ ⚠ ⌶ **Facilities:** ⌐ ⊙ ♉ ✳ & ℓ ⬚ ⬚ ⌂

Services: ⊡ ⬚ ♀ ⅃ ⬚ ⊞ ⒯ ✕ ⬚

→ ∪ ⌐ ▲ ⚌ ⅃ ⚶ 👄 🔲 🔲

ETTRICK VALLEY   Map 11 NT21

▶ ▶ ▶ **Honey Cottage Caravan Park (NT295164)**
Hope House TD7 5HU ☎ 01750 62246
Dir: Off B709
★ 🚐 fr £7.50 🚎 fr £7.50 ▲ fr £3
Open all year Booking advisable
This is a level, riverside site set in the remote and unspoilt Ettrick Valley. The site has modern facilities and is open twelve months a year. The

---

Facilities: ⚲ Bath ⌐ Shower ⊙ Electric Shaver ♉ Hairdryer ✳ Ice Pack Facility & Disabled Facilities ℓ Public Telephone
⚶ Shop on Site or within 200yds ⬚ Mobile Shop (calls at least 5 days a week) ⬚ BBQ Area ⌂ Picnic Area ⊀ Dog Exercise Area

enthusiastics owners are continually improving the site. A 3-acre site with 22 touring pitches and 40 statics.

Leisure: ⚠ Facilities: ♀⊙℄⚏⊼ Services: ☎◙🛢∅
→⤏

JEDBURGH   Map 12 NT62

▶ ▶ ▶ Camping & Caravanning Club Site (NT658219)

Elliot Park, Edinburgh Rd TD8 6EF ☎ 01835 863393
Dir: Entrance to site lies directly opposite the Edinburgh & Jedburgh Woollen Mills on the Northern side of Jedburgh on A68 Newcastle to Edinburgh Rd
★ ⊞ £9.80-£12.40 ⊞ £9.80-£12.40 ▲ £9.80-£12.40
Open 20 Mar-1 Nov Booking advisable bank hols & Jul-Aug Last arrival 21.00hrs Last departure noon
A touring site on northern edge of town, nestling at foot of cliffs close to Jed Water. Please see the advertisement on page 14 for details of Club Members' benefits. A 3-acre site with 55 touring pitches.

Facilities: ♀⊙℄☀⚘℄🛒 Services: ☎◙⊞
→∪▶⚠⤴⚏ ➲▦

▶ ▶ ▶ Jedwater Caravan Park (NT665160)

TD8 6PJ ☎ 01835 840219 & 7050 219219
Dir: Located 3.5m S of Jedburgh on A68
★ ⊞ £8-£9 ⊞ £8-£9 ▲ £8-£9
Open Etr-Oct Booking advisable high season Last arrival mdnt Last departure noon
A quiet riverside site ideal for touring Borders and Northumberland. A 10-acre site with 30 touring pitches and 60 statics.
Bike hire, trampoline, football field.

Leisure: ♠⚠❑ Facilities: ♀⊙℄☀℄⚏🛒⊼🛒
Services: ☎◙∅⊞Ⓣ
→∪▶⤴

KELSO   Map 12 NT73

▶ ▶ ▶ ▶ *Springwood Caravan Park (NT720334)*

TD5 8LS ☎ 01573 224596
Dir: Located on A699, signed Newton St Boswells
⊞⊞▲
Open end Mar-mid Oct Booking advisable bank hols & Jul-Aug Last arrival 23.00hrs
A very well-maintained site with a pleasant atmosphere, set in a secluded position on the banks of the tree-lined River Teviot about 1m west of town. The well-maintained mature parkland offers a

peaceful, spacious landscape in which to relax. The park is under the careful supervision of the owners, and offers a high standard of modern toilet facilities which are mainly contained in fully cubicled units with shower, washbasin and toilet. The park is close to the historic town of Kelso, and Floors Castle. A 4-acre site with 50 touring pitches and 260 statics.

Leisure: ♠⚠ Facilities: ♀⊙℄☀℄℄🛒
Services: ☎◙🛢
→∪▶⊙⚏⤴⚏ ➲▦▨

LAUDER   Map 12 NT54

▶ ▶ ▶ Camping & Caravanning Club Site (NT508533)

Carfraemill, Oxton TD2 6RA ☎ 01578 750697
Dir: From the town of Lauder, turn right at rdbt onto A697, then left at the Lodge Hotel. Site on the right behind Carfraemill Hotel
★ ⊞ £10.60-£13.90 ⊞ £10.60-£13.90
▲ £10.60-£13.90
Open 20 Mar-1 Nov
Meadowland site with facilities housed in pine lodge buildings, and pleasant surroundings. See advertisement on page 14 for details of Club Members benefits. 50 touring pitches.
Fishing

Leisure: ❑ Facilities: ♀⊙℄℄🛒 Services: ◙
→▶

▶ ▶ ▶ Thirlestane Castle Caravan & Camping Site (NT536473)

Thirlestane Castle TD2 6RU
☎ 01578 722254 & 0976 231032
Dir: Signed off A68 & A697, just S of Lauder
⊞ £8 ⊞ £8 ▲ £8
Open Apr-1 Oct Booking advisable Jul-Aug Last arrival anytime Last departure anytime   *contd.*

Services: Ⓣ Toilet Fluid ✗ Café/ Restaurant 🍟 Fast Food/Takeaway 🍼 Baby Care ☎ Electric Hook Up
◙ Launderette ♀ Licensed Bar 🛢 Calor Gaz ∅ Camping Gaz ⊞ Battery Charging

Mainly level grass site set in the grounds of the impressive Thirlestane Castle. A 5-acre site with 60 touring pitches.

Facilities: ⟁ ⊙ ↺ **Services:** ⊕ ⊡

→ ► ↲ ⚑

PEEBLES   Map 11 NT24

► ► ► ► Crossburn Caravan Park (NT248417)
The Glades, 95 Edinburgh Rd EH45 8ED
☎ 01721 720501
Dir: Situated 0.5m N of Peebles on A703
★ ⊞ £9-£10 ⊞ £8.50-£9.50 ⚑ £8-£10

Open Apr-Oct Booking advisable Jul-Aug Last arrival 22.00hrs Last departure 14.00hrs
A level site in a peaceful and relatively quiet location, despite the proximity of the main road which partly borders the site, as does the Eddleston Water. There are lovely views across the Edleston Valley, and the park is well stocked with trees, flowers and shrubs which lend it a particularly rural feel. Facilities are maintained to a high standard, and the site shop which is comprehensively stocked also keeps a large supply of caravan spares. Fully-serviced pitches are available, as well as a choice of grass or hard pitches. A 6-acre site with 35 touring pitches and 95 statics.
9-hole putting course & mountain bikes for hire.

Leisure: ⚲ ⋀ **Facilities:** ➔ ⟁ ⊙ ⦂ ⚹ ⚿ ↺ ⚑ ⊓ ☂
Services: ⊕ ⊡ ⚑ ⌀ ⊞ ⊤
→ ∪ ► ↲ ⬤ ▦ ▨ ⟳

► ► ► Rosetta Caravan & Camping Park (NT245415)
Rosetta Rd EH45 8PG ☎ 01721 720770
Dir: From N signed from A703, 1m S of Redscarhead, 2m N of Peebles
★ ⊞ £10-£10.50 ⊞ £10-£10.50 ⚑ £8-£9
Open Apr-Oct Booking advisable public & bank hols, Jul & Aug Last arrival 23.00hrs Last departure 15.00hrs
A pleasant parkland site set in hilly woodland country. The park offers good facilities and amenities which are well run and maintained. A 25-acre site with 160 touring pitches and 48 statics.
Bowling & putting greens.

Leisure: ⚲ ⋀ ⏣ **Facilities:** ⟁ ⊙ ⦂ ⚹ ↺ ⚑ ⊞ ☂
Services: ⊕ ⊡ ⚺ ⚑ ⌀ ⊞ ⊤
→ ∪ ► ⚹ ↲

SELKIRK   Map 12 NT42

► ► ► Victoria Park Caravan & Camping Park (NT465287)
Victoria Park, Buccleuch Rd TD7 5DN ☎ 01750 20897
Dir: From A707/A708 N of town, cross river bridge & take 1st left, then left again
⊞ £7.50-£8.50 ⊞ £7.50-£8.50 ⚑ £7.50-£8.50
Open Apr-Oct (rs 10-18 Jun site closed) Booking advisable Jul-Aug Last arrival 21.00hrs Last departure 14.00hrs
A consistently well-maintained site with good basic facilities forming part of public park and swimming pool complex close to River Ettrick. A 3-acre site with 60 touring pitches.
Mini gymnasium, sauna, sunbed.

Leisure: ⚲ ⋀ **Facilities:** ⟁ ⊙ ⦂ ⚹ ↺ ⚑ ▦ ⊡ ⊓ ☂
Services: ⊕ ⊡ ⓘ ✕
→ ∪ ► ↲

SOUTH AYRSHIRE

AYR   Map 10 NS32

► ► ► Heads of Ayr Leisure Park (NS300184)
Dunure Rd KA7 4LD ☎ 01292 442269
Dir: 5m S of Ayr on A719
★ ⊞ £9-£11.50 ⊞ £8-£10 ⚑ £8-£10
Open Mar-Nov Booking advisable bank hols & Jul-Aug Last arrival 23.30hrs Last departure 15.00hrs
A small family-run site with attractive, well-screened pitches, 0.5m from beach overlooking

HEADS OF AYR LEISURE PARK
Dunure Road, Ayrshire,
Scotland KA7 4LD
Tel: 01292 442269
Fax: 01292 500298

This park has been operated by The Semple family for over 30 years and caters for families and small parties. Entertainment to suit all ages. Activities close by include pony trekking, fishing, tennis, bowling, skating and golf. This site is an ideal base for your holiday.

Facilities: ➔ Bath ⟁ Shower ⊙ Electric Shaver ⦂ Hairdryer ⚹ Ice Pack Facility ⚿ Disabled Facilities ↺ Public Telephone
⚑ Shop on Site or within 200yds ⊡ Mobile Shop (calls at least 5 days a week) ▦ BBQ Area ⊓ Picnic Area ☂ Dog Exercise Area

Firth of Clyde. A new restaurant has been opened on the site. An 8-acre site with 36 touring pitches and 126 statics.

Leisure: ⚙ **Facilities:** ⬈⊙ℚ☀ℂ⚲ℾ
Services: ⊞⊟ℚⅈ∅⊞⊤✕⊯
➔∪▸⚌⤙

▶ ▶ ▶ **Windsor Holiday Park (NX216835)**
KA26 OPZ ☎ 01465 821355
Dir: On A714 between Newton Stewart & Girvan
⬛ £8.50-£9 ⬛ £8.50-£9 ⚠ £5-£8.50
Open all year (rs Nov-Feb open wknds only)
Booking advisable Jun-Aug Last arrival 22.00hrs
Last departure 16.00hrs
A small family-run site in a rural location, well-screened from A714 by small, mature trees. A 6-acre site with 30 touring pitches and 26 statics.
Leisure: ⚙ **Facilities:** ⬈⊙ℚ☀ℂ⊟⊞⊓ℾ
Services: ⊞ⅈ∅⊞⊤
➔▸⤙⚲ 💳 🔋 🔌

▶ ▶ ▶ **Sundrum Castle Holiday Park (NS405208)**
KA6 5JH ☎ 01292 570057
Dir: Set off A70
⬛ ⬛ ⚠
Open Mar-Oct Booking advisable all times Last arrival 23.30hrs Last departure 14.00hrs no cars by tents
A large family holiday centre, with plenty of on-site entertainment, just a 10 minute drive from the centre of Ayr. A 30-acre site with 52 touring pitches and 250 statics.
Amusement arcade.
Leisure: ⚑ ✎ ⚓ ⚙ ▢ **Facilities:** ⬈⊙ℚℂ⚲⊞
Services: ⊞⊟ℚⅈ✕⊯
➔∪▸⊙⚌⤙ 💳 🔋 🔋 🔌

▶ ▶ ▶ ▶ **The Ranch (NS286102)**
Culzean Rd KA19 8DU ☎ 01655 882446
Dir: Situated on left of B7023, 1m S of Maybole towards Culzean
★ ⬛ £8.45-£12.50 ⬛ £8.45-£12.50 ⚠ £5-£10
Open Mar-Oct & wknds in winter Booking advisable bank hols & Jul-Sep Last arrival 20.00hrs Last departure noon

A very attractive privately-run park with two distinct areas for statics and tourers, but all sharing the same excellent leisure facilities, including a heated indoor swimming pool. Touring pitches are fully serviced, and screened for privacy by shrubs and rose bushes. A 9-acre site with 40 touring pitches and 68 statics.
Mini gym, sauna & sunbed.
Leisure: ⚑ ✎ ⚙ **Facilities:** ⬈ℚ☀⚖ℂ⚲⊞ℾ
Services: ⊞⊟ⅈ⊞⊤
➔∪▸⊙↯⤙

▶ ▶ ▶ ▶ **Camping & Caravanning Club Site (NS247103)**
Culzean Castle KA19 8JX ☎ 01655 760627
Dir: From S on A77 turn L onto A719. Site 4m on left. From N on A77 turn right onto B7023. After 100yds turn left. Site 4m
★ ⬛ £11.80-£14.90 ⬛ £11.80-£14.90 ⚠ £11.80-£14.90
Open 20 Mar-1 Nov Booking advisable bank hols & Jul-Aug Last arrival 21.00hrs Last departure noon
A mainly level grass park with some gently sloping pitches and hard stands along the bed of an old railway, situated at the entrance to the castle and country park. The park is surrounded by trees on three sides and with lovely views over Culzean Bay. Please see the advertisement on page 14 for details of Club Members' benefits. A 10-acre site with 90 touring pitches.
Leisure: ⚙ **Facilities:** ⬈⊙ℚ☀⚖ℂ⊓ℾ
Services: ⊞⊟ⅈ∅⊤
➔∪▸⤙⚲ 💳 🔋

▶ ▶ ▶ **Middlemuir Park (NS439263)**
KA5 5NR ☎ 01292 541647
Dir: Located off B743 Ayr to Mauchline road
⬛ ⬛
Open Mar-Oct Booking advisable bank hols & Jul-Aug Last arrival 22.00hrs Last departure noon
A rural site in the partly-walled garden where Montgomerie House once stood. Set in rolling farmland. A 17-acre site with 25 touring pitches and 60 statics.
Leisure: ✎ ⚙ **Facilities:** ⬈⊙ℚ☀ℂℾ
Services: ⊞⊟∅⊞⊤
➔∪▸⤙

SOUTH LANARKSHIRE

▶ ▶ **Clyde Valley Caravan Park (NS868441)**
ML11 9TS ☎ 01555 663951 01698 357684
Dir: From Glasgow on A72, cross river bridge at Kirkfieldbank & site on left. From Lanark on A72, right at bottom of steep hill before going over bridge
⬛ ⬛ ⚠
Open Apr-Oct Booking advisable anytime Last arrival 23.00hrs Last departure noon

contd.

Scotland

Level, grass site with trees and bushes set in hilly country with access to river, adjacent to Clyde Walk footpath. A 5-acre site with 50 touring pitches and 115 statics.

Leisure: ⚖ **Facilities:** ⌂⊙⚲⌘ᴸ
Services: ⚑⊟ᵢ⊘⊞Ⓣ
→↻▶⌦♨⌿

STIRLING

PREMIER PARK

▶ ▶ ▶ ▶ ▶ **Trossachs Holiday Park**
(NS544976)
FK8 3SA ☎ 01877 382614
Dir: Access on E side of A81 1m S of junct A821
⚑ £9-£12 ⚑ £9-£12 ⚑ £9-£12
Open Mar-Oct Booking advisable anytime Last arrival 21.00hrs Last departure noon
An imaginatively designed terraced site offering a high degree of quality all round, with fine views across Flanders Moss. All touring pitches are fully serviced with water, waste, electricity and TV aerial, and customer care is a main priority. Set in 20 acres of ground within the Queen Elizabeth Forest Park, with plenty of opportunities for cycling off-road on mountain bikes, which can be hired or bought on site, Winner of Campsite of the Year for Scotland 2001. A 40-acre site with 45 touring pitches and 38 statics.

Cycle hire.
Leisure: ⚲⚖⌑ **Facilities:** ⌂⊙⚲☀ᴸ⚞⌘
Services: ⚑⊟ᵢ⊘⊞Ⓣ
→▶⌦♨⌿ ⬤⬛⬛⬛⬛ ⬛⬛ ⬛

▶ ▶ ▶ **Cobleland Caravan & Camping Site**
(NS531988)
FK8 3UX
☎ 01877 382392 (in season) & 0131 314 6505
Dir: On unclass road just off the A81, 1.5m S of Aberfoyle
★ ⚑ £7.50-£9 ⚑ £7.50-£9 ⚑ £7.50-£9
Open Etr-29 Oct Booking advisable bank hols & Jul-Aug Last arrival 20.00hrs Last departure noon
Set within the Queen Elizabeth Forest Park, this grass and tree-studded site offers seclusion, views, forest walks and free fishing on the River Forth which borders the camping area. An 8-acre site with 100 touring pitches.
Fishing & swimming in river.
Leisure: ⚖ **Facilities:** ⌂⊙⚲☀⚞ᴸ⚞⌘⌑
Services: ⚑⊘⊞Ⓣ
→↻▶⌦⌿ ⬤⬛⬛⬛⬛ ⬛⬛ ⬛

▶ ▶ ▶ *Auchenbowie Caravan & Camping Site*
(NS795880)
FK7 8HE ☎ 01324 823999
Dir: 0.5m S of junct 9 of the M9. Turn right off A872 for 0.5m, signposted
⚑ ⚑ ⚑

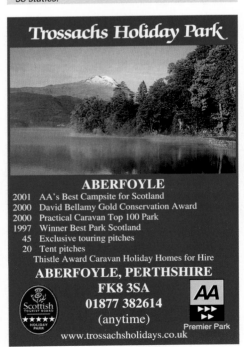

Trossachs Holiday Park

ABERFOYLE

2001	AA's Best Campsite for Scotland
2000	David Bellamy Gold Conservation Award
2000	Practical Caravan Top 100 Park
1997	Winner Best Park Scotland
45	Exclusive touring pitches
20	Tent pitches

Thistle Award Caravan Holiday Homes for Hire

ABERFOYLE, PERTHSHIRE
FK8 3SA
01877 382614
(anytime)
AA
▶▶▶
Premier Park
www.trossachsholidays.co.uk

Auchenbowie ▶▶▶
Caravan Site
by STIRLING FK7 8HE

Peaceful central situation in rural surroundings, offering an ideal base for touring. Pitches for caravans, motor caravans & tents. Electrical hook-ups available. Comfortable, well equipped static caravans for hire.

Open April to October

Rates on application.

Telephone: Denny (01324) 823999

Facilities: ⮩ Bath ⌂ Shower ⊙ Electric Shaver ⚲ Hairdryer ☀ Ice Pack Facility ⚞ Disabled Facilities ᴸ Public Telephone ⚞ Shop on Site or within 200yds ⊡ Mobile Shop (calls at least 5 days a week) ⌘ BBQ Area ⌑ Picnic Area ⌦ Dog Exercise Area

Open Apr-Oct Booking advisable mid Jul-mid Aug
Last departure noon
*A mainly level, grassy site in quiet rural location. A
3.5-acre site with 60 touring pitches and 7 statics.
Paddling pool.*
Leisure: ⚐ **Facilities:** ⚐⊙⚐⚐⚐⚐ **Services:** ⚐⚐⚐
→⚐⚐⚐⚐⚐⚐ ⚐⚐

BALMAHA   Map 10 NS49

▶ ▶ ▶ **Camping & Caravnning Club Site
(NN407927)**
Milarrochy Bay G63 0AL ☎ 01360 870236
*Dir: A811 Balloch to Stirling Rd, take Drymen turning. In
Drymen take B837 for Balmaha. After 5m road turns
sharp right up steep hill. Site 1.5m further on*
★ ⚑ £11.80-£14.90 ⚑ £11.80-£14.90 ▲ £11.80-£14.90
Open 20 Mar-1 Nov Booking advisable Last arrival
21.00hrs Last departure noon
*Situated on the quieter side of Loch Lomond next to
the 75,000 acre Queen Elizabeth Forest. Please see
advertisement on page 14 for details of Club
Members' benefits. A 14-acre site with 150 touring
pitches.*
Boat launching & fishing.
Leisure: ⚐ **Facilities:** ⚐⊙⚐⚐⚐⚐⚐⚐
Services: ⚐⚐⚐⚐⚐
→⚐⚐⚐ ⚐⚐

▶ ▶ ▶ **Cashel Caravan & Camping Site
(NS395940)**
G63 0AW
☎ 01360 870234 (in season) & 0131 314 6505
*Dir: Situated on the B837 Drymen to Rowardennan
road, 3m N of Balmaha*
★ ⚑ £7.50-£9.60 ⚑ £7.50-£9.60 ▲ £7.50-£9.60
Open Etr-Oct Booking advisable public hols & Jul-
Aug Last arrival 22.00hrs Last departure noon
*An attractive and well-wooded Forestry
Commission site, lying on the eastern shores of
Loch Lomond within the Queen Elizabeth Forest
Park, offering seclusion to campers and splendid
views over the loch. Caravanners should beware of
a steep hill at a sharp right turn when leaving
Balmaha. A 12-acre site with 100 touring pitches.*
Boating on Loch Lomond.
Leisure: ⚐ **Facilities:** ⚐⊙⚐⚐⚐⚐⚐⚐⚐⚐
Services: ⚐⚐⚐✕⚐
→⚐⚐⚐⚐ ⚐⚐⚐⚐⚐

CALLANDER   Map 11 NN60

▶ ▶ ▶ ▶ **Gart Caravan Park (NN643070)**
The Gart FK17 8LE ☎ 01877 330002
Dir: 1m E of Callander on A84
⚑⚑
Open Etr or Apr-15 0ct Booking advisable Bank Hols
& Jul/Aug Last arrival 22.00hrs Last departure noon
*A well-screened caravan park bordered by trees and
shrubs, near to the Queen Elizabeth Park amidst
ideal walking and climbing country. A feature of the
park is the careful attention to detail in the
maintenance of facilities, and the owners are very
helpful and friendly. A 25-acre site with 122 touring
pitches and 66 statics.*

Fishing on site.
Leisure: ⚐ **Facilities:** ⚐⊙⚐⚐⚐⚐⚐⚐
Services: ⚐⚐⚐
→⚐⚐⚐⚐⚐⚐ ⚐⚐⚐⚐⚐

LUIB   Map 10 NN42

▶ ▶ ▶ ▶ ▶ **Glendochart Caravan Park
(NN477278)**
FK20 8QT ☎ 01567 820637
Dir: 5m E of Crianlarich on the A85
⚑ £9.50-£10.50 ⚑ £9.50-£10.50 ▲ £9.50-£10.50
Open Etr-Oct Booking advisable Jul & Aug Last
arrival 22.00hrs Last departure noon
*A small, well-maintained site with imaginative
landscaping. Set on hillside in Glendochart with
glorious mountain and hill-country views. A new
sanitary block has transformed the facilities
here, and tree planting is part of an ongoing
programme of improvement. The site is well
located for trout and salmon fishing. A 7-acre
site with 45 touring pitches and 40 statics.*
Leisure: ⚐ **Facilities:** ⚐⊙⚐⚐⚐⚐⚐⚐⚐⚐
Services: ⚐⚐⚐⚐⚐⚐⚐
→⚐⚐⊙⚐⚐⚐ ⚐⚐⚐⚐

STIRLING

See **Auchenbowie**

Glen Dochart
Caravan Park

Luib, Crianlarich, Perthshire FK20 8QT
Tel: Killin (01567) 820637 Fax:(01567) 820024

A small, quiet touring and static holiday park,
nestling in the glen between Killin and
Crianlarich, overlooking the River Dochart.
Ideally situated for salmon & trout fishing,
hillwalking, exploring the central highlands or
just relaxing. The park offers cleanliness and
quality modern toilet, shower and launderette
facilities. Grass or hard level electric hook-up
touring pitches available.
Please telephone for brochure.

Scotland

Scotland

WEST DUNBARTONSHIRE

BALLOCH   Map 10 NS38

▶ ▶ ▶ ▶ *Tullichewan Holiday Park (NS383816)*
Old Luss Rd G83 8QP ☎ 01389 759475
*Dir: Turn right off A82, 17m N of Glasgow on to A811
Stirling to Balloch road. Park 0.25m in Balloch*
⌂ ⌂ Å
Open all year Booking advisable bank hols & Jul-
Aug Last arrival 22.00hrs Last departure noon
*A popular, well-equipped site at south end of Loch
Lomond with completely refurbished facilities.
Pitches are in well-laid out areas with good screens
of trees and shrubs, surrounded by woodland and
hills. There are two play areas and a games room.
Toilet facilities have been totally refurbished. The
park's main advantage is its location for touring this
delightful area. A 13-acre site with 120 touring
pitches and 35 statics.*
Leisure suite - sauna, spa bath, sunbeds.Bike hire.
Leisure: ♠ ⚒ ☐ **Facilities:** ➤ ♠ ⊙ ♋ ☀ ⟐ ⬡ ⬛ ☐ ♉
Services: ⬛ ⬛ ⬛ ⬛ ⬛ ⬛ ⬛
→ ∪ ▶ ⬡ ⤴ ⟋ ⬛ ⬛ ⬛ ⬛

WEST LOTHIAN

EAST CALDER   Map 11 NT06

▶ ▶ ▶ *Linwater Caravan Park (NT104696)*
West Clifton EH53 0HT ☎ 0131 333 3326
*Dir: Leave A720 to Wilkieston, turn N onto B7030, & left
in 1m onto unclass road signed Calder. Site 1m on the
right*
⌂ ⌂
Open late Mar-late Oct Booking advisable Last
arrival 21.00hrs Last departure 12.00hrs
*A farmland site in a peaceful rural area within easy
reach of Edinburgh, with very good modern
facilities. A 5-acre site with 60 touring pitches.*
Leisure: ⚒ **Facilities:** ♠ ⊙ ♋ ☀ ⟐ ⟍ ♉
Services: ⬛ ⬛
→ ∪ ▶ ⤴ ⟋ ⬛

ARRAN, ISLE OF

LAMLASH   Map 10 NS03

▶ ▶ ▶ *Middleton Caravan & Camping Park
(NS027301)*
KA27 8NN ☎ 01770 600251 & 600255
⌂ ⌂ Å
Open late Apr-mid Oct Booking advisable Jul-Aug
(for static caravans only) Last arrival 21.30hrs Last
departure noon no cars by caravans
*A grassy site sheltered by hills and mature trees,
with lovely views. Close to sea and village
amenities in a very pleasant location. A 3.5-acre site
with 70 touring pitches and 60 statics.*
Facilities: ♠ ⊙ ♋ ☀ ⟐ **Services:** ⬛ ⬛ ⬛ ⬛
→ ▶ ⬡ ⤴ ⟋

Middleton Caravan & Camping Park ▶▶▶

Lamlash, Isle of Arran
Telephone: (01770) 600251 or 600255

The park is flat and grassy, 5 minutes walk to the
village, shop, beach and most other amenities.
Laundry facilities on site. Electrical hook ups.

Open – 3rd week in April until mid October.

For hire – all modern caravans, fully serviced with
toilet, shower, fridge and TV. All mains electricity.
Gas cooking and heating. Caravans are fully
equipped.

LOCHRANZA   Map 10 NR95

▶ ▶ ▶ *Lochranza Caravan & Camping Site
(NR942500)*
KA27 8HL ☎ 01770 830273
*Dir: On A84 at N tip of island, beside Kintyre ferry and
14m M of Brodick for ferry to Ardrossan*
Open mid Mar-Oct
*Attractive park in a beautiful location, run by
friendly family owners. The park is adjacent to a 9-
hole golf course, opposite the famous Arran
Distillery between tree-lined hills on the edge of the
village. Golf and ferry packages can be arranged. A
2.5-acre site with 50 touring pitches.*

MULL, ISLE OF

CRAIGNURE   Map 10 NM73

▶ ▶ ▶ *Shieling Holidays (NM724369)*
PA65 6AY ☎ 01680 812496
*Dir: From the ferry, left onto A849 to Iona. After
400mtrs, left at the church, follow campsite signs
towards the sea*
★ ⌂ £10-£11.50 ⌂ £10-£11.50 Å £8.50-£11.50
Open Apr-Oct Booking advisable Spring bank hol &
Jul-Aug Last arrival 22.00hrs Last departure noon
*A lovely site on the water's edge with spectacular
views, and less than 1m from ferry landing. There is
a camper's shelter in a disused byre which is
especially popular in poor weather. Hardstandings
and service points are provided for motorhomes,*

---

and there are astro-turf pitches for tents. The park now offers bunkhouse accommodation for families. A 7-acre site with 30 touring pitches and 15 statics. Adventure playground, boat hire.

Leisure: ◆ ∧ ▢ Facilities: ⋔ ⊙ ⬛ ✳ ⬛ ⬛ ⬛ ⬛ ⬛ ⬛ ✝
Services: ⬛ ⬛ ⬛ ⬛
→ ▶ ⬛ ⬛ ⬛ ⬛ ⬛ ⬛ ⬛ ⬛ ⬛

FISHNISH   Map 10 NM64

▶ ▶ **Balmeanach Park (NM657415)**
PA65 6BA ☎ 01680 300342
Dir: On A849 Craignure to Tobermory road at Fishnish, 1m from Lochaline ferry landing & 6m from Craignure
★ ⚹ fr £9
Open Apr-Oct Booking advisable Last arrival 21.30hrs Last departure 11.00hrs
An attractive little park, family-run, set in 15 acres of woodland and well screened. Located at the rear of a tea room/nursery garden, but with its own touring toilet facilities, and some hardstands and electric points. A 1-acre site with 7 touring pitches.
Facilities: ⬛ ✳ ⬛ ⬛ ⬛ ✝ Services: ⬛ ⬛ ✕
→ ▶

SKYE, ISLE OF

EDINBANE   Map 13 NG35

▶ ▶ ▶ *Loch Greshornish Caravan Site (NG343524)*
Borve, Arnisort IV51 9PS ☎ 01470 582230
Dir: Situated by the loch-shore at Edinbane, approx 12m from Portree on A850 Dunvegan road
⬛ ⬛ ⚹
Open Apr-Oct Booking advisable Jul-Aug Last arrival 22.00hrs Last departure noon
A pleasant, open site, mostly level and with a high standard of maintenance. There is a campers' shelter in a disused byre which is especially popular in poor weather. A 5-acre site with 130 touring pitches.
Facilities: ⋔ ⊙ ⬛ ✳ ⬛ ✝ Services: ⬛ ⬛ ⬛
→ ∪ ⬛ ⬛

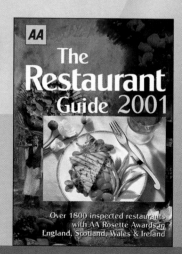
Services: ⊤ Toilet Fluid ✕ Café/ Restaurant ⬛ Fast Food/Takeaway ⬛ Baby Care ⬛ Electric Hook Up ⬛ Launderette ⬛ Licensed Bar ⬛ Calor Gaz ⬛ Camping Gaz ⬛ Battery Charging

Wales

WALES

ANGLESEY, ISLE OF

AMLWCH   Map 06 SH49

▶ ▶ **Point Lynas Caravan Park (SH474930)**
Llaneilan LL68 9LT ☎ 01407 831130 & 01248 852423
Dir: 1m N of Penysarn on A5025. Turn right at garage onto unclass road to Llaneilian. Site on left just before beach
★ 🚐 £6-£8 🚐 £6-£8 ▲ £5-£8
Open Mar-Oct Booking advisable bank hols Last arrival 22.00hrs Last departure noon
This very good site is near a sheltered rocky cove, safe for swimming.The facilities are always immaculate. A 2-acre site with 10 touring pitches and 44 statics.
Childrens sandpit & climbing bars.
Facilities: 🌬️⊙💧🍴🔭 **Services:** 🔌🔋⊘🖽
→▶🍴🔲🛒

BRYNSIENCYN   Map 06 SH46

▶ ▶ ▶ **Fron Caravan & Camping Park (SH472669)**
LL61 6TX ☎ 01248 430310
Dir: Off A4080 Llanfair to Newborough road, 1m W of Brynsiencyn
★ 🚐 fr £9 🚐 fr £9 ▲ fr £9
Open Etr-Sep Booking advisable Spring bank hol & Jul-Aug Last arrival 23.00hrs Last departure noon
Quiet family site in pleasant rural area, ideally situated for touring Anglesey and North Wales. A 5.5-acre site with 60 touring pitches.
Leisure: 🎣🌊⛰ **Facilities:** 🌬️⊙🍴🔭💧🛒🔭
Services: 🔌🔋⊘🖽⊤
→○▶🛒🔲

BRYNTEG   Map 06 SH48

▶ ▶ ▶ ▶ *Nant Newydd Caravan Park (SH485814)*
LL78 8JH ☎ 01248 852842 & 852266
Dir: Located 1m from Brynteg on B5110 towards Llangefni
🚐 🚐 ▲
Open Mar-Oct (rs May & Sep pool restricted)
Booking advisable Jul-Aug Last arrival mdnt Last departure 17.00hrs
Gently sloping grass site sheltered by mature trees and gorse bushes, set in meadowland in a small valley. The park is well landscaped with flower and shrub gardens and water features, and aims to cater for those seeking a quiet, restful holiday in near natural surroundings. A large heated swimming pool and small toddler pool are very popular, and the long sandy beach of Benllech is just three miles away. A 4-acre site with 30 touring pitches and 83 statics.
Satellite TV & licensed shop.
Leisure: 🎣🌊⛰🔲 **Facilities:** 🌬️⊙🔭🍴💧🛒🖽🔭🐾
Services: 🔌🔋🔋⊘🖽⊤
→○▶🔲🛒🐾🔲

▶ ▶ **Ysgubor Fadog Caravan & Camping Site (SH497820)**
Ysgubor Fadog, Lon Bryn Mair LL78 8QA
☎ 01248 852681
Dir: Turn off A5 onto A5025 for Benllech. After 7m turn left onto B5108. Outside 30mph limit take 3rd left turn. Site 400yds on right
★ 🚐 £6-£6.50 🚐 £6-£6.50 ▲ £5-£6.50
Open Etr-Sep Booking advisable Whitsun & school hols Last arrival 20.00hrs Last departure 18.00hrs
A peaceful and remote site reached along a narrow lane where care is needed. A 2-acre site with 15 touring pitches and 1 static.
Facilities: 🌬️⊙🔭🍴🔭 **Services:** 🔌🖽
→○▶⊘🔲🛒

DULAS   Map 06 SH48

▶ ▶ ▶ ▶ **Tyddyn Isaf Caravan Park (SH486873)**
Lligwy Bay LL70 9PQ ☎ 01248 410203
Dir: 0.5m off A5025 between Benllech & Amlwch
★ 🚐 £8-£13.50 🚐 £8-£13.50 ▲ £6-£11
Open Mar-Oct (rs Mar-Etr & Oct clubhouse limited, shut from mid Sept) Booking advisable May bank hol & Jun-Aug Last arrival 22.00hrs Last departure 11.00hrs
A beautifully-situated family park on gently rising ground adjacent to sandy beach, and with magnificent views overlooking Lligwy Bay. Access to the long sandy beach is by private footpath, or by car. Other footpaths along the coast lead to Dulas Bay and the small harbour village of Moelfre with its lifeboat station and seawatch centre. The park offers a superb toilet block, a well-stocked shop, and a clubhouse serving meals and takeaway food. A 16-acre site with 80 touring pitches and 50 statics.
Leisure: ⛰🔲 **Facilities:** 🌬️⊙🔭🍴💧🛒🔭🔭
Services: 🔌🔋♀🔋⊘🖽⊤✕🍴
→○▶🛒🐾✕🔲

Services: ⊤ Toilet Fluid ✕ Café/ Restaurant 🍴 Fast Food/Takeaway 🐾 Baby Care 🔌 Electric Hook Up
🔋 Launderette ♀ Licensed Bar 🔋 Calor Gaz ⊘ Camping Gaz 🖽 Battery Charging

Wales

ty newydd

►►►

LEISURE PARK

Proprietors: Mike & Gill Monger

Llanbedrgoch, Isle of Anglesey LL76 8TZ

Tel: 01248 450677 / 07071229148

Fax: 01248450 711

This small, select, family-run park is ideally situated for Benllech Bay with extensive views of Snowdonia. Facilities include licensed country club and restaurant serving meals for the family, well-equipped shop, excellent toilet facilities, free showers, disabled toilet, baby changing room, laundry room, children's playground and games room, heated outdoor swimming pool, health centre with spa, sauna, pool and gymnasium equipment, electric hook-ups and luxury fully-equipped caravans for hire.

Dogs on leads are welcomed.

Sailing, water skiing, fishing, climbing, walking, golf, pony trekking and safe sandy beaches are available on the island. 9 hole golf course within ½ mile.

LLANBEDRGOCH   Map 06 SH58

►►► **Ty Newydd Leisure Park (SH508813)**
LL76 8TZ ☎ 01248 450677 & 07071 229148
Dir: A5025 from Brittania Bridge. After passing through Pentraeth village bear left at layby. Site 0.75m along on the right
★ ⚑ £7-£19 ⚑ £7-£19 ▲ £7-£19
Open Whit-mid Sep (rs Mar-Whit & mid Sep-Oct club/shop wknds only outdoor pool closed) Booking advisable Etr, Whit & Jul-Aug Last arrival 23.30hrs Last departure 10.00hrs
A low density site with many facilities including a health centre. A 4-acre site with 40 touring pitches and 60 statics.
Health centre.
                See advertisement under BENLLECH BAY
Leisure: ⚐ ⚐ ⚑ ⚑ Facilities: ⚐⊙⚐☀⚑⚑⚑
Services: ⚑⚑⚑⚑⚑⚑⚑✕
→ ∪ ⚑ ⚑ ⚑ ⚑ ⚑ ⚑ ⚑ ⚑ ⚑ ⚑

MARIAN-GLAS   Map 06 SH58

►►►► **Home Farm Caravan Park (SH498850)**
LL73 8PH ☎ 01248 410614
Dir: Located on A5025, 2m N of Benllech, with park entrance 300mtrs beyond church
⚑⚑▲
Open Apr-Oct Booking advisable bank hols Last arrival 21.00hrs Last departure noon
A first class park with friendly, helpful owners. Home Farm is in an elevated and secluded position, sheltered by trees in a peaceful rural setting with

views of farmland, sea and the mountains of Snowdonia. The modern toilet block has helped it to win numerous awards, and there are excellent play for children both indoors and out. The area is blessed with sandy beaches, and local pubs and shops cater for everyday needs. A 6-acre site with 61 touring pitches and 72 statics.
Indoor adventure playground.
Leisure: ⚐⚑⚑ Facilities: ⚐⊙⚐☀⚑⚑⚑⚑⚑⚑
Services: ⚑⚑⚑⚑⚑⚑
→ ∪ ⚑ ⚑ ⚑ ⚑ ⚑ ⚑ ⚑ ⚑ ⚑

PENTRAETH   Map 06 SH57

►►► **Rhos Caravan Park (SH517794)**
Rhos Farm LL75 8DZ ☎ 01248 450214
Dir: Site located on left of A5025, 1m N of Pentraeth
⚑⚑
Open Etr-Oct (rs Mar shop & showers restricted) Booking advisable Spring bank hol & Jul-Aug Last arrival 22.00hrs Last departure 16.00hrs
Site on level, grassy ground off main road to Amlwch. A 15-acre site with 98 touring pitches and 60 statics.
Leisure: ⚑ Facilities: ⚐⊙☀⚑⚑⚑⚑
Services: ⚑⚑⚑⚑⚑⚑
→ ∪ ⚑ ⚑ ⚑ ⚑ ⚑

RHOSNEIGR   Map 06 SH37

►► **Ty Hen (SH323737)**
Station Rd LL64 5QZ ☎ 01407 810331
Dir: In Anglesey, on A5 take A4080 to Rhosneigr & park on left beyond railway bridge
⚑⚑▲
Open Mar-Oct Booking advisable Bank Holidays Last arrival 21.00hrs Last departure 11.00hrs
Attractive seaside position near large fishing lake and riding stables, in lovely countryside. Very friendly and considerate owners. A 7.5-acre site with 38 touring pitches and 41 statics.
Fishing, riding & beach.
Leisure: ⚐⚑⚑⚑ Facilities: ⚐⚑☀⚑⚑ Services: ⚑⚑
→ ∪ ⚑ ⚑ ⚑

CAERPHILLY

OAKDALE   Map 03 ST19

►►► **Penyfan Caravan & Leisure Park (SO189012)**
Manmoel Rd NP2 0HY ☎ 01495 226636
Dir: From junct 28 of the M4 follow A467 to Crumlin, turn left onto B4251 & follow signs towards site
⚑⚑▲
Open all year Booking advisable bank hols
A constantly improving site with good facilities for the whole family, including a licensed bar with bar meals. A 4-acre site with 75 touring pitches and 12 statics.

Facilities: 🛁 Bath ⚐ Shower ⊙ Electric Shaver ⚐ Hairdryer ☀ Ice Pack Facility ⚑ Disabled Facilities ⚑ Public Telephone
⚑ Shop on Site or within 200yds ⚑ Mobile Shop (calls at least 5 days a week) ⚑ BBQ Area ⚑ Picnic Area ⚑ Dog Exercise Area

Leisure: ♦ /△ □ Facilities: ľ ⊙ ※ ⅃ 悥 ⊞ ⼱
Services: ⚡ ⊡ ⚲ ✗ 墨
→ ▸ ☎ ⤙ ⅃ ⚡ ▦

CARDIFF

CARDIFF   Map 03 ST17

▶ ▶ ▶ ▶ **Cardiff Caravan Park (ST171773)**
Pontcanna Fields CF1 9JJ ☎ 029 20398362 20445919
Dir: Turn off M4 onto A48 through Cardiff. Turn left at lights at Llandaff & follow signs to Sophia Gardens & the Welsh Institute of Sport
⚡ £14.10 ⤙ £14.10 ▲ £6
Open all year Booking advisable Last arrival telephone Last departure noon
An excellent site with good amenities, and very close to centre of Cardiff. A 2-acre site with 95 touring pitches.
Facilities: ľ ⊙ ⚲ ⅃ ⚡ Services: ⚡ ⊡ ▮
→ ∪ ▸ ◎ ⚴ ⅃ ☎ ⌙

CARMARTHENSHIRE

LAUGHARNE   Map 02 SN31

▶ ▶ ▶ *Ants Hill Caravan Park (SN299118)*
SA33 4QN ☎ 01994 427293 & 427355
Dir: On A4066 entrance is on minor road to left
⚡ ⤙ ▲
Open Etr-Oct Booking advisable Jul-Aug & public hols Last arrival 23.00hrs Last departure 10.30hrs
A small, well-run touring site on sloping grass, located near the village, on the Taff estuary. Care should be taken on descent into Laugharne. A 4-acre site with 60 touring pitches and 60 statics.
Leisure: ⚘ ♦ /△ □ Facilities: ľ ⊙ ⚲ ⅃ ⚡
Services: ⚡ ⍰ ▮ ⌀ ⊞ ☎ 墨
→ ∪ ▸ ⅃ ⊡

LLANDDEUSANT   Map 03 SN72

▶ ▶ **Black Mountain Caravan & Camping Park (SN773259)**
SA19 9YG ☎ 01550 740621
Dir: Left off A40 at Trecastle, then right at Cross Inn
★ ⚡ £5-£6.50 ⤙ £5-£6.50 ▲ £4-£5

Open all year Booking advisable bank hols Last arrival 22.00hrs Last departure 10.30hrs
A very pleasant small site in a secluded position. A 5-acre site with 40 touring pitches and 20 statics.
Facilities: ľ ⊙ ⚲ ※ ⚡ Services: ⚡ ▮ ⌀ ☎
→ ⌙ ⤙ ▦ ▦ ⌙

LLANDOVERY   Map 03 SN73

▶ ▶ **Erwlon Caravan & Camping Park (SN776343)**
Brecon Rd SA20 0RD ☎ 01550 720332
Dir: 1m E of Llandovery alongside A40
★ ⚡ fr £6 ⤙ fr £6 ▲ fr £6
Open all year (rs Oct-Apr Limited pitches) Booking advisable bank hols Last arrival anytime Last departure noon
Long established family-run site set beside a brook in the Brecon Beacons foothills. An 8-acre site with 40 touring pitches.
Leisure: /△ Facilities: ľ ⊙ ⚲ ※ 悥 ⅃ ⚡ ⊞ ⼱
Services: ⚡ ⍰ ▮ ⌀ ⊞
→ ∪ ▸ ⌙

LLANGADOG   Map 03 SN72

▶ ▶ ▶ **Abermarlais Caravan Park (SN695298)**
SA19 9NG ☎ 01550 777868 & 777797
Dir: On A40 6m W of Llandovery
⚡ £7.50 ⤙ £7.50 ▲ £7.50
Open 15 Mar-15 Nov (rs Nov, Dec & Mar 1 wc, water point no hot water if frosty) Booking advisable bank hols & 15 Jul-Aug Last arrival 23.00hrs Last departure noon
An attractive, well-run site with a welcoming atmosphere. Set on grass in a wooded valley on edge of Brecon Beacons National Park, beside the River Marlais. A 17-acre site with 88 touring pitches.
Volleyball, badminton court & softball tennis net.
Leisure: /△ Facilities: ľ ⊙ ※ ⅃ ⚡ ⼱
Services: ⚡ ▮ ⌀ ⊞ ☎
→ ∪ ⌙

NEWCASTLE EMLYN   Map 02 SN34

▶ ▶ ▶ ▶ ▶ **Cenarth Falls Holiday Park (SN265421)**
Cenarth SA38 9JS ☎ 01239 710345
Dir: Off A484 on outskirts of Cenarth
⚡ £8-£15 ⤙ £8-£15 ▲ £8-£15

contd.

Wales

Open Mar-9 Jan (rs Mar-mid May & mid Sep-9 Jan swim pool closed, clubhouse wknds only) Booking advisable bank hols & Jul-Aug Last arrival 20.00hrs Last departure 11.00hrs
A very well run park with excellent facilities, in a spectacular setting overlooking the River Teifi cascading through the Cenarth Falls gorge. Beautifully landscaped, with a heated pool and country club. A 2-acre site with 30 touring pitches and 89 statics.
Club with bar meals, pool table, video games.
Leisure: 🎣 ♠ ⚙ Facilities: 🖍⊙🔍✳&🌙🍴🐾
Services: 🔌🖪🍴♿🚿⚑🅱🛢🇹
→🍽🍴♨ 🚬🚆🎦🕹

▶ ▶ ▶ ▶ **Afon Teifi Caravan & Camping Park (SN338405)**
Pentrecagal SA38 9HT ☎ 01559 370532
Dir: Signed off A484, 2m E of Newcastle Emlyn
★ 🚐 £7-£8 🚐 £7-£8 ▲ £7-£8
Open Apr-Oct (rs Nov-Mar when facilities limited, no toilet block) Booking advisable peak periods Last arrival 23.00hrs
A very attractive and well-managed park in the depths of the unspoilt and secluded Teifi Valley, alongside the famous salmon and trout river itself. Toilet facilities are of a high standard, and include a laundry room with washing, drying and ironing. A pub serving bar meals and a shop are within 100 metres of the park entrance. A 6-acre site with 110 touring pitches and 3 statics.
15 acres of woodland, fields & walks.
Leisure: ♠ ⚙ Facilities: 🚮🖍⊙🔍✳&🌙🍴🖼🏕🐾
Services: 🔌🖪🛢♿🅱🇹
→🍴📐♨🍴

RHANDIRMWYN   **Map 03 SN74**
▶ ▶ ▶ ▶ **Camping & Caravanning Club Site (SN779435)**
SA20 0NT ☎ 01550 760257
Dir: From Llandovery take A483 left at sign 'Rhandirmwyn 7', left at Post Office. Site on left before river
★ 🚐 £11.80-£14.90 🚐 £11.80-£14.90 ▲ £11.80-£14.90
Open 20 Mar-1 Nov Booking advisable bank hols & peak periods Last arrival 21.00hrs Last dep noon
On the banks of the Afon Tywi near Towy Forest and the Llyn Brianne reservoir, this first class site has superb views on all sides. Please see the advertisement on page 14 for details of Club Members' benefits. An 11-acre site with 90 touring pitches.

Leisure: ⚙ Facilities: 🖍⊙🔍✳&🌙🍴🐾
Services: 🔌🖪🛢🇹
→🍴🚬🚆🕹🍴

CEREDIGION

ABERAERON   **Map 02 SN46**
▶ ▶ ▶ **Aeron Coast Caravan Park (SN462633)**
North Rd SA46 0JF ☎ 01545 570349
Dir: On A487 coastal road on northern edge of Aberaeron. Filling station at entrance
🚐 £8-£11 🚐 £8-£11 ▲ £8-£11
Open Mar-Oct Booking advisable bank & school hols Last arrival 23.00hrs Last departure noon
A large site sloping gently towards the sea, run by enthusiastic owners. A 22-acre site with 50 touring pitches and 150 statics.
Indoor leisure rooms & entertainment hall
Leisure: 🎣 🎾 ♠ ⚙ 🖵 Facilities: 🖍⊙✳&🌙🍴
Services: 🔌🖪🛢♿🅱🇹🛁
→🍴⊙♨💲🍴 🚬🚆 🕹

ABERYSTWYTH   **Map 06 SN58**
▶ ▶ ▶ **Ocean View Caravan Park (SN592842)**
North Beach, Clarach Bay SY23 3DT
☎ 01970 828425 & 623361
Dir: Turn off A487 in Bow Street. Follow road to X-roads and carry on straight ahead. Ocean View is 2nd on right
★ 🚐 £6.50-£9.50 🚐 £6.50-£9.50 ▲ £6-£9
Open Apr-Oct (rs March Statics only) Booking advisable bank hols Last arrival 22.00hrs Last departure noon
A neat and tidy site on gently sloping ground in a sheltered valley with views to the sea. A 9-acre site with 24 touring pitches and 50 statics.
Leisure: ⚙ Facilities: 🖍⊙✳🍴🌙🍴🖼🐾
Services: 🔌🛢🅱🇹
→🍴⊙🚬🍴🍴🖪

BETTWS EVAN   **Map 02 SN34**
▶ ▶ ▶ *Pilbach Caravan Park (SN306476)*
SA44 5RT ☎ 01239 851434
Dir: S on A487, turn left onto B4333
🚐 🚐 ▲
Open Mar-Oct (rs Mar-Spring bank hol & Oct swimming pool closed) Booking advisable Spring bank hol & Jul-Aug Last arrival 22.00hrs Last departure 10.30hrs

Facilities: 🚮 Bath 🖍 Shower ⊙ Electric Shaver 🔍 Hairdryer ✳ Ice Pack Facility & Disabled Facilities 🌙 Public Telephone
🍴 Shop on Site or within 200yds 🅱 Mobile Shop (calls at least 5 days a week) 🖼 BBQ Area 🏕 Picnic Area 🐾 Dog Exercise Area

An exceptionally well-run small site set in secluded countryside. A 3-acre site with 65 touring pitches and 70 statics.
Leisure: ૨ ♣ ∕瓜 Facilities: ꭇ ⊙ ℛ ✳ ୧ ㏓ ㋡
Services: ⊞ 🖥 ♀ 📱 ⌀ 🛄 🅃 ✗ ⏧
→ ∪ ▶ △ ㋐ ↗ ⬤ ⇶ ▦ 🐾 ⬚

Wales

Leisure: ◣ ⚂ Facilities: ⋔⊙❋ℂ⊡⋔ ⊩
Services: ⊡⒝⊻⋔ℰ⊡✕
➔ ∪ ⋏ ⬥⋏ ⛺ ⤳ ⊾ ⬤ ⨯ ⧯ ⧉ 🌀

PENBRYN   Map 02 SN25

▶ ▶ ▶ ▶ Talywerydd Touring Caravan &
Camping Park (SN297507)
SA44 6QY ☎ 01239 810322
*Dir: Take 2nd turn off A487 signed Penbryn, & site
500yds on left*
★ ⬤ £7-£11.50 ⬤ £7-£11.50 ▲ £7-£11.50
Open Mar-Oct Booking advisable bank hols & Jul-
Aug Last arrival 22.00hrs Last departure 11.00hrs
*A small family park for the discerning visitor, with
sea views from every corner. All the usual facilities
are available to the individual pitches, and away from
the living areas there is a playing field for football
and other games. A popular club room serves meals,
and there is a covered, heated swimming pool. A
coastal path leads to attractive local hamlets and
villages, and a lane leads down to the sea at
Penbryn. A 4-acre site with 40 touring pitches.*
9-hole pitch & putt, microwave available
Leisure: ⚲ ◣ ⚂ ❑ Facilities: ⋔⊙❋ℂ⊾⊞⋔⊩
Services: ⊡⒝⊻⋔ℰ⊡✕⋔ ⬥
➔ ∪ ⋏ ⬤ ⬥⋏ ⤳ ⬤⧯ 🌀

CONWY

ABERGELE

See **Betws-Yn-Rhos**

BETWS-YN-RHOS   Map 06 SH97

▶ ▶ ▶ Hunters Hamlet Caravan Park (SH928736)
Sirior Goch Farm LL22 8PL
☎ 01745 832237 & 0421 552106
*Dir: A547 into Abergele. Straight through lights and 1st
left onto A548. After 2.75m right at X-roads B5381. Site
0.5m on left*
⬤ £9-£19 ⬤ £8-£10
Open 21 Mar-Oct Booking advisable bank hols &
Jul-Aug Last arrival 22.00hrs Last departure noon
*A delightful little site next to the owners' Georgian
farmhouse. An excellent purpose-built toilet block
with good quality fittings and furniture. A 2-acre site
with 23 touring pitches.*
Leisure: ◣ ⚂ Facilities: ⇥⋔⊙⚴❋⊾ℂ⋔⊩
Services: ⊡⒝⊡
➔ ⋏⤳⊾ ⬤⧯⧉ 🌀

CONWY   Map 06 SH77

▶ ▶ ▶ Conwy Touring Park (SH779757)
Trefriw Rd LL32 8UX ☎ 01492 592856
Dir: 1.5m S on B5106
⬤ £4.85-£11.08 ⬤ £4.85-£11.08 ▲ £4-£11.08
Open Etr-Sep Booking advisable public hols & Jul-
Aug Last arrival 19.00hrs Last departure noon
*An excellent site, with informally sited pitches set
high up above the Conway Valley, and a good range
of facilities. A 70-acre site with 319 touring pitches.*

Indoor playground monitored by staff.
Leisure: ◣ ⚂ Facilities: ⋔⊙❋⊾ℂ⬥⋔
Services: ⊡⒝⊻⋔ℰⓣ
➔ ∪ ⋏ ⛺ ⤳ ⬤⧯⧉ 🌀

LLANDDULAS   Map 06 SH97

▶ ▶ ▶ ▶ Bron Y Wendon Caravan Park
(SH904786)
Wern Rd LL22 8HG ☎ 01492 512903
*Dir: Take A55 W. Turn right at sign for A547, then sharp
right. Continue 200yds under A55 bridge. Park is on the
left*
⬤ £9-£11 ⬤ £9-£11
Open 21 Mar-30 Oct Booking advisable bank hols
Last arrival anytime Last departure 11.00hrs
*A good quality site with sea views from every pitch
and excellent purpose-built ablution block. An 8-
acre site with 130 touring pitches.*
Leisure: ◣ ❑ Facilities: ⋔⊙⚴❋⊾ℂ⬥⋔⊩
Services: ⊡⒝⊡
➔ ∪ ⋏ ⬤ ⬥⋏ ⤳ ⬤⧯⧉ 🌀

LLANRWST   Map 06 SH86

▶ ▶ ▶ Bodnant Caravan Site (SH805609)
Nebo Rd LL26 0SD ☎ 01492 640248
*Dir: S in Llanrwst, turn off A470 opposite Birmingham
garage for B5427 signed Nebo. Site 300yds on right,
opposite leisure centre*
⬤ £7-£9 ⬤ £7-£9 ▲ £7-£9

Facilities: ⇥ Bath ⋔ Shower ⊙ Electric Shaver ⚴ Hairdryer ❋ Ice Pack Facility ⊾ Disabled Facilities ℂ Public Telephone
⊾ Shop on Site or within 200yds ⊡ Mobile Shop (calls at least 5 days a week) ⊞ BBQ Area ⋔ Picnic Area ⊩ Dog Exercise Area

Open Mar-end Oct (rs Mar 1 toilet block open if weather very bad) Booking advisable Etr, May Day, Spring bank hol & Jul-Aug Last arrival 22.00hrs Last departure 11.00hrs
Small, well-maintained, level touring site. Twelve times winner of 'Wales in Bloom' competition for best kept touring caravan site in Wales. A 5-acre site with 54 touring pitches and 2 statics.
Leisure: ⚖ Facilities: ╟⊙℞✻╘⊡⌂
Services: ⊠🖩⌀⊞
→╟⅄⌿⊡⅋

TAL-Y-BONT (Near Conwy)   Map 06 SH76

▶ **Tynterfyn Touring Caravan Park (SH768692)**
LL32 8YX ☎ 01492 660525
Dir: 5m S of Conwy on B5106, road sign Tal-y-Bont, 1st on left
🚐 fr £5.30 🚐 fr £5.30 Å fr £5
Open Mar-Oct Booking advisable bank hols & Jul-Aug Last arrival 22.00hrs Last departure noon
Small, family site on level ground situated in the lovely Conwy Valley. A 2-acre site with 15 touring pitches.
Leisure: ⚖ Facilities: ╟⊙℞✻⌂
Services: ⊠🖩⌀⊞
→∪⅄⌿⅋

TOWYN (Near Abergele)   Map 06 SH97

▶ ▶ ▶ **Ty Mawr Holiday Park (SH965792)**
Towyn Rd LL22 9HG ☎ 01745 832079
Dir: On A548, 0.25m W of town
🚐🚐 Å
Open Etr-Oct (rs Apr (excluding Etr)) Booking advisable at all times Last departure 10.00hrs
A well laid out coastal site with very good leisure facilities. An 18-acre site with 348 touring pitches and 352 statics.
Free evening entertainment
Leisure: ⌇ ♦ ⚖ Facilities: ╟⊙℞✻⅋⌂℣⌂
Services: ⊠🖩℣⌀✕⅏
→∪⅄ 🔲🔳

TREFRIW   Map 06 SH76

▶ ▶ ▶ **Plas Meirion Caravan Park (SH783630)**
Gower Rd LL27 ORZ ☎ 01492 640247
Dir: On B5106, turn left opposite Woollen Mill, site 200mtrs on left
★ 🚐 £7.50-£10 🚐 £7.50-£10
Open Etr-Oct Booking advisable school hols Last arrival 22.00hrs Last departure 10.30hrs ✗
A small select park in the garden of the owner's house, set in the Conwy Valley and with mature trees. A 2-acre site with 5 touring pitches and 26 statics.
Facilities: ➡╟⊙℞✻⅋⌂ Services: ⊠🖩🖩⊞
→∪⅄⅄⅋

CORWEN   Map 06 SJ04

▶ ▶ **Glan Ceirw Caravan Park (SJ067454)**
Ty Nant LL21 0RF ☎ 01490 420346
Dir: 500yds off main A5, on unclassified loop road between Corwen & Betws-y-Coed. 1.5m from Cerrigydrudion
★ 🚐 £5-£10.25 🚐 £5-£10.25 Å £5-£8
Open Mar-Oct Booking advisable bank hols & Jul-Sep Last departure noon no cars by tents
A small riverside site in a rural location. A 4.5-acre site with 15 touring pitches and 29 statics.
Leisure: ♦ ⚖ ⌂ Facilities: ╟⊙✻⅋⏚⊟⌂
Services: ⊠℣🖩⌀⊞
→⅄⌿⅋

▶ ▶ **Llawr-Betws Farm Caravan Park (SJ016424)**
LL21 0HD ☎ 01490 460224 & 460296
Dir: 3m W of Corwen off A494 Bala road
★ 🚐 £6-£8 🚐 fr £6 Å £5-£10
Open Mar-Oct Booking advisable bank hols & Jul-Aug Last arrival 23.00hrs Last departure noon
Mainly level site with grass and mature trees. A 2.5-acre site with 35 touring pitches and 72 statics. Fishing.
Leisure: ♦ ⚖ Facilities: ╟⊙℞✻⅋⌂⊟⏚⌂
Services: ⊠🖩🖩⌀⊞⊤
→∪╟⅄⅏⅋

LLANDRILLO   Map 06 SJ03

▶ ▶ ▶ **Hendwr Caravan Park (SJ035386)**
Tyddyn Hendwr LL21 0SN ☎ 01490 440210 & 440252
Dir: From Corwen (A5), take B4401 for 4m. Turn right at sign for Hendwr. Site 0.5m down wooded driveway on the right
★ 🚐 £8 🚐 £8 Å £8
Open Apr-Oct (rs Nov-Mar no toilet facilities during this period) Booking advisable bank & school hols Last arrival 22.00hrs Last departure 16.00hrs
Level grass site with mature trees near river, hills, woods and moorland. A 10-acre site with 40 touring pitches and 80 statics.
Wet weather camping facilities.
Facilities: ╟⊙℞✻⅋⌂ Services: ⊠🖩🖩⌀⊞⊤
→∪⅋

LLANGOLLEN   Map 07 SJ24

▶ ▶ ▶ **Ty-Ucha Caravan Park (SJ232415)**
Maesmawr Rd LL20 7PP ☎ 01978 860677
Dir: 1m E of Llangollen. Signposted 250yds off A5
🚐 £7.50 🚐 £6.50
Open Etr-Oct (rs Mar toilet block closed) Booking advisable public hols Last arrival 22.00hrs Last departure 14.00hrs
A very well-run site in beautiful surroundings conveniently placed close to A5. Ideal for country and mountain walking, with small stream on its southern boundary. A 4-acre site with 40 touring pitches.
Leisure: ♦ Facilities: ╟⊙✻ Services: ⊠🖩⌀⊞⊤
→∪╟⅄⌿⊡⅋

Wales (side tab)

Wales

RHUALLT   Map 06 SJ07

▶ ▶ *Penisar Mynydd Caravan Park (SJ093770)*
Caerwys Rd LL17 0TY ☎ 01745 582227
*Dir: 2m NE of Penisar. From Chester take A55 west
beyond Prestatyn exit, take 2nd right turn in 2m. From
Llandudno take 1st left at top of Rhuallt Hill*
🚐🚐
Open Etr or Apr-Oct Booking advisable bank hols
*A beautifully situated site, close to seaside resort of
Rhyl. A 2-acre site with 30 touring pitches.*
Leisure: ⚠ Facilities: ♠⊙✳✆🛒 Services: 🚱🗑💧🏥
→▶◎🌙

GWYNEDD

ABERSOCH   Map 06 SH32

▶ ▶ ▶ ▶ **Bryn Cethin Bach Caravan Park**
(SH304290)
Lon Garmon LL53 7UL ☎ 01758 712719 & 712156
*Dir: Take A499 to Abersoch. Fork right at Lande Sea
Garage, Lon Garmon. Park 0.5m up hill on the right*
★ 🚐 £10-£12 🚐 £10-£12
Open Apr-Oct (rs Mar-May shop closed) Booking
advisable Spring bank hol & Jul-Aug Last arrival
18.00hrs Last departure noon
*A well-run family site within 0.5m of sandy beaches,
the harbour and all the facilities of Abersoch,
offering lovely views and a first class toilet block.
This small, select park is set in 22 acres containing
wooded areas and a picturesque fishing lake.
Tourers can choose between a sheltered terraced
pitch and a more exposed one with great views. All
pitches are individually marked, with water and
electricity. The toilets are housed in a number of
outbuildings, updated with state of the art
furnishings, and kept in immaculate condition. A 22-
acre site with 21 touring pitches and 53 statics.
Lake & fishing.*
Facilities: ♠⊙🔧✳✆🛒🗑🎋🐾 Services: 🚱🗑💧🏥🚽
→🔾▶🔺🔆🍽

─────────────────────

▶ ▶ ▶ **Seaview (SH305262)**
Sarn Bach LL53 7ET ☎ 01758 712052 & 713256
*Dir: Very sharp turn opposite the telephone kiosk in
Sarn Bach. Site 200yds on the right*
★ 🚐 fr £12 🚐 fr £12 ⚑ £6-£10
Open Mar-Oct Booking advisable from March Last
arrival 23.00hrs Last departure noon
*Gently sloping family site in quiet elevated position
near to Abersoch, on the Lleyn Peninsula. A 4-acre
site with 97 touring pitches.*
Facilities: ♠⊙🔧✳☆✆🛒🗑🎋🐾
Services: 🚱🗑💧⌀🏥🚽
→🔾▶🔺🔆🍽🌙🥤🍴📷

─────────────────────

▶ ▶ **Beach View Caravan Park (SH316262)**
Bwlchtocyn LL53 7BT ☎ 01758 712956
★ 🚐 £9-£12 🚐 £9-£12 ⚑ £8-£11
Open Mar-Oct Booking advisable Jul, Aug & Bank
hols Last arrival 21.00hrs Last departure 11.00hrs
A friendly family park which has benefited from

*enthusiastic new owners who have made many
improvements. It has fantastic sea views and is
within a six-minute walk of the beach. A 4-acre site
with 47 touring pitches.*
Facilities: ♠⊙🔧✳✖🐾 Services: 🗑💧⌀🏥
→🔾▶◎🔺🔆🌙🥤

BALA   Map 06 SH93

▶ ▶ ▶ ▶ **Camping & Caravanning Club Site**
(SH962391)
Crynierth Caravan Park, Cefn-Ddwysarn LL23 7LN
☎ 01678 530324
*Dir: A5 onto A494 to Bala. Through Bethal and Sarnau
villages. Pass Cefn-Ddwysarn sign. Right up lane before
red phone box. Site 400yds on left*
★ 🚐 £11.80-£14.90 🚐 £11.80-£14.90 ⚑ £11.80-£14.90
Open 20 Mar-30 Oct Booking advisable bank hols &
peak periods Last arrival 21.00hrs Last departure
noon
*A quiet pleasant park with interesting views and
high class facilities, set back from the main road in
a very secluded position. Lake Bala offers great
appeal for the water sports enthusiast, as does the
nearby River Tryweryn, a leading slalom course in
white water rafting. Please see the advertisement
on page 14 for details of Club Members' benefits. A
4-acre site with 50 touring pitches.*
Leisure: ⚠ Facilities: ♠⊙🔧✳☆✆🛒🐾
Services: 🚱🗑💧⌀🚽
→🔾▶🔺🔆🥤🌙 📞🚋

─────────────────────

Facilities: 🚿 Bath 🎋 Shower ⊙ Electric Shaver 🔧 Hairdryer ✳ Ice Pack Facility ☆ Disabled Facilities ✆ Public Telephone
🛒 Shop on Site or within 200yds 🖥 Mobile Shop (calls at least 5 days a week) 🎋 BBQ Area 🏥 Picnic Area 🐾 Dog Exercise Area

► ► ► ► **Pen Y Bont Touring & Camping Park**
(SH932350)
Llangynog Rd LL23 7PH
☎ 01678 520549 07971 116211
*Dir: From A494 take B4391 and site is located 0.75m on
the right*
★ ⊞ £8.45-£10.45 ⊞ £7.95-£9.95 ▲ £7.45-£10.45
Open Apr-Oct Booking advisable all year Last arrival
23.30hrs Last departure 13.00hrs
*A recently upgraded park offering first class
facilities in a woodland country setting, very close
to the River Dee and Bala Lake. Only the best
fittings have been used in the toilet block, and this
sets the standard for the rest of the park. Most
pitches have hardstandings with water and
electricity. Lake Bala is famous for its water sports,
with Afon Tryweryn catering for enthusiasts of
canoe slalom and white water rafting. A 7-acre site
with 85 touring pitches.*
Facilities: ｢❷⦶❋⬦╲⬟囲戸⽝
Services: ❷⬚⬤⬀⊞⊺╚➤
→ ∪ ┠⬦╳➈┛

► ► ► ► **Pen-y-Garth Caravan & Camping Park**
(SH940349)
LL23 7ES ☎ 01678 520485 & 0780 8198717
*Dir: Leave A494 in Bala and proceed onto B4391. After
1m fork right at sign to Rhosygwaliau. Site is 600yds on
right*
★ ⊞ £7.25-£8.95 ⊞ £7.25-£8.95 ▲ £7.25-£8.95

Open Mar-Oct Booking advisable bank hols & Jul-
Aug Last arrival 22.00hrs Last departure noon
*A level site with well-laid out pitches for tourers,
amidst attractive scenery with a wealth of wildlife. A
20-acre site with 63 touring pitches and 54 statics.*

Table tennis,10 acres recreation
Leisure: ❧⚠ **Facilities:** ｢❷❋╲⬟戸
Services: ❷⬚⬤⬀⊞
→ ∪ ┠⬦╳╪┛ ⬤╼⬛🚩🌀

BARMOUTH   Map 06 SH61

► ► ► ► **Hendre Mynach Caravan Park**
(SH605170)
Llanaber Rd LL42 1YR ☎ 01341 280262
★ ⊞ £6-£14.50 ⊞ £5-£12 ▲ £5-£12
Open Mar-9 Jan (rs Nov- Feb shop) Booking
advisable bank hols & Jul-Aug Last arrival 23.00hrs
Last departure noon

*A lovely site with immaculate facilities, situated off
the A496 on the northern outskirts of Barmouth and
near to railway, with almost direct access to
promenade and beach. Caravans should not be put
off by the steep descent, as park staff are always on
hand if needed. The toilet facilities are modern and
excellent, and pitches have TV and satellite hook-up
as well as water and electricity. A small café serves
light meals and takeaways. Winner of the Best
Campsite for Wales 2001. A 10-acre site with 205
touring pitches.*
TV & satellite hook ups.
Leisure: ⚠ **Facilities:** ｢❷❋╲⬟⽝
Services: ❷⬚⬀⊞╳➤
→ ∪┛ ⬤╼⬛🚩🌀

► ► ► *Trawsdir Touring & Caravan Park*
(SH596198)
Caerddaniel Caravan Park, Llanaber LL42 1RR
☎ 01341 280999 & 280611
Dir: 3m N of Barmouth on A496
❷⬞▲

contd.

Trawsdir Touring & Caravan Park
Open Mar-Oct Booking advisable Etr, Whitsun &
Jul-Aug Last arrival 21.00hrs Last departure noon
A recently developed park on a working sheep farm
with views to sea and hills, and very accessible to
motor traffic. The facilities are of a very good
standard. 50 touring pitches.
Leisure: ⚠ Facilities: ♠⊙ℚ☀♿💧🐾
Services: 🔌📶🔧🗑
→ ∪⊚◭🎿🛒

BEDDGELERT   Map 06 SH54

► ► ► Beddgelert Caravan & Camping Site
(SH578490)
LL55 4UU ☎ 01766 890288
Dir: 2m N of Beddgelert village on the A4085
★ 🚐 £6.80-£9.20 🚐 £6.80-£9.20 ⛺ £6.80-£9.20
Open all year Booking advisable bank hols & Jul-
Aug Last arrival 22.00hrs Last departure noon
Well-run and very popular Forestry Commission
site amidst trees and bushes. Set in mountainous
woodland country near to river and main road. A
25-acre site with 280 touring pitches.
Leisure: ⚠ Facilities: ♠⊙ℚ☀♿🛒🛒🌲
Services: 🔌🔧🗑🚾Ⓣ
→ 🎿🗑 📶🚫🗑

BETWS GARMON   Map 06 SH55

► ► ► ► Bryn Gloch Caravan & Camping Park
(SH534574)
LL54 7YY ☎ 01286 650216
Dir: Site on A4085 between Beddgelert & Caernarfon
🚐🚐⛺
Open all year Booking advisable school & bank hols
Last arrival 23.00hrs Last departure 17.00hrs
An excellent family-run site with modern toilets,
and all level pitches in beautiful surroundings. The
park offers the best of two worlds, with its bustling
holiday atmosphere and the peaceful natural
surroundings. The 25 acres of level fields are
separated by mature hedges and trees,
guaranteeing sufficient space for families wishing
to spread themselves out. There are plenty of walks
in the area, and a constant source of interest is the
babbling stream, Gwyrfai. A 12-acre site with 160
touring pitches and 14 statics.
Family bathroom & mother & baby room.
See advertisement under CAERNARFON
Leisure: ♠⚠🏊 Facilities: ➡♠⊙ℚ☀♿🛒🌲🐾
Services: 🔌🔧🗑🚾Ⓣ
→ ∪🎿⊚🎿🗑 📶🚫🗑🚫🗑

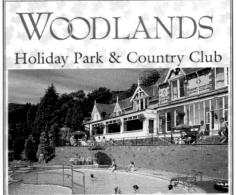

WOODLANDS
Holiday Park & Country Club

Situated within the Snowdonia National Park,
Woodlands offers good clean facilities on this well
established site. Country Club, outdoor swimming
pool, launderette, play area, amusements and
high-season entertainment.

New – full service hook-up points for electric,
water, T.V. and mains sewerage.

Three miles from the sandy beaches of Tywyn and
surrounded by beautiful countryside.

Telephone for colour brochure: (01654) 710-471
Bryncrug, Tywyn, Gwynedd LL36 9UH

BRYNCRUG   Map 06 SH60

► ► ► Woodlands Holiday Park (SH618035)
LL36 9UH ☎ 01654 710471
Dir: 2m from Tywyn on B4405 road to Tal-y-Llyn
★ 🚐 £6-£7.50 🚐 £6-£7.50
Open Etr & Apr-Oct Booking advisable Jul-Aug Last
arrival 22.00hrs Last departure 11.00hrs
A small touring park with hard pitches set apart
from the static/chalet section of this large holiday
park and country club. The park is partly
surrounded by trees. A 2-acre site with 20 touring
pitches and 122 statics.
Entertainment in high season.
Leisure: ♦♠⚠🏊 Facilities: ♠⊙♿🛒🚾🛁🌲
Services: 🔌🗑🚿❌
→ ∪🎿⊚◭🎿🎿 📶🚫

CAERNARFON   Map 06 SH46

► ► ► Cadnant Valley Caravan Park (SH487628)
Cadnant Valley Park, Llanberis Rd LL55 2DF
☎ 01286 673196
Dir: On the outskirts of Caernarfon on B4086 to
Llanberis
★ 🚐 £7.50-£9.50 🚐 £7.50-£9.50 ⛺ £7.50-£9.50
Open 15 Mar-Oct Booking advisable bank hols &
Jul-Aug Last arrival 22.00hrs Last departure
11.00hrs

Situated close to the main Caernarfon-Llanberis road and conveniently near the town. Level, terraced pitches in a secluded, landscaped, wooded valley with some near a stream. A 4.5-acre site with 69 touring pitches.

Leisure: ⚲ Facilities: ⬤⊙🏴❄⚓🏪🛢🚻🐕
Services: 🔌🔋🛢⊘⊞
→ ∪ ⏸ ◬ ↘ ✈

► ► ► Glan Gwna Holiday Park (SH502622)
Caeathro LL55 2SG ☎ 01286 673456 & 676402
Dir: Take A4085 signed Beddgelert. 1.5m from Caernarfon
★ 🚐 £10-£16 ▲ £10-£16
Open Etr-Oct (rs mid Apr-May & mid Sep-Oct some facilities are closed) Booking advisable bank hols & Jul-Aug Last arrival 23.00hrs Last departure noon
Beautifully situated on a bend in the Afon Seiont, and part of a large holiday complex with excellent facilities. A 7-acre site with 100 touring pitches and 130 statics.
Fishing.

Leisure: ⚲ ⚲ Facilities: ⬤⊙🏴❄⚓🏪🐕
Services: 🔌🔋🍽🛢✗🚽
→ ∪ ⏸ ◬ ↘ 🍴 🚆 🔧 🎿

► ► ► Riverside Camping (SH505630)
Seiont Nurseries, Pont Rug LL55 2BB
☎ 01286 672524 & 678781 eves
Dir: 2m from Caernarfon on the right of A4086
🚐 £8-£13 🚐 £8-£10.50 ▲ £3-£9
Open Etr-end Oct Booking advisable Jul-Aug Last arrival anytime Last departure 20.00hrs
A secluded park divided up by shrubs and trees, adjacent to the small River Seiont. A 4.5-acre site with 55 touring pitches.
River swimming.

Leisure: ⚲ Facilities: ⬤⊙❄⚓🏪🐕
Services: 🔌
→ ∪ ⏸ ◎ ◬ ↘ ✈ 🔋 🛢

► ► ► Ty'n yr Onnen Mountain Farm Caravan & Camping (SH534588)
Waunfawr LL55 4AX ☎ 01286 650281
Dir: At Waunfawr on A4085, turn down unclass road opposite church. Site is signposted
🚐 £7-£9 🚐 £6-£8 ▲ £6-£8
Open Spring bank hol-Oct (rs Etr & May Day bank hol open if weather premitting) Booking advisable Spring bank hol & Jul-Aug Last arrival 21.00hrs Last departure 10.00hrs
A gently sloping site on a 200-acre sheep farm, set in magnificent surroundings with mountain views. A 4-acre site with 20 touring pitches and 4 statics.
Fishing.

Leisure: ⚲ ⚲ ⬚ Facilities: ➡⬤⊙🏴❄⚓⚓🏪🛢🚻🐕
Services: 🔌🔋🛢⊘⊞⊤
→ ∪ ⏸ ◬ ↘ ✗ 🚆 ✈ 🔧 🎿

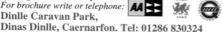

CRICCIETH

▶ ▶ ▶ Llwyn-Bugeilydd Caravan & Camping Site (SH498398)

LL52 0PN ☎ 01766 522235
Dir: Situated 1m N of Criccieth on B4411. Site is 1st on the right

Open Etr/Apr-Oct Booking advisable Etr, Whit & Jul-Aug Last arrival anytime Last departure 11.00hrs
A beautiful little site, well-maintained and in excellent condition, with sea and mountain views. A 6-acre site with 45 touring pitches.
Facilities: ⦿ ✳ Ⓔ **Services:** ⦿ Ⓔ
→ ∪

▶ ▶ Tyddyn Cethin Farm (SH492404)

LL52 0NF ☎ 01766 522149
Dir: N from Criccieth on B4411 & Tyddyn Cethin is 4th site on right
★ ⦿ £7-£9.50 ⦿ £7-£9.50 ▲ £5-£7
Open Mar-Oct Booking advisable Feb-Mar Last arrival 22.00hrs Last departure noon
A very good, quiet holiday site with enthusiastic proprietors, on banks of River Dwyfor. An 8-acre site with 60 touring pitches and 40 statics. Fishing on site.
Facilities: ⦿ ✳ **Services:** ⦿ Ⓔ
→ ∪

▶ Tyddyn Morthwyl (SH488402)

LL52 0NF ☎ 01766 522115
Dir: 1.5m N of Criccieth on B4411
★ ⦿ £5.50 ⦿ £4 ▲ £5.50
Open Etr-Oct (rs Mar & Oct) Booking advisable Spring bank hol & Jul-Aug Last departure 14.00hrs
A quiet, sheltered site with good level grassy pitches, ideal for families. A 10-acre site with 60 touring pitches and 22 statics.
Facilities: ⦿ ✳ **Services:** ⦿ Ⓔ
→ ∪

DINAS DINLLE — Map 06 SH45

▶ ▶ ▶ ▶ Dinlle Caravan Park (SH443568)

LL54 5TW ☎ 01286 830324
Dir: Turn right off A499 at sign for Caernarfon Airport. 2m W of Dinas Dinlle coast
★ ⦿ £5-£12 ⦿ £5-£12 ▲ £5-£12
Open May-Aug (rs Mar-Apr & Sep-Nov club, shop, swimming pool restricted hours) Booking advisable Spring bank hol & Jul-Aug Last arrival 23.00hrs Last departure noon
A very accessible, well-kept grassy level site, adjacent to sandy beach, with good views to Snowdonia. The park is situated in acres of flat grassland, with plenty of room for even the largest groups. A lounge bar and family room are comfortable places in which to relax, and children are well provided for with an exciting adventure playground. The beach road gives access to the golf club, a nature reserve and to Air World at Caernarfon Airport. An 11-acre site with 175 touring pitches and 167 statics.

See advertisement under CAERNARFON

Leisure: ⚓ **Facilities:** ⦿ ✳ ▲ **
Services: ⦿ Ⓔ
→ ∪

DYFFRYN ARDUDWY — Map 06 SH52

▶ ▶ ▶ Murmur-yr-Afron Touring Park (SH586236)

LL44 2BE ☎ 01341 247353
Dir: On A496 N of village

Open Mar-Oct Booking advisable bank hols Last arrival 23.00hrs Last departure 11.30hrs
A pleasant, family-run park alongside a wooded stream on the edge of the village, and convenient for large sandy beaches. A 4-acre site with 67 touring pitches.
Leisure: ⚲ **Facilities:** ⦿ ✳ **
Services: ⦿ Ⓔ
→ ∪

LLANBEDROG — Map 06 SH33

▶ Henllys Newydd (SH320320)

LL53 7RE ☎ 01758 740398
Dir: From A497 in Llanbedrog take B4413 & site is at the top of the hill

Open Mar-Oct Booking advisable Last arrival 21.00hrs
Gently sloping field with extensive views of distant mountains and nearby sea. A 1-acre site with 10 touring pitches.
Facilities: ⦿ **Services:** ⦿
→ ∪

Facilities: ⬤ Bath ⬤ Shower ⦿ Electric Shaver ⦿ Hairdryer ✳ Ice Pack Facility ♿ Disabled Facilities ☏ Public Telephone ⬤ Shop on Site or within 200yds ⬤ Mobile Shop (calls at least 5 days a week) ⬤ BBQ Area ⬤ Picnic Area ✝ Dog Exercise Area

LLANDWROG — Map 06 SH45

▶ ▶ ▶ ▶ **White Tower Caravan Park (SH453582)**
LL54 5UH ☎ 01286 830649 & 07802 562785
Dir: 1.5m from village along Tai'r Eglwys road. From Caernarfon take A487 Porthmadog road. Cross over rdbt, then take 1st right. Park 3m on right
⊞ £5-£10.50 ⊞ £5-£10.50 ▲ £5-£10.50
Open Mar-Dec (rs Mar-mid May & Sep-Oct bar wknds only) Booking advisable bank hols & Jul-Aug Last arrival 23.00hrs Last departure noon
A level, well-maintained site with lovely Snowdonia views, three miles from Caernarvon and two miles from the nearest sandy beach at Dinas Dinlle. The touring area is served by an immaculately maintained modern toilet block with key access, and the individual hardstandings have their own water and electricity. A well-stocked shop and a games and TV room, along with an outdoor heated swimming pool and lounge bar with family room are some of the popular amenities on this park. A 3-acre site with 52 touring pitches and 54 statics.
Leisure: ⊰ ◀ 瓜 ▢ **Facilities:** ♠ ⊙ ٩ ⋇ & ₡ ♨
Services: ♤ ▣ ♀ ▪ ∅ ⊞ ⊤ ➡
→ ∪ ▶ ♧ ⋇ ✈

LLANYSTUMDWY — Map 06 SH43

▶ ▶ ▶ ▶ **Camping & Caravanning Club Site (SH469384)**
Tyddyn Sianel LL52 0LS ☎ 01766 522855
Dir: From Criccieth take A497 W, 2nd right to Llanystumdwy, site on right
★ ⊞ £11.80-£14.90 ⊞ £11.80-£14.90 ▲ £11.80-£14.90
Open 20 Mar-1 Nov Booking advisable bank hols & peak periods Last arrival 21.00hrs Last departure noon
Well-maintained, attractive grassy site on slightly sloping land with a good range of facilities. Please see the advertisement on page 14 for details of Club Members' benefits. A 4-acre site with 60 touring pitches.
Playfield
Facilities: ♠ ⊙ ٩ ⋇ & ₡ ♨ ✚ **Services:** ♤ ▣ ▪ ∅ ⊞ ➡
→ ∪ ▶ ♧ ⋇ ✈ 🍴 📠

MORFA BYCHAN — Map 06 SH53

▶ ▶ ▶ **Gwyndy Caravan Park (SH543371)**
Black Rock Sands LL49 9YB ☎ 01766 512047
Dir: In Porthmadog turn at sign to Morfa Bychan. After 2m turn left after Spa, then 2nd right. Follow signs to park
★ ⊞ £11-£13.50 ⊞ £11-£13.50
Open Mar-Nov Booking advisable bank hols & Jul-Aug Last departure 11.00hrs
A quiet family site a minute's walk from the beach at Black Rock Sands. A 5-acre site with 15 touring pitches and 44 statics.
Facilities: ♠ ⊙ ⋇ ♨ **Services:** ♤ ▣ ▪ ∅ ⊞
→ ∪ ▶ ◎ ♧ ⋇ 🍼 ✈

PONTLYFNI — Map 06 SH45

▶ ▶ ▶ **St Ives Touring Caravan Park (SH432524)**
Lon-Y-Wig LL54 5EG ☎ 01286 660347
Dir: Off A499 along lane towards beach from village centre
⊞ ⊞ ▲
Open Mar-Oct Booking advisable all times Last arrival 21.00hrs Last departure noon
An immaculate little site with good facilities, within easy walking distance of beach. A 1-acre site with 20 touring pitches.
Facilities: ♠ ⊙ ⋇ & ₡ ▢ 瓽 **Services:** ♤ ▣ ▪ ∅ ⊞ ⊤ ♨
→ ∪ ▶ ◎ ♧ ⋇ ✈ ✈ ♨

▶ **Llyn-y-Gele Farm & Caravan Park (SH432523)**
LL54 5EL ☎ 01286 660283 & 660289
Dir: Located off A499
⊞ ⊞ ▲
Open Etr-Sep Booking advisable Jul-Aug Last arrival 22.00hrs Last departure 13.00hrs
Quiet farm site within 5-7 minutes' walking distance of the beach in the centre of the village. Centrally situated for touring the Lleyn Peninsula, Anglesey and Snowdonia. A 4-acre site with 6 touring pitches and 24 statics.
Leisure: 瓜 **Facilities:** ♠ ⊙ ⋇ ♈ **Services:** ♤ ▪
→ ∪ ✈ ♨

PONT-RUG

See **Caernarfon**

PORTHMADOG — Map 06 SH53

▶ ▶ ▶ ▶ **Tyddyn Llwyn Caravan Park & Camping Site (SH561384)**
Black Rock Rd LL49 9UR ☎ 01766 512205 & 514196
Dir: Turn by Woolworth, 0.5m from Porthmadog
★ ⊞ £7-£9 ⊞ £7-£9 ▲ £7-£9
Open Mar-Oct Booking advisable school hols Last arrival 23.00hrs Last departure noon
Set in an amphitheatre of wooded hills, with both level and slightly sloping pitches in beautiful countryside. The grounds include gentle sloping areas for vans, and there is plenty of space for tenters to find a secluded spot. The toilet blocks have been upgraded or rebuilt to provide excellent facilities. The park grounds are shared with a small hotel which can provide some gracious living for those in need. A 14-acre site with 153 touring pitches and 53 statics.
Leisure: ◀ 瓜 ▢ **Facilities:** ♠ ⊙ ٩ ⋇ ₡ ♈
Services: ♤ ▣ ♀ ▪ ∅ ⊞ ⊤ ✕
→ ∪ ▶ ◎ ♧ ♨ ✈ ♨

TALSARNAU — Map 06 SH63

▶ ▶ ▶ ▶ **Barcdy Touring Caravan & Camping Park (SH623368)**
LL47 6YG ☎ 01766 770736
Dir: From Maentwrog take left turn for Harlech, on A496. Barcdy 4m on the left
★ ⊞ £8.50-£10 ⊞ £8.50-£10 ▲ £8.50-£10

contd.

(side tab) **Wales**

Barcdy Touring Caravan & Camping Park
Open Apr-Oct (rs Etr-Spring bank hol & mid Sep-Oct
only two fields open, food shop closed) Booking
advisable from Feb ✍
*A quiet, picturesque park on the southern edge of
the Vale of Ffestiniog near Dwryd estuary. The
enthusiastic and hard-working owners maintain the
park to very high standards. Two touring areas are
available, one a large flat piece of land near the park
entrance, and the other with more secluded
terraced pitches running along one side of a narrow
valley. Footpaths through adjacent woodland lead
to small lakes and an established nature trail. A
12-acre site with 68 touring pitches and 30 statics.*
Facilities: ♠⊙♨✳ℭ❧✿ **Services:** ☺⬛⬛◫✸
➔∪♪ ⬛⬛⬛⬛

TAL-Y-BONT   Map 06 SH52

▶ ▶ *Benar Beach Camping & Touring Park
(SH573226)*
LL43 2AR ☎ 01341 247571 & 247001
Dir: 1m from A496, halfway between Harlech & Barmouth
☺⬛Å
Open Mar-3 Oct Booking advisable peak periods
*Friendly family site consisting of a large, level
camping field with much improved facilities.
Adjacent to sandy beach with view of mountains.
A 5-acre site with 40 touring pitches.*
Satellite & TV hook-ups.
Facilities: ♠⊙✳ℭ✿ **Services:** ☺
➔∪♪✿

TYWYN   Map 06 SH50

See also **Bryncrug**
▶ ▶ ▶ *Pant y Neuadd (SH592005)*
Aberdyfi Rd LL36 9HW ☎ 01654 711393
Dir: Situated off A493, close to the hospital.
Open Mar-Oct
*A secluded park on the outskirts of Tywyn within a
few minutes' walk of shops and amenities. The
excellent facilities are well-maintained by
enthusiastic owners. A 7.5-acre site with 24 touring
pitches and 65 statics.*

▶ ▶ ▶ **Ynysymaengwyn Caravan Park (SH601021)**
LL36 9RY ☎ 01654 710684
Dir: On A493, 1m heading towards Dolgellau
★ ☺ £7-£10 Å £6-£9
Open Etr or Apr-Oct Booking advisable Jul-Aug Last
arrival 23.00hrs Last departure noon

*This site is ideally situated with the full amenities of
the seaside on one hand and beautiful countryside
and hills on the other. A 4-acre site with 80 touring
pitches and 115 statics.*
Leisure: ⚠ **Facilities:** ♠⊙♨✳ℭ❧✿◫
Services: ☺⬛⬛◫
➔∪▶⊙⬛⬛♪

MONMOUTHSHIRE

CHEPSTOW   Map 03 ST59

▶ ▶ ▶ *St Pierre Camping & Caravan Site
(ST509901)*
Portskewett ☎ 01291 425114
*Dir: From Chepstow take A48 towards Newport, turn left
at 1st rdbt, then immediate left*
☺⬛Å
Open Mar-Oct Booking advisable bank hols Last
departure 18.00hrs
*Well-established site with immaculately kept
facilities and a peaceful atmosphere, overlooking
the Severn Estuary. A 4-acre site with 50 touring
pitches.*
Boule, croquet.
Facilities: ♠⊙♨✳ℭ❧✿✿ **Services:** ☺⬛⬛

DINGESTOW   Map 03 SO41

▶ ▶ ▶ *Bridge Caravan Park & Camping Site
(SO459104)*
Bridge Farm NP25 4DY ☎ 01600 740241
*Dir: Signposted from Raglan & located off A449, South
Wales-Midlands road*
★ ☺ £8-£10 ⬛ £8-£10 Å £8-£9.50
Open Etr-Oct Booking advisable bank hols Last
arrival 22.00hrs Last departure 16.00hrs
*An excellent site in a quiet village setting. A 4-acre
site with 94 touring pitches.*
Fishing.
Facilities: ♠⊙♨✳ℭ❧✿✿ **Services:** ☺⬛⬛◫◫
➔∪▶✳◫♪

MITCHEL TROY   Map 03 SO41

▶ ▶ ▶ *Glen Trothy Caravan & Camping Park
(SO496105)*
NP25 4BD ☎ 01600 712295
*Dir: Signposted on B4293. Site on right at entrance to
village*
★ ☺ fr £7 ⬛ fr £7 Å fr £7
Open Mar-Oct Booking advisable Bank hols & high
season Last arrival 21.00hrs Last departure noon
*New owners are modernising this site in a well
wooded area adjacent to the River Trothy. Three
large level fields. A 6.5-acre site with 80 touring
pitches.*
Leisure: ⚠ **Facilities:** ♠⊙♨✳ℭ
Services: ☺⬛◫◫
➔▶⊙⬛✳◫♪⬛⬛

MONMOUTH   Map 03 SO51

▶ ▶ ▶ *Monmouth Caravan Park (SO498135)*
Rockfield Rd NP5 3BA ☎ 01600 714745
Dir: From A40 take B4233 S of Monmouth, leading into
Rockfield Road & site is opposite fire station
🏕 🚐

Open Mar-Oct Booking advisable
Level grassy site adjacent to Offa's Dyke footpath
and within easy walking distance of town. A 3-acre
site with 40 touring pitches.
Facilities: ℝ ☉ ℂ 🎿 **Services:** 🔌

PEMBROKESHIRE

BROAD HAVEN   Map 02 SM81

▶ ▶ **Creampots Touring Caravan & Camping Park**
(SM882131)
Broadway SA62 3TU ☎ 01437 781776
Dir: From Haverfordwest take B4341 until reaching the
village of Broadway. Turn left signed Milford Haven.
Park 2nd entrance, 500yds on the right
🚐 £6-£9.50 🏕 £6-£9.50 ▲ £6
Open Mar-Oct (rs mid Jan-Feb) Booking advisable
mid Jul-Aug Last arrival 23.00hrs Last departure
noon
Large, well-maintained fields with a good toilet
block. A 5-acre site with 72 touring pitches and 1
static.
Milk, eggs & newspapers daily.
Leisure: ⚠ **Facilities:** ℝ ☉ 🜲 ☀ ♿ 🎣 🛉
Services: 🔌 🗑 ⊞
→ ∪ 🛆 ✕ 🍴 ☕ 🎿

▶ ▶ **South Cockett Caravan & Camping Park**
(SM879135)
South Cockett SA62 3TU ☎ 01437 781296 & 781760
Dir: 1.5m E off B4341
★ 🚐 £5.65-£8 🏕 £5.15-£7.50 ▲ £4.15-£6.50
Open Etr-Oct Booking advisable Jul-Aug Last arrival
23.30hrs
Small farm-style campsite rurally located and
offering high standards of modern toilet facilities.
Conveniently positioned close to the coastline and
a good touring base. A 6-acre site with 70 touring
pitches and 1 static.
Facilities: ℝ ☉ ☀ ℂ **Services:** 🔌 🗑 ⚫ ⊘ ⊞
→ ∪ ✕ ☕ 🎿

FISHGUARD   Map 02 SM93

▶ ▶ ▶ **Fishguard Bay Caravan & Camping Park**
(SM984383)
Garn Gelli SA65 9ET ☎ 01348 811415
Dir: 1m N of A487
★ 🚐 £9-£11 🏕 £9-£11 ▲ £8-£10
Open Mar-9 Jan Booking advisable Jul-Aug Last
departure noon
Well-run, part level and sloping grass site with
bushes, high up on cliffs with excellent views and
close to the sea. A 5-acre site with 50 touring
pitches and 50 statics.
View point.

Leisure: ⚓ ⚠ ⛶ **Facilities:** ℝ ☉ 🜲 ☀ ℂ 🎿
Services: 🔌 🗑 ⚫ ⊘ ⊞ 🔲
→ ∪ ✕ 🍴 ⚓ ☕ 🛢 📀 🔲 🔧

▶ ▶ ▶ **Gwaun Vale Touring Park (SM977356)**
Llanychaer SA65 9TA ☎ 01348 874698
Dir: From Fishguard take B4313. Site situated 1.5m on
the right
🚐 £7-£8 🏕 £7-£8 ▲ £7-£8
Open Mar-Oct Booking advisable Jul-Aug Last
arrival 22.00hrs Last departure 15.00hrs
A beautiful and immaculate site run by an
enthusiastic owner. A 1.75-acre site with 28 touring
pitches.
Free loan of Boules, video films, guide books.
Leisure: ⚠ **Facilities:** ℝ ☉ 🜲 ☀ ℂ 🎿 🎣 🛉
Services: 🔌 🗑 ⚫ ⊞ 🔲 ✕
→ ∪ 🛆 ✕ 🍴 ☕ 🗑

HASGUARD CROSS   Map 02 SM81

▶ ▶ ▶ **Hasguard Cross Caravan Park (SM850108)**
SA62 3SL ☎ 01437 781443
Dir: Approach to B4327 from Haverfordwest to Dale.
After 7m turn right at X-roads & site is 1st entrance on
the right
★ 🚐 £6.75-£8.75 🏕 £6.75-£8.75
Open all year Booking advisable Spring bank hol &
Jun-Aug Last arrival 21.00hrs Last departure
10.00hrs
A very clean, efficient and well-run site in
Pembrokeshire National Park with views of
surrounding hills. 1.5m from sea and beach at Little
Haven. A 3-acre site with 25 touring pitches and 35
statics.
Facilities: ℝ ☉ ☀ ℂ **Services:** 🔌 ⚟ ⚫ ⊞ ✕ 🚿
→ ∪ ▶ 🛆 ✕ 🍴 ☕ 🗑 🎿

HAVERFORDWEST   Map 02 SM91

▶ ▶ **Nolton Cross Caravan Park (SM879177)**
Nolton SA62 3NP ☎ 01437 710701
Dir: 1m off A487 Haverfordwest-St Davids at Simpson
Cross.
★ 🚐 £5.50-£7 🏕
Open Mar-Dec Booking advisable High season Last
arrival 22.00hrs Last departure noon
An established static site now accepting tourers,
1.5m from the sea. The site is exposed but high
banks give shelter. A 4-acre site with 15 touring
pitches and 30 statics.
Leisure: ⚠ **Facilities:** ℝ ☉ ☀ ℂ 🎿 🎣 ⛶
Services: 🔌 ⚫ ⊘ ⊞
→ ∪ 🛆 🍴

LANDSHIPPING   Map 02 SN01

▶ ▶ *New Park Farm (SN026111)*
SA67 8BG ☎ 01834 891284
Dir: 7m W of Narberth, along unclass road off A4075
🚐 🏕 ▲
Open May Day wknd-Oct Booking advisable peak
periods Last arrival 20.00hrs Last departure noon

contd.

Services: 🔲 Toilet Fluid ✕ Café/ Restaurant 🚿 Fast Food/Takeaway 🍼 Baby Care 🔌 Electric Hook Up
🗑 Launderette ⚟ Licensed Bar ⚫ Calor Gaz ⊘ Camping Gaz ⊞ Battery Charging

A nice, quiet site on a smallholding with basic but adequate facilities. A 2-acre site with 5 touring pitches and 30 statics.

Facilities: ⌐⊙☼ ⌂ 🛒 **Services:** 💬📶🖊⊘⊞🅣
→ ∪↳ ♪ 🛒

LITTLE HAVEN

See Hasguard Cross

LUDCHURCH   Map 02 SN11

▶ ▶ ▶ **Woodland Vale Caravan Park (SN140113)**
SA67 8JE ☎ 01834 831319
Dir: N of Ludchurch on unclass road, the continuation S of B4314
★ 🚐 £11-£15 🚐 £11-£15
Open Mar-Nov Booking advisable bank hols & Jul-Aug Last arrival 23.00hrs Last departure 12.00hrs
Site with informally sited pitches set between areas of water created in an old quarry. A 1.5-acre site with 30 touring pitches and 80 statics.
Free coarse fishing
Leisure: ⤜ ♦ ⚠ **Facilities:** ⌐⊙☼⌂ 🛒🎍🍴
Services: 💬📶♀🖊⊞
→ ∪ ▶ ♪

NARBERTH   Map 02 SN11

▶ ▶ ▶ ▶ **Noble Court Caravan & Camping Park (SN111158)**
Redstone Rd SA67 7ES ☎ 01834 861191
Dir: Located on B4313 between Narberth & A40
★ 🚐 £8-£15 🚐 £8-£15 ▲ £8
Open Mar-Nov (rs early & late season swimming pool closed) Booking advisable Jul-Aug Last arrival 23.30hrs Last departure 11.00hrs
A sloping park set in rolling countryside with lovely views from pitches, and a high standard of service. The park has its own fishing lake and picnic areas. A 25-acre site with 92 touring pitches and 60 statics. Walks & picnics 0.5 acres of course fishing lake
Leisure: ⤜ ♦ ⚠ **Facilities:** ⌐⊙☼☼⌂ 🛒🎍🍴🐕
Services: 💬📶♀🖊⊘⊞✕ ⛟
→ ∪ ▶ ♪ 🛒 ⬤ 🚲 🏴

ST DAVID'S   Map 02 SM72

▶ ▶ ▶ **Caerfai Bay Caravan & Tent Park (SM759244)**
Caerfai Bay SA62 6QT ☎ 01437 720274
Dir: At St Davids turn off A487 at the Tourist Information Centre. Follow signs for Caerfai Bay. Turn right at the end of the road
🚐 £7.50-£11.50 🚐 £6.50-£11.50 ▲ £5.50-£6.50
Open Etr-Oct Booking advisable school hols Last arrival 21.00hrs Last departure 11.00hrs
Gently sloping meadows with magnificent coastal scenery overlooking St Brides Bay - bathing beach 300yds from park entrance. A 10-acre site with 82 touring pitches and 33 statics.
Facilities: ⌐⊙☼☼⌂ 🛒 **Services:** 💬📶🖊⊘⊞
→▶ 🛒♪ ♪

▶ ▶ ▶ **Hendre Eynon Camping & Caravan Site (SM773280)**
SA62 6DB ☎ 01437 720474
Dir: 2m NE of St Davids on unclass road leading off B4583
★ 🚐 £5-£9 🚐 £5-£6 ▲ £5-£9
Open May-Sep (rs 27 Mar-Apr one toilet block & showers only) Booking advisable school hols Last arrival 21.00hrs Last departure noon
A country site on a working farm with a modern toilet block including family rooms. A 7-acre site with 48 touring pitches and 2 statics.
Facilities: ⌐⊙☼⌂ ⌂🐕 **Services:** 💬📶🖊⊞⛟
→ ∪ ▶ 🛒♪ ♪ 🛒

▶ ▶ **Camping & Caravanning Club Site (SM805305)**
Dwr Cwmdig, Berea SA62 6DW ☎ 01348 831376
Dir: S on A487, right at Glyncheryn Farmers Stores in Croesgoch. After 1m right following signs to Abereiddy. At x-roads left. Site 75yds on left
★ 🚐 £10.60-£13.90 🚐 £10.60-£13.90 ▲ £10.60-£13.90
Open 20 Mar-27 Sep Booking advisable bank hols & peak periods Last arrival 21.00hrs Last departure noon
Immaculately kept small grassy site in open country near the Pembrokeshire Coastal Path. Please see the advertisement on page 14 for details of Club Members' benefits. A 4-acre site with 40 touring pitches.
Facilities: ⌐⊙🍴⌂ **Services:** 💬📶🖊⊘⊞🅣♿
→ ∪ ▶ 🛒♪ ♪ 🛒 ⬤ 🚲

▶ ▶ *Tretio Caravan & Camping Park (SM787292)*
SA62 6DE ☎ 01437 720270 & 781359
Dir: On leaving St David's keep left at Rugby Football Club & carry straight on for 3m
🚐 🚐 ▲
Open 14 Mar-14 Oct Booking advisable bank hols & mid Jul-Aug Last arrival 23.00hrs Last departure 17.00hrs
A gently sloping touring site with well-converted facilities. A 4.5-acre site with 40 touring pitches and 10 statics.
4.5 acre pitch & putt, small animal farm corner.
Leisure: ⚠ **Facilities:** ⌐⊙🍴☼⌂ 🛒🎍🐕
Services: 💬🖊⊘⊞🅣⛟
→ ∪ ▶ 🛒♪♪ ♪

TAVERNSPITE   Map 02 SN11

▶ ▶ ▶ **Pantglas Farm Caravan Park (SN175122)**
SA34 0NS ☎ 01834 831618
Dir: On B4328 between Ludchurch & Tavernspite. At village pump take middle turning & site is signed on the right
★ 🚐 £6.50-£8 🚐 £6.50-£8 ▲ £6.50-£8
Open Etr-15 Oct Booking advisable Spring bank hol & Jul-Aug Last arrival 23.00hrs Last departure 11.00hrs
A quiet, family-run site in a rural setting, with a welcoming attitude towards children. A 7-acre site with 75 touring pitches.

Facilities: ⛟ Bath ⌐ Shower ⊙ Electric Shaver 🍴 Hairdryer ☼ Ice Pack Facility ♿ Disabled Facilities ⌂ Public Telephone
🛒 Shop on Site or within 200yds ⊞ Mobile Shop (calls at least 5 days a week) 🎍 BBQ Area 🍴 Picnic Area 🐕 Dog Exercise Area

Year round caravan weekly storage £2.50.
Leisure: ◀ /⚠ Facilities: ➡ ↾ ⊙ ⊕ ✳ & ⭑ ⊑ ⧕
Services: ⊕ ⊚ 🛢 ⌀ ⊞
→ ∪ ♒ ⚡

TENBY — Map 02 SN10

Kiln Park Holiday Centre (SN119002)
Marsh Rd SA70 7RB
☎ 01834 844121 08457 433433
Dir: On A4139
★ 🚐 £14-£19 🚙 £14-£19 ▲ £8.50-£19
Open Mar-Oct (rs Mar-mid May & Sep-Oct less
venues available) Booking advisable all times
Etr-Sep Last arrival 22.00hrs Last departure
10.00hrs no cars by caravans
*A large, commercial, touring, camping and static
holiday site, situated on level ground on the
town's outskirts. A short walk through dunes
leads to the sandy south-facing beach. The*

---

well-equipped toilet block is kept very clean.
A 103-acre site with 240 touring pitches and
620 statics.
Entertainment complex, bowling, putting green
Leisure: ⚲ ↖ ⚾ ◀ /⚠ Facilities: ➡ ↾ ⊙ ⊕ ✳ ⭑
⛴ 🍴 ⧕ 🐾 Services: ⊕ ⊚ ⛽ 🛢 ⌀ ⊞ ✕ ⯭
→ ∪ ♙ ⊙ △ ⚡ ⚉ ⛺ ♩ ⚌ ▦ ▦ ▦ ▦ ⑉

► ► ► ► **Trefalun (SN093027)**
Devonshire Dr, St Florence SA70 8RD
☎ 01646 651514 & 0500 655314
Dir: W of St Florence, 3m off B4318
★ 🚐 £7-£11 🚙 £7-£11 ▲ £6-£8
Open Etr-Oct Booking advisable bank hols & Jul-
Aug Last arrival 20.00hrs Last departure noon
*Set within 12 acres of sheltered, well-kept grounds,
this park nestles among some of Pembrokeshire's
finest scenery. This quiet country park offers well-
maintained level grass pitches separated by bushes
and trees, with plenty of space to relax in. Children
will enjoy the enclosed play area, and can feed the
park's friendly pets. Plenty of activities are available
at the nearby Heatherton Country Sports Park,
including go-karting, indoor bowls, golf and
bumper boating. A 7-acre site with 35 touring
pitches and 10 statics.*
Leisure: /⚠ Facilities: ↾ ⊙ ⊕ ✳ ⭑ ⊑ 🐾 🐎
Services: ⊕ ⊚ 🛢 ⌀ ⊞
→ ∪ ♙ ⊙ △ ⚡ ⚉ ⛺ ♩ ⚌ ▦

See advert on page 280

► ► ► ► **Well Park Caravan & Camping Site
(SN128028)**
SA70 8TL ☎ 01834 842179
Dir: On right of A478, approx 1m before reaching Tenby
★ 🚐 £7-£12 🚙 £7-£12 ▲ £6-£10
Open Apr-Oct (rs Apr-mid May & mid Sep-Oct)
Booking advisable Spring bank hol & Jul-Aug Last
arrival 22.00hrs Last departure 11.00hrs
*An excellent, well-run site with trees and bushes. A
10-acre site with 100 touring pitches and 42 statics.
TV hookups*
Leisure: ◀ /⚠ ⎅ Facilities: ↾ ⊙ ⊕ ✳ ⭑ ⊑ 🐾 🐎
Services: ⊕ ⊚ ⛽ 🛢 ⌀ ⊞ ⊡ ➡
→ ∪ ♙ ✕ ⚉ ♩

See advert on page 280

► ► ► ► **Wood Park Caravans (SN128025)**
New Hedges SA70 8TL ☎ 01834 843414
*Dir: At rdbt 2m N of Tenby follow A478 towards Tenby,
then take 2nd right & right again*
★ 🚐 £6-£13.50 🚙 £6-£13.50 ▲ £5-£9.50
Open Spring bank hol-Sep (rs Etr-Spring bank hol &
Sep-Oct bar & launderette may not open) Booking
advisable Spring bank hol & Jul-Aug Last arrival
22.00hrs Last departure 10.00hrs

contd.

Services: ⊤ Toilet Fluid ✕ Café/ Restaurant ⯭ Fast Food/Takeaway ➡ Baby Care ⊕ Electric Hook Up
⊚ Launderette ⚲ Licensed Bar 🛢 Calor Gaz ⌀ Camping Gaz ⊞ Battery Charging

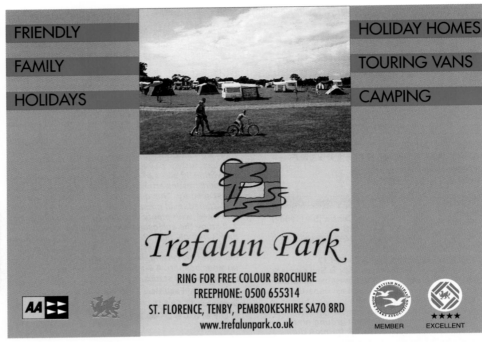
Wales

Wood Park Caravans

A well-run, slightly sloping, part-level grass site with trees and bushes. A 10-acre site with 60 touring pitches and 90 statics.

Leisure: ◕ ⚠ **Facilities:** ⌐ ⊙ ⌐ ✳ ⛺ ⚓
Services: ⊞ ⊞ ⚲ ⚡ ∅ ⊞
→ ∪ ▶ △ ⋏ ⚑ ⚒

POWYS

BRECON	Map 03 SO02

▶ ▶ ▶ ▶ **Brynich Caravan Park** (SJ071279)
Brynich LD3 7SH ☎ 01874 623325
Dir: 2km E of Brecon on A470, 200mtrs from junct with A40
🚐 £8.50-£10 🚐 £8.50-£10 ▲ £8.50-£10

Brynich Caravan Park
Brecon, Powys LD3 7SH
Tel/Fax: 01874 623325
E-mail: brynich@aol.com
Web: www.brynich.co.uk

Family run site with panoramic views of the Brecon Beacons. Well maintained, flat site with closely mown grass and large pitch sizes. Modern shower facilities with free hot water, including disabled and baby rooms – cleanliness a priority. Well-equipped licensed shop, telephone, adventure playground, recreation field and dog exercise field.

AA BEST CAMPSITE FOR WALES 1999

CALOR AWARD – MOST IMPROVED PARK IN WALES 1998

Open Etr-Oct Booking advisable bank & school hols Last arrival 23.00hrs

Very attractive and well-appointed site offering commanding views of the Brecon Beacons. Ideal as a touring base or for longer stays. A 20-acre site with 130 touring pitches.

Adventure playground, off-licence.

Leisure: ⚠ Facilities: 🕯⊙🍴※♿🔌🛒📮🐕
Services: 🔌🚿🍴⊘🔋🅣➡
→∪🍴⚖✕🎱🍴➜ 💳 🏧 📶 🌐

► ► ► **Bishops Meadow Caravan Park (SO060300)**
Bishops Meadow, Hay Rd LD3 9SW
☎ 01874 610000 & 622138
Dir: From A40 take A470 Hereford road. Turn left onto B4602
★ 🚐 fr £10 🚐 fr £10 ▲ £6-£10
Open Mar-Oct Booking advisable bank hols
Part of a large leisure complex with a wide range of facilities. A 3.5-acre site with 82 touring pitches.
Leisure: ⚲🔥⚠ Facilities: ➡🕯⊙※♿🔌🛒🐕
Services: 🔌🚿🍴⊘🔋🅣✕➡
→∪🍴⚖✕🎱🍴⊘🖥 💳 🏧 ⅅ 🌐

BRONLLYS   **Map 03 SO13**

► ► ► **Anchorage Caravan Park (SO142351)**
LD3 0LD ☎ 01874 711246 & 711230
Dir: 8m NE of Brecon on A438
🚐 fr £8 🚐 fr £8 ▲ fr £8

contd.

Services: 🅣 Toilet Fluid ✕ Café/ Restaurant 🍴 Fast Food/Takeaway ➡ Baby Care 🔌 Electric Hook Up ⊚ Launderette ⚖ Licensed Bar 🔋 Calor Gaz ⊘ Camping Gaz 🔋 Battery Charging

Open all year (rs Nov-Mar TV room closed) Booking advisable bank hols Last arrival 23.00hrs Last departure 18.00hrs
A well-maintained site. Touring pitches are on grassy slopes and level ground with good mountain views of the Brecon Beacons National Park. An 8-acre site with 110 touring pitches and 101 statics. Baby bath room, post office
Leisure: ⚬⬚ **Facilities:** ⬤⬀⊙⬀✳⬤⬤⬤⬀⬀
Services: ⬤⬤⬤⬀⬤⬤
→⬤⬀

BUILTH WELLS   Map 03 SO05

► ► ► *Fforest Fields Caravan & Camping Park (SO100535)*
Hundred House LD1 5RT ☎ 01982 570406 & 570220
Dir: From town follow signs to 'New Radnor' on A481, after 4m signed entrance on right
⬛⬛⬀

Open Etr & Apr-Oct Booking advisable bank hols & Jul-Aug Last arrival 23.00hrs Last departure 18.00hrs
A sheltered site in a hidden valley, with wonderful views. This peaceful park is set on a working farm, next to a mountain stream with shallow ponds for children to play in. There are plenty of delightful walks from, and over, the farm. A 7-acre site with 40 touring pitches.
Facilities: ⬀⊙✳⬤⬀ **Services:** ⬤⬤⬀⬀⬤
→⬀⊙⬤⬤⬀⬤

CHURCH STOKE   Map 07 SO29

► ► ► ► **Daisy Bank Caravan Park (SO303929)**
Snead SY15 6EB ☎ 01588 620471
Dir: From A49 at Craven Arms take A489 to Churchstoke. Turn off 1.5m after Bishops Castle
★ ⬛ £7.50-£9 ⬛ £7.50-£9 ⬀ £5-£7.50
Open Feb-Nov Booking advisable bank hols Last arrival 21.00hrs Last departure 17.00hrs
A first-rate park in an idyllic setting amongst the Welsh and Shropshire hills, with glorious views in all directions. The park is for adults only, and offers a peaceful environment in which to relax. The superb sanitary facilities are enhanced by the addition of fresh flowers and piped music, and they are always in excellent condition. A 9-hole putting green is a popular addition to the park. A 4-acre site with 40 touring pitches.
Putting green
Facilities: ⬀⊙✳⬤⬤⬀⬀⬀ **Services:** ⬤⬀⬤⬤
→⬤⊙⬀⬤⬤

► ► **Bacheldre Watermill Touring & Camping Park (SO243928)**
Bacheldre Watermill SY15 6TE ☎ 01588 620489
Dir: Located 2m W of Churchstoke on the A489. Site 50yds on right
★ ⬛ £6 ⬛ £6 ⬀ £6
Open Etr-Oct Booking advisable bank hols Last departure noon
Secluded little site in the grounds of a working water mill. A 2-acre site with 25 touring pitches.
Facilities: ⬀⊙✳⬤⬤⬀ **Services:** ⬤⬤
→⬀⬤

CRICKHOWELL   Map 03 SO21

► ► ► **Riverside Caravan & Camping Park (SO215184)**
New Rd NP8 1AY ☎ 01873 810397
Dir: On A4077, & well signed from A40
★ ⬛ fr £7 ⬛ fr £7 ⬀ fr £8
Open Mar-Oct Booking advisable for stays over 1 wk Last arrival 23.00hrs
A clean and well-maintained site, adjacent to the River Usk, in lovely tranquil surroundings. The site does not take children. A 3.5-acre site with 35 touring pitches and 20 statics.
Facilities: ⬀⊙✳⬤⬤ **Services:** ⬤⬀⬀⬤
→⬤⬀⬀⬀

CROSSGATES   Map 03 SO06

► ► ► *Greenway Manor (SO081651)*
LD1 6RF ☎ 01597 851230
Dir: Immediately off A44, 0.5m W of Crossgates
⬛⬛⬀
Open May-Oct
A small secluded site in the wooded and lawned grounds of a newly-refurbished hotel. A 2-acre site with 13 touring pitches.
Facilities: ⬀

► ► **The Park Motel (SO081651)**
Rhayader Rd LD1 6RF ☎ 01597 851201
Dir: 3m N of Llandrindod Wells on A44 on Rhayader Rd
★ ⬛ £6.75-£7.50 ⬛ £6.75-£7.50 ⬀ £6.75-£7.50
Open Mar-Oct Booking advisable bank hols Last arrival 22.30hrs Last departure noon
This quiet rural site, set in beautiful countryside, has flat pitches and is well-sheltered by trees. It is an ideal touring centre. A 3-acre site with 10 touring pitches and 15 statics.
Leisure: ⬤⚬ **Facilities:** ⬀⊙✳⬤⬤⬀
Services: ⬤⬤⬀⬀⬤✕⬀
→⬤⊙⬀⬀⬤⬀⬤

LLANDRINDOD WELLS   Map 03 SO06

► ► ► **Disserth Caravan & Camping Park (SO035583)**
Disserth, Howey LD1 6NL ☎ 01597 860277
Dir: 1m off A483, between Howey and Newbridge on Wye, alongside 13th-century church
⬛ £7.25-£8.50 ⬛ £7.25-£8.50 ⬀ £7.25-£8.50
Open Mar-Oct Booking advisable early as possible Last arrival 22.00hrs Last departure noon

---

Facilities: ⬤ Bath ⬀ Shower ⊙ Electric Shaver ⬀ Hairdryer ✳ Ice Pack Facility ⬤ Disabled Facilities ⬤ Public Telephone
⬤ Shop on Site or within 200yds ⬛ Mobile Shop (calls at least 5 days a week) ⬀ BBQ Area ⬀ Picnic Area ⬀ Dog Exercise Area

A peaceful site nestling in a beautiful valley on the banks of R. Ithon, a tributary of the R. Wye. A 2.5-acre site with 25 touring pitches and 21 statics. Private trout fishing.

Facilities: ſ⊙ℛ⚲⛽ Services: 🅴🆅♀🅰🅸⊡✕

→⊍⊍⦿⚤⚤⚤⚄⚄⚄ 🌐 🚍 🌐 🛞 🔵

► ► Dalmore Camping & Caravanning Park (SO045568)
Howey LD1 5RG ☎ 01597 822483
Dir: 1.5m S of Village
★ 🚐 £6.50-£7.50 🚐 £6.50-£7.50 ⛺ £5-£7.50
Open Mar-Oct Booking advisable Jun-Aug Last arrival 22.00hrs Last departure noon
A clean, tidy site located on A483 but screened from road and traffic noise by hedgerow. Wonderful views. A 2-acre site with 20 touring pitches and 20 statics.

Facilities: ſ⊙⚹⚲⛽✝ Services: 🅴🅰🅸⊡

→⊍⊍⦿⚤⚤⚄⚄⚄

LLANGORSE   Map 03 SO12

► ► ► Lakeside Caravan Park (SO128272)
LD3 7TR ☎ 01874 658226
★ 🚐 £7-£9 🚐 £7-£9 ⛺ £7-£9
Open Jun-Sep (rs Mar, Apr, May & Oct swimming pool, clubhouse, restaurant, shop) Booking advisable peak periods Last arrival 21.30hrs Last departure noon
An attractive park comprising two level fields, with areas of maturing vegetation. Located next to Llangorse Lake, and with its direct access to the water it makes an ideal centre for water sports enthusiasts. A 2-acre site with 40 touring pitches and 72 statics.
Boat hire & launching, windsurfing, fishing.

Leisure: ↘ ⚠ Facilities: ſ⊙ℛ⚹⚲⛽🐾✝
Services: 🅴🅱♀🅰⊡✕ 🔥

→⊍⚄⚤⚄ 🌐 🚍 🌐 🛞 🔵

MIDDLETOWN   Map 07 SJ31

► ► Bank Farm Caravan Park (SJ293123)
SY21 8EJ ☎ 01938 570526
Dir: 13m W of Shrewsbury, 5m E of Welshpool on A458
🚐 £7.50-£8.50 🚐 £7.50-£8.50 ⛺ fr £5.50
Open May-Oct Booking advisable bank hols Last arrival 20.00hrs
A grass site with two different areas - one gently sloping and the other mainly level. Immediate access to hills, mountains and woodland. A 2-acre site with 20 touring pitches and 33 statics.
Trout pool.

Leisure: ↘ ⚠ Facilities: ſ⊙ℛ⚹⚲⛽✝
Services: 🅴🅰⊡

→⊮⚄⚤

PRESTEIGNE   Map 03 SO36

► ► ► Rock Bridge Park (SO294654)
LD8 2NF ☎ 01547 560300
Dir: 1m W of Presteigne off B4356
🚐 🚐 ⛺
Open Apr-Oct Booking advisable public & school hols Last arrival 21.30hrs Last departure noon ⚹

Part-level, part-sloping grass site with trees and bushes, set in meadowland with access to River Lugg. A new bridge across the stream gives good access to nearby footpaths. A 3-acre site with 35 touring pitches and 30 statics.

Facilities: ſ⊙⚹⛽&ⵣ Services: 🅴🅰🅸⊡

→⊮⚄⚤

TALGARTH   Map 03 SO13

► ► ► Riverside International (SO148346)
Bronllys LD3 0HL ☎ 01874 711320 & 712064
Dir: On A479 opposite Bronllys Castle
★ 🚐 £8.50-£9.50 🚐 £8.50-£9.50 ⛺ £8.50-£9.50
Open Etr-Oct Booking advisable bank hols & Jul-Aug Last arrival 22.00hrs Last departure 16.00hrs ⚹
Well-appointed touring site with pitches available on riverside. Elevated position with magnificent views of the Black Mountains. A 9-acre site with 80 touring pitches.
Leisure facilities, sauna, jacuzzi, sunbed & gym.

See advertisement under BRECON

Leisure: ↘ ⚛ ⚠ ⬜ Facilities: ⬅ſ⊙ℛ⚹⛽&ⵣ⚲⛽
Services: 🅴🅱♀🅰🅸⊡🆃✕🔥

→⊍⚄⚤⚄ 🌐 🚍 🛞 🔵

SWANSEA

RHOSSILI   Map 02 SS48

► ► ► Pitton Cross Caravan & Camping Park (SS434877)
SA3 1PH ☎ 01792 390593
Dir: 2m W of Scurlage on B4247
★ 🚐 £8.50-£11.25 🚐 £6.50-£11.25 ⛺ £8-£11.25
Open Apr-Oct Booking advisable Spring bank hol & Jul-Aug Last arrival 21.00hrs Last departure noon
Constantly improving farm site within walking distance of the coast, with enthusiastic proprietors. A 6-acre site with 100 touring pitches.
Motor caravan service bay, baby bath

See advertisement under SWANSEA

Leisure: ⚠ Facilities: ſ⊙ℛ⚹⛽&⚲⛽✝
Services: 🅴🅱🅰⊡🆃 ⬅

→⊍⊮⚄⚤ 🌐 🚍 🌐 🛞 🔵

SWANSEA   Map 03 SS69

► ► ► Riverside Caravan Park (SS679991)
Ynys Forgan Farm, Morriston SA6 6QL
☎ 01792 775587
Dir: 1m NE of A48/A4067 unclass road 200mtr M4 junct 45
🚐 🚐 ⛺
Open all year (rs winter months pool & club)
Booking advisable bank hols & main school hols Last arrival mdnt Last departure noon
A large site close to the M4, an ideal base for touring Mumbles, Gower beaches and Brecon National Park. A 70-acre site with 120 touring pitches and 132 statics.
Fishing on site by arrangement.

Leisure: ↘ ⚛ ⚠ ⬜ Facilities: ſ⊙ℛ⚹⛽&⚲⛽✝
Services: 🅴🅱♀🅰🅸⊡🆃🔥

→⊍⦿⚤⚤⚄ 🌐 🚍 🌐 🛞 🔵

Services: Ⓣ Toilet Fluid ✕ Café/ Restaurant 🔥 Fast Food/Takeaway ⬅ Baby Care 🅴 Electric Hook Up
🅱 Launderette ♀ Licensed Bar 🅰 Calor Gaz 🅸 Camping Gaz ⊡ Battery Charging

WTB
★★★

Pitton Cross
Caravan Park

AA
▶▶▶

RHOSSILI, SWANSEA, SA3 1PH
Tel: 01792 390593 Fax: 01792 391010
www.pittoncross.co.uk
e-mail: Rogerbuttonmm@Tesco.net

We pride ourselves in providing excellent camping facilities over many years. In a superb location close to beautiful coves and sandy beaches and some of the finest countryside in Wales. **Over 50's discount when pre-booked Low/mid season.** A well deserving 3 star touring and camping park (WTB August 99).

VALE OF GLAMORGAN

LLANTWIT MAJOR   Map 03 SS96

▶ ▶ ▶ **Acorn Camping & Caravan Site (SS973678)**
Ham Ln South CF61 1RP
☎ 01446 794024 & 0589 421112
Dir: From Llantwit Major follow B4265 S. Approach site through Ham Manor residential park
★ ➡ £6-£7 ➡ £6-£7 Å £6-£7
Open Etr or 1st Feb - 8th Dec Booking advisable bank hols & Aug Last arrival 23.00hrs Last departure noon
A quiet country site on meadowland, with individual pitches marked out by hedges and shrubs. Within one mile of the sea, and offering ultra-modern facilities. A 4.5-acre site with 90 touring pitches and 15 statics.
Leisure: ◣ ⚠ Facilities: 🛈⊙🔫✳⛄🔧🛒 Services: 🖳🛈🖩⊞⚦⛟
→ ∪ 🖉 🍽 🗒 🥤

▶ ▶ ▶ **Llandow Touring Caravan Park (SS956713)**
CF7 7PB ☎ 01446 794527 & 792462
Dir: Signed off B4270
★ ➡ £7-£9 ➡ £7-£9 Å £5-£9
Open Feb-Nov Booking advisable bank hols & end Jun Last arrival 10.00hrs Last departure noon
A large level touring park with a new purpose-built toilet block, within easy reach of Glamorgan's Heritage Coast, and a short distance from Cardiff

and Porthcawl. A 6-acre site with 100 touring pitches.
Caravan Storage
Leisure: ⚠ Facilities: 🛈⊙🔫✳⛄🔧🛒🏕🐕 Services: 🖳🛈🖩⊞⚦⊞⊤
→ ∪ 🍽 🥤

WREXHAM

BANGOR-ON-DEE   Map 07 SJ34

▶ ▶ ▶ **Camping & Caravanning Club Site (SJ385448)**
The Racecourse, Overton Rd LL13 0DA
☎ 01978 781009
Dir: From A525 follow racecourse/camping signs through village, turn left immediately opposite Buck Hotel, site 1m on right
★ ➡ £9.80-£12.40 ➡ £9.80-£12.40 Å £9.80-£12.40
Open 20 Mar-1 Nov Booking advisable bank hols & peak periods Last arrival 21.00hrs Last departure noon
A mainly level, grassy site within the racecourse which lies in a bend of the River Dee. Please see the advertisement on page 14 for details of Club Members' benefits. A 6-acre site with 100 touring pitches.
Horse racing
Facilities: 🛈⊙✳⛄🔧🛒🐕 Services: 🖳🛈🖩⊞⚦⊞⊤
→ ∪ 🍽 🥤 🍽 🗒

EYTON   Map 07 SJ34

▶ ▶ ▶ ▶ **The Plassey Leisure Park (SJ353452)**
The Plassey LL13 0SP ☎ 01978 780277
Dir: Leave A483 at Bangor-on-Dee exit, along B5426 for 2.5m. Follow signs to site
★ ➡ £11-£13.50 ➡ £11-£13.50 Å £11-£13.50
Open Mar-Oct Booking advisable bank hols & school hols Last arrival 20.00hrs Last departure 18.00hrs

A lovely level grassy site set in 247 acres of quiet farm and meadowland. Adjoining the Plassey Craft Centre. A 10-acre site with 120 touring pitches and 80 statics.
Sauna, sunbed, badminton, table tennis,9-hole golf.
Leisure: 🔫 ◣ ⚠ 🖵 Facilities: 🛈⊙🔫✳⛄🔧🛒🏕🐕 Services: 🖳🛈🖩🍽⚦⊞⊤✖⛟
→ ∪ 🍽 ⊚ 🖉 🍽 🗒 🗒 🥤

Facilities: 🛁 Bath 🛈 Shower ⊙ Electric Shaver 🔫 Hairdryer ✳ Ice Pack Facility ⛐ Disabled Facilities 🔧 Public Telephone 🛒 Shop on Site or within 200yds 🖳 Mobile Shop (calls at least 5 days a week) 🏕 BBQ Area 🗒 Picnic Area 🐕 Dog Exercise Area

Ireland

NORTHERN IRELAND

CO ANTRIM

BALLYCASTLE   Map 01 D6

▶ ▶ ▶ *Silver Cliffs Holiday Village*
21 Clare Rd BT54 6DB ☎ 028 20762550
Dir: 0.25m W of Ballycastle, off A2
🚐 🚘 ▲
Open 17 Mar-Oct Booking advisable 11-25 Jul & 22-25 Aug Last arrival 20.00hrs Last departure 17.00hrs
A large seaside site with a swimming pool and bar. Close to the beach and River Glenshesk. A 2-acre site with 50 touring pitches and 250 statics.
Sun beds, sauna, spa & snooker.
Leisure: ₹ ♠ ⚑ Facilities: ⋔⊙✻ᚼ℄ᚼᚼᚼ
Services: ⚑⊠⚏⬦⊘⊟⊤✕⬥
➔ ∪ ▶ ⬥ ⟍ 🍴 💷

BALLYMONEY   Map 01 C6

▶ ▶ ▶ ▶ *Drumaheglis Marina & Caravan Park*
36 Glenstall Rd BT53 7QN
☎ 028 27666466 & 27662280
Dir: Signed off A26, approx 1.5m outside Ballymoney in direction of Coleraine off B66 S of Ballymoney
🚐 🚘 ▲
Open 31 Mar-1 Oct Booking advisable
Exceptionally well-designed and laid out park beside the Lower Bann River, with very spacious pitches and two quality toilet blocks. Ideal base for touring Antrim or for water sports enthusiasts. A 16-acre site with 52 touring pitches.
Leisure: ⚑ Facilities: ⋔⊙◔✻ᚼ℄ᚼᚼ⋔
Services: ⚑♦
➔ ∪ ▶ ⬥ ⟍ ⬦ ⊠ᚼ

BUSHMILLS   Map 01 C6

▶ ▶ ▶ ▶ *Ballyness Caravan Park*
36 Castlecatt Rd BT57 8TN ☎ 028 20732393
Dir: On outskirts of Bushmills on Dervock road, a short distance from town
Open 17 Mar-Oct
A quality park with superb toilet and other facilities, on farmland beside St Columb's Rill, the stream which supplies the famous Bushmills distillery. Several ponds provide good fishing, and the park is peacefully located close to the beautiful North Antrim coast. The friendly owners have built this brand new park with the discerning camper in mind. A 12-acre site with 45 touring pitches and 15 statics.
Leisure: ⚑ Facilities: ✻℄ᚼ Services: ♦⊟⊤
➔ ∪ ▶ ⟍ 🍴 💷 ⬦ ◑

CUSHENDALL   Map 01 D6

▶ ▶ *Cushendall Caravan Camp*
62 Coast Rd BT44 0QW ☎ 028 2171699
Dir: On A2, 1m S of town
🚐 🚘 ▲

Open mid Mar-mid Oct Booking advisable peak periods Last arrival 23.00hrs Last departure 14.00hrs
A pleasant site next to the beach and sailing club. A 1-acre site with 14 touring pitches and 64 statics.
Facilities: ⋔⊙◔℄ᚼᚼᚼ Services: ⊟♦
➔ ∪ ▶ ◎ ⬥ ⬦ ⟍ 🍴

CUSHENDUN   Map 01 D6

▶ ▶ *Cushendun Caravan Park*
14 Glendun Rd BT44 0PX ☎ 028 25761254
Dir: From A2 take B92 for 1m towards Glenarm, signed
🚐 🚘 ▲
Open Etr-Sep Booking advisable Jul-Aug Last arrival 22.00hrs Last departure 12.30hrs
A pretty little grassy park surrounded by trees, with separate secluded areas offering some privacy, and static vans discreetly interspersed with tourers. A 0.5-acre site with 15 touring pitches and 50 statics.
Leisure: ♠⚑⎄ Facilities: ➔⋔⊙◔℄ᚼ
➔ ∪ ▶ ◎ ⬦ ⟍ ⊟

LARNE   Map 01 D5

▶ ▶ ▶ *Curran Court Caravan Park*
131 Curran Rd BT40 1BD
☎ 028 28273797 & 277994
Dir: Site on A2, 0.25m from ferry. From town centre follow signs for Leisure Centre, opposite Curran Court Hotel
★ 🚐 £8.50-£10 🚘 £8.50-£10 ▲ £5-£6.50
Open Apr-Sep Booking advisable main season
A tidy and very clean council site ideal for the ferry and clearly signed. A 3-acre site with 40 touring pitches.
Bowling & putting greens.
Leisure: ⚑ Facilities: ⋔℄ᚼᚼᚼ⋔ Services: ⚑
➔ ▶ ◎ ⬦ ⚏ ⟍ ⊟ 🍴 💷 ◑ ⊜

PORTBALLINTRAE   Map 01 C6

▶ ▶ *PortBallintrae Caravan Park*
Ballaghmore Av BT57 8RX ☎ 028 20731478
Dir: Located in Portballintrae village, clearly signed from A2, 0.25m from Bushmills Distillery
🚐 🚘 ▲
Open Apr-Sep Booking advisable Etr & Jul-Aug Last arrival 20.30hrs Last departure 14.00hrs
Very tidy site, popular for Giants Causeway. A 12-acre site with 53 touring pitches and 150 statics.
Leisure: ⚑ Facilities: ⋔⊙✻ᚼ℄⋔ Services: ⚑⊟♦
➔ ∪ ▶ ⬦ ⟍

CO DOWN

CASTLEWELLAN   Map 01 D5

▶ ▶ ▶ *Castlewellan Forest Park*
BT31 9BU ☎ 028 43778664
Dir: Off A25, in Castlewellan turn right at Upper Square and turn into Forest Park which is signed
🚐 £7-£11 🚘 £7-£11 ▲ £7-£11
Open all year Booking advisable wknds & Jul-Aug Last arrival 22.00hrs Last departure 15.00hrs

---

Facilities: ➔ Bath ⋔ Shower ⊙ Electric Shaver ◔ Hairdryer ✻ Ice Pack Facility ᚼ Disabled Facilities ℄ Public Telephone
ᚼ Shop on Site or within 200yds ⊟ Mobile Shop (calls at least 5 days a week) ᚼ BBQ Area ᚼ Picnic Area ⋔ Dog Exercise Area

Attractive forest park site, situated down a long drive with views of the castle. Site broken up into smaller areas by mature trees and shrubs. A 5-acre site with 90 touring pitches.
Lake, arboretum, fishing on site. First aid.
Facilities: ▥ ☉ ✳ ᕼ Ꮮ ᎑ ᕱ 쿠 ᛘ **Services:** ⊞ ✕ ᛤ
➙ ∪ ▶ ᎎ ┘

NEWCASTLE   Map 01 D5

▶ ▶ ▶ *Tollymore Forest Park*
☎ 028 44722428
Dir: From A2 at Newcastle take B180, site signed on right
⊞ ⊞ ᗩ
Open 15 Mar-15 Nov (rs 16 Nov-14 Mar) Booking advisable Jul & Aug & wknds Apr-Sep Last arrival 21.00hrs Last departure 17.00hrs
Popular site with family field and large tent area, set in a large and beautiful forest park. A 7.5-acre site with 100 touring pitches.
Facilities: ▥ ☉ ᕼ Ꮮ ᎑ ᗮ 噕 ᕱ **Services:** ⊞ ᗙ � ⌀ ✕
➙ ∪ ▶ ◎ ◍ ᎎ ᛤ ┘

CO FERMANAGH

ENNISKILLEN   Map 01 C5

▶ ▶ *Blaney Caravan Park*
BT93 7ER ☎ 028 68641634
Dir: On A46, Enniskillen to Belleek road, approx 12km from Enniskillen
Open all year
Small park close to Lough Erne, ideal for touring, and offering adequate facilities. A 3-acre site with 26 touring pitches and 12 statics.

LISNASKEA   Map 01 C5

▶ ▶ ▶ *Mullynascarty Caravan Park*
BT92 0NZ ☎ 028 67721040
⊞ ⊞ ᗩ
Open Apr-Sep Booking advisable Jul-Aug Last arrival 21.00hrs Last departure noon
A pretty riverside site set in peaceful countryside. With well kept facilities and helpful owners. A 4-acre site with 43 touring pitches.
Leisure: ⅄ **Facilities:** ▥ ☉ ✳ ᕼ Ꮮ ᗮ 쿠 **Services:** ⊞
➙ ∪ ▶ ᎎ ᛤ ┘ ▣ ᛤ

CO LONDONDERRY

CASTLEROCK   Map 01 C6

▶ ▶ ▶ *Castlerock Holiday Park*
24 Sea Rd ☎ 028 70848381
Dir: From A2 to Castlerock, turn right before the railway station, site signed
★ ⊞ £8-£12 ⊞ £8-£12 ᗩ £8-£12
Open Etr-Oct Booking advisable Jul-Aug Last arrival 21.00hrs Last departure noon
A mainly static site at the seaside with a tidy touring area, 2 minutes from the beach. A 12.5-acre site with 20 touring pitches and 260 statics.

Leisure: ▲ ⅄ **Facilities:** ▥ ☉ Ꮮ Ꮮ **Services:** ⊞ ᎎ ⌀ ᎌ ᎗ ᛤ
➙ ∪ ▶ ᎎ ┘ ᛤ

CO TYRONE

DUNGANNON   Map 01 C5

▶ ▶ ▶ *Dungannon Park*
Moy Rd BT71 6BT ☎ 028 8727327
Dir: Situated 1m from A4 on A29, 1m from Dungannon
⊞ ⊞
Open all year Booking advisable
Brand new caravan park in 1999 in quiet area of public park with fishing lake and excellent facilities, especially for disabled. A 2-acre site with 12 touring pitches.
Leisure: ⅄ **Facilities:** ▥ ☉ Ꮮ Ꮮ 噕 ᕱ ᕱ
Services: ⊞ ᎌ ✕
➙ ∪ ▶ ᎎ ᛤ ┘ ▣ ᛤ

REPUBLIC OF IRELAND

CO CLARE

KILLALOE   Map 01 B3

▶ ▶ ▶ ▶ *Lough Derg Caravan and Camping Park*
☎ 061 376329
Dir: Take R463 N from Killaloe beside Lough Derg, site on right after a few miles
⊞ ⊞ ᗩ
Open 29 Apr-Sep Last arrival 21.00hrs Last departure noon ⍻
Well laid out wooded park with good screening, and frontage onto Lough Derg, with groups of spacious pitches in secluded plots. A 4.5-acre site with 57 touring pitches and 15 statics.
Boats for hire, boat slipway, fishing.
Leisure: ⌇ ◣ ⅄ **Facilities:** ▥ ☉ ᎗ ✳ Ᏼ ᎑
Services: ⊞ ᎌ ⌀ ᎌ ᎗ ✕ ᛤ
➙ ∪ ▶ ◍ ᎎ ┘

KILRUSH   Map 01 B3

▶ ▶ ▶ *Aylevarroo Caravan and Camping Park*
☎ 065 9051102
Dir: 1.5m before Kilrush on N67 close to Tarbert car ferry
⊞ ⊞ ᗩ
Open 24 May-13 Sep Booking advisable Last arrival 22.00hrs Last departure noon ⍻
A peaceful park in rolling countryside right on the edge of the Shannon Estuary. A 7.5-acre site with 36 touring pitches and 10 statics.
Basketball court.
Leisure: ⌇ ◣ ⅄ ▢ **Facilities:** ▥ ☉ ✳ Ꮮ
Services: ⊞ ᎎ ⌀
➙ ∪ ▶ ◎ ◍ ᎎ ᎎ ┘ ▣ ᛤ

Ireland

LAHINCH — Map 01 B3

► ► ► *Lahinch Camping and Caravan Park*
☎ (065) 81424
Dir: On N67
🚐🚐⚠

Open May-Sep Booking advisable mid Jul-mid Aug
Last arrival 23.00hrs Last departure noon
*Busy park in the seaside town of Lahinch, enclosed
by houses but close to magnificent coastal and
mountain scenery, including the towering Cliffs of
Moher. A 5-acre site with 115 touring pitches and 12
statics.*
Bicycle hire.

Leisure: ◔ 🅰 ▢ **Facilities:** ⋔ ☉ 🭮 ☀ ☍ 🝨
Services: 🖵 🗟 🖭
→ ∪ ▶ ⊚ ⌂ ⅄ ∿

CO CORK

BALLINSPITTLE — Map 01 B2

► ► ► ► *Garrettstown House Holiday Park*
☎ 021 778156 & 775286
Dir: 6m from Kinsale, through Ballinspittle village, past
school and football pitch on main road to beach. Beside
stone estate entrance.
★ 🚐 IR£9.50-IR£10.50 🚐 IR£9.50-IR£10.50
⚠ IR£8.50-IR£10.50

Open May-Sep (rs Etr-1 May No shop) Booking
advisable 10 Jul-15 Aug Last arrival 22.00hrs Last
departure noon
*Elevated holiday park with tiered camping areas
and superb panoramic views. Plenty of on-site
amenities, and close to beach and forest park. A
7-acre site with 60 touring pitches and 80 statics.*
Childrens club, crazy golf, video shows
Leisure: ◔ ◔ 🅰 ▢ **Facilities:** ⋔ ☉ 🭮 ☀ ⅋ ☍ 🝨 ✦
Services: 🖵 🗟 🖉 🖽 🖵 ✕ 🥄
→ ∪ ▶ ⊚ ⌂ ⅄ ∿ 💳 🎫

BALLYLICKEY — Map 01 B2

► ► ► ► *Eagle Point Caravan and Camping Park*
☎ 027 50630
Dir: 4m from Bantry, in Ballylickey, on N71, opposite
petrol station
🚐🚐⚠

Open May-Sep Booking advisable Last arrival
22.00hrs Last departure noon 🐾

GARRETTSTOWN HOUSE HOLIDAY PARK ► ► ► ►

**Garrettstown, Kinsale, Co Cork
Tel: 00 353 21 778156/775286**

Top class spacious park in old world setting of
Garrettstown estate near beach and forest. Ideally
located for touring, scenic, historic and amenity
areas of the south. Kinsale, gourmet centre of
Ireland is 6 miles. Cork/Ringaskiddy ferryport 25
miles. Numerous facilities and activities on site or
within 16 km.
*Recommended by all main camping clubs
including BFE 4 star*

*An immaculate park set in an idyllic position
overlooking the rugged bays and mountains of west
Cork. Boat launching facilities and small pebble
beaches, in an area of outstanding natural beauty.
A 20-acre site with 125 touring pitches.*
Leisure: ◔ 🅰 ▢ **Facilities:** ⋔ ☉ ☀ ☍ 🝨
Services: 🖵 🗟 🖭
→ ∪ ▶ ⌂ ∿ 💳 🎫

BLARNEY — Map 01 B2

► ► ► *Blarney Caravan & Camping Park*
Stone View ☎ 021 4385167 & 4382051
Dir: N20 from Cork or Limerick, then R617 to Blarney
🚐 IR£10-IR£11 🚐 IR£10-IR£11 ⚠ IR£9-IR£10
Open all year Booking advisable anytime Last
arrival 22.00hrs Last departure noon
*Attractive, well-kept grassy park in elevated position
overlooking countryside and Blarney Castle. Very
spacious and quiet, surrounded by hedging, with
adjacent pub and restaurant run by family. A 3-acre
site with 40 touring pitches.*
Mini golf, 18-hole golf course
Leisure: ▢ **Facilities:** ⋔ ☉ 🭮 ☀ ☍ 🝨 🀫 ✦
Services: 🖵 ⅄ 🖉 ✕
→ ∪ ▶ ⊚ ∿ 🗟 🎫 💳

Facilities: 🛁 Bath ⋔ Shower ☉ Electric Shaver 🭮 Hairdryer ☀ Ice Pack Facility ☍ Disabled Facilities ☍ Public Telephone
🝨 Shop on Site or within 200yds 🖽 Mobile Shop (calls at least 5 days a week) 🀫 BBQ Area 🀫 Picnic Area ✦ Dog Exercise Area

CROOKHAVEN   Map 01 A1

► ► ► ► *Barley Cove Caravan Park*
☎ 028 35302 & 021 346466
*Dir: Follow signs for Crookhaven on R592 from
Ballydehob, site on right next to sandy cove, after
Goleen*
⬙ ⬙ ⚠
Open Etr & Jun-1 Sep (rs May & Sep) Booking
advisable 7 Jul-17 Aug Last arrival 21.00hrs Last
departure noon ⬙
*Spacious holiday park in seaside location beside
two coves and lovely sandy beaches. A very rural
spot on the scenic Mizen Head peninsula. A 9-acre
site with 100 touring pitches and 50 statics.
Pitch & putt, children's playhouse*
Leisure: ⬙ ⬙ ⚠ ⬙ **Facilities:** ⬙ ⬙ ⬙ ⬙ ⬙ ⬙ ⬙ ⬙ ⬙ ⬙
Services: ⬙ ⬙ ⬙ ⬙ ⬙ ⬙ ⬙ ⬙
→ ⬙ ⬙ ⬙ ⬙

CO DONEGAL

PORTNOO   Map 01 B5

► ► *Boyle's Caravan Park*
☎ 075 45131 & 086 8523131
*Dir: Turn off N56 at Ardra onto R261 for 6m. Follow
signs for Santaann Drive*
★ ⬙ IR£10 ⬙ IR£10 ⚠ IR£10
Open 18 Mar-Oct Booking advisable All year Last
arrival 23.00hrs Last departure 11.00hrs
*Set at Banna Beach and close to a huge selection of
water activities on a magnificent stretch of the
Atlantic. This open park nestles among the sand
dunes, and offers well-maintained facilities. A 1.5-
acre site with 20 touring pitches and 10 statics.*
Facilities: ⬙ ⬙ ⬙ ⬙ ⬙ ⬙ ⬙ ⬙ **Services:** ⬙ ⬙ ⬙ ⬙
→ ⬙ ⬙ ⬙ ⬙ ⬙

CO DUBLIN

CLONDALKIN   Map 01 D4

► ► ► ► *Camac Valley Tourist Caravan &
Camping Park*
Naas Rd ☎ 01 4640644
Dir: Directly off N7, near Clondalkin village
⬙ ⬙ ⚠
Booking advisable Jul & Aug Last arrival anytime
Last departure noon
*A pleasant lightly wooded park with top class
layout, facilities and security, within a 30 minute
drive or bus ride of the city centre. A 15-acre site
with 163 touring pitches.*
Leisure: ⚠ ⬙ **Facilities:** ⬙ ⬙ ⬙ ⬙ ⬙ ⬙ ⬙ ⬙
Services: ⬙ ⬙ ⬙ ⬙ ⬙
→ ⬙ ⬙ ⬙ ⬙ ⬙

SHANKILL   Map 01 D3

► ► ► *Shankill Caravan Park*
☎ 01 2820011
*Dir: From Dublin, 10m S on N11. From Dun Laoghaire,
follow signs to N11, at N11 turn left. From Rosslare,
turn off M11 at Bray/Shankill sign*
⬙ IR£9-IR£10 ⬙ IR£9-IR£10 ⚠ IR£8-IR£8.50
Open all year Last departure noon
*Pretty tree-studded park with camping areas
divided into smaller plots, and offering generous
facilities. A 7-acre site with 82 touring pitches and 9
statics.*
Facilities: ⬙ ⬙ ⬙ ⬙ ⬙ ⬙ **Services:** ⬙ ⬙ ⬙ ⬙
→ ⬙ ⬙ ⬙ ⬙ ⬙ ⬙ ⬙

CO KERRY

ARDFERT   Map 01 A2

► ► *Sir Roger's Caravan & Camping Park*
Banna Beach ☎ 066 7134730
Dir: 3km from Ardfert, 9km NW of Tralee
⬙
Open May-1 Oct
*A well-maintained park next to a famous surfing
beach, with hire equipment available, and 'Blue
Flag' rating. This modern park is well equipped, and
run by friendly owners. A 3.5-acre site with 50
touring pitches and 20 statics.*

CAHERDANIEL   Map 01 A2

► ► ► ► *Wave Crest Caravan and Camping Park*
☎ 066 9475188
*Dir: On main N70 Ring of Kerry road, from Sneem
direction 1m before Caherdaniel on left*
⬙ ⬙ ⚠

Open 17 Mar-12 Oct Last arrival 22.00hrs Last
departure noon
*Seaside site, with pitches tucked away in the natural
contours of the hillside, and offering plenty of
privacy. Very good facilities, and an excellent shop.
A 4.5-acre site with 45 touring pitches and 2 statics.
Boat anchorage, fishing & pool room.*
Leisure: ⬙ ⚠ ⬙ **Facilities:** ⬙ ⬙ ⬙ ⬙ ⬙ ⬙ ⬙ ⬙ ⬙ ⬙
Services: ⬙ ⬙ ⬙ ⬙ ⬙ ⬙ ⬙ ⬙
→ ⬙ ⬙ ⬙ ⬙ ⬙ ⬙

Ireland

Services: Ⓣ Toilet Fluid ✗ Café/ Restaurant ⬙ Fast Food/Takeaway ⬙ Baby Care ⬙ Electric Hook Up
⬙ Launderette ⬙ Licensed Bar ⬙ Calor Gaz ⬙ Camping Gaz ⬙ Battery Charging

KILLARNEY　　　　　　　Map 01 B2

Fossa Caravan Park
Fossa ☎ 064 31497
Dir: 2.5m SW on N72W
★ 🚐 IR£9-IR£9.50　🚐 IR£9-IR£9.50
▲ IR£8.50-IR£9.50
Open Etr-Sep (rs Sep & Apr-May restaurant &
takeaway closed) Booking advisable Jul-Aug
Last arrival 23.00hrs Last departure noon
Attractive terraced park, in lightly wooded
grounds, with good screening and easy access
to main facilities. A 6-acre site with 100 touring
pitches and 20 statics.
Campers kitchens & bikes for hire.
Leisure: ☌ ♦ ⚠ ☐ **Facilities:** ⋔ ☉ ⌇ ✲ ⚅ ⛢ ⚒ ⊓
Services: ⛽ ⑤ ⌀ ✕ ⚱
→ ∪ ┣ ◉ ┿ ⚌ ✔ ▓ ▒

KILLORGLIN　　　　　　　Map 01 A2

▶ ▶ ▶ **West's Caravan Park & Mobile Home Hire**
Killarney Rd ☎ 066 9761240
Dir: 1m on Killarney road
🚐 IR£8-IR£9　🚐 IR£8-IR£9 ▲ IR£8-IR£9

Open Apr-Oct Booking advisable mid Jul-mid Aug
Last arrival 21.00hrs Last departure noon
Pretty little site on banks of the R. Laune, but safely
fenced off, offering trout and salmon fishing, and
good facilities for families. A 5-acre site with 20
touring pitches and 40 statics.
Salmon/Trout fishing.
Leisure: ☌ ♦ ⚠ ☐ **Facilities:** ⋔ ☉ ⌇ ✲ ⚅ ⛢ ⚒ ⊓
Services: ⛽ ⑤ ⊞ ✔
→ ∪ ┣ ✔ ▓ ▒

LAURAGH　　　　　　　Map 01 A2

▶ ▶ **Creveen Park**
Healy Pass Rd ☎ 064 83131
Dir: 1m SE on R574
🚐 IR£7-IR£9　🚐 IR£7-IR£9 ▲ IR£7-IR£9
Open Etr-Oct Booking advisable Aug bank hol Last
arrival mdnt Last departure noon
Wild and beautiful site on hill farm, with views of
sea and mountains. Good facilities including an
equipped kitchen for tenters. A 2-acre site with 20
touring pitches and 2 statics.
Leisure: ⚠ ☐ **Facilities:** ⋔ ☉ ✲ ⚅ ⊓ ⌇
Services: ⛽ ⑤ ⌀ ⊞ ✕
→ ⌇ ✔

WATERVILLE　　　　　　　Map 01 A2

▶ ▶ ▶ *Waterville Caravan and Camping*
Spunkane ☎ 066 9474191
Dir: 1km N of Waterville just off main N70, Ring of Kerry
road
🚐 🚐 ▲
Open Etr-Sep Booking advisable Jul-Aug Last
departure noon
Seaside park with a good range of facilities for
families, in very attractive countryside. A 4.5-acre
site with 59 touring pitches and 17 statics.
Playroom, cycle hire, campers' kitchen.
Leisure: ♦ ⚠ ☐ **Facilities:** ⋔ ☉ ⌇ ✲ ⚅ ⚒ ⛢
Services: ⛽ ⑤ ⌀ ⊞ ⓣ ⚱ ✔
→ ┣ △ ┿ ✔

CO KILKENNY

KILKENNY　　　　　　　Map 01 C3

▶ ▶ ▶ **Tree Grove Caravan & Camping Park**
Danville House ☎ 056 70302
Dir: 1km from Kilkenny on R700 New Ross road, on
right immediately past rdbt
★ 🚐 £10　🚐 £10 ▲ £7.50
Open Apr-Oct Booking advisable
A pretty park set in the hills of Kilkenny, with tiered
pitches and plenty of space. Friendly, welcoming
owners and good facilities. A 7-acre site with 30
touring pitches.
Campers kitchen & sinks.
Leisure: ♦ ⚠ **Facilities:** ⋔ ☉ ✲ ⚒ ⛢ ⚱ ⊓ ⟑
Services: ⛽ ▮ ⌀ ⊞ ⓣ
→ ∪ ┣ ◉ △ ⚌ ✔ ⑤

CO MAYO

KNOCK　　　　　　　Map 01 B4

▶ ▶ ▶ **Knock Caravan and Camping Park**
Claremorris Rd ☎ 094 88100 & 88223
Dir: Follow signs to Knock Shrine
🚐 IR£9.50-IR£10　🚐 IR£9.50-IR£10 ▲ IR£6-IR£7
Open Mar-Nov Booking advisable Aug Last arrival
22.00hrs Last departure noon
A pleasant, very well maintained caravan park
within the grounds of Knock Shrine, offering
spacious terraced pitches and excellent facilities. An
8-acre site with 75 touring pitches and 17 statics.
Leisure: ♦ ⚠ ☐ **Facilities:** ⋔ ☉ ⌇ ✲ ⚅ ⚒ ⊓ ⟑
Services: ⛽ ⑤ ▮ ⌀ ⊞ ⓣ
→ ∪ ┣ ✔ ⚒

Facilities: ⚱ Bath　⋔ Shower　☉ Electric Shaver　⌇ Hairdryer　✲ Ice Pack Facility　⚅ Disabled Facilities　⚒ Public Telephone
⛢ Shop on Site or within 200yds　⚌ Mobile Shop (calls at least 5 days a week)　⛢ BBQ Area　⊓ Picnic Area　⟑ Dog Exercise Area

CO ROSCOMMON

ATHLONE   Map 01 C4

▶ ▶ ▶ **Hodson Bay Caravan & Camping Park**
Hodson Bay ☎ 0902 92448
Dir: From Athlone, take N61 for 3m, at sign for Hodson Bay, turn right here for approx 1.5m, park at end of road
★ ⛟ fr IR£10 ⛟ fr IR£10 ▲ fr IR£9.50
Open Jun-Aug Booking advisable bank hols & last wk Jul-1st wk Aug Last arrival 22.30hrs Last departure noon ⊗
A lovely site in a superb location on the shores of Lough Ree, part of a 200-acre farm with a two-mile walk to be enjoyed through unspoilt countryside. A 2-acre site with 34 touring pitches.
Leisure: ☐ Facilities: ⋒☉❑❄⅋℄⊞☵
Services: ⊕⊠⓵⊘⊞⊤
→∪▶◉⧗⊁⚎♩⅃

BOYLE   Map 01 B4

▶ ▶ ▶ ▶ **Lough Key Forest Park**
☎ 079 62363 & 62212
Dir: Follow signs for Lough Key Forest Park, site within grounds, about 0.5m from entrance
⛟ IR£8.50-IR£9 ⛟ IR£8.50-IR£9 ▲ IR£6-IR£8
Open 13 Apr-2 Sep Booking advisable 3 wks before arrival Last arrival 22.00hrs Last departure noon no cars by tents
Peaceful and very secluded site within the extensive grounds of a beautiful forest park. Lough Key offers boat trips and waterside walks, and there is a viewing tower. A 15-acre site with 72 touring pitches.
Leisure: ⚠☐ Facilities: ⋒☉℄⅋⅃☵
Services: ⊕⊠✗
→▶◮⧗⚎♩

CO SLIGO

ROSSES POINT   Map 01 B5

▶ ▶ ▶ **Greenlands Caravan & Camping Park**
'Ardmachree', Larkhill Rd ☎ 071 77113
Dir: 5m NW of Sligo beside golf club
⛟ IR£12-IR£13 ⛟ IR£12-IR£13 ▲ IR£12-IR£13
Open Etr-mid Sep Last arrival 20.00hrs Last departure noon
Beachside park built on the sand dunes overlooking Sligo Bay, and two lovely bathing beaches. Spacious open camping areas, and good central facilities. On Rosses Point peninsula. A 6-acre site with 100 touring pitches.
Leisure: ⚓☐ Facilities: ⋒☉❄℄⅋☵
Services: ⊕
→▶◉⧗♩⊠⬤▭

STRANDHILL   Map 01 B5

▶ ▶ ▶ **Strandhill Caravan Park**
'Ardmachree', Larkhill Rd ☎ 071 68111
Dir: 5m W of Sligo, site at beach on Airport Rd
⛟ IR£12-IR£13 ⛟ IR£12-IR£13 ▲ IR£12-IR£13
Open Etr-mid Sep Last arrival 23.00hrs Last departure noon
Sand dune site overlooking Sligo Bay, with views of Knocknarea and Benbulben mountains, and offering plenty of seclusion and privacy. A 20-acre site with 72 touring pitches.
Leisure: ⚓☐ Facilities: ⋒☉❑❄℄⅋☵
Services: ⊕
→∪▶◮♩⊠⬤▭

CO WATERFORD

CLONEA   Map 01 C2

▶ ▶ ▶ *Casey's Caravan Park*
☎ 058 41919
Dir: Take R675 Dungarvan road, following signs to Clonea Bay. Site at end of road beside sea
⛟ ⛟ ▲

Open May-6 Sep Booking advisable May-Jun Last arrival 22.00hrs Last departure noon
Spacious, well-kept park with excellent toilet facilities, next to beach. A 4.5-acre site with 108 touring pitches and 170 statics.
Crazy golf & games room.
Leisure: ⚓⚠☐ Facilities: ⋒☉❑❄℄⅋
Services: ⊕⓵⊘➡
→▶❄⚎♩

Services: ⊤ Toilet Fluid ✗ Café/ Restaurant ⅋ Fast Food/Takeaway ➡ Baby Care ⊕ Electric Hook Up
⊠ Launderette ⅄ Licensed Bar ⓵ Calor Gaz ⊘ Camping Gaz ⊞ Battery Charging

CO WESTMEATH

BALLYKEERAN   Map 01 C4

► ► *Lough Ree Caravan and Camping Park*
☎ 0902 78561 & 74414
*Dir: Take R675 Dungarvan road, following signs to
Clonea Bay. Site at end of road beside sea.*
🏕🚐⚤

Open Apr-2 Oct Booking advisable bank hols
*Pleasant secluded grassy park on shores of Lough
Ree, with trees providing screening, and well-kept
facilities. A 5-acre site with 40 touring pitches and 2
statics.*
Pool table & campers kitchen.
Leisure: ⚠ **Facilities:** ☏⊙✳✆🛒 **Services:** 🖾🅱
➔∪▶◎⚤⚓🛁🍴

CO WEXFORD

KILMUCKRIDGE   Map 01 D3

► ► ► *Morriscastle Strand Caravan &
Camping Park*
Morriscastle
☎ 053 30124 & 01 4535355 (off-season)
*Dir: From Kilmuckridge follow signs for Morriscastle
Strand*
🏕🚐⚤
Open Jul-27 Aug (rs May-Jun & 28 Aug-Sep shop,
reception, games room, take-away food) Booking
advisable Whitsun wknd & mid Jul-mid Aug Last
arrival 22.00hrs Last departure 16.00hrs ⚇
*Popular holiday park beside a glorious stretch of
beach, with good facilities on site and in the nearby
town. A 16-acre site with 100 touring pitches and
150 statics.*
Leisure: ⚲♣ **Facilities:** ☏⊙🗑✳⚤✆🛒
Services: 🖾🅱🍴🖊🍴
➔∪▶◎⚓🛁

WEXFORD   Map 01 D2

► ► ► *Ferrybank Caravan Park*
Ferrybank ☎ 053 44378 & 43274
*Dir: Beside the bridge on the NW of Wexford Harbour,
off R741*
🏕🚐⚤
Open Apr-Sep (rs Etr & Sep no shop) Booking
advisable Whit wknd & Aug bank hol Last arrival
22.00hrs Last departure 16.00hrs
*An open site beside the sea and on the edge of
Wexford, with level grassy pitches. A 4.5-acre site
with 130 touring pitches.*
Leisure: ⚲♣⚠🖵 **Facilities:** ☏⊙✳⚤✆🛒🏊
Services: 🖾🅱🗙🖊
➔∪▶◎⚓🛁

Ireland

CO WICKLOW

DONARD   Map 01 D3

► ► ► **Moat Farm Caravan & Camping Park**
☎ 045 404727
Dir: Off N81 in village of Donard
★ 🚐 fr IR£10 🚐 fr IR£10 ▲ fr IR£10
Open all year Booking advisable bank hols & Jun-
Aug Last arrival 22.30hrs Last departure noon
*Quiet open parkland on an organic farm in the
foothills of the Wicklow Mountains. Plenty of grassy
space and a good area with hardstandings for vans.
Very attractive facilities. A 2.75-acre site with 40
touring pitches.*
Leisure: ⚠ ❑ **Facilities:** 🍴 ⊙ 🔍 ✳ ♿ ⚓ 🛒 🏪 🎠 🏕
Services: 🔌 🔋 🛢 ⌀ 🔋 ➡
➜ ∪ ▶ ⊚ ✦

ROUNDWOOD   Map 01 D3

► ► ► ► **Roundwood Caravan Park**
☎ 01 2818163
*Dir: From N11 Shankill by-pass take R755 at
Kilmacanogue for Glendalough. Park on left at entrance
to Roundwood village*
🚐 IR£11-IR£12 🚐 IR£11-IR£12 ▲ IR£11-IR£12
Open Apr-Sep Booking advisable Jun-Aug Last
arrival 11.00hrs Last departure noon
*Attractive touring park in the midst of the Wicklow
Mountains, with well-screened pitches and views of
Vantry Lakes. A 6-acre site with 71 touring pitches.
Campers kitchen & dining room.*
Leisure: ♦ ⚠ ❑ **Facilities:** 🍴 ⊙ ✳ ⚓ 🛒 🏕
Services: 🔌 🔋 🛢 ⌀ 🔋 🔋
➜ ∪ ▶ ✦

Ireland

Services: 🔋 Toilet Fluid ✖ Café/ Restaurant 🍔 Fast Food/Takeaway ➡ Baby Care 🔌 Electric Hook Up
🔟 Launderette ⚱ Licensed Bar 🛢 Calor Gaz ⌀ Camping Gaz 🔋 Battery Charging

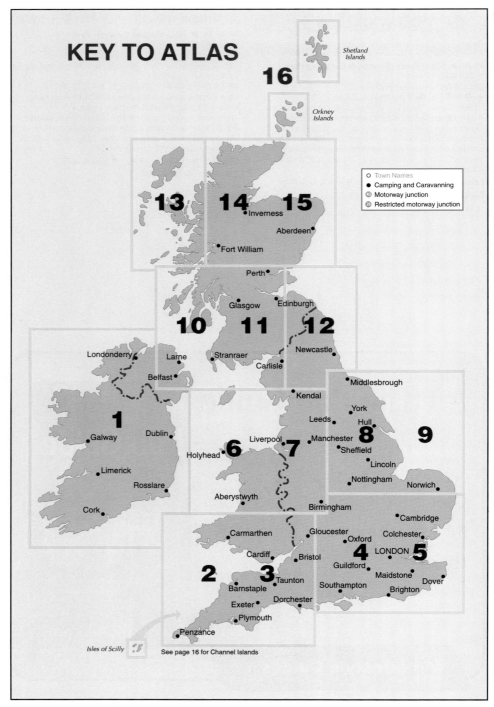

KEY TO ATLAS

16 Shetland Islands

Orkney Islands

○ Town Names
● Camping and Caravanning
⑩ Motorway junction
⑩ Restricted motorway junction

13

14 Inverness

15

Aberdeen

Fort William

Perth

Glasgow   Edinburgh

10   **11**   **12**

Londonderry   Larne   Stranraer   Newcastle

Belfast   Carlisle

Kendal

Middlesbrough

1   Leeds   York   Hull

Galway   Dublin   Liverpool   Manchester   **8**   **9**

Holyhead   **6**   **7**   Sheffield

Limerick   Lincoln

Rosslare   Nottingham   Norwich

Aberystwyth

Cork   Birmingham

Cambridge

Carmarthen   Gloucester   Colchester

Cardiff   Oxford

2   **3** Taunton   Bristol   **4** LONDON   **5**

Barnstaple   Guildford   Maidstone

Exeter   Dorchester   Southampton   Brighton   Dover

Plymouth

Penzance

Isles of Scilly   See page 16 for Channel Islands

© Automobile Association Developments Limited 2000

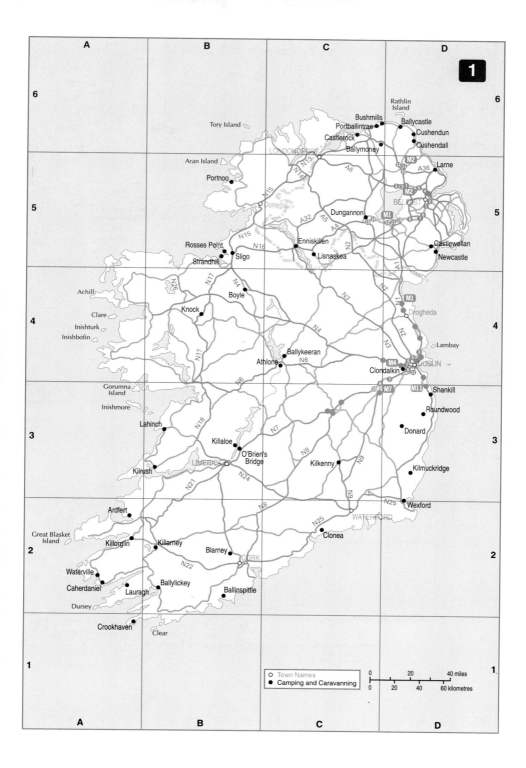

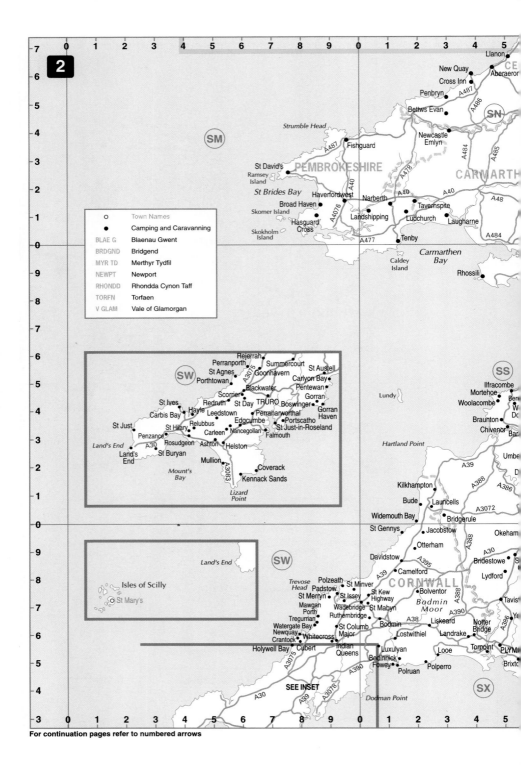

2

○	Town Names
●	Camping and Caravanning
BLAE G	Blaenau Gwent
BRDGND	Bridgend
MYR TD	Merthyr Tydfil
NEWPT	Newport
RHONDD	Rhondda Cynon Taff
TORFN	Torfaen
V GLAM	Vale of Glamorgan

SM

SN

SS

SW

SS

SX

Strumble Head

Fishguard

St David's
Ramsey
Island

PEMBROKESHIRE

CARMARTH

St Brides Bay   Haverfordwest

Broad Haven   Narberth

Skomer Island

Landshipping   Ludchurch

Hasguard
Cross

Skokholm
Island

Tenby

Llanon

New Quay   Aberaeror

Cross Inn

Penbryn

Bettws Evan

Newcastle
Emlyn

Tavernspite

Laugharne

CE

Carmarthen
Bay

Caldey
Island

Rhossili

Rejerrah
Perranporth   Summercourt
St Agnes   Goonhavern   St Austell
Porthtowan   Blackwater   Carlyon Bay

Scorrier   St Day   TRURO   Pentewan

St Ives   Redruth   Boswinger   Gorran
Carbis Bay   Hayle   Leedstown   Perranarworthal   Gorran
St Just   St Hilary   Relubbus   Edgcumbe   Portscatho   Haven
Penzance   Carleen   Nancegollan   St Just-in-Roseland
Land's End   Rosudgeon   Ashton   Helston   Falmouth
Land's   St Buryan
End   Mullion
Mount's
Bay   Coverack
Lizard   Kennack Sands
Point

Lundy

Ilfracombe
Mortehoe
Woolacombe

Braunton

Chivenor

Hartland Point

Kilkhampton

Bude   Launcells

Widemouth Bay   Bridgerule

St Gennys

Jacobstow

Davidstow   Otterham

Camelford

Bodmin
Moor

Okeham

Bridestowe

Lydford

Isles of Scilly

○ St Mary's

Land's End

SW

Trevose   Polzeath
Head   Padstow   St Minver
St Merryn   St Issey   St Kew
Mawgan   Highway   Bolventor
Porth   Wadebridge   St Mabyn
Tregurrian   Ruthernbridge
Watergate Bay   St Columb   Bodmin   Liskeard
Newquay   Major   Lostwithiel   Landrake
Crantock   Whitecross   Notter
Holywell Bay   Cubert   Indian   Luxulyan   Bridge
Queens   Bodinnick   Looe   Torpoint
Fowey   Polperro
Polruan

CORNWALL

Tavis

Ye

Notter
Bridge

PLYM

Brixto

SEE INSET

Dodman Point

SX

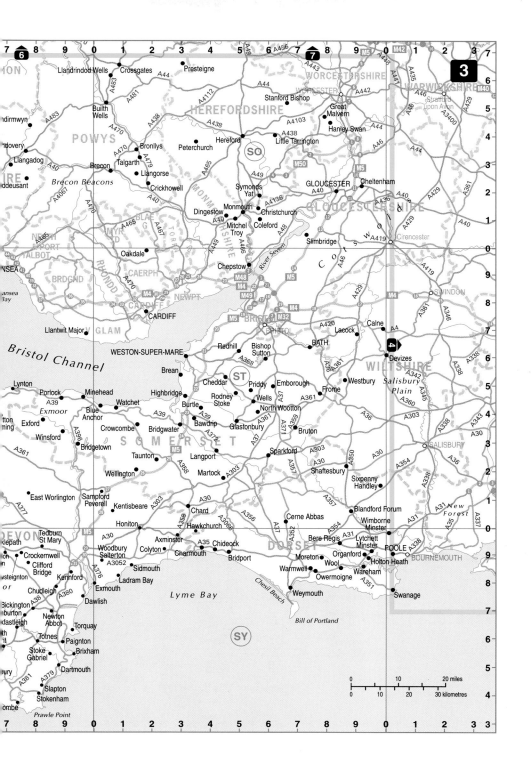

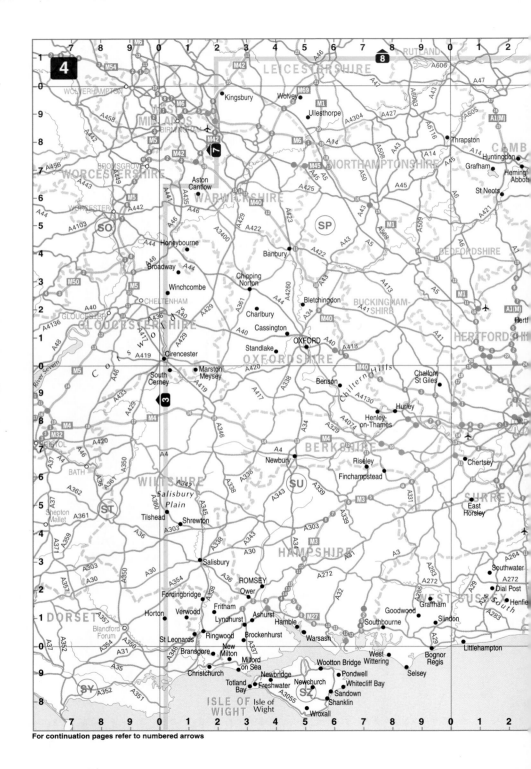

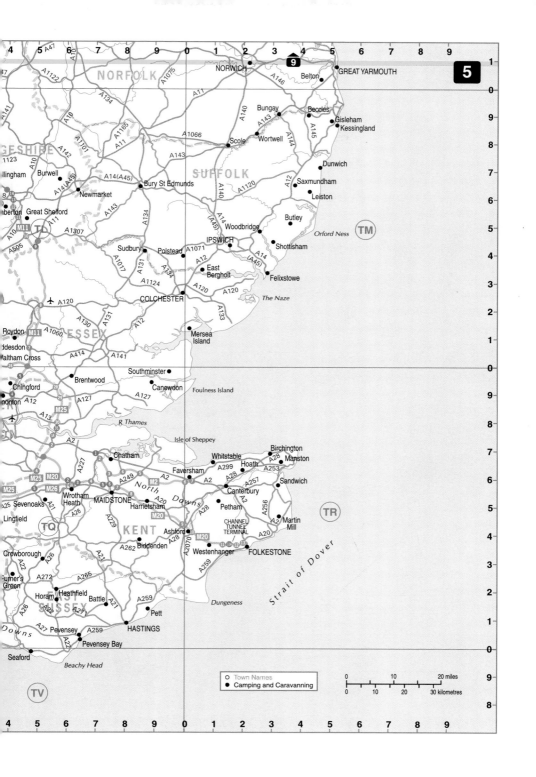

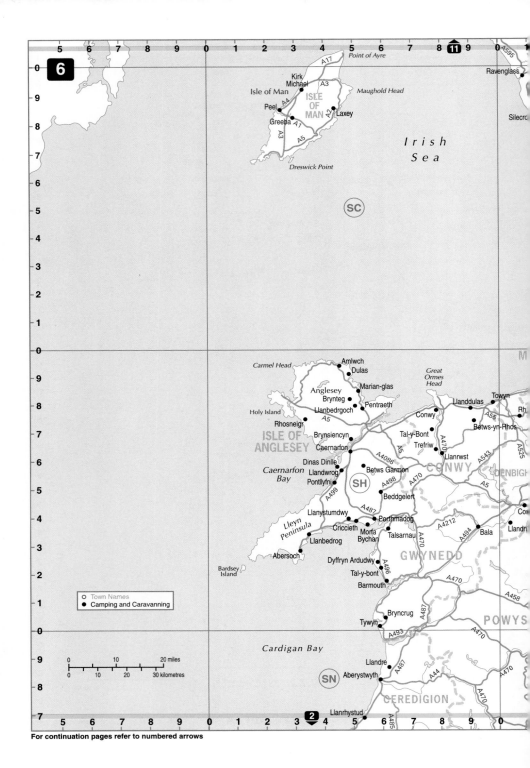

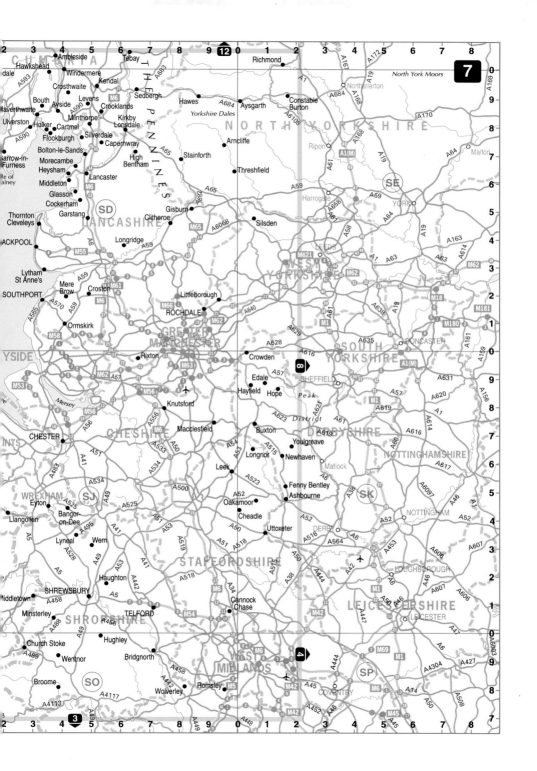

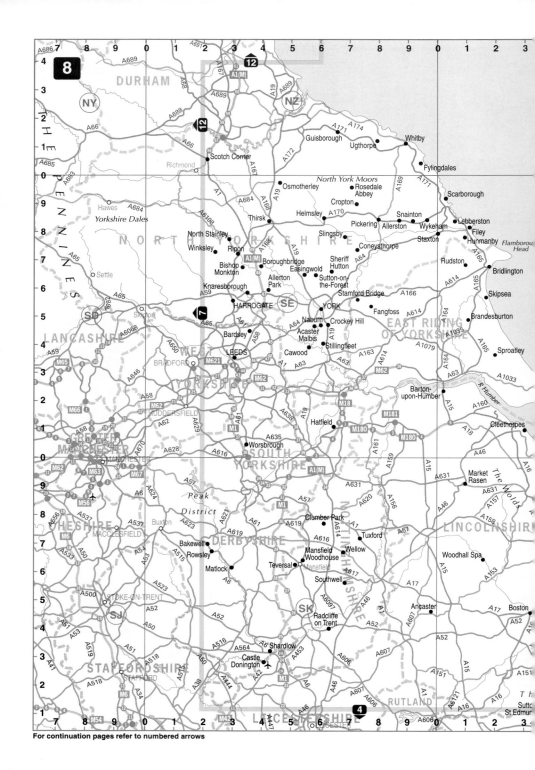

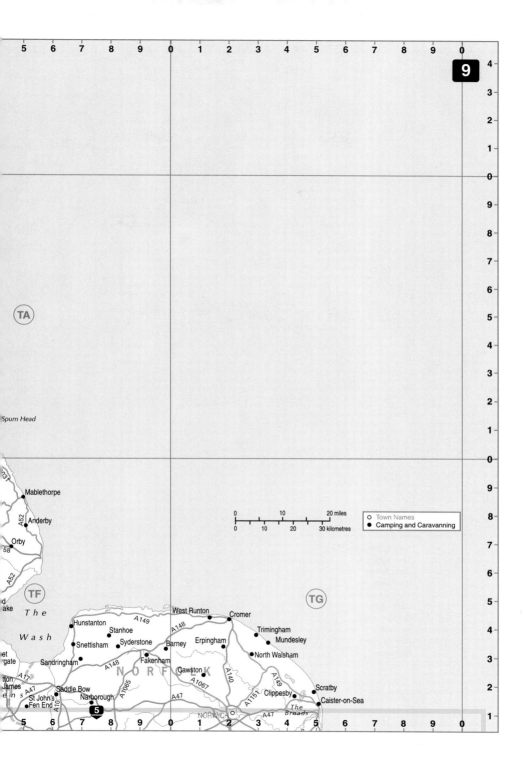

9

5 6 7 8 9 0 1 2 3 4 5 6 7 8 9 0

4
3
2
1
0

9
8
7
6
5
4
3
2
1
0

TA

Spurn Head

0

9
8
7
6
5

Mablethorpe

A52 Anderby

Orby
58

TF

d
ake   *The*

W a s h

et
rgate
tton
James A47
e n s

St John's
Fen End

5

Hunstanton
Snettisham

Sandringham

Saddle Bow
Narborough

Stanhoe
Syderstone

A149

A148

West Runton

Barney

Erpingham

Cromer

Trimingham
Mundesley

North Walsham

A1065

A1067

Cawston

A47

A140

Clippesby

A149

A1151

*The
Broads*

Scratby

Caister-on-Sea

NORWICH

A47

Fakenham

N O R F O L K

5

0	10	20 miles
0	10 20	30 kilometres

○ Town Names
● Camping and Caravanning

5 6 7 8 9 0 1 2 3 4 5 6 7 8 9 0

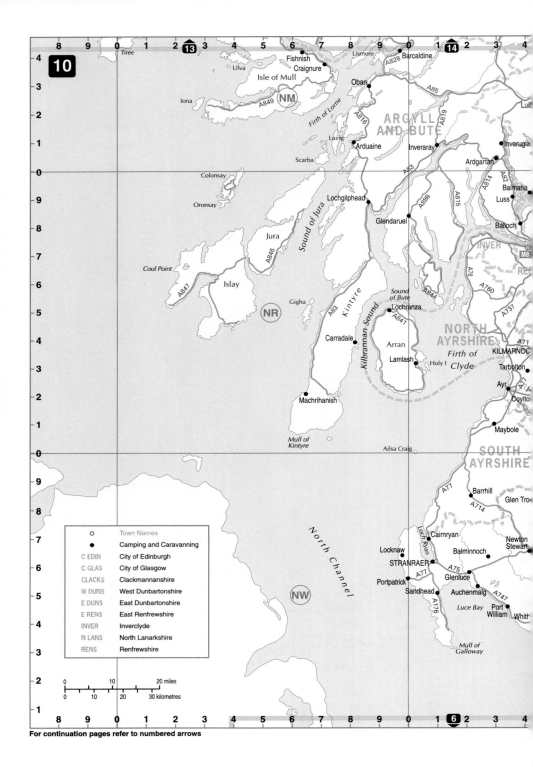

Tiree

Fishnish
Craignure
Ulva
Isle of Mull

Iona

A849 (NM)

Firth of Lorne

Lismore

A828 Barcaldine

Oban

A85

ARGYLL
AND BUTE

A816

Luit

A819

Inverugla

Luing

Arduaine

Inveraray

Ardgartan

Scarba

A83

Ardgartan

Colonsay

A814 A82

Balmaha

Oronsay

Lochgilphead

A886

A815

Luss

Glendaruel

Balloch

Jura

Sound of Jura

INVER

A846

A83

M8

Coul Point

Kintyre

REI

A847

Islay

Gigha

Sound
of Bute

A844

A760

A737

(NR)

Lochranza

NORTH
AYRSHIRE

A71

A841

Carradale

Arran

Firth of
Clyde

KILMARNOC

Kilbrannan Sound

Lamlash

Holy I

Tarbolton

Machrihanish

Ayr

Coylto

Mull of
Kintyre

Ailsa Craig

Maybole

SOUTH
AYRSHIRE

A77

Barrhill

Glen Tro

A714

North Channel

Loch Ryan

Cairnryan

Newton
Stewart

Locknaw

Balminnoch

STRANRAER

(NW)

A75

Portpatrick

A77

Glenluce

A747

Sandhead

Auchenmalg

Port
William

Luce Bay

A76

Whit

Mull of
Galloway

	Town Names
●	Camping and Caravanning
C EDIN	City of Edinburgh
C GLAS	City of Glasgow
CLACKS	Clackmannanshire
W DUNS	West Dunbartonshire
E DUNS	East Dunbartonshire
E RENS	East Renfrewshire
INVER	Inverclyde
N LANS	North Lanarkshire
RENS	Renfrewshire

0 — 10 — 20 miles
0 — 10 — 20 — 30 kilometres

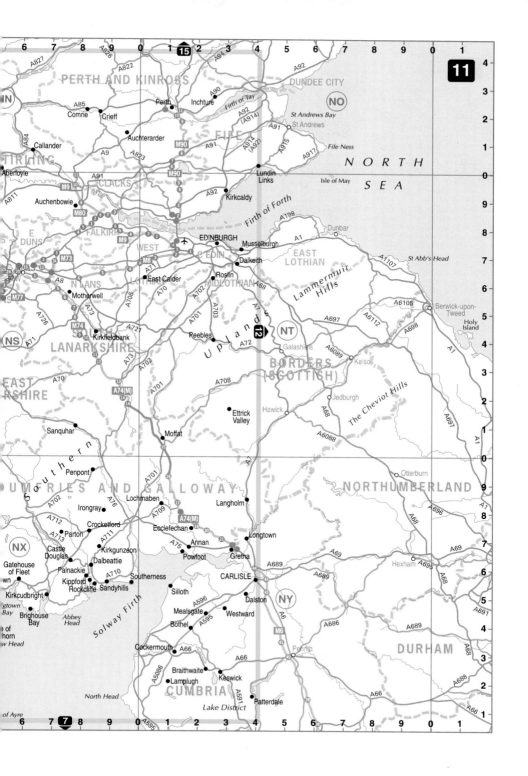

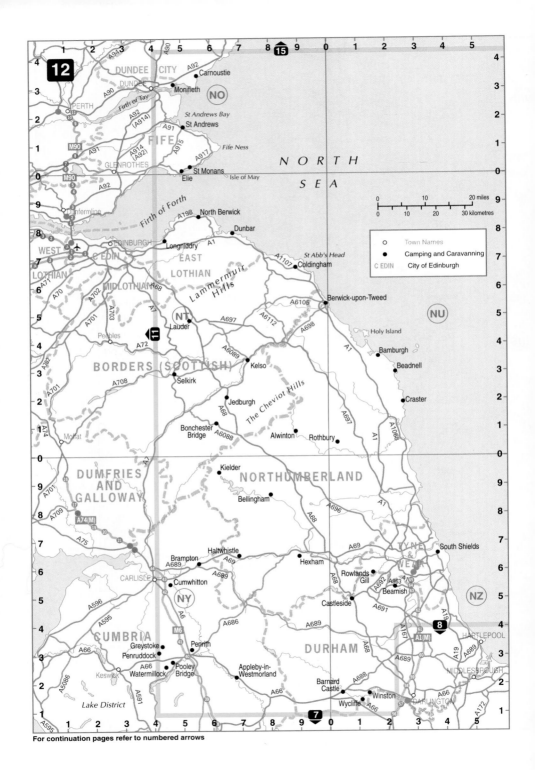

For continuation pages refer to numbered arrows

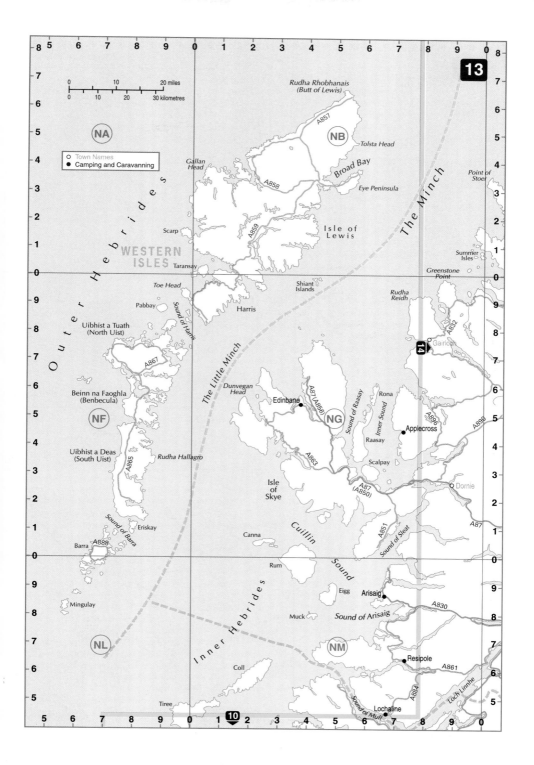

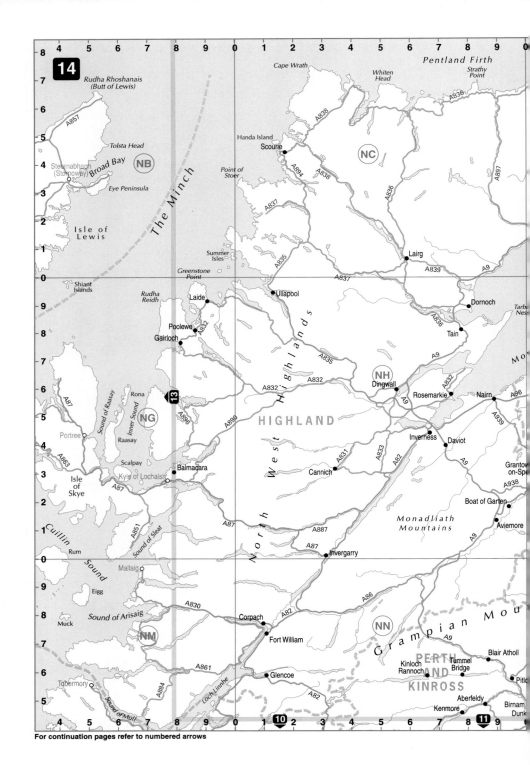

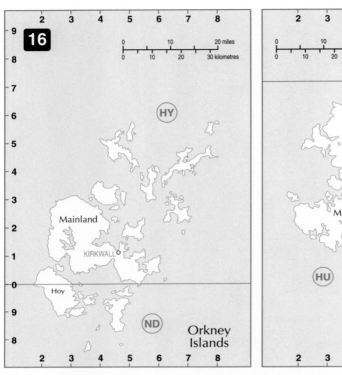

16

HY

Mainland

KIRKWALL o

Hoy

ND

Orkney
Islands

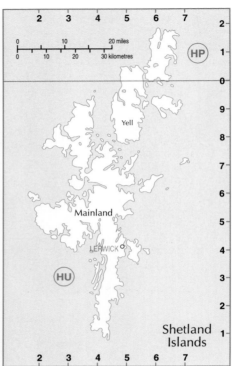

HP

Yell

Mainland

LERWICK o

HU

Shetland
Islands

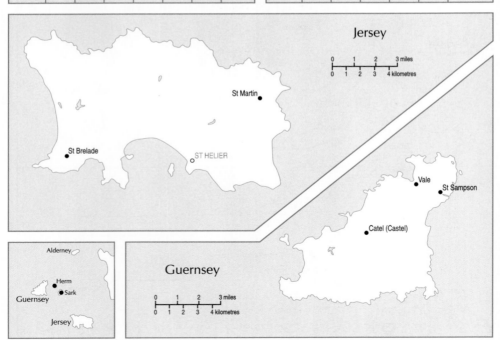

Jersey

St Martin ●

St Brelade ●

ST HELIER o

Vale ●

St Sampson ●

Catel (Castel) ●

Alderney

Herm ●
● Sark

Guernsey

Jersey

Guernsey

0   1   2   3 miles

0   1   2   3   4 kilometres

This is the checklist compiled by one of our campsite inspectors to ensure that he leaves nothing behind when he sets off either from home or from park visits with a towed caravan. We thought you might like to share his handy hints, and save yourself from embarrassment ... or worse.

- Check that all interior caravan items are safely stored, cupboards are closed, loos not full of moveable objects, all interior electrics set correctly. Remember that vase of flowers!

- Check roof lights are closed and windows secure.

- Corner steadies should be up tightly, blocks cleared away, steps stowed.

- Disconnect electric hook-ups to site and check that gas bottles are turned off.

- Make sure electrics to car are secure.

- Check that the tow-hook safety wire is clipped on, and, if used, that the anti-snake device is fitted correctly.

- Visually check that caravan number plate is secure – and that it reads the same as the one on the car.

- Using a second person to stand behind the caravan, check that all lights and indicators are working correctly.

- Move forward about 15 metres, then stop, get out and inspect your pitch for any items which have been left under the caravan.

- Check that the caravan door is locked and secure.

- Another useful and potentially life-saving tip is to always travel with a small fire extinguisher, fire blanket or both. Fires in caravans and tents are all too commonplace, and once started can take hold very quickly. By the time help has come, or you have gone to find the site's fire-fighting equipment, a tent in particular can already have burned down completely. Never treat fire lightly.

- If you use Calor Gas, they issue a free directory of stockists and dealers.
  Simply call free on 0800 626 626.

Before
You Go

AA **Hotel Booking Service**

Now you have a free, simple way to book a place to stay for a week, weekend, or a one-night stopover – The AA Hotel Booking Service

From farmhouse charm to five star luxury, we have just the place for you. Whether you wish to stay in a rustic farm cottage, a smart city centre hotel, a family lodge; or if you just want a cosy weekend for two – we can accommodate you.

If you are touring around Britain or Ireland and need accommodation, then just give the AA Hotel Booking Service a call. Provide us with your location and overnight requirements and we'll do the rest!

Why not try booking on-line. Full entries of AA recognised accommodation can be found and booked through the AA Hotel Booking Service via the AA Web Site

Telephone 0870 5050505

Office hours
Monday - Friday 9am - 6pm   Saturday 9am - 1pm
The service is not available Sundays or Bank Holidays

Book on-line: www.theAA.com

Please write to: Campsites Editor, AA Camping and Caravanning
Guide, Lifestyle Guides,
The Automobile Association, Fanum House,
Basingstoke RG21 4EA

Use this form to recommend any caravan and camping park with good touring pitches where you have stayed which is not already in our guide.

If you have any comments about your stay at a touring park listed in the guide, we shall be grateful if you will let us know, as feedback from readers helps us to keep our guide accurate and up to date. Please note, however, that the AA only inspects and classifies parks for their touring facilities. We do not inspect or grade static caravans.

If a problem arises during your stay on a park, we do recommend that you discuss the matter with the park management there and then so that they have a chance to put things right before your holiday is spoilt.

Please note that the AA does not undertake to arbitrate between you and the park management, or to obtain compensation or engage in protracted correspondence.

Readers Report form

Your name (block capitals) . . . .

. . . .

. . . .

Your address (block capitals) . . . .

. . . .

. . . .

. . . .

. . . .

. . . .

Comments . . . .

. . . .

. . . .

. . . .

. . . .

. . . .

CARAVAN AND
CAMPING
GUIDE 2001

....
....
....
....
....
....
....
....
....
....
....
....
....
....
....
....
....
....
....
....
....
....
....
....
....
....
....
....
....
....
....
....

CARAVAN AND
CAMPING
GUIDE 2001

Please write to: Campsites Editor, AA Camping and Caravanning
Guide, Lifestyle Guides,
The Automobile Association, Fanum House,
Basingstoke RG21 4EA

Use this form to recommend any caravan and camping park with good touring pitches where you have stayed which is not already in our guide.

If you have any comments about your stay at a touring park listed in the guide, we shall be grateful if you will let us know, as feedback from readers helps us to keep our guide accurate and up to date. Please note, however, that the AA only inspects and classifies parks for their touring facilities. We do not inspect or grade static caravans.

If a problem arises during your stay on a park, we do recommend that you discuss the matter with the park management there and then so that they have a chance to put things right before your holiday is spoilt.

Please note that the AA does not undertake to arbitrate between you and the park management, or to obtain compensation or engage in protracted correspondence.

Readers Report form

Your name (block capitals) . . . .
. . . .
. . . .

Your address (block capitals) . . . .
. . . .
. . . .
. . . .
. . . .
. . . .

Comments . . . .
. . . .
. . . .
. . . .
. . . .
. . . .
. . . .

CARAVAN AND
CAMPING
GUIDE 2001

CARAVAN AND
CAMPING
GUIDE 2001

Please write to: Campsites Editor, AA Camping and Caravanning
Guide, Lifestyle Guides,
The Automobile Association, Fanum House,
Basingstoke RG21 4EA

Use this form to recommend any caravan and camping park with good touring pitches where you have stayed which is not already in our guide.

If you have any comments about your stay at a touring park listed in the guide, we shall be grateful if you will let us know, as feedback from readers helps us to keep our guide accurate and up to date. Please note, however, that the AA only inspects and classifies parks for their touring facilities. We do not inspect or grade static caravans.

If a problem arises during your stay on a park, we do recommend that you discuss the matter with the park management there and then so that they have a chance to put things right before your holiday is spoilt.

Please note that the AA does not undertake to arbitrate between you and the park management, or to obtain compensation or engage in protracted correspondence.

Readers Report form

Your name (block capitals) . . . .

. . . .

. . . .

Your address (block capitals) . . . .

. . . .

. . . .

. . . .

. . . .

. . . .

Comments . . . .

. . . .

. . . .

. . . .

. . . .

CARAVAN AND
CAMPING
GUIDE 2001

CARAVAN AND
CAMPING
GUIDE 2001

Please write to: Campsites Editor, AA Camping and Caravanning
Guide, Lifestyle Guides,
The Automobile Association, Fanum House,
Basingstoke RG21 4EA

Use this form to recommend any caravan and camping park with
good touring pitches where you have stayed which is not already
in our guide.

If you have any comments about your stay at a touring park
listed in the guide, we shall be grateful if you will let us know, as
feedback from readers helps us to keep our guide accurate and up
to date. Please note, however, that the AA only inspects and
classifies parks for their touring facilities. We do not inspect or
grade static caravans.

If a problem arises during your stay on a park, we do
recommend that you discuss the matter with the park
management there and then so that they have a chance to put
things right before your holiday is spoilt.

Please note that the AA does not undertake to arbitrate
between you and the park management, or to obtain
compensation or engage in protracted correspondence.

Readers
Report form

Your name (block capitals) . . . .

. . . .

. . . .

Your address (block capitals) . . . .

. . . .

. . . .

. . . .

. . . .

. . . .

Comments . . . .

. . . .

. . . .

. . . .

. . . .

. . . .

CARAVAN AND
CAMPING
GUIDE 2001